CAUSES

OF THE

REDUCTION OF AMERICAN TONNAGE

AND THE

DECLINE OF NAVIGATION INTERESTS,

BEING THE

REPORT OF A SELECT COMMITTEE

MADE TO

THE HOUSE OF REPRESENTATIVES OF THE UNITED STATES ON THE 17TH OF FEBRUARY, 1870.

WASHINGTON:
GOVERNMENT PRINTING OFFICE.
1870.

CAUSES OF THE REDUCTION OF AMERICAN TONNAGE.

[To accompany bills H. R. No. 1261 and 1262]

FEBRUARY 17, 1870.—Ordered to be printed.

Mr. LYNCH, from the Committee on the causes of the reduction of American tonnage, made the following

REPORT.

The select committee appointed by resolution of the House of Representatives March 22, 1869, "to inquire into and report at the next session of Congress the causes of the great reduction of American tonnage engaged in the foreign carrying trade, and the great depression of the navigation interests of the country, and also to report what measures are necessary to increase our ocean tonnage, revive our navigation interests, and regain for our country the position it once held among the nations as a great maritime power," have considered the subject referred to it, and agreed to the following report:

Your committee, in prosecuting its inquiries, have, during the recess of Congress, held sessions at the cities of New York, Philadelphia, Boston, and Portland, receiving the statements of merchants, ship-builders, ship-owners, and insurance agents; gentlemen having practical knowledge and experience relating to the matter under investigation. The ship-owners associations of New York, Philadelphia, and Maine, and the board of trade of Boston were represented at the sessions of the committee, and presented the views of these various associations. Like information and evidence have been received in the sessions of the committee held at the capitol during the present session of Congress. Circular letters have been addressed to gentlemen engaged in the various branches of business connected with the shipping interests, requesting a statement of their views on the subject under inquiry, and also to American consuls at the principal ports of foreign countries, asking them to furnish information in regard to the condition of the mercantile marine of those countries.

The evidence elicited by these various modes of inquiry will be found under the head of testimony taken by the Special Committee on Navigation Interests, and appended to this report.

The committee would call special attention to the exhaustive paper furnished through the State Department by our consul at London, Hon. Freeman H. Morse, and also to the tables of statistics prepared for the committee by Mr. F. A. Walker, Deputy Special Commissioner of the Revenue, and by Joseph Nimmo, jr., of the Treasury Department, who has made the condition of our shipping interest a subject of special attention.

THE DECLINE IN AMERICAN OCEAN TONNAGE.

In order fully to comprehend the extent of the decadence of American shipping and the causes which have operated to produce that decadence, we must ascertain the points at which the prosperity of this interest culminated, and trace it thence back to the source of that prosperity, and forward to the present time of decay. It is obvious that whatever causes may have existed prior to the commencement of the late rebellion tending to produce the present condition of our shipping, their effects did not become manifest until that period. Previously there was a gradual, steady, and healthy increase of our ocean tonnage, fluctuating with the fluctuations of business, but constantly gaining until the year 1861.

The increase of our tonnage engaged in the foreign carrying trade from 1830 to 1840, was about sixty per cent.; from 1840 to 1850, seventy-five per cent.; from 1850 to 1860, sixty per cent. This latter is the first decade in which we find any reliable statistics of the registered tonnage of Great Britain, to enable us to institute a comparison between it and our own. In this decade the tonnage of Great Britain, employed exclusively in the foreign trade of that country, increased about forty per cent. Our own tonnage engaged in the foreign carrying trade, reached its highest point in 1861, being that year 2,642,628 tons, while that of Great Britain was at the same time 3,179,683 tons, giving us the second place in rank among nations in the extent of our ocean tonnage, while we were the acknowledged superior of all in the proficiency which we had attained in the science of naval architecture and in the efficiency of our mercantile marine.

It is difficult to realize that our country, which in little more than half a century ending in 1860, had reached the very foremost rank of maritime nations, has in less than a decade lost half its merchant shipping and all its maritime prestage, and that we now stand debating whether we shall without a struggle yield all, and become the mere commercial dependency of the nation for whose advantage we have been thus spoiled and reduced.

From 1861 to 1866 our tonnage engaged in the foreign trade decreased from 2,642,628 tons to 1,492,926 tons, a loss of 1,149,902 tons, or more than 43 per cent., while Great Britain, in the same time, gained 986,715 tons, or more than 30 per cent. Even this statement does not show the full extent of our relative loss as compared with Great Britain, a very large percentage of the increase of the latter in tonnage having been made in steamers, one ton of which class of vessels is equal in efficiency to at least three tons of sail vessels, while by substituting largely iron for wood, as building material, a still further advantage was gained over us in her much larger class of iron vessels, doubly as durable as those of wood. The increase of the steam tonnage of Great Britain during the period alluded to, was 275,988 tons, making an addition in efficiency over our sailing ships of at least 500,000 tons. So that, taking into account the durability and efficiency of the tonnage added by Great Britain to her merchant marine from 1860 to 1866, it would probably equal an increase of 50 per cent. of sail vessels.

RISE AND FALL OF THE MERCANTILE MARINE.

The following tables of statistics present a more forcible statement of the rise and fall of our mercantile marine, and furnish a more striking illustration the effect of the war upon our own shipping and that of Great Britain, engaged in foreign commerce, than any other language than that of figures can furnish.

Table showing the tonnage of United States and British registered vessels employed in the foreign trade of each country, during the years, respectively, 1830, 1840, 1850, *and from* 1860 *to* 1868, *both inclusive.*

Year.	United States.			Great Britain.*					
				In the foreign trade.			Partly in home and partly in foreign trade.		
	Registered sail.	Regist'd steam.	Total registered.	Registered sail.	Regist'd steam.	Total registered.	Regis'd sail.	Reg'd steam.	Total reg'td.
1830	575, 056	1, 419	576, 475	....	....	....	....	....	....
1840	895, 610	4, 155	899, 765	....	....	....	....	....	....
1850	1, 540, 769	44, 429	1, 585, 198	2, 143, 234	45, 186	2, 188, 420	222, 341	5, 298	227, 639
1860	2, 448, 941	97, 296	2, 546, 237	2, 804, 610	277, 437	3, 082, 047	226, 556	29, 803	256, 359
1861	2, 540, 020	102, 608	2, 642, 628	2, 866, 218	313, 465	3, 179, 683	219, 522	24, 924	244, 446
1862	2, 177, 253	113, 998	2, 291, 251	2, 993, 696	328, 310	3, 322, 006	246, 479	29, 463	275, 942
1863	1, 892, 899	133, 215	2, 026, 114	3, 246, 526	371, 201	3, 617, 727	284, 413	33, 547	317, 960
1864	1, 475, 376	106, 519	1, 581, 895	3, 532, 242	456, 241	3, 988, 483	268, 125	36, 944	305, 069
1865	1, 504, 575	98, 008	1, 602, 583	3, 629, 023	523, 698	4, 152, 721	282, 295	43, 225	325, 520
1866	1, 294, 637	198, 289	1, 492, 926	3, 612, 973	553, 425	4, 166, 398	278, 167	47, 194	325, 361
1867	1, 369, 917	198, 115	1, 568, 032	3, 641, 662	608, 232	4, 249, 894	199, 846	50, 201	250, 047
1868	1, 343, 703	221, 939	1, 565, 732	3, 646, 150	619, 199	4, 265, 349	240, 921	52, 150	293, 071

* NOTE.—This table includes Channel Island vessels but not those of the British plantations. The home trade signifies on the coasts of the United Kingdom, or to ports between the limits of the river Elbe and Brest. The foreign trade signifies to ports beyond such limits.

Registered tonnage of United States, 1860	2, 546, 237
Registered tonnage of Great Britain (exclusive of colonial)..	3, 082, 047
Total..	5, 628, 284
Registered tonnage of United States, 1868	1, 505, 732
Registered tonnage of Great Britain, 1868.................	4, 265, 349
Total..	5, 771, 081
If to this we add, for increase in steam tonnage..........	500, 000
	6, 271, 081

It will be observed that notwithstanding the check caused by the war upon the production of the crops of the South, which furnished so arge a percentage of our exports, the aggregate tonnage of the United States and Great Britain engaged in the foreign carrying trade has increased about 14 per cent., while from the position of nearly an equal in tonnage with that nation, our own tonnage had dwindled to less than one-third of that of Great Britain.

The change of the business furnished by our own country in exports and imports from American to foreign vessels is still more striking, as will be shown by the following table:

A table showing the amount of American and foreign tonnage entered the ports of the United States from foreign countries in 1830, 1840, 1850, *and from* 1860 *to* 1869, *both inclusive.*

Fiscal years.	American tonnage.	Foreign tonnage.	American in excess of foreign tonnage.	Foreign in excess of American tonnage.
1830	967, 227	131, 900	835, 327	
1840	1, 576, 946	712, 363	864, 583	
1850	2, 573, 016	1, 775, 623	797, 393	
1860	5, 921, 285	2, 353, 911	3, 567, 374	
1861	5, 023, 917	2, 217, 554	2, 806, 363	
1862	5, 117, 685	2, 245, 278	2, 872, 407	
1863	4, 614, 698	2, 640, 378	1, 974, 320	
1864	3, 066, 434	3, 471, 219		404, 785
1865	2, 943, 661	3, 216, 967		273, 306
1866	3, 372, 060	4, 410, 424		1, 038, 364
1867	3, 455, 052	4, 318, 673		863, 621
1868	3, 550, 550	4, 495, 465		944, 915
1869	3, 402, 668	5, 347, 694		1, 945, 026

VALUE OF TONNAGE.

The estimated value of the tonnage of the United States engaged in the foreign carrying trade was, in 1861, $108,347,748; the estimated gross yearly earnings of which was 33⅓ per cent., or $36,115,916. In 1869, the estimated value of the same tonnage was $70,488,945, and the estimated earnings, $23,496,315; a net loss in yearly earning of this interest, of $12,619,601. (Table No. XIV of the Appendix.)

The increase in gross earnings of this class of tonnage from 1850 to 1860, $14,719,397, or 73 per cent. Taking the same ratio of increase from 1860 to 1869, say 65 per cent., and we should have, in 1869, $57,417,643. The actual amount of gross earnings is $23,496,315, or a net annual loss, in consequence of the decline of our ocean commerce, of $33,921,328.

Add to these the table showing the relative proportion in value of the imports and exports by American and foreign vessels to and from the United States, (table No. XV in Appendix,) and we have a complete epitome of the deplorable condition to which our shipping interests has been reduced. The following, from the table referred to, shows the total foreign commerce of the United States in 1850, 1855, 1860, 1865, and 1869:

Fiscal year.	Exports and imports in American vessels.	Exports and imports in foreign vessels.	Total.
1850	$239, 272, 084	$90, 746, 954	$330, 037, 038
1855	405, 485, 462	131, 139, 904	536, 625, 366
1860	507, 247, 757	255, 040, 793	762, 288, 550
1865	167, 402, 872	437, 010, 124	604, 412, 996
1869	289, 950, 272	586, 492, 012	876, 442, 284

It will be seen by the foregoing that in 1850, 75 per cent. of our total exports and imports were shipped in American vessels. In 1855, 75 per cent. in American, and 25 per cent. in foreign vessels. In 1869, 34 per cent. in American to 66 per cent. in foreign vessels. Our exports have doubled since 1853, while the percentage carried in American vessels has fallen from 67 per cent. to 34 per cent.

Could there be a more striking refutation of the assumption that the revival of our shipping will follow the increase of our exports, than is furnished by the statistics referred to. The increase of our exports will only furnish an increased business to foreign ships unless we put our own vessels in a position to compete with them on equal terms. It is estimated that more than 60 per cent. of the registered tonnage of the United States is engaged in the carrying trade between foreign countries, on long routes carrying the bulky cheap freights, while, as has been shown by the foregoing table, our own exports and imports are passing in foreign bottoms, the freights going to enrich our commercial rivals, and to swell the foreign balances against us, which must be settled in gold.

VALUE OF IMPORTS.

The following are the values of imports into the district of New York during the fiscal year ending June 30, 1869, with estimated proportion in sailing and steam vessels:

Total value of imports	\$295, 137, 415
Of which estimated proportion in sailing vessels	57, 867, 025, or $19\frac{607}{1000}$ per cent.
Proportion in steam vessels	237, 270, 390, or $80\frac{393}{1000}$ per cent.
Total	295, 137, 415
Estimated proportion in American steamers	35, 441, 606
Estimated proportion in foreign steamers	201, 828, 784
Total in steamers	237, 270, 390

Or nearly seventy per cent. of the imports at the great commercial city of the country in foreign steamers.

There are now running regularly, to and from New York, 89 foreign steamships, the aggregate tonnage of which is 205,338 tons. The increase in this class of vessels, since 1860, has been 47 ships, 139,605 tons, or more than two hundred per cent., and the number is constantly augmenting to meet the increased demands of business. (See table XXV in Appendix.)

Estimating the freights paid at eight per cent. of the value of the cargoes and we have here paid to, foreign carriers of goods to a single port, in round numbers, sixteen millions of dollars, while the amount paid on outward cargoes will probably reach half that sum, making a grand total of twenty-four million dollars annually drawn from our own people to support the steamships of foreign nations, which steamships constitute the naval reserve of those powers.

STEAMSHIP LINES.

At present the whole tendency of the freighting business of the world is to seek direct routes, and by steam communication, to combine mail and passenger with merchandise transportation. The long and tedious voyages around capes are avoided by connecting oceans either by ship canals or railways. The advantage of this change in the mode of transportation, in addition to that of carrying passengers and mails, is that it furnishes a way business that cannot be commanded by sail vessels which can only carry advantageously between two points.

Great Britain availing herself of the use of steam has obtained control of the chief of these direct lines of ocean communication, and in doing so has occupied the shortest routes and those which, without loss of time or distance, afford the most points to touch and tap the trade belonging to them.

Between America, North and South, she has nine direct lines. Two carry the mails between the United States, British America, and England. Both lines start from Liverpool, touch at Queenstown, and sail direct to New York. One, however, calls at Halifax. To feed these lines the Cunard Company run a line from Halifax to Nassau, which is subsidized. There are also "way" steamers, if we may call them so, between Halifax and Newfoundland, the Bahamas and New York. There is a line between Liverpool, New Orleans, and Balize.

Three lines sail direct from Southampton to the Gulf of Mexico. One to Tampico, Mexico, another to Aspinwall, the third runs to Puerto Cabello, in Venezuella.

There are also three lines sail for the Atlantic coast of South America. One to Brazil, stopping at Rio de Janeiro, after calling at the leading ports to the north; another makes Buenos Ayres its stopping place. The third runs to Montevideo. These lines sail from Falmouth and Southampton direct, taking the shortest route across.

Panama is the starting point for four lines of British steamers. One down the Pacific coast of South America to Valparaiso, touching at all the chief ports. Another to the leading places in Central America. A third is a local line running to neighboring points, and the fourth direct to Wellington, New Zealand, connecting with an Australian line to Sydney and Melbourne.

There are two lines along the West coast of Africa, both starting from Southampton, one going to and from the Cape of Good Hope, touching at St. Helena and Ascension, the other tapping the coast, from Cape St. Vincent, Portugal, to Sierre Leone and other points.

Besides a number of short routes connecting different points, the greatest line of all is that of the Peninsula and Oriental Mail Steamship Company. Its point of departure is Southampton. From that port their vessels go to Gibraltar, through the Mediterranean, touching at different points, as Malta, &c., to Port Said, through the canal, the Red Sea, across the Arabian Sea, to Bombay and Ceylon. At the latter place a line runs to Australia; there connecting with a line already mentioned, running from Panama, and thus making the circle complete. The general route of the steamers takes in all the leading Indian ports, also Singapore, Penang, Hong Kong, and Shanghai. By following the indicated routes it will be at once seen that they leave out only two principal regions; Pacific North America and the lower portions of the Indian Archipelago. For the latter, short routes from point to point are being organized, while it is understood that this great company propose to unite the British steam marine at either end of our continental railroad system, by establishing a competing line with the Pacific Mail Steamship Company from Shanghai to San Francisco. This will inevitably be followed by another line from San Francisco to Panama. This extension of lines of steamers has been procured mainly by means of liberal subsidies paid by the British and French governments for carrying the mails.

For the postal service they perform Great Britain pays to twelve of her principal mail steamship companies, in the form of an annual subsidy, £903,750, or $4,392,244, besides the amounts collected for postage over from other principal routes and a number of connecting lines, amounting to enough more to make the entire payments at least $5,500,000. Of this large sum about $2,000,000 is paid to the lines connecting with the American Continents.

The French government is even more liberal than that of Great Britain, and the effect of their policy is seen in the establishment of several lines of the finest equipped steamships afloat, even rivalling the best British lines. The French government pays several million dollars annually to these lines. The French Transatlantic Company run three lines—to New York, to the West Indies and Vera Cruz, and to Gaudaloupe and Aspinwall. It receives all the money paid for postage and a direct annual subsidy of $1,000,000. Besides these amounts, the French government loaned it $5,000,000 for ten years without interest, which is being returned by the withholding ten per cent. of the postage paid. The subsidies to the other steamship lines are on the same scale, having received a loan as part of their capital, and all are paid the amounts collected on mail matter which they carry.

Other chief lines start from Marseilles and run to the various Mediterranean ports, the French colonies of Algiers; and one of the finest appointed lines in the world, Méssageries Imperiale, runs direct to Alexandria and Port Said, through the Suez Canal, down the Red Sea, communicating with the French colonies off the east coast of Africa, and thence to the leading ports in the Indian Seas direct to the two or three points which yet remain in French possession, thence to Saigoon in Cambodia or Cochin China. The present terminus is Shanghai.

By means of these lines France is tapping the chief sources of commercial prosperity: North America, the West Indies and Central America, Africa, and Farther Asia.

There are besides the great lines indicated others which are also extending rapidly. From Hamburg and Bremen there are finely-appointed transatlantic lines, which receive aid in heavy charges for carrying mail matter from Great Britain and the United States, besides direct aid from the North German government. Austria and Italy both have lines sailing from Trieste and Vienna, and carrying the mails for Mediterranean ports. One or both these lines are pushing toward India and China. Holland has a regular line to and from her East Indian colonies, and Spain one also to the Phillipine Islands. All these governments see the advantages derived from development of the "through route" steamship system. Even Japan, just waking up to the influences of Western material progress, is encouraging the formation of a mercantile steam marine, and owns and employs in her own waters, and in trade with China, twenty first-class steamers, paying liberally for the transportation of the mails between her own ports and islands.

In striking contrast with the activity displayed by foreign nations, is the want of it manifested by our own. During the year ending June 30, 1869, there was paid by the United States, for ocean mail service, $1,101,674, of which amount $336,163 was paid to foreign companies.

We have but two lines of mail steamers running on the Atlantic. One, monthly, runs to Rio de Janeiro from New York, stopping at St. Thomas and Pernambuco, the other, Pacific Mail, from New York to Aspinwall, making weekly trips. On the Pacific side we have from Panama, one line to San Francisco, and from there to Yokohama, and Shanghai. From the same port there is a semi-monthly line to Honolulu, Sandwich Islands, one to Vancouver's Island, carrying the mails to Oregon, British Columbia, and the Puget Sound country, and one, semi-monthly, to Mazatlan, Mexico. In all not more than thirty steamships are employed in this service, of which the Pacific Mail have fourteen. The British Peninsula and Oriental Company alone employ forty-nine large vessels, forty-six of which are mail carriers for the East and Australia.

Thus it appears that our shipping has declined absolutely and relatively with that of other nations; that not only the carrying trade between foreign nations, but between our own and foreign countries; the business furnished by our exports and imports is being transferred to foreign bottoms; and last, and most important of all to our prestige as a maritime nation and our influence in the affairs of the world, that we have allowed other nations to possess themselves of the most important lines of steam navigation connecting distant parts of the globe.

In consequence of this decline of our shipping the business of ship-building in the United States is at the present time at a complete standstill. The yards are empty, the workmen out of employment, and what capital has survived the wreck of disaster is either idle or turned to other channels.

CAUSES OF DECLINE.

It has been urged by some that this depression of our navigation interests is the result of general causes, such as an over-production of tonnage and a depression in the business of the world.

But such causes, if existing, would be temporary in their operation. If the shipping of the world were temporarily in excess of the business of the world, the equilibrium would soon be restored by the natural decrease of ships and the ever-advancing increase of commercial business. The period of prosperity would, as it always has, speedily follow that of depression. The facts stated, however, show a decline of our navigation interests running through a decade—a period too long to be affected by a mere depression of business or any over-production of tonnage.

Moreover, the decline has been wholly in the shipping of the United States. While that of other nations has been *depressed* from the causes alluded to, there has not only been no absolute *decline*, but, as has been shown, a constant increase in tonnage and in the efficiency of their vessels. In 1868, there were built on the Clyde alone 197 vessels, of 169,571 tons, more than one-half of which were steamers. The total of tonnage built and registered in the United Kingdom in 1868 was 316,197 tons—a larger amount than was built in any one year prior to 1863.

It is obvious from the foregoing that the causes operating to produce the present condition of the navigation interest are special—such as affect American tonnage only—and, as your committee believe, may be readily ascertained.

The steady increase of our shipping engaged in the foreign trade up to the commencement of the rebellion, and the sudden and rapid decline from that point, leads directly to the conclusion that its decadence is attributable mainly, if not solely, to incidents of the war. According to the best available data, 919,466 tons of American shipping disappeared from our lists during the rebellion. Of this amount, 110,163 tons were destroyed by anglo-confederate pirates, while 803,303 tons were either sold to foreigners or passed nominally into their hands and obtained the protection of their flags. Here was an actual loss to the private owners of less than five per cent., and a loss to the nation of about thirty-seven per cent. of the total of American tonnage engaged in the foreign carrying trade. The loss of this amount of tonnage would not of itself have produced such disastrous results as we have seen had not the value of what remained been virtually destroyed by the peril in which it was placed from English piratical vessels sailing under the confederate flag. The risk of sailing under the American flag was so great as to divert a large share of the carrying trade into foreign bottoms, principally those of Great Britain.

That changes which have occurred in naval architecture and in the materials of which ships are now being constructed operated anterior to the rebellion, and tended to produce a revolution in the shipping of the world, is undoubtedly true. Iron, as a building material for ships, was fast superseding wood, and screw steamers were, as we have said, crowding out sail vessels on all ocean routes where the carrying of passengers and mails could be combined with the general freighting business. But it by no means follows that this revolution in the character of the mercantile marine of the world would, if peace had continued, have prevented us from maintaining with foreign nations our relative position as a great maritime power. Our people, with their sagacity, enterprise, and aptitude for mercantile and mechanical pursuits, would doubtless have perceived and availed themselves of the advantages resulting from this progress in nautical mechanics.

Having invented the steamship and first navigated the ocean with this class of vessels, and taken the lead of all nations in the science of naval architecture, we should, it may be safe to assume, have held our way against the world in competing for supremacy on the ocean, had not our attention been diverted from the pursuits of peace to the preservation of our national existence.

The war not only deprived us of the advantages resulting from this change in the character of commercial vessels and the currents of trade affected thereby, but gave an impetus to all business connected with ocean navigation, in the hands of our great commercial rival, and an advantage over us, that but for the war she would not have possessed. The business thus diverted into new channels could not be immediately regained by American vessels even under the most favorable circumstances. But the disastrous effects of the war did not cease with the return of peace. They were rather aggravated by the burdens of taxation which the war had left imposed upon all the industries of the country, but which operated with peculiar hardship upon this particular interest, inasmuch as it is subjected to the unrestricted competition of untaxed foreign rivals, and this competition must be met not only at home in our own ports, but in all parts of the world.

In a contest so unequal there can be but one result, and that is the total loss of our foreign carrying trade and the destruction of our merchant marine. Under such conditions as these it is as impossible to revive our shipping interests, unaided by the government, as it would be to build up our manufacturing interests by imposing a heavy tax upon all raw materials, and at the same time admitting all manufactured articles free of duty.

REMEDIES.

The fact that our commerce is rapidly disappearing from the ocean has been mathematically demonstrated. The causes which have brought it to this condition can be traced with considerable certainty, but the remedy for the evil, the means best calculated to restore it, are more difficult to discover and apply.

The committee, in endeavoring to find the best method of remedying the evil, have considered the following proposed plans of legislation in relation thereto, which have been urged upon its attention and received its careful consideration:

1. The readmission of the vessels which sought the protection of a foreign flag during the war to American registry.

2. The modification of our navigation laws so as to admit foreign-built vessels to American registry, either free of duty or on payment of a moderate duty on the tonnage of such vessels.

3. The allowance of a drawback on imported material which is used in the construction of vessels, or an equivalent to the drawback where American materials are used.

4. Permission to withdraw from bond stores to be consumed by vessels on voyages to foreign ports.

5. Exemptions of tonnage from all taxes other than by the federal government. And

6. The granting of such government aid, by way of postage on mails and by subsidies, as will insure the establishment of lines of Amirican ocean steamers to the principal foreign ports of the world, thereby enabling our citizens to participate in the profits of the trade created by such lines.

REGISTRATION OF FOREIGN-BUILT SHIPS.

Your committee are of opinion that the readmission to American registry of vessels placed under foreign flags during the rebellion is against sound public policy. To allow citizens to avail themselves of all the advantages conferred by our government during peace, and escape all the risks of supporting it during war, by placing their property at such times under the protection of a foreign government, would be a dangerous precedent to establish. Most of the vessels which changed their nationality were placed under the flag of a nation that, under the guise of neutrality, was making war upon our commerce for the benefit of its own. They identified their interest with those of our enemy, and obtained all the advantages resulting from such connection; to readmit them now to the same privileges accorded to vessels which adhered to the flag and fortunes of the country through all the perils and under all the disadvantages incident to the war, would be to encourage desertion in times when the country most needed the aid of its citizens.

The argument in favor of the policy of admitting foreign-built vessels to American registry is based upon the assumption that the change which has taken place in the character of commercial vessels from wood to iron, and from sail to steam vessels, has given to foreign nations, particularly to Great Britain, such advantages in regard to the cheap construction of this latter class of vessels, as to make it impossible for us to compete with her; and that we are reduced to the alternative of either purchasing our ships of her or of surrendering to her the carrying trade. It is further urged that this trade contributes so greatly to the wealth of a nation that we should secure it, by purchasing and sailing foreign-built ships; to which end it is necessary that all restrictions to the purchase of such ships should be removed from our statutes.

The opposite policy of allowing only American-built vessels the privilege of the American flag and register was adopted at the formation of the government, and has been uniformly adhered to since, modified only by the act of December 23, 1852, which permits foreign vessels wrecked in the waters of the United States, and repaired in our ports, the repairs amounting to two-thirds of the value, to take out an American register. The best proof of the wisdom of this policy is the rapid and uninterrupted progress which we attained as a commercial nation under its operations. Great Britain became the first maritime nation of the world under a like policy, which she never relaxed until her merchant marine was strengthened beyond danger.

In order to understand and appreciate the practical operation of the policy of admitting foreign-built ships to American registry, and its effects upon the national wealth, we must consider somewhat in detail the manner in which the shipping of a country—and particularly that of our own—is built up and maintained. The shipping of the United States has never been built, and only to a limited extent has it been owned, by capitalists, but by men of moderate means, the lumberman, the mechanic, the ship-master, and the merchant, each having an interest in the production, the sailing, and the freight of the ship, independent of the profits to be directly derived from its earnings.

The lumberman to make a market for his timber, the mechanic to obtain employment in constructing, the ship-chandler for sale of his goods in furnishing, the ship-master to obtain business in his profession, and the merchant to secure the commissions resulting from the management of the business, all unite in building, owning, and sailing vessels. To use the expression of Mr. Loring, a practical ship-carpenter, largely interested in building and owning vessels, who testified before the committee at Portland: "The whole parish are often interested in building and owning vessels."

This associated effort not only supplies the capital but the practical knowledge and experience to construct and manage this description of property successfully, and also furnishes an incentive to produce it far greater than that of mere interest on investment of capital alone.

By purchasing our ships in foreign countries we transfer not only all the labor necessary to construct them, from the taking of the timber from the forests, and the ore from the mines, to the launching of the ship, but also all the business of furnishing the outfits and supplies for the voyage. It is estimated that more than sixty per cent. of the tonnage of the United States engaged in the foreign carrying trade is engaged in freighting between the ports of foreign countries, and many of these vessels never return after sailing from our ports. What advantage would it be to our country to have the real or nominal ownership of this class of vessels, built, fitted, manned, and provisioned for their voyage in a foreign port, touching only at the ports of the United States to obtain an American register, and then pursuing their voyage, perhaps never to return? If such vessels were really wholly owned in the United States it could be of no advantage to us.

It would not be tonnage, the production of which would aid in furnishing profitable employment to American mechanics and American agriculturalists and help to increase our national wealth. It would not multiply comfortable cottages nor create thriving villages of industrious workmen around busy American ship-yards in time of peace. It would be simply the investment of American capital in property out of the country, the dividend from which only would be returned to us. It would give no strength in time of war. Representing capital alone, it would partake of the timidity of capital, and whenever danger threatened, seek safety under a neutral or hostile flag.

Still further, we cannot build up a truly American merchant marine in a foreign country, for the reason that the countries in which we build will have every advantage over us in competing for the carrying trade which is to sustain such a marine. First, in the profits of the business of building and fitting out the vessels. Second, in the command of cheap capital. Third, in combining the building, owning, and manging interests, which can only be done in the country where the shipping is built. And fourth, in the prestige such countries would obtain by furnishing the vessels which Americans would own, and also those which were to compete for the business with American-owned vessels. Furthermore, it is not probable that American capital would be sent to Europe to build ships with which to compete on equal terms for business with the ships of those who build for them, unless these foreign-built vessels were allowed to participate in our coasting trade—a change in our policy which would not only entirely destroy every branch of mechanical industry in the United States dependent upon ship-building, but would ruin the present owners of coasting vessels. It would be admitting to the enjoyment of American business foreigners who pay no taxes to the American government, and who, by virtue of that exemption, would be enabled to drive American tax-payers out of employment.

The policy of admitting foreign-built ships to American register, on payment of a duty, has also been urged. The committee cannot recommend such legislation, for whatever duty might be so imposed, would operate only to the advantage of the foreign ship-owner, with whom the American purchaser and owner of such foreign-built ships would have to compete. If we were to admit foreign-built ships to American register at all, it would be with the view of enabling our ship-owners to supply themselves with vessels at a rate as low as that paid by foreign competitors. An American ship-owner must in such case be able to purchase as cheap as the foreigner, or he must obtain better ships; otherwise he is deprived of that equality of ability to compete, which is an essential quality of the success desired by those who engage in the carrying trade of the world. The statement is in itself a sufficient answer to the proposition.

But there are other objections more weighty than those referred to, that should prevent the adoption of either policy. They would deprive us of the mechanical skill requisite to build our navy in time of war, or oblige us to maintain it at great expense connected with the government works in time of peace, and would also compel the maintenance of a large naval force entirely useless as a peace establishment, but necessary to preserve and defend the national honor and interests in case they were menaced. It would be humiliating, indeed, to every American to see Great Britain employed and paid by us to build shipping to replace that which she so effectively aided to destroy during the rebellion. If we adopt a policy that will admit of such results, that nation could well afford to pay our most extravagant demands upon her for damages inflicted by the cruisers which from her ports made war upon our commerce during the rebellion.

Every consideration, whether of interest or of national pride, impels us to build upon our own soil the ships which are to bear the flag of our country to all quarters of the globe.

This result can only be accomplished by adopting a policy as liberal and enlightened as that of the nations with which we are to compete for the carrying trade of the world, which nations are now in possession of the field.

Those nations admit all the material entering into the construction of vessels free of duty; they also allow the withdrawal from bond of all stores used on the voyage of a ship sailing to a foreign port, the same as though such stores were exported; and they pay liberally to steamers for carrying the mails, and thus establish lines to all parts of the world.

SUBSIDIES TO STEAMSHIPS.

The subsidies paid by Great Britain and France to establish their steamship lines, and for the promotion of their general shipping interests, are returned to them many fold by the nations that pursue a more narrow and short-sighted policy. It is the United States that supports the foreign steamships which run to and from her ports, by the mail, passenger, and freight money which she pays to them, rather than to establish lines of her own. Worse still, while we carefully scrutinize every appropriation for our own navy, we pay annually more to support this most efficient arm of the navy of Great Britain than is asked for the support of our own.

The testimony taken by the committee is nearly unanimous that by offering to our citizens the same encouragement and protection as is afforded by other commercial nations to their citizens, our shipping can be built and lines of ocean steamers established as fast as the requirements of business demand, and that there would be a present demand for ships if they could be cheaply supplied.

That although the cost of iron and some other materials would be higher by the amount paid for freight, and the wages of labor are also higher with us than in Europe, yet we should have an advantage in the cost of timber, a large amount of which is used, even in the construction of iron vessels; and that the higher rates paid for American labor would be more than counterbalanced by its greater efficiency and skill. This leads us to the difficult question, as to the methods in which government shall endeavor to extend its aid to our decaying navigation interests. Your committee, after the most careful deliberation, impressed with the great importance of restoring our commercial marine, not only as a means of increasing the national wealth in time of peace, but also as one of the most efficient agencies for national defence in time of war, respectfully recommend the following measures as calculated to promote the desired object:

First. The remission of the duties imposed upon the raw material entering into the construction of vessels and steamers, limiting the amount to the minimum of duties per ton collected on the material required for certain classes of vessels; and where American iron is used in the construction of iron vessels, an amount per ton equivalent to the duties on a like amount of imported raw materials, limiting the amount to be paid.

Second. That all stores to be used by vessels sailing to foreign ports may be taken in bond free of duty; and

Third. Further to encourage investment in shipping, and to extend the aid to ships already built, and which have been sailed during and since the rebellion at great disadvantage, allowing to all sail vessels and to all steamers running to the British North American Provinces, one dollar and fifty cents per ton; on steamers to European ports, four dollars per ton; and on all other steamers running to foreign ports, three dollars per ton.

In view of the fact that the tax upon tonnage cannot be removed without relieving the vessels of all foreign nations of the same, while no such exemption is extended to American vessels in foreign ports, and in view of the further fact that the shipping interest of the country is to receive some relief by the passage of the proposed measures, the committee recommend only the removal of all tonnage, harbor, pilotage, and other like taxes imposed upon shipping by State and municipal authority, (most of which taxes have been declared by the Supreme Court unconstitutional,) and the readjustment of the present tax upon tonnage, so that it will fall more equitably upon the different classes of vessels affected thereby. The amount which will be received from this source is estimated by the committee to be more than three million dollars per annum, and will to that extent contribute to the relief which is proposed to be granted in aid of the shipping interest of the United States. For the purpose of carrying out the foregoing recommendations, your committee report herewith two bills for consideration.

In reporting the bills referred to, your committee are hopeful that in case of their adoption the shipping interests of the country may derive very considerable relief. That they will fully meet the expectations of the large class of our citizens connected with this interest they do not expect. Nor have they full confidence that the result will be the speedy restoration of our lost commerce.

Time will be required to organize the capital and labor necessary to embark extensively in the business of constructing iron sail and steamships; and still greater inducements must be offered to insure the establishment of lines of American ocean steamers which will relieve us from our present humiliating and disgraceful dependency upon foreigners.

It is but a few days since that our government was reminded by the managers of the English lines of steamers, the Inman and Cunard, of the disgraceful fact, that not a single merchant steamer bearing the American flag now crossed the Atlantic, and that we were entirely dependent upon them for the transportation of our mails, which they carry under temporary arrangements, to be terminated at their pleasure. While our government has with lavish liberality, in subsidies of lands and money, aided in extending railways through the West, and have appropriated large sums for the improvement of interior water communications, our ocean navigation has been left without either aid or protection. The prosperity of the country in time of peace, as well as its security in time of war, is largely dependent upon an efficient merchant marine, and it is worthy of the consideration of Congress whether by granting such aid as will secure the building up of a large part of this marine, in swift ocean steamers, readily convertible into cruisers in time of war, we are not providing a most economical and efficient means of naval defense. It was stated by Admiral Porter, before this committee, that with a few such ships converted into war vessels at the breaking out of the rebellion, such a blockade of the southern coast could have been established as would have prevented the rebels from sending out a pound of cotton or obtaining supplies or munitions of war, and the rebellion would have been strangled almost at its birth. Who can compute the loss in lives and in money consequent upon the want of a few such ships?

It is evident that our future wars with any of the great powers must be upon the ocean, and with an enemy that must cross the ocean to attack us, and whose vulnerable point to assail is the population and wealth which he has scattered on every sea.

Great Britain has, as we have seen, adopted the policy of subsidizing her lines of ocean steamers, and the result is that she has doubled the efficiency of her navy, and at the same time added immensely to her national wealth. These subsidized ships are subject at all times to the demands of the government. Our government has no such source to draw from, and must consequently depend entirely upon a navy supported in peace, to be available in war.

It would even be a matter of economy if our government should build vessels adapted to the uses of commerce in time of peace, and readily convertible into fighting ships in time of war, giving the free use of such ships in time of peace to merchants who would take care of and use them until required for the national defense. Under such circumstances the government would be relieved of the cost of taking care of the ships when not required for the public service, and the national wealth would be increased by their use for mercantile purposes. As the government can have the control of such vessels when needed, by paying only a small percentage of their cost, is it not clearly a matter of economy and sound public policy to legislate with a view to such results?

The policy here suggested, in regard to extending government aid to establish lines of steamers, should be entered upon only after such careful and thorough consideration of the whole subject as will lead to the adoption of a comprehensive system that will be permanent in its character and certain to secure the desired results.

Your committee have only had time to consider the general question relating to navigation interests, and leave this particular branch of the subject to be reported upon after considering fully the various bills relating thereto referred to them by the House.

OUR RIVER AND RAILWAY NAVIGATION.

The vast navigable rivers and extensive lines of railway of our country are so intimately connected with the subjects of ocean steam navigation that your committee cannot refrain from alluding to them in concluding this report.

The continental position and geographical features of this republic, lying in the direct route between Europe and Asia, washed on either shore by the two great oceans of the world, and interlaced with a vast net-work of interior navigable waters, affords in itself the grandest of all possible incentives toward determining the granting of such legitimate aid as may be accorded in the effort to revive our shipping interests, as well as to achieve that supreme maritime leadership to which we may reasonably aspire.

Our natural advantages are still further aided by the artificial means which scientific and material enterprise has afforded through the development of the railroad system, especially of those great lines which connect the Atlantic and the Pacific, and which, with their branches, are to intersect the whole territory between those oceans. They are like so many mighty rivers, furnishing capacity for unlimited transportation.

The mail route from London to Eastern Asia lies across the American continent, and passengers and valuable freights such as the trade of China and Japan provides will pass over the same lines. Yokohama, the principal port in Japan, and Shanghai and Hong Kong, in China, are all nearer in time and distance to London via New York and San Francisco than via the newly opened route of the Suez Canal.

The following comparative distances between London and New York and some of the principal ports of Eastern Asia illustrate the advantages of our position:

London to Yokohama (Japan) via Suez Canal	11,509
London to Yokohama (Japan) via New York and San Francisco	10,000
New York to Yokohama (Japan) via Pacific railroad and San Francisco	7,520
San Francisco to Yokohama (Japan) per steamer	4,520
London to Shanghai via Suez Canal	10,469
New York to Shanghai via Pacific railroad and San Francisco	8,555
San Francisco to Shanghai per steamer	5,555
Chicago to Yokohama	6,900

St. Louis about same distance as Chicago.

Nothing in the future is more certain than that the foreign importations of the West are to be made directly to her chief commercial cities, and distributed therefrom as they now are from the ports of the seaboard. The railways which are to supply them in part are but in their infancy, and by means of improvements yet to be introduced may ere long be able to compete successfully with steam transportation by water. Through such improvements, the routes across our continent, already the most direct, may become the cheapest routes from London to China and Japan. Between the western termini of these routes and the lands that are washed by the Pacific and Indian Oceans, nature has provided free of cost a great highway, which we have only to occupy with vehicles of transportation. No mountain barriers are to be scaled or leveled to reach them.

Those Asiatic countries are teeming with a busy, industrious population, skilled in the mechanic arts, and adepts in the science of agriculture. Abounding in wealth, with extensive internal, and little external commerce, their trade has been the prize for which all commercial nations have for centuries contended. The trade of the more important of these countries, India, China, and Japan, Great Britain now draws to herself, and distributes again from her stores to the rest of the world.

The silver products of the mines of America make nearly the circuit of the world to reach, via Great Britain, the countries of the East, while the products of those countries come back to America by the same circuitous route.

These far Eastern countries are at our very doors; their relations with us more friendly than with any other nation; their trade is at our command, if we will but stretch forth our hand and take it.

The advantages to result from the revival of our commerce and navigation, and especially from our obtaining possession of the Pacific trade, are confined to no one section of the country. With the Sandwich Islands in our possession, and by the adoption of a wise and liberal commercial policy, we can control the trade of Eastern Asia and the commerce of the Pacific, and pour their wealth directly into the valley of the Mississippi, which is to be the center of population in the future of our country. Chicago, St. Louis, and other cities of the West are, as we have said, to become ports of entry, and distributors of the products of Asia as well as of Europe. Thus, the great West has the same interest in reviving and maintaining the ocean commerce of our country under the American flag that the Atlantic States have in opening up internal lines of commerce, whether by the building of great lines of railway, or by the improvement of lake or river navigation.

Shall we, after having expended millions in opening this opportunity of controling the commerce of the world by uniting the two great oceans that wash the opposite shores of the continent—after astonishing the world by our energy and wisdom in carrying through such a gigantic commercial enterprise while in an armed struggle for national existence—surprise it still more by our supineness and folly in neglecting to avail ourselves of the greater advantages which nature has opened to us without cost?

JOHN LYNCH.
JAS. BUFFINGTON.
CADWALADER C. WASHBURN.
GILES W. HOTCHKISS.
DAN'L J. MORRELL.
HERVEY C. CALKIN.
ERASTUS WELLS.

Mr. LYNCH, from the Select Committee on the Causes of the Reduction of American Tonnage, reported the following bill:

A BILL to revive the navigation and commercial interests of the United States.

Whereas the mercantile marine of the country was nearly destroyed during the late rebellion in consequence of the inability of the government to protect it; and now, while bearing its share of taxation, has no such protection from foreign competition as is afforded to other great national interests and industries, and is therefore steadily declining; and whereas the restoration of our commercial marine, constituting as it does, one of the most efficient means of defense in time of war, is of great national importance and essential to the maintenance of our position as a first-class power: Therefore,

Be it enacted by the Senate and House of Representatives of the United States of America in Congress assembled, That upon all imported lumber, timber, hemp, Manila, and composition metal, and upon iron not advanced beyond plates, rod bars and bolts, which may be used and wrought up into the construction of steam or sail vessels built in the United States, whether for the hull, rigging or equipment, or machinery of such vessels, there shall be allowed and paid by the Secretary of the Treasury, under such regulations as he may prescribe, a drawback equal to the duties which may have been paid on such material: *Provided,* That the amount of such drawback shall not exceed on wooden vessels, eight dollars per ton; on iron vessels, twelve dollars per ton; on vessels known as composite, that is, vessels composed of iron frames and wooden planking and sheathing, ten dollars per ton; on wooden steamers, ten dollars per ton; on composite steamers, composed of iron frames and wooden planking, twelve dollars per ton; on iron steamers, fifteen dollars per ton: *And provided further,* That where American material is used in the construction of iron or composite vessels or steamers, there shall be allowed and paid, as aforesaid, an amount equivalent to the duties imposed on similar articles of foreign manufacture when imported, the full allowance on American and foreign materials not to exceed the amounts per ton, on vessels of each class respectively, hereinbefore specified.

SEC. 2. *And be it further enacted,* That all ship stores and coal, to be used and consumed by any vessel on its voyage from any port of the United States to any foreign port, may, in such quantity and under such regulations as the Secretary of the Treasury may prescribe, be taken in whole packages in bond, and disposed of for such purposes, free of import and internal duty and tax.

SEC. 3. *And be it further enacted,* That the owner of any American registered sail or steam vessel which shall be engaged for more than six months in the year in the carrying trade between American and foreign ports, or between the ports of foreign countries, shall, at the end of each fiscal year in which such vessel has been so engaged, be paid by the collector of the port where such vessel is registered, upon exhibiting satisfactory evidence, in form to be prescribed by the Secretary of the Treasury, that such vessel has been so engaged, upon every sail vessel, one dollar and fifty cents for each registered ton; and upon every steamer running to and from the ports of the North American Province, one dollar and fifty cents for each registered ton; and upon every steamer running to and from any European port, four dollars for each registered ton; and upon every steamer running to and from all other foreign ports, three dollars for each registered ton.

Mr. LYNCH, from the Select Committee on the Causes of the Reduction of American Tonnage, reported the following bill:

A BILL imposing tonnage duties, and for other purposes.

Be it enacted by the Senate and House of Representatives of the United States of America in Congress assembled, That in lieu of all duties on tonnage now imposed by law, a duty of thirty cents per ton is hereby imposed on all ships, vessels, or steamers entered in the United States; but the receipts of vessels paying such tax shall not be subject to the tax provided in section one hundred and three of an act approved June thirty, eighteen hundred and sixty-four, nor by any act amendatory thereof: *Provided,* That no ship, vessel, or steamer having a license to trade between different district of the United States, or to carry on the bank, whale, or other fisheries, and no vessel or steamer to or from any port or place in Mexico, or from any port or place south of Mexico, down to and including Aspinwall and Panama, or from any port or place in the British Provinces of North America, or the West India Islands, and employed regularly in these trades and no others, shall be required to pay the tonnage tax contemplated by this act more than once in each fiscal year.

SEC. 2. *And be it further enacted,* That no harbor dues, pilotage fees, or other taxes on imports levied, or pretended to be levied, on the tonnage, merchandise, trade, imports, or cargoes of any vessel, by virtue of the authority of any State or municipal government, except wharfage, pierage, and dockage, shall be collected; and the collection of, or attempt to collect the same, or any portion thereof, shall be a penal offense, to be punished as hereafter provided.

SEC. 3. *And be it further enacted,* That any person who, by virtue of any authority or pretended authority derived under any State or municipal government, shall collect any such illegal tax, fees, or dues, or shall attempt to collect the same, shall, upon the conviction of each offense, be fined in a sum not exceeding one hundred dollars for each offense, the amount of which fine shall be paid into the Treasury of the United States to the credit of the judiciary fund, and he shall further be liable to pay a sum not exceeding double the amount of the illegal taxes, fees, or dues thus collected, or attempted to be collected, one-half to be paid to the informer, and the other to be placed to the credit of the appropriation for light-houses.

SEC. 4. *And be it further enacted,* That any captain or master of a vessel, or any other person being the duly authorized agent of any vessel, line of vessels, or transportation company, who shall pay, with or without protest, any such illegal taxes, fees, or dues as are prohibited by this act, may recover the sum from the person collecting the same by action in appropriate form in the district court of the United States of the district where the collection was made, and the courts of the United States shall have full jurisdiction in all cases arising under this act.

NAVIGATION INTERESTS.

TESTIMONY TAKEN BY THE COMMITTEE.

NEW YORK, *October* 14, 1869.

The committee met in a room in the custom-house.

Present: The chairman, Messrs. Buffinton, Morrell, Wells, Calkin, and Holman.

The chairman stated the objects for which the committee was appointed, and said that he had been notified that committees had been appointed by the Ship-owners' and Ship-builders' Associations, of New York, to present the views of those associations, and that the committee would now be pleased to hear from the New York associations.

The New York Ship-owners' Association was represented by Messrs. Gustavus A. Brett, Edward Hincken, Ambrose Snow, James W. Elwell, William Nelson, jr., and Allston Wilson.

Mr. HINCKEN, as one of the representatives of the New York Ship-owners' Association, stated that there were one hundred and eighty members on the rolls of that association, and that almost every man owning a ship in the city of New York was represented by the association. The matter before the committee had been discussed by that association, and it believed that there was but one salvation for the shipping trade, and that that consisted in Congress permitting the purchase of ships where they could be bought cheapest. He thought that, with one or two exceptions, that was the unanimous opinion of the ship-owners of New York. The ship-builders of Maine would present their own views of the case. The ship-owners saw no other means of competing with foreign nations for the carrying trade unless they could buy their ships in the same market. The cost of sailing-ships, after they came under the American flag, would be greater than their cost would be to foreign ship-owners; but it was believed that the ship-owners of America had sufficient energy, enterprise, and ability to overcome that difference, just as the ship-builders of Maine thought that they could overcome the difference in the cost of labor, &c., if the materials that entered into the building of their ships were free of duty. The ship-owners of New York were for buying their tools where they could buy them cheapest, because a ship was but a tool, and it was the only tool that was prohibited from being imported. As to the amount of duty that was to be paid on imported ships, that would be a question for Congress to decide. They claimed as carriers that they ought to have the right, if the carrying trade of the country was of any advantage, to buy their tools wherever they could buy them cheapest. England had bought her ships here when she could not build them so cheaply herself; but England was now building iron ships, and France and Germany and Belgium were buying their ships in England. Before the French had entered into this commerce there were sixteen regular packets running from New York, which sailed as regularly as the day of sailing came round, whether they were full or not full. But what was the case now? The house which he (Mr. Hincken) represented was the sole survivor of four similar houses, and it was reduced to two ships. The trade of France had gone into foreign steamers. And why? Because American houses could not buy and sail foreign-built vessels. Certainly, they might go to England and buy steamers and run them under the English flag; but he asked that those vessels should be allowed to run under the American flag, if there was any national importance attached to the fact that the carrying trade of the country should be done under the American flag.

The CHAIRMAN. Cannot ships be built in the United States as cheaply as in Europe, provided the materials used in the construction are obtained free of duty?

Mr. HINCKEN. I only know by what our ship-builders say—that, if they had the materials duty free, they would compete with the cheaper labor on the other side; but they could not compete with the greater cost of the materials. I am told that England allows drawbacks on everything that enters into the construction of ships, and I know that she does upon ship stores. If I take a cask of sugar out of the custom-house in this city, it will cost five or six dollars for custom-house fees besides the duty, whereas in England such stores are admitted free of duty and of fees; so that this operates very much against American navigation interests. There is no provision for so provisioning ships under our revenue laws.

Mr. AMBROSE SNOW, also representing the New York Ship-owners' Association, said that, as to the matter of cost of building ships, that could be very well explained by the gentlemen who would come before the committee as builders, but that he and the gentlemen with him, representing the Ship-owners' Association, confined themselves simply to the difficulties that they met in the prosecution of their business. They were prepared to answer any questions that might be put to them in that connection.

The CHAIRMAN said that he had asked the last question because he supposed that the gentlemen who were members of the Ship-owners' Association knew the relative cost of building vessels on both sides of the Atlantic.

Mr. SNOW remarked that they were all more or less familiar with it, but that they were disposed to confine themselves to the difficulties which they had to contend with as ship-owners, and to the condition of the ship-owning interest. It was very apparent that the foreigner was taking away that trade, and they had cast about to see where the trouble lay. They could see that there was no way for them to compete with the foreigner, unless they were able to buy ships as cheaply as foreigners bought them, and they had settled down on the proposition that a free navigation law, similar to the law passed in England some twenty years ago, was what would relieve the ship-owners of the United States. It seemed rather paradoxical that the ship-owner who was interested in protection should at the same time be in favor of free trade. The ship-owners of the United States had now the whole coasting trade, and yet they asked for free trade in their ships. It might seem natural for them to oppose free trade, but they did not; they found that every nation in the world was encouraging free trade in ships; they found that all nations had been forced, from one cause or another, to recognize that their interests lay in that sort of free trade. The ship-owners of New York had had a great deal of discussion on the subject, and they had come to the conclusion that a free navigation law, similar to the law passed in England some twenty years ago, would relieve the shipping interest more than any other thing. If American ship-builders could compete with foreign ship-builders upon the allowance of a drawback, then the free navigation law which the ship-owners advocated would not hurt the ship-builders. The question was not so much one of building wooden ships in Maine as it was a question of occupying the ocean routes, which he compared to railroad routes. The route of the Peninsular and Oriental Steamship Company, which started from Southampton, touching at Marseilles, and which went from Marseilles to Alexandria, then across the Isthmus of Suez, then down the Red Sea and to Hong Kong, and from Hong Kong across to San Francisco, and from San Francisco to Panama, and then back to Southampton, making a complete circuit of the world, might be considered as a railroad track round the world. That company was putting on just as many steamers as could be employed in the trade, and was thus absorbing the trade. As American ship-owners could not build ships to compete with such companies, they held that free trade in ships should be made the law, so that they could buy ships where they could buy them cheapest. Another line of ships, starting from Southampton and touching at Bordeaux and the Canary Islands, going thence to Valparaiso, was taking possession of those avenues of trade. This was almost like laying a railroad track across a continent. Once a railroad track was laid to San Francisco, there was not any great encouragement toward laying another railroad track near it. The New York ship-owners were simply asking for a law to enable them to occupy, as it were, railroad tracks across the Atlantic Ocean, and they had settled down to the belief that the only relief which they should ask from Congress was the passage of a free navigation law. He remembered very well the passage of a similar law in England some twenty years ago. He recollected very well the discussion on that law. The ship-owning interest had opposed it very much. They had said that England, of all other nations, should keep the shipping trade to herself. She had her colonies then the same as she had now, and could build cheap ships. She had a very large colonial trade, and the English government opened the whole of that trade to competition. And yet, during the twenty years since then, the English shipping trade had increased enormously, so that that navigation law proved to be one of the most beneficial measures of legislation. If Great Britain were to do with this country what this country was doing with her, and refuse to Americans a participation in her colonial trade, American ship-owners would be obliged to put a large portion of the ships they now own under the British flag, in order to get employment for them. The conclusion that American ship-owners had come to was, that unconditional free trade in ships was what they must have.

Mr. MORRELL. Do you not think it better that we should, if possible, build our ships in this country?

Mr. SNOW. We have thought of that a good deal, and there are many gentlemen, particularly ship-builders, who entertain that opinion.

Mr. MORRELL. Will it not in the end be likely to produce the same result as it produced in England, namely, build up an interest which will eventually cheapen the cost of ships? The proposition seems to me, so far, rather beneficial to English ship-builders and English interests than in favor of American interests and American ship-builders.

Mr. SNOW. If American ships could be built cheaper than English ships, we admit that that would be a help. We also think that a bonded warehouse system, such as they have in England, would be of much advantage to us. Prior to the war, and prior to having any internal revenue tax upon our goods, we did not feel the want of a bonded warehouse system; but now we do. If a ship is taking among her stores a barrel of whisky, for instance, instead of buying it here out of bond, at cost price and free of duty, she has to go to England and buy it there; because there she can get it free of duty and here she cannot. In England, all ships going abroad take their stores out of bond free of duty, which lessens very much the cost of the outfit of the ship. Here there is no such provision, and we need it very much. We have thought that such a system might be inaugurated here with a great deal of profit. The trade of ship-chandlers in this city has been almost ruined by the difference between the two countries. It would take four hundred sailing ships of one thousand tons each to do the work which the European lines of steamers to this port now do; and those steamers buy nothing here except their fresh stores. They buy in their own ports our products which go from here abroad, because they get them cheaper than they can get them here. It will be seen that the laws governing our commerce in this respect require modification. They require first-class talent to be brought to their examination, and they require complete modification. It is the defect in our laws that is putting us behind other nations in the carrying trade. A few years ago American ships always got the preference in fine goods and fabrics going to the East; but now American ships get no fine goods for trade; they get nothing but the coarsest articles. In England, ship-building has been so much improved that England is now a first-class nation in the carrying trade. Heretofore, in the cotton ports, our ships always got one-sixteenth of a penny per pound more than English ships did; but now we do not get any such preference.

Mr. MORRELL. That is to be attributed to the introduction of steam, is it not?

Mr. SNOW. No, sir; it is to be attributed to the improvement that the English have made in the building of their ships. From being a first-class carrying nation we have become a second or third-class carrying nation.

The CHAIRMAN remarked to Mr. Snow that he supposed that in the matter of ship stores the disadvantage was one more to the general trade than to ship-owners especially.

Mr. WELLS inquired as to the relative cost of iron ships and wooden ships.

Mr. BRETT, one of the committee of the New York Ship-owners' Association, remarked that he found that question answered in the New York Times of this morning, in a letter from a correspondent, who was sent to Europe for the purpose of inquiring into the ship-building business. He (Mr. Brett) read a portion of the letter, and asked that it be incorporated in the proceedings of the committee.

As the author of this letter was not before the committee, it was not deemed proper to introduce an anonymous paper into the report.

Mr. HINCKEN replied that it affected ship-owners also, and that if the disbursement bills of foreign ships at this port were examined it would be seen that their disbursements for ship stores were confined to articles of positive necessity. Ship-owners would buy wherever they found stores the cheapest.

The CHAIRMAN. The point is, whether an American master provisioning his ship in a foreign port is placed upon the same footing as the masters of vessels belonging to that nation?

Mr. HINCKEN replied that he was. American ship-masters bought their ship stores abroad on the same terms as foreign ship-masters. In regard to the building of iron ships in this country, he remarked that it would not do to suppose that they could be built here at first as good and as cheap as they were now built upon the Clyde. The first building of them here would necessarily be an experiment, and very few ship-owners were willing to try that experiment.

Mr. MORRELL. Do you not consider it an advantage that we should acquire the skill and facility to build iron ships here?

Mr. HINCKEN. Certainly.

Mr. MORRELL. Would it not be better for us to so legislate as to make that possible, rather than to drive our ship-owners abroad to obtain ships?

Mr. HINCKEN. I believe it would be much better if we could so legislate that ships could be built here; but it would take four or five years to acquire that facility in building iron ships as cheap and as good as they are now built on the Clyde, and that period of four or five years might be very fatal to the interests of commerce in this country.

Mr. BRETT read a letter which he had received some time since from a very intelligent ship-master, and which had been recently published in the Journal of Commerce, of New York.

The letter is as follows:

SAN FRANCISCO, *September* 10, 1869.

DEAR SIR: As an old friend, I take the liberty of writing you a few lines in regard to a matter in which I know you take a deep interest—that is, our "shipping." I see that the Ship-owners' Society of New York, of which you are a prominent member, have made a movement, which I hope will lead to the repeal of the navigation laws; laws so ancient that the far-famed "oldest inhabitant" does not remember when they were made. That our shipping interest has declined no one will deny. The cause, most ascribe to the war; but I do not think this a correct assumption. The war I consider an accessary after the fact only. The main cause for the decline of our shipping interest I ascribe to the wording of our reciprocity treaties and the existence of our navigation laws. Many years ago Congress passed an act admitting into our ports, on the same terms as American vessels, the vessels of all foreign nations that would extend to us the same privilege in their ports. By the wording of these treaties foreign nations are allowed to bring into our ports, on reciprocal terms with an American vessel, all vessels sailing under their flag. Now the American is not allowed, by his government to hoist the United States flag on any but an American-built ship, and at the present day all foreign nations allow their subjects to nationalize vessels without regard to where they are built, whether at home or in a foreign country; and these vessels can then enter a United States port on the same terms as an American-built vessel. If when these treaties were made our *diplomats* had understood the matter in hand, they would have considered that as the American flag could only be hoisted (legally) on an American bottom, so must reciprocity exact the same of the foreigner, and only those foreign vessels be admitted to reciprocity that were built in the country of the flag under which they sailed.

As the case now stands the Hamburger can go to England or Scotland, buy a steamer, put her under the North German flag, and run her between any foreign port and any port in the United States with all the privileges of and in effect as an American vessel. This with the consent of our own government. At the same time the American is not allowed by his laws to purchase this steamer and hoist on her the American flag And even gives the Hamburger further encouragement by giving him the European mails to carry from our country. Here we see our government, by its laws and acts, encouraging foreigners, to the detriment of its own citizens. I suppose no one will dispute at this time that iron steamers are much better than those built of wood, for ocean navigation, as regards strength, speed, capacity, and economy. The high cost of iron steamers and vessels in the United States precludes our building them, and if not allowed by our government to purchase them abroad, we must go without them and see all foreign-carrying trade pass out of our hands. Ship-owners can, and have the right to, demand of our government that they be placed by our laws on the same equality as the foreigner, or else that the reciprocity laws be repealed, and no vessel of any nation or flag be allowed to come into our ports on terms of reciprocity, unless it be those built in the country of the flag under which they sail. Almost all the iron steamers or sailing vessels are built in Great Britain; they can be built much cheaper there than in any other country. A first-class iron ship, to class A 1 for twenty years, with an East India outfit, which includes two suits of sails, three bower chains and anchors, and in fact everything belonging to the ship, except provisions and cabin stores, can be built for £14 10*s*. per ton register, and guaranteed to carry one and a half tons weight per register ton; also to attain a speed of twelve knots. The insurance on such a ship out to Calcutta and back is two and a half per cent. I know you are fully aware of the advantage of iron in the construction of ships, and I merely mention the above as facts that have come under my own observation. There is another matter I would wish to call to your notice. Last summer Mr. Seward made an arrangement with Great Britain whereby vessels under that flag could enter at the custom-house in the United States under their English register and not be remeasured, American ships to enter the customs in England under their American register. This is another example of the smartness of our *diplomats*. Now, in England American ships almost invariably measure less than they do (honestly) at home. For instance, the Norway, that I now command, measures in England 1,983 tons; United States register says 2,107 tons, a difference of 124 tons. By this American register now dock dues, pilotage, steam hire, &c., are paid, and our government, in its great desire to reciprocate with foreign nations, obliges me to pay the above dues on 124 tons more than I ought or would, provided the above arrangement had not been made. The Ne Plus Ultra, that I commanded before this ship, was 1,534 tons American and 1,450 English; and, if necessary, I could give you many other instances of the same kind. I complained to the English officials, but they told me to go to my own government; it was it that made the arrangement. To that I could make no reply. I was really in hopes that when we got a new Secretary of State it would be one who knew how to make a bargain, and who would get value equal to what he gave. Of Hamilton Fish I have not much hope. All our laws relating to seamen abroad want revising as they now stand. Consuls can do as they please, and ship-masters are obliged to submit.

Excuse this, if uninteresting, for the good of the cause.

With many regards, I remain yours, truly,

J. T. WOODBERRY.

G. A. B., Esq.

The CHAIRMAN. It has been a question with some whether we really sail our vessels as cheaply as foreign vessels are sailed, on account of our higher-priced provisions and higher wages to officers and men. I want to get at the views of you, gentlemen, as to whether we do not really stand on the same footing with foreign vessels in that regard, as we have the privilege of buying at foreign ports, and as foreign vessels are subject to the same disadvantages as American vessels in buying at American ports; in other words, whether that thing does not equalize itself, and whether we do not really provision our vessels as cheaply as foreigners provision theirs; and also, whether we do not man them nearly as cheaply as they do, we having the privilege of manning our vessels with foreign crews to a certain extent the same as they have.

Mr. SNOW. When our vessels are in the same trade as foreign vessels, of course we have the same facilities in those respects. If a foreign vessel was in our port bound from here to an English port, she would have no advantage which our vessels would not have; but if we are fitting out a ship to go from here to the East Indies, we cannot take out of bond, duty free, the ship stores that we want for that voyage, but we have to pay internal revenue tax upon them; whereas an English ship going to the East Indies would provision herself duty free.

The CHAIRMAN. Suppose, for instance, that an American line of steamers or of sailing vessels were running between Liverpool and New York, with an English line running alongside of it, would not both buy their stores in England at the same rates?

Mr. SNOW. Certainly.

Mr. CHAIRMAN. And both would buy on this side at the same rates?

Mr. SNOW. Certainly.

The CHAIRMAN. The vessels of both lines are assumed to be in port and out of provisions the same number of times. Are they not, therefore, really equal in respect to the purchase of ship stores, except in their first outfit?

Mr. SNOW. I presume so.

The CHAIRMAN. Then the cost of provisions is, in the long run, no greater to an American vessel than to an English vessel?

Mr. SNOW. That is so when they are trading between here and England, but it is not so when they are trading between here and Rio Janeiro, or Buenos Ayres, or Havana. The vessels that get their stores here do not get them free of duty, whereas the English vessels going to those ports get their stores free of duty. I grant you that when trading directly to England, American vessels would be on the same footing precisely as English vessels.

The CHAIRMAN. But the foreign and American vessels that pursue the same trade stand on precisely the same footing?

Mr. SNOW. Precisely; if English ships were running from here to Havana, they would be on the same footing precisely as American ships in the same trade. As to ship-building, capital is being diverted from that branch of industry to something else. Take an eastern ship-building town where the people have been in the habit of investing their capital in ships. They find now that that business has become unremunerative, and little by little, as their ships are sold off, their capital is diverted into something else, and the town ceases ultimately to be a ship-owning town. There are towns in Maine that have ceased to be ship-owning towns in consequence of the depression in commerce. When you do not protect the ship-owner, the ship-builder has no market, and the matter of first importance is to make a market. If you want to protect the ship-builders, there must be somebody for them to sell to. Now, if all the capital is driven out of that business and diverted into other channels, most of the people engaged in ship-building will in ten years have gone out of the business; the father will die and the sons will not be brought up in it. If it is a matter of importance that our commerce shall be retained, something must be done for that purpose sooner than it can be done by the means of granting drawbacks to the builders.

The CHAIRMAN. If you buy your ships as cheap, can you sail them in competition with foreign ship-owners?

Mr. SNOW. I think we can; there is no doubt of it; but if we want to run a line of steamers between here and England, in competition with the English, we must have vessels fully equal to theirs in every respect. They recently built two steamers in Boston which cost fourteen hundred thousand dollars. One of them went one voyage, and the other never has been at sea. One of the owners talked with me the other day about buying those ships at six hundred thousand dollars. He said to me that if I would take a half interest in them, he would take the other half, and I could keep the management of them and run them in the Liverpool trade. Now that seemed to be a very good opening, the ships being cheaper than English ships; but I venture to say that you cannot run those ships by the side of the existing lines of steamships, because you would have to contend with all the adverse influences that would be brought to bear by the first-class iron ships in that trade. That is the position we are brought to. There is no use in looking at it in any other way.

The CHAIRMAN. Could not that be on account of the want of adaptation of those ships to that particular business?

Mr. SNOW. They are very fine wooden ships; but those foreign ships occupy the ground. You cannot, for instance, put another line of railroad alongside of the Pacific railroad after the present line has got the start. Any other company going in would have to meet with so many disadvantages, as would be ruinous to them.

The CHAIRMAN. You mean that a regularly established line has advantages?

Mr. SNOW. Yes, it has all the advantages. But what I wish to impress upon the mind of the committee is, that we are letting foreign ship-owners take possession of all those routes, and that when once they have possession, we cannot, even though we may get vessels as cheap or cheaper than theirs, cut inside of them with any prospect of success.

The CHAIRMAN. Does that apply to the general freighting business as well as to established lines of steamers?

Mr. SNOW. Not so much; but a general revolution in business has been going on, and we are being run out of the business. We are sailing wooden ships, and cannot participate in the business of running iron ships.

Mr. MORRELL. Are these Boston ships unfit to enter into competition with foreign vessels?

Mr. SNOW. We build the finest wooden vessels. When the Cunard folks withdrew their line to Boston, the Boston people felt a great deal of pride in having a line of their own, and they built those two ships, hoping to get a subsidy from the government, and intending to build other ships, and to have a successful line.

Mr. WELLS. Are not the English steamers that are running here mostly subsidized by the English government?

Mr. SNOW. No, sir; there are a few lines subsidized by the government. Speaking of subsidies, our ship-owners, as a rule, would oppose with all their influence any subsidy, because it would be building up the interests of a few to the prejudice of a great many. In England they have subsidized steamers, and the result has been, perhaps, up to this time, profitable; but subsidies would not be favored by the ship-owning interest in this country.

The CHAIRMAN. I understand you to give it as your opinion, that in the general freighting business, if an American ship-owner could procure his ships as cheaply as the foreign ship-owners procure theirs, he could run them in competition with foreigners, except in regard to those established lines?

Mr. SNOW. I would not individually go so far as to say what we could do in that way; but after all the discussion that we have had on the subject, we have come to the conclusion that if there is anything that will help us, this one thing is what will help us, namely, giving us the benefit of free trade in ships. I do not believe that ship-owners generally claim to be sure that that would relieve them entirely. It is possible that the foreigner, having still other advantages, may do better than we can do, but we have faith to suppose that we should compete successfully with foreigners in that trade. We want a law giving us the privilege of purchasing where we can purchase cheapest. There is no other nation in the world that does not purchase ships wherever she can purchase them to the best advantage.

Mr. WELLS. Do you believe that a drawback of the small duty of twenty per cent. or ten per cent. on materials entering into ship-building would remedy the evil?

Mr. SNOW. I think it would help.

Mr. BRETT expressed the belief that if American ship-owners could procure their vessels as cheaply as foreigners do they could compete successfully with any foreign line. Although it cost more to sail American vessels, still, the superiority of the American ship-masters was more than an equivalent for that. He mentioned the case of an Austrian vessel which recently arrived at this port, taking one hundred and twenty-nine days to come from Bordeaux. She was manned by Austrians, who received only $8 a month, her captain receiving only $40 a month;

whereas American crews received from $25 to $30 a month, and an American captain from $125 to $150 a month. But with all that difference in the cost of running, he believed that the American vessels could compete with foreign vessels, on account of the greater activity and intelligence of the Yankee officers and seamen.

The CHAIRMAN. Let me ask you if that same superiority is not manifested by American mechanics and workmen?

Mr. BRETT replied that it was. He said that mechanics in this country now demanded five dollars a day for their labor, whereas in England they obtained only five shillings sterling a day; and he thought that, having to pay five dollars a day for skilled workmen in the building of ships, American ship-builders could not successfully compete with English ship-builders. That was the reason why the Ship-owners' Association asked the privilege of buying vessels where they could buy them cheapest, and of having such vessels, when purchased, navigated under the American flag.

The CHAIRMAN. What I want to get at is whether, although American labor costs more than foreign labor, its greater efficiency does not overcome the difference in the rate of wages.

Mr. BRETT. Our labor is no better, so far as mechanical skill and work are concerned, than it is in England.

The CHAIRMAN. But do not our workmen accomplish more in the same time.

Mr. BRETT. No; English laborers do more work. They work a greater number of hours, and do much more labor in a day than the mechanics in our yards do, because our workmen are so independent that unless the boss allows them all the privileges which they demand, they immediately knock off work and go to some other yard; and the demand for skilled labor in this country is so great that we cannot successfully compete with England.

Mr. MORRELL. Is that the case in the ship-building business?

Mr. BRETT. It is.

Mr. MORRELL. Then I would infer from that that the ship-building business is not so very much depressed.

Mr. BRETT. So far as this city is concerned, our ship-workmen demand the same rate of wages that they did during the war.

Mr. HAYDEN, of Bath, Maine, representing the ship-building interest of Maine, addressed the committee in reference to the question of obtaining ship stores free of duty, and as to whether that privilege was reciprocal between other nations and ours. So far as the direct trade between this country and England was concerned, he admitted that the advantages were reciprocal, but showed that in regard to the trade from New Orleans, Savannah, Norfolk, and other southern ports, the advantages were not reciprocal. American vessels going to those ports had to pay duty upon all their stores, whereas British vessels going to British ports had their stores free of duty, and came directly into competition with American vessels for the freights from those ports. The advantage, therefore, was evidently with the foreign vessels, and against American vessels. So it was with the trade to Cuba, and the West Indies, South America, and all over the world, except in the direct line from this country to England.

Mr. BRETT read to the committee a resolution which he had submitted last evening to the Ship-owners' Association, and which it had been thought prudent to lay over for the present. The resolution is as follows:

Resolved, That the committee of this association appointed to confer with the congressional Committee on Commerce and Navigation be instructed to express the views of this association as desiring for American citizens the right of purchasing vessel property in any part of the world where they may find it most advantageous to do so, which vessel or vessels, when so purchased, shall be entitled to all the privileges of United States registry.

Mr. MORRELL. Can you tell how much more per ton it costs to build an iron ship here than it costs to build one in England?

Mr. SNOW. Iron ships are now built in England, classed A No. 1, for from £12 10*s*. to £14 a ton. Steamers will cost about £20 a ton.

Mr. WELLS. What do they cost in this country?

Mr. SNOW. There have been very few iron ships built here, and I do not know what they cost. The ship-builders will be able to answer that question.

Mr. WELLS. What does it cost to build wooden ships here?

Mr. SNOW. Wooden ships, classed A No. 1 for about nine years, are costing now about $80 in currency per ton.

Mr. BRETT. These questions are answered in the communication from the Journal of Commerce, to which I have already directed the atten- of the committee.

Mr. SNOW remarked, in speaking of iron ships, that an American ship captain had mentioned to him the other day the case of the iron ship Richard Cobden, which had been built about thirty years ago, and which had been registered in England some time since for ten years longer, making her classification run for forty years. He mentioned in that connection that the life of a wooden ship is usually considered as ten years, although by extensive repairs they are sometimes made to last twenty years.

The CHAIRMAN. Have you ever got any proposals from American iron ship-builders, so as to know what iron ships could be built here for?

Mr. SNOW. No, sir; I am not prepared to say what they can be built for here. There is only one yard in this country that builds iron ships that I know of; that is the yard of Harlan & Hollingsworth, in Wilmington, Delaware. I understand that they would contract to build iron ships on English specifications at the same price as they are built in England.

Mr. BRETT. That has been rumored here for some time, but I understand it has never been carried out. I understand that they did build one iron ship, the Costa Rica, for the Panama Railroad Company.

Mr. MORRELL. How does the ship compare with foreign-built iron ships?

A MEMBER OF THE SHIP-OWNERS' ASSOCIATION. She went down to Aspinwall, and was wrecked within three months after her arrival.

The CHAIRMAN understood that there was one American-built iron sailing ship in this port now.

Mr. SNOW had heard of it, but did not know the particulars. But if it were a fact that American builders can build iron ships as cheaply as the English can, that was no argument against free trade in ships, because that fact would be all the more in their favor. If American builders can build as cheaply as English builders can, we should not go abroad to get ships, only in such measure as our own builders cannot supply them fast enough.

The committee from the Ship-owners' Association thereupon, having submitted their views, withdrew from the committee room.

Mr. JOHN HAYDEN, of Bath, representing the Ship-builders' Association of Maine, remarked that he had now very little interest in ship-building, as, owing to the effect of the present laws upon that trade, he had gradually got out of it, so that the position which he took upon the subject he took upon national considerations, not on personal considerations. If the disabilities that were now imposed upon American shipping, and which prevented the building of ships in this country as cheap as they could be built in other countries, were removed, the ship-building trade would be revived in a very short time, and ships would be built in this country as cheaply as in any other country; instead of Americans going abroad to buy ships the people of other countries would be coming here to buy them, as they did before the war. He regarded the remedy proposed by the New York Ship-owners' Association as one which would be disastrous to the ship-building interest. He argued that if the government should take the present burden off American ship-builders, and still should allow them no time to fill the void existing in the American shipping trade, but would give the ship-owners time to fill up that void with the refuse ships of Europe, American ship-yards would be rendered inactive for all time to come. But if a little time were allowed (two or three years would be sufficient in his estimation to give American ship-builders all the start they wanted) they could fill this void that had been created, and things would go on as smoothly as before. Why did Great Britain own such a large amount of shipping as she now owned? It was because, during the late contest in this country, American ships had been sold to England. He himself had gone over to England and sold two of his ships. England had thus filled up her trade, while Americans had been depleting theirs; besides that, the extra cost of ship-building in this country was now so great as almost, not quite, to annihilate American ship-building. The British kept on building, and now they had four or five times the tonnage engaged in the foreign carrying trade that Americans had. The remedy for the evil was to remove those disabilities. He suggested that a certain amount per ton, the exact figures to be obtained by estimates, should be allowed as a drawback upon every vessel built in this country, as an equivalent for the duty paid on the copper, iron, cordage, sail-cloth, &c., used in her construction. He thought that with these allowances American ship-builders could compete with foreign nations. He put this on high national grounds. It was of the utmost importance that the country should be in a position, in regard to her mercantile marine, to deter other nations from going to war with her. If she put herself in that position she would insure peace, and thereby prevent the cost of war. It was incumbent on this country to have a large mercantile marine, and to have American sailors to man her ships, and to have skilled mechanics of every kind on hand; and all this could not be secured if the ship-building interest was allowed to decay. He considered that if the other course were to be adopted, namely, the course proposed by the New York Ship-owners' Association, the mechanics skilled in ship-building would either leave that business and turn to some other branch of industry, or would leave the country and go where they could profitably pursue their business, and that, consequently, in the time of emergency, we would not have skilled mechanics to extemporize a defensive or offensive fleet. He held that it was of vast importance that this country should retain the carrying trade and the profits arising therefrom.

Mr. WELLS. What do you propose?

Mr. HAYDEN. I propose the allowance of drawbacks on the amount of materials used in ship-building. I think that nothing else would be requisite. Let us have this and we can build ships as cheaply as other nations can. The ship-owners of New York, who have one particular view of the question, would be in a very short time satisfied, because things would return to the condition they were in ten years ago. They would have no more cause of complaint than they had then. It is not necessary that we should always have a navy on hand, but it is necessary that we should always have skilled mechanics to construct a navy.

Mr. HOLMAN inquired of Mr. Hayden as to the extent to which Great Britain had been engaged in the purchase of American vessels before the war.

Mr. HAYDEN said that he was not able to state that definitely, but he had been in ports of Great Britain and of the Continent, and had seen a great many ships, which he knew to be American-built ships, under the flags of foreign nations. Still he would not state in what proportion other nations were purchasers of American ships.

Mr. HOLMAN inquired to how late a date citizens of other nations had been purchasers of American-built ships.

Mr. HAYDEN replied that the last one he had himself sold in England was sold in 1864.

Mr. HOLMAN inquired whether ships had been built in the United States for foreign capitalists upon contracts.

Mr. HAYDEN replied that he did not think they were, except in some few instances. The rule generally was to send them abroad with freight, or in ballast.

Mr. HOLMAN inquired whether up to 1860 wooden ships had been built as cheaply in the United States as in England or on the Continent.

Mr. HAYDEN. Undoubtedly; and they could be sold so as to compete with foreign-built vessels.

Mr. HOLMAN. Labor was higher in the United States?

Mr. HAYDEN. Yes, sir.

Mr. HOLMAN. But materials were cheaper?

Mr. HAYDEN. I do not know that; but persons who have seen our mechanics at work in this country, and have seen mechanics at work in other countries, cannot help appreciating the vast difference there is between them. On this point Mr. Hayden proceeded to give some illustrations.

Mr. WELLS. Is the skill of American laborers so much superior to that of English laborers?

Mr. HAYDEN. I will not say as to England. The illustration I have given had reference to France.

Mr. HOLMAN. Your theory is that American labor, considering its quality, is actually cheaper than foreign labor?

Mr. HAYDEN. Exactly so.

Mr. HOLMAN. And you think that if drawbacks were allowed on materials entering into the construction of ships, ships could be built as cheaply in this country as abroad?

Mr. HAYDEN. I have no doubt of it.

Mr. HOLMAN. Supposing that policy were adopted, how many years would be requisite to construct any considerable number of ships so as to materially increase our mercantile marine?

Mr. HAYDEN. So far as wooden ships are concerned, a good deal might be done in one year; but I can't say as to iron ships. Iron ships have been laid and constructed in this country—in Boston and in Wilmington—and I cannot entertain a doubt that, if due encouragement were given, the building of iron ships here would succeed as well as in any other nation.

Mr. HOLMAN. Suppose that the policy were adopted of allowing American registrations to foreign-built vessels, either without the payment of any duty, or with the payment of a small duty, imposed upon the tonnage; and suppose at the same time that a drawback were allowed upon the materials entering into the construction of ships in this country, what would be the effect of that policy on the shipping interest of the country?

Mr. HAYDEN. The immediate effect would be that the ships already built by other nations would flow in here at first and fill the void so as to deprive our mechanics of the opportunity to do so.

Mr. HOLMAN. Suppose that such vessels as were purchased abroad were excluded from the coastwise trade, and that American-built vessels had the exclusive coastwise trade, how would that policy affect both the commerce of the country and the ship-building interest?

Mr. HAYDEN. In reference to the coastwise trade, I do not think that we derive any advantage now from the discrimination in our favor. What American who is concerned in shipping at all, and who wishes to invest money in it, would invest his money in coasting vessels rather than in foreign trading vessels? What little of the foreign trade we have is better to us than the coasting trade, so that I do not see any objection at all to removing altogether the restrictions on the coastwise trade.

Mr. MORRELL. Is the foreign trade better than the coasting trade?

Mr. HAYDEN. There is more money made out of it.

Mr. MORRELL. The coasting trade is entirely in our own hands?

Mr. HAYDEN. Yes; but that is a trade which requires but little capital, and the competition is already complete, so that there is no room for foreigners to get into that trade.

Mr. HOLMAN. But by persevering in that policy some encouragement and protection would be furnished to ship-builders.

Mr. HAYDEN. Let the whole matter remain as it is for a few years, (in my judgment three years would be sufficient,) and let American ship-builders be allowed drawbacks on the materials, and then I shall be perfectly willing, as one interested in shipping and as a citizen of the United States, to repeal all navigation laws, and to make them just as the British navigation laws now are. But if we admitted free trade in ships at once, the effect would be to crowd in all the refuse vessels of foreign nations, so that it would take some time before we could have anything to do. It would be a blow to ship-building worse than anything that we have yet received.

Mr. HOLMAN. Can those inferior vessels compete with the foreign lines already established?

Mr. HAYDEN. Of course we would want equally good vessels to compete with them. The British have the whole run now.

Mr. HOLMAN. As to the ordinary carrying trade, would not the preference be given to, and a lower rate of insurance required on, the superior vessel? As a commercial adventure, would there be any advantage in purchasing those inferior foreign-built vessels?

Mr. HAYDEN. No; but a great many would be brought in for general business. In reference to the letter published in the Journal of Commerce, to which the attention of the committee has been called to-day, it was written by a gentleman of San Francisco, and it is not necessary, I presume, to say anything about it, because the testimony amounts to nothing. He says that iron ships can be built at £14 10*s.* a ton; but I am very incredulous on that point, as I think it costs very much more. Any letter written in that way is a very loose kind of evidence.

Mr. HOLMAN. Do you know how long it is since any European nation has imposed restrictions on the granting of registers to foreign-built vessels entering into their commercial marine?

Mr. HAYDEN. I do not recollect, myself, except by what has been already stated here as to Great Britain, which removed such restrictions about twenty years ago.

Mr. HOLMAN. Has any nation, within the last twenty years, adhered to that policy?

Mr. HAYDEN. I do not know; I cannot testify on that point.

Mr. HOLMAN. You spoke of the importance of protecting the ship-building interest, as a national measure, on account of the necessity of being prepared for emergencies in case of war. How far has the experience of this country, say from the beginning of the war of 1812 up to this time, demonstrated the facilities of improvising an effective navy for war purposes out of the commercial navy of the country?

Mr. HAYDEN. I suppose I know no more on that point than any other person; but I suppose it will be conceded by every one that we were in a good condition at the beginning of the late war. At the beginning of the war of 1812 we were not in so good a condition, because the embargo had almost annihilated our shipping interest.

Mr. HOLMAN. In a national point of view your argument would be in reference to the facilities for building ships for war purposes.

Mr. HAYDEN. Exactly; and to the advantages which the country would have from the carrying trade.

Mr. HOLMAN. Would not that result follow as well from American citizens being the owners of foreign-built vessels?

Mr. HAYDEN. Yes, sir; undoubtedly.

Mr. HOLMAN. So that the other is the real advantage for encouraging that particular industry?

Mr. HAYDEN. Yes, sir. It will be recollected that in the war of 1812 the frigate which took the principal part in the action on Lake Erie was built in eighteen days from the time that her keel was laid. If we had not had skilled mechanics, such a thing could not have been done.

Mr. P. M. WETMORE, of New York City, made some remarks to the committee in reference to a proposition which had been made by him during the late civil war, to send out privateers against British commerce, and said that if that had been done British commerce would have been swept from the seas to a greater extent even than the American commerce had been. He also advocated the subsidizing of American lines of steamships, giving some facts in reference to former subsidies to the Collins line, and to the two lines owned by Mr. Law and Mr. Aspinwall. He declared his belief that whenever the United States government would restore the system of giving a reasonable subsidy to mail steamers on the ocean, it would be a happy day for the commerce of the country. Americans to-day could not send a letter to any nation in Europe without hiring a foreign steamer to carry it. He did not think that creditable to the intelligence, the enterprise, or the public spirit of the country. He gave an illustration of the injury to the American trade with China, caused by the necessity of our sending, some years since, American letters destined to China through the English mails.

Mr. WELLS inquired whether there was not an American line subsidized to Rio Janeiro, and one to Hong-Kong.

Mr. WETMORE replied that that was so, but that it was a very small affair, and that when the commerce of the nation is spoken of it is not South American commerce, but the Atlantic commerce that is meant.

Mr. WELLS inquired whether those subsidies did not operate beneficially to the trade between this country and South America.

Mr. WETMORE replied that they did, and that he should not like to live to see the day when they would be withdrawn; but that was only one point in the common system of commerce. He believed that a mail line on the ocean could not be supported by the mere carrying of mails and passengers, but that there must be subsidies, and that the United States government could well afford to give subsidies.

Mr. HOLMAN inquired whether there had not been many successful American lines prior to 1860 that were not subsidized.

Mr. WETMORE replied that if there had been he was not acquainted with them. The Collins line had had a subsidy of $385,000, Mr. Law's line a subsidy of $290,000, and Mr. Aspinwall's line a subsidy of $199,000.

Mr. HOLMAN. These lines were in the direct trade with Europe?

Mr. WETMORE. Yes, sir.

Mr. HOLMAN. Had we any subsidized line to South America prior to 1860?

Mr. WETMORE. No, sir; none to South America, nor was there any subsidy to any line on the Pacific Ocean. I think that the granting of a subsidy to the Pacific Mail Steamship Company was a beneficial public measure. I think that that company has committed the same fault that Mr. Collins committed, in making its ships too costly; in other words, I think that there has been a want of economy in the management of the concern.

Mr. N. G. HICHBORN, president of the Maine Ship-owners' Association, next addressed the committee. He said that the ship-owners of Maine simply asked the committee to recommend such measures of relief as would unfetter that interest, and bring back the mercantile marine of the country to its former position. Up to 1860 the Maine ship-builders constructed sailing ships for England cheaper than the English could build them, but under the disabilities which the ship-building interest was now laboring under, that trade had languished. The representatives of that trade asked this committee to recommend to Congress the passage of such laws as would facilitate their efforts in building up commerce, and such as are granted to the same interests in other commercial nations. A ship now costs sixty or seventy dollars a ton built in this country, whereas in the Provinces it only costs forty-five or fifty dollars a ton, and the two ships when afloat were brought into competition with each other. He spoke of the importance of having a merchant marine that could, in case of emergency, be used for the defense of the sea-coast, and remarked that during the late civil war a single British gunboat could have destroyed all the towns upon the Penobscot Bay and along the coast of Maine, whereas if the government had authorized it to be done, the people of Maine could have created a floating defense in three weeks that would have defied attack from abroad. He spoke of the commander of the Kearsarge having been educated in the mercantile marine in Boston, and said that though an army might be extemporized in three or four months, sailors could not be extemporized in that way. He asked that the ship-building trade be unfettered, and that it have the opportunity to use iron and coal and wood and all other materials as cheaply as it can procure them, and there would then be no fear of foreign competition, and there would be, in a time of national peril, a fleet and sailors ready to defend the country. If the mercantile marine were increased, the ships of the navy, which were now maintained at great cost, could be brought home, and the commerce of the country would be better protected through the evidence of the strength and power and civilization of the country, manifested by the fleets of the American mercantile marine. He understood that there were to-day in the port of New York some sixty barks, forty-three of them being foreign vessels, and only seventeen American vessels. Those vessels were principally engaged in carrying western grain to European markets; and he showed how it was to the interest of the western producer to have his grain sent to the market in American bottoms rather than in foreign bottoms. Valuable as was the guano of the Chincha Islands, the carrying of that guano was of more value, so that if Peru continued to own those islands, and if Americans owned all the shipping engaged in the transportation of the guano, they would get more value out of it than Peru would. The East India trade was now being carried on almost entirely by foreigners. He had been informed recently by an intelligent American master that in his voyage to and from Yokohama he had only spoken two American vessels. It was of vast importance that this nation should have as much of that business as it could possibly have. As to the inquiry whether Americans could compete with foreigners in the sailing of vessels, he thought that they could. American masters and seamen were superior to foreigners. He related an instance of the master of a small vessel of six hundred or seven hundred tons which was lying some time since at Boston, there being lying on the other side of the wharf at the same time a British iron ship which was understood as a fourteen-knot ship and of about one thousand five hundred tons. They were both bound for Melbourne. The merchants of Boston were invited to put their cargoes into the iron ship, because she would be at Melbourne before the wooden ship. But the young American master (who had come to him a barefooted boy some fifteen or eighteen years before) said that he would do the best he could to get there before the other, and the result was that he delivered his cargo seventeen days before the iron ship arrived, so that the Boston merchants who shipped by his vessel had saved more than the cost of the freight in having their merchandise arrive first at Melbourne. The same principle of American superiority held true in the line of ship-building. As to the question of labor, labor was now in excess in Europe, and the ship-builders there did not use machinery to the same extent as the ship-builders here did. He did not like to be over-sanguine, but he believed that if the ship-builders of Portland could not learn to build an iron ship in two years they would have forgotten their skill. They only wanted two or three years, and they would then take care of the ship-building interest.

Mr. WELLS inquired how Mr. Hichborn proposed to remedy the evil. Was it by drawbacks?

Mr. HICHBORN. Yes, sir; we want a drawback on the articles entering into the construction of ships. He did not want to antagonize the interests of Pennsylvania or any other interest; but simply asked that if it took one thousand dollars to pay the duty on iron entering into the construction of ships, that duty should be refunded whether the iron was procured from abroad or from Pennsylvania. He spoke of the English insurance companies combining against the American shipping interest, by requiring a premium of from eight to ten per cent. upon American wooden vessels to Calcutta, and requiring only two and a half per cent. upon English iron vessels. Whereas if he were to decide which style of vessel was the most competent to take a cargo to Calcutta, he would say that the wooden vessel was at least as competent as the other. He did not believe that the time had come for the end of wooden ships, or for the disappearance of sailing ships. Ships of wood and ships of iron would both be continued, propelled by steam and propelled by sails. The ship-building interest of Maine called upon Congress simply to unfetter it in the matter of ship-building, and it would then meet all the demands upon it.

Mr. HOLMAN inquired what the present condition of ship-building in Maine was?

Mr. HICHBORN replied that it was a great deal depressed now, owing to the fact that the late war had troubled the exchange of the world, and that a very large amount of shipping had been transferred, together with the fact that more iron vessels were being built now.

Mr. HOLMAN inquired whether any iron vessels had yet been built in the Provinces?

Mr. HICHBORN replied that very few, if any, had been.

The CHAIRMAN inquired whether the yards where the government iron-clad vessels had been built were prepared to build mercantile iron vessels, and whether the same kind of work and machinery would answer for both classes?

Mr. HICHBORN replied that at all events the same kind of workmen would answer, and that the difference between the two classes was about the same as the difference between the building of steamships and of sailing-ships. There was a very fine yard in Wilmington, Delaware, for the building of iron vessels, and such vessels could easily be built in Maine, if they could have the iron in Maine as cheap as they had it on the Clyde. American mechanics would simply need the time to learn how to rivet, and they would get out of four days' labor as much as they would get out of six days on the Clyde. He would say to his New York friends that both the ship-owning and ship-building interests were aiming at the same subject, but in a different direction. They both wanted cheap ships, and the ship-builders of this country would supply them if Congress would only unburden the ship-building interest.

Mr. HOLMAN. If you are allowed drawbacks on the materials entering into the construction of ships, what is gained in a national point of view between the building of ships here and the purchase of ships abroad? Is there anything else gained than the value of the labor which goes into the construction of the ship?

Mr. HICHBORN. Yes, sir. First we have our ship-yards kept intact in case of the emergency of war with a foreign country, and that I think a very essential point. Secondly, we have our sailors trained and formed; but if we get our ships abroad, we will get our sailors there too, and they will be men on whom we would have no claim, and who would have no love for this country in case of danger. Perhaps a great many of the masters also would be from Europe, and they would be men who would have no love for our flag and no disposition to spread our civilization and sentiments.

Mr. HOLMAN. Up to 1860 had the ship-building interest of Maine steadily increased from the time it commenced?

Mr. HICHBORN. Yes, sir; very steadily. You will understand me to admit that it had its intermittent spells.

Mr. HOLMAN. Was it greater in 1859 and 1860 than it had been previously?

Mr. HICHBORN. I do not think that it was. Our great ship-building years were 1852, 1853, 1854. They were wanting ships on the other side, and they discovered that we could build them very cheaply, and we did build for ourselves and for the world.

Mr. HOLMAN. Between 1848 and 1860 was any large number of vessels built in Maine on contracts with foreign capitalists?

Mr. HICHBORN. Not extensively so. Our people constructed ships and sent them abroad, some in ballast and some with freight, and there they were sold. There were, however, some built on contract;

but yet we did not get acquainted with each other enough to go into that business extensively.

Mr. HOLMAN. What is the present condition of the ship-building interest in Maine?

Mr. HICHBORN. At this time I should think that about three-fifths of our ordinary capital is at work. The inquiry may be made, how we can do so much work as that under the circumstances? The answer is that those towns of ours which have been used for ship-building have that business as a specialty and have nothing else that they can do. The people who have followed it understand it and understand nothing else; and they are now building more than they can afford to do, simply because the workmen must have something to do, and they must have some employment themselves. I built a ship this year, and I cannot get 85 per cent. of what it cost. The ships now being built in Maine will not sell for more than 85 or 90 per cent. of their cost.

The CHAIRMAN. What are the rates that are paid now to mechanics in ship-building?

Mr. HICHBORN. From $2 to $2 50 a day for skilled mechanics and ship-carpenters. I have not paid over $2 50, and I have had a great many at $2.

Mr. CALKIN. What were the wages before the war?

Mr. HICHBORN. I am quite certain that in 1854 I have paid $3 50.

The CHAIRMAN. Is not the decrease in wages in consequence of the depression in business, and is not labor as low in that branch of business as it was before the war?

Mr. HICHBORN. Yes, sir; we have two applicants for labor where we can only employ one.

Mr. CALKIN. Do you know anything about the price of labor of machinists, as to how it rates now in comparison with what it did before the war?

Mr. HICHBORN. I think that a good machinist to-day gets from $3 50 to $4 a day. I fell in this morning with a friend of mine who wanted some stone-cutters to send to Maine, and the man with whom he was talking told him that if he could not give more than $4 a day he need not seek any here, because they were getting $4 50 a day here, and yet our very best mechanics in ship-yards can only get $2 50 a day.

The CHAIRMAN. Then I understand you that in regard to labor you can build ships as cheaply now in currency as you could before the war in gold?

Mr. HICHBORN. Certainly we can. In 1854 I have paid $3 50 in gold to the same men that I am now paying $2 50 a day in currency; but that was in an emergency.

The CHAIRMAN. How did the average rate of wages then compare with the present rate of wages?

Mr. HICHBORN. My judgment would be that it would not vary twenty-five cents to-day from the average for ten years before the war.

Mr. CALKIN remarked that in New York good machinists could be had for $2 a day, on account of the depression in business.

Mr. BUFFINTON remarked that in his city (Fall River, Massachusetts) good machinists received $3 50 a day, and that there was plenty of work for them.

Mr. CALKIN said that Mr. Roach was hiring them in this city at $2 a day.

Mr. BUFFINTON remarked that house-carpenters in Fall River received thirty-five cents an hour, and that common dirt-diggers in the street got $2 50 a day.

Mr. WELLS inquired from Mr. Hichborn what amount per ton should be allowed for duty in the shape of drawbacks.

Mr. HICHBORN replied that the estimate was about $8 per ton upon wooden vessels.

Mr. WELLS inquired what it would be on iron vessels.

Mr. HICHBORN replied that it would be something more—perhaps $10 or $12 a ton.

The CHAIRMAN. Is that for the hull alone?

Mr. HICHBORN. No, sir; it is for the hull and spars and rigging.

Mr. MORRELL. Do you think that a bounty equal to $10 or $12 a ton on iron vessels, and $8 a ton on wooden vessels, would put you on an equality with foreign ship-builders?

Mr. HICHBORN. Yes, sir; I am clearly of the opinion that $8 a ton would do it on wooden vessels, but I am not so clear as to iron vessels.

The CHAIRMAN. If that is the case, why is there so much difference between the cost of building in the Provinces and in Maine.

Mr. HICHBORN. The ships in the Provinces are not so well constructed as ours are, though they will get the same rate as we do through English houses. They make ships entirely of spruce, which is a light and cheap quality of timber. If we built ours of spruce we could build them at $8 or $10 a ton less; but we use oak and hard pine and hackmatack. I had a vessel of five hundred tons at Boston, and on the other side of her was a British vessel built entirely of spruce inside and outside. My vessel was discharging sugars at perhaps $15 or $20 expense of cooperage on her cargo, whereas the other vessel was also discharging sugar at $200 or $300 expense of cooperage, and you could have scraped up cart-loads of sugar. I think my vessel had twice the strength of the other. She cost $20 or $30 more per ton.

In conclusion Mr. Hichborn extended an invitation to the committee to visit Portland in the pursuance of its investigation.

Mr. WETMORE addressed the committee in defense of wooden vessels as against iron vessels. He believed that if a careful calculation were made it would be found that from two to three iron-built steamers were wrecked off Newfoundland for the one wooden steamer that was wrecked there. He spoke of Admiral Farragut having put the bow of the wooden frigate Hartford dead upon the iron ram in Mobile Harbor; and about the Star of the West, also a wooden vessel, placing herself alongside of Fort Sumter and bringing back her flag in safety. He believed that the public interest of the country required that its commerce should be extended wherever it could be done without infringing upon any of the great principles of the Constitution.

The committee adjourned till to-morrow, October 15.

NEW YORK, *October* 15, 1869.

The committee met at 10 o'clock a. m. Present, the chairman, and Messrs. Morrell, Holman, Calkin, Buffinton, and Wells.

Mr. A. C. STIMERS addressed the committee. He said that he was interested in seeing ships built and run under the American flag, which was not done now to any extent. If there were the same laws on the subject of shipping in this country as there were in other countries the result would be the same—the growth of American shipping and commerce. He understood the law of England to be, that all materials entering into the construction of a ship were free of duty, and that all stores subsequently put into her were also free of duty. With such a law in this country ships could be built and run in competition with any nation. Americans were superior in the arts of ship-building and navigation to the French, Germans, and Spaniards, and were certainly equal to the English. Labor cost more here, but it was also worth more, in consequence of the superior intelligence of American mechanics; so that if the duty were taken off materials a ship would not cost any more here than in England. The tax should come off iron used in the construction of iron ships.

Mr. MORRELL remarked that there was not much tax now on manufactured iron, except the mercantile tax.

Mr. STIMERS replied that that was one of the taxes which he wished to see taken off. Ships could be built here now cheaper than was generally supposed. He had noticed that it had been stated yesterday before the committee that iron steamers could not, for the present, be built here as well as they were abroad. He did not agree to that. During the late war iron steamers had been built for the government under his general superintendence, and Mr. Rowland, now present, had built as good iron ships as ever had been built.

Mr. MORRELL inquired whether it would not be desirable to use American materials in the construction of ships when they could be got as cheap as foreign materials.

Mr. STIMERS replied that American iron was much better than English iron. Shippers and shipping merchants always paid a higher price for American iron than for English iron.

Mr. MORRELL inquired whether it would not be better to allow a drawback on iron equivalent to the duty, so as to allow the ship-builder to use American iron.

Mr. STIMERS replied that it would, and that ship-builders would always prefer American iron on account of its superiority. If it were made free it would come to that. At first English iron might be imported, but builders would soon come round to American iron. He had been government inspector of the iron-clads, which had been constructed under his supervision, in various parts of the country. The machinery for government iron-clads and for iron mercantile vessels was just the same. The armature of the iron-clads would be heavier, but the construction of the hulls would be the same. Vessels with iron hulls had been built for the government at Portland, Boston, New York, Jersey City, Greenpoint, Chester, Wilmington, Baltimore, Pittsburg, Cincinnati, and St. Louis. He had been abroad, and had seen nothing there to surpass the American iron work. The iron here was better than is made in Europe, and, therefore, the ships were better. These iron-clads had been to sea, and had pounded on sand-banks, and not a hole had been made in one of them. Americans had not to learn how to build iron ships. They knew to-day how to do it. Give them a chance and they would build fleets of them. As to the low insurance on English iron ships, the insurance would be equally low on iron ships built here. The latest works on naval architecture were obtained and studied in this country, so that American ship-builders knew all that English ship-builders were doing, and would not produce work inferior to the English work.

The CHAIRMAN. Do I understand you as saying that the difference is simply the difference in duties on materials, and that in all other respects we can compete with foreign ship-builders?

Mr. STIMERS. Yes, sir; decidedly.

The CHAIRMAN. How would you overcome the difference in the cost of labor?

Mr. STIMERS. The labor here is worth more. You can get more out of an American mechanic than you can out of an English mechanic.

The CHAIRMAN. Is there more machinery used here?

Mr. STIMERS. No, sir. We use similar machinery. In a great many cases we have more ingenious arrangements for saving labor; but more attention has been paid to that in England recently than used to be. In 1854, when I was in England, their ships were, as a rule, inferior to ours in New York; but now, I think, they are rather superior, because we have had so much discouragement, and have been running down.

The CHAIRMAN. Do the builders of wooden ships adapt themselves readily to the building of iron ships?

Mr. STIMERS. Yes, sir. The change is very simple. My opinion is, that when iron ships come to be made here, it will be found that the builders are those who have been building wooden ships. It requires only a different arrangement of materials, which is very easily learned. In fact, the art of ship-building is simple if you understand naval architecture, and that the wooden ship-builders understand. I have seen men acting as common laborers, carrying iron about, and have seen them in six months afterwards driving rivets, which is the most particular thing. If you have the head man right the labor part is easily learned, as is proved by the building of all these iron ships all over the country. Of course the knowledge how to direct all to be done requires a labor of years; but, after the plans and specifications are completed, the other parts of the work are easy.

Mr. MORRELL. I suppose you would apprehend no difficulty in supplying the demand for all the iron ships needed if you were sure of the demand after the ships were built?

Mr. STIMERS. I would apprehend no difficulty at all.

Mr. MORRELL. That was proved by the ability to supply the demand during the war?

Mr. STIMERS. Yes, sir. That is the best proof of it. Mr. Fox, the Assistant Secretary of the Navy, complained to me that the South was building ships faster than we were. I said, "Yes; but when the ships meet, what becomes of the southern ships? We not only build a number of ships, but we build good ships."

Mr. MORRELL. What you want is to be secured possession of the American market for ships?

Mr. STIMERS. We want to be on a par with Englishmen. That is all.

Mr. MORRELL. You would prefer to be able to use American materials?

Mr. STIMERS. Yes, sir; they are better. American iron will always command a better price than English iron. It is worth more.

Mr. HOLMAN. The vessels built by the government during the war would be too costly for commercial purposes?

Mr. STIMERS. Their cost was not on account of their being government vessels, but on account of the disturbed condition of labor and finances. They were made after the rules of building iron vessels.

Mr. HOLMAN. But a capitalist could not think of expending anything near the amount of money for a ship for commercial business that the government did for its vessels.

Mr. STIMERS. No; but he would have equally good vessels. The difference is that labor now is cheaper, and materials are cheaper, and the finances are in a better state. The machinery for building iron ships is simple.

Mr. HOLMAN. Your experience only goes to the question of the practicability of building such vessels in this country.

Mr. STIMERS. I know the cost of all the vessels that we were building then. I saw how they were being built. I saw how the process was carried on, and how it was carried on abroad. The processes are quite similar, except that an American workman will always get off more work.

Mr. HOLMAN. I understand you to say that, with relief from the payment of taxes, internal and external, on the materials entering into the construction of ships, they could be built in this country, of wood or of iron, so as to compete with foreign builders?

Mr. STIMERS. Yes, sir; but then I also want the inducement of letting all stores be put on board ship free of duty. That would be an additional inducement to build ships, because it would afford profits.

Mr. HOLMAN. Is that the practice of all commercial nations?

Mr. STIMERS. It is the practice of England. A passenger on board a Cunard steamer gets his bottle of champagne for three shillings; whereas on an American ship he has to pay three or four dollars for it.

Mr. HOLMAN. Does that policy of furnishing goods from bonded warehouses extend any further than Great Britain?

Mr. STIMERS. I do not know. I notice, however, that other continental nations are adopting the liberal policy of England in reference to ships. Ships that are built in England are imported into France, Germany, and other countries, and enter into navigation under their laws.

Mr. HOLMAN. That is the policy of all the commercial continental powers.

Mr. STIMERS. I understand that it is.

Mr. HOLMAN. There is no government except ours that prohibits the sailing under its register and flag of vessels built in foreign countries.

Mr. STIMERS. I do not know of any.

Mr. HOLMAN. Suppose that ship-builders were allowed a drawback of duties, internal and external, on all materials entering into the construction of ships, what would be the gain to the country between that policy and the policy of letting our merchants buy their ships abroad?

Mr. STIMERS. I think our ships would pay better profit than English ships would. My opinion is that the American ship will earn money where the English ship will be simply paying expenses. There are technical reasons why I think that is so. The vessel that is constructed here is owned here, and our people make the profit resulting from running her.

Mr. HOLMAN. Would not that result follow if the ship were built abroad and owned here?

Mr. STIMERS. Yes, except that if we build our own vessels we will make more money than by buying foreign vessels. Ours are more profitable vessels to run. We have always led all other nations in the construction of ships, both naval and mercantile. The French vessels used to be superior to the English, but the French had not the aptitude for going to sea that the English had, and they were consequently driven from the sea by the English.

Mr. MORRELL. Is there not another and a higher reason for building our own ships—and that is that we may be able to supply our navy in time of need?

Mr. STIMERS. Yes, that is a further consideration which should be kept in view by statesmen. During the war we derived great advantage from the fact that our people were able to construct ships.

Mr. HOLMAN. Vessels purchased abroad by Americans would be likely to be manned by American citizens.

Mr. STIMERS. If you buy a ship abroad you would be very apt to put people aboard of her there. Ships now are owned here, as nearly as they can be owned, running under the American flag, that are commanded and manned by Englishmen.

Mr. HOLMAN. Sailors are admitted to vessels without regard to nationality.

Mr. STIMERS. Yes, sir. I think it has been always so. I never heard of any restrictions on that account either as to officers or crews.

The CHAIRMAN. I believe that a certain proportion of the crew has to be American.

Mr. STIMERS. Perhaps so. I do not know about that.

Mr. HOLMAN. Then your view of the matter is, that the advantage to be gained by the United States from relieving ship-builders of the duty on materials is that resulting to labor from the construction of the vessel here, and that of keeping up our ship-yards with a view to any national exigency that may occur, and also the fact that you think our ships are better than foreign-built ships.

Mr. STIMERS. Yes. These are the advantages that I had in my mind.

Mr. HOLMAN. Taking the present condition of our commerce into consideration, would the advantages to labor resulting from the construction of vessels here countervalue the advantages of allowing our merchants to buy their ships abroad and have them registered here, thus stimulating our commerce immediately? In other words, which would employ the largest number of persons?

Mr. STIMERS. I suppose that the building of ships here would. I should like to see the whole thing left free—to see the duties taken off materials entering into the construction of ships, and then to let our merchants go and buy ships abroad if they chose. I think that very few would buy their ships abroad.

Mr. HOLMAN. And American commerce and ship-building would be promoted to a large extent?

Mr. STIMERS. Yes, sir. In the first year, no doubt, there would be quite a number of ships bought abroad; but merchants would soon find out that they could do better here. The comparison would be in favor of our ships. And after the first year, I think there would be few ships purchased abroad by our ship-owners.

Mr. HOLMAN. Then you think that the true end would be obtained by allowing foreign-built vessels purchased by American citizens to obtain American registers, and, at the same time, by removing all duties from the materials entering into the construction of ships here.

Mr. STIMERS. Yes, sir.

Mr. HOLMAN. You think that both these plans would improve our commerce?

Mr. STIMERS. Yes, sir.

Mr. HOLMAN. Without any injury to the ship-builder?

Mr. STIMERS. Yes, sir. I do not think he would suffer at all. I am interested in it myself, because I am a ship engineer.

Mr. HOLMAN. Would you make any distinction between vessels built abroad and those built at home as to their right to engage in the coastwise trade?

Mr. STIMERS. I would throw the coastwise trade open to all ships under the American flag, wherever they were built.

Mr. HICHBORN, of Maine, remarked that it seemed to have been the sentiment of those who had appeared before the committee yesterday that, even with a remission of duties, iron ships could not be constructed here at once to compete with those built on the Clyde or the Tyne, but that it would require two or three years for the American iron shipbuilders to get ready.

Mr. STIMERS replied that Americans could proceed at once in the construction of iron ships. There were several establishments ready now to go right ahead and build iron ships, and large numbers of such ships could be supplied in the first year. He thought that they could be produced here quicker than they could be procured abroad.

Mr. MORRELL. Do you think that if you had a demand for iron ships at this time you would be able to build them of American materials as quickly as you could by importing the materials?

Mr. STIMERS. Yes, sir. We have rolling mills that are prepared to roll such iron if they only get the order.

Mr. MORRELL. You found no trouble during the war in supplying the demand after a few months?

Mr. STIMERS. No, sir. The mills sprung up to meet the demand. I superintended the construction of our first iron vessel, the little Monitor, and we got the iron from Baltimore for the armature. It was supposed at that time that it could not be obtained anywhere else; but just as soon as more vessels were wanted the whole country was ready to supply the article.

Mr. MORRELL. If the duty on iron were remitted and there were no provision made for the use of American iron on our ships, do you suppose that those American mills could live? Do you not suppose that all the American vessels would be built of foreign materials?

Mr. STIMERS. It is impossible to say how cheaply the American mills could produce the article. My opinion is that they would soon come to the point of producing it as cheaply as it could be imported.

Mr. HOLMAN. Were all those monitors and iron vessels built of American iron?

Mr. STIMERS. Yes, sir. All of their iron was rolled here. There never was a pound of English iron imported for the purpose.

Mr. MORRELL. You experienced no trouble in getting anything you wanted of American manufacture when you were able to give the order?

Mr. STIMERS. No, sir; not at all. This country can produce anything required for ships. There was competition throughout for the supplying of these things.

Mr. WELLS. What material used in the construction of a ship is not produced in this country?

Mr. STIMERS. I believe we import Manila hemp; but that is a very small matter, particularly in steamships. Most of the ships built hereafter will be, I think, iron steamers. That is the tendency.

Mr. WELLS. Then the drawback would be principally on iron and on the stores that go into the ship after its construction?

Mr. STIMERS. Yes, sir.

Mr. HOLMAN. Were any new navy yards established during the war?

Mr. STIMERS. No, sir. All those vessels were built in private yards. There were naval stations established, but not what we understand as navy yards. Those at Cincinnati and St. Louis and other points were just improvised ship-yards. Mr. Rowland, who built the first monitor for us, had already a ship-yard.

Mr. WELLS. The iron vessels at St. Louis were built on the open levee?

Mr. STIMERS. Yes, sir.

Mr. HOLMAN. All that was needed to secure the prompt construction of vessels for the government was to have the skilled workmen?

Mr. STIMERS. Yes, sir. The only difficulty about skilled workmen was the needs of the army. Many of them were drafted into the army, and employers had to look around and make them out of common laborers, which they soon did. At present we could not have any such difficulty.

Mr. HOLMAN. Any man skilled in iron-work can readily be trained in that kind of work?

Mr. STIMERS. Certainly, sir. The head man, of course, wants to understand naval architecture. We have men enough in the country to build hundreds of iron ships very soon.

The CHAIRMAN. Were not a majority of the iron-clad government vessels built at private yards?

Mr. STIMERS. Yes, sir; all having iron hulls were. We did not attempt iron hulls at the navy yards. Mr. Fox asked me how long it would take to build them at the navy yards. I told him that it would probably take a couple of years; and that, therefore, we must build them at private yards. A few iron-plated vessels, with wooden hulls, were built in the navy yards: but the iron vessels proper were built in private yards. I went into a ship-yard on the river Clyde. It had been a meadow eighteen months before, and yet they had already launched fourteen ships from it; so that you see it does not take long to establish an iron ship-building yard.

Mr. HOLMAN. In case of emergency, would there be any difficulty in constructing any number of vessels that might be required, with a reasonable degree of promptness?

Mr. STIMERS. No, sir. I really think we could get the vessels more promptly than by going abroad for them.

Mr. CALKIN. Are there not concerns in Wilmington, New York, and Boston, that would be prepared at once to build iron steamers?

Mr. STIMERS. Yes, sir. At Wilmington, Delaware, Chester, Pennsylvania, Philadelphia, New York, and Boston, they can go right to work at once, as soon as they get contracts; you would see the riveters at work in a week.

Mr. MORRELL. The difficulty is the want of demand, rather than of means to supply it?

Mr. STIMERS. The want of demand is the entire difficulty. That is why I want to see ship-building encouraged here by the withdrawal of duties.

Mr. CALKIN. Do you not think that the talent of this country in the way of building iron ships is equal to that of Europe?

Mr. STIMERS. Yes, sir. We build better ships than they build abroad; ships that earn more money. I refer to iron ships, as well as wooden ones.

Mr. T. F. ROWLAND next addressed the committee. He said that he was the proprietor of the Continental ship-yard at Greenpoint, Brooklyn. That yard was established in 1859—about two years before the war broke out. Previous to the war he had only built some three or four iron vessels there—coasters running between New Orleans and Mobile, and one or two for the Sound trade. After the breaking out of the war Captain Ericsson took a contract to build what was afterward called the Monitor, and as he (Mr. Rowland) was the only man in the business in New York, Captain Ericsson applied to him to do the work. That vessel was built in just one hundred and one days from the day she was started. She happened to be successful, and the government wanted some more of the same kind, and Captain Ericsson got a contract to build six, somewhat larger. There were only twelve months allowed to build the whole six. Captain Ericsson sent for him, and he told Captain Ericsson that he would undertake three of them. He subsequently became sick, and his foreman called to see him, and proposed that if he should get ten per cent. of the profits he would stay; otherwise he would strike. He (Mr. Rowland) told him to strike and to clear out; and he cleared out the whole tribe of workmen who had been with him two or three years. After clearing out the whole party of experts, he went to work and laid the keels of the Passaic, Montauk, and Catskill. Not a man struck a blow upon them who had ever struck a blow on an iron ship before. He built those vessels with house-builders, molders, and all kinds of mechanics. There were no ship-carpenters among them. Mr. Badger, a house-carpenter in New York, helped him a good deal. Mr. Badger's business had given out, and he had a good number of German mechanics—good fellows—with whom the work was done and the vessels got out. The other three, which were built in Wilmington, Delaware, came out after his. After that the government had given orders for two large monitors, the Dictator and Puritan, and he (Mr. Rowland) took the Puritan. He thought he would send to England for some workmen, and he got eleven of them from the Tyne, agreeing to pay them two dollars a day. These men staid but three weeks with him. They were not worth their two dollars a day, and they cleared out. He was better without them than with them. He built the Puritan and launched her, and he believed that there never was a piece of iron work done to excel the work on her. He did not know the cause of the present decline in the shipping interests. During the last year, at least once a week, he had made propositions to build iron sailing vessels at not exceeding ten per cent. in currency over their cost on the other side; but people did not want ships. Mr. Low had sent for him, and he had made drawings and a contract to build a ship for the China trade, but just then the recent troubles in Wall street occurred, and consequently the ship had not been built. He had offered to build her as cheap as she could be got in England. He had seen by the paper to-day that Mr. Low had stated before the committee yesterday that they did not know how to build iron ships in this country. He himself, however, had built a good many. The Americans were a peculiar people, but the English were still more peculiar. The English never learned anything without immediately running to some printing office and publishing it all. The Yankee never did that; but he knew enough to read up and keep posted. The Yankee thus had the benefit of his own experience and of the Englishman's too, and had sense enough to pick out the good and to throw away the bad. The iron planing machine, which had long been in use here, had only recently been adopted by the English; and that was one reason why they were doing better work. But yet the English could not build a ship much cheaper than Americans could. Iron sailing ships cost about £16 sterling per ton, and steamers from £22 to £24.

It was in England as here. One could get a vessel for almost any price. The idea of using English iron was all moonshine. Ships could not be built in this country of English iron, but the American iron would have to be rolled to order, for by the time that iron could be procured from England rolled to order, the Yankee would want his ship launched. During the war the Passaic had come into New York wanting some repairs done. He had gone into Mr. Wells's store with an order for about thirty plates of iron, saying that it was life and death to have them; that the vessel was in the dock, and that they must be got. Mr. Wells hadn't them in the store, but said he would have them rolled. This was about eight o'clock in the morning, and the same evening a cart drove into his yard with one load of that iron, which had been rolled in Jersey City, sheared and delivered at Greenpoint, and the rest of it came the next day. If it had been necessary to send to England for a lot of iron, he would have had to wait a long while to get it, and price was no object in such a case as that. All that he had ever seen of English iron was perhaps thirty or forty per cent. poorer than American iron in regard to its ductility and strength.

Mr. MORRELL. Do you not think that those English ships that are built so cheaply are built of iron that is vastly inferior to American iron, and that it is an unfair competition for American builders to be brought into contact with them?

Mr. ROWLAND. The kind of iron that I have seen from England is mighty poor stuff.

The CHAIRMAN. Do not the insurance companies in Europe discriminate against a poor quality of iron in ships?

Mr. ROWLAND. No, sir. According to Lloyds' regulations a certain weight of iron per ton measurement must be put into a ship. That iron must have a strength of twenty thousand pounds to the square inch, and there is no difference made. If we put into our ships iron of one hundred thousand pounds to the square inch, we would have to put in the same weight of iron as if it was only twenty thousand pounds to the square inch. Until that regulation of Lloyds' is changed, I do not see how we can enter into competition with the English. I will make a contract to build an iron ship at less than they can produce it in England, if regard is had to the strength of the iron, not to its weight.

The CHAIRMAN. You would use a lighter quality of iron and get the same strength?

Mr. ROWLAND. Yes, sir. I would use not more than five-eighths the weight of iron and get greater strength. I do not propose to build a ship out of English iron. I would rather leave the business. I could not do it.

The CHAIRMAN. Your experience in iron ship-building was during the war, when you were obliged to have everything at once, without any regard to its cost. The only question is whether you could afford to pursue that mode of doing business in regard to mercantile ships?

Mr. ROWLAND. You could not build ships of any magnitude without ordering the iron rolled at the mill and cut to shape. You cannot afford to have it rolled except on pattern, because if you had afterwards to cut it into shape you could not stand the waste.

The CHAIRMAN. Would not the iron be all of a certain shape, and if the business were pursued would not the result be to come down to those certain shapes and certain sizes, and to have them imported and kept on hand?

Mr. ROWLAND. No, sir, I think not.

The CHAIRMAN. If you were building several thousand-ton ships, would you not necessarily build them on the same model, so as to have the patterns and sizes of plates alike; in other words, would you not follow the mode of building them all pretty much in the same way?

Mr. ROWLAND. I have been an engineer for about twenty-two years. It is about that length of time since I first started in the building of locomotive and marine engines. Our marine engines that go to sea, and that all look alike to the eye of a layman, do nevertheless differ from each other. I do not recollect making two engines that were precisely alike. We are always making alterations and what we call improvements, though they are only sometimes improvements. I never built two engines precisely alike. I built three ships for the government, all apparently alike; but if you came to measure them, you would find them entirely different.

The CHAIRMAN. Do I understand you that the plates are necessarily cut to shape?

Mr. ROWLAND. They are cut to shape. We generally allow a half inch for the edges and use the shears.

Mr. MORRELL. You order the plates to be cut to pattern?

Mr. ROWLAND. Yes, sir.

Mr. MORRELL. And the rolling mills cut the plates to pattern?

Mr. ROWLAND. Yes; and a half inch is allowed for irregularity in the shearing. That makes a waste of a quarter of one per cent., whereas if you order plates promiscuously, there will be a waste of five per cent. and the labor of cutting, and no ship-builder could stand anything like that.

The CHAIRMAN. What, in your opinion, is the remedy for the present depressed condition of the ship-building interest?

Mr. ROWLAND. That is a pretty hard question to answer.

The CHAIRMAN. What would be requisite in order to revive the ship-building interest?

Mr. ROWLAND. Taking the duty off iron might help us some. It would make those Pennsylvania people come down in their prices, and then, instead of building ships at the same prices or at greater prices than they are built in England, I think we could build them ten per cent. cheaper. It looks to me like a lack of enterprise among our merchants. When an Englishman makes three or four per cent. on the capital invested, he is quite well satisfied; but our people do not look at it in that light.

The CHAIRMAN. Do you not know that Americans are negotiating to buy ships in England, and are sailing them under foreign flags, in consequence of their inability to procure vessels here at cheaper rates?

Mr. ROWLAND. No, sir; I do not know that.

Mr. BUFFINTON. Do I understand you to say that you are prepared to-day to build an iron ship as cheaply as it can be built in Europe?

Mr. ROWLAND. I said I would do it at a difference of not exceeding ten per cent. over the cost in England. On a large specification I would build a ship for less money. I do not want anything but the contract.

Mr. BUFFINTON. You would build a ship as good, in your opinion, as it could be obtained abroad for the same money?

Mr. ROWLAND. Yes, sir.

Mr. WELLS. But under Lloyd's regulations it would cost you ten per cent. more?

Mr. ROWLAND. Yes, sir.

Mr. BUFFINTON. Then if that statement is correct, it is not the duty on the iron and on the materials that go into ships that causes the depression in the trade?

Mr. ROWLAND. I think not, myself; but I want the duty taken off iron, so as that we can build ships under Lloyds' rule and build them as they are built in England.

Mr. MORRELL. Would you not consider it rather a disaster than an advantage if by legislation you compelled the iron masters of this country, in order to compete with English manufacturers, to reduce the standard of their quality of iron?

Mr. ROWLAND. I do not want it reduced any more than it is now. Our American iron is poor enough now, to say nothing of the English iron. The trouble is that we do not always get the Pennsylvania iron when we think we do. At the present time there are four thousand tons of scrap iron in port here, which will be rolled and sold for American plate iron.

Mr. MORRELL. If you want plates rolled to specification, you must have American bloom iron, and can afford to pay more for it; but if you compel American iron masters to sell their iron as cheaply as foreign iron is sold, you will break down the business?

Mr. ROWLAND. I do not know. I have got an idea that iron masters like to make a great deal of money.

Mr. MORRELL. There is probably some money made in the business; but there are rolling mills that are standing idle now for want of orders. The best mill in the United States to-day, and the one most able to make those plates, is comparatively idle, has not made money, and has not declared a dividend. I refer to Abbott's, at Baltimore. We want to save this work to our own country. We do not want extreme profits, but simply to be able to earn interest on the capital invested.

Mr. ROWLAND. It seems to me that if we were to go abroad to buy our vessels, and if English vessels were allowed to come here on the same basis as American vessels, American capitalists would cease to be interested in commerce on the seas, and would put their money in railroads, so that we would lose our coasting trade also. If that kind of policy is pursued it seems to me that we might as well give up our ship-yards altogether. The ship-yards and ship mechanics of the country must be taken care of. History says that the time has been when the English would not sell us vessels. That may be again. We had better be ready to do our work at home. Without knowing much of the policy of the government, it seems to me that if the government should give up all its navy yards and should have its ships outside, it would be better for the government in case of an emergency. The navy yards were not worth the room they took during the war. They never built an iron-clad during the war. The government had to take for that purpose to poor fellows like myself. As to the cost of machinery here, that can be constructed by the horse-power for the same money as is paid in England. Mr. Delamater and Mr. Roach, of the Morgan Iron Works, would take a contract to-day to do it.

Mr. HOLMAN. Then you are inclined to attribute the decline in our ship-owning and ship-building commerce to the fact that American capitalists are not satisfied with the small rate of interest that English capitalists are satisfied with?

Mr. ROWLAND. Yes, sir. There is to-day, in our port, an iron ship that was built in Wilmington, Delaware, and she lies here without any business. I do not know why it is. She has been here three or four weeks, and there is no business to be found that would pay her. She is a ship of eight hundred tons, as splendid a vessel as ever entered the port of New York. There is apparently no business for her. She lies at the dock paying wharfage, waiting for freight, I suppose.

Mr. MORRELL. Do you not think that there are certain combinations of great shipping lines to divert freight into the channels in which these foreign vessels are chiefly employed?

Mr. ROWLAND. No; I guess that merchants go where they can get things cheapest. These Englishmen carry for less money than we do. They are satisfied with less profit upon their investments.

Mr. WELLS. Is it your opinion that the allowing of drawbacks on the materials used in ship-building would facilitate and encourage the building of ships here?

Mr. ROWLAND. It would make a ship cost fourteen or fifteen dollars a ton less, and that would help us some; there is no doubt of it.

Mr. CALKIN. You spoke of building ships of a lighter class of iron, using a better quality, of course not giving so great a weight. Please to state that again.

Mr. ROWLAND. An inch square bar of English iron is supposed to hang up 20,000 pounds without breaking. I suppose that would be the test of a bar of English iron. A bar of American iron of the same size would be considered rather poor if it did not hold up 40,000 pounds.

Mr. MORRELL. The average is 60,000 pounds?

Mr. ROWLAND. Yes, sir. The Abbott Company iron will carry 40,000 pounds sure. Under Lloyds' rules we are bound to put quite as much of that 40,000 pounds iron into a ship as an Englishman puts in of the 20,000 pounds iron. The one costs about two and a half cents a pound in gold, and we pay from four and a half to five cents a pound in currency, so that really our iron does not cost a great deal more than theirs, if you take it by the real value. But if you take it by the thickness, they can beat us to death. But where we do beat them is in our labor. They pay a great deal less for labor than we do; but we do more in one day than they do, and what we lose in iron we gain in labor.

Mr. HOLMAN. Do you pretend to say that the English capitalist is satisfied with less profit and a less rate of interest as well on the building as on the earnings of ships?

Mr. ROWLAND. I think so.

Mr. HOLMAN. And you attribute the decline in ship-building and in American commerce largely to that fact?

Mr. ROWLAND. I think that the American people got pretty well discouraged during the war by having their vessels taken away, and they went into other speculations in which there is a great deal more gain with less risk.

Mr. HOLMAN. Speaking of Lloyds' regulation in regard to the weight of iron in ships, that has only reference to the insurance?

Mr. ROWLAND. That is all; but the insurance of a ship is the life of her. If we cannot insure our ships there is no use in building them.

Mr. HOLMAN. To what extent does that rule act?

Mr. ROWLAND. It acts the world over. An American ship to-day would not pass Lloyds' muster. To-day there are American vessels in China lying up for want of trade, while there is freight waiting for English vessels built under Lloyds' rule.

Mr. HOLMAN. English vessels as well as American vessels are insured here in the same way?

Mr. ROWLAND. Yes, sir.

Mr. MORRELL. Would it not be an advantage to American commerce if our merchants could establish something like Lloyds regulations here?

Mr. ROWLAND. Yes, sir; and if we could make Englishmen come under it at this end of the route, it would hurt them some; there is no doubt of it.

Mr. MORRELL. Is it not time that, we, as a nation, should establish our own registration of ships?

Mr. ROWLAND. Yes, sir.

Mr. HOLMAN. How long has this evil been felt?

Mr. ROWLAND. It is about twelve years since Lloyd's rule was originally established. Four years ago, after the Royal Charter and other vessels were lost, they went to work and got up a new set of rules requiring more iron than before, and the inspection since then has been more rigid than it was before.

Mr. HOLMAN. Has this question ever been a subject of diplomacy between this government and the English government?

Mr. ROWLAND. Not that I am aware of. I do not know than any

effort was ever made by the United States to relieve American ship-owners from the effect of the English rule in reference to insurance. This rule has existed ever since iron vessels have been in vogue.

Mr. L. A. SMITH, of the Continental Iron-works, New York, next addressed the committee. He said that there appeared to be a discrepancy between the ship-owners and ship-builders. The ship-owner wanted his ship free; but if absolute free trade in ships were established, he believed that the ship-builder could not keep his business going. There should be absolute and unconditional free trade for all or for none. If the manufacturing interests of the country were to be protected, the ship-building interest should be protected. As to allowing iron ships built in England to be brought in here duty free, and to run under an American registration, it would simply amount not only to allowing English iron to come in duty free, but also to allowing English labor to come in duty free. He had been at some little pains within the last day or two to ascertain the cost of a thousand-ton iron sailing-ship, built in New York, to comply with Lloyds' specification, and fitted out ready for sea, excepting stores. It would cost $121,000. The same vessel would be built in England at £16 per ton, which, allowing currency and exchange to be at $1 40, would make it cost in our currency very nearly $116,660. That would be a little over 4,000 less than the American-built ship, and that showed about the extent of the relief that American ship-builders wanted. The duty on iron averaged about thirty-five per cent. The duty on the iron in such a ship would be about $21,000; so that if that duty were taken off, it would give the American builder an advantage of between $16,000 and $17,000.

Mr. MORRELL. You mean pound for pound of iron, making the American ship of the same weight as the English?

Mr. SMITH. Exactly. As to the question of steam, they are paying in England from £45 to £50 per horse-power. At that rate American engines could be built at good profit, though not English engines, perhaps.

Mr. MORRELL. Does that include the boiler, &c.?

Mr. SMITH. Yes; it includes the engine complete, ready to propel the ship. The Pacific Mail Steamship Company is running its ships with a consumption of about forty tons of coal a day, and making between eleven and thirteen knots. They are about three-thousand-ton ships. The Clyde-built steamers, I believe, are using from fifty to seventy tons of coal per twenty-four hours, and are making about the same rate of speed.

The CHAIRMAN. The Pacific Mail Company's ships are American-built?

Mr. SMITH. Yes; they are American-built, and with American engines; they are built of wood; they are not as good ships as the Clyde or Tyne built vessels; that is, they are not such shapely ships, but their engines appear to be superior.

The CHAIRMAN. Do I understand you to say that American engines can be built as cheaply here as in England?

Mr. SMITH. Yes, sir.

The CHAIRMAN. The difference, then, is only in the hull of the vessel?

Mr. SMITH. The difference would not be even in the hull if we could put in American iron according to its real merits. They build ships in England of steel or semi-steel; it is not a very good material—it is rather treacherous; but where they have built those ships and shown a tensile strength of sixty or seventy pounds to the square inch, a reduction has been allowed in their scantling; if that same reduction could be allowed to American-built ships, that would sustain from one-third to one-half more tensile strength than the English iron, then the enhanced cost of the American iron would be made up practically to the builder and the owner of the ship. If we had an American insurer as reliable all over the world as Lloyds, then we should have no difficulty in the matter.

Mr. BUFFINTON. Has there been any recent improvements in steam-engines?

Mr. SMITH. Yes, sir; a good many.

Mr. BUFFINTON. I suppose you know the machinery and engines of the Old Colony, the Newport, the Providence and the Bristol steamboats?

Mr. SMITH. Yes, sir.

Mr. BUFFINTON. Do you know that the Providence and the Bristol consume in a trip from ten to fifteen tons less coal than the other two boats, while they are much larger boats?

Mr. SMITH. I do not know that; I have no information on the subject.

Mr. BUFFINTON. If it is so, it is not the result of the model of the boats?

Mr. SMITH. No, sir; the Old Colony and the New Bedford are as good models of boats as the Bristol and the Providence; if that is the fact, it arises from the construction of the motive power, either in the engines or in the furnace.

Mr. WILLIAMS, of the firm of Williams & Guion, ship-owners, next addressed the committee. He said that the great difficulty in the way of our navigation was, he supposed, pretty apparent. The English had got the tools to work with and we had not; and the English were running away with our business. The English had started with iron steamers years ago, had followed it up, and had arrived at a great degree of perfection. The Americans had not done so; they were just making a commencement, he might say. There were very few iron vessels built here; he believed that there was only one square-rigged iron sailing vessel built here, and that one was built recently. Iron vessels, both of steam and of sail power, were generally approved by shippers. They were much the superior class of vessels; underwriters would insure them at much less rates, and of course that was operating against wooden vessels and against the American shipping interest. That was the whole thing, and the question, he supposed, was how to overcome that difficulty.

The CHAIRMAN. Have you had vessels built in England?

Mr. WILLIAMS. Yes, sir.

The CHAIRMAN. Have you made any comparison as to the cost of building on each side? Have you got any proposals from parties here to build iron ships?

Mr. WILLIAMS. I cannot say that we have had proposals. We have had specifications made out, and some approximation to the cost.

The CHAIRMAN. Do you regard the difference in the cost between American and English built ships as being the main difficulty in the way?

Mr. WILLIAMS. I do not know what the difference is; but, of course, that is a very important point. But we have not been prepared here to build iron ships; we have had no works here to enter on that large business of building iron steamers of two thousand tons and upward. We have not had experience in it to do it to a large extent on an economical basis. During the war a great many iron vessels were built here;

but I do not think that they would meet the economical wants of our commercial interests.

The CHAIRMAN. How many English ships have you running in your line?

Mr. WILLIAMS. We have six running now.

The CHAIRMAN. What is about the cost per ton of that class of vessels in England?

Mr. WILLIAMS. They are not all the same price. They cost perhaps, on the average, about £22 or £23 per ton. They are three thousand ton ships, some a little less and some a little more. They are iron propellers running from two thousand eight hundred to three thousand five hundred tons. That price includes all the outfit of the ship ready for sea.

The CHAIRMAN. Do you know whether the English have any advantage over ourselves in the sailing of their vessels outside of the government subsidy?

Mr. WILLIAMS. I think they have. I think that generally they man their ships more economically. I do not know that there is any principle which shows that that should be so, except simply that we have not had the experience. We have a great many American sailing ships, but not steamers, engaged in the foreign trade. Sailing between Liverpool and New York, the trade that we are engaged in, the foreign vessel would have no advantage over the American in regard to fuel, although you get fuel in England cheaper than you get it here. But when vessels are sailing from both ports their facilities for getting cheap fuel are the same. I think that the officers and crews of English ships generally sail at less rates. I think it is certainly so at present, and has been so up to this time.

The CHAIRMAN. Do you officer and man your vessels principally with Englishmen?

Mr. WILLIAMS. Mainly so. We have a great many Americans.

The CHAIRMAN. About the same proportion of Americans, I suppose, as there would be of Englishmen in an American ship?

Mr. WILLIAMS. Yes, sir.

The CHAIRMAN. But the character of the vessel and crew is English?

Mr. WILLIAMS. Yes, sir; necessarily so.

Mr. CALKIN. There is also an advantage in being able to buy your liquors and stores in bond on the other side?

Mr. WILLIAMS. There is a very great advantage in that; but that advantage we would have with an American vessel as well as with an English vessel.

Mr. WELLS. The English government gives you the same advantage in that respect under the American flag as under the English flag?

Mr. WILLIAMS. Precisely. There is no distinction at all. We go in there with American ships, and we take our stores out of bond duty free.

The CHAIRMAN. I understand, then, that your vessels are substantially English vessels?

Mr. WILLIAMS. Yes, sir; we have nothing but American captains.

The CHAIRMAN. Would not the effect of building our vessels in Great Britain be, in the ordinary course of business, to have them substantially English vessels, manned, officered, and fitted out—would it not substantially transfer the business, except as to the ownership, to Great Britain?

Mr. WILLIAMS. O, no; that would not be so. If we put them under the American flag of course we should be subject to United States laws, and could not have a foreign crew. We might, perhaps, have English engineers; but as to officers, captains, and mates, they should be Americans. I think that this thing is all in a nut-shell. What we are seeing now was as apparent to me fifteen years ago as it is to-day. I saw that we were going to lose our commerce simply from the effect of the advantage which Great Britain had over us in the building of iron steamers. They had seen the advantage of those steamers before we did, and had facilities for building them, and pressed the business ahead.

The CHAIRMAN. Did that advantage become manifest before the commencement of the war?

Mr. WILLIAMS. It was manifest to me fifteen years ago.

The CHAIRMAN. When did it develop itself?

Mr. WILLIAMS. It had commenced to develop itself in 1858. I went to England expressly for that purpose, seeing that we could not get American iron vessels here, and could not get foreign iron vessels registered under the American flag. The war only hurried on the development.

Mr. WELLS. From your experience, what remedy of legislation would you recommend?

Mr. WILLIAMS. I am, myself, a free-trade man. I go for free ships. That policy would certainly have saved our commerce to a very great degree, if it had been adopted fifteen years ago.

Mr. WELLS. That policy was adopted in Germany and France as well as in England?

Mr. WILLIAMS. Yes, sir.

Mr. WELLS. As I understand, they buy their ships wherever they can get them cheapest, and run them under their own flag?

Mr. WILLIAMS. Yes, sir. Most of the vessels in the French and Bremen lines have been built in England.

Mr. WELLS. Are all the lines of steamers between this port and the ports of Great Britain subsidized lines?

Mr. WILLIAMS. No, sir; the only subsidized lines are the mail lines. The Cunarders run two boats a week. One of them is subsidized and the other not. The Inmans run one boat weekly here, which is subsidized, and one fortnightly, by way of Halifax, which is subsidized; but a large part of the tonnage is not subsidized.

Mr. HOLMAN. What restrictions are imposed upon a foreigner in England as to obtaining a registry on a vessel which he purchased there? Can he hold the title himself and obtain the registration?

Mr. WILLIAMS. I apprehend not.

Mr. HOLMAN. The title of the vessel must be in a British citizen?

Mr. WILLIAMS. Yes, sir; I think so.

Mr. HOLMAN. The fact of a foreigner being an owner constitutes no impediment to obtaining the registration?

Mr. WILLIAMS. I really cannot answer as to that. As regards our own case, we are only part owners. We are shareholders in an incorporated company.

The CHAIRMAN. Have not these lines been established under subsidies?

Mr. WILLIAMS. No, sir; the largest amount of tonnage between here and Liverpool has never been subsidized. One boat each week of the Cunard line and one of the Inman line are subsidized; but the Inman line ran for a dozen years without being subsidized. It is only recently, within a year or two, that they got that contract. The Cunard freight line, and the National line, and our line, have never been subsidized.

Mr. WELLS. Are not the French and German steamers that run to this port subsidized?

Mr. WILLIAMS. Yes, sir; they have mail contracts; they all get more or less compensation from their own governments, and some of them from our government, for the mails that they carry; and they get some from the British government for the letters that they carry to England. Vessels stopping at Southampton and Plymouth get a certain portion of the mail money.

Mr. HOLMAN. Is there any commercial nation except ours that inquires into the fact of where a vessel is constructed, for determining the question as to granting registration?

Mr. WILLIAMS. Yes, sir; I presume that they all do. In England transfers are made without impediment; but in France there is a duty of, I think, ten per cent. imposed on foreign-built ships.

Mr. HOLMAN. Is there a duty imposed by most other nations?

Mr. WILLIAMS. I am not advised as to that.

Mr. NELSON, a member of the Ship-owners' Association of New York, next addressed the committee. He thought that the question before the committee was one which concerned the whole country, not one particular portion of it. All were directly interested in this matter of ship-building. Ship-owners were clogged and dragged down by what he considered an obsolete and a fossil law—a law which compelled them to buy their vessels in this country alone. It was a law copied, he thought, from the enactments of the time of Cromwell, and yet the American government was still sticking to that old law. Our commercial rival, Great Britain, had known the effect of that law and had twice altered it, the last time in 1854. In that year the American tonnage was 5,100,000 tons, equal to that of Great Britain; but now what was it? It had declined within the last ten years fifty per cent., whereas the tonnage of England had increased to about 7,500,000 tons. The whole tonnage of the world, outside that of Great Britain, was something like 9,800,000 tons. Deducting from that all the river tonnage and lake tonnage, fishing boats and canal-boats, and reducing it down to ocean tonnage, it would be found that the tonnage of Great Britain at this day was equal to that of the rest of the world. The business of entering and clearing from British ports had so increased that statistics showed that they carried last year from sixty to seventy per cent. of the whole business, while all other countries carried only about thirty-three per cent. They were all seeking about to find where the trouble lay, and it was a ray of light to see the appointment of this committee. They had nearly given up every hope, but they now trusted that this committee would make such a report and would so sift the thing down as to find a solution of the trouble.

There were three important things necessary to increase American tonnage: first, the vessels; second, marine insurance; third, negotiability, based both on the vessel and on marine insurance. They first wanted to get the vessels, but American capital was now invested in lands, houses, bonds, and all other interests that give a better return than shipping gives. He would leave it to any ship-owner in New York and vicinity to say whether or not the owning of tonnage for the last three years had not been a grievous thing to his pocket. The knowledge that a man was keeping race-horses would probably not help his character as a business man, but really the character of owning ships was about equal to that. After the Crimean war he had been in London and he found the docks there full of transports, vessels that were owned by doctors, clergymen, ladies, bishops, apothecaries, tin-smiths, and all classes of the community. Every one owned a little piece, and many of them made large fortunes during the war; but since the war had closed they were very glad to get rid of their vessels. He had seen some very fine boats there for sale, and thought it would be a good thing if they could be bought and owned here; but the collector at New York informed him that they could not be owned and registered here. He had asked the collector whether he could not own them and put them under somebody else's name. The collector said: "Mr. Nelson, if you can swear that no person except a citizen of the United States owns them, or is directly or indirectly interested in their profits, you can take them." He (Mr. Nelson) had, therefore, to drop that idea, and he presumed that there were others at the same time willing to do the same thing. But the Germans saw the chance, bought two or three of those boats, fitted them up as passenger boats and sent them to this country as a nucleus for new lines, and they had now grown into extensive steamship lines. Gentlemen had said that the English people were contented with less profit than Americans would be. He did not admit that that was so; they were not contented with small profits. Some years ago the Anchor line to Glasgow consisted of one solitary ship, and now that same line had thirty steamers, all built out of the profits of their business. To this day the Chinaman was operating under the same navigation law that he was operating under thirty centuries ago, and the Americans were just following that example, wanting to shut out everything. He did not think that that was a proper mode to pursue. If nature had placed iron and coal and a superabundant population in one portion of the world, enabling iron vessels to be built cheaper than elsewhere, Americans should take advantage of that and buy their vessels where they could get them cheapest. Mr. Rowland had said that he could build an iron vessel within ten per cent. as cheap as it can be built in Great Britain, and yet for two years he had been trying to get an order and could not get one. That gentleman thought that American capitalists wanted more return for their money than the Englishmen did, and that, therefore, they would not invest in ships; but surely the business of New York was open to the capitalists of the whole world on the other side of the water. However, they had the business so nicely digested and so nicely arranged that capitalists were always ready to come forward and advance money upon any steamship line. But what was the case here? There was no security to be had on wooden vessels. Wooden vessels had had their day. In Maine, to be sure, there had been considerable money made in the building of wooden vessels; but they had lost a great many such vessels. The loss from 1854 to 1858 had been one thousand two hundred, and the loss for the last five years was about one thousand eight hundred. Many gentlemen on the committee were probably not familiar with the ship-owning interests. It was absolutely ridiculous for a man to spend his time now in going around among capitalists and soliciting them to invest money in ships. An old ship-owner had said to him a day or two ago, that a man who would invest money in ships here was deemed a lunatic. And why? Because there was no security in lending money on a vessel. Americans could not build up their tonnage unless they could buy their ships where they could buy them cheapest. He supposed that there must be more or less shipping consisting of sailing-vessels; but the great desideratum now was speed, and therefore the great bulk of the commerce would be done in steamships. If the Englishman, the Frenchman, or the German could come to New York and do business between New York and New Orleans cheaper than he could do it, let them do so, and let the people of the country receive the advantage of it. Six years ago there were between thirty and forty large ships being built in New York alone. Now there was but one. Two years ago, for the space of four months, there was not a single American ship or vessel going from New York to Liverpool, whereas there used to be six or eight great lines of ships in that trade. American sailors were all going into other avocations, and, in a short time, there would be very few American sailors left. He should like to see this committee take up this question of supplying American ships with sailors; because, in case of foreign war, sailors would be wanted. He should like to see every ship obliged to carry a certain number of apprentices. He should also like to see all the local pilot laws of the country repealed, and one general statute passed to cover all the points.

The following letter was received from Mr. Allston Wilson:

NEW YORK, *October* 15, 1869.

Hon. John Lynch, Chairman of Committee, &c.:

DEAR SIR: As a member of the committee of the Ship-owners' Association, and having been prevented from attending the conference held yesterday, I desire to call your attention to a collateral branch of the subject which does not appear to have been discussed before you by my colleagues. While fully agreeing with those gentlemen in their statements that the only salvation for the shipping interest under our flag is to admit to free registry all vessels upon their becoming the property of American citizens, I would add that free ships require free sailors, and therefore suggest the removal of all restrictions as to the nationality of officers and men serving in our mercantile marine. It is an admitted fact that our navigation laws are behind the times, and that we require a new code that will not suffer in comparison with that of Great Britain, which passed in 1854 an act known as the merchants' shipping act, many of the provisions of which might be adopted to advantage in this country, to assure the better protection of seamen, and to secure an organized system of shipping and discharging by proper officers, with forms of certificates of capacity and conduct. The mercantile community being alive to the alarming decrease of their tonnage, it becomes those of us who have the ear of your committee to present our opinions for suitable legislation.

Very truly, yours,

ALLSTON WILSON.

Mr. WILLIAM H. WEBB next came before the committee. He said that he was not prepared to make any statements, but would answer any questions that might be asked. He did not see the ship-owners of New York represented before the committee. He did see some members of the Ship-owners' Association, but in his opinion they did not represent the ship-owners of New York. He had heard the sentiment expressed by some ship-owners that they would be very glad if the meeting of the committee could be postponed for a little time, until they could get together and put their views in some shape to lay before the committee.

The CHAIRMAN intimated that the committee would be very glad if the ship-owners would do so.

Mr. WEBB repeated that the principal ship-owners of New York were certainly not represented by the Ship-owners' Association. Those who were most largely engaged in the business were not connected with that association.

Mr. WELLS. I understand you to be a ship-builder as well as a ship-owner?

Mr. WEBB. Yes, sir; I have been long engaged in the building of ships, and I have been heretofore very largely interested in sailing ships; and I suppose that to-day I have as large an interest in steamships as any other man in the country.

Mr. WELLS. What remedy would you recommend for the present depressed condition of commerce and ship-building?

Mr. WEBB. My general views are that if Congress would pass a law freeing all materials that enter into ship-building from the payment of duties, we could then begin to build ships and could compete with any foreign ship-builders. It has been said that that would open the door to a great many frauds upon the government. To avoid that, I would suggest that the materials when purchased and when used in the ship should be ascertained by the government in such manner as might be deemed best for its own security, and that then the drawback should be made upon the materials that were absolutely used in the ship. I think that that would enable the government to adopt this plan without being defrauded.

The CHAIRMAN. I understood you to say that you are not now engaged in the construction of vessels, but that you are merely a ship-owner?

Mr. WEBB. I have a ship-building establishment, and keep it open, but unfortunately we do not do much business there. I am sorry to say that in that yard, where we built a great many ships, the grass is now growing.

The CHAIRMAN. As a constructor of vessels, do you give it as your opinion that you can build ships in competition with the ship-builders of Great Britain if you are allowed a draw-back to the amount of the duties on the materials entering into the construction of vessels?

Mr. WEBB. I do, under the protection that the ship-building interest has in the prohibition of foreign bottoms being owned and registered in this country. We built ships in this country, from here to Maine, so cheaply and so well that we absolutely obliged foreign ship-owners to come to this country and buy our ships, and I think I may say, without fear of contradiction, that there is no other production known in this country, or perhaps in any other, where that thing has been accomplished. The English came here to buy ships, the Germans, the French, and the Italians came here to buy ships. And why? Simply because they could buy better ships and cheaper than they could at home. And yet the wages of our operatives then were nearly double the wages of the same class of operatives abroad; but we managed our business so as to be able to do that. Put us on the same footing as we were then, and we would be able to compete again with the rest of the world in ship-building. It is true that the cost of operating ships is much greater in this country than on the other side, but I trust that that will eventually find its proper level. Wages were always higher here. At present we have to pay firemen on board our steamers more than twice as much as they are paid in Europe.

The CHAIRMAN. Is there any greater difference now than there was before the war?

Mr. WEBB. Yes, sir; there is a greater difference. The difference against us is from forty to fifty per cent. greater than it was then, and it has been as high as from sixty to seventy. But notwithstanding the difference of wages, if we could get the materials of our ships at about the same as they have them on the other side, we could compete with them successfully; at any rate, I should be willing to go in and invest my money in ships and make the trial; but as it is now it is entirely hopeless. I have a place where I built more than one hundred ships within the last thirty years, and, as I said, the grass is growing there now. I have attempted to build a ship recently, and I have lost money by it.

The CHAIRMAN. Do you believe that if the draw-backs were allowed to the amount of the duties paid, the ship-building business of the United States would revive immediately?

Mr. WEBB. Yes, sir; immediately.

The CHAIRMAN. And that a vessel could be built as cheaply here as in England?

Mr. WEBB. Not quite so cheap, but the difference would not be so great as that we could not compete with them. We might not have so good a return for our money, but the return would be such as would induce our people to go in and build ships, and I think that in a comparatively small number of years we would regain the position that we have lost. We have always had much to contend with in this country against foreign ship-building. One considerable item was that a ship-owner was always taxed more or less on his shipping interest as personal property, whereas in Great Britain there was no personal tax on shipping. A ship-owner in Great Britain does not pay any personal tax on his shipping interest; he pays income tax, but that is all. We have always had much of that to contend with, and yet we competed with them successfully. That was due to the fact that we built better ships and on better models. The same talent exists in the country now; and I do not hesitate to say that if we had the same help from our government that the foreign steamship owners and builders have from theirs, we would be able to compete successfully with them in building and running steamships. I am entirely satisfied that we can surpass them in the model of our ships.

The CHAIRMAN. What would be the effect on the ship-building and general navigation interests of the country of amending the navigation laws, and allowing the purchase of foreign ships, while at the same time allowing a draw-back of duties on the materials entering into ship-building in this country? What would be the effect of having the two measures go into operation at the same time?

Mr. WEBB. That is a question which I have not deliberated enough upon to be able to give a satisfactory answer.

The CHAIRMAN. Would the vessels probably be contracted for here, or would they be contracted for in England?

Mr. WEBB. I think, without giving the thing due reflection, that the operation of that would be that the ship-owners of this country would buy ships that are already built to such an extent as they could, and that beyond that they would be obliged to contract for new ships. I think it would take all the ship-building business from this country, and for such a length of time that it would die out. I think that all the ship-yards of the country would die out under that system.

The CHAIRMAN. Do you think that if drawbacks on materials were allowed for three years, and that then the navigation laws were amended so as to admit foreign vessels to register, the American ship-builders would be in a condition to compete with foreign ship-builders?

Mr. WEBB. It would take a much longer time than two or three years. Time soon runs away. It would take a much longer time than that. The navigation laws might have been abrogated any time between 1850 and 1860 without injury to the American ship-builders. Then we had enough of the field to ourselves to have enabled us to have continued to compete with foreign ship-builders. Our labor was at a moderate rate, and everything was going on successfully. All kinds of materials for building ships could be obtained then at much less rates than they can be now. The business was extensive, and the supply was very great. Now the supply is limited and irregular.

Mr. WELLS. I understood you to say that American-built ships were superior to foreign-built ships?

Mr. WEBB. Yes, sir.

Mr. WELLS. Do you not believe that American merchants would

give the preference to American-built ships sufficiently to overcome the difference that you speak of?

Mr. WEBB. Yes, sir; an American ship-owner will give more money for a first-class American-built ship than he will for any other ship. He would be induced to do that because the underwriters of this country would certainly give the preference to American-built ships.

The CHAIRMAN. I suppose that they have been gaining on us in that regard in Great Britain while our business has been depressed?

Mr. WEBB. Certainly; not only in one direction, but in all the ramifications of the shipping interest they have been gaining ground upon us until they have got the field pretty nearly to themselves, and if the thing runs on as at present for one or two years longer, not only the ship-yards of this country will be all closed, but the skilled operatives will have gone away or left the business, and we will have no men to build our ships. For the last ship that I built, last year, I found more difficulty in getting skilled operatives to work upon her than upon any vessel I ever built.

Mr. MORRELL. Do you believe that if the Alabama, and the other confederate privateers, had not been permitted to prey upon American commerce we would have been able to have held our supremacy, notwithstanding the war?

Mr. WEBB. No, sir; I do not think we would. These vessels, of course, aided very much in injuring our commerce; but the high price of labor and of materials has been perhaps the principal drawback. I do not expect that labor will ever come to the level that it was at many years ago; but it will fall sufficiently, I think, to enable us to build ships if we can buy our materials cheap.

Mr. NELSON, speaking for the Ship-owners' Association, asserted that it represented three-fourths of the tonnage visiting the port of New York, and that that fact could be proved if Mr. Webb denied it. He presumed that Mr. Webb was not putting a stigma upon that association.

Mr. WEBB said he had no desire of that kind. He had given what was his impression, and he still thought that the older ship-owners of New York, who had had the most experience in the business, were not represented by the Ship-owners' Association.

Mr. WESTERVELT next addressed the committee. He expressed his belief that very much of the trouble was owing to the fact that the American standard of mechanical labor was very greatly reduced, and that we were paying very much more for the amount of labor performed than we used to do in former years. He thought that the ship-builders had neglected their own interests. Twenty years ago it had been the custom for each ship-builder to educate a certain number of boys to the business, and to make them familiar with the mysteries of ship-building; but he believed that there had been no apprentices taken for many years past. The result was that the mechanics employed by ship-builders now knew very little about their business, and that ships cost a great deal more to build than they used to cost. Probably the bosses themselves had not kept up with the times, and he did not think that they had. He thought, however, that the days of wooden ships were ended. He believed that iron ships possessed all the qualities that wooden ships did, and possessed besides many qualities that wooden ships did not. In almost all respects iron ships were superior to wooden ones, and it was no longer worth while to talk about their respective merits. There had been very little experience in the building of iron ships in New York. He understood that in other parts of the country iron ships could be built almost as cheaply as they could be abroad. He thought that we might be able ultimately to compete with foreign ship-builders, but not for some years; because the foreigners had got men educated to the business, and Americans were not so well skilled in the art of iron ship-building as the English were, and that, for the best of all reasons, because very few iron ships had been built here in comparison with the immense number of iron ships built in England. There were very few establishments in the country in which iron ships could be built. He believed that it cost more to build ships in New York than in any other place in the world. There had been a time when New York built ships which were equal and superior to the ships of any part of the world; but now they were turning out ships in England which, in his opinion, were equal to anything that New York had ever done in that way.

The CHAIRMAN. If you obtained the materials free of duty, could you construct ships in competition with the English?

Mr. WESTERVELT. I cannot speak of iron vessels, because I am not conversant with them, and to build wooden ships I think would be labor lost.

The CHAIRMAN. How much higher are the wages that are now paid to ship-carpenters than they were before the war?

Mr. WESTERVELT. Before the war we paid $2 25 per day; we are now paying $4. At that time a first-class ship cost $55 a ton to build; to-day it costs $110 a ton.

Mr. WELLS. What proportion of the expense of building wooden ships is in the labor?

Mr. WESTERVELT. I can hardly state that, for I have built no ships for several years. I have got the cost of ships recently built in Boston, and I am told that they cost about $110 a ton. I have not built ships for several years.

Mr. MORRELL. Would the cost per ton for a ship of eight hundred tons be the same as for a ship of sixteen hundred tons?

Mr. WESTERVELT. The cost per ton would be rather greater in the small ship than in the large one. As a ship increases in size the rate per ton would be less. I am speaking about ships of fifteen hundred tons costing about that much per ton.

Mr. WILLIAM H. WEBB was again called before the committee.

Mr. CALKIN. As Mr. Webb has had experience in running steamers to Europe, I desire to ask him whether, if Congress should pass a law relieving the shipping interest so that iron steamers could be built as cheap in this country as abroad, and if Congress should subsidize them to a small amount, could a line of steamers then compete with the present Enropean lines and pay a fair dividend to the owners?

Mr. WEBB. I have had some experience in running steamships in different directions—in the past year to Europe. Judging from that experience, I should say that if Congress should pass a law relieving the construction of steamships from the onerous duties now paid, and should also grant a liberal subsidy—I cannot say a small subsidy, but a liberal subsidy, no more than European governments have heretofore granted to their ship-owners—we could run steamships and compete successfully with any of the foreign lines.

Mr. CALKIN. In reference to immigration, do you know whether the immigrant coming to this country usually prefers to come in an American ship and under the American flag rather than in a foreign ship?

Mr. WEBB. Heretofore they gave a decided preference to American ships; but from the fact that American ships have almost died out, that preference, as a matter of course, has also died out. I have sent two ships last year, and the preference was given to them simply because they were American ships. I do not mean to say by that that the preference has been given to them over any foreign ships, but I mean over foreign ships of the same class. And I know from my recent traveling in Europe that a sympathy exists there, especially among emigrants, in favor of American ships, and a desire that American ships should be put into the business again.

Mr. FRANCIS COBB, of Rockland, Maine, largely interested in ship-building, next appeared before the committee and was inquired of in reference to the wages paid to ship-carpenters. He said that ship-carpenters in Maine were now being paid from $2 50 to $3 a day.

The CHAIRMAN. How do their wages now correspond with what they were before the war?

Mr. COBB. There has not been that advance with that class of labor that there has been with other classes, for the very reason that there has been less ship-building than there was formerly. We used to get men at perhaps half a dollar a day less before the war. There was one statement made here to-day in reference to the cost of ships, which I desire to correct. It has been stated that first-class ships cost, in New York, at the rate of $110 per ton. I can say that first-class ships are built in Maine (nine-year ships of the very first class of oak and pine) at $55 per ton. They can be fitted out ready for sea, with all their fittings, at from $70 to $75 per ton.

The CHAIRMAN. What did the same class of ships cost before the war?

Mr. COBB. The cost of such ships before the war was about $40 per ton, without spars. Similar ships are now being built at from $50 to $55 per ton. I saw a contract recently for a large ship at $55 per ton. That is about thirty or forty per cent. more than they were before the war. That is the price that ship-builders are selling them at, and I suppose they would not build them without making some profit on them.

Mr. R. P. BUCK, of New York, next addressed the committee. He said he rose principally to corroborate what Mr. Cobb had just said relating to the present cost of ships. He had just sent to sea a new ship which had cost, coppered, $73 per ton, and he should launch another of one thousand four hundred tons within a week, which would cost $75 a ton without copper. She is more of a white-oak ship, and cost a little more money on that account. She is rigged with wire rigging, which is a little cheaper than hemp rigging, although I am inclined to think it is not quite so good. As to the remedy for the present evil, it has puzzled my head for the last fifteen years. I do not know where the remedy is. Most certainly we cannot throw open our whole coastwise trade to foreign ships unless we have free trade in everything, and that we cannot afford to have under the present circumstances. I think that if the matter is sifted down it will be found that most of the men who want free trade in ships are men who are directly or indirectly interested in ships built in the provinces, and who would like to get those ships registered here so as to put them into the coasting trade. The very moment that foreign ships are admitted to registration here those ships will do all our coasting trade instead of the ships that are built in Maine. It will produce what Mr. Webb has described, a dearth of mechanics, and we will have no ship-builders in time of war. It will also make our sailors extinct, because they will not go to sea in foreign ships. I have known American captains, during the war, who were so loyal that they would rather stay at home than go to sea in foreign ships that were offered them. I think that if we had a reduction of the duties on all the materials going into the construction of ships, whether the materials be American or foreign, and if we could also be freed from the taxation on ships, as is the case, I understand, in other countries, we could then afford to build our ships in this country and to compete with any other nation. I do not believe that there is any more ingenuity in Glasgow or any other ship-building place than there is in this country; nor do I believe that there is any more energy among the foreigners than among Americans. I think that if we are put upon the same footing we will be able to compete on the ocean with the rest of the world. We have a greater ocean front than any other nation, and it would be a terrible disgrace if we allowed ourselves to be driven from the ocean. It has been wisely said that the nation which controls the ocean controls the world; and since we have the Pacific and the Atlantic, we are destined to do that. That is what we will do if we have sufficient encouragement from the government, or rather if the government withdraws its restrictions upon us. The tariff renders the cost of materials so great that we cannot build ships. I do not think that the ship-owners of New York are represented extensively in the Ship-owners' Association. I am free to say that I believe that if you could call together the men who have been twenty or forty years in the ship-owning business in this city, you would not find the majority of them ready to throw the business open to foreigners and to have our ships purchased abroad. I saw that it was stated here yesterday that British vessels are insured at two and a half per cent., while the rates on our ships are from eight to nine per cent. I have made inquiry this morning at the office of the Atlantic Insurance Company, and I was informed that insurance is just as cheap on an American vessel as on a foreign vessel.

The CHAIRMAN. The statement was that the low rate of insurance is only charged upon iron ships abroad, and the high rate of insurance upon wooden ships.

Mr. BUCK. They may insure on what they like abroad, but we want our insurance done at home. They may insure iron ships cheaper there; but I do not believe that they insure cargoes any cheaper in an iron ship than they do in a ship built by Mr. Webb. Just think how the balance of trade is against us. If we bought our ships abroad, paying gold for them at thirty per cent. premium, we would be impoverished so speedily that we would never be able to get back to specie payments.

The committee adjourned till to-morrow, 16th October.

NEW YORK, *October* 16, 1869.

The committee met.

Present, the Chairman and Messrs. Wells, Holman, and Calkins.

Mr. A. A. Low appeared before the committee.

The CHAIRMAN. The committee would like to hear from you in regard to the general policy of building our ships at home or buying them abroad, as we understand that you are a ship-owner and importer. What should be the policy of the government to protect and foster our shipping interest and to bring it back to the standard position it held before the war?

Mr. LOW. Individually, I have always been in favor of protecting American interests. I have been inclined to sustain our own architects, builders, and mechanics, and to rear our own sailors and advance the interests of commerce generally in that direction. Most of our laws are formed with a view to protecting our various industries; but the laws which protect our general industry bear oppressively upon this particular interest, so that the laws which are designed for the protection of American industry are really a burden upon our shipping industry.

The CHAIRMAN. We would like you to give the committee your views as to the causes which have operated to produce the present depressed condition of affairs in our shipping interests.

Mr. Low. In the first instance we have a depreciated currency. I think that militates against the building of ships. We have very high prices of labor, and high prices of all the materials that enter into the construction of ships. These prices are increased by the laws which are designed to protect other branches of industry, and of course they all tend to increase the cost of the ships in the first instance, and the cost of the sailing of the ship after she is built. I think that the American shipping interest suffered before the war came on. The California trade had caused the building of a vast number of ships, especially of the class known as clipper ships. Then the steam lines began to multiply and to take the valuable traffic on the Atlantic. That forced sailing ships upon distant courses, and the freight was very low for several years before the war—so low as to be wholly unremunerative. When the war came on, the privateers burned our vessels and added to the cost of sailing by increasing the rates of insurance upon our ships. Our ships were destroyed, and there is no motive to replace them at the increased cost. Nor do I see how we can recommence building ships unless the ship-building interest is relieved from the taxes put upon all the materials that enter into the construction of vessels. My own belief is that the policy of England, in subsidizing lines of steamers to the various ports of the world, has given her a prestige which is almost insuperable. Her mechanics have been trained in the construction of iron ships and of all the machinery requisite for the purpose, and it would seem to me that it would take our mechanics a long time to get into a condition to compete with England. We have just now but one important steam line, and that is the Pacific Mail Steamship line, and it seems to me that all the subsidies which our government has ever given to all the steam lines that we have ever had would not be equal to the amount of loss inflicted upon that single remaining line by the Pacific railway. We gave fifty or sixty million dollars, and lands extending for miles on either side, to that railroad—an internal line of communication to the Pacific, which has cut off all the support that hitherto belonged to the Pacific Mail Steamship line—so that during the little time that that Pacific railroad line has been opened that single line of steamers must have suffered an injury of from six to eight million dollars. The capital of the Pacific Mail Steamship line is twenty million dollars. Two years ago its stock was worth from one hundred and forty to one hundred and fifty; now it is down to fifty-six. It has fallen within a year from one hundred and twenty-five down to fifty-six, which would represent about fourteen million dollars. I do not know why the Pacific Mail Steamship line would not be as good property to-day as it was before if Congress had not given fifty or sixty million dollars, and immense quantities of land, to that line of railroad, and so built it up at the expense of the only single line of steamers remaining to this country. There does not seem to be a law upon our statute books which does not inflict an injury upon our commercial interests. Then, again, the policy of England in reference to subsidies has been different from our own. The English have engrossed the traffic from almost every country. They have manufactures in abundance to supply the distant markets. They have their distant colonies to incite them to effort. Occupying an insular position as they do, there is not a man in England that does not appreciate the importance of commerce; so that all the English laws are for the benefit of commerce. Our country is so large, and the opportunities for the employment of capital are so diverse, that our legislators do not give that attention to commerce which the statesmen of England do. I think the English statesmen have been wiser than ourselves in subsidizing largely, in the first instance, all their ocean lines, until they have trained their mechanics perfectly in the creation of steamships. There is a very interesting article in the Times this morning which shows what the English are doing in that line. It is easier to explain the causes of our decline than it is to suggest a remedy. If there is any way of relieving the ship-building interest from the duties imposed upon it for the protection of other American industries, that would certainly be a step in the right direction. If a subsidy could be given to ocean steamers that would be an offset to the extra cost of building our steamers, that would be another mode of meeting the difficulty. My own impression has been that large subsidies should be given as an inducement, and that those subsidies, while they would cost the government something in the beginning, would cost the government nothing in the end, because the materials used in the construction of ships would pay back in taxes to the government whatever is paid in subsidies. At present we build no steamers—we can build none. We cannot build steamers, I suppose, because iron has taken the place of wood. We abound in wood but not in cheap iron. The screw steamers have taken the place of the side-wheelers, and wooden vessels cannot bear the action of the ocean upon the screw; so that we are inevitably driven upon iron in the construction of our ocean steamers, and we have not the cheap iron to compete with the cheap iron of England and with the skilled labor of England. I see that Mr. Webb and others express great confidence in the ability of our mechanics to compete with English laborers. I must say that I have not that same confidence in the superiority of our workmen. They work a shorter time than the English workmen do, and demoralization seems to have extended into the department of labor to a greater degree perhaps than to almost any other. Our labor generally is very much demoralized, and any one who undertakes to build a house or anything else will soon find it out. I have no doubt that we can command as skillful workmen as any in the world, but that we can command better workmen than are in England I do not believe. Certainly the ships that they send here are superior to any that have ever been made hitherto. They are excellent in model and in workmanship. Any one who has made a passage across the Atlantic in one of their ocean steamers will be satisfied of their stability and excellence as well as of their great speed. It seems to me that the English have attained to the utmost excellence in that line, and that although our mechanics may be of the best order, we should be weak and foolish to think that we can excel the English in any of those respects. We should be put to our mettle to hold our own with them until we have had a good many years to study the art and to practice it.

The CHAIRMAN. Can you give us any information as to the amount of subsidies paid by our government and by the English government?

Mr. LOW. I cannot give you the particulars of the different subsidies paid by Great Britain or by this country. I only know that the English have adhered to the policy of sustaining their ocean lines of steamers by sufficient subsidies. They have never shrunk from the necessity of paying whatever was needed to continue a line to distant countries. For instance, if a line of steamers were formed to Australia and were unsuccessful, and if it were found that a larger subsidy was necessary to continue it, they would liberally give what was sufficient for the purpose. In a word, the English have always, in peace and in war, manifested a determination to hold the supremacy on the ocean; and the supremacy which they acquired by arms in war they have in peace acquired by subsidies. They have, deliberately and intentionally, driven the Americans from the ocean by paying subsidies which they knew our Congress would not pay. I believe it has been the deliberate purpose on the part of England to maintain her supremacy on the ocean by paying larger subsidies than any other nation as long as subsidies were necessary to preserve their control. I believe that when the Collins line was running, the subsidy to the Cunard line was renewed for the express purpose of enabling it to run off the Collins line. It was renewed several years before the expiration of the subsidy already granted, so that the Cunard line might enter upon contracts for new ships; and a committee of the English Parliament similar to this committee was employed to make the most minute investigation into the matter. It was after the most careful inquiry by that committee that the contract with Cunard was renewed, for the express purpose of enabling that line to run the American steamers from the ocean; and they have driven us from the ocean by that policy just as effectually as they ever did drive an enemy from the ocean by their guns.

Mr. WELLS. From your experience of the mode of conducting steamship lines, do you not think that the English run their lines at much less expense than the Americans, and that if Collins had run his line at the same expense as Cunard it could have been sustained?

Mr. LOW. The English protect their ships, but we burden ours. We burden every supply that goes on board our ships. Every pound of tea and every pound of sugar is burdened with heavy tariff charges. The English exempt the stores that are put on board their ships from such charges. In every way they increase their shipping interests, and in every way we depress ours. In the time of the war the shipping interest was the only interest that suffered. The privateers burnt our ships or subjected them to heavy rates of insurance; and so far as foreign insurance companies were concerned, they turned their faces against insuring our ships.

The CHAIRMAN. In your opinion are ship-owners generally in favor of amending the navigation laws, so as to allow the purchase of ships abroad and nationalizing them here?

Mr. LOW. I dare say that those who are not fully American in their feeling would be in favor of bringing foreign-built ships here, and of putting them under the American flag; but I, individually, would prefer to see our mechanics encouraged as hitherto, to build those vessels. I think that we should be relieved from the burdens which now stand in the way of ship-building, so that we shall not only have ships to sail, but men to build them. Still, it would be better to go abroad and buy our ships and put them under the American flag rather than to be ruled out off the sea altogether, as we now are. The shipping interest has been so unprofitable in this part of the country that capital has been diverted from that branch of commerce to more inviting fields.

The CHAIRMAN. In your opinion, if the American ship-builders and ship-owners were put upon the same footing and offered the same encouragement as the ship-builders and ship-owners of Great Britain, would we be able to compete with them?

Mr. LOW. If it were possible to put them on the same footing, of course there is an aptitude among our people in the pursuit both of building and sailing vessels that would soon manifest itself, unquestionably.

Mr. WELLS. In other words, you think that if drawbacks were allowed on the materials entering into ship-building in this country, and if the disabilities in reference to buying ships abroad and putting them under the American flag were removed, our commerce would revive?

Mr. LOW. I have said that there are many things in the way of the restoration of our commerce, and one of the first difficulties is the condition of the currency. That aggravates everything.

Mr. WELLS. That cannot be remedied for the time being. But as to the more immediate relief, what do you think would be its result?

Mr. LOW. Our mechanics say that if the materials that enter into the construction of ships were relieved from taxes they could go to work, and I have no doubt that that is so. I have no doubt that we have iron equal to any other for the construction of ships, and that we have the skill to construct them. We have not the experience; but I have no doubt that that will come.

Mr. WELLS. And we have national pride, too.

Mr. LOW. We have the pride.

Mr. WELLS. That, together with the subsidies, you think would probably be the only policy to relieve us for the time?

Mr. LOW. Yes, sir.

The CHAIRMAN. You speak of the currency being an impediment. Where we compete with England upon gold prices, would the condition of our currency make any real difference?

Mr. LOW. Inasmuch as the traffic is carried on in gold prices, we would be on a par with them; we should have the same remuneration as they have.

The CHAIRMAN. Then, really, what effect does the currency have on the question?

Mr. LOW. It is the parent of a great deal of demoralization. Everything is high—rents, and labor, and materials. We have exaggerated prices for everything.

The CHAIRMAN. Above the difference between gold and currency?

Mr. LOW. Apparently. Labor is certainly out of proportion to the difference between gold and currency. Where we used to pay eleven dollars a month to sailors, we now pay twenty-five dollars. That exhibits more than the difference between gold and currency. I speak of the sailors in the China trade, where the rates are lower than in the European trade. We used to pay eleven dollars where we now pay twenty-five dollars. Commerce now is threatened in another way. The trade that we have hitherto done in ships to China shall be lost to us through this Pacific railroad, after awhile. The teas that now come by ships may come from San Francisco over the road; and I presume they will do so before long. Then, again, we are threatened through the Suez Canal, and through the competition of steamers with sailing vessels. I understand that the English are already making inquiries here in relation to the cost of transportation of teas by steam from China; so that the commerce which we have carried on with the East is threatened the whole way by the land route across the continent, and by the steam route through the Suez Canal. I do not, myself, believe in the transportation of teas by so expensive a route. At present there is no profit in the importation of teas, and there has not been for two years past. And inasmuch as there is no profit with the inconsiderable cost of bringing them by sailing vessels, there would be no warrant for the higher cost in bringing them by steam vessels, as steamers cannot transport freights so cheaply as sailing vessels can.

The CHAIRMAN. I understand you, then, to be in favor of an attempt to restore our shipping by building it at home rather than by buying it abroad?

Mr. LOW. Certainly, sir; my feeling is to have our ship-yards revived. The skill acquired there would make us independent of foreign labor. That has always been my feeling. I always had a desire to see our own ship-yards restored to their usefulness, and to see men trained up in this country so to make us independent of foreign skill and labor in that regard. I suppose that it is the natural feeling of every one who has an interest in American commerce to see American industry thrive in that direction. Still, I think it would be better to resort to England for steamers, rather than be ruled out entirely from the benefits of a very profitable pursuit.

The CHAIRMAN. What effect do you think it would have on our commercial interests if we were to amend our navigation laws and go abroad to buy our vessels?

Mr. LOW. It seems to me that at present the English can build much more cheaply than ourselves, and that that policy would put off the time when we should be independent of other nations. It would be pursuing a course in reference to that particular industry of ship-building at variance with that which is adopted in reference to all other American interests. In regard to all other internal pursuits, we adhere to the policy of protection; but in reference to ship-building, we adhere at present to one of oppression. We protect all other industries at the expense of commerce.

The CHAIRMAN. Would the effect of purchasing our ships abroad be to make them foreign in their character to a considerable extent?

Mr. LOW. They would be foreign ships; and I think they could build them at present so much more cheaply than we can that there would be little hope of reviving that industry among ourselves.

The CHAIRMAN. What I mean is, whether there would not be interests of ownership on the other side which would make those ships to a great extent foreign—whether it would not necessitate a change of laws as to officering and manning our ships, and whether our ships would not be finally pretty much under the control of foreign interests?

Mr. LOW. If Americans should buy ships abroad and put them under the American flag, we have men enough to command and man them, and I do not know whether there would be any tendency to employ others instead of Americans.

The CHAIRMAN. Why I ask that question is, that was submitted by the Ship-owners' Association of New York, in favor not only of foreign ships, but of foreign officers and crews.

Mr. LOW. I think that that is the sentiment of an alien, not of an American. I cannot imagine that any American should wish to see foreign ships where we hitherto had American ships, and to see foreign commanders and sailors in place of Americans. Our sailors have been always very largely foreigners, but our ship-masters and mates have been generally Americans. There are enough of them awaiting employment now, and every patriotic sentiment would urge their employment.

The CHAIRMAN. I suppose that that was a question of economy, as it is in the purchase of ships?

Mr. LOW. We have many men now idle who would be glad of employment at a very moderate compensation. In former times we had no disposition to employ foreigners in preference to Americans, when the laws allowed it. We always had good commanders, and when wood was employed in the manufacture of our ships, we had the sea. It was only when the new condition came into force, steam instead of sailing ships, and iron instead of wood, that we lost it, and then, I think, through the policy of England in subsidizing steam lines, which took all the valuable traffic and all the passengers. The English maintain their steamers by ample subsidies; our government does not. And, as I said before, the propeller has taken the place of the side-wheeler, and the wooden ship cannot bear the propeller; therefore England now engrosses almost the whole building of steamers.

The CHAIRMAN. You say that wooden ships cannot bear the propeller. Is that on account of the strain?

Mr. LOW. The action of the propeller, I am told, is such that no wooden vessel can stand it on the ocean. They do very well along the coast and in still waters; but I was told that on the Atlantic a wooden vessel cannot stand the action of the propeller. I think that Mr. White will tell you the same thing. Therefore our steamers are driven from the ocean. I do not think myself that wooden fabrics would stand the strain.

Mr. CALKIN. I do not understand you to be in favor of abrogating the present navigation laws?

Mr. LOW. I have been always in favor of American interests.

Mr. CALKIN. You are one of our leading merchants, and I should like that expression from you.

The CHAIRMAN. He has already given it while you were out.

Mr. LOW read some proof-sheets of an article contributed by him to Putnam's Magazine for December, which article is hereto annexed, as follows:

SOVEREIGNTY OF THE SEAS.

An idea extensively prevails that the contest for supremacy on the ocean was virtually closed with the victories of Trafalgar and the Nile. After the destruction of the French fleets in the Mediterranean, it was indeed evident enough that no single nation, nor all the maritime powers in the world combined, could successfully cope with Great Britain on the sea. Throughout the waters of the globe the British ensign waved triumphantly, the undisputed and unquestioned symbol of sovereignty. Down to the time when the wars of Napoleon ceased the naval arm was used more as an auxiliary to contending armies battling for dominion on the land than as a means of controlling the commerce of the world. As an agent for crippling the strength of an adversary the navy has always been employed; while the lust for gain has stimulated an active crusade against private property in aid of a more direct national aim. Even now, when commerce is so much extended, and the interests of all countries and all peoples are so blended as to be inseparable, every effort to abolish privateering fails, and, when nations resort to war, merchant-ships, doubtless, will continue to be the prey of the national cruiser and privateer alike.

The purpose of this article, however, is not to consider the "usages of war," nor the abuses to which war gives rise. Friend and foe have taught the United States a lesson in this regard that will not soon be forgotten. It is our aim, rather, to show in this paper that supremacy on the ocean in the interests of commerce was not so directly sought, nor so effectually gained, by the vast and costly armaments of Great Britain in the wars that preceded the present century, as it has been by the more peaceful and inexpensive method steadfastly pursued by that country during the last thirty years. Or, without undertaking to show, what it might be difficult to prove, that the contest on the ocean has not always been waged by Great Britain to advance the interests of her foreign commerce; or, admitting this to have been the ultimate aim, and open communication with her distant colonies a *sine qua non*, demanding the utmost exertion of her naval power, it is still of paramount importance to mark the policy that has governed her statesmen since the cessation of the continental wars. Whether for coast defense, or as a means of hostile attack, or to keep pace with the growing navies of other maritime powers, England steadily adds to the number of her ships of war, never faltering in her purpose of holding, at any cost, the dominion of the sea. Let any who doubt this visit her dock-yards and her channel fleets, and behold the majestic iron-clads, formidable for their size, their armor, and their armament, as well as for their great propelling power. The superiority of England in this class of vessels for purposes of attack and defense it is not popular with us to admit. We are vain enough to assume that against armored ships of the greatest magnitude and the most powerful batteries, our slowly-moving monitors, with two and four heavy guns, are a safe reliance. Be it so!

Monitors have answered the purpose for which they were created; and it is not in the direction of her naval armaments that the policy of England demands our present attention or imitation. Were it otherwise, our naval officers are abroad—they are intelligent and observing—and we can safely leave to the verdict of their judgment such problems as only experts can solve.

From 1815 to 1835 peace reigned throughout the world, affording an opportunity to all the nations bordering on the sea to enter into a friendly competition for the carrying trade of the nations. In the ensuing struggle the United States acquired a prestige that was unexcelled; and such was the skill of our mechanics, the abundance of our material for the construction of ships, and the aptitude of our sons for the life of a sailor, that our republic gained the command of the trade to and from Europe, and was a bold and successful competitor with Great Britain for the traffic between her own colonies and the mother-country, as well as for that from China and other portions of the East. A little later on, our clippers, outsailing the old-fashioned vessels, became models for merchantmen; and, notwithstanding the proverbial obstinacy of the English and Scotch, they were alert enough to accept and adopt them.

But what a change since then has taken place, commencing in 1837 and 1838, but not patent to the common eye till ten or fifteen years later on. England's maritime supremacy is so manifest now as to reflect our national humiliation! How this is to come to pass it is not difficult to explain; but the explanation is mortifying and painful.

Many things have combined and worked together to produce the revolution. In the chain of events resulting in the rapid decline of our commerce may be cited the following, viz:

1st. A substitution of steamships for sailing-vessels; this commenced about 1837-'38.

2d. The use of iron instead of wood in the construction of ships and steamers.

3d. The reaction from high rates of freight, because of the vast increase of tonnage which the trade of California brought into being, the expulsion of sailing-vessels from short ocean routes, and the consequent overcrowding of distant ports.

4th. The war of the rebellion, which raised up an insidious foe, and for five years rendered the building and sailing of American ships a worse than profitless pursuit, and which finally imposed a burden of taxes on all the material that enters into the construction of vessels, and so enhanced the price of labor and of seamen's wages as to make competition with our great rival most unequal.

When it is borne in mind that the shipping interest was the only important interest at the North that suffered by the war, and that other great interests have been benefited rather than injured by the enactment of import and internal revenue laws, it seems strange that Congress has done little or nothing to mitigate the burden on our external commerce; failing utterly to relieve it from the operation of laws that bear unjustly on the mercantile class, and hence, injuriously on the community at large.

Under four distinct heads we have now stated what seem to be secondary causes of the decline of our national commerce. The disturbed condition of our currency might have been named after the fourth of the series, because it is the direct consequence of our civil war. It is too important to be overlooked; it is too well understood, and too keenly felt, to require comment. Would that there were any disposition in the people at large to correct what so many profess to deplore, and yet do nothing to amend! Unless a better spirit appears than hitherto has marked the deliberations of Congress, this fruitful source of demoralization and disability must continue and stand out as a harm and a hinderance to our commercial progress. The depreciation of the national currency, considered in connection with the other reasons for the depression of our commerce, serves to intensify the claim on our government for the renewal, on a more generous scale, of *subsidies to ocean mail steamers.* Assuming, as we do, that the contest for supremacy on the ocean did not cease in 1815, but has taken a new form, nothing has transpired to signalize the wisdom of British statesmen more striking than the plan so successfully pursued of subsidizing lines of mail steamers to all important parts of the world. The wisdom on their part would be manifest enough if not contrasted with our own folly; and our folly would be more endurable if we had not been misled by the arguments of our free-trade adversary, plausibly presented, instead of being guided by his example.

The astute Emperor of France disdains not to listen to English counsel, but, with a judgment better than our own, imitates English example. Indeed, it is beautiful to behold two hereditary foes, in loving obedience to the doctrine of "free trade," steaming side by side, in quest of the silk of China and Japan—competing in generous rivalry for the trade of the East. And observe the consequences! By degrees Lyons becomes the distributing mart instead of London, and English manufacturers close their doors in view of the French competition. France returns the chalice to the lips of England! In the face of such results it must have amused the friend of Cobden—the renowned Emperor—when it was declared in Parliament that to receive proposals from the Messageries Impériales for the transportation of her Britannic Majesty's mails would be "free trade run mad," and the sentiment was applauded to the echo! England was for free trade just so long as England could profit by it, and no longer.

The application of steam as a motive power to ships on the ocean about 1837 and 1838 inaugurated a new era in maritime history, and the statesmen of England were quick to discern the importance of the epoch. Almost immediately a contract for the transportation of British mails to the United States was entered into, being the first of a system of contracts which has been persistingly extended till it has become world-embracing. Lines of steamers to Canada, to the West Indies, to Brazil, to the Cape of Good Hope, to Australia and New Zealand, to British India, China, and Japan, are among the most important of those hitherto established. These have not all been uniformly successful. In the loss of ships at sea several have been unfortunate, and financial disaster sometimes has been imminent; but under every discouragement the British government has been faithful, sustaining by large and larger subsidies the waning fortunes of the weak, and by most liberal concessions strengthening others to resist either threatened or actual competition. From the outset, the vivifying effect upon the commerce of England of these swift messengers to different countries was too apparent to escape observation. It was seen that under another name an international express system had been established which was taking to Great Britain the "quick orders" and also the most enterprising traders, to seek in the well-supplied warehouses of England the merchandise they needed, while returning steamers conveyed goods and buyer, at once, to his own doors at home.

The results of this extended, well-organized, and regular system of international transportation were soon apparent:

1st. In the creation of a class of unsurpassed steamers.

2d. In raising up a select body of seamen, loyal adherents to the service in which they were reared, and ready both to man the transports so useful in peace, and to sustain the honor of their flag in the emergencies of war.

3d. In educating a corps of accomplished officers, all the while acquiring familiarity with the navigable waters, ports, and harbors constantly visited and revisited.

4th. In perfecting the skilled mechanics of the realm in the use of iron, and its adaptation to the rapidly-growing steam marine.

5th. In imparting a stimulus to the manufacturing industries of the kingdom, so abounding in resources and talent, garnered up and held in reserve for new and enlarged uses.

6th. In drawing to the bonded warehouses of London and Liverpool the products of every country and every clime, to be distributed, through largely increased facilities, to the less favored nations and the waiting markets of the surrounding world.

It were easy enough to extend the recital of advantages immediately resulting from the adoption of a policy in the pursuit of which British statesmen have never wavered. But the record is long enough and amply suggestive.

When ten years or less had borne abounding testimony to the success of this policy on the other side of the Atlantic, the American Congress was awakened from its slumbers, and manifested a willingness to follow a lead that was so full of promise, and to strike for a share in the prize that was not yet beyond our grasp. A subsidy was finally granted to the "Collins line," and we recall, with melancholy pleasure, the outgoing and incoming of those noble ships, the Atlantic, Pacific, Baltic, Arctic, and Adriatic, as they entered on their brief, brilliant, unfortunate, disastrous career. The time of service was long enough to establish their excellence as sea-going vessels, and the record of their passages will compare favorably with any similar number made in later years. But misfortunes came apace. The Arctic and Pacific both foundered at sea—the Arctic in consequence of a collision with a French steamer; the Pacific, probably, in consequence of a collision with an iceberg. There was bad management on shore, and it is said injudicious applications were made to Congress for increased pay. These things disheartened and disgusted the friends of the enterprise, and it came to an untimely end. The failure of this line to justify public expectation proved a death-blow to the hopes of all who had looked to Congress for a more generous support. Unlike British statesmen, our own had yielded a reluctant assent to a pressing popular demand. The statesmen of Great Britain embraced with ardor a great opportunity, and adhered to it with courage and fortitude as in the prophetic strength of a grand inspiration. All are familiar with the sequel. Three hundred thousand immigrants come annually to our shores in British-built steamers; and thirty to fifty thousand Americans cross and recross the Atlantic, paying tribute in gold to the superior genius of British statesmanship; and it is come to pass, in the great contest for supremacy on the ocean, that the "stars and stripes" droop beneath the cross of St. George.

It is disheartening to pursue the topic; but hope is not wholly banished. Amid the host of lawyers, farmers, and politicians that throng the halls of Congress there are many men of enlarged minds and noble impulses—American in name and in heart. It is not too late for them to ponder the lesson so dearly learned, and to fight out the battle once more on the old line.

Brazil shares with our country the merit of sustaining by a feeble subsidy a number of steam-packets, which, sailing monthly, touch here and there along the South American coast. The Pacific mail, stretching out seven thousand miles across the ocean whose name it bears, being subsidized by Congress, still lives, fulfilling all reasonable expectations. But the subsidy it receives from the Post Office Department of $500,000 is wholly inadequate to an extension of the service. At any time it may be driven from the field by the Peninsular and Oriental line of steamers, whose contract with the British government for carrying her Majesty's mails has lately been renewed, with the subsidy increased to £500,000, a sum greater than $3,000,000 of our currency. In this connection, let it not be forgotten that when Cunard wanted to build the Persia and Scotia to run off the Collins steamers, after a careful investigation by a parliamentary committee, the contract with his company was renewed years in advance of the period of its expiration. Some "blue book" that is yet to meet our eyes may enlighten us in regard to the spirit and arguments that animated her Majesty's ministers in this increase of pay to the Peninsular and Oriental line.

The recent completion of our great continental railway imparts a fresh interest to the subject of this article. The munificent appropriation of sixty millions of dollars in aid of a single work of internal improvement, a work, too, that comes in direct competition with the Pacific Mail Steamship Company, presents in niggardly contrast the annual appropriation of less than one million dollars to facilitate the transmission of the mails on all the great highways of the ocean, when, as we have seen, so much else depends upon the venture.

About two hundred millions in gold, annually, are derived from duties on imports; fifteen or twenty millions are voted, annually, for the maintenance of a navy; and one of the declared purposes of the national income is to protect our external commerce.

Indirectly much good results from the expenditure of this income in ways that have been suggested in the course of this paper; but far better returns would be obtained if subsidies were largely and wisely bestowed in building up and sustaining lines of steamers on all the great ocean routes. Let the national money be so spent as to restore, if possible, our lost prestige on the sea.

The foe to our commercial development is in cabinets, and not in hostile cruisers; money, instead of guns, is the instrument employed to secure supremacy on the ocean; and, in these modern days, victory is won under the banner of peace.

When our legislators cease to be mere politicians and learn to be statesmen, they will heed the voices that come up from the sea. Then the "stars and stripes," floating at the peaks of our transatlantic steamers, will once more gladden our eyes, and the mortification of the present hour will give place to a pride like that of our fathers, in which some of us shared in our youthful days!

Mr. POILLON made a statement to the committee. He said that he was a ship-owner and ship-builder in New York. He was engaged in the construction of wooden vessels, and was part owner in some twenty-four vessels. His views had been fully expressed previously by Mr. Stimers. The views expressed by Mr. Stimers were generally correct in relation to the conduct of our shipping interests and the mode of its revival. He should like, however, to correct the impression that the Ship-owners' Association reflected the views of the ship-owners generally of New York. That was not so. He had in his hand the constitution and by-laws of the Ship-owners' Association, which contained all the names of its members, to the number of one hundred and forty-one. Of that one hundred and forty one there were forty who owned foreign ships entirely, and whose interests were not identical with American interests in any way whatever. Although among the remainder there were some of the most respectable ship-owners of New York, yet there were also many others whose business was confined entirely to the consignment of foreign vessels, and who were thus identified with foreign ships. He therefore considered that that association was not a fair exponent of the ship-owners of New York or of the country. Many of the most respectable ship-owners, among others Messrs. Low, Nesmith & Sons, R. P. Buck & Co., and many others whose names he could not now recall, had no connection with that association. Several ship-owners connected with the association entertained entirely different views from those expressed yesterday, and were most strongly opposed to the repeal of the navigation laws. He thought that all that the ship-building interest of the country required was a drawback of duties on all the materials that enter into the construction of ships, particularly of the duties on iron, copper, and cordage. The duty on copper at present was a prohibitory duty, preventing any importation of copper, and compelling American ship-builders to pay some seven or eight cents per pound for copper more than the English ship-builders paid. The duties on iron, he believed, were from thirty to thirty-five per cent., operating to that extent against the American ship-building interests. As to labor, although the American workmen were paid more than the English, yet he thought that the superior skill of the American mechanics more than offset the difference in wages.

Mr. HOLMAN. You say that the duty imposed on copper results in actual prohibition?

Mr. POILLON. Yes, sir; the act of last winter is a prohibitory tariff so far as copper is concerned. It acts very seriously on the ship-repairing interest. The ships that require to be recoppered will take a freight which they know is not profitable, and sometimes where they know that there will be real loss upon it, for the purpose of getting to England in order to make a saving on their copper; thus not only cutting off the revenue that might be derived by this country from a moderate tariff such as existed before the war, but also seriously injuring our mechanical interests in the coppering work being done in England which should be done in this country. Not only was the coppering work thus lost to this country, but also a large amount of repairs, which generally go with the coppering of vessels, such as rigging and carpenter work. It strikes at a dozen different kinds of mechanical interests.

Mr. HOLMAN. How does that occur, inasmuch as the duty on copper does not exceed that on iron?

Mr. WELLS. It does exceed that on iron.

Mr. HOLMAN. Very slightly.

Mr. WELLS. The duty on iron is thirty-three or thirty-four per cent., and on copper seventy-five per cent.

Mr. POILLON. The copper is furnished in England at about 7½*d.* per pound, whereas here it is twenty-seven cents.

Mr. HOLMAN. Then the practical result is actually to exclude copper from importation?

Mr. POILLON. Yes, sir. It operates also very seriously against our docking interests. We have the best docking facilities in this port that there are in the world. We can take up the largest vessels with the most expedition. There are millions of dollars invested in the docking interests in this port, and this prohibitory tariff on copper strikes them very seriously.

Mr. WELLS. What effect would the imposition of a duty upon all foreign-built ships coming to this country have upon our commerce?

Mr. POILLON. That would cause great excitement, and foreign governments would be inclined to put the same duty upon American ships, so that I think it would not have the desired effect.

Mr. WELLS. Then the only remedy, you think, is to allow drawbacks upon the materials used in the construction of ships?

Mr. POILLON. Yes, sir; to put our mechanics on the same footing with the English mechanics.

Mr. WELLS. In the event of Congress passing a law of that kind, what would be your opinion as to the expediency of removing all obstacles in the way of purchasing ships abroad and affording them American registration?

Mr. POILLON. I think that, after we once got a start, we would require out a short time to be able to compete with England in ship-building, and American ship-owners would find that ships could be built as cheaply here as in England; and, wherever that has been so, American vessels have always been preferred.

Mr. WELLS. Under our present law a great number of ships owned by Americans are sailing under the English flag, and that would bring those ships back under the American flag, and would, of course, give our commerce more respectability abroad as well as at home?

Mr. POILLON. It occurs to me that all that the ship-building interest of this country requires is to be put upon the same footing with the English. If free trade in foreign bottoms were to be allowed, and not free trade in ships' materials at the same time, so that the two should go hand in hand together, the result would be that our coasting trade would be swamped with English bottoms before we could defend ourselves. They would be nominally held by Americans, but in reality they would be held by British subjects and would be controlled by British capital; and our immense coasting trade, the only thing of value left to us, would be swept entirely from us.

Mr. HOLMAN. Mr. Stimers expressed the opinion that if drawbacks were allowed to the extent of the duty on materials entering into the construction of ships, and if free trade in ships were allowed at the same time—those two measures going together, without any reference to admitting foreign-built bottoms to our coasting trade—our commerce and ship-building interest would revive. What would be your view on that point, taking those two measures together?

Mr. POILLON. I think that they ought not to go together at the same time. I think that the ship-building interest ought to have the preference, so as to give sufficient start to put itself on a fair footing, so as to make the responsibility equal. After the ship-building interest having this advantage for two or three years, then the whole trade should be opened; but I think we should have a little chance first to recover ourselves.

Mr. CALKIN. Let us have your idea of the time required again more definitely.

Mr. POILLON. Two years would be ample. What Americans cannot do in two years they never can do.

Mr. HOLMAN. If you connect these two measures, free trade in foreign-built vessels and drawbacks on materials entering into ship-building, and if you give American-built vessels exclusively the whole coastwise trade, how would that affect commerce, the whole three going together from the beginning?

Mr. POILLON. I think that that is all that our people could reasonably ask for.

Mr. WELLS. Do you not think that allowances of reasonable subsidies to new lines of steamers, in connection with those other measures, would have a tendency to increase our commercial interests?

Mr. POILLON. I think that that is the only way we can ever recover the European trade; but it would not be requisite in regard to other trade. The English have such an immense start over us in the European trade that that is the only way we can ever place ourselves even with them, even if we should build ships as cheaply as they do.

Mr. WELLS. Do you not think that our business men here would give American bottoms the preference?

Mr. POILLON. American merchants have not the same unity of action that the English merchants have. Capital is more abundant in England, and the English are content with less interest for their money. For any enterprise that looks like paying at all there never is any lack of capital there. The English and French have pursued the same policy in the South American trade. They subsidize vessels to a large extent in the Brazilian trade and in the trade to the west coast of Africa, and wherever there is an opening to build a commerce, there they subsidize ships. The result is that in the Brazilian trade the French lines are superior to the English, as they have more encouragement.

Mr. WELLS. The French subsidize their ships heavier and have finer ships?

Mr. POILLON. Yes, sir; that is the opinion I have heard expressed by Brazilians of them—that the French ships are preferred to the English.

Mr. CALKIN. Then I understand from you that the English and French governments are subsidizing their steamers running to South America and to other ports more than they do those running to this port?

Mr. POILLON. Yes, sir; that is done to get this Brazilian trade. That has always been the policy of England. It was so in relation to this country. It was the means employed to crush out the Collins line—together with the opposition of Vanderbilt, who failed to get a subsidy for his line at that time, and then turned and helped to crush the Collins line.

Mr. CALKIN. The English government formerly subsidized the Cunard line more than it does now?

Mr. POILLON. Yes; the line is now more able to take care of itself. But the English government would have supported that line to any extent rather than see it broken down.

Mr. HOLMAN. You are not able, I suppose, to state the extent to which the English encourage shipping by subsidies?

Mr. POILLON. No, sir; I have seen the amounts that are paid by the mail department, but I have not them in my mind at present. The English government is more liberal with lines to South America and other countries, than with lines to this country at present.

Mr. HOLMAN. You are not able, I suppose, to state the extent of its subsidies to this trade?

Mr. POILLON. No, sir; I am not. We would require something more than free trade in ships in order to put us on a par with England. Their policy is to allow a drawback upon all the articles that a ship requires for her outfit. They are taken out of bond duty free. An English ship would still have a very great advantage over our vessels if our vessels were not entitled to the same privilege.

Mr. HOLMAN. Does that system prevail generally among commercial nations?

Mr. POILLON. I am not prepared to state how it is in France; but my impression is that it does, because the French have been copying in a measure the English laws so far as they relate to commerce.

Mr. HOLMAN. Would that system naturally exist with any nation that was not peculiarily a commercial nation?

Mr. POILLON. I think not.

Mr. HOLMAN. Where commerce is the main object, such a policy would be natural and proper enough?

Mr. POILLON. Yes, sir. The fostering of commerce has been the source of England's wealth, and they have always had that in view.

Mr. HOLMAN. I understood you to express the idea that if free trade were allowed in foreign-built vessels at the same time as a drawback of duties on the materials used in the construction of ships here, and if a preference were given in the domestic trade to American-built vessels, those three measures going together would revive our shipping and commercial interests?

Mr. POILLON. Yes, sir.

Mr. George Opdyke, banker, and vice-president of the New York Chamber of Commerce, came before the committee.

The CHAIRMAN. The committee would like to hear any suggestions that you may desire to make in reference to the subject of inquiry, which is as to the causes operating to depress our navigation interests and as to the remedies needed in order to revive them.

Mr. OPDYKE. My reflections on the subject of the depression of our shipping interest have led me to the conclusion that the present depression is mainly due to three causes: The first is—and perhaps in as large a degree as any other—the substitution of iron for wooden vessels, and of steam for sailing vessels. Great Britain has a great advantage over this country in the lower cost of iron and in her larger experience in its manufacture. The English can build of iron much cheaper than we can. When vessels were built mainly of wood we had the advantage of the English in consequence of the superior abundance and cheapness of that material in this country. In machinery, as well as in steam, they have the advantage. The cheaper labor there for running vessels gives them also another advantage. The second cause is the high duty charged upon such foreign materials as enter into the construction of our ships. Ships, after they are built in this country, have to compete, without any protection, with the ships of other countries. If we charge a high duty on the materials used in the construction of our ships, their cost is necessarily enhanced to that extent. And after they are finished, unlike our domestic manufactures that are sold at home, our ships enter on the ocean and have to compete, even, without any protection, with the vessels of other countries. That I regard as a most onerous exaction upon our shipping interest, and one that has done much to cripple it. Then there is another cause, which is probably temporary, but which, for the time being, has been more potent than either of the others named: It is the effect of the premium upon specie. We know that everything bought with our currency at home, including real estate, commodities of all kinds, and the price of labor, which is the best criterion of all, is on an average at least seventy-five per cent. higher than it was under our convertible currency; so that we are building ships and paying for materials in currency at an enhanced cost of seventy-five per cent., and sending them out to a trade where the business is done upon a coin basis, but where we do it on a currency basis. You see at once what an enormous disadvantage we labor under in competition with ships built for coin, and the earnings of which are in coin. The difference between the premium on gold and the depression of currency—some thirty-five or forty per cent.—is an absolute loss to that interest. That, after a time, will be corrected. The difficulty has existed since the war in consequence of our dropping the use of coin as currency, save in a few of our transactions, and lessening the demand for coin at home. Our securities have gone abroad to pay the adverse balance of trade, so that the demand for the precious metals in this country has not been equal to the supply, and this has kept the premium far below the price of other things. That, in brief, is my view of the cause of the present depression.

The CHAIRMAN. What measures would you suggest for the improvement of the navigation interest?

Mr. OPDYKE. The first advantage to the shipping interest would be to exempt from duty all materials entering into the construction of ships. I have long felt that that was due to the shipping interest, and without it I do not think that we can ever fully or successfully compete with foreign-built vessels. The last cause will correct itself very soon. It does not need any legislation. The other cause is more difficult to overcome, and I fear it will be very many years before we can build steamships of iron, such as are now controlling nearly all the ocean trade, as cheaply as they can be built in Europe. One remedy has been suggested, and that is to permit foreign-built vessels to have American registration, and to make absolute free trade in ships. As a free-trader, I am inclined to believe that that would be the true policy; but so long as protection is the policy of the country, we can scarcely expect an exception to be made in favor of the shipping interest. It is one of the last things that the American mind will accept. But if we had a policy of absolute free trade, which I think would result in great benefit to the country, (not to do it at once, but to do it gradually,) then I would embrace with it ship-building, and the purchase and the sale of ships abroad. The granting of subsidies is another remedy. While I am opposed in theory to all government subsidies, it would seem to be essential, if we desire to control the maritime commerce that properly belongs to us on important lines, that our government should, to some extent, follow the policy of Great Britain in that respect, as otherwise we cannot probably successfully compete with her. How far that policy should go I am not prepared to say. In theory I am opposed to it altogether But from the present crippled condition of our commerce, if we desire to regain the position that we once held, I am inclined to believe that it would be good policy for the government in proper cases, where valuable lines of steamers should be established between this and other important ports of other nations, to meet Great Britain with her own weapons and grant subsidies in some form.

The CHAIRMAN. I understand you to say that you are in favor both of exempting materials used in the construction of ships from duty, and also of amending the navigation laws, so as to allow the registration of foreign ships?

Mr. OPDYKE. As an ultra free-trader I should be in favor of that; but that is not the policy of our country, and I should not be in favor of it unless it is adopted prospectively as the policy of the government in reference to other things. I mean absolute free trade.

The CHAIRMAN. At first you would be in favor of the exemption of materials used in ship-building, and you would let all the other things follow?

Mr. OPDYKE. Yes; my policy would be to abandon gradually the whole protective policy of the country—not suddenly, which would be disastrous to many interests and unjust to them, but by a system of gradations extending over ten or twenty years, so as ultimately to get out of this false system altogether. The navigation laws stand upon the principle of reciprocity and are an absolute necessity for every maritime nation. We cannot, for example, permit other vessels to come and join in our coasting trade, and to come into our ports and be exempt from the charges and duties to which our vessels are subject in the ports of other countries, except on the principle of reciprocity. It would never do, therefore, to repeal the navigation laws, even with absolute free trade. They are always necessary.

Mr. HOLMAN. Taking those three subjects in connection: the rebate of the taxes, internal and external, on materials entering into the construction of ships; free trade in ships built abroad; and the giving to ships built in America the preference in our domestic trade—what effect would those three measures together have, probably, upon our commerce?

Mr. OPDYKE. I take it that they would give us the supremacy of the sea. The American people have more aptitude for maritime commerce than any other people in the world, and all that they want is an open field and fair competition to win that supremacy. I mean by the "supremacy of the sea" that we should have a larger maritime commerce than any nation in the world.

The CHAIRMAN. What effect would those measures have upon our ship-building interests?

Mr. OPDYKE. My impression is that they would greatly diminish the building of ships in this country for a period. How long that period would last would depend on circumstances.

The CHAIRMAN. In your opinion, is there not some protection needed for a period to our ship-building interest from foreign competition, in order to overcome the disadvantages under which it has labored for a few years past, and the advantages which foreigners have acquired by that condition of things?

Mr. OPDYKE. In my opinion there is no means of protecting the ship-building interest successfully except by the granting of bounties. Our ships have to compete with the ships of other nations, and inasmuch as we have not the same advantages for building ships as cheaply in this country as they have in Europe, the only way that the government, by its interference, can annul that advantage possessed by foreigners, would be by the granting of a bounty.

The CHAIRMAN. You mean by "the granting of a bounty," the exemption from duty of the materials employed in the construction of ships?

Mr. OPDYKE. That in itself would not be sufficient at present, on account of the superior advantages of Europe in the construction of iron vessels and of steam machinery, and in consequence of the cheaper labor there, and also in consequence of the marked difference between the value of coin and paper money. The purchasing powers are different.

The CHAIRMAN. The statement of steam engineers yesterday was that we can now build steam-engines as cheaply as they can be built in Europe.

Mr. OPDYKE. I am not sufficiently informed in regard to that; but judging from all other fabrics of metal, such as rails for railroads, and a thousand other things of import paying a very heavy duty on them and competing with our home productions, I am satisfied that England has great advantages over us. The rebate of duties upon foreign materials entering into the construction of ships is no protection whatever. It simply puts the American builder upon the same platform with his foreign competitor. The ships would cost our people precisely the same as they cost the people of England. And then, besides, we labor under the disadvantage of a difference of thirty-five per cent. between the purchasing power of gold and of paper money.

Mr. HOLMAN. Do the nations which admit foreign-built vessels to their registration exclude them from their domestic trade?

Mr. OPDYKE. I am ignorant of the policy of other nations in regard to registration; but if England and France do admit foreign-built ships to registration, I suppose they put them on the same basis as their own ships in regard to the coasting trade.

Mr. HOLMAN. Supposing that to be a fact, taking into consideration the extent of our coasting trade in connection with our foreign commerce, if you exempt from duty the materials entering into the construction of ships, and give American-built ships the exclusive control of the domestic trade, and supposing the duty on the main material entering into the construction of ships amounted to thirty-five per cent., would not the protection to the American builder be equal to forty-five per cent. in the construction of ships?

Mr. OPDYKE. If I properly apprehend the question, I cannot say that it would. There is another view, suggested by your question, which is a very important one: If we should admit foreign-built vessels to register here and put them on an equality with our own American-built vessels in our coasting trade, I think the effect would not fail to be injurious to American ship-building.

Mr. HOLMAN. Can you state the relation which our domestic shipping interests bear at this time to our foreign shipping interest?

Mr. OPDYKE. I suppose that our coastwise trade is at least three-fourths of our whole trade, because our shipping interest in foreign commerce is very small.

The CHAIRMAN. Have you ever had anything to do with the building of ships, or have you ever contracted to have them built for you?

Mr. OPDYKE. No, sir.

The CHAIRMAN. Have you ever owned or sailed ships?

Mr. OPDYKE. I have had a very small interest in ships, but I have not at present. I believe if anything is done in the way of admitting foreign-built vessels to registration, it should be on the condition that they should be only employed in the foreign commerce. I do not believe that the government or the people will ever permit foreign-built vessels to participate in our domestic trade. That is a prize of our own which we have a right to make the most of.

Mr. HOLMAN. Agricultural people, however, may take one view of that subject, and the strictly commercial and manufacturing interests of the country may take a different view.

NEW YORK, *October* 16, 1869.

Mr. HOWLAND, of the firm of Howland & Frothingham, shipping merchants of New York, stated as his opinion that the loss of American commerce resulted from various causes: First, that there is less carrying than heretofore; second, that there is a superabundant supply of tonnage in proportion to the business; and third, on account of the accident of the late civil war, which gave to foreigners an advantage in shipping business, and in fact gave them the track for the time being, and which he believed they would always keep. He did not see anything to prevent it. Foreigners could build their ships cheaper than Americans, and could sail them cheaper, and their ships, he thought, were better managed. They had better seamen, and better officers, as a class, than Americans. Their iron ships were improving, whereas American wooden vessels were growing old and out of date. Iron was superseding wood for ships, and must take the place of wood for the reason that it was much more economical. It would be some years, he thought, before the United States would be able to cope with Great Britain in building iron ships, because the English had had a long time to organize and to systematize their business, so that they could now build ships almost in a day. He was a ship-owner and had been a ship-master. His ships had always sailed under the American flag. They were American-built wooden ships. He had no iron ships.

The CHAIRMAN. What advantage do you consider the iron ship has over the wooden ship?

Mr. HOWLAND. Economy throughout. An iron ship carries her cargo much safer and with less damage. The only inconvenience is the not being able to metal the bottom. But there is no wear and tear. They are twenty-year ships.

The CHAIRMAN. Is not the matter of fouling the bottoms of iron ships a serious one?

Mr. HOWLAND. Yes; but they are getting over it. Barnacles will grow on the bottoms of iron ships very rapidly in tropical climates.

The CHAIRMAN. Do I understand you to say that the English sail their ships cheaper than we do?

Mr. HOWLAND. No, not cheaper. They carry more men than we do. They are required by law to have twenty-five per cent. more men than we carry. They can sail cheaper because they buy all their outfits in bond, free of duty; and not only that, but their wages are lower. I do not see that it is possible for us to compete with them under our present federal and State laws. So long as sailor landlords here have charge of manning our ships they have it all their own way, and we cannot expect wages to be any lower than now. A ship-owner has no control of his vessel in that respect. My impression is that it will be some years before we can compete fairly with foreign countries.

The CHAIRMAN. Do you believe that if the materials entering into the construction of vessels were admitted free of duty, we could build ships here in competition with English ship-builders?

Mr. HOWLAND. We could, after a certain length of time; but I think it would require a few years first, to build up our prestige again. We must use machinery in building iron ships, and it will be some time before we are fairly started. Then, again, there is another difficulty to contend with. The shipping interest is not a favorite interest with investors. On the contrary, it is probably the poorest interest. No man will invest in a ship unless it pays him at least as much interest as other investments; and as to outsiders, who used to own small interests in ships, you can hardly find any person now in the city of New York to make such an investment, because it is considered a poor one. A man puts his money into a ship, and there it must remain. He puts it entirely out of his own hands, and has not the least power over it.

The CHAIRMAN. Has it not been usual for ship-builders to get up parties to make a company for the ownership of the vessel?

Mr. HOWLAND. That was done not so much by the builder as by the agents. The agent would endeavor to make up capital for the ship. The builder would generally take an interest in it. There would be generally eight or ten owners of the ship; but now it is almost impossible to get any man, who knows the history of our shipping interests for the last six or eight or ten years, to put his money into a ship. There is nothing to warrant him in doing it. There is no encouragement. I think, however, that if all the duties were removed from ship-building materials, and if ship's stores could be taken out of bond free of duty, these measures would be the best that could be adopted.

Mr. CALKIN. Previous to the war, when ships could be built as cheap here as in England, and when the carrying trade was good, is it not a fact that, all along our sea-coast and in our large seaport cities, there were many men who amassed large fortunes in running ships?

Mr. HOWLAND. Not large fortunes. Many have made comfortable fortunes. I do not know of any one who made a large fortune in this city by running ships, whatever may have been the case in the East. But what *has been* is evidently not what *is now*, or what is likely to be. I do not see any encouragement for building ships, except we can build them and sail them as cheap as other nations. And we are worse off in that respect in regard to steamers than we are in regard to sailing vessels, for there is the strongest competition in steamers.

The CHAIRMAN. Would you be in favor of an abrogation of the navigation laws as a means of restoring our shipping interest?

Mr. HOWLAND. I should not. I should be in favor of throwing off all restrictions and duties on building materials.

The CHAIRMAN. You would be in favor rather of building ships at home than of buying them from abroad?

Mr. HOWLAND. Certainly. The foreigners have got our carrying trade now; and if we pay them for making our ships, and even after that cannot compete with them for the carrying trade, we would be worse off than we are now. Then, again, that would endanger our coasting trade, for, once they get in the entering-wedge, we do not know where they would stop. The right to buy and register foreign-built ships would benefit a certain class of people, such as commission merchants and shipping agents for British ship-owners; but it would not benefit our mechanics or ship-owners. On the contrary, it would be a prejudice to our coasting trade, which has saved our shipping interest for the last five or six years.

Mr. HOLMAN. What would be the effect on our commerce alone (without reference to the question of ship-building) of allowing foreign-built vessels to obtain American registers, and of excluding them from the coastwise trade?

Mr. HOWLAND. It would increase competition.

Mr. HOLMAN. Would it increase largely ship-owning in the United States?

Mr. HOWLAND. I do not think it would; because I think there is already tonnage enough for the business of the world. I do not believe that we would increase our tonnage; but, at the same time, many vessels might come under the American flag.

Mr. HOLMAN. Suppose that a duty of twenty-five per cent. (the lowest average of duties on manufactures) were imposed on vessels purchased abroad by American citizens, so as to entitle them to American registry, would such a policy increase the ship-owning interest in the United States?

Mr. HOWLAND. I should think not, because that would bring ships quite as high as they could be built for at home.

Mr. HOLMAN. Do you know any good reason why a different protective policy should be extended to the ship-building interest from that extended to any other manufacturing interest in this country?

Mr. HOWLAND. I do not. I think myself that the allowance of drawback of duties on ship-building materials would be inconsistent, and an exception to the general rule. I do not think that we have a right to claim free trade in ships more than in anything else.

Mr. HOLMAN. Is there any national interest connected with the subject at all, except it may be that of having facilities for the construction of vessels for war purposes in case of emergency? Is there any other reason to discriminate in favor of that particular branch of industry in preference to others?

Mr. HOWLAND. I do not see any.

Mr. HOLMAN. To what extent ought it to be the policy of a nation like this to afford peculiar protection to the ship-building industry, with reference to securing available means for the prompt construction of war-vessels?

Mr. HOWLAND. I should think to no great extent at this time, because high wages will bring all the men that we want for our navy.

Mr. HOLMAN. Supposing that iron vessels supersede entirely wooden vessels, (as may possibly be the result in the course of time,) in the event of an emergency and necessity for the rapid construction of ships—taking into consideration the various branches of industry connected with iron manufactures—if the government did not specially pro tect its ship-building interests, would there be a trouble in the construction of ships resulting from the absence of skilled workmen in that branch of industry?

Mr. HOWLAND. Yes; I should think that that might have an effect, because it would spread into other pursuits all over the country the mechanics now engaged in ship-building, so that the government could not avail itself of their services.

Mr. HOLMAN. Is the art of ship-building so peculiar and exclusive that you could not readily get together bodies of skilled workmen to construct ships, even if they had not been specially employed in that particular branch of industry?

Mr. HOWLAND. I take it for granted that all house carpenters, after a little practice, could go in and assist in building ships. Still, every man to his business and trade. I do not apprehend, however, that it would affect the government much, one way or other, whether we build iron ships or wooden ships. If ships were to be built rapidly, they would be probably wooden ships, because iron ships cannot be built so rapidly.

The CHAIRMAN. If I understand Mr. Holman's question, it is whether there is any real necessity for a nation to have an educated class of skilled workmen for the construction of ships, or whether that is a matter that can be improvised at once, at any time—whether ship-building is really an art to be cultivated and that requires time and experience, or whether workmen in any other business can be set to work at it?

Mr. HOWLAND. I should think it necessary to have men trained to the business.

The CHAIRMAN. We have always been a ship-building nation?

Mr. HOWLAND. Always.

Mr. HOLMAN. And would be, under any policy?

Mr. HOWLAND. Undoubtedly.

Mr. JAMES W. ELWELL, a member of the Ship-owners' Association, stated that he had been a ship-owner and a ship-agent for over thirty years. During the Mexican war and the famine in Ireland there had been a great stimulus given to ship-building, and American tonnage had increased very rapidly, because the few ships then employed were finding remunerative business. Up to 1854–'56 so many people entered into the building of ships that the market became overstocked and the owners suffered great losses. Then the commercial panic of 1857 depreciated the shipping business very much. Afterward a market was found for American shipping in England, on the continent, and in the East Indies. This, and the business resulting from the new article of guano, again stimulated the building of ships. Up to the commencement of the late war the size and number of American ships had been increasing, and finer ships were being built. During the war the foreign demand for American ships increased, owing, a good deal, to the difference in the value of gold and currency, and a large number of ships, especially those advanced in years, were sold abroad. Very few ships were built here at the same time, on account of the great cost of materials and labor; and as, in addition to these causes, many ships had naturally been lost, American tonnage had decreased very materially—perhaps fifty per cent. The burden of the ship-owners now consisted in the increased cost of building and equipping vessels, and in the increased expense of running them. The present expense of the labor part—loading and unloading vessels—and of the mechanical part, for repairs, was, on an average, two hundred or three hundred per cent. over what it was before the war. For instance, the stevedore's bill, which used to be, say, $500, would be now from $1,200 to $1,500.

The CHAIRMAN remarked that that applied to all vessels, native and foreign.

Mr. ELWELL assented, but remarked that foreign vessels kept their own crews, and did the work with them, whereas American vessels did not. Then the cost of repairs had increased so largely that the yearly insurance on a ship, which was formerly from seven to eight per cent., was now from twelve to fourteen per cent. The cost of building vessels now was not so great in proportion as it was during the war. Ships that cost, during the war, $100 per ton in currency, could now be built for from $65 to $70. His impression was, that if there were a drawback of duties allowed on all ship-building materials, American ship-builders could build ships and make a small profit on them. Then the ship-owner should be allowed, as in other nations, to buy his outfit and equipments, including provisions, in bond. Then he thought that Americans could compete with foreigners in the carrying trade of the world. At present the largest proportion of the repairs of American ships is done abroad, and outfits of all kinds were purchased abroad, thus causing large American expenditures to be made on the other side instead of at home. Every two or three years a ship required a general overhauling, and this was done abroad now, as well by American as by foreign vessels, taking a large amount of employment from American mechanics and giving it to foreign mechanics.

The CHAIRMAN inquired whether foreign vessels had any advantage in that respect over American vessels running in the same trade, inasmuch as the former had to employ American mechanics just as much as the latter had to employ foreign mechanics.

Mr. ELWELL replied that the ship-owner made repairs on his ship where he could do them most cheaply, but that still, as a general thing, an American ship-owner preferred to have his repairs done, if possible, at home, even at an advanced cost, because he could have them done under his own eye and supervision. The item of drawing stores and supplies free of duty was a very important matter to ship-owners. Americans had that privilege in England, but were liable to be called upon at home to pay duty on any excess of stores that they might have on board.

The CHAIRMAN. Do you think that the remission of duties on ship-building materials would tend to restore American shipping?

Mr. ELWELL. I think it would, very materially. It would produce an interest in ship-building which would grow as fast as the country would require it.

The CHAIRMAN. Are you in favor of the repeal of the navigation laws as a means of restoring our commerce?

Mr. ELWELL. Not at present. I do not think that the country is prepared to take that measure yet. I think it could have been done years ago with more propriety than it could be now. And it may again, years hence. Still, there might be an import duty imposed on vessels the same as on merchandise. But even that would be objectionable, as it would burden commerce with a great many old vessels at low cost, unless there was a specific duty imposed of so much per ton, without regard to the age or quality of the vessel. This, too, would be liable to a great deal of fraud and of objection.

Mr. HOLMAN. To what extent, under that policy, would our people become ship-owners more than they are now?

Mr. ELWELL. It is difficult to answer that question, as I think that a large portion of our ships might be owned in other nations, though really sailing under the American flag.

The CHAIRMAN. Then you think that it would lead to foreign ownership?

Mr. ELWELL. Yes, sir.

The CHAIRMAN. For the purpose of obtaining the benefit of our coastwise trade?

Mr. ELWELL. Yes, sir.

Mr. HOLMAN. Supposing our coastwise trade to be at present equal to three-fourths of our entire commerce carried on by American citizens, how would these three measures, taken together—the relief to the ship-builder to the extent of a rebate of internal and external duties on all materials entering into the construction of ships, free trade in foreign-built vessels, only excluding them from the coastwise trade, and giving to the home-built ships the exclusive right to that trade—affect, first, the commerce of the country, and second, the ship-building interest? Would they promote or diminish either?

Mr. ELWELL. They would promote the commerce of the country, and they would promote the ship-building interest, if the time for allowing foreign-built ships to be owned and registered here were postponed until our own ship-builders could commence operations. If that time were not postponed, foreigners would come in at once and fill up all the gaps in the way of commercial lines from place to place, before our people were prepared. I think that, in the course of a few years, our people would be prepared, and that then we could compete with other nations in building ships, whether with free trade or not.

Mr. HOLMAN. Taking into account the rebate of tax on materials entering into the construction of ships—internal revenue as well as external—and the exclusive benefit of the domestic commerce to American-built vessels, what would be the approximate extent of protection to the American ship-builder resulting from these two things together?

Mr. ELWELL. It would vary from ten to fifteen per cent. on the value of the ship. It would be more on iron vessels than on wooden ones, because there would be a greater rebate of duty on the former. It would not be over from ten to fifteen per cent. Our labor here is higher than it is abroad. Our ship-builders are ready to contract for a ship of one thousand tons, and would be satisfied with a profit of from $2,000 to $3,000 for their superintendence and the use of their tools and yards.

Mr. WELLS. Have you any means of knowing the proportions of our domestic and foreign commerce?

Mr. ELWELL. I should think that forty per cent. of our tonnage goes to foreign ports, and that sixty per cent. is engaged in the domestic trade. The coastwise trade is not of so much importance for the last two or three years as it was formerly. There used to be ten or eleven lines to New Orleans, each line employing five or six ships; whereas now there is not a regular line of sailing-ships to New Orleans. The domestic carrying trade is now done a good deal by the land lines of transportation instead of by sea.

Mr. HOLMAN. Is not the tonnage employed in the domestic trade increasing?

Mr. ELWELL. I should think it is. Since the close of the war a good deal of trade has been opened in the South. So far as large ships are concerned, our domestic trade, except the California trade, is of very little consideration. The California trade employs large ships, otherwise there would be very little business for them. The domestic trade is mostly done by a small class of vessels, and by steamers.

Mr. HOLMAN. But these vessels require the ship-yards to be kept up, and enter largely into the profits of ship-builders?

Mr. ELWELL. Our coasting trade has not been profitable.

Mr. HOLMAN. Do you attribute the falling off in that trade to inland land transportation?

Mr. ELWELL. Yes, sir; there has been an entire change. We used to bring all our tobacco, cotton, lead, &c., from St. Louis and Cincinnati by water, and *vice versa*, but now they all go by land.

Mr. HOLMAN. Suppose that our tonnage in 1860 was something over five million tons, what proportion of that would naturally, in these nine years, have been taken off by the use of inland land routes?

Mr. ELWELL. I should say that the coastwise trade is not over one-half of what it was previous to the war. It may not be over a third.

The CHAIRMAN. I understand you to represent the Ship-owners' Association?

Mr. ELWELL. Yes.

The CHAIRMAN. That association had a meeting and passed some resolutions, and appointed a committee, of which you were a member?

Mr. ELWELL. Yes.

The CHAIRMAN. How many were present at that meeting?

Mr. ELWELL. Perhaps between a dozen and twenty—about as many as generally attend the meetings of the Chamber of Commerce—out of a thousand members.

The CHAIRMAN. My object is to ascertain how full an expression of opinion it was. To what extent do the ship-owners of the country (not the ship-builders) favor a more liberal policy with regard to granting American registry to foreign-built vessels?

Mr. ELWELL. I should think they were about equally divided. They are all unanimous in favor of some legislation to relieve the shipping interest; but I should think there was not a majority of them in favor of free trade in ships.

The CHAIRMAN. Suppose the policy were adopted of relieving the materials entering into the construction of ships of all duty, what then, in your judgment, would be the opinion of the majority of the ship-owners in reference to admitting foreign ships to American registry?

Mr. ELWELL. I do not think that at present there would be a large majority in favor of it. The one measure would, of course, increase the number in favor of the other; but I do not think that that would satisfy all parties.

The CHAIRMAN. But you think there would be a majority in favor of excluding foreign ships from American registry?

Mr. ELWELL. I do; but I think that, after a few years, it could be done with greater unanimity of feeling among the ship-owners and ship-builders, and all connected materially with the interest of ship-building. Their attention is turned now to the building of iron ships; and it will require two or three years to get up all the machinery and appliances to build them.

Mr. PAUL M. SPOFFORD, ship-owner, expressed the opinion that there were various causes operating to produce depression in the American shipping interest. Among them were the system of subsidies granted by foreign governments to their lines of mail steamers, which had built up their steam marine at the expense of that of the United States, and the very great cost of constructing and navigating American ships. He did not know but that these were among the chief causes. If it were the policy of this government to revive the commerce of the country, he thought that it would be conducive to that end to allow Americans to purchase ships wherever they could be bought cheapest, and to allow those ships to American registry. He thought that the American ship-owner should not be compelled to use American ships at the high price that he has now to pay for them, when he had to come into competition for trade with foreign ships. He thought it also desirable that on the materials used in ship-building there should be a rebate of duty. The duty should either be entirely taken off, or only a small duty charged, so that American ship-builders might have an opportunity of competing on more favorable terms than they had at present.

The CHAIRMAN. I understand you to be in favor of the abrogation of the navigation laws?

Mr. SPOFFORD. I should be in favor of the abrogation of the navigation laws so as to permit American citizens to purchase foreign-built ships and run them wherever they pleased. But I should not be in favor of allowing the foreigner to engage in the coasting trade with a foreign ship.

The CHAIRMAN. If foreign-built ships were admitted to American registry, and if three-fourths of the vessel were owned by English and the other fourth by the nominal owner, an American, would not three-fourths of that ship's profit in the coasting trade go to the other side of the water?

Mr. SPOFFORD. I presume so.

The CHAIRMAN. Would there be any practicable mode of preventing that result?

Mr. SPOFFORD. I do not know that there would be.

The CHAIRMAN. And might not the entire ownership, by some little evasion of the laws, be on the other side, just as the entire ownership of some vessels under the English flag is here?

Mr. SPOFFORD. Yes, sir. I presume there would be methods of evading the laws and giving the benefit of the coastwise trade to foreigners.

Mr. HOLMAN. There is nothing now to prevent a foreigner being the actual owner of an American vessel engaged in the foreign trade?

Mr. SPOFFORD. No, sir. There is that disadvantage at present. If I purchase a British ship and wish to employ her in the English coasting trade, it is my impression that I must get a registry in the name of an Englishman. The English grant registers only to citizens. That is what I am in favor of. We should grant to our citizens a registry which would enable them to purchase their ships wherever they pleased, and to engage in our coasting trade or in any other trade; and if foreigners reap any side advantage, or if in benefiting our own citizens we also benefit foreigners, I do not think that the small advantage which we thus confer on them would counterbalance the great advantage which we would be conferring on our own citizens. I am speaking now with reference to the general advantage to the commerce of the country. I do not suppose that, so far as the mere ship-building interests are concerned, a measure of that kind would be particularly beneficial to them. But if, in addition to that measure, ship-building materials were relieved from duty, I think that there is that preference for American-built ships, and that there is that skill and industry in this country, to enable our ship-builders to compete favorably, and that they would eventually carry the day.

The CHAIRMAN. Do you believe that if the duty on ship-building materials were taken off, the demands of American ship-owners for ships could be supplied by our ship-builders at as low a cost as they could be got by purchasing them abroad?

Mr. SPOFFORD. I think that it would require some little time to get things organized. Our commerce has received too severe a blow, not only by direct but by indirect causes. Take, for instance, the case of the Collins and Cunard lines of steamers. The Cunard line has been in the receipt of a very heavy subsidy, while the subsidy to the Collins line was discontinued. We find that the English government is paying subsidies for its mail service all over the world. Of course that gives the recipient of such subsidy a very great advantage. I do not say that it is an insuperable advantage. I think that talent and attention to business will sometimes overcome this advantage. But, all other things being equal, it certainly gives a very great advantage. Government subsidy has been the English idea for many years, and it seems as if it was now being followed up by the French. The French and English are building up a magnificent marine, and ours is all going to decay. Within a comparatively few years the business of ocean commerce has been much changed. Steamships have taken the place of sailing-vessels. That alone is one cause of the decay of the business of building sailing-ships. Take our own case. A few years ago we had a line of packets from New York to Liverpool, comprising five or six of the largest ships sailing out of port. We could not run those packets now in opposition to the steamers. We have been obliged to send them to the Pacific. It is not because they are under the American flag as much as it is because we come right into competition with steamers which, on these short voyages, can carry their freight at a less rate. The English steam marine has been built up by subsidies in the mail service, and by the efforts which have been made in every way to develop that interest.

Mr. CALKIN. You now own steam-vessels?

Mr. SPOFFORD. Yes.

Mr. CALKIN. I believe that it is a fact, conceded by the merchants of New York, that the Collins line was extravagantly and badly managed. Do you not think that the merchants of New York have learned very much, in running steamship lines, to economize and run them cheaper?

Mr. SPOFFORD. I think they have.

Mr. CALKIN. They can manage them more economically now than they could when they first got into the business, so that, with a little help, they would be able to compete with foreigners better than they could ten or twelve years ago?

Mr. SPOFFORD. It may be a little egotistical in me to make the remark that my father, the senior of the firm, was engaged in the first ocean steamboat line in this country, and we have thus far, until within a few years past, found our steamship interest profitable. We have continued the business steadily up to the present time.

Mr. CALKIN. Then I understand your answer to be that they do manage the business with more economy than formerly, and are, of course, getting more knowledge of the business?

Mr. SPOFFORD. Yes, sir; so that with some subsidy we should be able to compete with foreigners.

Mr. HOLMAN. Your theory is that three measures are necessary to give new impetus to American commerce: first, the drawback on materials entering into the construction of ships to the extent of the duty, external and internal; second, free trade in ships; and third, subsidies from the government to encourage American lines in competition with foreign lines?

Mr. SPOFFORD. Yes, sir; these three measures I am in favor of.

Mr. HOLMAN. As to the coastwise trade, you think that whatever vessel sails under the American flag, without reference to the nationality of its birth, should be at liberty to participate in that trade?

Mr. SPOFFORD. Yes.

The CHAIRMAN. If the policy of admitting foreign ships to American registry were adopted at once, do you not think that the tendency would be to have our navigation interests owned, in a few years, very largely by foreigners, and that, after a short time, our commerce would not be essentially a foreign interest?

Mr. SPOFFORD. I am hardly prepared to give an opinion on that subject. So long as we keep the control of it under our flag, I do not know that there would be any more disadvantage in that than in allowing foreigners to own large interests in our railroads.

Mr. HOLMAN. Would they own in our shipping to the same extent?

Mr. SPOFFORD. I think not. Of course foreigners cannot be directly interested in our shipping, on account of the oath required of the American ship-owner, but they might be indirectly interested.

The CHAIRMAN. Is not the tendency to have ships owned and controlled where they are built?

Mr. SPOFFORD. I am hardly prepared to give an opinion on that subject. My impression is that the mere building of the ship does not give the control. I do not know that the people of Maine, a large ship-building State, control vessels as much as the citizens of New York do.

Mr. HOLMAN. Is it not a fact that foreign capital is to some extent, interested in American shipping now, not only in ownership but in running vessels?

Mr. SPOFFORD. That is my impression. I know cases were it has been so in former years. I am not prepared to say that that is any great disadvantage. If we wish capital for the prosecution of other public works, so long as we retain the management of it, I do not know that it is any great disadvantage for us to have it.

Mr. WILLIAM WHITLOCK made some remarks to the committee on the change that has taken place in substituting steamers for sailing vessels. He said that to a large extent the coastwise trade was done by steamers. The lines of packets between New York and the Gulf were now almost unknown. So with the Liverpool packets. Steamers were superseding them. He held that the application of all laws should be made universal. If the navigation laws were repealed it would be for the benefit of a class, thus introducing a species of class legislation in order that the capitalist might invest his money to the best advantage. He had no objection to that, but the principle should be carried out to its logical conclusions. He believed, however, that if the restrictions which now interfere with the building of ships here were removed, capitalists could invest their money in ships here as well as they could abroad. He was in favor of the latter solution of the difficulty, but was not in favor of the former, He had been a ship-owner and had been more or less intimately connected with ships for some years. He thought that all who were engaged in commerce, and who wanted to be able to carry freight at the minimum price, would undoubtedly favor for the time being the abrogation of the navigation laws, but he believed that the true American policy was to continue to foster every interest which would enable ships to be built in the United States rather than have them purchased abroad. He did not see what harm could be done (but rather benefit) by the investment of foreign capital in American shipping interests.

Mr. NESMITH, ship-owner, remarked that they had been very much puzzled by the question, What ought to be done to restore American commerce—whether that could be best accomplished by allowing drawbacks to ship-builders, or by allowing ship-owners to buy their vessels where they could buy them cheapest? They had thought that the idea of allowing drawback could not possibly be carried through, and they had therefore about made up their minds that free trade in ships was the only course that could give the country a commercial position. In order to show the condition of things—in the East Indies, for example—he had brought with him, and he submitted to the committee, the last Calcutta Freight Report, which showed that out of 101 ships in port only 6 were American, and that three-fourths of them were iron ships. He also submitted the specifications for an iron sailing ship of 1,030 tons, with a proposal from a Glasgow firm to build such a ship, with outfit and all ready for sea, at £14 10*s*. sterling per ton. They had had such ships offered, ready for sea, with double outfit, as low as £12 sterling per ton.

The CHAIRMAN. If the American ship-builder could obtain his materials, whether for an iron or a wooden ship, free of duty, could he, in your opinion, build his ships to compete with foreign ship-builders, and supply the demand as fast as ships are required here?

Mr. NESMITH. I should think so; but I do not think that, whatever you do—whether you open the door to free trade in ships or allow a drawback on ship-building materials—you can increase our commerce largely at present.

The CHAIRMAN. You think, however, that whatever ships are required to supply the demands of American ship-owners can be supplied by American ship-builders as cheaply as by English ship-builders, if they have the materials free of duty?

Mr. NESMITH. As to wooden ships I should say that there is no question but that they can do better; but as to iron ships I am not so well satisfied. In the first place, we must be able to get our material as cheap, which we cannot do, even with the drawback. I think, however, that if the American ship-builders were placed on the same footing with regard to materials as the English ship-builders are, they could furnish ships, whether of iron or wood, as fast as they are required, and better ships, too.

The CHAIRMAN. You then do not believe it necessary to buy our ships abroad for the purpose of supplying the demand—providing the other measure can be carried out?

Mr. NESMITH. I should say not. We are altogether Americans, and we want American ships and American everything. We do not wish to be compelled to step out of the business because we cannot have iron ships, and prefer that something should be done, either through free trade in ships, or in some other way, to enable us to procure and run ships in competition with other nations.

The following is the specification referred to in the statement of Mr. Nesmith:

SPECIFICATION OF AN IRON SAILING SHIP.

DIMENSIONS.

Length for tonnage 208 feet.
Breadth of beam, 34 feet 9 inches.
Depth of hold, 21 feet 2 inches.
Break, 45 feet by 20 inches.
Tonnage register, about 1,030 tons.
To class A A 1 at Lloyds, and twenty years in the Liverpool underwriters' book.
Keel to be of forged iron, 8½ by 3 inches, in long lengths, scarfed together.
Stem of forged iron, 8½ by 3 inches, scarfed at least 7 feet into the keel.

Stern post of forged iron, $8\frac{1}{2}$ by 4 inches, with solid forged gudgeons on back for rudder braces.

Center keelson to be box form, 16 by 17 inches, of $\frac{10}{16}$-inch plates, with angle irons $3\frac{1}{2}$ by 3 by $\frac{8}{16}$ inches, riveted to double-reverse bars on top for floors.

Frames of angle iron, 5 by 3 by $\frac{9}{16}$ inches, spaced 21 inches to center, to be in one piece from keel to gunwale.

Reverse frames of angle iron, $3\frac{1}{2}$ by 3 by $\frac{8}{16}$ inches, extending to gunwale and lower deck beams on alternate frames.

Floor plates, on every frame, 24 by $\frac{10}{16}$ inches, extending up to the bilges to the 4-feet water line.

Bilge keelsons, four in number, of angle iron, 5 by $4\frac{1}{2}$ by $\frac{9}{16}$ inches, riveted back to back and to double-reverse angle irons, and to be connected together at ends by breast hooks.

Intercostal keelson to be fitted on at each side at half-floor for two-thirds the vessel's length, of $\frac{10}{16}$-inch plates, connected to floor-plates by angle irons $3\frac{1}{2}$ by 3 by $\frac{8}{16}$ inches, and to project above floor-plates to form a keelson, riveted between double-angle irons 5 by $3\frac{1}{2}$ by $\frac{9}{16}$ inches, to have iron wash-plates.

Main deck stringers, 34 by $\frac{10}{16}$ inches in midships, reduced at ends to 26 inches, to be fitted close to the sheer strake, and secured thereto by an angle iron 5 by $4\frac{1}{2}$ by $\frac{9}{16}$ inches, with a flange formed round the scuppers. An angle iron 4 by 3 by $\frac{9}{16}$ inches, to be riveted to the stringer plates, forming a gutter water-way 16 inches broad. The butts of stringer plate in midships to be triple riveted.

'Tween deck stringers, 25 by $\frac{10}{16}$ inches, riveted to top of beams, and connected to reverse bars on frames by an angle iron 5 by $4\frac{1}{2}$ by $\frac{9}{16}$ inches.

Main and 'tween deck beams, of Butterby iron, $8\frac{1}{2}$ by $\frac{9}{16}$ inches, spaced $3\frac{1}{2}$ feet to centers with double-angle irons $3\frac{1}{2}$ by $3\frac{1}{2}$ by $\frac{3}{8}$ inches riveted on top edge, secured to side of vessel by the ends of the beams being turned down and formed a knee of, which is to be riveted to the frames 21 inches deep; hatch beams and fore and afters to be $9\frac{1}{2}$ inches deep.

Deck tie plates, $12\frac{1}{2}$ by $\frac{10}{16}$ inches, to run fore and aft on each side of hatchways on main and lower deck beams. Diagonal ties to be fitted, where practicable, on main deck beams, and in wake of masts, on 'tween deck beams. Mast partners to take three beams in length with bulb-iron combings.

Bulkhead—One collision bulkhead, to be fitted forward, of $\frac{7}{16}$-inch plates, riveted between double frames, and stiffened with angle iron $3\frac{1}{2}$ by 3 by $\frac{8}{16}$ inches, spaced 30 inches apart. All stringers to be continued through the bulkhead, and collars fitted round them to be perfectly water-tight.

Stanchions in lower hold $3\frac{1}{2}$ inches diameter, 'tween decks 3 inches diameter. Double stanchions to form iron ladders at main hatch, to have option of hollow stanchions, extra size.

Plating—

Garboard strakes, $\frac{13}{16}$ inch;
From garboard bilge, $\frac{12}{16}$ inch;
From bilge to three-fifths depth of hold, $\frac{11}{16}$ inch;
From three-fifths depth of hold to sheerstrakes, $\frac{10}{16}$ inch;
Sheerstrake, $\frac{12}{16}$ inch;
} To be reduced at ends, as allowed by Lloyds.

Butts of sheerstrake and main deck stringers to be triple riveted in midships.

Bulwarks to be of iron $\frac{6}{16}$ inch in way of break and forecastle, and $\frac{5}{16}$ inch in body of ship; to be stayed with H-formed stanchions, $1\frac{3}{8}$ inch. Top-gallant bulwarks to be neatly paneled with teak, varnished, and to have cast lead ornaments.

Main rail, of angle iron, $7\frac{1}{2}$ by $3\frac{1}{2}$ by $\frac{3}{8}$ inches, riveted to bulwarks with angle iron on inside edge, $2\frac{1}{2}$ by $2\frac{1}{2}$ by $\frac{3}{8}$ inches, for fixing greenheart pin rail, say 7 by $3\frac{1}{2}$ inches, or teak rail, owner's option, and greenheart pin rail.

Top-gallant rail, of teak $7\frac{1}{2}$ by $3\frac{1}{2}$ inches, fixed to an angle iron $2\frac{1}{4}$ by $2\frac{1}{4}$ by $\frac{5}{16}$ inches, riveted to bulwarks and caulked.

Rudder stock, of forged iron, $5\frac{3}{4}$ inches diameter at head and 3 inches diameter at heel, with two short stays forged to the frame, and plated with $\frac{6}{16}$-inch plates.

Riveting—To be double riveted throughout, bevel necked rivets to be used on the outside plating.

Decks, of yellow pine: main deck 5 by 4 inches, break-deck 4 by $3\frac{1}{2}$ inches, fastened with galvanized iron bolts and nuts let well into the decks, and plugged with well-seasoned turned plugs dipped in white lead. Decks to be well free from knots, and have two coats of raw oil. Teak plank next water-way, 8 inches broad, and one for ring bolts on each side of hatches 10 inches broad; cabin deck 6 by 3 inches.

Half deck, laid on 'tween decks, 8 feet from side and from after-hatch to break bulkhead; full deck also from fore bulkhead till afterpart of fore-hatch, 6 by 3 inches.

Hatches to be in size according to plan approved of by owners, with iron combings standing 15 inches above the deck. The fore and after hatches to have teak booby hatches on top. Main hatch 17 by 12 by 6 feet; lower hold 21 by 12 by 6 feet, with loose beams bolted with screw bolts. Fore and after hatch 6 by 5 feet.

Ceiling, to turn off bilge, of red pine, 2¾ inches thick; the flat of bottom to be laid in hatches, with rings to lift; the ceiling at bilge and ends where no hatches are formed to be properly caulked; the side, from top of bilge to main deck, to be sparred with 2¼-inch battens, spaced 10 inches apart, the battens to be properly planed and beaded on both edges.

Sweat boards—The gunwale stringer to be fitted with movable shutter boards, to carry off sweat from cargo. Shutters to be made of 1-inch pine and fastened with battens.

Chain lockers, of sufficient size to contain the chains, fitted according to plan approved by owners, to be made of greenheart.

Hawse pipes—Two on each bow, of cast iron, fitted in hard wood chocks, with iron sliding shutters.

Timber heads, of cast iron, to answer for ventilators, with brass tops and elevators; also all necessary mooring pipes of cast iron.

Windlass to be fitted with a patent, say 23 inches purchase, with fluting whelps and patent stoppers, spindle to run through the entire length of windlass; the windlass bitts to be of iron or greenheart; pall bitt of iron.

Winches—One at main-hatch with triple purchase, and one at fore-hatch with double purchase, and chain lifters; one small, portable, for cargo.

Capstan—Two on main-deck of the large size, and one smaller on forecastle-deck, to have brass plates on top and brass mountings round the holes; capstan plates to have ship's name and port engraved.

Store-decks in fore and after peaks as required by owners.

Galvanizing—All wrought and cast iron work connected with the hull, on deck, to be galvanized.

Tanks, two in number, to contain 4,500 gallons, placed where required by owners. Bread tanks, six in number, to contain 10 cwt. each, placed where required; or if required by owner, one tank fitted in run to hold 20 cwt.

Pumps, of Wilson & Formby's patent, 7 inches diameter, with fly-wheel motion. Bilge pumps, 5 inches diameter, to work of same spindle as main pumps. One small pump to be fitted between main pumps, 4 inches. One head pump to be fitted, and one pump in fore-peak. One brass or copper pump for water tanks, with all necessary pipes, &c.

Deck house to be fitted between main hatches and foremast for officers, crew, and boys, and galley store-room, &c., to be strongly built, and neatly finished outside with teak pilasters and moldings, and have carved moldings round top.

Forecastle—Fitted up in a plain style, for the accommodation of crew, with store-rooms, if required.

Cabin—Fitted in mahogany and maple, polished, with gilt moldings, and trusses between skin and ceiling to be filled with cork shavings. Captain's room to be fitted with mahogany bed, front drawers, book case, sofa, &c. Chief officer's room to be fitted in a comfortable style and painted oak. Pantry to be fitted with dresser with lead top and brass basin, with all necessary racks and lockers, lined with zinc. State-rooms to be fitted according to plan, with wash-hand basin with marble top in each room. The plan of the cabin to be approved by owners, and all to have first-class finish.

Companions and skylight to be of teak, varnished. The cabin skylight to have stained glass, and all locks and hinges to be of brass.

Painting—To have three coats of paint, inside and outside, to owner's satisfaction; the bottom inside to be cemented with the best Portland cement. McInnes's or other approved composition to be put on the bottom; the ship to be tested with water before cemented.

Boats, as required by board of trade. Boats' beams to be fitted, also chocks for long-boat, with swivel and a set of davits, with gear complete on each side. Boats' beams to be covered on top, and paneled on sides with teak wood, to owner's approval.

Masts—Fore and main and mizzen masts, also bowsprit, lower yards, and lower top-sail yards, of best iron. The other spars of red and pitch pine, owner's option. The smaller spars of spruce. The dimensions of masts and spars to be mutually agreed on, and masting plans to be approved by owners. All the spars to be of first-class quality.

Rigging—Standing rigging of best charcoal iron wire rope, 4¾ inches circumference, to be parceled and served over with small strings, the rest in proportion. The running rigging of European or best St. Petersburg clean hemp, to be fitted with a complete suit of ropes and blocks, brace halyards, and principal blocks to be patent roller bushes and steel pins. Blocks and bushes to be to owner's satisfaction. Dead eyes of lignumvitæ 10 inches, brass caps for end of stays. In addition to the above, the vessel to be supplied with spare gear, as hereafter mentioned. Jibstays to be fitted in wake of booms with chain.

Anchors and chains according to Lloyds' and underwriters' rules, and admiralty test. Anchors to be of Rodgers's patent. An anchor davit to be fitted on forecastle deck;

90 fathoms of 1-inch mooring chain to be supplied, together with all necessary small chain for rigging; one box chain punches to be supplied.

Generally—The whole to be of best workmanship and materials, as required for an A A 1 iron ship by Lloyds, and for the twenty years' class in red, in Liverpool underwriters' book.

GENERAL OUTFIT.

WARPS, ETC.

1 towline, 11 inches, 90 fathoms.
1 warp, 8 inches, 90 fathoms.
1 warp, 7 inches, 90 fathoms.
1 warp, 5½ inches, 90 fathoms.

BOATS, ETC.

1 long boat, 26 by 8 by 3 feet 8 inches, bottom coppered, and round stern, } Carrel.
1 skiff, 24 by 5 feet 9 inches by 2 feet 9 inches, } Carrel.
1 gig, 24 by 5 feet 9 inches by 2 feet 4 inches, } Clencher.
1 dingy, 18 by 5 feet 6 inches by 2 feet 3 inches, } Clencher.

Rowlocks brass for gig and dingy. Brass yoke do., and with rudders for each boat. Boats to be of larch, and thoroughly copper-fastened. Necessary back boards, gratings for boats, &c. Long boat to have cover over top, with teak-wood topsides, and fitted under on deck for live stock. Iron rowlocks for long boat and skiff.

SAILS.

1 flying jib.
1 standing jib.
2 small jibs.
2 foretopmast stay-sails.
1 fore stay-sail.
2 fore-sails.
2 sets foretop sails.
2 foretop-gallant sails.
1 fore royal sail.
2 mainsails.
2 sets maintop sails.
2 main top-gallant sails.
1 main royal sail.
1 main stay-sail.
1 top-gallant stay-sail.
1 main topmast sail.
1 royal stay-sail.
1 main spencer.
2 mizzens.
1 cross jack.
2 sets mizzen top-sails.
1 set mizzen top-gallant sails.
1 set mizzen royals.
1 mizzen stay-sail.
1 mizzen top-mast stay-sail.
1 mizzen top-gallant stay-sail.
3 topmast studding-sails.
2 lower studding-sails.
3 top-gallant studding-sails.
2 royal studding-sails.
2 wind-sails.
1 set awnings to mainmast and foremast, with stanchions and ridge chain complete; also, forecastle awnings, with same.
6 bolts canvas, Nos. 1, 2, 3, 4, 5, and 6.
24 pounds seaming twine.
18 pounds roping twine.
1 set boat sails and spars for long boat and skiff. (Owners to be allowed to make sails at 1*s.* 10*d.* per yard, dropping ½*d.* each number.)
2 sets fids.
6 palms, assorted.
6 dozen sail needles.

6 sail hooks.
2 iron rubbers.
Canvas covers for skiff, gig, and dingy.

CARPENTER'S AND BOATSWAIN'S STORES.

1 hand copper pump.
4 pump spears.
4 lower boxes.
1 break and weegee and wheel motion.
1 pair rigging screws.
2 sounding-rods.
1 spare top-gallant mast or yard.
1 spare top-mast or lower yard of red pine.
1 spare jib-boom or topsail yard of red or pitch pine.
4 spare Norway spars.
1 full set studding-sails, booms, and yards, with blocks and gear complete.
1 side accommodation ladder, fitted and mounted complete, of teak wood.
1 Jacob's ladder, complete.
1 hold ladder.
1 half-deck ladder.
1 forecastle ladder.
1 store-room ladder.
1 larzarette ladder.
1 set hatch bars with brass padlocks.
2 sets tarpaulines.
6 handspikes.
2 sets tarpaulines for small cargo hatches.
2 log chips. Full set capstan bars, fitted in rack where required.
1 pitch pot and ladle.
1 booby hatch for half-deck and fore hatch, teak wood.
30 gallons lamp oil.
35 gallons raw oil.
3 gallons turpentine.
5 gallons olive oil.
10 oil tanks, 10 gallons each.
2 five-gallon tanks. All to be fitted where required.
1 bladder patty.
1 leaf hog's lard.
1 brass bell and stand with ship's name and port on.
1 small brass bell for quarter-deck, with stanchions complete and ship's name and port on.
Mahogany wheel and teak-wood cover, and ship's name carved and gilded on each side of cover, and bound with brass, and ship's name engraved.
Screw steering apparatus, with spare tiller and blocks and chain, to owner's approval.
3 forecastle lamps.
1 cook's lantern.
1 shark hook.
1 portable filter.
1 medicine chest, with ship's name on brass plate, mahogany or teak, fitted complete for India or China voyage, say 30 inches by 17 inches.
1 ensign.
1 union jack.
1 burgee.
Ship's name.
1 house flag.
1 set signals and halyards and book, Maryatt's, and commercial code complete, in addition to full set of gear.
1 coil 1¾-inch rope, 120 fathoms.
1 coil 2½-inch rope, 120 fathoms.
1 coil 3-inch rope, 120 fathoms.
1 coil 3½-inch rope, 120 fathoms.
1 coil 3¾-inch rope, 120 fathoms.
1 coil 18 thread.
1 coil lanyard rope, 5-inch.
1 coil 2 yarn-spun yarn.
4 skeins amberline, }
4 coils marline, } say 2 hundred-weight.
4 coils house line, }

2 buoys and ropes.
2 patent life buoys.
1 spare shackle for each anchor.
2 dozen assorted forelocks.
2 dozen washers for bolts.
Fids for masts, iron.
1 hundred-weight nails, assorted.
1 axe.
1 adze.
1 saw.
1 mall.
1 hammer.
4 cork fenders, large size, to be worked over with hemp ropes by hitching.
1 set boat's chocks, complete.
1 pig-house, with iron bars.
2 dozen assorted connecting shackles.
2 dozen small shackles.
Iron check blocks on lower yards for top-sail sheets.
Iron hoops on lower yard for jack-stays, and quarter hoops for top-sail sheets, with rollers for studding-sail booms.
1 portable forge.
2 hundred-weight rivets, assorted.
1 set riveting jacks.
1 ratchet.
Set of drills from ½ inch to 1 inch, with knee.
4 chisels.
1 screw wrench, with patent spanner.
1 chain-purchase sling.
2 pairs skeets for ship's side, with covers for the rail in way of fore and main hatches.
60 feet hard wood, 12 by 3.
8 scrapers.
400 feet red fir planks.
4 spare ash oars.
4 iron crowbars.
2 dozen hooks and thimbles, assorted.
2 dozen clip hooks.
4 large ventilators, to be properly placed.
6 deck scrubbing brushes, with weegee.
1 register box and locks, with ship's name.
8 paint scrubbing brushes.
2 whitewash brushes.
18 paint brushes, assorted.
4 pencil brushes.
48 birch brooms.
4 joiner's scrapers.
2 plumber's scrapers.
2 cabin sweeping brushes, long and short.
12 hundred-weight paint, assorted.
1 cask M'Innes's paint, or tallow, say 3 hundred-weight.
40 gallons paint oil.
1 transparent compass, fitted on tripod, or some other suitable place.
1 azimuth compass.
1 steering compass, fitted complete in brass dolphin binnacle, all properly adjusted.
Compass fitted with 10-inch card and storm gimble center, owner's approval.
1 cabin compass, transparent.
2 spare compass cards marked with degrees.
1 thermometer.
1 barometer, } combined.
1 sympiesometer, }
1 pair glasses.
1 telescope, to be approved of.
4 log glasses.
1 patent log and line.
1 half-hour glass.
2 mops and handles.
1 log slate.
1 log book.
1 log reel and line.
1 patent deep-sea lead line and reel, 200 fathoms.

1 patent sounding machine.
2 hand leads and lines.
1 harpoon.
1 pair grains.
1 side pump leather.
1 side service leather.
Brass signal lamps, to be fitted up per board of trade requirement, say 4.
1 flash light.
12 fishing hooks.
1 box blue lights.
1 box rockets.
3 fishing lines.
2 spare log lines.
1 brass speaking trumpet.
1 fog horn.
Gratings between skylight and wheel; also, between cabin doors and skylight, with gratings front of poop, and gutter waterway on poop, all of teak wood.
1 grindstone and trough.
4 long tar brushes.
2 short tar brushes.
1 set ash oars to each boat.
½ cask pitch.
½ cask rosin.
1 cask Stockholm tar.
2 hundred-weight oakum.
18 chain hooks.
7 luff-tackle blocks, say 13 inches double.
7 luff-tackle blocks, say 13 inches single.
18 spare blocks.
2 spare dead-eyes and pins.
2 spare cargo pennants, with blocks and fall.
2 chain stoppers.
2 shank-painters.
2 chain claws.
1 spun-yarn winch, iron.
2 double 21-inch purchase blocks.
1 triple 21-inch purchase block.
2 cat-blocks.
2 top blocks, say 5 and 6 each rope.
3 snatch-blocks.
1 purchase gin and chain.
1 gaff fitted to mainmast.
1 ballast gin and chain.
1 anchor fishhook.
2 boat-hooks.
2 watch tackles.
12 marline spikes, flat pointed.
6 serving mallets.
3 serving boards.
2 pair chain can-hooks.
2 pair chain nippers.
1 pair chains for puncheons.
1 pair chain-purchase slings.
9 ballast shovels.
9 coal shovels.
16 feet hen-coops, teak.
1 fire-engine and hose, with teak cover.

COOPER'S STORES.

4 water casks, 100 gallons.
2 breakers, 20 gallons each.
2 oval harness casks.
12 deck buckets.
1 water can.
1 wash deck tub.
12 mess kids.
1 water funnel.
2 draw buckets.
4 bread boxes.

1 cask for flour.
3 vinegar casks, 20 gallons each.
2 lime casks, 20 gallons each.
1 molasses cask, 15 gallons.
All casks and 12 buckets to have galvanized iron hoops; also, 12 buckets and 2 harness casks which are to have brass hoops, and to be of teak.

CABIN STORES.

1 iron tea-kettle.
1 copper tea-kettle.
1 britannia metal tea-pot.
1 britannia metal coffee-pot.
12 table-spoons, E. P. No. 1.
12 tea-spoons, E. P. No. 1.
1 dozen table knives and forks, with white ivory handles.
1 dozen table forks, E. P. No. 1.
1 dozen dessert knives and forks, with white ivory handles.
1 dozen forks, E. P. No. 1.
1 basket for electro-plates.
1 metal tureen and ladle.
1 electro-plate tureen and ladle, No. 1.
12 electro-plate dessert spoons, No. 1.
1 electro-plate mustard-pot spoon, No. 1.
2 electro-plate salt spoons, No. 1.
6 common knives and forks, with 6 table and 6 tea-spoons, britannia metal.
1 carving knife and fork.
1 steel, ivory handle.
1 set castors, E. P. No. 1.
4 dish covers, E. P. No. 1.
1 black jack.
4 brass candlesticks.
4 pair snuffers and tray.
4 dozen plates, assorted.
1 dozen dishes.
6 vegetable dishes.
1 dozen mugs.
2 butter boats.
2 butter pots.
1 dozen egg-cups.
2 glass salts.
2 sugar basins, (1 glass.)
Crockeryware to have ship's name on.
½ dozen basins.
1 wash-hand basin and jug to be fitted up in each state-room.
2 water jugs for cabin.
2 dozen cups and saucers.
4 decanters.
1 dozen tumblers.
1 dozen wine glasses.
1 dozen champagne glasses.
2 brass cocks.
4 chamber pots.
1 pair flour scales and weights.
1 pair steel-yards.
1 set weights and scales complete.
2 coffee mills.
1 candle box.
1 spice box.
1 flour dredger.
1 set pewter measures, say 6
1 plate basket.
1 corkscrew.
1 dust pan.
1 hand bell.
2 fancy bread baskets.
1 cabin lamp, to be approved.
1 brass bar, to be fitted in skylight, with swing tray attached
1 berth lamp to each state-room and pantry.
Damask curtains in each room.
1 cabin stove, with copper funnel complete.

Iron funnel inside of copper, to be approved.
1 coal box, japanned.
1 set fire-irons.
1 chair for end of table.
1 stool for each room.
1 forecastle stove and funnel.
1 teak or mahogany table, to draw out.
1 stove for house on deck, and funnel.
Settees on each side of cabin table, with swinging backs.
All hair-cloth to be covered with hollands and bound with red.
Sideboard to be fitted in cabin of Spanish mahogany and marble top and brass rail.
Sofa, drawers, and book-case of teak in captain's room, with small table for chronometer.
Settees and after-lockers to be covered with best hair-cloth.
All hinges or locks in cabin or elsewhere to be brass.
Furniture for locks to be glass, owner's approval.
1 cloth for cabin table.
1 oilcloth for cabin table.
1 carpet for cabin floor, and oilcloth for each state-room and pantry, with runners.
Carpet for captain's room, with oilcloth and all necessary table-cloths and towels for the voyage.
1 side light in each room, and all to be approved by owners.
Steward's pantry and lazarette to be properly fitted up, with all necessary pease and other lockers, lined with zinc throughout.
1 water-closet and bath to be fitted in cabin, to have double-action valves, and 1 in wing of monkey, forecastle.
Cabin stairs to be leaded, and to have brass diamond step plates, fitted with brass rods from deck to cabin.
All small ladders on deck to have diamond brass plates.
1 looking-glass over sideboard, and one in each room, to owner's approval.
1 time-piece to match mirror.
2 guns complete, with carriages of teak, say 4-pounders.
24 rounds cartridges, ammunition, 24 shots for the voyage, with copper magazines.
6 muskets.
6 pistols.
6 bayonets.
6 cutlasses.
6 hand-cuffs.
Ship to have female figurehead.
The poop skylight companion grating over wheel.
12 buckets and harness casks and forecastle scuttle to be of teak.
All cooking utensils to be supplied, with caboose of first-rate quality for East India voyages, to owner's approval.

COOKING RANGE, (to be sufficiently large to cook for 24 hands.

2 copper boilers and steamer.
3 lined oval pots.
4 saucepans.
1 fish pan.
1 cullender.
2 frying pans.
1 cook's ladle.
1 basting spoon.
1 cook's knife.
1 cook's axe.
1 saw.
1 cleaver.
1 steel.
1 tormentor.
1 mincing knife.
1 bread grater.
2 pudding pans.
3 bread tins.
3 pudding molds.
2 roasting pans.
2 gridirons.
1 pepper box.
1 slice.
6 skewers.
3 baking dishes, enameled.

It is understood that anything enumerated twice is only to be singly supplied. No extras to be supplied without the same be given in writing to any party appointed by the owners, and having their approval by signing the notice, a copy of which is to be sent to

Anything left out of this specification which it is customary to supply to this class of vessel, it is understood that the same will be supplied by the builders. And anything left out of this specification must be supplied in this case in accordance with contract, and everything to be carried up to Lloyds' and underwriters' rules.

Everything of first-class material and of the best workmanship. Delivery at the Broomielaw, Glasgow, after being in graving dock, on the , or before, if practicable.

Model to be approved of before laying the vessel down, and finished model sent to purchasers during the building.

Builders' present price, as per specification, £14 10*s*. per register ton.

Mr. WILLIAM H. WEBB suggested that the committee should, before adjournment, request the ship-owners of New York, and the underwriters, to communicate their views in writing on the question before the committee. He himself would be prepared to do so, and could give more information in that way than he could orally.

The CHAIRMAN stated that the committee intended to address circulars to gentlemen interested in the various branches of the business, and to get all the information that it could, in writing as well as orally. The committee would be very glad to have Mr. Webb communicate his views in writing.

Mr. WEBB said he should be very glad to do so.

The following was received, and ordered on file:

MR. CHAIRMAN AND GENTLEMEN OF THE CONGRESSIONAL COMMITTEE: I have heretofore been quite a vessel owner and builder, but not so now, and therefore cannot complain much; but I feel proud to think that there has been enough evidence before your honorable body by the merchants and ship-builders of the United States to convince you that the taxes and tariffs on ships and ship-building materials ought to entirely cease, for the protection of commerce. But there is another branch of taxes which I wish to call your serious attention to. I have been for the last three years contesting the illegality of State and municipal taxes on the commerce of the United States. Those sort of taxes on vessel property are enormous, and attended with obstructions, delays, and damage. I hope, Mr. Chairman, you and your committee will not be unmindful in assisting us in pressing our claims at the next session of Congress to abrogate and finally break up the different and various State and municipal taxes that are imposed upon and exacted from commerce at the various ports in the United States, as partially set forth in this petition, which has been presented to Congress, but which has not been acted upon at present.

I also wish to state to you that within the walls of this edifice the collector of the port of New York has collected millions of dollars, and up to this date is collecting State and municipal taxes and tonnage dues from commerce, in violation of the Constitution of the United States; in violation of the Congress of the United States; in violation of the supreme court of the District of Columbia in a case decided October 24, 1867, (Nautilus case;) in violation of the Supreme Court of the United States, decided December term, 1867, (steamship Charles Morgan—New Orleans case;) and, last, in violation of the orders of N. Sargent, Commissioner of Customs at Washington, dated August 13, 1869.

C. F. BARNES.

The committee adjourned to meet in Boston on Monday, 18th October.

BOSTON, TUESDAY, *October* 19, 1869.

The committee met in the rooms of the Board of Trade.

Present: the Chairman and Messrs. Buffinton, Morrell, Calkin, Wells, and Holman.

The CHAIRMAN stated the object of the committee, and invited the gentlemen appointed by the Board of Trade to express their views in reference to the cause of the depression of American commerce and navigation

Mr. EDWARD S. TOBEY, chairman of the Board of Trade, welcomed the committee to the city of Boston and to the rooms of the board, and said that the Board of Trade hailed the meeting of this committee as an auspicious omen to the interests of commerce, and as showing that Congress had become impressed with the importance of doing something to restore the shipping interest of the country. It was not his purpose now to present at length any views that he might hold on the subject, but rather to call upon other members of the Board of Trade to present their views, and in the course of the investigation he would endeavor to take some proper opportunity to give a statement of facts which had come within his own knowledge, and such deductions from those facts as might suggest themselves to his mind. He mentioned the presence in the room of one of the prominent representatives of the iron steam-ship-building interest, the treasurer of the Atlantic Works of East Boston, Mr. Smith, who was already known extensively throughout the country by his very able communication on the subject of iron steam-ship construction.

Mr. FRANKLIN W. SMITH, treasurer of the Atlantic Iron Works of Boston, addressed the committee. He said that he would not take up the time of the committee by repeating what it was better informed of than himself, the history of American commerce, its prosperity and decline. Nor would he trouble members of Congress with statistics, among which they were buried for a great part of the year. He only wished that a moiety of the intelligence possessed by members of Congress on this matter were possessed by the people. If that were so this committee would not be in session to-day. He need not recall how, in 1861, the American tonnage was greatly in excess of the tonnage of any other nation. Nor need he recall the record of the decline of that commerce. In 1868 there were but six iron vessels built in the United States, and at present he believed that there was not one iron vessel on the stocks in this country. A bark of six hundred or seven hundred tons, and the iron bark Novelty, built by the Atlantic Works, were the only iron sailing vessels built in this country. As to wooden shipping he was not able to follow its decline, the decline being so rapid. What was the reason for this? The answer might be given in one word—the tariff. The contrast on this matter between the United States and Great Britain was most painful. In 1867, out of two hundred and twenty-seven ships built upon the Clyde, there were but fourteen of wood, and these averaged only one hundred and sixty tons each. He held in his hand a slip from the Glasgow Herald of August 7, 1869, detailing the launches which had taken place during the previous month. There were thirteen of them, amounting in all to thirteen thousand nine hundred and ninety-one tons, averaging nearly eleven hundred, and all of iron. Why could not this be done here? Because of the tariff. He was indebted to one of the able articles of the New York Evening Post for a record of the changes in the tariff, and of the pressure which those changes had brought to bear upon the ship-building interest. In 1857, common rounds and squares of iron, such as are used in the wooden ship-building interest, and which were then the great item to be taxed in ship-building, were taxed twenty-four per cent. ad valorem. In 1861 they were taxed fifty per cent., and in 1864 one hundred and twelve per cent. ad valorem. It was stated that by the proposed bill introduced by Mr. Moorhead in 1868, those very bars of iron, essential in wooden ship-building, were struck at for a rate of one hundred and sixty-eight per cent. He held in his hand a list showing the charges to-day of an iron ship of one thousand tons burden, supposing that all her materials of foreign construction were imported. He submitted it in detail to the committee, as follows:

Duties on materials for a 1,000-ton iron ship.

IRON.

53 per cent., plate	530,000, duty, 1½ cents	$7,950 00	
18 per cent., refined iron and rivets,	180,000, duty, 1 cent	1,800 00	
23 per cent., T. and angle or beams,	230,000, duty, 1¼ cents	2,875 00	
3 per cent., forgings	30,000, duty, 2 cents	600 00	
3 per cent., castings	30,000, duty, say 1 cent	300 00	
100 per cent.	1,000,000 lbs., divided by 3,	13,525 00	
		4,508 33	
			$18,033 33

RIGGING.

35,000 pounds chain cable, duty, 2½ cents, gold 8,000 pounds small rigging-chain, duty, 2½ cents, gold	$1,075 00	
8,000 pounds anchors, 2¼ cents, gold	180 00	
8½ tons Russian hemp, $40 ton, gold duty; or if cordage be imported, 10 tons, 2,000 pounds each, 20,000 pounds, 3 cents	600 00	
5 tons Manilla hemp, 2,240 pounds, at $25 ton, gold; or if cordage be imported, 12,000 pounds, at 2½ cents	300 00	
	2,155 00	
Add 33⅓ per cent	718 33	
		2,873 33
		20,906 66

If wire rigging be used, 5 tons, cost 22 shillings sterling for 112 pounds, duty 35 per cent. ad valorem; costs now 7½ cents, gold, for galvanized, duty paid.

That was about twenty-five per cent. extra on the cost of an iron ship of one thousand tons in England. The Atlantic Works had recently invented a tank vessel for the carriage of molasses in the bulk—a peculiarly difficult liquid to carry, because of its expansive and fermenting qualities. A vessel for this purpose must be constructed of iron, so far as experience went, because it had been found impossible to get a wooden vessel strong enough and fixed enough in its joints to hold those tanks under all conditions. Those tanks, therefore, were constructed with the ship, adding strength to the ship. That vessel had been invented here and had been patented both here and in England, and had made two voyages which had been deemed to have been an absolute and unqualified success. He might state with entire safety that there had been a saving of five per cent. on each of those cargoes of molasses. The saving might have been much more. That vessel would bring five cargoes in the season, which would be a saving in a single season of twenty-five per cent. The molasses imported into Boston alone in a single season employed fifteen vessels, and one concern in New York employed fifteen vessels in the trade. The Atlantic Works had built one such tank vessel, and the firm for which they built it, as well as other parties, desired to have more such vessels. They were ready to build two on their own account; but, singularly enough, they had been actually stayed in the building of them, by the expectation of the benefits which they were now asking at the hands of Congress. They did not dare to build those vessels, in the expectation that Congress would strike off the duty and reduce the valuation next spring from $10,000 to $15,000. The building, therefore, of at least three of those vessels had been postponed to another season. But meanwhile the Atlantic Works Company finding their hands tied, as iron ship-builders, and finding it impossible to build those brigs themselves, wrote to England and had an offer from England to build them on the Clyde at twenty-five per cent. less than they could build them themselves. They were seriously debating the building of those brigs abroad, and having them under a foreign flag. This would probably be the case next year unless the necessary relief were granted. He had no doubt that the American merchants' interest in the molasses trade would insist upon this saving of $5,000 per cargo. If America could not supply those vessels England would; and if American merchants were too patriotic or too timid to put their vessels under the English flag, they would go abroad and give to England, not only the building of the ships, but the transportation besides. All that the Atlantic Works asked was a royalty on their patent which was registered abroad.

He had given the committee the rates on bars and plate iron, but there was another item to which he should call especial attention. The duty on beams and angle-irons was practically prohibitory. They were now rolled in this country by only three concerns. In iron ship-building they constituted twenty-three per cent. of the entire work, and the committee would see the disadvantage of a monopoly even in the hands of the best of men, from this fact, that no matter what rate of tariff was imposed, so long as the construction of those beams paid a profit—as they had paid a large profit for many years—those three mills had only to raise their scale of prices up to just below the cost of importation; and the consequence was that at present all beams and all angles had their prices adjusted by the rate of importation. It was natural that this should be so, and he did not wish to be understood as reflecting, in the least degree, upon the patriotic impulses or business course of any concern that might pursue this policy. Doubtless every concern in the country would consider it perfectly legitimate; but with our commerce to-day depending upon the closest possible competition and upon the most advantageous circumstances both as to material and labor, it was certainly a most discouraging feature that twenty-three per cent. of the materials that enter into the construction of iron ships should be absolutely in the hands of a monopoly of manufacturers. It was not so with pig or other descriptions of iron.

He had placed in a pamphlet, which he had had the honor to submit to Congress, the reasons, drawn from most experienced authority, showing why wooden ships were to-day practically superseded by iron ships. In Calcutta and San Francisco iron ships commanded five shillings sterling a ton premium in charters, because of their durability, because of their increased capacity, because of the fine condition in which merchandise could be transported in them, and because of the rates of insurance. While America had in her magnificent forests the monopoly of material, and thus gained her prestige on the ocean, England was at the disadvantage that America was at now. Now things were reversed; the advantages of coal, iron, and labor England had to-day, and she was building ships and selling them all over the world. Prussia was protecting her iron interest by charging ten per cent. upon the iron ships bought abroad, while she charged only five per cent. upon the wooden ships. But England, despite that, was building for all the world. J. S. Forbes & Co., of Boston, had, last March, sent to the Atlantic Works specifications for a first-class iron ship for Chinese waters. The Atlantic Works had not pretended to do any better than build the ship at cost. They had got one contract from the Boston and Baltimore line of steamships, and were glad to get it at cost, because such establishments as theirs were better kept running. To stop them causes great deterioration. They had received those specifications from Messrs. J. S. Forbes & Co., and had endeavored to figure them down to the necessary point; but they had despaired at the outset of getting the contract. While they were at it they had received a note from Forbes & Co., stating, "Gentlemen: We are informed by cable that this ship is ordered in England."

A few days since he had gone to New York to meet a gentleman who would have ordered an iron ship for the trade between New York and Mexico. This gentleman had said that his judgment was that in every respect iron ships were preferable to wooden ones, and that he intended to build of iron, but that when he came to figure out the cost and found that the absolute taxes on the materials entering into the construction of such a ship would be from $40,000 to $50,000, he had determined to build a wooden ship, take the chances, and let her rot out in ten or fifteen years, considering that the interest on the difference would build another ship. These were the facts as to the entire and absolute suppression of iron ship-building in the United States. As to a remedy, he should not suggest that American ports should be thrown open to foreign produce. For his own part he should be glad to see American products used in preference to foreign; they were better. He desired to see, through the influence of Congress, or through an organization of the merchants of the country, the establishment of the authority of the American Lloyds in rating ships equal to the authority of the British and French Lloyds. They should then have the opportunity to take into account the admitted and unquestioned superiority of American iron, and could make out a gain of twenty per cent. in the cost of iron ships. He had been astonished to see that with the American prestige, they had not before this time asserted an authority which should be equally authoritative before the world in the matter of rating ships. He could not understand why the underwriters should compel American ship-owners, who a few years ago owned more ships than any nation in the world, to bring everything up to a standard of British or French engineering. It seemed to him that Americans had proved in the history of the last war that the judgment of their mechanics as to what was strong and as to what was required to give strength, was equal to the judgment and intelligence of foreign engineers. If Congress could secure for American ship-owners the privilege of having their ships rated by underwriters as authoritatively as they are now rated by English or French companies, Americans could go into their own mines and dig out an iron superior, by from twenty-five to thirty-three per cent., in strength to English iron, and they could thus, with a modified tariff, be in a position to ask no favors from any source for the restoration of their commerce.

Mr. SAMUEL HALL, of East Boston, ship-builder, made a statement to the committee. He said that the wooden ship-building interest had been much depressed since the war. He had built but one ship since the war, and had one upon the stocks now. This depression was owing wholly to the high cost of the ships. The high duties upon the materials entering into the construction of ships, made ships cost from fifty to sixty per cent. higher than they did previous to the war. Iron which they used to buy for not exceeding forty dollars per ton was now eighty dollars per ton; rigging which they used to buy at eight cents per pound was now sixteen cents per pound; duck which they used to buy at twenty-eight cents a pound was now worth fifty-six cents; and everything else was in the same proportion. Unless there was something done to relieve ship-builders they would have to give up their business entirely.

Mr. MORRELL. The prices that you speak of now are in currency, as compared with gold prices before the war?

Mr. HALL. Yes, sir. Formerly we used to take ships to England and sell them. I believe that I took the first ship to England from this country and sold her there. Now I presume that if the trade were thrown open so that the English could send their ships here to be sold, there would be no ships at all built on this side. We cannot compete with them. They can build iron ships cheaper than we can build wooden ones.

Mr. CALKIN. How does the mechanical labor here compare with the mechanical labor of England?

Mr. HALL. It is much higher here than it is there.

Mr. CALKIN. Do our ship-carpenters here do any more work than their ship-carpenters do?

Mr. HALL. I think they do.

Mr. CALKIN. What would the average be?

Mr. HALL. I think that we are degenerating very fast on that point in this country, so far as my experience goes.

Mr. CALKIN. The reason why I ask the question is because the builders of New York gave it as their opinion that the American mechanics were superior to the English mechanics and did more work; and I want to get the opinion of a Boston builder on that point.

Mr. HALL. I think that they do, as a general thing. I think that the English hold on to their own notion of doing things. I do not know but that their workmen work as hard as ours; but the means that they take to accomplish the work is different. Their tools are not so good as ours. I think that if Congress would relieve the ship-builders by removing the duties on the materials that enter into the construction of ships, it would be a great advantage to them. Unless they do so, I think, in the course of a few years, there will be no more ship-yards in this country.

Mr. WELLS. I understood you to state that it costs to build a ship now from fifty to sixty per cent. more than it did before the war?

Mr. HALL. Yes, sir.

Mr. WELLS. By removing all the duties and allowing a drawback on the materials entering into the construction of wooden ships, would you then be able to compete with ships built in the provinces, where timber is equally as plenty as it is here?

Mr. HALL. If they used the same quality of timber that we do, we could build as cheap as they can in the provinces; but they build their ships out of cheaper timber, such as spruce and birch. I have worked in the provinces and know the manner in which they do their work.

Mr. WELLS. You have been carrying on that business for many years?

Mr. HALL. About forty-six years.

Mr. WELLS. What is your opinion as to the necessary legislation of Congress in order to enable ship-builders in this country to compete with foreign ship-builders?

Mr. HALL. I think that if all the articles used in ship-building were admitted duty free, American ship-builders would be able to go on as formerly.

Mr. WELLS. Suppose you were able to go on, would you find a market here for your ships?

Mr. HALL. I see no reason why we should not. Nothing but the high prices prevents our finding a market now. Enough of people want ships but cannot pay the prices for them.

Mr. WELLS. I notice several ships lying idle here, and also in New York, as if they had not any business. How do you account for that?

Mr. HALL. There is not a large amount of tonnage now, I think not near as much as there was before the war. There are not half the ships in New York now that there were formerly. If it were not for the coasting trade I do not know that there would be hardly an American ship to be seen. If our ports were thrown open to other nations and our coastwise trade opened to them, we should not have any use at all for our ships.

Mr. WELLS. Your opinion is that if Congress should remove all the obstructions in regard to duty, allowing ship-builders a drawback, and at the same time should throw open the purchase of ships in Europe, the mechanics in this country could compete with English mechanics in the building of ships?

Mr. HALL. I do not think they could. If the English were allowed to put their ships into the market, and if our navigation laws were repealed, I do not think there would ever be any more ships of any kind built here.

Mr. WELLS. American merchants are free now to go and buy ships abroad and to sail them under the English flag?

Mr. HALL. Yes; and I am told that quite a number of them are doing it.

Mr. MORRELL. Do you understand that the business as now carried on by the English nation is profitable; that they are making money to-day in their commercial marine?

Mr. HALL. I cannot say as to that. I should not think that the business is depressed there as it is here, because they build much more there, and people are not apt to follow a losing business a great while.

Mr. MORRELL. But they are willing to keep their ships running even when they are not making money?

Mr. HALL. I cannot say as regards the English whether their shipping is depressed or not; but I know that in this country it is very much depressed.

Mr. CALKIN. The question was asked you whether, if the drawback on the materials were allowed, and if the navigation laws were repealed so that capitalists could go abroad and buy ships, American mechanics could compete with English ship-builders, and you answered that they could not. Do you think that if the time were extended—for instance, if the drawback were allowed, and then in the course of four or five years the navigation laws were repealed—the ship-builders of this country could get themselves in a position by that time to compete with foreign builders?

Mr. HALL. I do not think they could.

Mr. CALKIN. You think it would take a longer time?

Mr. HALL. Yes. If the navigation laws were repealed almost all the ships in the world would be built in England.

Mr. CALKIN. You understand my question. It is whether, if a drawback were allowed for four or five years before the navigation laws were repealed, the American mechanics would then be in a position to compete with the English mechanics?

Mr. HALL. I think not.

The CHAIRMAN. How long a time would it take for American ship-builders to compete with foreigners?

Mr. HALL. I do not think they ever can. If Congress anticipates repealing the navigation laws it may as well do so to-day as wait for five years hence. The result would be the same.

The CHAIRMAN. What are the wages paid at present to ship-carpenters and mechanics here?

Mr. HALL. About three dollars a day in currency.

The CHAIRMAN. What were they paid before the war—say from 1854 to 1860?

Mr. HALL. Not exceeding two dollars a day—from that to one dollar and seventy-five and one dollar and fifty cents. I built the first clipper ship, I believe, that was built in Boston, the Surprise, in 1850, and I then paid one dollar and seventy-five cents a day.

The CHAIRMAN. 1850 was a year of great depression. How was it in 1854, which was a year of great activity in the building of ships?

Mr. HALL. Not so much as in 1852. In 1852 we had the greatest activity in ship-building in this country that we ever had. I recollect that I built four ships from March to December of that year, of eleven hundred tons each.

The CHAIRMAN. What were the average rates of wages paid to first-class mechanics from 1850 to 1860?

Mr. HALL. It would fall below two dollars. I should say that one dollar and seventy-five cents would be about the average, and sometimes it went down to one dollar and fifty cents for first-class mechanics.

The CHAIRMAN. So that there has been an advance of fifty per cent. in wages?

Mr. HALL. Yes, sir. The carpenter work on a ship which would then cost about seven thousand dollars would now cost about twelve thousand or thirteen thousand dollars.

The CHAIRMAN. You think, then, that something more than the admission of the materials entering into the construction of ships duty free is necessary to enable American ship-builders to compete with foreigners?

Mr. HALL. As long as things remain as they are now, the cost of labor will not recede much. Mechanics are going out of the business and seeking other employment, and there is great scarcity even now of mechanics in ship-building. That, of course, enhances the cost of wages.

The CHAIRMAN. Do you think, from your knowledge of the character of workmen here, and in Europe, that the difference in labor would be overcome or nearly overcome by the greater efficiency of the American workmen?

Mr. HALL. I do. It takes the English a great while to do a little work. They are diligent men, but they are very slow.

The CHAIRMAN. How would the cost of materials that enter into the construction of ships stand now free of duty as compared with the price of materials before the war, making an allowance for the difference between gold and currency?

Mr. HALL. The cost would be considerably higher now.

Mr. MORRELL. Does that refer to timber as well as to iron?

Mr. HALL. No, sir; to nothing but the iron; the wood we get here.

Mr. MORRELL. What is the value of the iron in wooden ships as compared with the value of the other materials?

Mr. HALL. A ship of one thousand three hundred and fifty tons, such as I am building now, will take about seventy-five tons of bolt iron and square iron.

Mr. WELLS. Do you not use a great deal of copper in the building of wooden ships?

Mr. HALL. Yes, sir.

Mr. WELLS. What is the difference between the cost of copper now and its cost previous to the war?

Mr. HALL. We do not now use clear copper.

Mr. WELLS. You cover the outside with copper?

Mr. HALL. That is sheathing copper. Before the war it was worth seventeen cents a pound; now it is worth twenty-seven cents.

Mr. CALKIN. In case of a repeal of the navigation laws, what would be the effect upon ship-carpenters' labor in this country in the course of four or five years?

Mr. HALL. There would not be any at all.

Mr. CALKIN. Can you take a house-carpenter or a wood-worker of any kind and make a ship-carpenter of him readily?

Mr. HALL. No, sir; no more than you can take a common mechanic and set him to make a watch.

Mr. HOLMAN. What will be the policy of ship-builders hereafter in regard to the building of wooden vessels? Are wooden ships likely to be built hereafter to any extent, or will iron ships supersede them?

Mr. HALL. I do not think that iron ships at present, unless they are built much cheaper, will compete with wooden ships.

Mr. HOLMAN. Take the commerce of the world.

Mr. HALL. I think the tendency is toward iron vessels.

Mr. HOLMAN. Supposing that Congress should adopt a more liberal policy by admitting foreign built vessels to American registration, only excluding them from the coastwise trade, and supposing that a rebate were allowed upon all the materials entering into the construction of ships, what effect would these measures, taken together, have upon our commerce and our ship-building? Would they promote the one and injure the other, or would they promote both?

Mr. HALL. I should think you would not promote the ship-building interest by throwing the trade open to foreign vessels.

Mr. HOLMAN. By giving the coastwise trade exclusively to American-built ships?

Mr. HALL. I do not think that there is enough of that to make it worth while building ships.

Mr. HOLMAN. In 1860, when our commercial marine was much larger than it is now, was not our domestic trade equal to fifty per cent. of the whole of our commerce?

Mr. HALL. Congress can tell better than I can about that.

Mr. HOLMAN. You had no occasion to inquire into that question?

Mr. HALL. No, sir.

Mr. HOLMAN. You think that the advantages resulting from the domestic trade to American-built ships are not very important, and that the reservation of that trade to American-built ships, combined with the use of free materials in the construction of ships, would not promote our ship-building, if registration were granted to foreign-built vessels?

Mr. HALL. No; I do not think that these measures would be of any great benefit; I think that ship-building here would finally die out. If the government does not do something to protect the ship-building interest it certainly will die out, and that very soon.

Mr. HOLMAN. And you think that this would be done in two ways: first by preserving the navigation act; and secondly, by allowing materials exempt from internal and external taxes to be used in the construction of ships?

Mr. HALL. Yes, sir.

Mr. HOLMAN. Are American capitalists willing to employ their capital at as low rates of interest in ship-building as English capitalists are?

Mr. HALL Yes, I think so.

Mr. BUFFINTON. Can you tell whether the business of building wooden ships in the provinces is about as much depressed as it is here?

Mr. HALL. I cannot tell you. I think there is very little business doing there.

Mr. BUFFINTON. Have you any means of knowing whether it is depressed there as much as it is here?

Mr. HALL. I have not.

Mr. JOHN TAYLOR, ship-builder of Chelsea, next made a statement to the committee. He said that he agreed in the main facts that had been stated by Mr. Smith and by Mr. Hall. What had been said in regard to iron ships was equally applicable to wooden ships, so far as half or more of the whole cost of the ship was concerned. He would not add to or take from what had been already stated. There was great depression here in the ship-building interest. The cause of that depression had been stated, and he did not know that he could add anything to the statement. He had been thirty-five years engaged in ship-building, and had constructed over one hundred large ships. He was not constructing any ships at present, nor did he contemplate doing so, as he had made up his mind to abandon the business altogether, and never to build another ship. This was for the simple reason that it could not be done; that American ship-builders could not compete with the ship-builders of other nations so long as the difference in the cost of materials existed. He believed that there were two ships at present on the stocks in this port, but that in two weeks from this time there would not be a ship on the stocks in Massachusetts. He accounted for the fact that there was any ship-building going on now in Boston, by saying that it was in order to keep the yards in existence and to employ the mechanics. He himself had done as little as he could possibly do, so as to employ his materials and workmen, hoping ere long that some assistance would come to the ship-building interest.

The CHAIRMAN. Can the ships which are now being built be sold at profit to the builder?

Mr. TAYLOR. No, sir; they are being built merely on account of the mechanics, and for the purpose of using up the materials and keeping the men together, in the hope of better times.

The CHAIRMAN. Where have you constructed heretofore?

Mr. TAYLOR. In East Boston for the last few years.

The CHAIRMAN. How long is it since you have built any ships?

Mr. TAYLOR. I have one now just about finished.

The CHAIRMAN. Please state to the committee the rates of wages which you are paying to first-class mechanics.

Mr. TAYLOR. From three to three and a quarter dollars a day.

The CHAIRMAN. What were the average rates of wages for the same kind of mechanics previous to the war—say from 1852 to 1860?

Mr. TAYLOR. In 1852–'3 wages were very high. In 1850 and 1851, and again in 1856–'7–'8, they were low. My experience would vary a little from Mr. Hall's. I think that the average would reach quite as high as to-day, and perhaps a little higher for first-class mechanics. For second-class mechanics wages would be very much below that. A great portion of them would be hired at from nine shillings a day to one dollar and seventy-five cents.

The CHAIRMAN. Reduced to gold, the present rate of wages would be about thirty-five per cent. higher than the rate of wages then?

Mr. TAYLOR. Yes, about that. There has been a great deal of tampering with labor here, and that, in my estimation, has injured the cause a great deal. These societies here have formed laws regulating labor, determining the hours of labor, &c.

The CHAIRMAN. How many hours do your mechanics work now?

Mr. TAYLOR. We have worked ten hours. The navy yard here employs about seven-eighths of all the ship-carpenters in this vicinity. There they work for only eight hours, and are paid three dollars and twenty-four cents a day, so that all the ship-carpenters are flocking to the navy yard.

The CHAIRMAN. What hours did your mechanics work previous to the war?

Mr. TAYLOR. Ten hours.

The CHAIRMAN. What effect does the navy yard have upon labor? Does it tend to increase the rates of wages in the neighborhood of the yard?

Mr. TAYLOR. Yes, sir; it always does.

The CHAIRMAN. So that a ship cannot be built as cheaply in the neighborhood of a navy yard as remote from it?

Mr. TAYLOR. No, sir; men will always seek employment in a navy yard even at lower rates of wages than they can get at private yards.

The CHAIRMAN. How does the price of materials at the present time (keeping in mind the difference between gold and currency) compare with the price of materials before the war—say from 1852 to 1860?

Mr. TAYLOR. If we used white-oak plank it would be very much higher; yellow pine would be very little higher.

The CHAIRMAN. How would it be, taking the materials for a ship right through by the ton?

Mr. TAYLOR. All the outfits, everything like spars and rigging, sails, iron, copper, and all finishing work, trimmings, brass work, and everything of that kind, is more than one hundred per cent. higher in currency.

The CHAIRMAN. Reduce it to gold and take the duty off, and how would the price of materials then compare with the prices previous to the war?

Mr. TAYLOR. If the duties were all taken off, I do not think there would be a great deal of difference, with the rates reduced to gold.

Mr. CALKIN. Do not navy yard commandants send to the different manufacturing establishments in the community and base the price of labor in the yard upon the price of labor outside?

Mr. TAYLOR. I do not think that they do. That is to say, I do not think that they get a fair representation of labor outside. Labor is always higher in the navy yard than it is out of it. We have several classes of labor. There is the repairing of ships. That labor fetches a higher price than new work does. For instance, if new work were paid at the rate of three dollars a day, old work would be paid at the rate of four dollars. The navy yard people are more inclined to take that kind of labor as a criterion; or, at all events, they take that kind of labor and the new, and they draw a line between them which would make the labor on the new ships higher than is paid outside.

Mr. CALKIN. Do you think that ship-carpenters get any higher wages than they ought to according to the price of everything?

Mr. TAYLOR. I do not think they do. I do not find any fault with the price of labor. We do find some fault with the time that mechanics propose to labor.

Mr. MORRELL. You say that you believe that the vessels now being built cannot be sold at a profit to the builder. Do you think that they could be sold at a profit, provided the duty on all the materials were refunded or a drawback allowed?

Mr. TAYLOR. I do.

Mr. MORRELL. Do you think that an additional number of vessels could be profitably put into the service and run at this time?

Mr. TAYLOR. Yes, I think we can run our ships against the world.

Mr. MORRELL. Is there a demand at this time for ships at any price?

Mr. TAYLOR. Perhaps not at the present moment.

Mr. MORRELL. Do you not think that the want of a demand for vessels has something to do with the depression in the business just now?

Mr. TAYLOR. Undoubtedly; there is no question about that.

The CHAIRMAN. I suppose that you experienced periods of depression before the war?

Mr. TAYLOR. Oh, yes.

Mr. MORRELL. You have seen dull times in ship-building before?

Mr. TAYLOR. Yes, sir; very dull indeed.

Mr. MORRELL. Do you not think that the introduction of iron vessels and of vessels of larger capacity propelled by steam has had a great deal to do with the depression of the ship-building business?

Mr. TAYLOR. It may have; I should think, however, very little now.

Mr. MORRELL. One vessel of large capacity takes the place of several vessels of smaller capacity and makes quicker trips?

Mr. TAYLOR. Yes, that affects the coastwise trade and perhaps the trade between here and Europe. It has been asked whether iron ships would finally supersede wooden ones entirely. There are some trades which iron ships are not fit for. For instance, the China trade. There they prefer wooden ships. In Calcutta and Bombay iron ships have quite the preference over wooden ones—some half dollar a ton, I think, in freight. The question was asked about our competing with foreign labor. I am inclined to think that we can do so. I am satisfied in my own mind that we can. Three years ago I was in Liverpool and had some large repairs done upon a ship there, and I made up my mind that so far as the labor was concerned we could do the work quite as cheap. Two years ago I was in Bremen, where labor was very low—only sixty cents a day for the best mechanics. I am satisfied that labor there costs more than it does here in Boston, although we pay four dollars a day and they only pay sixty cents.

Mr. WELLS. Why do they prefer wooden ships to iron ships in the China trade?

Mr. TAYLOR. I do not know. I think that I know the fact, but why it is I do not know.

The CHAIRMAN. If you have any other suggestions to make, the committee will be pleased to hear them.

Mr. TAYLOR. In reference to repealing the navigation laws, it occurs to me that in that case the government would be more seriously affected than even ship-builders or merchants, for, as Mr. Hall says, the ship-carpenters would become extinct in a short time, there would be scarcely enough left to repair old vessels, and then in case of a war like the last one, or in case of a war with England, (and such a thing may be,) we should be in no position whatever to provide ships of war, because our mechanics would be all gone.

Mr. WELLS. Is not the navigation law virtually repealed already?

Mr. TAYLOR. I think not.

Mr. WELLS. There is nothing to prevent American ship-owners buying ships in England and running them under the English flag?

Mr. TAYLOR. No, sir; but that has its disadvantages.

Mr. WELLS. It has been shown before the committee that it also has its advantages, as they get their stores cheaper and labor cheaper.

Mr. TAYLOR. Perhaps so.

Mr. WELLS. I suppose that the disadvantages are with reference to the title to the property and to the management of it?

Mr. TAYLOR. That is the disadvantage that I have spoken of.

Mr. MORRELL. Would not the allowance of a drawback of duty on all the materials going into the construction of a ship operate to exclude the use of American materials?

Mr. TAYLOR. No, sir; it would affect the prices of American materials, as Mr. Smith represented.

Mr. MORRELL. Do you not suppose that other interests are affected by legislation the same as your own? Do you not suppose that other interests can be entirely wiped out, as well as the ship-building interest, by adverse legislation?

Mr. TAYLOR. Yes, sir; there is no question about that.

Mr. MORRELL. If you render it impossible to produce those materials in the country profitably—that is, if the labor that produces them can be employed more profitably in other pursuits than in producing materials for ship-building—would it not operate to prevent their production here, and to compel you to buy foreign materials?

Mr. TAYLOR. Yes, sir; that would be the tendency, beyond a doubt.

Mr. HOLMAN. It is a fact, however, that certain interests have been rather protected by the events of the war?

Mr. TAYLOR. Yes, sir.

Mr. HOLMAN. Has not ship-building been entirely depressed by the war?

Mr. TAYLOR. Very much so. It was effectually destroyed. Those who were engaged in it were carrying it on under great disadvantages and loss; whereas the iron trade has been protected, so that the people engaged in it have been making money.

Mr. CALKIN. Do you think that if you were able to build ships cheap in Boston the Boston merchants would put their money in them?

Mr. TAYLOR. Yes, sir, I do.

Mr. HOLMAN. At as cheap a rate as foreign capitalists? For instance, will not an English or a French or a Prussian capitalist invest his money in ships at from four to five and six per cent.? And with the various advantageous modes of investing money in the United States, will American capitalists do that?

Mr. TAYLOR. I think they will. I think that a certain class of American capitalists would prefer to invest in ships rather than in anything else.

Mr. HOLMAN. That would be the case, perhaps, in commercial centers and in ship-building districts?

Mr. TAYLOR. Yes, sir.

Mr. PAUL CURTIS, ship-builder, next made a statement to the committee. He said that he could not add much to what had been already said. It was very evident that under the existing tariff ships could not be built in this country. If a ship-builder should go to a merchant and ask him to buy a ship, the merchant would say, "No, our ships are taxed too much. I cannot invest money in them." He thought that there would not be any ship-building done in Boston, at present, were it not for the purpose of keeping up the ship-yards. He himself was not building any at present. He had built a ship this summer of 1,418 tons, new measurement.

The CHAIRMAN. Please state to the committee the difference in the cost of the labor on that ship now, and what it would have been before the war—both in gold.

Mr. CURTIS. If you take gold at one-third higher than currency, I do not think there would be any great difference. Ship-carpenters are working probably as cheap as they can work.

The CHAIRMAN. What were the average rates of wages paid to ship-carpenters before the war, say from 1852 to 1860?

Mr. CURTIS. In California times we were paying a great deal more than we are paying now. That was from 1852 to 1854. There was a great deal of building then, and frequently when we got a ship built she would fetch ten thousand or twelve thousand dollars more than the contract price. Now it is quite the reverse. We get a ship built and there is no chance to sell her so as to make anything out of her. Lately I have not built any ships except on contract. This ship that I built was built on English account. They sent over word that if we could build a ship at so many pounds sterling we might go ahead and build her. We could not meet them at first, but finally we did get together and took the ship very low and built her. One of the parties in England, however, thought that he preferred an iron ship, and he requested us to sell her on his account. That ship was built at some four thousand or five thousand dollars less than we could duplicate her for, and yet we would not find a merchant who would buy that ship. She was offered here at two and a half per cent. on the cost, and there was no one to step forward and buy her.

The CHAIRMAN. Have you made any estimate as to the difference in the enhanced cost of materials at present and before the war?

Mr. CURTIS. Hard pine is about a third higher. Before the war we could get hard pine at twenty-five cents, and now we are paying from thirty-six cents to thirty-eight cents.

The CHAIRMAN. How is it as to the cost of iron?

Mr. CURTIS. Iron is a great deal higher.

The CHAIRMAN. How much is the total cost of iron to-day that is put into a thousand-ton ship all fitted for sea?

Mr. CURTIS. I do not know exactly. All that I know is that the lowest ever paid for iron was thirty-seven dollars a ton, and now we are paying somewhere about eighty dollars.

Mr. MORRELL. When did you buy iron at that price?

Mr. CURTIS. I guess four or five years before the war. I imported it.

The CHAIRMAN. You were going on to state the cost of all the materials entering into the construction of a ship?

Mr. CURTIS. Mr. McKay says that he went into a careful calculation, and that he made out the difference in the cost of a thousand-ton ship, caused by the tariff, to be from eight thousand to ten thousand dollars.

Mr. WELLS. What does it cost to build a wooden ship of that tonnage?

Mr. CURTIS. We can build her for about eighty dollars a ton in currency.

Mr. MORRELL. What would she have cost from 1855 to 1860?

Mr. CURTIS. You would have got her for about fifty-five dollars a ton.

The CHAIRMAN. Do you mean fitted out for sea?

Mr. CURTIS. Yes, sir. I have rigged many a ship for eleven thousand or twelve thousand dollars. This ship which I have just sent away cost us twenty-five thousand dollars for rigging, over and above the hull.

The CHAIRMAN. That is a great deal more than the difference which you have just stated as the difference on all the materials.

Mr. CURTIS. These ships may not have been quite as large; but for a number of years the price of rigging a ship did not vary a thousand dollars. It would be from eleven thousand to twelve thousand dollars. At present they are using iron with the rigging, and they would probably use it more than they do if it were not for the high tariff on it.

The CHAIRMAN. Is it used to any great extent upon wooden ships?

Mr. CURTIS. There have been three or four lately rigged with it; this one which I have just sent away was rigged with iron rigging; but I believe our merchants think that they would rather have the hemp rigging, because the old hemp will sell for enough to pay for the wear; they use the hemp here for some time, and then they go to England and put in wire rigging, and the hemp is then worth as much to sell as the wire costs in England.

Mr. HOLMAN. Prior to 1860 to what extent were vessels built by ship-builders of Boston for foreign capitalists?

Mr. CURTIS. When we built ships on our own account, if we could not sell them here we sent them to Europe; and there were a great many built here and sold in that way.

Mr. HOLMAN. Do you know of any having been built by contract with foreign capitalists prior to 1860?

Mr. CURTIS. Yes, sir; I built some myself, and I believe two or three since 1860 for the firm of Warren & Co.; four years ago I built a wooden ship for them of one thousand three hundred or one thousand four hundred tons; two or three years before that I built one of one thousand one hundred or one thousand two hundred tons for them. I do not know whether we can compete with the English in iron-ship building; we cannot at present; but I am satisfied that we can in wooden-ship building if we could have some relief on the tariff on our materials.

Mr. HOLMAN. You think that if the materials were relieved from taxation our ship-builders could compete with English ship-builders as to wooden vessels?

Mr. CURTIS. Yes, sir.

Mr. HOLMAN. But you think it doubtful as to iron-ship building, supposing that iron were relieved entirely from duty?

Mr. CURTIS. We should want a little more experience than we have got; the English are building their iron ships very scientifically—that is, they have got fairly under way, and it would require some time for us to do so.

Mr. HOLMAN. Is it not an advantage to the English ship-building interest that the rate of interest for capital in England is low?

Mr. CURTIS. Undoubtedly; at the same time I have built three ships for an English house within the last six or seven years.

Mr. CALKIN. Where does the government get its mechanical labor from for the navy yards—ship-carpenters, calkers, engineers, boiler-makers, &c.?

Mr. CURTIS. It gets them, of course, from private yards.

Mr. CALKIN. The government does not educate mechanics of any kind in the navy yards?

Mr. CURTIS. No, sir; apprentices are very seldom taken.

Mr. MORRELL. I understood you to say that a ship which formerly cost fifty-five thousand dollars would now cost about eighty thousand dollars?

Mr. CURTIS. Yes, sir; it would not vary much from that.

Mr. MORRELL. That is eighty-thousand dollars in currency against fifty-five thousand dollars in gold before the war?

Mr. CURTIS. Yes, sir.

Mr. MORRELL. That is twenty-five thousand dollars in currency over the gold cost?

Mr. CURTIS. Perhaps eighty dollars a ton is a little more than a ship would cost now.

Mr. MORRELL. I think it was stated in New York that a ship could be built for seventy-five dollars a ton.

Mr. CURTIS. We took an account of stock before we commenced to build this last ship, and we took an account of stock after we got through. We took the contract for less than eighty dollars a ton; but we lost money on it. For a thousand-ton ship I should say that eighty dollars a ton was a fair price; but for a larger ship it could be done cheaper. It does not cost so much a ton to rig a large ship as it does to rig a small one.

Mr. MORRELL. If all the duties were taken from the materials that entered into the construction of that ship, how much cheaper could you have constructed her?

Mr. CURTIS. I have not gone into that question; I only know, from what Mr. McKay says, that on a thousand-ton ship the difference would be about eight thousand dollars.

Mr. MORRELL. About eight dollars a ton?

Mr. CURTIS. Yes, sir.

Mr. MORRELL. Would the cheapening of a ship eight dollars a ton enable you to find work for it in this port?

Mr. CURTIS. I think it would; I think our merchants would give considerably more for an American-built ship than for a foreign-built ship.

Mr. MORRELL. Then it seems that the whole matter lies in the cheapening of a thousand-ton ship from eight thousand dollars to ten thousand dollars; would it not be a greater boon to the ship-owner if he could get the supplies of that ship relieved from duty rather than have the cost cheapened to that extent?

Mr. CURTIS. The ship-owner would evidently want some other things off. For instance, if Mr. McKay is going to carry his ship to New York, he has got to pay a year's license on her in order that he may carry her to New York and sell her. I understand that it costs six hundred dollars to get a ship sent there.

Mr. MORRELL. Is not that tax in itself more important than the duty on the materials?

Mr. CURTIS. All these things go to depress the business.

Mr. HOLMAN. After the vessel is constructed can the American owner run her as cheap as the English or the French owner?

Mr. CURTIS. I have no doubt that he can, and cheaper; he pays a little more to his men; but he takes less of them, and they are more efficient.

The CHAIRMAN. Do you run ships as well as build them?

Mr. CURTIS. I am to some extent a ship-owner. We are often obliged to take one-eighth of a vessel for the sake of getting the contract to build her.

The CHAIRMAN. Do ship-builders here generally own interests in the ships that they build?

Mr. CURTIS. There has been very little of that business done here. Ship-builders have depended upon the merchants. There is where we have not done so well as the people of Maine have. The ship-builders in Maine have owned parts of the ships, and there is more money made in running ships than there is in building them.

Mr. HOLMAN. Do our merchants attach any importance to the custom that prevails in some European countries of allowing ships' stores to be taken out of bond free of duty? Is that a matter of any importance in any of our lines of trade?

Mr. CURTIS. That is not a subject with which I am familiar.

The CHAIRMAN. Please state the effect on the ship-building interest of the tariff on copper.

Mr. CURTIS. I hear it stated that you can get your yellow-metal some seven or eight cents a pound cheaper in England than we can get it here.

The CHAIRMAN. What is the general practice of ship-builders and ship-owners in reference to the coppering of vessels? Is it generally done here or on the other side of the water?

Mr. CURTIS. If vessels are going to California, they are coppered here. If they are going to a cotton port and thence to Europe, they wait till they get over there.

The CHAIRMAN. If the cost of a ship at the present time is eighty dollars per ton here, would it be as low as that if there was the usual amount of ship-building being done? In other words, is not the cost reduced by the limited amount of business?

Mr. CURTIS. Probably wages would go higher if there was much work doing; but they are repairing vessels at the navy yards and are employing a great deal of labor. That, however, is local and temporary.

The CHAIRMAN. If the navy yard were not in operation would the rates of wages be lower?

Mr. CURTIS. Yes, sir.

The CHAIRMAN. And on the other hand, if ship-building for mercantile purposes were increased, that would increase the cost?

Mr. CURTIS. That would bring it up again, probably.

The CHAIRMAN. If there were ten or fifteen ships building here when you were building yours, would it have cost you any more for the labor; and if so, how much more?

Mr. CURTIS. Undoubtedly, if there were more ships building with the same state of things in the navy yard, there is no doubt but wages would be higher; but that is merely local and confined to the neighborhood of navy yards. Of course the more business that there is doing, the more wages we have got to pay.

The CHAIRMAN. Does not that thing always regulate itself? Does not the increased business always enable you to pay the increased cost of labor?

Mr. CURTIS. Certainly.

The CHAIRMAN. Do you think that you could build a ship for eighty dollars a ton if labor was in as large a demand at present as it was in 1860?

Mr. CURTIS. I do not suppose that I could. I suppose that that would increase the cost of the ship.

Mr. MORRELL. Was there not a time previous to the war when there was a large demand for ships, and when you could not produce them for fifty-five dollars a ton?

Mr. CURTIS. In California times, when everybody went on ships, and when they could get freight enough to pay for the ship, they wanted ships built in a hurry, and then wages were high; but just before the war the business was very much depressed; labor was low, and materials and everything. That is the time when ships could be built at fifty-five dollars per ton.

The CHAIRMAN. In your opinion, providing the materials that enter into the construction of ships were admitted free of duty, you could then build ships in competition with foreign ship-builders?

Mr. CURTIS. We could build wooden ships; I have no doubt of that.

As to iron ships, I have no experience that would enable me to answer the question.

The CHAIRMAN. But you think there is no doubt that the remission of the duties would enable you to build wooden ships here as cheap as before?

Mr. CURTIS. I have no doubt of it.

The CHAIRMAN. Do you believe there would be the demand for the ships in case they were built at that reduced rate?

Mr. CURTIS. I can only say that that is what the merchants estimate.

Mr. MORRELL. Is it not more the tax to which the ship is subjected after she is built that merchants object to, rather than the enhanced cost of the ship itself?

Mr. CURTIS. That is a question which had better be answered by the merchants.

Mr. WELLS. Speaking about coppering those ships, what is the expense of coppering a thousand-ton ship? How many tons of copper does it require?

Mr. CURTIS. I do not know that I can answer that question. Coppering is an extra charge, and it is not very often that we copper ships ourselves.

The CHAIRMAN. If the price of a ship is eighty dollars per ton fitted out for sea, does that include a copper or metal bottom?

Mr. CURTIS. No, sir.

The CHAIRMAN. How much would that increase the cost of a vessel of one thousand tons?

Mr. CURTIS. I suppose about $4,000 or $5,000, or four dollars and fifty cents a ton.

Mr. E. H. DERBY next addressed the committee. The committee was aware that the American tonnage, when it culminated in 1851, had reached the point of about five and a half million tons. It had risen just above the tonnage of England. Now, American tonnage had decreased to 4,300,000 tons, and the English tonnage had risen to 7,300,000, and was at present about seven millions. During the late war, and while England drew the great bulk of her cotton from India, the voyage occupied nearly a year; but, when the war ended and England again drew her cotton from America, the voyage was shortened more than half, so that less than half the tonnage was required for that business. That had some effect in diminishing English tonnage, and an immediate check was given to ship-building in England, which had been exceedingly rapid during the war, the tonnage having nearly doubled. Many American vessels had been placed under the English flag, and the consequent increase of English tonnage and decrease of American tonnage had been very great. With the close of the war, when American ships again entered into the field of commerce, there was a great check given to English tonnage; from the end of the war to the present time there had been rather a diminution than increase of English tonnage; but still the disparity between that and the American tonnage was very great.

By referring to statistics of American tonnage it would be found that now the coasting trade preponderated greatly over the foreign trade. By analyzing the returns of about nine months of the past fiscal year—from June to April—he found that the arrivals and clearances in the domestic trade were fifty-one million tons, and the arrivals and clearances in the foreign trade only seventeen millions, showing that the amount of business done in the coasting trade (the voyages being shorter) was nearly three times as great as in the whole foreign trade. When he came to analyze the foreign trade he found that of this seventeen million tons (of which, in former times, two-thirds were American and one-third foreign) two-thirds were foreign and one-third American, the American dwindling from year to year, and the foreign increasing. He found that, during those nine months which he had examined, the increase in the foreign tonnage was at the rate of fourteen per cent., and the diminution in the American tonnage was at the rate of twenty-eight per cent.; so that it would be seen that the American tonnage engaged in the foreign trade was being very rapidly extinguished, and was being driven from the ocean.

There was on the files of Congress at Washington a very valuable report on the commerce of the United States, which contained the reports of the United States consuls at all the foreign ports. That of Mr. Morse, consul to London, showed that before the war the American tonnage engaged in the carrying trade of the world was two and a half million tons, of English shipping very nearly an equal amount, the aggregate of all the rest not coming up either to the American or English. He (Mr. Derby) entertained no doubt that that two and a half millions of American tonnage was now reduced to five or six or seven hundred thousand tons, (less than one-third of what it had been,) and that that small proportion was rapidly diminishing.

The condition of American shipping at present was, that in the coastwise trade it was gradually and slowly increasing, particularly on the rivers and lakes, and a little on the coast; and that in the foreign trade there was an immense diminution. While the schooners, brigs, and small steamboats were increasing there was a great diminution in the construction of ships. For instance, before the war there were on the average three hundred and fifty ships a year built; now that three hundred and fifty had dwindled to sixty, and those were employed almost entirely in the coastwise trade. It had become apparent from the course of events that American vessels were being driven from the ocean in competition with foreign vessels, that Americans could not hold their own in the foreign trade, and that all they could do was to cling to the coastwise trade.

What had caused this, and how was it to be remedied? It had been said that the diminution in American shipping was due to the war. They had lost by privateers and British pirates between one and two hundred thousand tons of shipping, but that did not explain the loss of tonnage. The explanation was in the diminution in ship-building, and in the departure of vessels from the American flag to the British flag. Thus the tonnage of England had been increased, and that in the United States very materially diminished.

The difficulty in which commerce was at this moment was that, by the legislation of Congress, American vessels were shut out from the foreign trade. First, the vessels that had gone under a foreign flag were forbidden by law to return. They could not come back again. If a sheep were lost it might be recovered and brought back to the fold, but the ship once gone was gone forever. Such was the legislation of Congress. He would say a word for those parties who had parted with their ships. He regarded them as among the most meritorious merchants of the country. The duty of the sailor was to save his ship, to cling to his ship, and to bring her safe back to port. From time immemorial it had been the custom in time of war to put ships under a neutral flag, and it had always been considered perfectly legitimate to do so. During the late war the United States navy could give no protection to commerce. No armed ships could be spared to take care of American commerce on the open sea. He believed that there had not been a convoy during the war, the armed ships being employed in blockading southern ports, and properly so employed. The question that addressed itself to the committee and to Congress was a question of common sense. Was it to the interest of the country to save its ships? He held that it was to the interest of the country to save the ship, and to bring her safe to port. She could now return safe to port if Congress would only permit her. The question was whether Congress would compel an American owner to continue still to sail his vessel under the English flag, or permit him to bring her back to her own country. These ships could still make good whalers, and render good service in carrying oil from the Pacific and Atlantic. They could render good service in the Pacific trade, carrying lumber from Washington Territory to California. He did not represent one of them directly, but he would respectfully ask that the door be opened to them and that they may be brought home to diminish by so much the tonnage of England and increase that of the United States.

He presumed that at the end of the war there were nearly a million tons of American shipping sailing under the British flag. He did not suppose that there were now more than four or five hundred thousand tons, and he would ask that every American-built ship be permitted to come back. If the government did not take care of them during the war was it not proper that they should take care of themselves, and should they not now have the opportunity to return?

Passing from that subject to the subject of those duties that precluded the building of ships in the United States, he would say, in the first place, that by the navigation act foreign-built ships are prohibited from getting an American registry. He suggested that it would be politic to permit some foreign-built vessels to be owned and registered in the United States on the payment of a duty. If iron ships could be built cheaper in England than in America let them come—not freely, so as to break down American mechanics, but under a duty of ten or fifteen per cent., or $10 or $15 per ton; and then let a remission of duty to the same amount be made to the American ship-builder. He would not be in favor of taking the duty directly off the foreign commodity used in ship-building, but would make a general remission of duties to the amount of $10 per ton. That was Mr. McKay's estimate of the difference in the cost of a thousand-ton iron ship caused by the tariff, not $8 per ton, as had been mentioned to-day. He would let that sum go to the American ship-builder, and let it go to buy American goods instead of foreign. He had been lately in the provinces, (having made four reports on the subject of reciprocal trade,) and he found that labor there was little less than in the United States; that ship-building materials were inferior in quality, but were suitable for building a cheap class of vessels that would endure for only two-thirds or one-half the length of time that the white-oak vessels built in the United States last. Still, they made them very cheap, and, for certain purposes, they came in competition with the vessels built in the United States. Formerly those vessels had carried lumber to England, Ireland, and Scotland, but, under the free-trade system, they were now excluded from all but the western coasts. Norway, Denmark, and Prussia were sending supplies to the eastern coasts, and were getting round to the Bristol Channel, where the competition was about equal. He entertained the very confident opinion that if the duty on ship-building materials were virtually taken off, by making a concession of so much per ton, American merchants and ship-builders would be enabled not only to supply their own wants but to go into the market and again sell ships abroad. There should be a remission of $10 per ton, and at the same time there should be another change which he had seen foreshadowed the other day in California—the restoration of gold and silver as the circulating medium. A specie currency was needed to relieve the shipping interests. If a man were now to build or buy a ship at $85 per ton, and if next year the country were to go back to the gold currency, he would find his investment reduced to $60 per ton. Therefore it was necessary to get back to the gold currency as soon as possible, because the present condition of the currency deterred men from going into that kind of investment.

Another view of the subject was, the change produced by substituting steam for sails and iron for wood. They had undertaken recently in Boston to build two magnificent steamers, two of the finest vessels in the world. But Congress had virtually provided, by refusing to grant subsidies, that the United States should have no steamers carrying the mails across the ocean. The only subsidies allowed were to a few vessels running to Brazil and China, not half the number that ought to run between China and California. How could Americans under such circumstances run lines of steamers in competition with English and French lines which were largely subsidized? England had a fleet of a hundred sail of steamers running to the east, to Bombay, Calcutta, Japan, and China. And how was this immense fleet supported? How was it that England had to-day something like 500,000 tons engaged in steam navigation, and a navy more powerful than the navies of all the rest of the world? It was by her subsidies. She gave one, two, three dollars a mile to steamers, and, if necessary, was prepared to give four dollars. France had put on a line to China, and had begun to press the English line a little; but the English government had come forward and said, "We will give you $3 a mile on condition that your profits shall not get up beyond a certain sum; but you shall run your steamers and not be put down by the French." When other governments pursued the policy of granting liberal subsidies, why should not the American government do the same? Not one of the great steamship lines could have paid expenses without a subsidy, and the subsidy had been the sole basis on which they had run. If that were the case, if they could not run without subsidy, how could American lines run without subsidy, and with all the duties imposed upon them? Were Americans prepared to abandon the ocean? They were abandoning it to-day. If they wished to win fame and wealth on the ocean, as their fathers had done, their steam lines must be subsidized. They must be put on an equality with foreign lines, and then they would compete with the rest of the world.

It had been suggested that navigation should be made free, and that foreign vessels should be admitted to American registry. In theory that might seem to do very well, but would not Congress have to go a step further? When it dealt with navigation in that way, would it not have to go further and take the high duties off manufactured goods, and off iron and other things? If Congress took the high duties off ships, and kept them on everything else, who would want to own ships? What seemed essential to him was that a great reduction should be made in the cost of American-built ships, without doing injury to American manufactures, and that a tax should be put upon foreign-built vessels.

He had been in California the other day, and had seen that there was a competition between the Pacific railroad and the Pacific mail steamers, but he was certain that if the steamers running to Panama could be diverted to China, the diversion of each of the tri-monthly steamers would be worth a million dollars to the railway. In the one case the steamship line was an opponent, in the other case it would be a feeder. He thought it would be extremely desirable to have a line of propellers established between San Francisco and China, and he understood that the English were thinking of it. It seemed to him that there was so much need of some iron screw propellers for that trade that, if they could not be built cheaply here, some of them should be let in from England, and run on American account.

He had to say a word on another point in this connection. If they were to have shipping, the shipping must have something to carry. But Congress, by its legislation, provided that the foreign business should be to a great extent destroyed. He was rather inclined to give some protection to manufactures; but he thought there were certain limits to the protection which should be given. When duties were higher than thirty per cent. they encouraged smuggling. He found that there was a large amount of smuggling going on from the provinces, which operated in weakening and impairing the force of the United States duties. In the article of woolens particularly there was a very great amount of smuggling. He wished Congress to take off the duty on foreign wool, and to have the wool come in free, as it does in Europe, so as to give American shipping something to do in the way of carrying wool. He had been to California, and had learned something there about the manufacture of wool. The current price of a three-quarter pluck wool—nearly up to the full-blood grade—was twenty-one cents a pound; and he was told they could raise it a good deal cheaper than that. A gentleman, Colonel Halliday, had crossed the mountains in 1854 with a flock of twelve hundred sheep, and lost four hundred on the way.

Mr. WELLS. I understood that it was eight thousand, and that he had lost two thousand.

Mr. DERBY. "I tell the tale as it was told to me" at the Pioneer Woolen Factory in San Francisco; but whether the flock was eight thousand or twelve hundred will not matter materially, because the result is so prodigious that either will answer. That flock has increased to sixty-four thousand, and is yielding $100,000 a year to him, with wool at twenty-one cents a pound. And yet we have gentlemen from Ohio and Iowa saying that they must have forty or fifty cents a pound on wool, while here is a man making $100,000 a year out of what was originally worth little or nothing, by selling wool at twenty-one cents a pound in California.

That carries me to the story of La Plata wool. They have on those plains seventy-five million sheep, yielding a large amount of wool. In 1865 we received, principally from that country, Australia, and Africa, eighty-seven million pounds of wool. While we were receiving this large quantity of wool the government threw on the market some army clothing. Probably the country was a little overstocked with woolens. Wool fell in price; an excitement was got up; and a duty equivalent to thirteen or fourteen cents was put on foreign wool. The result was that the importation of wool was reduced from eighty-seven million pounds to twenty-three or twenty-four million pounds, and that sixty million pounds were excluded from the country by that duty. I want to show its effect on shipping. That wool gave employment to several hundred thousand tons of shipping. The vessels engaged in the trade carried back flour, furniture, fish, domestics, and a great variety of commodities from this country. They were exchanged for wool, and the wool was brought here and manufactured. The duty on wool was put up; and what became of La Plata? They sent their wool to England, France, and Belgium, where it was sold very cheap. We who give away our land to the settlers have put on a duty of fourteen cents a pound on an article which has since been selling in Liverpool at ten cents a pound—a duty of one hundred and forty per cent. The effect is that, in La Plata, they are getting out of the wool business, and are raising cattle instead of sheep. They have advertised a great fair, and have invited our government to send out specimens of all the machines of Yankee invention. They are abandoning the sheep business and are going into the cultivation of wheat and the raising of cattle. We are excluding them from the sheep business, and now they are going to take the cattle business and the wheat business out of our hands. Instead of shipping our wheat from California, England is going to get it more or less from La Plata, because we have excluded her wool.

You are sitting here on the question of ships, but let me say we do not want the ships unless we give them something to do. If you are going to destroy the foreign trade, and to say that foreign wool shall not be imported, what occasion have we for shipping? If the importation of wool employed three or four hundred thousand tons of shipping, and if you say that no more can be imported, we do not want the ships. Give us the trade.

Take the article of salt. I passed the other day through the very flourishing village of Syracuse, where salt is made. They have a protection of two hundred per cent. on salt. After the Revolution our ancestors put on duties of ten per cent., thinking that that was sufficient. We put on two hundred per cent. The result is that Syracuse is a flourishing village. They are said to have made $5,000,000 from salt since the war. But the salt trade and the navigation that should bring the salt home is very much broken down. In New Brunswick the duty on salt is three per cent., in the United States two hundred per cent. We compete with New Brunswick and Nova Scotia in the fisheries. Some relief was given by Congress. It was provided that all the salt which our fishermen could buy in New Brunswick (and no thanks to Congress for that, for our fishermen could stop at the Nova Scotian ports and take the salt) should be free of duty. And what do you think the Syracusans do? They determined that we should not have a salt trade with the West Indies. They come to Gloucester and say, "We have two prices of salt—that which is used on shore and that which is used on sea. We will take the duty off the price of that used at sea." They go over to Canada and sell salt, duty free, at a certain price; but if New York wants to buy salt it must pay two hundred per cent. additional in order to get it. The Syracusans go to Saginaw and say, "Gentlemen, you are trying to get salt out of your springs; we will undertake to supply you with what you want cheaper." Thus they monopolize the salt business of the country under a duty of two hundred per cent. The result is that they have come here to Boston, and stolen one of our clergymen and made him a bishop in their country. They are showing an unbounded prosperity, as I understand, on this basis of two hundred per cent. duty on salt. We ought to have a million tons of salt imported over what we do import to-day. The sun makes it gratuitously, and you can put it on board ship in the West Indies for eight cents a bushel or two dollars a ton. All the salt that you want you can get at the West Indies, or Cadiz, or up the Mediterranean to Sicily at about two dollars per ton, made by solar evaporation; while we put the duty at two hundred per cent., and burn up our forests for the purpose of benefiting Syracuse, and deprive our shipping of its legitimate business.

What I would suggest in regard to shipping is this: Take off the duties on ship-building materials. The question is, can you afford it? Mr. Wells told us a year or two ago that the surplus revenue was one hundred and twenty million dollars. Mr. Wells is a very careful man. He always underrates. He does it habitually. He holds a responsible office and does not want to be deceived. I feel confident, from looking over the same figures, that our customs are paying to-day two hundred million dollars a year, and our internal revenue two hundred million dollars. We are also running from twenty to thirty per cent. ahead of last year on our incidental revenue. We are selling every week one or two millions of gold at about thirty, and putting into the treasury from this source about thirty millions a year. There is a revenue of four hundred and thirty millions. Our estimated expenditures are two hundred and ninety millions, leaving a surplus of one hundred and forty millions. By reducing the duty on a few articles, such as Spanish cigars, spirits, spices, and wines, you can actually increase that surplus up to one hundred and eighty millions. Just as by reducing the tax on whisky from two dollars to fifty cents a gallon you increased the revenue from it from eight millions to eighty. So that, with our revenue capable of being made, by reduction of duties, equal to one hundred and eighty millions surplus, you can make very large reductions in these foreign duties, and so aid shipping. You will aid shipping more by reducing the duties than in any other way. I speak as one in favor of protection incidental to revenue. I do not speak as a free-trader. I do not go to those extremes. Perhaps I am not wise in not going further than I do. But I stand on moderate protection. Your protection to-day is forty-eight per cent. on the average on everything that you import. How was it before the war? Fourteen and a half per cent. was the average. Is Congress aware of that great disparity? Is Congress aware that we have crept up from fourteen and a half per cent. to forty-eight per cent. duty on everything that we import? Does Congress believe that forty-eight per cent. is a proper stage of duties, or that we are to maintain them at that rate? Is it just for this nation to do it? I respectfully submit that it is not wise nor just for this nation to do it.

In reference to the facilities for smuggling from the provinces into the United States, Mr. Derby related an incident which came within his own knowledge, of a merchant tailor in Halifax who showed him his order-book containing orders for suits of clothes from a large number of Americans, some of them wealthy residents of Boston, and which were delivered in Boston free of duty and at the same price as if they had been delivered in Halifax. He said that the only way was to do what the English and French and Belgians had done, that is, to go back to free trade in wools. The man who had his land gratuitously, or who could get it with scrip at seventy cents an acre, certainly did not need protection as against the Frenchman whose land cost him four hundred dollars an acre, or against the Englishman whose land cost him three hundred dollars an acre. Some employment must be given to American shipping, and if Congress was going to favor the shipping interest, the duties on imports should be at such a rate as that goods could be imported into this country.

The CHAIRMAN. Speaking of the vessels which sought protection under the English flag during the rebellion, you say that it has been the policy of all nations in times of war to allow their subjects to put their ships under a neutral flag. Do you think that during our late war Great Britain occupied the position of a neutral toward us?

Mr. DERBY. Only nominally. I do not think she was really a neutral, but she was nominally so, and the merchants had a right to consider her so.

Mr. CALKIN. In regard to subsidies, can you inform the committee how much money the English government is now paying for subsidies?

Mr. DERBY. The London Times of April 1, 1869, states that the Cunard Company was paid prior to 1868 £178,000 a year for one weekly service, and then £80,000 a year, and all the postages on letters from America. Seventeen lines of steamers have made during the last year 1,322 voyages between England and America. The Inman line is now paid for one weekly service. Three lines of British steamships subsidized for the carriage of the mails, viz., the Cunard, the Royal, and the Peninsular and Oriental Steamship Companies, employ more than 200,000 tons of shipping propelled by steam. The amount paid them has ranged from $1 to $3 per mile. In addition to these many other lines were subsidized from England, viz., a line to Montreal, a line to the coast of Africa, the Inman line, a line to Brazil, a line to Australia, and a line to the coast of Chili and Peru. The last named has fourteen steamships. The trade between Liverpool and the Mediterranean, chiefly conducted by them, amounts to 600,000 tons a year. In 1843 the Cunard line had four steamers, of 5,000 tons. In 1865 it had thirty-seven steamers, of 67,000 tons.

Mr. MORRELL. I infer from your remarks that a large proportion of the seeming decline in American commerce is only nominally so, and that the difference consists in vessels sailing under a foreign flag but still belonging to American citizens?

Mr. DERBY. That element, however, is diminishing. As these ships perish they are not supplied, and when the owners can sell them they do so. They are reluctant to have foreigners hold a trusteeship of their property.

Mr. MORRELL. At the present time the apparent falling off has not been entirely real?

Mr. DERBY. Not entirely. I think that we own still four or five hundred thousand tons sailing under the British flag; but I think that that tonnage is diminishing at the rate of 100,000 tons a year.

The CHAIRMAN. What is the average life of a wooden ship?

Mr. DERBY. There is a difference of opinion upon that. It depends very much upon the class of ship. A good white-oak built ship will last sometimes twenty or thirty years; but taking the chances of life, I suppose that twelve or thirteen years would be the average duration of a wooden ship. The average duration of the wooden ships built in the Provinces is not more than six or eight years. I have seen a ship that was built by my grandfather, and which, I think, was run after being forty or fifty years old. Ships are like individuals; some of them have greater longevity than others.

Mr. HOLMAN. Is there any commercial power that entirely excludes from its registration foreign-built vessels?

Mr. DERBY. I am not aware of it.

Mr. HOLMAN. What is the most general policy? Do any of the continental powers admit foreign-built vessels to register except on the payment of some duty? And what is the average of that duty?

Mr. DERBY. My knowledge does not extend that far. I know that there is a disposition among continental nations to increase their marine. Their duties are very low.

Mr. HOLMAN. What would be the effect on our commerce (disconnected with ship-building) of allowing foreign-built vessels an American registration on payment of a duty of ten or fifteen per cent., and at the same time excluding them from the coastwise trade?

Mr. DERBY. I am inclined to think that that would be the best policy.

Mr. HOLMAN. If Congress should allow foreign-built vessels to obtain an American registration on payment of, say, ten per cent., relieve the ship-building interest of the United States from the taxes on the materials entering into the construction of ships, and secure to American ship-builders the coastwise trade, what effect would these three measures, taken together, have both upon commerce and ship-building?

Mr. DERBY. If you allow me to make one modification, and instead of ten per cent. duty on foreign vessels, say $10 per ton, I would go for the measure heartily and think it a most beneficial one.

Mr. HOLMAN. Would it, in your judgment, promote our commercial interest, and at the same time afford a reasonable protection to the ship-building interest?

Mr. DERBY. With the modification I have suggested, I think it would. I would allow ten dollars per ton on wooden ships, and from fifteen to eighteen dollars a ton on iron ships. I am fearful of taking off the duties on the materials. In the Provinces there is a very strong disposition to join the United States, particularly in the maritime provinces; but if you let in their vessels free, or at a duty of ten per cent., they would not join us. They would stay where they are. I would have the duty high enough to induce them to come.

The CHAIRMAN. Do you know of any nation which puts a duty on the raw materials that enter into the construction of ships?

Mr. DERBY. I do not recollect any. I think that these materials ought to come in free, either by a remission of duty or in some other way. I think the remission of duty would be the fairest way. I am very much impressed with the importance of subsidies to steamers; so much so that I volunteered to speak before the Post Office Committee at Washington on that subject.

Mr. CALKIN. Is it your opinion that we cannot support steamship lines without subsidies?

Mr. DERBY. I do not see how we can.

The CHAIRMAN. I understood you to say that steamers were superseding sailing-vessels, and that that was one of the causes of the decline of our tonnage. How do you account for the fact that in the whole foreign commerce of New England, neither a foreign nor an American line of steamships has been able to sustain itself in competition with sailing-vessels? Does not this prove that steamers, standing on the same footing, cannot compete with sailing-vessels in long voyages, and in foreign commerce, unaided by any subsidy?

Mr. DERBY. I am inclined to that opinion, that steamers require the aid of subsidies to compete.

Mr. MORRELL. Are not subsidies confined to vessels that are required to make quick time?

Mr. DERBY. I understand that of late they have been building a class of vessels at Glasgow—cheap vessels—that will run for twenty-four hours with one ton of coal to the hundred tons, or ten tons of coal to the thousand-ton ships. I presume that that class of vessels running slowly would be able to compete with sailing-vessels; but I believe that the great increase in the steam navy of England has been due to the subsidies which have given it a stimulus. Congress did give a subsidy to one European line, the Collins line; but the vessels of that line were so expensive that even with the subsidy they could not get along. If they had followed the policy of the Cunard line, with a liberal subsidy of Congress, they would have been sucessful. One of the mistakes of our countrymen is, in undertaking to strike out new paths instead of following others which have already been discovered. Since the introduction of screw steamers, the English government has reduced the subsidy.

Mr. WELLS. But only a portion of the English lines are subsidized.

Mr. DERBY. I believe that that is so; but the steamship lines have been built up by the aid of previous subsidies. I think that that class of screw steamers which I have just alluded to might possibly be built to run slowly, carrying merchandise which would make money without a subsidy.

Mr. WELLS. It has been stated that not only in England but also in Germany and France ships' stores are taken out of bond without payment of duty.

Mr. DERBY. That is the case in England. I know that their wines and supplies of that kind are taken out of bond duty free; and with respect to coal, I believe that the foreign coal was taken out of bond here duty free by the Cunard line, under a certificate that it is consumed at sea.

The CHAIRMAN. Is that the case now?

Mr. DERBY. It was the case some years ago.

The CHAIRMAN. It is the same, I suppose, with American vessels; they would have the same advantage as the foreign vessels?

Mr. DERBY. Yes, sir; I am told that in the matter of coal the Cunard line had ultimately to refund the duty. They gave bond to have the question passed upon afterward. I am told that they made a test case of it, and that the decision was against them.

The CHAIRMAN. In either case, whether they paid the duty or obtained it free, the American and foreign vessels would be on the same footing?

Mr. DERBY. Certainly. The question has been asked to-day, whether ship-owners should not be favored in getting their supplies free of duty, so as to compensate for the duties on the ship-building materials. I should apprehend that the compensation would not be sufficient. The great expense of ship-owners is in fuel.

Mr. WELLS. Which would be the better policy; to remit the duties on the materials entering into the construction of ships, or to make an average allowance per ton?

Mr. DERBY. The difficulty that I see in allowing a drawback upon the materials actually used would be that American ship-builders would use no American iron; they would use nothing but foreign materials.

Mr. WELLS. So that in reality your suggestion is in favor of a bounty to ship-builders, rather than a remission of duties?

Mr. DERBY. Yes, sir; an inducement to build.

Mr. WELLS. Would not the opening of ship-yards for building iron vessels in Massachusetts, Maine, and New York, actually stimulate the manufacture of iron materials that enter into the construction of iron ships? There is none of that material of any consequence made in the United States.

Mr. DERBY. There is a certain amount of it made, because we are building ships for the coasting trade.

Mr. WELLS. Would not the industry in the manufacture of iron for the construction of ships be actually increased by adopting a more liberal policy in reference to the use of foreign materials for ship-building?

Mr. DERBY. I think it would give a great stimulus to the industry of the country. We can build vessels for the coastwise trade ten dollars a ton cheaper, and we can carry the iron and coal cheaper, and thus stimulate the iron industry. There is one suggestion which I have omitted. It is this: If you can enlarge American shipping and build a half million tons every year, as we did a few years ago, you make an immense market for American products. If a Hamburg ship does the business, or if an Italian ship does the business, they get most of their supplies from Germany and from Italy. But if an American ship does the business its supplies are got here almost entirely, and you thus make a great market for the produce of the farm by reviving the navigation interest. All that market is now lost, and the men who have been sailors, and who have been using the products of the West, are now liable to become farmers in the West.

Mr. WELLS. In making this remission of duty or this bounty, should vessels for the inland commerce have the same benefits as ships for foreign commerce?

Mr. DERBY. That question is in my mind. It is not so essential for vessels in the coastwise trade as it is for vessels in the foreign trade; because in the foreign trade we meet foreign competitors; but in the domestic trade we meet only domestic competitors.

Mr. WELLS. Do we not meet the foreign competitor in our coastwise trade as competing with the railroad interest owned by foreigners?

Mr. DERBY. There is a competition there with the railway, unquestionably.

Mr. WELLS. And the more steamboats we can build, and the greater facilities, and the more drawbacks we can give them, the cheaper we get our wheat to market.

Mr. DERBY. Certainly, sir. But I am so much of a railroad man myself, that if we do anything for steamers I should like the same thing to be done for railroads, which are a benefit to them. But I was looking at the foreign competition which is driving us from the ocean.

Mr. CALKIN. I take it that this question resolves itself down to a question of developing the labor of the country generally on all points?

Mr. DERBY. Yes, sir; to a great extent the promotion of navigation benefits the whole country.

Mr. CALKIN. Exactly. Your whole argument has been that if we build ships we encourage all the other interests of the country?

Mr. DERBY. We do; and I think that by discouraging ship-building we are building up a competition with our farmers and depressing the labor of the West.

Mr. HARRISON LORING, iron ship builder, argued against the policy of a rapid contraction of the currency and return to specie payments, and submitted citations and figures from an English atlas (Tullock's) to show the effect in Great Britain of expansions and contractions of the currency—expansions being followed by general prosperity and contractions by stagnation in business.

He also called attention to the high rate of interest paid by the United States government as being injurious to business interests. Six per cent. was a rate that was above the labor of the country; and he thought he was safe in saying that, somewhat in proportion as the rate of interest is above the labor of the country, so will money go with increased rapidity from the hands of the masses of the people to those of the rich and to the great cities. At compound interest money at six per cent. would double in eleven years; and it was not possible for labor to produce the same result. He was inclined to think that one of the first steps toward relieving commerce would be the reduction of duties as far as possible.

Mr. CALKIN. You are an iron-ship builder?

Mr. LORING. Yes, sir.

Mr. CALKIN. Have you any information to give the committee as to the cost of building iron ships, and as to your ability to compete with foreign builders?

Mr. LORING. In 1857, '58, '59, '60, and '61 I could deliver a ship in India or China at the same price as English ship-builders could, but without profit, while the English ship-builder would have from five to ten per cent. profit. In 1857 I built one steamer for parties in Calcutta, and in 1858–'59, one for parties in China. The chairman asked Mr. Derby if steam could compete successfully with sailing-vessels. I believe Mr. Derby did not answer that question. I will say that steamers are competing successfully with sailing-vessels without a subsidy. In fact, most of the business with the principal cities on the coast is done by steamers.

Mr. CALKIN. They are really running off sailing-vessels?

Mr. LORING. Yes; from the trade between Boston, New York, Baltimore, Norfolk, Charleston, New Orleans, and Savannah. That is a question which will take care of itself. American steamers can compete successfully with American sailing-vessels in our waters.

Mr. HOLMAN. What, in your judgment, can the government do to revive the ship-building interests of the country?

Mr. LORING. I did not come here prepared to take up the different points and discuss them, and whatever I say will be said in a desultory manner. We all know that no nation can become wealthy on manufactures or on agriculture or on commerce alone, and that nations, to increase in wealth, must encourage two or more of those interests. My idea is, in relation to the whole business of the country, that we must aim to furnish the labor of the country with everything that it consumes, outside and inside, at the lowest possible cost, with a view of reducing the cost to commerce. An additional cost of one per cent. will prevent millions of exports.

Mr. HOLMAN. A nation may promote its commerce at the expense of the manufacturing industry engaged in the construction of ships. That can be done, of course, by allowing the purchase and registry of foreign-built vessels. But, looking at the question in connection with ship-building alone, and as only a mere agent of commerce, can the government do anything to promote the interests of the ship-builders except by relieving ship-building materials from the payment of internal and external duties?

Mr. LORING. Of course the best way would be a reduction of duties on imports; but no one expects that we are coming to free trade.

Mr. HOLMAN. Take only those materials that enter into the construction of ships in which foreign labor comes in competition with our own.

Mr. LORING. That, as Mr. Derby remarked, would interfere with American manufactures. It seems that the only way would be the allowance of a drawback.

Mr. WELLS. What drawback would you suggest for the purpose of encouraging the building of iron ships here?

Mr. LORING. No more than the amount paid in duties.

Mr. WELLS. How much is that per ton?

Mr. LORING. I have not gone into a computation. I presume that ten dollars per ton on wooden vessels is about correct. Wooden ships cost about eighty dollars a ton, and iron ships one hundred and twenty or one hundred and thirty dollars. To encourage iron-ship building of course a drawback should be allowed in proportion to the extra cost.

Mr. WELLS. Would a drawback of twenty dollars per ton be sufficient?

Mr. LORING. It is easily computed. I do not know what the cost of iron ships in England is. It is some three years since we have given up all idea of building. I have all the facilities for building. I am keeping up an establishment and organization in hopes of having some relief.

Mr. WELLS. It was stated before the committee in New York that twelve dollars per ton would be sufficient to justify the building of iron vessels in this country.

Mr. LORING. I think it was set too low. That would be discriminating in favor of wooden vessels. If ten dollars per ton be allowed for a wooden ship, the amount for an iron ship should be in the proportion to the cost, which is one hundred and twenty-five dollars per ton to eighty dollars for a wooden vessel.

Mr. WELLS. It was remarked there that a wooden ship could be built in England at from fifty-five to sixty dollars, and here at about seventy dollars, and that an iron ship cost in England about one hundred and twelve dollars a ton, and here from one hundred and twenty to one hundred and twenty-five dollars—the difference being from ten to fifteen dollars.

Mr. LORING. If these are the facts, of course an allowance of twelve dollars per ton would be sufficient.

The CHAIRMAN. In your opinion, as an experienced iron-ship builder, if the duties on iron were remitted, could American ship-builders then compete with foreign ship-builders?

Mr. LORING. There is no question as to that; we have one great advantage in this—that an American ship of the same weight of metal would be very much stronger than an English vessel, and would have a better reputation all over the world.

The committee here took a recess for dinner.

AFTERNOON SESSION.

Mr. ANDREW T. HALL, of Boston, ship-owner, said that there could be no question as to the very positive decline in the shipping interests of New England. This had always been a great point for building ships. There was no time within the past fifteen years that ships on the stocks could not be counted by dozens in and around Boston. Now there were none on the stocks. Iron was so very heavily taxed that, without something in the nature of a drawback, American ship-builders could not compete with English ship-builders. Iron ships had been recently introduced in England for commercial purposes, and would enter largely into the carrying trade of the world. Americans could not begin to compete with the English in iron-ship building. As to wooden ships, they were still trying to keep the business alive. He had, himself, built a large wooden ship within the last few weeks, but there was very little opportunity for profit in the business. What ship-builders wanted, he thought, was a drawback of duty on the iron used in the manufacture of ships. There was a good deal of iron rigging used now in ships, which had not been the case heretofore, and a drawback of duty upon it would be a material help.

Mr. CALKIN. Do you make a specialty of the iron, or do you require a drawback on all the articles entering into the construction of a ship?

Mr. HALL. Iron is the principal object, because the wood we have ourselves, and the copper also.

Mr. CALKIN. Do you speak of iron ships particularly?

Mr. HALL. I am speaking of iron ships. There is not so much difference in the foreign and American value of copper as there is in that of iron. We are producing such a large quantity of copper that the price has been reduced somewhat.

Mr. HOLMAN. To what extent, if it should be done at all, do you think this government should adopt a more liberal policy than its present one with reference to the admission of foreign-built vessels to American registry?

Mr. HALL. I should think that that would be the means of driving every ship mechanic out of the country.

Mr. HOLMAN. What effect would it have on the commerce of the country alone, apart from the ship-building interest?

Mr. HALL. We should have no commerce but in foreign-built ships.

Mr. HOLMAN. Suppose that all articles entering into the construction of ships were relieved from taxation, that the coastwise trade was reserved exclusively to American-built vessels, and that foreign-built vessels were admitted to American registry on the payment of a small duty, say ten or fifteen per cent. on the value, what effect would these three measures, taken together, have on our commerce as well as on our ship-building?

Mr. HALL. I have not thought of it in the view that you present it. I should suppose, however, that any mode which would introduce foreign-built ships into our mercantile marine would be adverse to American interests.

Mr. HOLMAN. Our policy, however, up to the present time, has been more restrictive than that of any other commercial nation?

Mr. HALL. Yes, sir. We have a reputation in New England of building good ships—ships that last. The reputation of the Provinces in that respect is far inferior. Their ships will rarely last over four or five years, whereas New England ships frequently last from fifteen to twenty-five years.

Mr. HOLMAN. If the materials used in the construction of wooden vessels were relieved from taxation, how far do you think that would enable the American ship-builder to compete with the foreign ship-builder?

Mr. HALL. I think it would enable him to compete entirely.

Mr. HOLMAN. And as to iron vessels?

Mr. HALL. As to iron vessels also.

Mr. HOLMAN. As successfully?

Mr. HALL. It would take us some time to compete with England in iron vessels. We would have to get up large establishments like theirs. There are establishments in England where they are building fourteen or fifteen iron ships at a time. We could hardly expect to go into the business so extensively at present, but we would arrive at it in course of time.

Mr. HOLMAN. What probability is there, in the immediate future, of iron vessels superseding wooden ones?

Mr. HALL. Judging from what they have done in England, I should think that half our ships for the foreign trade would be iron ships. There are objections to iron ships which do not apply to wooden ships—as, for instance, if an iron ship gets on a rock she is gone, whereas a wooden one, although injured, may be got off. But, keeping them off the rocks, the iron ship lasts much longer than the wooden one. In England they class iron ships for insurance at twenty years. At the end of that time she is examined and is classed for twenty years more, so that they run on a low rate of insurance for forty years. Then they require no calking. They require, once a year, to go into dock to be cleaned. And they run at much less expense than wooden vessels. I cannot say what the difference in the rates of insurance between an iron and a wooden vessel is. The difference is in favor of the iron vessel.

Mr. CALKIN. Is there any difference in the insurance here?

Mr. HALL. I do not know.

Mr. CALKIN. You spoke of their having advantages in England over us in building iron ships. Is their machinery for constructing iron ships superior to ours?

Mr. HALL. They have a greater magnitude of machinery. They have larger establishments. We could come to it here if we had a demand for the ships. There is an immense capital employed in the business there, which in this country we are hardly able to furnish. Mr. Laird's concern, opposite Liverpool, is almost a town. All along the Clyde, in Glasgow, there are immense establishments. Where we commence with dollars they do with pounds.

The CHAIRMAN. What preference do iron ships have over wooden ones in freight?

Mr. HALL. They have no advantage in carrying except that they can be sailed cheaper.

The CHAIRMAN. Do iron vessels command higher rates of freight than wooden vessels?

Mr. HALL. I should think not. I should think that, if anything, the reverse would be the case. I think that wooden ships would have the preference for our East India voyages. There are some cargoes, salt for instance, that cannot be brought as well in iron as in wooden ships.

The CHAIRMAN. Do you think that the cargo is generally carried as well in wooden as in iron ships?

Mr. HALL. I should think so. I should give the wooden ships the preference.

Mr. HOLMAN. Can you suggest any other means by which the American shipping interest can be improved than what you have mentioned—the abatement of the duty or internal and external tax on the materials used?

Mr. HALL. I know of no other advantage that we should have the right to claim. I do not think that the ship-builders of New England would call on the government for any other aid.

Mr. HOLMAN. That would be more practicable, you think, than bounties?

Mr. HALL. Yes, sir. I am not in favor of any bounties for American ships. We want to be allowed a chance of competing with foreign ship-builders by having the materials that enter into the construction of ships free of duty. It would be very beneficial to the ship-owner, and would increase the production of our own iron founderies.

Mr. HOLMAN. Would you regard it as consistent with the interests of other branches of industry to encourage the production of iron to a greater extent than at present, and at the same time to relieve ship-builders from the duty imposed on that article?

Mr. HALL. I am not prepared to advocate that. I only regret, as an American, that we are so dependent on abroad for the immense supply of iron that we should furnish ourselves. It is for Congress to suggest a remedy.

Mr. CALKIN. Do you think that the iron interest is protected sufficiently to warrant the construction of other founderies?

Mr. HALL. I do not know enough of the trade to answer the question.

Practically speaking, it does not appear to be, judging by the enormous quantities landed on the Constitution dock here from Liverpool. That is all that I judge by.

The CHAIRMAN. To what extent would allowing vessels to take ships' stores in bond, as is done in England, relieve the shipping interest?

Mr. HALL. I think it would be proper to allow ships going on foreign voyages to take goods in original packages free of duty.

The CHAIRMAN. How much of an item would that be? Would it be any measure of relief to the ship-owner?

Mr. HALL. Not to a very great extent, except in packet-ships, where they carry a large number of passengers. There it would be quite a relief. It would be a very great advantage to the steamship lines. You can get a bottle of champagne on the English steamers cheaper than you can get it in Liverpool, although they put on large profits on board ship. It might lead to abuse; but I think that where goods can be taken out of bond in original packages—bags of coffee, barrels of sugar, &c.—it would be a very important relief to the shipping interest to allow it to be done. I regret very much to see mooted the subject of admitting foreign ships to registry in this country. I think that it would be, if anything, more destructive than the high duty on ship-building materials.

The CHAIRMAN. Do you think that the admitting foreign ships to American registry would have a tendency gradually to transfer the shipping interests to the other side of the water, and make our ships largely foreign and only nominally American?

Mr. HALL. I think it would. I think it would be a death-blow to ship-building in this country.

The CHAIRMAN. And that the ownership, as well as the building, would go to the other side?

Mr. HALL. In a great measure.

Mr. HOLMAN. No nation, I suppose, allows a foreigner to hold the title to a ship registered there?

Mr. HALL. I think not.

Mr. HOLMAN. So that, if the American government adopt a more liberal policy, the title would have to be in an American citizen?

Mr. HALL. Yes. During the war many of our citizens put their ships under the English flag, put in captains, and took mortgages on the ships. I was told in England that those mortgages were of no legal effect, as being in violation of the law.

The CHAIRMAN. Do you not understand that there are a great many Americans owning ships that do sail under a foreign flag?

Mr. HALL. I do not think it is so to a great extent. I have no means, however, of knowing.

Mr. HOLMAN. And, on the other hand, I suppose there are foreign capitalists interested in our vessels sailing under an American register?

Mr. HALL. Unquestionably, to some extent. All the lines of steamships to this country are owned by foreigners. I take it that the amount owned by Americans in those ships is a mere bagatelle, if any at all.

Mr. HOLMAN. Is it your opinion that the commercial interests of the country are promoted by adhering to our present policy in regard to the nationalizing of foreign bottoms?

Mr. HALL. Decidedly so.

Mr. HOLMAN. You think that it would promote the permanent commercial interest of the country to adhere to that policy?

Mr. HALL. I do.

Mr. HOLMAN. Yet it is not the policy of any other commercial power?

Mr. HALL. No, sir.

The CHAIRMAN. Do you know how long Great Britain adhered to the policy of excluding foreign ships from English registry?

Mr. HALL. No, sir, I do not.

Mr. HOLMAN. Has not the policy of Great Britain rather been to increase and enlarge her carrying trade than to promote specially ship-building; and has not the ship-building interest been promoted by her more liberal commercial policy?

Mr. HALL. I have not seen any evidence of it. I judge that the commercial activity of the English has arisen solely from their having advantages over us in building iron ships. They certainly have not increased their wooden ships. It is the iron marine that has been affected most. That has been increased many hundred thousand tons.

Mr. HOLMAN. Up to 1860 we had considerable advantage over Great Britain in the construction of wooden vessels?

Mr. HALL. I think we had. American ships had always the preference all over the world for freight. There was no port where English and American vessels were together that the American vessels had not the preference. There was some difference in the China trade, for which their ships were built with a great deal of care and elegance.

Mr. CALKIN. It has been advocated here this morning that those ships which were once under the American flag, and that went under the British flag, should be allowed to come back. What do you think?

Mr. HALL. I should hope that it will never be done. An American who put his vessel under the English flag should be let keep her there. I have some national feeling about it.

The CHAIRMAN. How many ships did you own during the war?

Mr. HALL. About six.

The CHAIRMAN. Did you sail them under the American flag under all the disadvantages?

Mr. HALL. Entirely. I had one ship which was unfortunately put under the English flag without my knowledge. I owned half of her. She lay at Hong-Kong four months and could get no freight. We sent out a power of attorney to sell her. The captain put her under the English flag, brought her to Australia, and there sold her. I am too much of an American to want to have a ship of mine sailed under the English flag.

The CHAIRMAN. You sailed your ships under great disadvantages in keeping them under the American flag? Those who put their ships under the English flag had a great advantage over you in insurance and rates of freight?

Mr. HALL. Decidedly. I had to pay double insurance all through the war, which I could have avoided by putting my vessels under the English flag as others did theirs.

Mr. MORRELL. Do you not consider the present depressed condition of American commerce largely due to the unfriendly action of England during the war, in permitting the departure from her ports of such ships as the Alabama?

Mr. HALL. It had an influence, but to what extent I am not prepared to say.

The CHAIRMAN. I understand you to say that if the materials entering into the construction of ships were relieved from duty you could compete successfully with the English ship-owner in the foreign carrying trade.

Mr. HALL. I believe entirely so. I believe that we build better ships, more convenient and sightly ships, than the English do, and I believe that we could have a large share in the carrying trade of the world.

The CHAIRMAN. You have to pay higher rates of wages, I presume, to officers and crew than the English do?

Mr. HALL. I should think that our officers are better paid; but I think we sail our ships quite as well as the English do, and with as little expense.

The CHAIRMAN. You think that, on the whole, you sail them as economically as they do?

Mr. HALL. I do.

The CHAIRMAN. In sailing them with a less number of men?

Mr. HALL. No, I think there is better care taken of the ships. I think that American ship-captains are men of a higher grade than English ship-captains—that they are men of more understanding and more mind.

The CHAIRMAN. You think that the greater efficiency of American officers and crews overcomes the difference in the rates of wages that you have to pay?

Mr. HALL. I do.

The CHAIRMAN. So that, on the whole, you can compete with the English in sailing your ships?

Mr. HALL. I think that our intelligence is such that we can manage our ships to better advantage than the English do. Of course there are exceptions; but it is a well-known fact that the captains of American ships are altogether a grade higher than the captains even of English ships. Many of our American captains are part owners of the vessels. The crews are supplied with better provisions than in foreign ships.

Mr. CALKIN. The ship-owners of New York complain on account of the assessment or tax put upon them by the State authorities of New York, as being quite a detriment to the shipping interest. How does that affect it here in Massachusetts? Is there a tax here on the shipping interest?

Mr. HALL. Individual taxation. If a man owns a ship he pays a tax on it as on other property; but there is no special tax on ships. Every man is assessed according to his property, whether it be in ships or anything else.

Mr. MORRELL. Is not that species of property taxed abroad as other property is taxed? Would a ship-owner in England be exempt from paying the same rate on ships as he pays on real estate?

Mr. HALL. I do not know how that is.

Mr. HOLMAN. Is not the decline in our ship-building interest partly attributable to the fact that there are so many other more profitable modes of investing money in this country?

Mr. HALL. I do not think that that enters into the question at all.

Mr. CALKIN. In case the government relieves the ship-building interest and enables American ship-builders to compete with foreigners, do you think that the merchants and capitalists of Boston will put their money in ships again, and go on and build as usual?

Mr. HALL. They will, the moment they see that they can get a return for their money. Show them a probability of success, and there will be capital enough invested in the business.

Mr. HOLMAN. Can a capitalist in this country afford to invest money in ship-building unless he has a profit of eight or nine per cent.?

Mr. HALL. If he is sure of his eight or nine per cent. he will go in; but as a general thing shipping pays better than that.

Mr. CALKIN. Ought it not certainly to pay ten per cent., to make allowance for the deterioration of shipping?

Mr. HALL. Yes, sir; it must be a very badly managed ship that does not pay it.

Mr. HOLMAN. Yet there is a material difference between ship-owning and ship-building—the one is merely an agency of commerce, while the other is but an article of manufacture.

Mr. HALL. There is a difference—to what extent I do not know. I am not able to say what the profits of ship-building are, but I know that ship-builders are men who acquire a handsome competency in course of time. You will find that the ship-builders in Maine are all more or less interested in the ships that they build. It is so in London also.

Mr. HOLMAN. Do you think that it is the policy of the government rather to protect the interests of ship-building than to look to the promotion of commerce at the expense of the ship-building interest?

Mr. HALL. I do not see how you can separate them.

Mr. HOLMAN. The United States might be a very powerful commercial nation and yet its vessels might be built elsewhere, as is the case with some continental nations.

Mr. HALL. I have not thought of that subject, but my impression is that the two interests are so connected that you can hardly separate them.

The CHAIRMAN. Speaking of the profits of ship-building, so far as your knowledge and observation extend, have not ship-builders, prior to the war, been as successful in proportion to the amount of capital employed as any other class of manufacturers?

Mr. HALL. They appear to me to have done as well. Now that their yards are idle they are living, of course, on what they made before.

The CHAIRMAN. I understand you to give it as your opinion that it is necessary to revive the ship-building interest in order to revive the ship-owning interest, and that the building of our ships abroad would carry the ownership and business abroad?

Mr. HALL. It would have that tendency. You revive our commercial interest by creating ships. We do a large carrying trade all over the world. We have three or four ships in the guano trade. That trade employs two or three hundred American ships. I would venture to say that more than half of that guano trade has been done by American ships.

The CHAIRMAN. Do the ships that are in that trade go back in ballast?

Mr. HALL. No, sir; after landing their cargo of guano at a port in Ireland, England, or Scotland, or at Antwerp or Rotterdam, they generally go to Cardiff, where they take a load of coal, which they carry to Rio Janeiro or some other South American port, and then go to Peru for the guano. They generally get enough from the cargo of coal to pay their expenses round to where they get the guano.

The CHAIRMAN. Is there much of that guano trade done with the United States now?

Mr. HALL. Not so much as formerly. I have not noticed any of it coming this way of late years.

Mr. CHAIRMAN. Before the war it was carried principally to the southern ports?

Mr. HALL. Yes; and a good deal of it went to New York at one time.

Mr. HOLMAN. There is, then, an actual profit resulting to American citizens in a commerce that has no direct relation to the United States. Now, would you not consider it a wise measure of national policy, if both the ship-building and the commercial interests cannot be revived together, to promote the commercial interests of the country without reference to the kindred question of ship-building; and can that be done by adopting a more liberal policy with reference to the registry of foreign-built vessels in the United States?

Mr. HALL. I think the two are so combined that you can hardly separate them. If you want to revive the commercial interests of the country you must do it by creating ships.

Mr. HOLMAN. We have a separate and peculiar industry connected with commerce and disconnected from ship-building?

Mr. HALL. Yes, sir.

Mr. HOLMAN. And we have a peculiar industry connected with ship-building and not connected with commerce?

Mr. HALL. Exactly.

Mr. HOLMAN. Now if ship-building cannot be revived—if, from the nature of the impediments thrown in its way by the national debt, by the opportunities for making more profitable investments and other causes, it cannot be revived—would it not be the policy of the United States (supposed to have peculiar advantages as a commercial power) to adopt a more liberal policy with reference to nationalizing foreign-built vessels?

Mr. HALL. No, sir. I should think that we were throwing all the advantages to the foreigners which should be retained to our own citizens. The commerce of the country and the ships of the country are so identified that you can hardly separate them. It is only a small proportion of our ships that are always abroad.

Mr. WELLS. If there is nothing done to relieve the ship-building industry here, and if foreign-built ships be allowed to come under the American flag, how long will it be before there will be no American vessel in the foreign carrying trade?

Mr. HALL. It would not be many years before the foreigners would monopolize the whole of it.

Mr. CALKIN. Outside of the point of view of national pride, would it have any particular effect on the commerce of the country if those vessels that struck their own colors and hoisted the English colors were admitted back?

Mr. HALL. It would deprive us of the building of just so many ships.

The CHAIRMAN. Are there many of those ships in existence at the present time?

Mr. HALL. There are probably a good many of them.

Mr. CALKIN. I speak of commerce, not of the ship-building interest. Would it have any particular effect on the commerce of the country if those ships were allowed to be brought back?

Mr. HALL. It would prevent the commercial interests of America from receiving the profits they now get from their own ships.

Mr. CALKIN. Would it be beneficial or not?

Mr. HALL. It would not be beneficial to the commerce of the country. I am unquestionably opposed to their being brought back.

Mr. WELLS. During the late war more than half of the vessels engaged in commerce on the Mississippi River went down into rebellion and hoisted the confederate flag. When the blockade was removed from time to time those vessels came back under the American flag. There was no objection to that. But, according to your doctrine, that property should have been sacrificed?

Mr. BUFFINTON. If I understand it, those vessels are now under the American flag?

Mr. WELLS. Certainly.

Mr. HOLMAN. What flag would they get under?

Mr. WELLS. (To Mr. Hall.) Are you aware of the fact that blockade-runners which were captured by the government were sold and are now under the American flag?

Mr. HALL. I was not aware of it.

Mr. E. S. TOBEY. Those vessels were sold under a decree of the United States district court, which entitled them to registry.

Mr. THEODORE NICKERSON next addressed the committee. He said he was associated with one of the largest ship-owning firms in the city. They were ship-owners and ship-builders. They could not afford to buy ships, and therefore they built them. They could not afford to pay another man to build ships for them, and therefore they built them for themselves, saving thus so much. They had been long of opinion that the remission of the duties on materials entering into the construction of ships would be a decided advantage, and would enable them to compete successfully with foreign tonnage. The prosperity of English ship-building was coincident with their iron ship building. For himself and his firm, they would prefer wooden ships; but the question seemed to turn really on the point whether they would be allowed to build iron ships and to compete with England in that respect. Iron ships were sought for, and higher rates of freight were paid to them, and lower rates of insurance charged. A prominent Calcutta merchant had given him as a reason why he preferred to ship goods by an iron vessel that, if an accident happened, that was the last of her, and he was paid his insurance, whereas a wooden ship would go into port and be repaired, and after a lapse of time he would get his goods to market. He (Mr. Nickerson) believed that the matter of iron shipping would decide whether Americans could successfully maintain their commercial marine. Although wages were higher in the United States than in England, he thought that the superiority of American labor counterbalanced the nominal difference in wages. He thought that, in coppering vessels, the relative cheapness of the copper in England was offset by the greater difficulty of having the copper put on in a workmanlike manner.

As to admitting foreign-built vessels to American registration, it occurred to him that, aside from the question of embarrassing American ship-builders, the demand for ships from this side, added to the demand at home, would necessarily increase the price, and eventually make the cost of ships greater than they could be built for at present in the United States.

As to the coasting trade, he thought that if English ships were admitted to it, under ever so great a tax, (unless it amounted to prohibition,) the only avenue open to the employment of the American merchant marine would be closed. Fully half the tonnage of the United States ships was employed in the trade between Boston, New York, and San Francisco; and if that avenue were closed, American tonnage would not be worth fifty per cent. of its present value.

As to admitting back the ships that were put under the English flag during the war, he was opposed to it. Although his firm held a great many ships during the war, it had not put one of them under a foreign flag. He could not agree with the argument of Mr. Derby in that respect, and he failed to see any advantage that would result from restoring them to the American flag.

Mr. EBEN HOUSE, an underwriter and representative of the French Lloyds, next came before the committee. He said that his business was more particularly to examine the quality and merits of ships, and to classify them for the benefit of underwriters. He inspected ships during their construction to see that they had all the requirements which the rules and regulations prescribed to make them sea-worthy. His impression was that there was no difference in this country in the rates of insurance charged on iron and on wooden vessels of the same class. He presumed that in England they did make such a difference. His experience in England, which country he frequently visited, was that there had been an effort made there to create a prejudice against wooden ships and in favor of iron ships for many years past, the reason being that the English had iron to build ships and had not wood. That was one reason, and, he presumed, a very proper one.

The CHAIRMAN. Your business has led you to observe the revolution that has been spoken of in the construction of ships. What is your opinion in reference to iron ships superseding wooden ships?

Mr. E. HOUSE. I have no doubt that that will be the case when we get out of wood to build ships, and when they can be built cheaper and to better advantage of iron. Previous to 1862–'3 we could compete with any nation in the world in the building of sailing-vessels. We asked no favor from the government then; we wanted none. We were having a fair chance and could compete with all the world. Since that time, and since the high duties have been put on, we have not been able to do so. There is the simple fact. Everything is so high in building a ship, and in sailing her, (that is, in regard to provisions,) that we cannot compete with England. In England they get all their supplies out of bond free of duty, and this advantage amounts to a good deal.

The CHAIRMAN. What relief, in your judgment, would be sufficient to enable us to restore our commerce?

Mr. E. HOUSE. Simply put us back where we were previous to 1861 in reference to duties on the materials in ship-building.

The CHAIRMAN. You think that the exemption of ship-building materials from duty would be sufficient?

Mr. E. HOUSE. I have no doubt that it would help a great deal. We try to struggle along to build a ship now and then; but it is a very poor business.

Mr. MORRELL. In the examination of wooden ships for registration you take into account the materials of which they are built as well as the manner in which they are built?

Mr. E. HOUSE. Certainly.

Mr. MORRELL. Do you take into consideration, in the examination of an iron ship, the quality of the iron of which the ship is built?

Mr. E. HOUSE. That is always taken into consideration. The iron has to bear certain tests.

Mr. MORRELL. What are those tests?

Mr. E. HOUSE. I really do not know. I have had very little to do with iron-built vessels, and I would have to refer to the rules and regulations respecting iron-built vessels.

Mr. MORRELL. It was tested in New York that the English Lloyds require iron vessels to be built at a certain weight per ton, and that they make no requirements as to the quality of the iron except that it should bear a test of twenty thousand pounds to the square inch; and it was stated that the iron which would stand two or two and a half times that tensile test would not require to be of so much weight.

Mr. E. HOUSE. It depends upon the length and depth and breadth of the ship. The weight of iron must be according to that.

Mr. MORRELL. It was stated there that if the American ship-builders were permitted to use an iron of the same strength, yet lighter in weight, they could build American iron ships, of the same tensile strength, as cheap as English iron ships.

Mr. E. HOUSE. I presume that it is according to the goodness of the iron.

Mr. MORRELL. It was stated there that the fact of the greater strength of the iron was not considered in the insuring of a vessel in England. Is that considered here?

Mr. E. HOUSE. I really do not know what rules they have here in regard to iron ship-building.

Mr. MORRELL. I believe it was stated there that they would not rate a vessel A No. 1 that did not weigh so many pounds to the ton measurement, regardless of the strength of the iron.

Mr. E. HOUSE. I have not attended to the statistics about iron-built vessels. I have asked the question several times at headquarters in Paris, where I get my instructions from. They had a meeting in Liverpool this last year to revise the rules and requirements of ship-building, and to try to get a uniform regulation, and I have not got the result yet.

The CHAIRMAN. Are you aware that, so far as English iron vessels are concerned, the question of their insurance rests on the rules and specifications prepared by the English Lloyds as an English requisite to pass those ships?

Mr. E. HOUSE. Yes, sir; that is the fact. I believe that the French and English engineers have now entered upon one uniform mode of building iron ships.

Dr. OSBORN HOUSE next addressed the committee. He said that he was a ship-owner in the foreign trade. His vessels were entirely wooden ships, trading to California, the East Indies, and Europe. He had some interest in iron steamers running between Boston and New Orleans. There were two English-built iron steamers on the line.

The CHAIRMAN. What measures would you suggest to be adopted in order to revive our navigation interests?

Mr. O. HOUSE. I think, if we were placed as we were formerly, with but little if any duties on our ship-building materials, we could compete with foreigners. Formerly we felt that we could take care of ourselves. I think that until quite recently ship-owners have never asked any aid or assistance from the government. They have always said, "Let us alone and we can take care of ourselves." But for seven or eight years past we found it pretty hard work to get along, on account of the high duty on many articles used in the construction of ships. The cost of ship-building materials in this country is double the cost that they have to pay in England.

The CHAIRMAN. How would it be if the iron of which you manufacture were duty free?

Mr. O. HOUSE. It would be a great saving to us, of course. Then there is Manila hemp, for which there is no substitute, and that article pays a duty of twenty-five dollars per ton in gold. It does not come in competition with any hemp raised in this country.

The CHAIRMAN. Does it not come in competition with Kentucky hemp?

Mr. O. HOUSE. Not at all; for it is used for running rigging, and Kentucky hemp is never used for that purpose.

The CHAIRMAN. Do you think that the exemption from duty of all the raw materials that enter into the construction of a ship—hemp, iron in a crude state, bars, bolts, sail-cloth, and duck—would enable American ship-builders to compete with foreign ship-builders?

Mr. O. HOUSE. I think so.

The CHAIRMAN. Would you ask any exemption on manufactured duck?

Mr. O. HOUSE. The price is much higher here than cotton duck. During the war we were obliged to use foreign duck altogether, as cotton was so high, and we got a very poor article at that.

The CHAIRMAN. You think that the exemption of duty on the raw materials would be sufficient to revive American ship-building?

Mr. O. HOUSE. I think that with that we would be able to compete with foreigners.

The CHAIRMAN. Have you any interest at all in ship-building?

Mr. O. HOUSE. None at all.

The CHAIRMAN. As a ship-owner, would you be in favor of granting American registration to foreign-built vessels?

Mr. O. HOUSE. I think not. I think that would be a great injury to our mechanical industry.

The CHAIRMAN. What effect would it have upon our navigation interests, aside from the ship-building interest?

Mr. O. HOUSE. It is impossible to say. It would have a very serious effect upon the ship-building interest; there is no doubt about that.

The CHAIRMAN. Suppose that the two measures were put together, the exemption from duty of all the materials entering into the construction of a ship, and the free registry of foreign-built ships, what effect would they have upon the ship-building interest?

Mr. O. HOUSE. Since the English have commenced building iron ships I think they have rather an advantage over us. It is possible that if the duties were taken off, or a drawback of the duty allowed on iron, we might successfully compete with them; but we probably could not at first. It would take some time to get things properly arranged so that we could build iron ships as cheaply as they can. They can build an iron ship almost as cheaply as we can build a wooden one.

Mr. CALKIN. How is the coasting trade now?

Mr. O. HOUSE. It has not been very profitable these few years past.

Mr. CALKIN. A law relieving the ship-building interest would help very much the present ships in the matter of their repairs.

Mr. O. HOUSE. It would in their repairs. I think that most of the repairs that are now done on the other side would then be done here.

Mr. HOLMAN. If the policy were adopted of giving to the American ship-builder the benefits that may arise from the exemption of his materials from internal and external taxes, and if American-built ships were given the exclusive benefit of the domestic trade, as they have now, and if at the same time Congress were to allow the registration of foreign-built vessels purchased by American citizens on the imposition of a duty of ten or fifteen per cent., what effect would these three measures combined have on ship-building and on commerce? How would they affect the ship-building interest on the one hand and the commercial interest on the other?

Mr. O. HOUSE. I should think they would have a favorable effect; it strikes me so. I never thought of that mode of dealing with the question.

Mr. HOLMAN. Two of those measures would be friendly to the ship-building interest, and the other one to the promotion of commerce?

Mr. O. HOUSE. Yes, sir.

Mr. HOLMAN. Would not these three measures taken together have the effect of increasing the ship-owning of the country, at least?

Mr. O. HOUSE. I should think they would.

Mr. HOLMAN. And might they not have that effect without necessarily impairing the interests of the ship-builder?

Mr. O. HOUSE. I do not see how they would injure him.

Mr. HOLMAN. Looking at the subject as a ship-owner, you think that these three measures connected together, if they should become the policy of the government, could not be justly objected to by either the ship-building interest on the one hand or the commercial interest on the other?

Mr. O. HOUSE. My impression is that they would be well received; I should think so.

Mr. FREDERICK NICKERSON, ship-owner, said that he concurred generally in the expression of opinion by the ship-owners and ship-builders as to the necessity of relief in the shape of drawbacks. The only point that he would like to draw the attention of the committee to was to the relief to steam navigation in the matter of coal. He suggested whether, if the duty on coal were not to be repealed, an arrangement might not be made by which coal should be allowed to be brought from abroad, entered in bond, and exported for consumption on the high seas. He said that coal could be bought in Pictou at $2 05 a ton in gold. The duty here was $1 25 in gold. If that coal could be brought here and landed in bond, and could be shipped for consumption on steamers and consumed at sea, with a proper guard against its being relanded, it would be a very great relief to the steam commerce of the country.

Mr. MORRELL. I think that that would be entirely satisfactory to the coal-producing interest of the country.

Mr. F. NICKERSON remarked that it seemed to him that that relief to the steam commerce of the country was as much needed as any other matter. It was a matter of very great importance. The high price of coal was very much against the encouragement of steam commerce. That system would naturally follow, on the same principle as allowing ships to take their stores for consumption at sea, as is done in England. In fact, there had been some little correspondence with the Secretary of the Treasury on that very point. It had been thought first that it was a point that might be decided by himself; but there had been afterward nothing done about it, as it had been considered that it might lead to opening the door to some other matters, such as taking ships' stores out of bond. This privilege seemed to him a very reasonable thing to be asked for and granted.

Mr. NATHANIEL MCKAY submitted a written statement of the cost of building iron steamships both in this country and abroad.

The letter is as follows:

BOSTON, *October* 18, 1869.

GENTLEMEN: * * * The cost to build an iron ship in England ready for sea is (£14) fourteen pounds per ton; in this country it would be (£22) twenty-two pounds per ton. He says that there are now building on the Clyde one hundred vessels, all of iron, upward of one hundred thousand tons, twelve thousand horse-power; last year (1868) they built 171,126 tons of steam and sailing vessels, 15,940 horse-power, and still the business is on the increase, and several new ship-yards are starting up. A steamship arrived in London in the month of September with three thousand tons of tea, sixty-five days from China, and still another with a freight valued at thirty thousand pounds, or one hundred and fifty thousand dollars. He says the steamships will use up the tea sailing clippers in the China trade, and owners of iron sailing ships are much alarmed at the progress of steam over sailing vessels in the China as well as other trades. A new ship in Scotland, built of iron, 387 feet long, 43 feet beam, 30 feet deep, speed ten knots, cost seventy-eight thousand pounds. This ship has made sixteen and one-quarter voyages to New York in twenty-four months, an average of forty-four and one-fourth days to the round voyage. Carries of crew, all told, one hundred and ten persons. This same company are now building another vessel to run to New York from Liverpool. She is to be 415 feet long on deck, 43 feet beam, 30 feet deep, speed twelve knots, costing complete, ready for sea, without provisions, eighty-five thousand pounds. The engine for this ship cost eighteen thousand pounds. We could not build the same ship here for twice that amount of money. A steamer, with a compound engine, has just arrived from China, with two thousand four hundred tons of tea, in sixty-two days. She is a ship 309 feet long, 28 feet deep, 39 feet wide, register 2,280 tons gross, net 1,550 tons—2,400 tons of fifty feet to the ton; sails nine knots; bark-rigged; main yard sixty-two feet; burns twenty-four tons of coal per day; cost fifty-two thousand pounds. The same company are building four others for the China trade. The Chinese tea clippers are used up on account of the steamers doing such wonders. The cost of the angle iron for the frames of ships, in England, cut to lengths, seven pounds ten shillings; the cost of plates, cut to shape for an entire ship, is eight pounds five shillings; wire rigging twenty-one pounds per ton; chain cables ten pounds per ton. Cost of American angle iron for a ship $134 40 per ton, a difference in favor of England of $89 40, or four cents per pound. Cost of plates in America $112 per ton; in England $49 50; difference in favor of England, $62 50, or three cents per pound. Cost of chain cables in this country is $134 40 per ton; difference in favor of England $57 20. Cost of wire rigging in America, $291 20 per ton; difference in favor of England, $89 60. * * * * * * *

I have many more figures that I could give you, but will not tax your patience.

I remain, cordially yours,

NATH'L McKAY.

To JOHN LYNCH.
Chairman Committee on Commerce.

The CHAIRMAN asked Mr. McKay whether his firm had built any iron sailing or steam vessels.

Mr. McKAY replied that his firm could not afford to build them.

Mr. CALKIN inquired who had built the Merrimac.

Mr. McKAY replied that it had been built by Mr. Loring, who had been before the committee to-day.

The CHAIRMAN. In your opinion, if the duties were taken off from the materials entering into the construction of iron and wooden vessels, could the American ship-builder compete successfully with foreign builders in the construction of both those classes of vessels?

Mr. McKAY. I think he could; but if we go to work to have a bill passed repealing the duty on iron alone it will kill the whole thing, for we will have all Pennsylvania in Washington. And if we try to have the tax withdrawn on cotton duck, we will have the mills of Lawrence and Baltimore represented at Washington.

Mr. BUFFINTON. And if you say hemp, you will have my constituents acting against you?

Mr. McKAY. Yes, sir. We cannot specify any one thing. But we must have the duty remitted on everything that goes into the construction of a ship and into its repairs, whether it be a sailing ship or a steam-ship.

The CHAIRMAN. Do you know any ship-owner who has gone entirely out of the business?

Mr. McKAY. Yes, sir; I know one gentleman who was appointed on the committee of the Board of Trade, but who would not attend, he was so much disgusted with the business. He was a very large ship-owner; but his money is invested to-day in railroads.

Mr. BUFFINTON. Do you think that railroads pay him a better percentage than ships would?

Mr. McKAY. I think they do. The government has aided them more than it has aided the ship-yards. I asked one member of Congress from Boston, the other day, who used to be one of the largest ship-owners in the country, in reference to this drawback on ship-building materials. Well, he did not know. He thought it might be done. The committee was very much in favor of it, but for himself he had very much doubt about it. If we do not have this relief we are going to be wiped from the ocean. We do not want American ships that went under the English flag taken back to this country; nor do we want foreign ships enrolled in this country. If we adopt that policy, the honest men who learned the ship-building trade will have to pack up, go west, and buy farms, or get the government or some of the railways to give them farms. To-day you cannot hire a joiner in Boston to work on a ship at less than four dollars. The mechanics who have worked side by side with me are to-day driving potato carts through the city.

Mr. CALKIN. If the government does not protect the shipping interest all the mechanics will be driven out of it, and in five or ten years there will be none left?

Mr. MCKAY. There will be still some left to keep up the coastwise trade.

Mr. CALKIN. Various opinions have been expressed in regard to the capability of American mechanics competing with foreigners in the construction of iron ships. Do you not think that they are ready to go to work and to build iron ships without waiting one or two years to learn how?

Mr. MCKAY. I do not think that any man on the other side of the water can beat a Yankee any way. That is my idea. I am a good deal of the opinion of John Bright, who said in a speech that every other Yankee you find has got a patent of some kind. I do not think that any class of mechanics can beat the American mechanics. Of course, we have got to have some experience in building iron steamers. We have built but few iron ships, and most of them have been failures. The government spent one hundred millions during the war and got no navy. All that New York is doing in the way of merchant marine is in the coastwise trade. The New Yorkers pride themselves on the number of steamers in their port; but John Bull owns them. As to the Pacific Mail Steamship Company, the English have got ships on the same line that are burning only thirty tons of coal a day, when these New York side-wheelers are burning sixty-five tons, and the English will eat them all up.

Mr. CALKIN. Allow me to say that the Pacific Mail Steamship Company is running large steamers on a consumption of forty tons a day.

Mr. MCKAY. Well, they run very slowly. But you will find that when they come to run fast they burn from fifty to sixty tons a day. If the government will only go to work and relieve the ship-builders and give us some subsidy for mail lines of steamers, you will see the hammers and axes at work in every ship-yard. The government gives millions of subsidies to railroads, and for want of a subsidy to steamships it allows all our trade across the ocean to be carried on in foreign bottoms.

Mr. WELLS. In your communication to the committee have you stated the comparative cost of an iron ship here and in England?

Mr. MCKAY. Yes, sir; I say that it costs nearly as much again here.

Mr. WELLS. Are you now engaged in the building of ships?

Mr. MCKAY. No, sir; there are no ships to be built now; and I think I shall spend the rest of my days in the city of New York, where all business goes.

Mr. E. S. TOBEY, of the Boston Board of Trade, said that it had been remarked by a distinguished member of Congress, and not without apparent truth, that every interest in the United States had its friends, but that the American shipping had none. He did not wonder at that remark, judging from the standpoint at Washington, where the representatives of the American shipping interest had seldom or never appeared. It had been stated before the committee that that interest had never needed relief. Up to 1861, when the war commenced, that was true, so far as related to sailing vessels, but not so far as related to steamers—

because the Collins line of steamers did ask and did receive aid from the government. He submitted that it was specially the interest of the United States government, for its own sake, to restore the American flag to the ocean. It was pre-eminently a national question. Capital could very well take care of itself. The only thing on the part of Congress was to see that it did not take too good care of itself. It was a rare and exceptional thing to find a large capitalist who could be called a ship-owner; ships were generally owned by several persons. Capitalists who had money in ships could sell their ships to England and put their capital in western railroads and mortgages. Thus capital would take care of itself. But that was not for the interest of the government, which should encourage, maintain, and develop the mechanical industry of the country, as the cheapest way in which to maintain its navy power. If the ship-building interest were not encouraged, the mechanics engaged in it would be dispersed; and once dispersed, how could they ever be got back again? The trade of a ship-builder was not learned in a day. Naval architecture was perhaps one of the finest sciences that could be named; and the time might come when the country would need another Ericsson. If the business were to be transferred to the rival of the United States on the other side of the Atlantic, by admitting foreign-built vessels to American registry, it was not to be expected that the few ship-builders now attempting to carry on their business would continue that fruitless attempt. It was, therefore, a matter of the highest importance for the government itself, that the ship-building mechanics should be sustained, not for the sake of capital, but for the sake of the nation. Every American ship-owner could better afford to transfer his ship to Great Britain and invest his capital how he chose, than the United States government could afford to allow that to be done.

As to the decline of the shipping interest of the United States, he would merely refer to Mr. Wells's report, in which it is stated that whereas, in 1853, American commerce on the high seas was fifteen per cent. greater than that of Great Britain, and maintained a close competition until 1861, it had fallen in 1864 to less than one-half as much, and was now probably not more than one-third. The causes of this decline he attributed, first, to the operation of confederate cruisers, by which many vessels were destroyed and many more transferred to the English flag, to the natural termination of ship's lives, and to the fact that American currency had become inflated to such an extent that it was impossible, during the war, to replace those ships. American commerce had thus declined, not through any want of enterprise on the part of American citizens, but from natural causes which the government itself could not control, and for which it was in no degree responsible up to this time. He regarded the appointment of this committee as one of the most encouraging features that he had seen for a long time, because it showed that Congress meant to obtain information on the subject, and to address itself to the remedies by which the shipping interests of the country could be brought up to a point in competition with other maritime nations.

The simple question was, how it could be done. He submitted, as a logical proposition, that if the United States would do just as England and other nations had done to promote their commerce, the same results would follow, and American shipping would again come to the front and claim its share in the carrying trade of the world both by steam and sailing vessels. This country was to-day paying from twenty to thirty million dollars a year to foreign nations for the mere transportation of merchandise in foreign bottoms.

If the government adopted the policy of permitting foreign-built vessels to be purchased and registered in the United States, what, he asked, would be the effect on the finances of the country—to say nothing of its effect on mechanical industry? It would take from the country another vast sum of gold, and hand it over to the commercial rival of the United States to build up its mammoth steamboat interest and utterly to crush out that of the United States. It seemed to him entirely suicidal to the interests of the United States to think for a moment of transferring to the American flag vessels of foreign construction. A ship was a sort of national institution; and the men to build ships must be kept at home. Steamers and ships amounting to three hundred sail had been put in requisition to blockade the southern coast during the rebellion; and if there had not been American artisans to draw upon, where would these ships have been built and repaired?

Secretary Stanton had said to him, in the early part of the war, "I want you to go home and, by private enterprise, push our iron-clads forward. Bring everything into requisition, and give us something to contend with this Merrimac, or we are gone. Even the southern women are selling their trinkets to build up a navy, and here we are relying on the navy yards, and no results." Fortunately the ship-yards and the skill were to be obtained. This country was liable to be at war again. If that war were to be with Great Britain, and if Americans had gone to work and built up her navy at the expense of the iron ship-building interest, what would be the result?

He found that there was a very prevalent notion abroad that Americans did not know how to build iron steamships. There was no greater fallacy than that. The Collins line had proved the ability of American steamers to compete with English steamers in point of speed. Mr. Collins had made a mistake, however, in undertaking to surpass the English in that respect. It cost too much, and that cost was not counterbalanced by the subsidy. He (Mr. Tobey) was chairman of the committee which had the Mississippi and Merrimac steamships built recently at South Boston, and he had been informed by the man who made the model that he was paid six hundred dollars to duplicate the model and send it to Liverpool. These ships proved the ability of American mechanics to model a ship equal to anything that floated. Why should that ability not be cherished and encouraged?

American seamen should also be kept up and encouraged. During the late war the government had drawn from the merchant marine thirty or forty thousand men to blockade the southern ports. Without that blockade the war would have terminated speedily in the success of the rebellion; and, without the merchant marine, the blockade could not have been maintained. The government could not afford to see the American merchant marine crushed out. That merchant marine was indispensable for the maintenance of the national maritime power, and it must be constructed by American mechanics, conducted by American citizens, and owned by American capitalists.

The English government had increased its subsidies to steamship lines. It had increased that of the Peninsular and Oriental line from about two hundred thousand pounds sterling originally to five hundred thousand pounds. England claimed to be a free-trade country; but what did she do with her foreign commerce—her steamship interest? She protected it to a degree that no other interest there ever was protected. And why? Because it was the most potent means of developing every other commercial interest, and because it was the cheapest way of sustaining her navy. Earl Gray had said that one of the reasons why he was in favor of subsidizing steamships to all parts of the world was, that swift ships bring back swift orders for manufactured goods. And, as illustrating the force of that remark, in less than five years after subsidizing the line to Brazil, the exports from England to Brazil increased three hundred per cent.

While England possessed the natural advantage of cheap coal, cheap iron, cheap labor, cheap capital, she was not content with them as a means of competing with other nations; but she very wisely took a still further step, and, for the purpose of drawing capital to the development of her steam commerce, she had commenced in 1838 to pay four steamers, running from Liverpool to Boston, eight hundred thousand dollars a year for carrying the mails. She had commenced, the same year, the subsidies to the Peninsular and Oriental line, and increased them till they now reached five hundred thousand pounds sterling per annum. The course which England pursued in subsidizing her foreign commerce he regarded as wise.

Just as soon as the policy of the United States government would allow American ship-builders to construct vessels as cheaply as they are constructed in England, by remitting the duties on materials, and would then compensate steamship lines for carrying the mails to the same extent and for as long a period as England did, and would then remit the duties on all ships' stores as England did, and would then omit to tax American ships internally as England omitted to do—when the United States government accepted those ideas and acted on them, it would be found that the enterprise and skill of the people of the United States would enable them to compete with any other people.

The policy of subsidizing had not been pursued by England alone. The Emperor of the French had seen the results achieved, and had said that he was not going to have such a powerful neighbor without competing with her, and he had commenced to subsidize a line to New York, which to-day received twenty-six thousand dollars in gold for every round trip. And the result was that the last New York enterprise, the line of the Arago and Fulton, had had to surrender. Although the United States government had given them the postal service, they were compelled to withdraw and to give up the whole route to the French. The Pereire and Ville de Paris had been built in Scotland, but it was because the Emperor knew very well that France had not the experience in naval construction to compete with England or with the United States in the merchant marine. It was just the same with Germany and with Holland. They were subordinate naval powers, and therefore had no objection to allowing foreign-built vessels to their registration. They saw their advantage in transportation interests. They had acted wisely and well in the matter. But the United States, occupying a great central position, holding to the continents of Asia and Europe, claiming even to be the rival of England and France as a naval power, could not afford to do so. The navy and the mercantile marine of the country had done, prior to the late war, more than anything else to raise the reputation of the nation before the maritime nations of the earth, and to make the American flag respected; and every American citizen wanted to see that flag flying again in every foreign port. In the war of 1812, New England owned seven-eighths if not a larger proportion of the tonnage of the United States. The merchants of Salem had contributed out of their own pockets to build the Essex frigate, which chased hundreds of British ships from the seas, which went into the mouth of the English Channel, and which so pestered and restrained the commerce of England that the rates of insurance went so high as practically to exclude their ships from the sea; and this had been one of the most potent means of bringing England to terms. He had adverted to these facts to show the intimate relations that existed between the naval power and the mercantile marine, and to show that the one cannot be maintained without the other. The men who constructed ships were needed as well as the men who navigated them; and he believed that everything possible should be done to cherish the ship-building interest. He felt encouraged and hopeful that when the facts were fully investigated and understood it would be found that the interests of the country, irrespective of section, demanded the restoration of the American flag not only on sailing-vessels but on steamships on the ocean.

It had been assumed, erroneously, that the people of the West had no particular interest in the matter of shipping. But he proposed to show that they had absolutely more interest in it than the people of the East had. The latter could better afford to dispose of all their ships and to invest the proceeds in western railroads, where they could get a better return to their capital, than the people of the West could afford to dispense with the facilities for getting their produce to foreign markets at a low rate of transportation. If the United States government should pay a subsidy for carrying the mails across the Atlantic as large as England pays—so large as to compensate entirely the ship-owner for the whole voyage, and so large that he could say to the producer or shipper, "We can afford to carry your goods for nothing, we are so liberally compensated by the government"—who would be deriving the most advantage from it? The producer in the West. He could have his goods transported at a very low rate, because the ship-owner could afford to do it, and competition would induce him to do it. Therefore the subsidy paid out of the treasury of the United States and assessed on the general interests of the country would be one of the best means of developing the agricultural interests of the country, by aiding to cheapen transportation from the place of production to the place of consumption on the other side of the Atlantic. Hence, as a mere practical question, the people of the West had as much interest in promoting lines of steamships and sailing vessels as the people of the East. He had never met the first man in his intercourse in Washington, or in a convention of two hundred and forty members held in Boston two years ago, who dissented from the general proposition that it was of the greatest national importance to restore American commerce under the American flag. That convention had unanimously voted a resolution to that effect, which had been transmitted to Congress.

In conclusion, Mr. Tobey stated, in reply to a remark by Mr. Calkin, that American ship-owners must be put on the same footing as foreigners. They must have all the encouragement that foreign governments give to their commerce; and even then the American ship-owners would be placed under the disadvantage arising from the condition of the currency.

Mr. Franklin W. Smith, treasurer of the Atlantic Iron Works, made some additional remarks. He said that the revenue was now receiving nothing from the taxation of ship-iron, because none was imported. Therefore the government would be no loser by allowing a drawback on iron used in ship-building. The iron men of Pennsylvania were making no sales of ship-iron to-day, and therefore they would not be the losers. It would be remembered that the subsidies to the British lines were at first looked upon with great jealousy in the United States because that navigation would be making the entire coasts of the United States familiar to British pilots. He remembered that when the Cunard steamer Unicorn came into the port of Boston there was great alarm, because the pilotage of the port was being made known to British pilots. But to-day there was scarcely a port of the American coast that was not as familiar to British ship-masters and British pilots as to any American pilots. The object of the British subsidies had not been simply to keep up a mercantile marine, but had been also to keep afloat in the cheapest possible way a naval force; and England had done it. She could throw fifty thousand men upon any point of the globe to-day earlier than any other nation. It seemed to him that there was no interest to be injured by a change in the present condition of affairs. The iron men of Pennsylvania should join instantly with the shipping and commercial interests, and let the ports be open to English iron, but let the ship-builders have the choice to use American iron. And if they used American iron, let them have a drawback equal to the duty on English iron.

Mr. MORRELL. That is all that the iron men have asked.

Mr. SMITH. That is all we want. We certainly would use American iron, and the incidental demand for American iron would be very great. The government would certainly lose nothing by it; for it is getting no revenue to-day from ship-building iron. The western interest would be benefited by it, because the ship is the continuation of the western lines of railroad around the globe.

The committee adjourned to meet in Portland on the 21st of October.

PORTLAND, *October* 21, 1869.

The committee met in the collector's room in the custom-house.

Present: The chairman and Messrs. Morrell, Buffinton, Wells, and Calkin.

Captain WASHINGTON RYAN submitted his views to the committee. He said that he had noticed newspaper reports of the statements made before the committee, and he agreed with most of them. There was another thing, however, which he thought tended to the depression of our commerce, and which he had not seen touched upon. That was the deterioration of the men who sail American ships. He thought that they had been in the down-hill road for some years from one end of the ship to the other—masters, officers, and crew. He thought that that was owing in a great measure to the apathy of the ship-owning interests, or perhaps to the want of public spirit. He had never known any ship-owner who seemed to him to take any interest in improving the condition of the men who sailed his ships. He thought that the American merchant marine law, if there was such a law, needed a thorough and complete revision. In fact, he might say that there was no mercantile marine law in this country. Masters and officers of ships came up like Topsies. There was no board of examination, and nobody knew whether an officer, when he came on board a ship, could determine the latitude and longitude of a ship by meridian observation. There was what is called a Ship-masters' Association in New York, which gave certificates to officers, but did so without making any examination. He considered an association like that an absolute and positive injury to the shipping interest, because it encouraged a bad state of things. And it was astonishing to him that the underwriters of New York would take a risk at one-half per cent. less on the strength of a certificate from such an association. He favored such a revision of the mercantile marine law as had been proposed in the Senate of the United States by Mr. Fish, of New York, in 1853. He thought that, had that bill become a law, it would have produced a very different state of things. As it was, respectably brought up young men, who might have imbibed a passion for the sea, went now for a voyage or two, and became so disgusted with the business that they invariably quitted it. He thought that the navigation laws of England and of the southern European nations was such as to keep their best men in their own navies, leaving only the refuse to American ships. The consequence was that the sailors on board American ships were, in a great measure, the refuse of the maritime nations of Europe. He approved of the government shipping offices that were to be found in every seaport in England. Sailors were shipped and paid off in those offices. The names of the sailors shipped there were kept upon the registry with memoranda of their characters; so that unless a sailor had a good character he could not get employment at one of those offices.

The CHAIRMAN. Do I understand you to say that the character of American seamen is below that of the seamen of Great Britain?

Mr. RYAN. No, sir; I do not mean to say that; but we were so far above them years ago, that we had some room to fall and still to be fully equal to them.

The CHAIRMAN. Do you mean to say that American seamen have deteriorated, and are not as good as they were formerly?

Mr. RYAN. Yes; and the causes of the deterioration are going on every year.

The CHAIRMAN. How is it with the English sailors? Are they improving?

Mr. RYAN. I should judge so. I should judge that the inevitable consequences of the shipping act, which has not been long in operation, must be to keep their best men for their own ships, and to send off the refuse.

The CHAIRMAN. How is it with the officers? How do they compare with our officers?

Mr. RYAN. Our officers compare favorably with them, and perhaps they always will; but I do not think they are what they were some years ago.

Mr. CALKIN. I understood you to say that it is no great credit to a captain to procure a certificate from the Ship-masters' Association of New York.

Mr. RYAN. No, sir. The last application that we had from a captain, he was told by the chartering party that he was required to have a certificate from the Ship-masters' Association of New York, and his exclamation was, "Humbug! I have been a master for ten or a dozen years, and I have gone along safely. What is the use of one of those things?"

Mr. WELLS. Are not these certificates given under oath?

Mr. RYAN. No. sir.

Mr. WELLS. Well, what harm can it be to have a certificate?

Mr. RYAN. The harm lies in this: that that board is presumed to be a duly constituted and properly qualified board of examiners, and so long as it is in existence it tends to prevent the formation of a proper board, which should be under the authority of the government.

Mr. WELLS. How long have you been a ship-owner?

Mr. RYAN. I was a sailor for twenty-eight years, and twenty years of that time I was a master. I have been on shore for the last fifteen years; but I have been interested more or less in vessels since 1853.

Mr. WELLS. Are you familiar with commerce?

Mr. RYAN. Yes, sir.

Mr. WELLS. I understood you to say that, in your opinion, the grade of officers and men employed at present is not up to the same standard as it was some years ago.

Mr. RYAN. I do not think it is.

Mr. WELLS. Is it your opinion that that is one of the causes of the depression in our commerce?

Mr. RYAN. Yes, sir; my opinion is that that is one of the causes of the depression in our commerce. Take the matter of insurance. The premium of insurance has increased thirty per cent. within twenty years back, and I think it is mainly due to that cause.

Mr. MORRELL. Are not vessels that are running with American crews insured as cheaply as other vessels?

Mr. RYAN. I think so.

Mr. MORRELL. Were American vessels formerly insured at less rates at corresponding times?

Mr. RYAN. Yes.

Mr. MORRELL. What legislation would you recommend to encourage the building up of a better class of seamen?

Mr. RYAN. I would recommend a thorough revision of the mercantile marine law by practical men. I would have sailors shipped in every considerable port in the country by a government shipping officer. I would have the men mustered under the eye of that government officer on board the ship, before she proceeds to sea. These details are carried out fully in the bill introduced by Mr. Fish, to which I have already referred. On every vessel bound on a foreign voyage I would require that there should be an examining surgeon, and that every one of those men should be examined, as men are examined in the navy before they go to sea. Our ships go to sea with the least possible number of men, and if one of the men becomes sick or disabled it affects all the rest. I would have the men paid off at the government office when the ship returns, as is the custom in England. I think that that is the only way to break up the sailor landlord system, which is the curse of our mercantile marine. I would have this board of examiners appointed by the government, and every application for the position of master or first or second officer examined by that board, and then, when the vessel returned from sea, I would have the ship paid off at that government shipping office, and every man's character recorded—whether there was any trouble on board the vessel, any fighting, quarreling, &c.

Mr. CALKIN. In other words, you would have a government espionage on the mercantile marine of the country?

Mr. RYAN. Call it espionage or what not, I would have the same kind of a court as they have in England, before which cases of collisions, &c., are tried—such a court as that of Dr. Lushington in London, assisted by two experienced naval officers.

Mr. CALKIN. Would you have that only for the foreign trade, or to cover our coastwise trade also?

Mr. RYAN. I would have it for every case occurring on board a vessel, and for this reason, that discipline is necessary, and that it cannot be maintained by bringing those cases before the civil courts.

Mr. MORRELL. Do you not think that our whaling business of former times contributed to build up a better class of seamen by the co-operative system of paying the seamen and officers a percentage on the profits of the voyage?

Mr. RYAN. Yes, sir.

Mr. BUFFINTON. That system is carried on to-day in the whale-oil trade?

Mr. RYAN. Yes; but there are not so many whalemen as there used to be, and consequently there are not so many seamen drawn to the ocean by that business. I think the principle is a correct one, and the tendency would be certainly to improve the class of seamen.

Mr. CALKIN. Are not many of the captains now in our foreign trade and in our immense coasting trade interested in their vessels?

Mr. RYAN. A great many of them are—probably more than half of them.

Mr. CALKIN. Does not that have a tendency to make them more diligent and vigilant in their business?

Mr. RYAN. Certainly. That is the only reason why the owners of vessels require masters to have an interest. But at the same time there is a disposition, especially in certain ports of Massachusetts, not to permit masters to have an interest in their vessels, but to manage the vessels by merchants and agents at each end of the route, the master being merely the navigator. I am told that that is becoming more and more common, except down on the Cape.

Mr. CALKIN. When you spoke of the depression of our commerce being the fault of the sailor, did you intend to apply that to the coasting trade?

Mr. RYAN. It has its effect upon all branches of trade.

Mr. CALKIN. But our coasting trade has increased?

Mr. RYAN. Yes; but the same men who may be on an East Indiaman one voyage may be in the coasting trade the next voyage.

Mr. MORRELL. Do you not think that the building up of these extensive lines of foreign steamers, principally owned by foreigners, having their agencies at both ends of the route, was calculated to interfere very much with the ordinary American commerce, and that the tendency is to force the business into these channels, and to deprive the individual ship-owner of getting his ordinary share of business?

Mr. RYAN. Freight will go where it can be carried cheapest. If these great lines can carry freight more expeditiously and more cheaply than single ships, whether propelled by steam or sail, I suppose that freight will go there, and thus co-operation thoroughly organized and well managed may, I suppose, monopolize the greater part of the trade.

Mr. CALKIN. What is the sentiment in Portland in reference to the navigation laws? Are you in favor of repealing the navigation laws?

Mr. RYAN. No, sir.

Mr. CALKIN. Are you in favor of Congress passing a law allowing a drawback or bounty to the ship-building interest?

Mr. RYAN. I am.

Mr. WELLS. Are you in favor of repealing the navigation law, of allowing a drawback on the materials used in ship-building, and at the same time of retaining the coastwise trade exclusively for American-built vessels? What effect would those three measures, taken together, have upon the commercial and ship-building interests of the country?

Mr. RYAN. I do not know whether one of those measures would offset the other. The benefit that would be derived from the remission of duties on the materials entering into the construction of ships would be offset by the privilege given to our merchants to buy foreign-built ships.

Mr. BUFFINTON. Suppose that there were nothing done excepting to allow a drawback upon the materials going into the manufacture of a ship, do you believe then that there would be an increase of ship-building, or that the American ship-builders would be able to compete with foreign ship-builders, taking into view the whole state of the country at present, the capital invested in other business, and the interest that is received from that capital?

Mr. RYAN. I am satisfied that the ship-building and commerce of the country would be increased.

Mr. BUFFINTON. But if the navigation laws were repealed you think that that would offset the drawback?

Mr. RYAN. So it seems to me, so far as I have given the subject thought.

The CHAIRMAN. You gave it as your opinion that our sailors and officers have deteriorated, and that the character of foreign officers and seamen has improved. Do you believe that that is the cause or the effect of the decline in our ship-building interest?

Mr. RYAN. I think it is probably the cause. I think that the advance in the rates of insurance may be traced more directly to that than to any other cause. James Brown, a well-known Liverpool merchant, a man to whom I used to apply for advice when I was in the Liverpool trade, remarked to Captain Schofield of Brunswick six years ago, "You American masters are not what you were in years past. You are going down every year; I can see that plainly." I think that one reason of it is owing to ship-owners crowding down the rates of wages to masters.

Mr. CALKIN. You are not an old resident of Portland?

Mr. RYAN. I have been here fifteen years.

Mr. CALKIN. In case Congress passed a law allowing a drawback on the materials used in the construction of ships, so that iron steamships might be built in this country for the European trade, and also allowing them a fair subsidy, somewhat in keeping with the subsidies allowed by the English government, do you think that you could support an American line of steamers from this port, running, say, monthly at first, and getting down to weekly?

Mr. RYAN. I do not think we could; but when we come to get our railroad completed, connecting us with the West by way of Ogdensburg, I think we can do it.

Mr. MORRELL. Do you think that a line of steamers across the ocean could be supported depending chiefly upon passengers and mail service for its business?

Mr. RYAN. I have no knowledge of the management of steam lines, and I have not sufficient information to answer your question.

Mr. JOSEPH W. DYER, ship-builder, submitted his views to the committee. He said he had no doubt but that the ship-building interest would be revived by the exemption from duty of the articles entering into the construction of ships. He thought that then ships could be built in this country as cheaply as they are built in Europe.

The CHAIRMAN. What rates of wages do you pay now to ship-carpenters?

Mr. DYER. From two dollars and fifty cents to three dollars a day.

The CHAIRMAN. What were the average rates of wages from 1852 to 1860?

Mr. DYER. From one dollar and fifty cents to one dollar and seventy-five cents and two dollars a day.

The CHAIRMAN. Were your wages as low as that in 1854, 1855?

Mr. DYER. Yes, sir; they were two dollars a day. We now pay three dollars for first-class carpenters.

The CHAIRMAN. The advance is about fifty per cent.

Mr. DYER. Yes, sir.

The CHAIRMAN. Do you think that the difference in the cost of labor between here and Europe would not prevent your building ships here as cheaply as they are built in Europe?

Mr. DYER. No, sir; we should not ask any odds there. I think that our mechanics are sufficiently better than theirs to make up that difference.

The CHAIRMAN. You think that you get as much work for the money you pay as they get?

Mr. DYER. That is my opinion. That has been my experience all through life.

The CHAIRMAN. Have you built ships recently?

Mr. DYER. Not very recently. I have built some small vessels within the year. In the course of the war I built two. Previous to that I built one or two ships a year.

The CHAIRMAN. Do you know what the difference would be in the cost of a thousand-ton ship between the present time and what it was from 1852 to 1860?

Mr. DYER. Previous to the war we could build a thousand-ton ship, first-class, at from fifty-five to sixty dollars a ton, and since then from seventy-five to eighty dollars.

Mr. MORRELL. Does that increase consist chiefly in the enhanced cost of labor or of materials?

Mr. DYER. There is something of it in the labor, of course. The cost of labor on a ship will probably reach from seven thousand to eight thousand dollars.

The CHAIRMAN. I understood you to say that vessels which cost sixty dollars a ton before the war cost seventy-five dollars now?

Mr. DYER. Yes, sir; from seventy-five to eighty dollars.

The CHAIRMAN. So that, making an allowance for the difference between gold and currency, vessels can be built as cheaply now as before the war?

Mr. DYER. About the same.

The CHAIRMAN. A vessel all fitted out for sea costs no more at present than seventy-five dollars a ton?

Mr. DYER. From seventy-five to eighty dollars.

The CHAIRMAN. What effect do you think it would have upon the ship-building interest of the country to exempt from duty the materials entering into the construction of ships and at the same time to admit foreign-built ships to American registration?

Mr. DYER. I do not think the effect would be very good.

The CHAIRMAN. Do you think that the ship-building interest could be revived under that system?

Mr. DYER. I think that if you allow foreign ships to come in here and obtain American registration you cannot revive our ship-building interest.

The CHAIRMAN. Do you think that the ship-building interest could be revived if these two measures were passed at the same time?

Mr. DYER. I do not.

Mr. WELLS. I understood you to say that by a remission of the duty on the materials you can build a ship now as cheaply as you could before the war?

Mr. DYER. No, sir; there is an increase in the price of labor.

Mr. MORRELL. You are speaking of wooden ships now?

Mr. DYER. Yes, sir.

Mr. WELLS. What would be the amount of saving per ton in the building of a ship by the remission of duty on the materials?

Mr. DYER. I never went into any calculation of that kind. I know what it costs us to build a vessel and what it cost us before the war.

Mr. WELLS. What would be the advantage of the remission of the duty?

Mr. DYER. We could build so much the cheaper.

Mr. WELLS. But you could not build as cheaply as they do in England?

Mr. DYER. Probably not. We never could. Still we competed with them successfully. We considered our vessels much better than theirs.

Mr. WELLS. If you cannot build as cheaply as they, do you not think that American merchants will buy their ships abroad?

Mr. DYER. Perhaps some will if they can buy them at five dollars a ton less.

Mr. WELLS. Then what would be the advantage to the ship-building interest to have a remission of the duty if they cannot then compete with ships built in other countries?

Mr. DYER. We can compete with them if the navigation laws are not repealed. So far as my knowledge goes our laboring men are many times better than theirs. We make better ships here and have better materials. The quality of materials that enter into ships here and in the provinces is very different.

The CHAIRMAN. I understood you to say that you thought you did not pay any higher for the amount of service you obtained than is paid abroad?

Mr. DYER. Yes, sir.

The CHAIRMAN. So that there really is no difference in the cost of labor?

Mr. DYER. I do not think there is.

Mr. CALKIN. In case there is nothing done to relieve the shipping interest what effect is it going to have within the next five or ten years upon the mechanical labor connected with ship-building?

Mr. DYER. There is no other course for the mechanics except to go out of the country or leave the business.

Mr. CALKIN. Are there as many ship-carpenters to-day in Maine as there were previous to the war?

Mr. DYER. No, sir; there are not.

Mr. CALKIN. How many hours a day do your mechanics work here?

Mr. DYER. Ten hours a day.

Mr. CALKIN. Is there any difficulty in getting them to work ten hours?

Mr. DYER. None at all.

Mr. CALKIN. Can you easily make a ship-carpenter out of a house-carpenter, or out of a wood-worker of any kind?

Mr. DYER. I should prefer to get a green hand and make a ship-carpenter out of him.

Mr. BUFFINTON. I think you did not fully understand a question put to you by the chairman. I understood the chairman to ask you whether, if our currency was equal to gold, you could build a ship as cheaply now as you could before the war, and I think you answered, yes.

Mr. DYER. I did not mean to.

The CHAIRMAN. The difference that you give between the present cost of a ship in currency and the cost of a ship before the war, which was in gold, is only about the percentage of the difference between gold and currency?

Mr. DYER. From fifty-five to sixty dollars before the war, and from seventy-five to eighty dollars now.

The CHAIRMAN. That would be in the neighborhood of thirty per cent. advance.

Mr. DYER. Yes, sir.

The CHAIRMAN. Well, as there is now a difference of thirty per cent. betweeen gold and currency, that would be the only difference in the cost of a ship between now and before the war. In point of fact, the answer you gave would have that result; so that you build a ship to-day, according to that statement, as cheaply in gold as you did then?

Mr. DYER. Yes, provided we have the drawback. What I mean to say is that if this drawback were allowed us we could build a vessel as cheap as we ever did.

Mr. WELLS. If you have the drawback and the gold currency as you had previous to the war, do you think you would have any market for your ships, after you had them built?

Mr. DYER. I think we would have the same market that we always had.

Mr. WELLS. Previous to the war you had no steamers to compete with you in the domestic trade, and our foreign commerce was more extensive; the products of this country were carried to foreign countries, which is not the case now.

Mr. DYER. Not now; but I trust they will be.

The CHAIRMAN. What has been the practice usually in reference to the coppering of vessels built in the United States? Has it been done in this country or in Europe?

Mr. DYER. Of late years vessels go to the other side to copper.

The CHAIRMAN. What is the common practice in building a vessel here? Is the coppering done here?

Mr. DYER. No, sir. With a new vessel it is generally preferred that she should make a voyage first, except she is going a long vogage, such as to the Pacific. In that case they copper her here; but if a vessel is going into the southern trade and then to Liverpool or France, they do not copper her until they get on the other side, where it is cheaper.

The CHAIRMAN. When you speak of the cost of a vessel you mean her cost fitted out for sea without coppering?

Mr. DYER. Yes, sir.

Captain CHARLES M. DAVIS submitted his views to the committee. He said that he disagreed somewhat with his friend Captain Ryan about the trouble in the depression of American commerce. He thought that it was necessary to go further back than Captain Ryan did to get at the bottom of the trouble. They had got no ships now, comparatively speaking, with which to make sailors. American ships had almost disappeared from the ocean, and for very obvious reasons. During the late war the pirates destroyed many American ships, and many were transferred to foreign flags. Shipping would have to be brought back and then discipline would follow. If the United States had shipping equal to that of England or France, he would guarantee that American ship-masters could compete with the French or the English in discipline and in the sailing of their ships. He had yet to learn that American ship-masters did not take as good care of their ships and did not make as good passages as any foreign ship-masters. American ships used to be preferred to foreign ships in the carrying trade. American shipping must be built up, and in order to do that the ship-builders must have something to help them or else they could not compete with foreign ship-builders. He had letters in his pocket, which he had received lately from Quebec and from St. John, showing that he could buy ships there—first-class ships of a thousand tons—at from thirty-seven thousand to thirty-eight thousand dollars in gold, all fitted out for sea. Adding thirty per cent. to that price for the difference between gold and currency, would make their cost in the neighborhood of fifty dollars per ton in currency. They built pretty good ships in Quebec—rather better than in St. John. They had oak and hackmatack there and they built good ships. Ship-builders on this side could not compete with them in price. Mr. Dyer had said that a thousand-ton ship at present would cost seventy-five dollars a ton. He could buy such a ship to-day in Quebec for fifty dollars a ton. That was a great difference; but he thought that if American ship-builders could have the advantage of a remission of duty on the materials used in the construction of ships, and if ship-owners could get their outfits out of bond free of duty, as they did in England and France, American ship-builders and ship-owners could compete with the world, provided that there was business for them. There was a change in the freighting business. Steamers were taking the place of sailing-vessels. These latter only got heavy cargoes to carry, such as tobacco, coal, salt, &c. Only let American ships be built as cheaply as the ships of other nations, and American ship-owners would ask no odds.

The CHAIRMAN. Would we labor under any greater disadvantages now than we did prior to the war, provided the materials entering into the construction of ships were admitted free of duty? Could we then as successfully compete with foreigners on a gold basis as we did before the war?

Mr. DAVIS. I do not know why we should not, if business was the same.

The CHAIRMAN. Were there not always these periods of depression in the shipping business prior to the war, some years prosperous and some unprosperous?

Mr. DAVIS. Yes, sir; some years we could not run our ships except at a loss, and then again the business would revive, and we would make money.

The CHAIRMAN. That business is not so regular and steady as other branches of business?

Mr. DAVIS. No, sir; it is dependent upon the crops and upon a great many other things, on which other branches of business are not dependent. I take it that if you will give us a fair chance, we will build our commerce up again, and I think that when it is built up discipline will follow. I do not think that we can undertake to have discipline when we have no ships. As for our ship-masters, there is a change in them as there is in every profession, and in all classes, ministers, lawyers, doctors, &c.

Mr. BUFFINTON. Are you acquainted with Cape Cod?

Mr. DAVIS. Not on shore.

Mr. BUFFINTON. The tonnage of Cape Cod is far greater than it was formerly, and I want to ask you if you think that the seamen of Cape Cod have deteriorated at all, and if ship-owners have not seen that while the interest has kept up, the seamen have kept up?

Mr. DAVIS. I think so.

Mr. BUFFINTON. I think that if you go to Cape Cod you will find as good captains and seamen there as ever were there.

Mr. DAVIS. Yes, sir; that is true. When the interest is kept up you will find no deterioration in the officers and men.

The CHAIRMAN. You are considerably acquainted with the business on the other side of the water?

Mr. DAVIS. I am conversant with it.

The CHAIRMAN. What do you know about the business of building ships upon the Clyde and Tyne? what is the condition of the ship-building business there?

Mr. DAVIS. I can give you the price of first-class iron ships at Glasgow. First-class iron ships of a thousand tons fitted for sea, and rated for twenty years, can be had at fourteen pounds ten shillings per ton. I present to the committee the specifications and some letters on the subject. [The letters are attached to Mr. Davis's statement.] There is no use in talking of a demand for ships this year; there is no demand for ships. It is pretty hard to charter a ship for a long voyage; but that does not stop the building of ships on the other side, because there will be a demand for ships. Give us a fair chance to build ships and to run them by allowing a drawback of duty, and by allowing outfits free of duty, and we cannot be driven off the water.

The CHAIRMAN. What do you think would be the effect of such modification of the navigation laws as to admit foreign-built ships to American registry?

Mr. DAVIS. My own opinion is that it would be better for our commerce. Some interests would not be benefited by it; but I think that, on the whole, it would be generally benefited. I do not see why, if I can buy a ship at St. John for fifteen thousand dollars less than I can buy her here, I should not be allowed to do so. What difference does it make to the government when I am going to sail her under the American flag?

The CHAIRMAN. What effect would that have on the ship-building interest of the country?

Mr. DAVIS. I think it would rather head them off a little.

Mr. WELLS. I infer that you would be in favor of repealing the navigation laws and letting our merchants buy ships wherever they can buy them cheapest?

Mr. DAVIS. Yes, sir; that is my opinion.

Mr. WELLS. You are a ship-owner?

Mr. DAVIS. I have been a ship-owner. I have been retired from the business for some time. I built some ships and owned some. I have not owned any ships since the war.

Mr. WELLS. What did you have to pay for ships of a thousand tons previous to the war?

Mr. DAVIS. They cost us about fifty to fifty-five dollars a ton. Before the war I could get a good ship fitted out with a single suit of sails for a European voyage (not for the East Indian voyage) at fifty-five dollars a ton.

Mr. WELLS. The same class of ship as you can get at Quebec now for thirty-eight dollars a ton?

Mr. DAVIS. I think rather a little better.

The CHAIRMAN. Do you believe that if the duties were taken off the materials entering into the construction of ships, our ship-builders could compete with those in Europe?

Mr. DAVIS. I think so.

The CHAIRMAN. Do you believe that ships could be built here as fast as the demands of business required them?

Mr. DAVIS. Yes, sir; no doubt of it.

The CHAIRMAN. Then why are you in favor of the admission of foreign-built ships to American registry if we can build them here as fast and as cheaply?

Mr. DAVIS. You would be opening a larger market to competition. If you do not the ship-builders will put their prices up.

The CHAIRMAN. Will not competition on this side settle that as well as it settles other business?

Mr. DAVIS. Perhaps it may. We have always lived under our home competition and done very well by it; but I would rather have a larger field if I could have it.

The CHAIRMAN. I understood you to say that if we should do that, it would be rather hard upon ship-builders here. That means, I suppose, that they could not build ships if the navigation laws were repealed.

Mr. DAVIS. I do not think it would go to that extent. I think the case would rather level itself. I do not see why, if we had the same chances to build a ship here with the duties off all the materials, we would not do so as well and as cheaply as they do on the other side. If we can, so be it; then we will buy our ships at home; but if we can buy them cheaper abroad, I would prefer to be at liberty to do so.

The CHAIRMAN. What would be the effect upon the general interest of the country of allowing that?

Mr. DAVIS. I think it would be better for the whole of the country.

Mr. CALKIN. If Congress should repeal the navigation law and allow American merchants to go abroad and buy their ships, and at the same time allow a drawback to the builders here, do you think that the builders here could live and compete with the foreign market at once, and that our ship-building interest would grow up side by side with the ship-building interest of England?

Mr. DAVIS. In regard to wooden ships I think so; I do not know why it should not be so. As to iron ships we cannot compete with the English in ten or twenty years. We cannot learn to build ships here as they do on the Clyde. I do not think that we can compete with the iron ship-building interest of England for the present; I think we can compete with them in wooden ships.

Mr. CALKIN. What effect would it have to repeal the navigation law and to allow a drawback—what effect on the whole general interest of the country, on the wealth and labor of the country? Would it advance or deteriorate it?

Mr. DAVIS. I think it would advance it. It would give us a stimulus and a life which we have not seen for some time.

The CHAIRMAN. I believe you have stated that it was a very common practice for masters of vessels to be interested in their vessels. Is it also a very common practice for the builders of vessels to be interested as owners?

Mr. DAVIS. Yes, sir; here in our State it has been always so.

The CHAIRMAN. What would be the tendency of building ships abroad and bringing them here? Would it be to create a foreign interest in the vessels and to build up a really foreign interest in our navigation? While our ships were nominally American, would they not be really foreign?

Mr. DAVIS. I do not know why it should be so. If I want to buy a ship I buy her and run her for my own purpose and under my own flag; I do not know why there should be any foreign interest in her.

The CHAIRMAN. If you build a vessel here the builder has generally an interest in her. Now suppose you bought your ship abroad, would not that be the operation of the thing—that the foreign ship-builder would retain an interest in her?

Mr. DAVIS. I should not think so. I should not want to have foreigners owning with me. My experience and observation here are that our folks do not like very much to own ships with foreigners.

The CHAIRMAN. That is because we cannot own them with foreigners. But suppose that condition of things should cease?

Mr. DAVIS. I do not know why it should be more so here than in France or Germany or other places. They have always had the privilege of buying their ships abroad, and they never have filled up their commerce with American ship-owners or British ship-owners.

The CHAIRMAN. Have they ever really been in the condition that we are in?

Mr. DAVIS. They have been in a condition that they can buy our ships and put them under their own flag.

The CHAIRMAN. Have we ever had that advantage over them that they have over us now?

Mr. DAVIS. No, sir; I do not think so. They have got us where they can handle us just as they have a mind to.

Mr. CALKIN. Do you believe that it is the policy of the government to encourage iron ship-building?

Mr. DAVIS. No, sir; I do not think so. I should think it would be costing the country too much to undertake now to build iron ships so as to compete with other nations. I should rather husband our own resources and wait until we get stronger.

Mr. MORRELL. You believe that a large proportion of American commerce across the ocean is done in iron ships?

Mr. DAVIS. Yes, sir.

Mr. MORRELL. Then are you prepared to surrender that ocean commerce entirely to foreign-built vessels?

Mr. DAVIS. No, sir; I would buy them and put them under our flag. The ships are yours when you buy them.

Mr. MORRELL. Do you not think that it is the policy of the government to encourage that interest, and to have mechanics to build iron ships as well as wooden ones?

Mr. DAVIS. No, sir; I do not think it public policy to build iron ships here and to protect them by a protective tariff. If we can build iron ships here as cheaply as they do in England, let us build them. I go a good deal for free trade, and to let the smartest take the lead. I believe that this young country will do better in that way than in the other way. I do not like so much red tape, so much tied-up business. I think we should do better if we had more liberty.

Mr. MORRELL. Then you believe it better to sacrifice that interest, at present, as you know we cannot immediately compete with iron ship-builders abroad?

Mr. DAVIS. There is no sacrifice if we cannot do it.

Mr. MORRELL. Iron ships have been built in this country, and can be built now to some extent.

Mr. DAVIS. Time will bring it along, no doubt. We cannot build iron ships here now at anything like the price that we can buy them for across the water. If we undertake to build iron ships who is going to pay the bills?

Mr. CALKIN. Are you in favor of admitting back vessels that were once under the American flag, and that were put under a foreign flag during the war?

Mr. DAVIS. No, sir. Let them die off; they will soon die off, the general age of a ship is from six to eight years.

Mr. Davis submitted to the committee the following business letters:

ST. JOHN, N. B., *September* 27, 1869.

DEAR SIRS: I have your note of 23d instant. In reply, beg to say that the last sale of a seven year veritas classed ship was, hull and spars, twenty-five dollars, gold, per ton, and outfits, with wire rigging, would cost not over ten dollars per ton, gold. This sale was made under peculiar circumstances, and was rather *under* the market; but no doubt a ship of similar class could be contracted for at twenty-six dollars per ton, anything from one thousand tons and upwards. Six years' class at veritas can be produced at twenty-four dollars per ton, outfits at the same rate as dearer vessels.

I am yours, truly,

WM. THOMSON.

Messrs. C. M. DAVIS, *Portland.*

English measurement about the same as American new measurement.

C. M. D. & CO.

QUEBEC, *September* 30, 1869.

DEAR SIRS: In reply to your favor of September 23, we have ascertained that the cost of building ships in this place is as follows: A 1, seven years, 1,000 tons, not coppered, but copper fastened up to the lower deck stringers, and the usual Quebec outfit, $38 gold per registered ton; for a 1,500-ton ship as above, the cost would not exceed $37 per ton.

The highest price any of our first-class builders have named is $39 per ton, and we are satisfied that, at these figures, you could contract to build a really first-class ship.

Yours, truly,

For R. R. DOBELL & CO.,
T. BECKETT.

Messrs. C. M. DAVIS & CO.,
Portland, Maine.

English measurement about the same as American new measurement.

C. M. D. & CO.

Mr. CYRUS F. SARGENT said that he had been building ships for some fifteen years, but had never sailed any himself. He had been no ship-owner.

The CHAIRMAN. Do you believe that if the duties were taken off ship-building materials the ship-building interest of this country would revive?

Mr. SARGENT. Undoubtedly it would.

The CHAIRMAN. Do you think that we can compete with Great Britain in building wooden ships?

Mr. SARGENT. I think we could if we had a drawback upon all the materials that enter into the construction of ships. As it is, after a ship is built here we cannot copper her here, on account of the expense. We take a lower rate of freight than we would otherwise take, for the purpose of sending her to Europe to have her coppered.

The CHAIRMAN. Do they copper a ship on the other side as well as they do here?

Mr. SARGENT. Yes, sir, I think they do.

Mr. WELLS. What is the cost per ton of coppering a first-class ship?

Mr. SARGENT. To copper a thousand-ton ship would cost, I think, about six thousand dollars. That includes the docking of the ship, the cost of the copper, and putting it on.

The CHAIRMAN. Do you believe, if the materials entering into the construction of vessels were exempt from duty, that ships could be built as fast as the demands of business required them?

Mr. SARGENT. Yes, sir, wooden ships could be. I have talked with ship-builders from Quebec and St. John, and the information I received from them is somewhat different from that which Captain Davis has stated. My understanding is that ships there cost more than Captain Davis has stated, and I think we can build better ships than they can; we have better materials. Our southern pine is one of the best articles that goes into the construction of a ship, and we can get it cheaper than any people in the world.

Mr. WELLS. Can you get it any cheaper than they can get it in the provinces? Have they not the right to go to North Carolina for it, and take it into the provinces free of duty?

Mr. SARGENT. I do not know whether there is any duty on it or not.

The CHAIRMAN. Do you think that we sail our ships as cheaply as the English sail their ships? Do you think that an American ship-owner could afford to run a ship in competition with foreign ship-owners, provided he can obtain her as cheaply?

Mr. SARGENT. It is my opinion that the English sail their ships for less than we do. They have a larger number of men, and they pay them higher wages than we do. But we ship our men in Liverpool or London, and they get the best men. The American ship only gets the rejected men that the English ships will not take.

Mr. WELLS. What is the policy of shipping the poorest men they can find?

Mr. SARGENT. Before a sailor in Liverpool can go on board an English ship, he must have a certificate from the last master that he was under; he must have a certificate of good moral character and efficiency. The consequence is that the English ships take all the good men, and leave the American ships only the "runaways" and desperate men, whom it is hard to manage. They come right on board, and no questions are asked, and the American ships take them.

Mr. MORRELL. What is your opinion in reference to the repeal of the navigation laws? Do you believe it best for American commerce?

Mr. SARGENT. I should not think it would be, except all the tariff laws are repealed together, and let us have free trade in everything.

Mr. CALKIN. What do you mean by that?

Mr. SARGENT. I mean, to have general free trade all over the country in everything.

Mr. CALKIN. What effect would the repeal of the navigation laws have upon the general interest of the country?

Mr. SARGENT. That alone, I should think, would operate against the ship-building business of the country.

Mr. CALKIN. Would it not eventually transfer our ship-yards to foreign countries?

Mr. SARGENT. As Mr. Dyer remarked, it would shut up the ship-yards here; but if you make it free trade in all things, I think we can compete with foreigners.

Mr. CALKIN. I suppose it is simply a question whether our laboring men shall be reduced to the level of the laboring men of other nations. Would not that be the effect?

Mr. SARGENT. I should not think it would.

Mr. CALKIN. Are you well acquainted with most of the ship-owners of Portland?

Mr. SARGENT. I know quite a number of them—perhaps the majority.

Mr. CALKIN. Can you tell what their sentiment is in regard to the repeal of the navigation laws?

Mr. SARGENT. I have never exchanged views on the subject with the ship-owners of Portland. I built, during the war, a ship of about eleven hundred and fifty tons, ready for sea, and I believe she only cost me $41,000 in gold. That was in 1864 or 1865, I believe.

The CHAIRMAN. The premium on gold was very high at that time?

Mr. SARGENT. Yes. I am of opinion that a ship can be built for gold now cheaper than she could be before the war. It seems to me that the great difficulty is the depreciation in the currency.

The CHAIRMAN. Do you mean to say that you can build a ship cheaper now than you could then, paying the duty on the materials?

Mr. SARGENT. Yes, sir; other gentlemen may differ with me, but that is my opinion. The last ship I built was fifteen hundred odd tons. She was ready for sea, (not coppered,) had eighteen months' provisions on board, and she only cost about sixty dollars a ton. She went to sea two years ago.

The CHAIRMAN. Then, according to your present statement, we really do build our ships as cheap as we ever did?

Mr. SARGENT. I think so; there is the trouble about this depreciated currency. It is a speculating matter. When one wins another loses.

That was the reason why the ship we built during the war cost such a small amount in gold; for exchange was then at two hundred and fifty.

Mr. WELLS. Did you build her on English account?

Mr. SARGENT. No, sir; but I made a contract with some of the owners that the account should be made up in gold.

The CHAIRMAN. What, then, do you consider to be the difficulty under which we labor at present in reviving our commerce? Why do we not build ships?

Mr. SARGENT. The great trouble is in the depreciated currency. People say, "I can get a better interest for my money than I can by putting it in a ship." They do not wait to consider that they are really paying only seventy cents on the dollar. They deceive themselves in the matter of the currency, and you cannot get them to build a ship that would cost eighty or ninety dollars a ton in currency.

The CHAIRMAN. Then there is only an imaginary difference in the price; it is not a real difference?

Mr. SARGENT. Only an imaginary difference.

Mr. CALKIN. Do you live in Portland?

Mr. SARGENT. No, sir.

Mr. CALKIN. Where do you reside?

Mr. SARGENT. In Yarmouth.

Mr. CALKIN. That is a ship-building place?

Mr. SARGENT. Yes, sir.

Mr. CALKIN. What is the sentiment of the ship-owners of Yarmouth in reference to the repeal of the navigation laws?

Mr. SARGENT. I do not know that I have ever talked with them about that; but we have talked a good deal in reference to free trade for everything and for everybody. And as to our ship-building interest, we feel satisfied that we could compete with any other people, so far as we are concerned, if we had free trade.

The CHAIRMAN. Then you do not want the principle of free trade applied to ships alone?

Mr. SARGENT. No, sir.

Mr. WELLS. Do you not find from experience that gentlemen who have heretofore had their money invested in ship property make more interest now by putting their money in the national banks and railroads, and other speculations, and that that is a reason for the depression of the ship-building interest?

Mr. SARGENT. Yes, sir. The English ship-owner will be satisfied with four or five per cent. interest on his money; but here in America nothing will satisfy people less than eight per cent., and many of them put their money in bonds and securities. The English are easier satisfied.

Mr. WELLS. Prior to the war were not ship-owners making more than eight or ten per cent.?

Mr. SARGENT. Yes, sir.

Mr. CALKIN. What is the average life of American ships?

Mr. SARGENT. I believe underwriters state it at about eight years.

The CHAIRMAN. What is the life of ships built in the Provinces?

Mr. SARGENT. I do not know.

Mr. CALKIN. Have we not had the reputation always of building better ships here than they do in the Provinces?

Mr. SARGENT. We always had.

Mr. CALKIN. Does not the English capitalist calculate more closely on his percentage on the loss being a total loss than an American does on his investment in an American-built ship?

Mr. SARGENT. In the north of Europe and in England, and many

European countries, they only insure against a total loss. If a ship touches bottom they pay a partial loss; but if any other damage results, that is unless she touches bottom, the underwriter does not pay any loss.

Mr. BUFFINTON. How much more do you pay for the materials that go into a ship now than you had to pay for them before the war?

Mr. SARGENT. I have never made a calculation about that.

Mr. CALKIN. Do you not pay more for iron and more for duck than you did before the war?

Mr. SARGENT. Yes, sir.

Mr. BUFFINTON. Do you not really pay from ten to thirty per cent. more for every article that goes into the construction of a ship than you paid before the war?

Mr. SARGENT. Taking all the materials, I should say that they would not cost thirty per cent. more than they did before the war.

Mr. BUFFINTON. I say from ten to thirty per cent.

Mr. SARGENT. Yes, they would.

Mr. BUFFINTON. I ask you, then, this question, because it is thought that there must have been an error in a remark you made, and that you could not have intended to say what you did. You said that you could build a ship to-day just as cheap with gold as you could before the war. How could you do it with labor higher, and materials higher?

Mr. SARGENT. The difference in labor and the difference in the cost of materials do not amount to the difference in value between gold and paper.

Mr. BUFFINTON. But before the war, iron and all the materials that went into the construction of ships were from ten to thirty per cent. less than they are now. Do you mean to say that after paying the increased cost of these articles you can still build a ship as cheaply as you could before the war?

Mr. SARGENT. Either you or I do not understand it. The increased price of the materials that go into the construction of a ship does not amount to the premium that there is on gold, say thirty-five per cent.

Mr. BUFFINTON. Iron costs a great deal more; sail-cloth costs a great deal more; and in fact every article costs more.

Mr. SARGENT. Yes, more in paper money.

Mr. BUFFINTON. Do they not cost more in gold?

Mr. SARGENT. No, sir; southern pine costs less in gold.

Mr. BUFFINTON. How about iron?

Mr. SARGENT. All the difference is just the duty.

Mr. BUFFINTON. If you are correct I do not see that the country needs any legislation on the subject.

The CHAIRMAN. How much do the duties on the materials in a thousand-ton wooden ship amount to?

Mr. SARGENT. I have never seen the figures made. I have talked with a number of ship-owners on the subject, and they have put the amount from $10,000 to $15,000; perhaps $12,000 might come nearer to it.

The CHAIRMAN. The cost of labor is somewhat higher here than in England.

Mr. SARGENT. I suppose so.

The CHAIRMAN. I understood you to say that we can really build a ship now as cheap in gold as a ship can be built for in Great Britain in gold.

Mr. SARGENT. That I do not know. I did not make that statement.

The CHAIRMAN. I understood you to say that the difference was only about the difference in currency.

Mr. SARGENT. I made the statement that we could build a ship here in gold as cheaply as we did before the war.

The CHAIRMAN. The tariff has been increased very largely. Do I understand you to say that ships can be built, paying the duty on the materials, as cheaply now as when there were no duties paid?

Mr. SARGENT. That is the question you all want to know. I answer as I did at first, that if you let the duties go just as they are, we can build a ship now as cheaply in gold as we could before the war.

The CHAIRMAN. Then how do you overcome the disadvantage resulting from the increase in the tariff?

Mr. SARGENT. A good deal of it comes out of the labor. We paid for good men before the war from one dollar and seventy-five cents to two dollars a day. Two dollars would be the average price. Now we pay only two dollars and fifty cents.

The CHAIRMAN. Then you pay quite as high in gold now as you did before the war?

Mr. SARGENT. No, sir; we do not. If you add thirty-five per cent. to what we paid before the war, you will find we do not pay so much now.

Mr. WELLS. I understood you to say that in 1864–'65 you built a ten-hundred-and-fifty-ton ship at a cost of forty-one thousand dollars?

Mr. SARGENT. Yes, sir. That was in the time of the war, when gold was very high. Exchange was selling for about two hundred and fifty.

Mr. WELLS. Can you tell me what the duty on iron and the duties on the materials that go into ship-building are now, compared with what they were in 1860?

Mr. SARGENT. I do not think I can.

Mr. WELLS. The difference is not over ten per cent., is it?

Mr. SARGENT. I do not recollect. Before the war I recollect buying iron for about forty-two dollars per ton.

The CHAIRMAN. What effect would it have on our navigation interest if Congress were to admit foreign-built ships free? Would it have a tendency to carry the ownership partly abroad?

Mr. SARGENT. I do not know. I should hardly think it would; for all owners like to have the other owners as near home as they can get them. If you are connected in business with men, you want them where you can see them occasionally; and that would be the case with ship-owners.

The CHAIRMAN. Do you mean to say that, as a general rule, we pay less to our sailors than the English do?

Mr. SARGENT. Yes, sir; the wages of sailors are lower in an American ship than in an English ship.

The CHAIRMAN. I understood you to say that the duty is from ten to fifteen dollars a ton in gold on all the materials that enter into the construction of a ship, and yet you say that notwithstanding that, you can build ships as cheaply as they can build them on the other side?

Mr. SARGENT. Not on the other side; you confound that thing; but I say that we can build them as cheaply as we built them before the war.

The CHAIRMAN. Did we build our ships as cheaply before the war as they built them on the other side?

Mr. SARGENT. We built them cheaper.

The CHAIRMAN. Then, of course, we still build them cheaper than they do on the other side. That is a very remarkable statement; and what I want to get at is, how you account for that condition of things, that we can pay an increased duty of ten to fifteen dollars a ton in gold, and still build not only cheaper here, but cheaper than where all the materials are free of duty.

Mr. SARGENT. It is because our greenbacks are worth only seventy cents on the dollar.

The CHAIRMAN. Put the two in gold. Suppose that you build for gold, and that your foreign competitor builds for gold?

Mr. SARGENT. Yes, but we do not build for gold; we build for paper, and then we reduce the cost to gold.

The CHAIRMAN. And you build for less on this paper basis?

Mr. SARGENT. When it is reduced to gold, the ship does not cost any more than it did before the war.

The CHAIRMAN. Then there is great advantage to ship-builders to build for paper?

Mr. SARGENT. Yes, sir.

The CHAIRMAN. Then, instead of the currency being a disadvantage, it is an advantage?

Mr. SARGENT. It operates against the laborer; it comes out of him.

The CHAIRMAN. I understood you to say that you paid about two dollars a day on the average in 1860, and that you now pay two dollars and a half. Is not that an increase of twenty-five per cent.?

Mr. SARGENT. Yes, reckoning gold and paper equal.

The CHAIRMAN. He can take his paper and sell it, and still get two dollars in gold?

Mr. SARGENT. O no; you must take off thirty-five per cent., which will leave him less than two dollars in gold. If he got two dollars in gold before the war, that gold would cost now two dollars and sixty cents, and we only give him two dollars and a half.

The CHAIRMAN. That makes ten cents a day difference, and that certainly cannot account for all the other differences.

Mr. SARGENT. There is other labor connected with ship-building besides the carpenter labor. I do not think that ship-carpenters are in as good a condition now as they were before the war.

The CHAIRMAN. Does not that result from the fact that they are not employed fully?

Mr. SARGENT. I don't know about that. They are employed about the same. In Yarmouth they are.

The CHAIRMAN. Do you mean to say that ship-building is as prosperous now in Yarmouth as it was before the war, and that there is as much doing there now as there was before the war?

Mr. SARGENT. More. There has been more doing for the last year than there had been before the war.

Mr. WELLS. What class of ships do they build there?

Mr. SARGENT. Ships for the coastwise trade, and for the European trade, both.

Mr. WELLS. What did ships cost before the war?

Mr. SARGENT. A thousand-ton ship would be built for from fifty-five thousand to sixty thousand dollars.

Mr. WELLS. What would you build the same class of ship for to-day, in paper money?

Mr. SARGENT. I should think it could be built for eighty thousand dollars. I was told the other day that one was built in Kennebunk of a thousand tons, and was sold to a party in Boston for seventy-six thousand dollars. There are some materials which would be worth more in gold than they were before the war.

Mr. GILES LORING, of Yarmouth, stated that he was a practical ship-builder. That had been his business for quite a number of years. He had acted as a boss carpenter and contractor. He had built ships before the war, and had built some during the war, and some since the war. He could hardly agree with his friend, Mr. Sargent, and he could not exactly agree with his friend Mr. Davis, in his answer to one question about foreign capitalists. He (Mr. Loring) thought that if Americans bought their ships abroad, foreign capitalists would certainly have an interest in them. The lumber which he used to get before the war from Canada, for the floor and frame of the ship, at from ten to thirteen dollars a ton, delivered in the cars at Portland, he had now to pay eighteen and twenty dollars a ton for. He had got one floor and top from there at ten dollars, and this year he had to pay nineteen dollars for the same. Therefore, Mr. Sargent's idea that ships could be built just as cheap now as before the war, on a gold basis, he certainly could not agree with.

The CHAIRMAN. What is the difference in the cost of a thousand-ton ship now and before the war?

Mr. LORING. I should give it as my idea, that the difference amounts to about twenty per cent. more now than before the war.

The CHAIRMAN. Do you mean in gold?

Mr. LORING. Yes, sir, in gold. But still I may be mistaken. Gold and paper were one and the same thing before the war. He disagreed with his friend Mr. Sargent in stating that as many ships were built now as before the war. The money which used to be invested in ships was now invested in government bonds, because the owners could do better in that way. All that worked against the ship-building business. It seemed to him that if there were not drawbacks allowed, (although he was not able to say what they should be,) it would be but a few years before all the ship-builders would have to leave Maine and go out West.

The CHAIRMAN. State your opinion as to what ought to be done.

Mr. LORING. I should rather leave that to my friend, the chairman of the committee, because he is a more practical man in that business than I am.

The CHAIRMAN. What relief would enable you to build ships in competition with foreign ship-builders?

Mr. LORING. If you take the duties off everything that we have to use in ships, we can compete with any other nation.

The CHAIRMAN. Do you think that that would revive the ship-building interest?

Mr. LORING. I think it would. The great trouble now is that ships cost so much, and that people are not willing to put their money into them.

The CHAIRMAN. You then give it as your opinion, that if the duties were taken off all the materials that enter into the construction of ships, the ship-builders of this country would be able to build ships as cheaply as they are built abroad. And you think that if ships could be built as cheaply here as abroad men would invest their money in them, and that that would tend to revive the business?

Mr. LORING. That is my idea; and if something is not done, it will be the ruin of Maine; for when our ship-building interest is gone, Maine is gone.

The CHAIRMAN. What would be the effect upon the ship-building interest if foreign ships were allowed to come in and be nationalized, provided at the same time that you were allowed drawbacks on the materials entering into the construction of ships? Could you then compete with foreign ship-builders?

Mr. LORING. I should hardly think we could.

The CHAIRMAN. If you were protected from that competition for a number of years, do you think that then you could do it?

Mr. LORING. I think we could, if we had protection until we got a start.

The CHAIRMAN. Could you have stood such competition prior to the war?

Mr. LORING. I should hardly know how to answer that question. My opinion is that we could at that time, but that we cannot now.

The CHAIRMAN. But you think that after a few years you could?

Mr. LORING. I think that, after getting once started again, we could.

The CHAIRMAN. What rate of wages do you pay now?

Mr. LORING. I paid this year all the way from two dollars and a half to three dollars.

The CHAIRMAN. What did you pay to the same class of mechanics before the war?

Mr. LORING. All the way from one dollar and seventy-five cents up to two dollars. I built one vessel on which I paid only one dollar and seventy-five cents. That was eight years ago. At that time I paid a cent and a half a pound for iron.

The CHAIRMAN. How was it from 1852 to 1854?

Mr. LORING. I worked as a carpenter then, and at that time wages were all the way from one dollar and a half to two dollars. Wages at that time were pretty high.

The CHAIRMAN. What wages were you paid as a carpenter at that time?

Mr. LORING. Two dollars and a half.

The CHAIRMAN. Were you a master carpenter?

Mr. LORING. No, sir; I was a common carpenter at that time.

Mr. CALKIN. When did you commence as a master builder?

Mr. LORING. In 1855.

Mr. CALKIN. How many vessels have you built since that time?

Mr. LORING. Speaking of the cost of coppering vessels, a few years ago I had a ship of seven hundred tons coppered abroad. The cost of the coppering of that vessel was just about equal to the cost of coppering one of four hundred tons here. I know that, because I had at that time one coppered abroad and one coppered in New York. A great many of our New York ship-owners prefer to have their ships coppered at home.

Mr. CALKIN. Do they think that the work is done better here?

Mr. LORING. I do not know that it is done better; but I believe they would get it done just as cheap, notwithstanding that they pay higher wages here than are paid abroad.

The CHAIRMAN. Are you a ship-owner now?

Mr. LORING. Yes, sir.

The CHAIRMAN. As a general thing, do those who build ships in your section retain an interest in the vessel?

Mr. LORING. As a general thing they do. That is the way I have worked. A captain comes to me sometimes with one-fourth and sometimes with one-half the cost of a vessel, and I have to look out to make up the difference. Sometimes I have one-fourth of it entered in my name; sometimes more, and sometimes not so much.

The CHAIRMAN. How many vessels are you interested in?

Mr. LORING. Only four.

The CHAIRMAN. How large a class of vessels are you owning in?

Mr. LORING. The vessels I have built have been from four hundred to nine hundred tons.

The CHAIRMAN. Is it the practice of ship-masters also to own parts of the vessel?

Mr. LORING. Yes, sir.

The CHAIRMAN. Then the ownership is divided between the ship-builder, the ship-master, and the merchant who does the business?

Mr. LORING. Yes, sir; and as they say with us, "all the parish." Sometimes the joiner has an interest; sometimes the calker, the blacksmith, the farmer, and the trader. In fact, everything of that kind with us is brought into the shipping interest.

The CHAIRMAN. So far as you know throughout the State, is that the manner in which ships are built and owned?

Mr. LORING. I should suppose it was, but I do not pretend to say that it is. There is one thing which works a little against the ship-builder; in the first place, the government established eight hours for a day's labor. Now, for a ship-builder to employ men in that way is rather out of the question. Perhaps it is right for the government to do so; but the consequence is that Mr. A, Mr. B, Mr. C, and Mr. D, ship-carpenters, will say, "I must get into the government employment, because I have only to work eight hours, and I can get a little more pay than by working ten hours in private employment." I should say that this year from four to six of our best carpenters have gone to the Kittery navy yard. We thus lose from this class some of our best men.

The CHAIRMAN. I supposed that the navy yard being so far off would not have had much effect on you?

Mr. LORING. I think the effect is considerable. The distance does not make any difference; they will go sometimes to Boston and sometimes to New York to get into the navy yards. People do not like to work ten hours a day if they can get the same wages by working only eight hours.

Mr. MORRELL. As a ship-builder, ship-carpenter, and master-builder, what is your opinion as to the eight-hour law? Do you think it calculated to benefit ship-carpenters or not?

Mr. LORING. I should give it as my opinion that it was of no benefit at all to them, unless it was so arranged that the ship-carpenter could work after hours and get pay for extra time. Then it would be a benefit.

Mr. MORRELL. Do you believe that any United States law regulating the price of labor, or the hours of labor, is of any benefit to the laboring man?

Mr. LORING. I do not think it is.

Mr. CALKIN. Do you mean to say that it is no benefit to him physically, mentally, or financially?

Mr. LORING. I do not think it is in any way. When I began to work, we used to work, I may say, from sun to sun. I was opposed to that, after a while, and then we got the ten-hour system. I was in favor of that and am now. I believe ten hours long enough for a man to work; but when you reduce the hours of labor below that, I think you are cutting them down too much.

Mr. CALKIN. Do you not believe that the government gets the pick of the mechanics in the ship-yards—ship-builders, calkers, iron workers, &c.—by adopting the eight-hours system?

Mr. LORING. Without doubt the government gets many of the best men by adopting that system, but still, if you take these best men, put them into the government service, and let them work awhile there, they will soon get so that they do not do much work. I am not saying that for the purpose of coming down on my friends the carpenters, but it is perfectly natural for men, when they get into the government service, to do so. The tonnage dues have been rather severe upon ship-owners. If there could be something done to help the ship-owners and ship-builders in Maine, I think that Maine would actually come up again. But if things go on as they have been going for some years back, Maine will certainly be depreciated, and it must necessarily be so.

Mr. JAMES E. SIMPSON said that he was a ship-builder, and had been engaged in the repairing of ships up to 1863. He then went to Boston to construct a dock for the South Point Dry Dock Company of Boston. He had gone into the business of building and repairing in 1848, and from that time he had more or less to do with ships, both in repairing and constructing, and in the construction of docks and the docking of ships.

The CHAIRMAN. What disadvantages do we labor under in the repairing of ships in comparison with other countries?

Mr. SIMPSON. In 1853–'54–'55–'56 we could get yellow material for about eighteen to twenty cents a pound. Now it is from twenty-seven to thirty cents a pound. It is so with all the materials that enter into the construction of ships. We could then have bolts, spikes, &c., at from three and a quarter to three and a half cents a pound. Now we cannot buy the raw material short of five or six cents a pound. Ships will not be coppered on this side when they can be coppered much cheaper on the other side. In 1859–'60 and 1861 the docks of New York were employed all the time, and ships were entered three, four, five, and six weeks ahead for their turns to get on the dock. Now, the reverse is the case, the docks lie five and six weeks without a ship. What is the cause of it? The natural depression in the shipping business which is caused by the tariff. The commerce of the country is conveyed in foreign bottoms. There are to-day some eighty or ninety steamers running to New York, all foreign vessels. Do they ever dock in New York? No, unless it is for mere temporary repairs. A statement had been made by an Englishman that there were no mechanics in this country who understood their business. He (Mr. Simpson) considered that that was a slur. An English vessel had been recently taken into the Erie basin and repaired in just half the time it would have occupied to repair her in England. Where six men were employed in this country the English required to use sixteen. As to the difference in labor, he (Mr. Simpson) thought that, although the nominal price of labor was cheaper here than abroad, there was more work got out of mechanics in this country in proportion to the wages paid.

The CHAIRMAN. What rates of wages are paid in New York?

Mr. SIMPSON. Wages there now are four dollars a day.

The CHAIRMAN. What are the rates here in Portland?

Mr. SIMPSON. I think the prices are from \$3 50 to \$4. I have, while constructing a dock here, paid from \$2 25 to \$3 25. The average is about \$2 50 per day, and four dollars in New York. That is on old work. On new work I should judge that it is somewhat in the neighborhood of \$3 50 a day in New York. They work one hour more on new work than they do on old. In Boston they work ten hours on new work, and eight hours on old. In New York they work nine hours on old and ten hours on new work. I helped to dock the first ship that was ever docked in the Charlestown navy yard—the Constitution.

The CHAIRMAN. You have become a contractor and a patentee of docks?

Mr. SIMPSON. I started and constructed a dock on my own idea, and on my own patent; and I have now superintended the construction of six of them.

The CHAIRMAN. You are one of the owners of the new dock here?

Mr. SIMPSON. Yes.

Mr. CALKIN. How do you account for the difference in labor between New York and Maine? Is there the same supply of mechanics in New York as there is in other places?

Mr. SIMPSON. It is a point of strike. At the time they struck in Boston the merchants undertook to hold out the same as they did in New York. They held out for some time; but finally they made a compromise to give the men four dollars a day if they would go to work, and they allowed them to work only eight hours. There had been a half hour allowed for lunch time, which they did away with. The ship Archer went to Boston to be repaired from New York, and when she got there the men in Boston struck because they were helping to support the New York society. I think that ship-builders, repairers, &c., are suffering a great deal to-day by the eight-hour system in the navy yards. I have had men leave me in New York, and men have also left Mr. Poillon and other master-builders to go to the navy yards, because they have to work less time, and thus the best class of men are taken away from the outside business.

The CHAIRMAN. Have you any knowledge of the building of iron ships?

Mr. SIMPSON. I was connected with the building of the first iron ship in this country. She was built by Holden & Gallagher, at East Boston, for the Egyptian government. She was contracted for by George H. Stone. I have seen the construction of her. She was about as thoroughly well constructed a ship as I have ever seen. Since that I have watched more or less the construction of iron vessels. I built in 1867 two iron gates for the last dock I constructed, which were equal to about a two hundred and fifty or a three hundred ton iron vessel; and I am satisfied in my own mind that iron vessels can be constructed in this country, with proper facilities, and we having the materials at the same price that they have them abroad. I think we can compete with any nation upon any kind of ship, either wooden or iron. Let the government protect us as the English government protects its ship-builders, and in less than five years this country can compete with the world in building ships.

The CHAIRMAN. Iron ships?

Mr. SIMPSON. Any ships. Iron ships have been built at Delaware and at Chester, and at the Atlantic Works, in East Boston. They are built to-day as cheaply for gold as they can be got for gold in Europe, taking the duty off.

The CHAIRMAN. You overcome the difference in the rates of wages paid by the greater efficiency of the workmen on this side?

Mr. SIMPSON. Yes; we pay more wages, but I think we get more work for it. I think that, with the tariff off, we can build ships as cheaply as they are built on the Clyde; but as the tariff is, we cannot do so. We used to get yellow pine down South for $25 to $27 a thousand, and our white oak for three and a half to four cents a foot, or $30 to $40 a thousand. We have now to pay from $65 to $75 and $80 for white oak, and from $35 to $50 for yellow pine.

The CHAIRMAN. Is there much American iron used either in building or repairing a vessel?

Mr. SIMPSON. Not a great deal, unless we want it for strength; because the English iron is of a poorer quality. The Ulster iron commands the best price.

Mr. CALKIN. Are you in favor of repealing the navigation laws so as to allow foreign-built vessels to be brought here?

Mr. SIMPSON. No, sir.

Mr. CALKIN. If the navigation laws should be repealed, and at the same time a drawback should be allowed, could the ship-builders in this country compete successfully with the ship-builders of foreign countries?

Mr. SIMPSON. Yes, sir.

Mr. CALKIN. I mean, if we repeal the navigation laws, and at the same time take off all the duties on materials entering into the construction of ships, can we commence right there and then to compete with foreign builders?

Mr. SIMPSON. Not just to-day.

Mr. CALKIN. How long a time should the builders of this country be protected if a law of that kind should be passed?

Mr. SIMPSON. I think that if they were protected for five years they then could compete with any nation.

Mr. WELLS. I understood you to say that previous to the war the docks in New York were overtaxed, and that ships had to wait for weeks for their turns to come on the dock; but that now that is reversed. Is not that because iron vessels are used instead of wooden ones?

Mr. SIMPSON. That is somewhat the cause, but not entirely. It is not that we cannot put an iron ship on. Our government has never protected our iron ship-building, and the foreigners have taken that business from us; and for that reason our docks are lying idle.

Mr. WELLS. Is it not a fact that one steamer will do the business of four or five vessels in the European trade, and will at the same time last two or three times as long without repairs?

Mr. SIMPSON. I do not think that one steamer will do the business of four sailing vessels. A Liverpool packet ship generally makes the round voyage in from seventy-five to ninety days, and the steamer takes on an average about five weeks to make the round voyage. The steamers take the place of a little over double the number of sailing ships.

Mr. WELLS. Do you know, of your own knowledge, the cost of building steam vessels in this country?

Mr. SIMPSON. No, sir. Of course the cost varies somewhat. I think that we spend more money on our merchant ships in finish and style than is generally spent on merchant ships of other countries, and of course they cost more on that account. But if foreigners were to build ships of the same materials and finish that we do, we having a drawback on the materials, I think we could build the vessel for less than they can.

Captain J. B. COYLE, president of the Portland Steam Packet Company, said that he was interested in coasting steamers, and that they now cost nearly double what they did before the war, on account of the high duties levied on everything. Then, again, if they got the steamers, they were taxed to death to run them. Every little thing that could be stuck on in the way of taxes was stuck on. The tonnage dues were increased. They had to pay for every passenger they carried, so that after they paid all the government dues the owners had very little left, and the consequence was that people were going out of that kind of business.

Mr. CALKIN. You think that the coasting trade should be relieved by the remission of duties and taxation?

Mr. COYLE. Yes, sir.

Mr. CALKIN. The public generally would be relieved by it?

Mr. COYLE. Certainly. If we were relieved we could do better by the traveling public; we could take freights less and passengers less.

Mr. WELLS. Are you taxed more onerously than railroads are?

Mr. COYLE. I think so. I think that the government discriminates against floating property. On all our coasting steamers, if we take an alien and carry him to Boston, we must pay two dollars a head upon him; but if he goes by railroad, he goes free. The English vessels carry their paupers and emigrants into Canada, and they come down here on the railroads free. But if one of our coasting steamers brings them here, she has to be taxed so much a head for them. That is one thing against us which presses pretty hard upon steamboats. The moment we get into port a revenue officer comes on board of us, and every man and woman who is an alien is marked and has to be paid for. Queen Victoria, if she came in that way, would have to pay head money. But if you take all the paupers that were ever raised in the old country and send them here by railroad, there is no such tax levied.

Mr. WELLS. Would you be in favor of repealing the navigation laws?

Mr. COYLE. If you took the duties off, I certainly would not be in favor of having the navigation laws repealed.

Mr. WELLS. You are in favor of encouraging home industry?

Mr. COYLE. By all means. I think that is our strength as a nation, particularly in our seaports. Our best men are drifting to the West. A great many of them are leaving our seaports, particularly our mechanics, who are the bone and muscle of the country.

Mr. WELLS. Do you not think that if that law were repealed, and if American merchants were allowed to go abroad and buy their vessels, it would have a tendency to drive all the mechanics of the country out the business?

Mr. COYLE. Certainly.

Captain CYRUS STURDIVANT made some remarks in favor of removing the duties from the materials entering into the construction of ships, and thus encouraging ship-building. He trusted that Congress would give the ship-building and ship-owning interest some relief, and thus prevent the best men of Maine from going elsewhere for a living. As to steamboats they were taxed to death. They had to get their license renewed every year and to pay thirty cents on the ton for new measurement. Then the internal revenue collector exacted two and a half per cent. on all the income they receive from passengers; and when the season came round they had to pay exorbitant prices for coal. He hoped that coal would be permitted to come in free, and said that unless the ship-owning and ship-building interests had some relief in this direction all engaged in them would have to emigrate elsewhere.

Mr. PUTNAM, mayor of the city, remarked that although Portland was a leading ship-building port in the State, it was deeply interested in navigation, and he thanked the committee for the patient labor with which it was investigating this matter. He trusted that the report of the committee would convince Congress of the necessity of granting the relief so earnestly needed by the great interest of the country, ship-building.

The committee adjourned to meet in Philadelphia on the 1st of December next.

PHILADELPHIA, PA., *December* 2, 1869.

The committee met at 10 a. m.

Present, Messrs. Buffinton, Washburn, Morrell, and Mr. Lynch, chairman. Committees appointed by the Commercial Exchange, Board of Trade, and Ship-builders' Associations, of Philadelphia, Wilmington, and Baltimore, to represent those associations, were present.

FRANCIS R. COPE, of the Commercial Exchange, Philadelphia, stated that there was no business coming so directly in competition with foreign industry as the shipping interest. A foreign vessel will encounter the same difficulties, and earn the same freight as an American vessel in the same trade, and the reason why we cannot compete with foreign vessels must be either from the increased cost of building American vessels or the expense of sailing them.

With regard to the cost of building, timber is cheaper and labor cheaper in the provinces, and wooden vessels can be built cheaper there than in the United States. It is also true that iron vessels can be built at Liverpool and on the Clyde cheaper than Americans can build them.

After the first outfit of a vessel her expenses are very nearly the same, whether American or foreign. If she has to undergo any repairs, it must be at the next port, after the accident or disability occurs, whether it be in a foreign country or our own; and with regard to wages we find that the rate is regulated to a great extent by the wages of other persons employed in other branches of business; and in that respect a great increase has taken place in this country within the last few years. Some twelve or fifteen years ago the rate of wages of seamen in this country was about fifteen dollars a month, while that in England was about two pounds ten shillings. At the present time we are paying sailors thirty dollars per month, while they are paid in England about two pounds fifteen shillings. We are now sailing about four vessels between this port and Liverpool, and the difference between the cost of wages we have to pay and the cost at the rate paid in England amounts to about twenty thousand dollars a year for the four vessels.

Now, as to the cure for these evils, my opinion is that it must lie in a reduction of the tariff, which will reduce the price of everything.

The CHAIRMAN inquired whether American vessels are manned with as large crews as foreign vessels.

Mr. COPE replied there was not necessarily any difference. American vessels are frequently better manned than British, but that is a mere question of economy. Most American owners consider that it is better economy to man vessels more fully and make quicker passages than the British vessels make. As a rule, English vessels carry more apprentices than American, but not larger regular crews. As a general rule now, the crews of American sailing-vessels are perhaps more efficient than those of English vessels, but the crews of British steam-vessels are generally much more efficient than in former years.

In regard to the wages of sailors, the rate is determined by the port from which the sailor ships. A man who goes out in an American vessel at thirty dollars per month, and leaves his vessel at Liverpool or London, and again ships on another American vessel, must do so at a much lower rate. While professedly from one-half to two-thirds of our American crews are American in point of fact, there is no more than one American to five or six foreigners. If you could discharge your crew as soon as you reached a foreign port and reship a crew from an English port, the difference in the cost of wages would amount practically to very little; but the law requires you to carry your crew for the round trip, unless they leave voluntarily.

The CHAIRMAN inquired whether, if we could build our ships as cheaply as foreign ships are built, we could compete for the carrying trade of the world.

Mr. COPE replied that that was his opinion; certainly if the tariff were reduced so as to reduce the rate of wages.

Mr. MORRELL asked whether that remedy would not be worse than the evil.

Mr. COPE responded that that was for the committee to judge. We have lost our commerce to a great extent, and are losing more every year. No doubt a part of it would be regained by a return to specie payment, and he did not know of any remedy short of that and a reduction of the tariff. He wished, however, in this matter to be understood as speaking for himself alone, and not for the committee which he represented. It seemed to him that if you are to protect one interest and then to protect another to counteract that, there would be no end to it. It was the high price of wages, the high price of food, and the high price of everything else which was in the way of our regaining our old prosperity in respect to the shipping interest.

Mr. WASHBURN inquired whether woolen goods and breadstuffs were not now as cheap as before our departure from a specie basis.

Mr. COPE replied that food was as cheap, but that woolen goods were not as cheap in this country as in England and France.

The CHAIRMAN asked whether the labor employed in the old country was as efficient as that employed in this, and whether the greater skill of our mechanics did not, to a certain extent, overcome the difference of price.

Mr. COPE replied that it furnished a certain amount of compensation without doubt, but there was not the same difference there used to be, nor was there the same difference in the vessels produced in the two countries, British steam vessels being now much superior to what they used to be, and our officers of steam vessels probably not quite as good as in former years. Business having declined in this regard, the best class of men had, to a great extent, sought other occupations.

The CHAIRMAN inquired whether the masters of American vessels were not, as a general rule, in part owners of the vessels.

Mr. COPE said that those employed in the coasting trade probably were.

Mr. WASHBURN asked whether it would be possible so to construct lines of steamers for mercantile purposes as to be readily converted into vessels of war when needed for that purpose.

Mr. COPE said he could not give any opinion upon that subject, as he had paid no attention to the building of iron vessels.

Mr. HENRY WINDSOR, of the Philadelphia Board of Trade, remarked that he had no doubt steamers could be built suitably for both purposes; it being true of modern war steamers that only a few guns were required, and those of long range, and that it might be practicable to devote a portion of the very large amount now expended on ships of war for the purpose of building mercantile vessels capable of being converted into naval vessels in time of war.

HENRY R. EDMUNDS, chairman of committee of ship-owners for Pennsylvania, New Jersey, and Delaware, said he intended to have prepared statistics and statements affecting the shipping interest of the country, but having failed to receive the notice sent him, he had been unable to do so. The association with which he was connected was more directly interested in the coasting trade than in the foreign ocean mercantile service, and he knew comparatively little in regard to building ships for foreign commerce. It was found in building vessels for the coasting trade that an onerous tax was encountered on all materials from the commencement of construction until the vessel was ready to go to sea. Everything entering into the construction of a vessel was taxed. If the tax was taken off vessels could be built profitably in this country, although they might not be built quite as cheaply as in Europe; yet American shippers would prefer to employ vessels sailing under an American register. Another difficulty to be met with was, however, in the fact that all important British foreign lines of steamers were subsidized by that government; in fact, Great Britain had subsidized almost every line of ocean steamers which had asked for it, and this country had allowed her mails to be carried in foreign bottoms simply because the government is not willing to lend a helping hand.

It seemed to him very feasible to construct mercantile vessels which should be capable of being converted into war vessels in time of war, although until the suggestion was made by Mr. Washburn to-day it never had occurred to him. Labor in Europe was much cheaper than in this country, but the men employed do not work nearly so intelligently; they are merely men driven around by masters like machines, while in our country a majority of our workmen employed on every grade of work were men of more or less intelligence.

The association with which Mr. Edmunds was connected has applied itself more particularly to get rid of such taxation as in their judgment was not only onerous but unlawful, such as half pilotage and harbor-masters' fees, and charges of that kind, where no service is rendered. They had already succeeded in procuring a decision of the courts that harbor-masters' fees were illegal, and they were now testing the question in regard to half pilotage, which was required to be paid by every vessel hailed by a pilot, although the services of a pilot were not required. This tax was considered especially onerous to parties engaged in the coasting trade.

The CHAIRMAN inquired whether the matter of the cost of repairing vessels had been brought to the attention of this association.

Mr. EDMUNDS said there was great difference in the cost of repairs. A vessel in the neighborhood of Galveston or New Orleans might almost as well be given away as to undertake to pay the cost of repairs in those ports. It was generally found cheaper to float her back to Philadelphia.

PHILIP FITZPATRICK, also a member of the committee of ship-owners, stated that since 1853 he had been connected with a house for which a great many vessels had been built. In his opinion if the cost of building could be reduced twenty or twenty-five per cent., this branch of industry would again revive. He had been connected with foreign trade, but had been compelled to discontinue it and engage altogether in the coasting trade. He had conversed with builders of foreign vessels, and was of the opinion that the difference in the cost of construction in this country and Great Britain was about thirty per cent. But if twenty or twenty-five per cent. could be taken off, the superiority of American vessels would enable our ship-builders again to commence the construction of ships.

The CHAIRMAN inquired what effect the employment of a large number of men in the navy yard in Philadelphia had upon the mechanics of the city not so employd.

Mr. FITZPATRICK replied that when there was plenty of work in the navy yard the best mechanics went there, and only scrubs, or the poorest class of workmen could be obtained by private parties.

The CHAIRMAN asked what effect the adoption of the eight-hour law had upon the men employed outside of the navy yard.

Mr. FITZPATRICK replied that the effect was very injurious; that men outside were exceedingly anxious to get employment in the navy yard for the purpose of obtaining the benefit of two hours a day less labor, and they would go hunting around for the influence of every person who was supposed to be able to give any assistance in getting employment in the navy yard.

Mr. LYNCH asked whether the rates paid in the navy yard were not regulated by rates outside.

Mr. FITZPATRICK said that was the law, but the practice was exactly the reverse, and that it operated very much to the prejudice of private parties employing this class of labor outside.

The CHAIRMAN inquired what the effect would be of allowing ship-stores being taken in bond, as they are in Great Britain and some others of the European nations.

Mr. FITZPATRICK replied that it would be an assistance, and in his opinion commerce ought to be assisted in some way by the government. We might not, if our vessels were built as cheaply, be able to compete with foreigners in sailing them; but as a general thing our vessels made quicker voyages and were preferred over foreign vessels. In time of war preference was given to English vessels in consequence of less rates of insurance. Whenever the cost of living was cheaper the price of wages would come down. Men could not work cheap while the cost of living was so high.

Mr. WASHBURN asked how much it would reduce the cost of ship-building if the duties were remitted upon all articles entering into their construction.

Mr. EDMUNDS thought it would probably work a reduction of twenty per cent. Wood was much cheaper in the Provinces, although the timber here is better; and we could afford to pay a little more than the cost of building there in consequence of the preference given to American vessels.

Mr. COPE remarked that, to give some idea of the difference in the cost of repairs in this country and Europe, he would state that a short time ago his house had a vessel repaired in Liverpool. On the return of the vessel his carpenter made an estimate of the amount the same repairs would have cost in Philadelphia, and reported that the work had been done for one-third less than it ought to have cost in this country, although the timber used had to be carried from this country to England.

The CHAIRMAN asked whether on account of this increased expense of repairs it was customary to repair vessels engaged in a foreign trade in a European country as far as possible.

Mr. COPE replied that such was the custom; that in the instance just referred to his house had saved five thousand dollars by having the repairs made in Liverpool.

HENRY WINDSOR, of the Philadelphia Board of Trade, said he would only refer to one of the causes for the decline of the American shipping interest, which was the great change that had taken place within the last few years in the increased number of steam ocean-going vessels. Formerly the preference was given to American sailing vessels, in consequence of their greater speed and the superior energy of their masters and crews. Now, for the same reasons, preference was given to steamers, which secured nearly all the better class of freights, while our American sailing vessels were compelled to take freights formerly rejected by them and carried in English vessels. In fact, nothing is left to us except the lowest class of freights formerly carried by foreign ships; and that is a difficulty that cannot be removed by any legislation in regard to sailing vessels; it must be done by lines of ocean steamships.

It is also true that the English have of late years constructed their steamships from much better models than formerly, and that they have evinced greater energy and brought themselves more upon an equality with our masters and crews than formerly, and the result has been that almost all the foreign trade worth having has gone into the hands of foreigners; and it is not only a matter of importance with us in regard to the carrying trade, but it is also true that the commerce of the world follows to a great extent the carrying trade, and foreigners will soon have control of the commerce of the world on land as well as on the ocean, unless something is done to revive our shipping interest.

A remission of the duties on imported articles entering into the construction of ships, and a subsidy upon those of American production used, would to a certain extent remedy the difficulty. Unfortunately, the manufacturers of the country think their interest is directly opposed to that of the ship-owners of the country. Such is not, in fact, the case. The difficulty is that the nature of the shipping interest is exceptional. We can protect our domestic industry on our own soil by a tariff; by the prohibition of imports if they think proper; but we can give no such protection to the American shipping interest, because the ocean is the great common field for all nations; and if we assist our ship-owners to compete with foreign nations it must be by reducing the cost of building ships and the cost of running them. If we cannot do it in that way it cannot be done at all. Give us the same privileges given by the British government to their ship-owners, and if we cannot get our share of the carrying trade we do not deserve to have it; but the same principle applied for the protection of American industry can be applied to the shipping interest, which is a branch of American industry as much as any other. It is very plain that it must be applied in a different way, but there is no reason why the advocates of protection to American industry should not be in favor of giving protection to this branch of industry because it must be reached through a different process. There is no departure from the principle; it is merely a difference of application.

Mr. LYNCH remarked that at the commencement of the war we were increasing our foreign tonnage more rapidly than Great Britain was hers, and asked whether the increase of steam vessels from 1850 to 1860 was not about as great as since that time.

Mr. WINDSOR said, perhaps so, but during the war the British and other foreign nations got possession of our foreign trade, and it is now very difficult to oust parties who have possession.

It is also true in regard to the increased efficiency, relatively, of the crews of British vessels that, during the war, our foreign commerce having been almost destroyed and our sailors diverted to other branches of industry, our capitalists now find more profitable avenues of investment.

It may also be worth stating that the capitalists of this country are not willing to engage in the carrying trade for the same profits as will satisfy those of other nations. The rate of interest is higher here and our people demand larger profits. English ship-owners are satisfied, after making due allowance for the deterioration and wear and tear of their vessels, with a net profit of six per cent. upon their profit, while

American ship-owners are not satisfied with that rate, because they can do better in their investments.

Mr. WASHBURN inquired if the attention of the witness had been drawn to the effect of opening the Suez Canal upon the shipping interest of this country or of the world.

Mr. WINDSOR said that his attention had not been drawn much to that subject, the success of that enterprise being problematical. If in the event it proves successful, it will have an important influence upon the carrying trade of the world; much fewer vessels, certainly for the European trade, will be required. Whether it will also affect our trade with the East Indies is uncertain. The navigation of the seas beyond the termination of the canal is very difficult.

HENRY TATUM, also of the committee of the Philadelphia Board of Trade, remarked that in 1860 William S. Lindsey, of London, was in this country and appeared before the different boards of trade on our seaboard, bringing to their attention a good many things, and among others he placed in the hands of the Philadelphia board a volume containing a large mass of information bearing upon this subject. This volume, Mr. Tatum said, he would place in the hands of the committee, it being a report made by Mr. Lindsey to Parliament upon the subject of shipping in 1860. Mr. Tatum had been, during the war, very active in urging upon the government the acceptance of League Island, for the purpose of having one large ship-yard in this country. He was satisfied that the idea of constructing merchant ships of such models as to be available as ships of war was a pure fallacy. Vessels so constructed as to be serviceable in the merchant marine could only be made available in war as privateers.

Mr. TATUM also stated that there was no port on our coast which is not to-day at the mercy of the British navy. Neither New York, Boston, nor any other port has any adequate means of defense against such war vessels as the British government may send. The whole policy of the British government during the war was to destroy our commerce, and in that enterprise they were very successful, and Mr. Lindsey, probably, as much as any other man, was instrumental in bringing about that result. For instance, what motive could the rebels have in sending out one of their best vessels at a very large expense when they had no money to spare, for the purpose of destroying our northwestern whale trade? Mr. Tatum believed it was done with the secret service money of Great Britain. The number of vessels and the number of the crews which on the average were at Honolulu was well known in Great Britain, and it was known that sailors belonging to these ships were the best seamen in the world, and if hostilities had occurred, as there was at one time imminent danger, between the United States and Great Britain, one of the first acts done by Great Britain would have been to have destroyed that fleet of vessels.

Mr. TATUM believed that if the American ship-builders were placed upon the same basis as those of Great Britain, ships could be profitably constructed in this country. With a drawback on all material entering into the construction of ships our ship-builders could profitably construct ocean-going vessels, as may be seen from the fact that the builders at Wilmington, Delaware, and at Chester, Pennsylvania, now compete very closely with foreign ship-builders.

CHARLES H. CRAMP, engaged in ship-building, said that Great Britain now had the advantage of this country in the carrying trade of the world, not because the vessels constructed were superior to ours in model, but because of the great superiority of their marine engines.

The English have built the finest and best marine engines in the world. We have always been inferior to her in that respect. Our models are the best, but our marine engines are poor copies of British engines. The British government have developed their iron ship-building interest by encouraging the skill of private ship-builders, notwithstanding her enormous ship-yards. Ninety per cent. of her iron-clads have been constructed at private establishments. It requires very little capital to embark in the building of wooden ships. Since the commencement of the war, the house with which Mr. Cramp was connected has been engaged in building both iron and wooden vessels, but has built no foreign iron steam-vessels since 1857, and none have been built in Philadelphia since that time. The same class of mechanics who in 1857 worked for a dollar and seventy-five cents a day, now receive three dollars a day. With the materials entering into ship-building, our ship-builders can compete with those in foreign countries in building iron ships; and very few wooden vessels will hereafter be built, iron ships being superior in every respect. Mr. Cramp's firm had built the largest ships ever built in Philadelphia. The ship Chamberlain, which in 1855 was built for sixty dollars per ton, can now be built for eighty dollars, and an iron ship of the same model for about one hundred and ten dollars. Timber is becoming higher and scarcer every day, and that is one reason for stating that the time for building wooden ships has gone by. It is impossible to state the length of time iron vessels will last. Some of the first built in England are still in good condition. The character of American wooden ships has been reduced every year in order to compete with the province-built vessels. There is a difference of about thirty dollars a ton between the cost of iron and wooden vessels, but the iron is really cheaper in the end. To enable the business of building iron ships to become firmly established in this country, a very large amount of very large machinery must be supplied, and some aid from the government must be rendered. Great demoralization among the mechanics in the government yards has been produced by the frequent changes made for political reasons. At the beginning of the war nobody but republicans could be employed. During the war they were turned out and all democrats put in; and since then still another change has taken place, and the character of the workmen employed has been constantly running down. Large numbers of men at times are forced upon the yards by politicians when there is no work for them to do. This has become a great evil, and Mr. Cramp hoped the committee would give it their attention. The eight-hour system has also done very much to render the mechanics not in government employ dissatisfied, and it has not improved the condition of anybody. Most of the best men were opposed to it in the first place, and it was only supported by some blatherskytes who were good talkers but bad mechanics. The repeal of that law is required. Men do not work as hard now as they used to—so much more machinery is employed.

Mr. Morrell inquired what was the average rate of duty now paid upon materials entering into the construction of ships.

Mr. Cramp supposed the average rate would be about forty per cent., and if our ship-builders could be relieved from that they could compete successfully with foreign builders. The difference in the cost of labor would be overcome by the superiority of American mechanics. The British workmen are a degraded set of beings, and the course pursued by their employers toward them tends still further to degrade them. Mr. Cramp had been informed that their men were frequently paid off at taverns, and that it was distressing to see women and children waiting to get what remained after a portion of the wages had been spent at the tavern. It would not be desirable to bring the wages of our men to as low a rate as those paid in England, if it could be done. American iron in the construction of iron vessels would always be preferred at the same price as foreign. It would be very inconvenient to send abroad for the iron plates. It is necessary to get the form of every plate before it is ordered, and if, after doing that, we must send abroad to have them made, very great inconvenience and delay would result. It was admitted, too, that American iron is of much better quality for this purpose than English. If the plates are of the same thickness and the same price, you get a great deal more valuable article for the money in using American iron. The same thickness of plates which the English adopt is not necessary if American iron is used, although the Lloyds will not insure unless the vessel is built according to their standard. It is an advantage in every way to use American materials in the construction of our ships. The reason English marine engines are superior to ours is not because our workmen are inefficient, but because they are more cloister engineers, as we call them, or fancy men. The engines in which we excel are the weak-beam engines, and if we are encouraged a little by the government we will excel them in the construction of every description of marine engines. The establishment of a large government ship-yard in any city is a calamity to that city, as these yards are now managed.

LEWIS C. MEDARA stated that his interest had been mostly in chartering vessels. He had always given the preference to American vessels, because more care was taken of the cargoes and less time consumed on the voyage. During the war he was obliged to charter foreign-built vessels, but found that great delay and long voyages was the result. He knew nothing about the cost of constructing vessels except what he could infer from the repairs made upon the vessels chartered. The eight-hour law was a most unfortunate measure for the government to adopt, and has affected the cost of repairing vessels very much. He was not able to say whether American-built vessels, if they could be profitably constructed now, could be sailed as cheaply as foreign vessels. That was a question belonging to the owner of the vessel, he chartering the vessel, knowing nothing of the expenditures or disbursements. He knew that American vessels made their return voyage in much shorter time than English vessels. The vessels chartered by him were employed principally in the Cuban and South American trade.

Captain J. S. CLARK, for many years the master of a vessel, remarked that he could generally get work done cheaper in America than abroad. The price of labor was less in England, but it took a great deal longer time. The men would leave their work first to get their beer, then their tobacco, and then their dinner, and accomplish very little in the course of the day. One great difficulty was, in having to advance moneys to the crews, which money was all absorbed by persons who harbored the sailors on shore.

Another difficulty was in the cost of provisions. In Europe they are allowed to take goods out of bond for use on ship-board. When in Antwerp, two years ago, the rope-rigging of his vessel was taken out, and an iron rigging put in, at a cost of nine hundred dollars in gold, while it would have cost not less than two thousand dollars to have done the same work in this country.

Mr. LYNCH inquired what proportion of foreigners were ordinarily in the crews of vessels.

Mr. CLARK replied that very often there would not be one native-born American in the whole crew, although a large portion of the men would ship as Americans. The officers are generally native-born men. We are laboring in this country under a great disadvantage by being obliged to ship the rubbish of Europe under the name of American seamen. In Europe there is a black-list of seamen kept at every port, on which any seaman misbehaving during the voyage is entered, and the result is they get good men there, while the bad men come to this part of the world and ship on our vessels as Americans. At one time, before the war, in a crew of sixty, Captain Clark said, he had but two men who could steer. Since the war he had been able to get a little better class of men. Another great advantage possessed by English steamers was that they employed their men at so much a week—the men finding themselves. He hoped something would be done to restore the prestige of American shipping on the ocean to where it was previous to the war.

John W. Everman, engaged in shipping, remarked that among the difficulties in the way of competing with other nations in our carrying trade, was the great amount of expense imposed upon shippers, for which no services were rendered. The port warden fees were not now collected, but under the laws of Pennsylvania, vessels now are compelled to pay half-pilotage if they do not take a pilot, and whole pilotage if they have an assorted cargo. At this rate, a vessel of three hundred tons has to pay thirty dollars for going past the breakwater, although she employs no pilot. At Norfolk her expenses for pilotage would be about one hundred and twenty dollars, whether a pilot is employed or not, and in Mobile, one hundred and forty dollars, or one hundred and fifty dollars. These charges are unjust.

He was not in favor of allowing vessels from the Provinces or foreign ports to come in here and have their stores placed in bond in the custom-house with the privilege of withdrawing them. For instance, a vessel coming from Italy will deposit at the rate of a quart of wine a day for each man on board, and they will in this way bring in fifteen or twenty thousand gallons of wine as a three-years' supply, and then go down the river and trade it off for anything they want.

Pilotage is one of the greatest evils our coasting trade has to contend with, although it is less in Philadelphia than almost any other city, and the owner of the vessel has no protection, as they have in going into a port in Cuba, and any other foreign ports where, if the pilot sinks the vessel, the government pays for it. Here, there is no such provision, and a captain coming in from a long voyage, understanding the river perfectly, will be much more likely to take a vessel safely, because he is sober, than the pilot, who is lying by among the islands, very likely intoxicated, and yet, if the captain does not hear the orders of the pilot and the vessel is sunk, the insurance will not be paid. The general practice for coasting vessels is to sail them on shares, the officers having a proportion of the earnings of the vessel. No vessel owner wants to reduce the wages of the men, unless the cost of living is also reduced. A couple of years ago, Mr. Everman wrote to Montreal to ascertain the cost of building a vessel of the dimensions given by him, and ascertained that it could be built for twelve thousand dollars. He found that it cost about twenty to twenty-five per cent. more, taking gold at forty, than to build it here; but an American-built vessel would sell at public auction for forty or fifty per cent. more, so that after all it is really more economical to build our own vessels.

Mr. Morrell asked what would be the cost of building a schooner of six hundred and fifty tons.

Mr. Everman thought that without being copper-fastened she would cost twenty-eight or twenty-nine thousand dollars. A large proportion of the vessels now being built in this country are schooner-rigged, and they are so built because they can be sailed with less men than a ship can. A very large number of three-masted schooners are now being built. Almost all schooners are iron-fastened, the duty on copper being so heavy that the cost of copper-fastening is too great.

JOHN F. STUMP, formerly harbor-master at Philadelphia, and afterward engaged in the custom-house, was under the impression that one of the great difficulties in the way of competing with foreign ships was the difference in the currency. He thought the difference in cost between sailing an American vessel, or an English or German vessel, was about fifty per cent.

AFTERNOON SESSION.

The committee again met at 3 o'clock.

WILLIAM G. GIBBONS, ship-builder, in Wilmington, Delaware, stated that for the past four years the business of the firm with which he was connected had been largely engaged in building iron river steamers to be used on the rivers in South America and Mexico; having constructed boats for nearly all the rivers in South America emptying into the Caribbean Sea or Atlantic, and also several for those emptying into the Pacific. The reason why they were able to build these boats in competition with the English, was that their character was such as to make them unfit to cross the Atlantic, the English builders being required to take them to pieces, ship them over, and then put them together again. The boats were shipped by St. Thomas, touching at Demarara and various points on the coast, and had all passed safely to their destination. His firm had never succeeded in getting an order to build a ship for ocean navigation purposes. They had recently built, for a line of steamers to run from St. Thomas, two screw steamers adapted to passengers and freight, of about seven hundred tons. The parties very much preferred to put their steamers under the American flag, the company being composed largely of citizens of New York; but the English bids were about twenty thousand dollars lower on an estimate of one hundred and twelve thousand dollars for each vessel, gold being the basis in each case, and of course the English obtained the order. In the construction of iron vessels about six-tenths of the entire cost is labor, and four-tenths material, and the tax now required to be paid upon every material entering into the construction of a ship, from the laying of her keel until she is finished, is a matter of vital consequence to American ship-builders. Our rates of labor are higher than those in any other country in the world, and this has compelled our people to exert their ingenuity for machinery and mechanic appliances to save labor whenever it is practicable. We have always excelled both the English and Scotch in this respect, and we have only been able to compete with them by economizing labor as we have done in the larger use of machinery, but they buy their machinery for about one-half in gold what it costs us in currency. For instance, forty-five dollars in gold will buy a ton of plate or bar iron in England, which here costs eighty-eight or ninety dollars for plates and eighty-five dollars for bars. When this is worked up we find that they have the advantage of us of about two-tenths in material. If the firm with which Mr. Gibbons was connected could get iron put down in their yard at the prices paid by the English ship-builders, they could furnish ships for anybody, and would give them their orders at as low rate as the English or Scotch could build them. They have never received any drawback on materials used in building vessels to be sent out of the country. In one or two instances the excise tax had been remitted, but it caused more trouble to obtain the remission than the saving amounted to.

JOHN TUCKER, vice-president of the Reading railroad, said that last winter the Reading Railroad Company contracted for two iron colliers, at a cost of fifty-nine thousand dollars and sixty thousand dollars, respectively. He sent the specifications to a friend in London to ascertain at what price they could be duplicated there. The first reply was that they would not build a collier according to the specifications given, and returned their criticisms upon the specifications. After my reply explaining the specifications they acknowledged that the colliers would be quite as efficient as if built in accordance with their usual specifications. They then sent a communication, which Mr. Tucker said he would furnish to the committee. Since that time the Reading works had contracted for eight more steam colliers, of larger dimensions, to be built at Chester, Pennsylvania, where the first two were constructed. Taking gold at thirty-three and one-third per cent., the difference between the cost of building these colliers at Chester and in England would be about four thousand dollars each. The same specifications were furnished to the American and English builders. American iron is much stronger than English, and a less quantity may be safely used in the construction of an iron vessel. One of the colliers built last summer in passing Hell Gate, New York Harbor, struck a rock, cutting about ten feet in her bottom. The vessel was raised and the injured piece of iron was exhibited here, attracting some attention. In accordance with their request, that strip of iron was sent to the Lloyds' underwriters, in France, as a specimen of the superiority of American iron, and since that time we have been able to effect our insurance there at ten per cent. per annum lower than we were doing it before. Previous to that time the cost of insurance was about eighteen per cent. per annum. The insurance is now effected there at seven and one-half per cent. The first two vessels were built as an experiment and for the purpose of taking coal all along the coast. For this class of vessels the cost of building is not very much more than on the other side. He was surprised to find so little difference. In fact, taking into consideration the superiority of American iron, they are really built cheaper in this country than they could be in England. The cost of building those now ordered is one hundred and five thousand dollars each for a thousand-ton collier. Mr. Gibbons remarked with regard to the question of screw colliers just referred to, that it was the opinion of his firm the prices at which they were being built were not remunerative. His firm had bid for the same vessels; but their bid was very much higher. In regard to the legislation ship-builders would like to have, there is a difference of opinion among different parties; but one thing is pretty clear, that if American builders can obtain their material at the same rates paid by the English and Scotch builders they will be able to compete with them in building ships. The cost of labor is of course greater in this country, but the additional skill obtained more than compensates for it. The English have old-fashioned ideas. The law referred to by Mr. Tucker just now speaks of two engines, and they frequently put four into one of their ships. Our ship-owners mostly prefer only one engine. The parties of whom Mr. Gibbons had already spoken, who desired to contract for building ships to run to St. Thomas, said they were willing to give considerable more money to an American than to an English builder, for the reason that the American builders provided greater comfort for passengers than the English, and passengers would follow the route which was provided with the most comfort. The boats built for the South American rivers are a sort of cross between the

Hudson River boat and the Mississippi River boat. They are side-wheel and built to run in shoal water. The peculiarity of the climate in South America is such as to require very different accommodations for passengers from anything required in this country. The boats built by the English for those rivers are of a different model, and more analogous to those used during the war for running the blockade. They do not carry very much freight and are exceedingly expensive. The boats built in Wilmington are equally as fast, draw a great deal less water, and have made a great deal of money for their owners, which is, after all, the test of success.

In regard to ocean steamers it is now universally considered that there is a great advantage in screw steamers over side-wheel steamers, for the reason that in rough weather it very often happens that one wheel is so much submerged as to waste almost all the power used, while the other will be almost out of water. This difficulty is obviated to a certain extent while the side-wheel steamers are immensely large, as in case of the Pacific mail steamers running between San Francisco and Hong Kong, but these ships are always very slow. The English seem to understand the principle of building screw ships, building them very narrow and very deep, so that unless the sea is very heavy they push their way across the ocean, rolling very little and being disturbed very little by an ordinary sea.

Another difficulty with side-wheel ships is that in a voyage from New York to Southampton' you must load the vessel with coal almost beyond her proper capacity, sinking the wheels too deep in the water on this side, and leaving them about four feet out on the other side as the coal becomes expended. The only remedy that can be asked by American ship-builders is that such scheme may be devised by which they may receive their materials at a lower rate than they do now. It is impossible to state any ordinary rate per ton for building an iron ship. The vessels are so different in their construction, and so many different considerations come into the cost of constructing different models of, vessels are built upon specifications, and taking given specifications, we are able to calculate the cost by the number of pounds of iron required. The tonnage is of course determined by the model of the ship itself as much as by the size. A thousand-ton iron ship built according to the requirements of the Lloyds, with reasonable passenger accommodation, would probably cost one hundred and fifty or one hundred and sixty thousand dollars. The colliers spoken of have very limited power, and would be nowhere if employed in the merchant service. For instance, between New York and New Orleans they have a cylinder of forty-four inches of diameter, while a merchant ship of the same capacity would have a cylinder of sixty inches. Their steam power is accessory only, but they are strong, first-rate vessels in all that relates to their carrying capacity. The English make their passenger ships cost just about as much as our American ships. It is only on their coarse, common work that they beat us. Where a great amount of labor is to be expended on fine work we can beat them; because they have to import their lumber, and because they use hand labor for a very large portion of their fine work, for which we employ machinery. Take the Adriatic, for instance, one of the Collins line of steamers now owned in Russia. Her inside work was a complete mass of elegant carving, which could not be done in England for anything like the amount it cost in New York. The same may be said of the St. John's and Dean Richmond, on the Hudson River, or of the Providence steamers. All this work is now woven out by machinery and costs very little. Ship-builders would like to have the tariff on iron taken completely off, although they know that, as a general proposition, is impracticable at present, and they would like to see it done by adopting a sliding-scale which at some distant period should reach zero, and be an end to the duty on iron. A good deal has been said of pauper labor on the other side of the ocean; that it is not applied to the mechanical pursuits; it is applied to the agricultural pursuits, where the labor is in excess of the amount of available land to cultivate; while in this country the supply of labor for that purpose is not equal to the demand; but for skilled labor the relative rates paid in England and France is not very largely below that paid in this country, taking everything into consideration. In this country, in many instances, our laborers are paid too much. In the stock and mining districts many of them get ten dollars a day, and coal enters largely into the cost of building ships. So in our foundries, puddlers, when they will work a whole week, get about sixty dollars; but the prices have so demoralized labor that they can scarcely ever be induced to work a whole week. The last advance upon the tariff rates on iron did not go into the hands of the manufacturers, but, to a great extent, into the hands of the laborers, who were already paid too much.

Mr. MORRELL asked, where in this country puddlers were paid the sixty dollars per week.

Mr. GIBBONS replied, in Wilmington.

Mr. MORRELL stated that in Pennsylvania puddlers were not earning more than four dollars per day.

Mr. LYNCH inquired whether, if ship-builders were allowed drawback upon the iron used by them, and also a subsidy to the same amount upon American iron used, the effect would not be that American iron would generally be used.

Mr. GIBBONS replied that it would be used for the reason that our ship-builders preferred to obtain their iron at home, both because of its superiority and because the work can be done promptly. It would be considered a great nuisance if they were compelled to wait, before furnishing their patrons, to send them abroad for the plates to be made. As a general rule, the party who wants a ship wants it now, and would not be willing to wait for the two months that would be required to send abroad to get the material. They could turn out a thousand-ton iron ship in about nine months, or, commencing in the spring, so as to have the benefit of the summer months, probably in less time than that.

Mr. MORRELL inquired the number of builders of iron ships in Wilmington.

Mr. GIBBONS replied that there was one other firm. His firm had formerly built large ships, and within the last two years, finding it more profitable, had confined themselves to river steamers.

The CHAIRMAN inquired the cost of building a thousand-ton sailing ship.

Mr. GIBBONS said it would cost about ninety thousand dollars in currency, built according to our American specifications. The cost would be more than that if built on the Lloyd specifications, they crowding much more iron into a vessel than we do. The cost of building under their specifications would probably be fifteen thousand dollars more—a vessel that under our specifications would be just as good for every practical purpose—but the Lloyds would not insure at the same rate.

The CHAIRMAN inquired whether, if our ship-builders were enabled to build American ships as cheaply as foreign builders, there would be a foreign demand for these vessels.

Mr. GIBBONS replied that it would not come immediately, because the channel of business in this respect is nearly all foreign, in the direction of Scotland, and it would take two or three years, and possibly more, to change it. Currents of trade, like currents of water, when they are or have once set in a given direction are difficult to change. We could control in a great degree the South American trade much sooner than we could that of the Mediterranean or the China trade.

The CHAIRMAN asked what description of vessels the Spanish gunboats were, of which we have heard so much recently in New York.

Mr. GIBBONS replied that they were constructed very much like our tug-boats, only larger, and built to cross the ocean. He said that Mr. Ericsson, who was intimate with the authorities at Madrid, obtained the order and gave it to his next friend, Mr. Delamater. It was through Mr. Ericsson that the order came to the United States.

The CHAIRMAN asked the witness if his firm did anything toward building vessels for the government during the war.

Mr. GIBBONS answered that they did.

The CHAIRMAN asked whether a class of iron vessels suitable for the merchant marine could be constructed so as to be converted into vessels useful to the government in time of war.

Mr. GIBBONS said they would require a great change, for the reason that the requirements of the two branches of service are so different. A merchant vessel would have to be turned inside out before she could be converted into a man-of-war. For privateersmen they would be just the thing.

Mr. WASHBURN asked whether, in case of a war with England, these would not be just such vessels as we would need.

Mr. GIBBONS said they would, because they are fast. Heavy ships, as a rule, are slow. The ships built in England during the war for blockade-runners, and captured by us, which have been sold into the merchant service, have one and all greatly disgusted their purchasers. They burn a great deal of coal and carry but little freight. They were constructed to run fast, but only the high freights they carried made them profitable, and when freights came down they would not do at all.

Mr. WASHBURN inquired whether, if we build vessels as cheaply as they can on the Clyde, there would be any difference afterward in the cost of keeping them in repairs.

Mr. GIBBONS said there would not, because the ship would be repaired wherever it was most convenient and it could be done the most cheaply; that even now vessels in this country destined for the East Indies often get freight from the United States to some European port, where they are repaired at a very much less expense than in this country, and the officers then get freight from that port to the East Indies and come home. Our vessels managed mostly to get their repairs done out of the United States, so as to economize, and that is the reason why we have but little to do in the way of repairing. If our ship-builders could have a subsidy from the government they could build ships, but it would be a dangerous precedent, because every other interest would want the same kind of protection.

The CHAIRMAN inquired how many hands were employed in the ship-yards in Wilmington.

Mr. GIBBONS said his firm employed about two hundred and fifty. The other firm built railroad cars as well as ships, and employed from four hundred to seven hundred hands. The other firm used to build boats for the American trade, but they are now building larger vessels. They were the builders of the steamship Champion, running between New York and Charleston; of the two iron ships running to Savannah;

of the American line of steamers running from New Orleans to Galveston, Texas. They built two very splendid vessels for the Panama company, one of them on the larger specifications, taking them at very near the quotations in Scotland. This was a vessel of two hundred and sixty feet in length, about thirty-three feet beam, and measuring two hundred tons. She was finished about a year and a half ago.

The CHAIRMAN inquired at what other ship-yards in the country iron steamships were built.

Mr. GIBBONS said there was one at Chester, and they were built at the Atlantic Works, Boston. During the war there were establishments in New York that built iron vessels, but they have since abandoned the enterprise. The rates are greatly higher than at Wilmington. At Wilmington mechanics are employed to work upon the hulls of vessels, and a few of them are paid fifteen dollars a week, but the average of them not more than nine and a half or ten dollars. The same class of workmen were paid about ten dollars a week before the war. A large grade of mechanics are employed to work upon iron vessels for the reason that a few skilled workmen can get along very well with a good many other of the lower grade. There is more difference in the cost of building marine engines between this country and Scotland than there is in the cost of building ships. They had not gone into competition with them in Wilmington in building engines. The only instance, Mr. Gibbons said, in which his firm had bid in competition was for the steel works in Pennsylvania, and then they were beaten fifty per cent. It might be, however, that their bids were too high and the bids in Scotland too low.

Letter from Samuel Harlan, of the firm of Harlan & Hollingsworth, iron ship-builders.

WILMINGTON, DEL., *December* 1, 1869.

Hon. D. J. MORRELL, *of Congressional Committee, &c.*

DEAR SIR: We are very much obliged for your invitation to be present at the meeting of your committee, in Philadelphia, but regret that absence from home will prevent our attendance.

If agreeable to your committee, we would be glad to present our views in writing in subjoined paper. We trust this will be acceptable to you, as the subject is one in which we are most vitally interested, and feel that the only hope for relief lies in the action of Congress.

Very respectfully, your obedient servant,

SAM'L HARLAN, JR., *President.*

We would present our views under the following heads, viz:

1. As to the present condition of the iron ship-building interest.
2. The causes which have led to its depression.
3. Our views as to the remedy or relief desired.

On the first point we would state that at no time since 1857 has the iron ship-building interest been so depressed as it has within the last twelve to eighteen months. During the time named we have scarcely been without contracts for iron boats and steamers until within the past twelve months, when the business has fallen off greatly, in fact, almost coming to a stand-still a good part of the time; yet, during this time, we have had more inquiries for iron ships from parties wishing to build than ever before, but owing to the cost of building being beyond what they could afford to pay, and greater than the same ships would cost in England, the negotiations have ended with mutual regrets, and the parties resolving to wait for a more favorable condition of affairs. What work we have taken to keep our men employed, has been at rates not remunerative, and in some instances, at positive loss.

Second. The causes which have led to its depression, &c.:

The principal one is the great advance which has taken place since 1860 in the price of labor and materials, ranging from forty to seventy-five per cent. In many instances where parties were convinced of the superiority of iron ships, as compared with wood, they were compelled to build of wood because the cost of the iron ship was so much greater. This difference in cost is due, in a great measure, to the fact that iron, more than wood, is the production of skilled labor, and is affected more by the various causes producing the advance referred to, as well as suffering more from taxation.

Third. As to the relief desired, &c.:

We cannot hope for a reduction in the price of labor, as we find it is more difficult for our workmen to support themselves and their families on the present rate of wages, with the greatly enhanced cost of everything consumed by them, than it was when their wages ruled the lowest, and, until the cost of living is greatly reduced, we cannot hope that the wages of the mechanic and laboring man will rule much below what it is at present; in fact, it cannot be, without being oppressive upon them. It remains, therefore, to reduce the cost of the materials entering into the construction and equipment of iron ships, as the only remedy left. Can this be done to an extent equal to the reduction in cost desired? We think not, without throwing off all the protection now given to the manufacturers of the various materials referred to. While this might relieve the ship-building interest it would be ruinous to other interests, and would meet with great opposition.

We cannot recommend a more simple and effectual remedy than the one already concurred in by a majority of ship-builders and ship-owners who have been before your board, viz: to remit the duties on all imported articles entering into the construction and equipment of both wood and iron, steam and sailing ships, or a drawback be allowed on all articles of domestic manufacture equivalent to the duties named above on the imported article.

This latter clause is especially desirable, that ship-builders may not be obliged to use the foreign article exclusively, and thus break down the American manufacturers.

The English and Scotch iron ship-builders have the advantage over the American ship-builders only in their enlarged experience from the greater number of large sea-going steamships which they have built; but in the quality of iron, and energy and skill of our workmen, we feel that we have decidedly the advantage, while our facilities in tools and machinery adapted to the purpose are quite equal to theirs. The foreign builders have no advantages over us except in the cheapness of their iron and other materials, and the greatly reduced rates of wages paid their workmen, but not in the superiority of their workmen, nor quality of their iron, nor their ability to build better ships.

What was done by American ship-builders at the commencement, and during the war, in building up our American marine, is a sure guarantee of what they can do in building up a mercantile marine, if they can be relieved from the causes producing the present great depression.

Timely relief will not only allow the ship-owners to procure vessels as cheaply as they can be built in foreign countries, but the stimulus thus given to the ship-building interest will produce ships equal to any in the world in our judgment.

The repeal of the navigation laws would enable the ship-owner to procure cheap ships, the refuse of every foreign country, and even good ships at a low figure, as the ship-building interest in England and Scotland is in a depressed state since the opening of the Suez canal has become an established fact. Yet it would effectually close up our ship-yards except to the building of small vessels which could not safely cross the Atlantic, and give to England the building of our mercantile marine as she now has our carrying trade.

The statement has been freely circulated in the papers that we could build iron ships as cheaply at our works, with the payments made in gold, as they could be built on the Clyde; but such is not the case with the difference in cost of labor and materials so greatly against us.

The advantages we have from long experience in building iron steamers, favorable location, experienced workmen, every facility in the way of machinery, &c., will not enable us to compete with foreign builders, at the present cost of labor and materials, but let Congress give relief in the shape asked for above, and the ship-owner will not have cause to complain that he cannot have ships built equal to those of any nation, and at as reasonable prices.

WASHINGTON, D. C., *December* 15, 1869.

Committee met. Present, all the members.

T. F. Rowland, ship-builder, of New York, appeared, and stated that he was present, with others, representing the ship-yard workingmen—carpenters, sail-makers, spar-makers, iron-workers, and other representatives of the labor required to produce a finished ship; that they came to Washington to see if something could not be done to relieve their interests; that they had reduced their views to writing, and the statement would now be made by Mr. Westervelt, the chairman of the committee.

Mr. D. D. Westervelt, ship-builder, of New York, thereupon read and presented to the committee the following written statement:

NEW YORK, *December* 14, 1869.

To the Hon. JOHN LYNCH,
Chairman of the Special Congressional Committee on Navigation Interests.

SIR: The undersigned, a committee appointed by the "New York Association for the restoration of American shipping interests," respectfully beg leave to call your attention to the following facts, with the view of setting forth the past and present condition of American commerce, and for the purpose of impressing upon Congress, through the action of your committee, the absolute necessity of some action being immediately taken to prevent the total destruction of American international commerce; and also to set forth the principle that the true policy of our government is to foster and encourage American ship-builders, as we believe that a nation's prosperity is reflected in the prosperity of its commercial marine.

As evidence of the condition of our commerce during the last thirty-two years, we respectfully call your attention to the accompanying exhibit A, which is a true copy of the record at the New York custom-house. It will be observed that during the year 1836 there entered the port of New York 407,096 tons of shipping, the handiwork of American craftsmen, and only one-third of that amount of tonnage entered under the head of foreign. The American builders sustained their prestige for twenty years thereafter, and specimens of their workmanship were seen and respected in every port, and carried our emblem on every sea.

In 1858 the English commenced the substitution of iron for wood in the art of ship-building, and since, by a chain of circumstances fortunate to them but disastrous to us, the record shows for 1868 that nearly two tons of foreign tonnage to one of American was recorded at the port of New York. Many of these vessels, notwithstanding they appear under a foreign flag, are productions of our American ship-yards, having changed their record for protection during our late internal struggle.

Previous to the year 1868, the port of New York sustained not less than twenty prominent ship-yards, employing with the collateral trades, such as joiners, spar-makers, sail-makers, &c., not less than twenty thousand skilled mechanics, in addition to one thousand young men as apprentices learning the various trades. To-day these yards have either ceased to exist, or are lying dormant, not one thousand skilled mechanics finding employment, and so small are the inducements for young men to learn the profession that apprentices are no longer to be found.

It is in the interest of the country at large, who in time of war must have ships to sustain its dignity, and mechanics to build them, that we appeal to your honorable committee to recommend to Congress some potent measure for the relief of our profession.

We would respectfully and most earnestly recommend that some action be immediately taken by our government to foster and encourage the art of ship-building; and, in consideration of the fact that all governments gain power and respect by the proficiency of their seamen and mechanics, we believe it would be eminently fit and proper that Congress should legislate to allow to the American ship-builder an equivalent on all American materials used by him in the construction of the finished ship, equal to the amount of duty which the government would receive should such raw material be of foreign production.

Regarding the proposition to modify or abrogate the United States registry laws, and allow foreign-built ships to register on equal footing with American productions, we most respectfully desire to protest. Nearly every native American, and, we believe, the great majority of our adopted citizens, are possessed of a certain amount of pride, and rejoice in the growth and success of our naval and mercantile marine; and, though at the present time the people at large may appear to be indifferent and lukewarm upon the subject, it is our united opinion that could a full expression be obtained, it would be found to be their unanimous desire that the principles inaugurated by the founders of our institutions in regard to our registry laws should be undisturbed, and that all vessels partaking of its benefits should be constructed on American territory.

D. D. WESTERVELT,
T. F. ROWLAND,
L. H. BOOLE,
WILLIAM FOULKE,
JOSHUA YOUNGS,
THOMAS STARK,
JOHN E. HOFFMIRE,
WILLIAM ROWLAND,
DAVID J. TAFF,
ROBERT A. RUSSELL,

Committee of the New York Association for the restoration of American shipping interests.

A.—*Tonnage entered at New York from foreign ports during the year* 1868.

	No. of vessels.	Tonnage.	Seamen.
American vessels	2,084	1,033,396	31,551
Foreign vessels	2,734	1,867,591	68,201
Total entered in 1868	4,818	2,900,987	99,752
Total entered in 1862	5,406	2,552,481	81,817
Total entered in 1852	3,847	1,709,988	58,867

Number of arrivals, amount of American and foreign tonnage, and the total tonnage entered at the port of New York, during the years below specified.

Year.	No. of arrivals.	American tonnage.	Foreign tonnage.	Total tonnage.
1836	2,285	407,996	149,634	556,730
1846	2,292	496,761	185,404	682,165
1856	3,861	1,684,596	386,263	2,070,859
1866	4,827	990,116	1,776,318	2,766,434
1868	4,818	1,033,396	1,867,591	2,900,987

DOMESTIC TONNAGE.

The returns for the past nine months show that the arrivals and clearances in the domestic trade amounted to upwards of fifty million tons, or about three times that of the foreign trade. It has been only moderately prosperous during the present years, barely paying insurance and depreciation.

Statement of the foreign trade of the city of New York, including the value of imports and exports, and showing the proportion under the United States and foreign flags, for the periods named.

Year.	In American vessels.	In foreign vessels.
1857	$239,565,610	$104,354,631
1867	123,687,012	367,508,647
1868	113,313,303	371,849,274

From the foregoing statement, it will be seen that the rapid increase of foreign tonnage is most startling, as we discover that in the year 1868 nearly two-thirds of the whole tonnage entered in the port of New York was foreign, whereas during the year 1856 it was scarce twenty per cent. of the total.

If we look at the cargo values respectively carried in American and foreign vessels, we find that during the year 1868 seventy-five per cent. were carried in foreign vessels; and it may be safely asserted that more than eighty per cent. of all the value of goods imported and exported from the port of New York during the present year has been carried in foreign vessels.

In the year 1857, out of a value of $536,000,000, carried to and from *all* our domestic ports, only $131,000,000 went under a foreign flag. In 1867, out of $864,000,000 at all the ports, $577,600,000 were carried in foreign vessels.

Mr. WM. FOULKE, of the same committee, made the following statement:

As will be seen by this document, we feel as if our business had gone from us, and that we were left desolate. In our ship-yards we have nothing to do; and we shall have nothing to do unless the government does something to protect us. I would like to see a return of the same prosperity in our ship-yards which we enjoyed years ago. I think we are capable of regaining our former prestige if we have a chance. We do not think we have lost our ability or our skill; and we will show that we have not, if an opportunity is given us to compete with foreign builders.

By Mr. WASHBURNE:

Q. Do you think that if you can obtain the materials that enter into the construction of a ship as cheaply as they do abroad, you can compete successfully with foreign builders, notwithstanding the high cost of labor?

Mr. D. D. WESTERVELT, (ship-builder.) That is the opinion of the gentlemen composing this committee. Labor is higher here, but we think American labor is sufficiently superior to foreign labor to compensate for the additional price it costs. We believe our workmen are superior to those of any country in the world. In former years we came into competition in this industry with Great Britain, and we almost swept her ships from the China Seas, by our superiority of model; our clipper ships were the best in the world, and to this day Great Britain has never known how to build the model of a ship except as she has been taught it by us. With all her superior and powerful engines, her ships were almost always slow, because the models were bad. At present we recognize the fact that the days of wooden ship-building are over. We may in this country, as they have in Great Britain, enter upon the construction of composite vessels, i. e., iron vessels, the bottoms of which are covered with plank, and again covered with copper. But we know that the great bulk of ships being built for the ocean are iron ships; and we believe that if the opportunity is afforded us, we can begin almost immediately to compete with Great Britain in building iron ships. All that we ask is, that we may have the materials as low as they are furnished to her ship-builders.

Q. What I understand you want, then, is this: That the government shall give you a bounty upon American materials used, equal to a drawback of duties on foreign materials, if they were used?

Mr. WESTERVELT. Yes, sir; that is about it. We prefer to use our own iron, and that the government will pay to us, on the American iron we use, an amount equal to the duty we should receive if a drawback were allowed on an equal quantity of foreign iron.

Q. Is there not this difference between giving a bounty and giving a drawback: That the drawback applies to money which has never gone into the treasury, never been in the possession of the government, and, therefore, is not an actual loss of revenue, while the bounties you ask require money to be paid directly from the treasury?

Mr. WESTERVELT. That is true; but our idea is to promote the interests of our own people, by building American ships of American materials.

WM. ROWLAND, (ship-builder,) of the same committee, made the following statement:

I would like to take exception to the expression used by Mr. Westervelt, that we were asking a bounty. It is a well understood principle that when money paid out brings back an equivalent consideration, the money so paid is not a bounty. Now, we propose to give a consideration in return for the money we ask the government to pay us. A great many people think that the best thing to be done to revive the ship-building interest is to take the duty off from iron. But that would not give us present relief at all in this country; it might ten years hence, but that would not answer our purpose. Our relief must come within the next twelve months, or the ship-building interests are gone. The consideration which we shall give the government in return for the money we ask is, the education of her seamen and mechanics for the ships required in time of war. Certainly if the government ever gets into trouble with a foreign nation, she will need us. To-day the government has not a ship of war that would not be a laughing-stock if sent abroad as a first-class naval vessel. During the last war, I had the honor of building the first monitor and the first iron-clad for the government; and I should very much dislike to think that those vessels were to be taken to England as an exhibition of what American skill can produce. And we cannot build vessels unless we have workmen; and I think government can well afford to educate the workmen of this country, as well as States can afford to build public school-houses and support schools for the education of the children. If the school-house is locked up, and the schoolmaster abroad, education will deteriorate. And so will ship-building, if ship-yards are closed and the workmen dismissed.

Mr. MORRELL inquired whether the government would not receive a greater benefit than the money now asked to be paid, by the additional employment this protection would give to our people.

Mr. ROWLAND. The compensation which we furnish is direct. It is just as directly for the benefit of the government as to cast cannon at your arsenals in time of peace, and wait for war to break out before using them. These ships, and men who know how to build the ships, are absolutely necessary for the safety of the government. They are of as much consequence to the navy of the country in time of war as the men you employ in the army. I do not like the word "bounty" to be used in this connection.

Mr. HOLMAN. Would not the simple allowance of a drawback upon the foreign material used furnish sufficient encouragement to revive the ship-building interests of the country?

Mr. ROWLAND. I cannot see how a drawback upon iron would be of any value to us at present. The iron that goes into the construction of an American ship must be rolled in this country. The raw material might come from England, but it must be rolled within five hundred miles of where the ship is to be built, or else the material will never go into the ship. Every vessel is built on its own model; and plates could not be rolled in England for one vessel which could be made available for other vessels here. Notwithstanding our great facilities of communication with England, I do not believe it would be possible to obtain the plates for a thousand-ton iron ship from England within three months after they were ordered.

Mr. LYNCH inquired whether the business of ship-building was not so perfected that a vessel could be built here of the same class of those to be built in England, and the iron received for them within a reasonably short time.

Mr. ROWLAND. No, sir; I think not. Plates are rolled to fit, without being cut at all, though I always allow for an inch. The iron scrap, or waste, of a three-thousand-ton ship amounts to about two per cent.

of the whole weight. This consists of the trimmings of the plates and what is punched out of the rivet holes. This should be reduced to one per cent., and undoubtedly will be, when we have had sufficient experience. The frames are also all rolled, and cut to a particular length.

Mr. WASHBURNE inquired what would be the cost of the raw material upon which a duty is paid for building a three-thousand-ton ship.

Mr. ROWLAND. I am not prepared to state to you what the cost would be. There would be about twelve hundred tons of materials of all descriptions in the ship, mostly of iron; very little copper is used. Even in the construction of engines much less copper is used than formerly. We find that iron is better. The loss of material caused by galvanic currents formed by the combination of iron and copper is prevented when only iron is used.

Mr. HOLMAN inquired whether the duty on copper affected the cost of ship-building very much.

Mr. ROWLAND. It affects the cost of building wooden ships materially, and let me say that I think Mr. Westervelt is very much mistaken when he thinks the days of building wooden ships are over. I doubt very much whether that day has arrived.

Mr. WESTERVELT. I make that statement from data which I think will convince any one. For instance, the average lifetime of a wooden ship is not more than twelve years, and there is always an uncertainty as to the time the vessel will live. During the war, gunboats were built which are already unfit for service; whereas a first-class iron ship will last for twenty-one years, without any difficulty. And although I am a wooden ship-builder, and never built an iron ship in my life, I am still of the opinion that the days of wooden ships are at an end. I never expect to build another. I believe that composite ships will be introduced into this country, as they have been into Great Britain. During the war we built for the government the Brooklyn, and some of the first batch of double-enders.

Mr. LYNCH inquired what were the advantages of composite ships.

Mr. WESTERVELT. The trouble with iron ships is, the bottoms soon become foul, covered with barnacles and sea-grass, so as greatly to impede their progress through the water; while ships the bottoms of which are covered with wood and coated with copper will remain in the water a long time without becoming foul. These composite ships will last as long as iron. The frames *are* iron; the planks being attached to the iron frames. The ventilation is so complete that there is no danger of the planks rotting. Wooden ships rot where the planks come in contact with the wooden frames. Inside the planking, five or six inches distant, slats are fastened, to prevent the cargo from coming in contact with the planking. The cost of composite ships, too, is considerably less than that of iron ships; and our ship-builders in this country would have this advantage in their construction, that wood is cheaper here. They are exceedingly useful in long voyages, particularly the tea trade. I have seen one of these vessels, after returning to Liverpool from China, with her bottom so clean that you would scarcely suppose she had been out more then ten or fifteen days.

Mr. LYNCH inquired as to the cost of insurance upon this class of ships.

Mr. WESTERVELT. I cannot answer that question accurately. I should suppose they would not rate quite as low as an iron vessel, although they are really as safe in every respect. They are no more liable to burn up, and the chance of the crew escaping in case of fire would really be greater. There is not very much difference in the strength; for the frame is iron, and the thickness of the planking is sufficient to give it the proper amount of strength.

Mr. WASHBÜRNE inquired what percentage of the whole cost of vessels it would be necessary for the government to pay to enable builders in this country to compete with those abroad?

Mr. WESTERVELT. I am not able to answer accurately. I should say, in sailing ships, thirty-three and a third per cent. would probably be sufficient. Sailing ships are now constructed in Great Britain for about fourteen pounds sterling per ton, and steamships for about twenty-three or twenty-four pounds sterling per ton. Ship-builders in this country, I think, would be able to construct better ships, because the materials here are better, in respect to both wood and iron. Iron steamships, in Great Britain, are constructed according to what is called Lloyd's specifications, and are required to conform to those specifications in order to enable the owners to effect their insurance. A certain thickness of the plates is required for a vessel of a certain tonnage; and, indeed, the specifications enter into so great a variety of details that anybody who can read can build a ship according to Lloyd's specifications. They are based upon the supposition that all iron is of the same strength; although the iron in this country is very much stronger than theirs, so that a considerably less thickness of plate would give the same strength as required by their specifications, when made of English iron. In fact, a less thickness of iron of our superior quality makes a better ship. Many parts of a ship are subject to a tension strain rather than a pressing strain. If only the latter were to be guarded against, cast iron would be very much better than wrought iron; for you can subject it to a great pressing strain without injury. Nor is it necessary that the iron should be of such thickness as not to yield, to a certain extent, under pressure. In fact, a ship which will yield a little, under a heavy sea, may be stronger and safer than one perfectly unyielding, as all of us know is true in the case of a bridge.

Mr. LYNCH inquired whether these composite ships usually have iron masts and rigging?

Mr. WESTERVELT. Most of them have iron masts, and some have iron yards also. Iron masts are made hollow, like a stove-pipe, with a hole at the top extending through to the bottom.

Mr. HOLMAN asked whether American ship-builders had not protection and encouragement in the fact that a very large percentage of the tonnage of the whole country was in the coasting trade, which, by law, is exclusively in the hands of American builders?

Mr. WESTERVELT. Yes, sir; and that is the only encouragement and safety we have. But for that the entire ship-building interests in the United States would inevitably be lost; but even that is changing very rapidly. Steam is monopolizing the coastwise trade, just as it has the foreign trade; and if we allow foreigners to compete with us in the coastwise trade, it will not be five years before we shall not have an American ship upon our waters. We are already losing rapidly in this respect, under our present laws; and if foreign-built ocean ships are permitted to have an American register, it will not be long before, having American crews, and being in fact then American ships, we shall find them transferred to our coastwise trade. I do not think there is any safety whatever to the commercial interests of this country in allowing foreigners to compete with us in building ships which are to have an American register, either for the foreign or the coastwise trade. We must keep them off. The most of our ship-builders are already quitting the business, and it will not be long before none will be left, unless something is done to encourage ship-building in this country. We are doing nothing in our own yard; we have employed hardly five men a week during the last six months.

Mr. LYNCH inquired whether the tendency now was not to crowd our vessels out of the foreign trade altogether, and force them into the coastwise trade, in which there was no competition?

Mr. WESTERVELT. Yes, sir; very greatly so. The only ocean trade left us, which is at all profitable, is the California business; and that only pays a few favorite ships, which have the reputation of great speed; and the competition has been so great among them for the past year that freights have been taken out at ruinously low rates, at which, of course, the vessels made ruinous voyages. I do not think a single dollar has been made by any American ship-owner, in any voyage to Liverpool, within the last five years. Still, we have ships that are continually running in the hope of occasionally making a paying voyage, and in the hope that something will occur to encourage them in this trade. Our ships are being worn out, and very few are being built. Some few are built to the eastward, but there is very little sale for them. They are often brought to New York and sold greatly below cost.

Mr. WASHBURN inquired whether the ship-builders of this country could construct steamers able to compete with the Cunard and Inman lines, and which at the same time would be useful as war vessels in time of war?

Mr. WESTERVELT. I think not. I think that great speed is rather antagonistic to the elements required for an efficient fighting vessel.

Mr. WASHBURN. Would not a great many ships, in case of a war—with Great Britain, for instance—be employed to prey upon the enemy's commerce, and would not great speed be required for this?

Mr. WESTERVELT. Yes, sir; and also for transportation, as was the case in the Crimean war. We built ships years ago capable of greater speed than any other nation could build; and we can do it now, if we have the proper encouragement. There are plans and drawings now in existence of a ship that will cross the Atlantic within seven days, I think, without doubt. We are ahead of all other nations with respect to models, and have always been. Wherever we have come into competition with the English in this respect we have always beaten.

Mr. WASHBURN asked whether war vessels could be built as well in private ship yards as at the government yards?

Mr. WESTERVELT. I think the private yards can build better ships. If the United States government desired to get war vessels that should exceed in excellence those of any other country, it should call upon the ship-builders of the country for models, plans, and drawings. When we made our contract for the ship of war Brooklyn, almost all the naval men said she would be a failure. But Admiral Farragut told me, in the presence of a number of gentlemen, that he considered her the most efficient vessel in the United States Navy. There are very few vessels now in the navy which can properly be called good vessels. I do not know of a single one built during the war that it would be desirable to duplicate for our navy. There are still good vessels in the navy, however, built before the war.

Mr. LYNCH inquired whether the plans and drawings to which the witness referred as being those of fast steamers were for screw propellers or side-wheel boats.

Mr. WESTERVELT. Side-wheelers. The great hindrance in crossing the Atlantic has been the great draught of water. Here our English friends have made their great mistake—in increasing their draught in proportion to the size of their vessels. A ship, to sail rapidly, must draw as little water as possible. We now recognize the fact that the Atlantic Ocean is simply a ferry, and that ships of one class are to be built simply to take passengers and their baggage, while ships of an entirely different class are to take the freight.

Mr. L. H. BOOLE, of the same committee, made the following statement:

There are one or two things I would like to say. In the first place, a great deal has been said, and written, and sent to this committee in the shape of letters and reports, by men who ought to have known and done better; letters of condemnation of our ship-builders, holding them up to ridicule. Now, it is true we cannot compete with the Clyde builders. Our materials are high, our labor very high. But these very men to whom I have referred—the ship-owners, who say in their report that there has been no improvement in ship-building in this country for the last ten years—are thus condemning the very men who in years past have furnished them the finest models of ships that ever floated on the ocean. One of the difficulties we have had to contend with is that the most of the ships we build are built by contract. The parties for whom we build furnish a superintendent, who is constantly present to see that the ship is built to suit their notions. This necessarily involves an increased cost of building. If the builders were allowed to exercise their own judgment, and their own ingenuity, they could build as good or better ships for fifteen or twenty per cent. less money.

The ships built upon the Clyde are not to be compared with our ships in either joinery or finish, in any respect. And yet these ship-owners, who require us to finish our ships in the best style of joinery, and to expend a great amount of labor upon the finish, are ready to go abroad and buy those cheap Clyde-built ships. I call your attention to a letter, which is already in your possession, stating that the working men of the Clyde have their minds so thoroughly made up upon running this business out of this country that they are willing to submit to any reduction of wages, and to any amount of sacrifice necessary to prevent our competing with them. Not more than four or five shillings a day is now paid there for skilled workmen; and yet these men are working day after day, and are willing to submit to greater sacrifices in order to compete with us in this country. It has often been remarked that, when you go on board these English steamers, you do not find any such finish, nor any such joinery, as you will find on our ships.

I would like to say just one word in regard to the coasting business. Our American builders not only want to compete for the coastwise trade, but they want to compete with the world in the building of ships. The people abroad could not build wooden ships equal to our models, and were, therefore, driven, from necessity, to build ships of iron. They have not the wood; they have the iron, and they can now turn out very good iron ships from our models. The commerce upon our lakes is just about the same as the coasting trade, and the extent of that commerce may not be known. In the years of 1856, 1857, and 1858, it is stated that the lake commerce amounted to about six hundred millions of dollars per annum. In the year 1856, the commerce which passed the St. Clair flats, exclusive of the coasting trade of the lake, amounted to upwards of four hundred millions of dollars. It was then something of a novelty for a Canadian vessel to come into one of our ports. Now, you see, a majority of the vessels in our lake ports are from Canada; and many of our ship-builders, formerly in Boston, have gone to Montreal and Quebec. It has been said very often of late by the British, that our weak spot was in the dwindling of our shipping. Only a little while ago a committee was endeavoring to make arrangements for carrying the freight from the Pacific railroad over the Grand Trunk railroad to Portland; and, in their way, they seemed to be working with success to draw our trade away from us.

I do not think the day for wooden ships is past, by any means. Our forests in Florida, Texas, Wisconsin, Michigan, and Maine, contain too large an amount of excellent ship-timber for that. The wooden clipper ships of this country can still go abroad with good profit. The idea was some years ago conceived by western men of building ships in the woods, loading them with grain, and sending them abroad to be sold. We found that the plan was feasible; and the only thing that prevented its being carried out was, that the Welland Canal was not sufficient to enable sea-going vessels to go through. Then parties from Boston and Chicago undertook to see if something could not be done for the enlargement of that canal. But they met with no encouragement from the Canadian authorities. Now, when the success of the enterprise would be for their benefit, they propose to enlarge the Welland Canal so as to enable *them* to build wooden ships, and send them abroad, as *we* formerly proposed to do.

Mr. HOLMAN inquired whether the ship-building interests of Canada were more prosperous than on this side of the line.

Mr. BOOLE. Yes, sir. Within the last three years that business has been very prosperous in Canada. I was not long since in a Canadian ship yard, in which six or seven vessels for the upper lakes were being built; and the price paid to the workmen was from sixty to seventy cents a day, in silver. This industry has been rapidly progressing, within the last two or three years, at Quebec, Montreal, and Three Rivers; and many of the men now employed there were formerly employed in Boston and other points in the United States. A few years ago you could tell a "Kanuck" vessel as far as you could see it; now, they have so improved in their construction that you cannot tell one until you get on board—though our vessels are still superior to theirs, when you examine them closely.

Mr. HOLMAN inquired whether an allowance equal to a drawback on the materials used, in spite of our higher rates of wages, would enable American ship-builders to compete with foreigners.

Mr. BOOLE. I think it would, if the law was so positive that ship-builders could be assured it would not soon be repealed. My judgment, after a very close calculation, is, that there is about thirty per cent. difference in the cost of building here and abroad. I think that if the government would pay to the ship-builders one-third the costs, in the shape of bounty, or whatever you choose to call it, it would enable them to compete with foreign ship-builders.

Another difficulty is, the higher rate of interest upon capital in this country than abroad. But if the business were rendered permanent, I think our ship-builders would be ready to enter vigorously into the competition. Formerly, ship carpenters commanded a higher rate of wages than those employed in building houses, &c. We then paid them five dollars a day, while they now command but three, or three and a half. House carpenters have the advantage, that houses cannot be built abroad and brought here, as railroads cannot be built abroad and brought here; while ships *can* be built abroad and brought here. Formerly, apprentices were glad to work for nothing, or at very low wages, in order to learn the art of ship-building, knowing that as a journeyman he could make good wages at that business; now there are no apprentices employed in our yards. I have four boys, and I would rather they would go into almost anything else than into a ship-yard—although I would be proud to bring them up in that business, if it could be established upon a basis such that ship-builders could live.

An English gentleman, who came to this country some years ago, could not understand how it was that we could send our lake and river steamers through the water at the rate of twenty miles an hour. He traveled up the Hudson, and from Buffalo to Cleveland, at that rate; but such boats are not now in existence. The tonnage of American vessels on the lakes is decreasing rapidly, while that of Canadian vessels is increasing as rapidly.

Iron vessels, so far, have not succeeded on the lakes as grain carriers.

Mr. HOLMAN inquired whether wooden vessels could not be built in this country as cheaply as in Canada.

Mr. BOOLE. No, sir; at the breaking out of the war we were getting the finest quality of timber at twelve or fifteen dollars a thousand, in the West. So large a quantity was then called for to be taken down the river to repair forts, and for other purposes connected with the war, that the price went up to twenty-eight or thirty dollars a thousand; and now it is about twenty or twenty-two dollars a thousand. We of course can get all the lumber we want in this country; but in Canada labor is so low that they make it into ships cheaper. There is a difference in the amount of labor a Canadian and an American will do; still, two Canadians will do more work than one American, although they together receive about the same pay as the American. In Canada no duty is paid on any article entering into the construction of a vessel, if the builder imports it himself. Very little copper is used in Canadian-built vessels, and in other respects they are built different from ours; they are built almost altogether of straight timber. Again, there are underwriters, who have gotten up specifications for ship-building, as the Lloyds have in England; and the builders are required to conform to these specifications in order to effect insurance.

I think it has been estimated in this country that the duties paid on a thousand-ton iron ship amount to about eleven or twelve thousand dollars; that is, about eleven or twelve dollars a ton. Vessels can now be built in Canada at a cost about forty per cent. less than in this country. We used to estimate an A No. 1 vessel at about a dollar a bushel; that is, a vessel carrying sixteen thousand bushels of grain would cost about sixteen thousand dollars; but now, I think the cost in this country is about one dollar and seventy-five cents per bushel; while Canada builders are able to construct their vessels lower than ever before.

Mr. WELLS inquired what proportion of the war vessels were built at private yards during the war.

Mr. WESTERVELT. I cannot answer that question with accuracy. The double-enders were built at private yards; and the first batch of gunboats, and several monitors; also a number of cutters; but what proportion of the whole I am unable to say.

WASHINGTON, *December* 16, 1869.

Committee met. Present: The chairman, and Messrs. Calkin and Holman.

Mr. JOHN ROACH proprietor of the Morgan Iron Works, New York, appeared, and made a statement to the committee. He said that he had been connected with the iron business for thirty-five years; and had also been engaged in building all parts of ships of every kind, from the smallest to the largest.

Immediately after the late civil war, he gave the matter a great deal of consideration.

He had made up his mind, from the prospects which he saw ahead, and from the cost of building ships in America, that something must be done; and had therefore sent some of the most competent persons connected with ship-building in New York, and some competent engineers, to Europe, procuring for them letters of introduction from the Secretary of State, which gained for them admission into all the dock-yards of England and France, and other countries where ship-building was carried on to any extent. He sent them at his own expense, in order that they might furnish him with information in regard to ship-building, and as to the superiority of iron ships over wooden ones. By this means he had probably acquired more information in detail upon this subject than was possessed by any one man in England or this country.

The instructions which he had given those persons were to obtain, not *newspaper* information, but *practical* information.

He had made up his mind that, sooner or later, Congress would discover, and would act upon the discovery, that no nation could be truly and permanently great which had to depend upon another nation for its ships, particularly when itself possessed abundant resources for building ships.

But aware that no man would have any right to come to Congress and ask for protective legislation unless he had first adopted every means in his power to protect himself, he had determined to spend a quarter of a million of dollars in perfecting machinery.

The consequence was that his alone, out of ten large marine-engine shops which had been in operation in the city of New York before the war, had been able to survive the present state of affairs. He had thus far been able to keep his shops open without sinking capital.

By a personal investigation of the matter, going around to different establishments, he had ascertained that the number of men engaged in the construction of ships, and in the various trades connected therewith, before the war, was about twenty thousand, besides about two thousand young men then engaged in learning the business.

To-day, out of the ten marine-engine shops that were in existence in New York at the commencement of the war, his was the only one remaining in existence. Some of them had been turned into small mills, some of them into stables. The ship-yards had all been closed except one, which was engaged in building a coasting vessel. He had no doubt that a similar state of things existed in other parts of the country.

The question was asked, whether all this had been brought about because the carrying trade was diminished?

He thought not; on the contrary, he believed that the carrying trade had increased. He had found out, by personal examination within the last year, that there were one hundred and nineteen iron steamships plying between the ports of America and of Great Britain. Of that number, one hundred and ten were running to the port of New York, with an aggregate tonnage of 311,600 tons. But of all these, with the exception of the Pacific Mail Steamship Company's steamers, of which two a month ran from New York, there was not a single steamship in the great commercial city of America, engaged in the foreign trade, carrying the American flag.

The last one that had crossed the ocean was the steamship Fulton, and he had taken her, last week, for a debt, for the purpose of breaking her up.

And this was the present condition of American commerce.

He had no doubt that a great pressure would be brought to bear upon Congress in regard to the introduction of foreign ships. But he was prepared to meet that question, and to show that such a policy was not consistent with the welfare of the United States.

In the one hundred and nineteen ships to which he had alluded, there was a capital of eighty millions of dollars invested. The greater portion of the earnings of these ships came from the carrying of American mails, American passengers, and American commerce.

Upon a close calculation, the repairs of all these ships, embracing their hulls, furniture and machinery, would amount to about nine millions of dollars per annum. Of that sum there was not one hundred thousand dollars per annum spent in this country, although the greater portion of the earnings of these ships was collected from citizens of the United States. They bring with them their own boats, their own putty, their own red lead, and everything connected with the repairing of a ship, and have those repairs done by their own crews; and it is only in case that general repairs are needed that they call upon the New York engine shops for a little aid. Here is an item of eight millions of dollars, for repairs alone, turned away from this country and sent abroad.

America had lost her commerce; and what had she obtained in exchange for it?

Simply the right for a few men to charge nine dollars per ton, in gold, on the importation of pig iron!

Pig iron was the basis of all other metals connected with the making and repairing of ships. There had been a revolution in ship-building, and iron was the material from which they were now built. The high cost of iron, produced by the tariff upon it, was one of the principal difficulties that our commerce had to contend with.

It might be said that Americans had protection in the coasting trade; but he could show the committee that that amounted to nothing.

There was probably no man in America who had more at stake in this matter than himself. He had a million of dollars in property dependent upon the building of ships, and, so far as he was concerned, he did not care how soon the coasting trade was thrown open to foreigners.

The men engaged in the coasting trade can now scarcely live and pay their bills. On account of the high duty on the materials used, it now costs fifty per cent. more to repair ships in America than in other countries, and on this account, and from the fact that this country is now so intersected and cut up by railroads, the coasting trade by sea is, to a large extent, done away with. Even the New Orleans trade is disappearing, because vessels are sent down there from England to carry the cotton to Europe. The Mobile trade is also passing away; so is the Baltimore trade. Foreign steamers frequent these ports, and thus this coasting trade of which so much has been said, after all, does not amount to anything.

There had been three propositions before the committee in regard to the mode of relief of American commerce. The first of these, as he understood it, was to permit Americans to go abroad and buy ships. The men who had suggested this idea were mostly men who had come to this country since American commerce had been transferred to England; who had opened shops in New York and were doing a foreign trade. He thought there were enough ships now to carry the trade. The trouble was, they belong in the wrong direction—they are owned by men over the water. If this privilege were granted, he regarded it as being nothing more nor less than permitting the one hundred and nineteen steamers now plying in the port of New York to do so under the American flag.

They would be owned abroad, in order to avoid American taxation, but their business would be transacted on this side.

A gentleman from the New York Chamber of Commerce called upon him a few weeks since and inquired what objection there could be to having ships built on the other side of the water. In reply, he asked the gentleman the simple question what he wanted to accomplish by buying ships abroad? The gentleman answered, "Nothing more than to bring commerce back to where it was before the war." He, Mr. Roach, then asked the gentleman, "Do you know where it was before the war? With what portion of commerce would you be satisfied?" The gentleman replied, "Nothing less than we then had, which was nearly one-third the entire commerce of the world." If this were to be undertaken, and if it were attempted to be brought about by buying ships to replace those which carried the American commerce before the war, it would require an expenditure of one hundred and fifty millions of dollars; and this money would be paid to England, the only great ship-building country in the world; and the effect would be to increase the price of ships at least twenty per cent. Besides, by so doing, all the American ship-yards and founderies would be closed, and the materials of American mines would remain unused. Again, everybody will recollect the difficulties experienced during the war from the want of ships; and American ship-yards and engine-shops were in a much better condition at the breaking out of the war than they are now. Yet it was found that when the government called upon private establishments, and gave them contracts for building ships and engines, the work that should have been done in one year was not done in four years. The ship-yards and founderies were not prepared to do the work. Had the American founderies and ship-yards and machine-shops been in the efficient condition in which such establishments then were and now are in Great Britain, he actually believed that the rebellion could have been put down at half the expense, if not in half the time, it really was.

Congress was much excited regarding the depredations committed by the Alabama. The Alabama was only one ship let loose upon American commerce; but here were to-day, coming into the harbor of New York, a hundred and twenty ships, each one of them more formidable and of greater speed than the Alabama, built by English builders, owned by English merchants, and to some extent under the supervision of English naval officers; so that, while now engaged in the peaceful pursuits of commerce, in forty-eight hours they could be converted into most effective ships of war.

If any one should inquire what American ship-builders were to give in return for the favors they asked, he would reply that one of these days the Navy Department would be asking Congress for an appropriation of fifty or sixty millions of dollars for the purpose of making a more efficient navy; and a very large proportion of that amount might be saved by encouraging American merchants in time of peace to build say a hundred steamers. The hundred and twenty English steamers now carrying our commerce were double the tonnage of the whole American navy. This fact he stated from authentic information; it was no loose and careless statement. And they were ready to be set at work at any time and for any purpose for which Great Britain might want to use them.

Again, if America were to close up her ship-yards and marine engine shops, and depend upon Great Britain to build her ships, she would be in the most helpless condition conceivable. The day is not far distant when it will concern the men who have capital invested in the prairies of the West, and the cotton plantations of the South, as much as the merchants of New York, to take an interest in and to protect the commerce of America. The people of the United States should be in a position to take that advantage of English commerce, in case of a war between England and France, that England took of American commerce when the United States were at war. The island of Great Britain is of no greater extent than the State of New York or Pennsylvania; and if her commerce were taken from her, what would be left of her? She would become one of the most helpless nations on the face of the earth. He, Mr. Roach, could not understand why nine dollars a ton duty should be paid on pig-iron, or why there should be any duty at all upon it. American iron and American engine-shops are as much American manufactures and were as essential to the prosperity of the nation as American rolling mills or other property; and yet American ship-yards and American engine-shops have no protection at all. The iron ore can be taken from the mines, and with ordinary, uneducated labor can be converted into pig-iron in forty-eight hours; but no nation would ever know the value of her ship-builders and mechanics of that class until she needed skilled workmen. The material is easily obtained; but it is of very little use without skilled workmen to work it. With the ship-yards and marine engine shops closed, and with these men, who had spent their lifetime in learning and becoming skillful in these trades, gone into other pursuits, it would be impossible to educate workmen in their stead. There would be as much possibility of educating children in the sciences with the school-houses locked up and the school-teachers gone away.

The CHAIRMAN. What remedies do you propose?

Mr. ROACH. In view of these one hundred and twenty steamers now engaged in carrying our commerce, I have looked at the matter in this light: What would be considered a healthy growth of American commerce? I think that the annual production of twenty such ships would be a healthy growth. They would cost from twelve to fifteen millions of dollars. In five years that would cause an outlay of, say one hundred million of dollars, which would seem to me to be a very simple and easy burden for this country to carry. My idea is that Congress should settle upon a percentage to be given the ship-builders, by way of bounty; not letting it go into the hands of speculators or mail contractors, but providing that, on every vessel built for the foreign trade, a certain amount should be allowed to the party building the ship. I think that at present twenty per cent. would be about a fair allowance. That percentage of twenty million dollars, which is my estimate of what would be a healthy growth of American commerce, annually, would be four million dollars. Can no way be found to distribute that four million dollars per annum over other interests that will not feel it, and thus help revive a most important interest that is utterly crushed? By helping to build ships, instead of sending one hundred and fifty millions of dollars abroad to buy ships, you develope your own iron mines, you give employment to your own workmen, you stimulate your own manufacturing interests.

The question may be asked, what is the country going to get back for this outlay? I answer, we would save you almost that much in the service which these vessels would be to your navy.

The CHAIRMAN. How would you apply your idea more in detail? In what shape should the money be given?

Mr. ROACH. In the shape of a percentage to every merchant, or other person, who should build a ship for the foreign trade; so much per ton upon the tonnage of the vessel as registered in the custom-house.

The CHAIRMAN. If a certain amount, equal to the duties paid on the materials entering into the construction of the vessel, were remitted, would there then be a demand for vessels to be built here?

Mr. ROACH. I think so. I make this statement upon accurate information as to the comparative cost of ship-building here and abroad. Whenever you resume specie payments, and as the tariff is gradually reduced, the amount necessary to be paid by government to put American ship-builders on an equal footing with foreign ones will gradually decrease, until the building of ships will cost the government nothing.

I saw a statement recently that our government was scarcely able to procure sailors; and that reminded me of what a gentleman remarked to me the other day. Said he, "Mr. Roach, if I wanted to destroy New York by a fleet of ships, I do not know but that I would have to get Englishmen to do it; they know our channel now much better than we do ourselves."

Mr. HOLMAN. During the last twenty years has not the tonnage employed in domestic commerce been equal to at least fifty per cent. of the entire tonnage of the country, and is not at this time the tonnage engaged in the domestic trade equal to seventy per cent. of the whole?

Mr. ROACH. Our domestic tonnage has increased, but you will find that it will largely decrease. Previous to the completion of the Pacific railroad, the Pacific Mail Steamship Company sent out four ships per month from New York, and the North American Steamship Company three ships; in all seven ships a month. Now there are but two ships engaged in that trade, instead of seven; and it would hardly be fair to expect that our coasting tonnage would keep on increasing in the future as it has increased in the past, because our railroads, intersecting the country everywhere, have cut into that trade to a very great extent. The New Orleans trade is not more than half what it formerly was. There used to be three or four large lines of steamers plying between New York and New Orleans. Now there are five English lines between New Orleans and England, and four English lines to Baltimore.

Mr. HOLMAN. Do you think that allowing the American ship-builder a drawback, or rebate of the duties and taxes, external and internal, on the materials entering into the construction of ships, would be sufficient to revive ship-building?

Mr. ROACH. I think there is no possible doubt of it. I am speaking from accurate information, when I tell you that things are not represented to you by the other side in their true light, because in every move that we make in Congress, we are striking at the seventy or eighty millions of capital invested in those one hundred and twenty steamships plying to New York; and it is a death-struggle whether the one hundred and fifty millions of dollars that are to be invested in American steamships, shall be expended in this country, or on the Clyde. I have been trying to get this very information, which I have placed before you, published in the New York press, but I could not do it. There is now on the one side, the interests of the broken down ship-builders, and broken down merchants of America, applying to Congress for relief; and there is on the other side, this capital of seventy or eighty millions of dollars concentrated in opposition. We have the facilities for ship-building in America. Our ship-builders and our engine-builders, amid all their discouragements, have not been idle. Tney have been closely watching the movement and the progress of the trade on the other side. And we can go to work to-day and build a faster ship than England can, and that will carry one-third more cargo, while it consumes no more fuel.

Mr. HOLMAN. I see that your mind favors the idea of the government paying to the ship-builder a bounty equivalent to the taxes imposed upon the materials; that is, equivalent to the taxes which *would* be imposed upon the materials, providing they were imported. Now, if instead of paying to the ship-builder a bounty, which would be equal to perhaps thirty per cent, the policy were to be resorted to of returning to him all the duties on the articles entering into the coustruction of the ship, what would the effect be?

Mr. ROACH. I did not come here to ask a bounty. I came here to tell you that, while all other articles of American produce are protected to a great extent, there is no protection for American ships. If Congress will take off all the duties from American iron, reducing it to tho price of foreign iron, then we are prepared to compete with foreign ship-builders. The labor question is misstated. We are prepared to meet that difficulty, and to ask no further legislation on the subject.

Mr. HOLMAN. You think, then, that a rebate of the taxes would be a sufficient encouragement to ship-building?

Mr. ROACH. Yes, sir; if we could avail ourselves of the benefits of it. But there is a practical difficulty in the way, right here. Iron has come to supersede wood in ship-building. The ships of the future will be built of iron. There is a class of iron manufactured, and imported, and converted into general use all over the civilized world; it is from the thickness of four inches to the thickness of a wire; but only about one-tenth of the iron we use in the building of a ship, is this imported iron; so that by the rebate of duties we would get no relief except to the extent of about one-tenth of the materials used. The question may arise, why not import the whole of the iron used in the ship? Simply because that would involve almost or quite three times the capital required to carry on the business, and when a man conducts his business upon such a plan that it requires three times the capital that ought to be required, he cannot conduct that business successfully. For instance, if a man makes a contract with me to build a ship, in agreeing upon the terms of payment, I say to him, the first payment is to be made when the keel and the first tier of plates connected with it are laid; and the second payment when the next tier of plates is laid; and so on dividing the payment into ten distinct parts. Now, if I am obliged to import my materials, I must make my drawings, and send them to Scotland, and import all those tons of iron *at once*, and pay for them; which will require a much larger capital than it would otherwise have been necessary for me to use. Besides, it is impossible for one ship-builder to compete with another, when the one is obliged to bring so heavy a material as iron from a distance of three thousand miles, and across the ocean. The freight on iron is a good deal more than it was some years ago, when it was transported in sailing-vessels; it is now transported in steamers. Some is yet transported in sailing-vessels; but the pig-iron, transported in steamers, is to-day worth in New York two dollars per ton more than that transported in sailing-vessels. A great proportion of all the pig-iron sold in New York is sold to consumers "to arrive." The purchaser can tell to a day when a steamer will arrive with his iron on board, and make his arrangements accordingly; but he cannot tell within weeks or even months the time when a sailing-vessel will arrive.

Mr. HOLMAN. Is there much pig-iron imported into this country?

Mr. ROACH. Very little, in comparison with what has been imported.

Mr. HOLMAN. And this duty of nine dollars per ton in gold, is an obstacle right in the way of that importation?

Mr. ROACH. Yes, sir.

Mr. HOLMAN. Would not the policy of allowing a rebate to the ship-builders of the duties on the materials entering into the construction of a ship, have the effect to bring down the cost of iron in this country? In other words, would not the American dealers be compelled to reduce the price of their iron, in order to prevent ship-builders from going abroad for it?

Mr. ROACH. I think it would have that effect. I think the ship-builders themselves would become the manufacturers of iron for their own ships. If such relief is given as will enable us to build ships, I will guarantee to put a rolling-mill in my ship-yard, and then I will be prepared to say to a man without regard to Pennsylvanian or other monopolies, "I will build you a ship for so much."

When gold was at 140, I could buy foreign pig-iron at a small price over what I could buy American iron for. To-day I can buy Scotch iron for seven dollars a ton less than I can buy American iron; the difference being in the premium on gold. I am really of the opinion that this difference in currency is used as a cloak for the advance of all commodities; for I find that nothing has sympathized with gold in proportion to the reduction of the premium.

WASHINGTON, D. C., *December* 21, 1869.

The committee met, all the members present.

Admiral PORTER appeared before the committee and made the following statement in reply to interrogatories: He said that the European governments had taken away entirely the American commerce on the Atlantic, and that we had now no steamships in the foreign trade, except one or two running to Brazil. If the United States possessed the steamships plying between New York and Europe, the government would have a better navy than it ever had. There was not a ship in the American Navy that could compare with the best ships on the English and French lines in point of speed, stability, or for carrying guns. The ship that would carry merchandise would carry guns. All those vessels could be fitted with masts in a very short time and rigged completely. They could keep the ocean three years without burning a pound of coal. This remark applied to the European screw-ships, of which he thought there were now sixty-five engaged in the New York trade, while the United States had not one. All the American mails were now carried in foreign steamships, which realized a very heavy profit from carrying the mails, particularly the French steamers. Each of those vessels carried from thirty to forty thousand letters a trip, and, as the French postage was double the English rate, it could be seen what a heavy profit they realized.

The CHAIRMAN. I understand you to say that a class of vessels can be built for commercial purpose that can be readily converted into vessels of war?

Admiral PORTER. Yes, sir; nearly every ship that was used during the war was a merchant ship. He went on to say that this diversion of the trade was driving from the American service all its naval engineers. The foreign vessels were all run by foreign engineers; there were not many American engineers on board of them.

When the rebellion broke out, all the American ships that were engaged in the European trade got such heavy profits from the government that they were at once absorbed in the navy. If the United States had possessed half the number of steamships now engaged in the European trade with New York, he did not think that the rebels would ever have got a bale of cotton from a southern port, and that the rebels would have had to submit long before they did. The American Navy at present was made up of tugs and old converted ships. It possessed ten or twelve or fourteen vessels that were planned to suit Isherwood's machinery, and at a cost which nobody knew. There had been $480,000,000 expended by the navy during the war, and he thought that $280,000,000 of that sum had been expended in the steam department, yet the navy had not much to show for it. Those ships, designed and built for Isherwood, were lying in navy-yards entirely useless. The department was trying to convert one of them into something, but it did not know whether it would succeed or not. It had been found necessary to take out half of her engines to make room for the people to live on board of her, and for the coal necessary to be carried. She was so filled with machinery and boilers that there was no place in her to carry coal or men. He referred to the Wampanoag. When that vessel went on the trial trip and came back into port, she had to send her crew on board the New Hampshire receiving ship, because she had no place to put them. There were twelve or fourteen of those vessels in the navy, and they were practically of no use. The navy also possessed about thirty tugs, the largest of them about three hundred and fifty tons. Two of them had been sent to sea the other day to take care of the iron-clad Dictator, going to Key West, and they had got into a gale of wind, and she had to take care of them; and these were two of the best of them. Then the navy had also a lot of little vessels, not inaptly described as canal-boats; vessels of five hundred tons. He believed that thirty ships such as the Pereire, on the French line, would make a better navy than the United States possessed to-day. There were a great many iron-clads on the navy list, but twenty-six of them had been condemned as being unfit for anything, except for old iron, and no one would buy them for that. There were about thirty good vessels in the navy altogether, fit for war purposes, and these were wooden vessels, and about ten monitors.

The CHAIRMAN. I understand you to say that if we had, at the commencement of our late war, thirty such vessels as you speak of—the best European steamers—they would have been as efficient as was our entire navy.

Admiral PORTER. Twice as efficient; I say that without any hesitation. The ships that we had could catch nothing. We never had a vessel that could run down a blockade-runner during the whole war, except the Vanderbilt and two others. Whenever we caught blockaders it was either with one of those fast tugs—vessels of fifty or sixty tons—or by the machinery of the blockade-runner breaking down, or by her getting into a fog and being surrounded by four or five of our vessels, when she would surrender rather than be fired at. I do not think that during the war we caught 30 vessels by fair running; that I am quite satisfied of. Any one of those vessels on the European lines can run away from anything we have got in our navy, and can run them out of sight in seven hours, and that is not saying a great deal. The iron-clads that we have are for home defense. They cannot go to sea. We send them to sea now and again, because we have nothing else to send, but they all require two or three vessels to go with them, in case they should break down or get out of coal. They are therefore of no use, except for harbor defense. In case of war with a foreign nation, such as Great Britain or France, our great power would be in cutting up their commerce. Great Britain could not stand a war six months with a fleet of vessels that we would send out after her commerce. They would break her up root and branch, and that kind of warfare would be more apt to bring about peace than fighting with iron-clads or heavy war vessels. The Alabama and another confederate vessel destroyed one hundred and eighty-six American vessels, amounting, I think, with cargoes, to about seventy millions of dollars. Now, if two vessels could do that, imagine what 200 could do. I think that one screw-propeller, which would use sail power, and when necessary put on steam, to chase or to be chased, would do more harm to a foreign enemy than all our iron-clads put together. We have other means of defending our coast, by torpedo-boats, obstructions, &c. But we want a good many fleet cruisers. Great Britain subsidizes all her foreign steamships. The profits of the Cunard line amount to twenty-two per cent. a year. I think that Great Britain has about three thousand steamships altogether, and, I suppose, that there must be at least three hundred of them subsidized.

Mr. CALKIN. You spoke about the decrease of American engineers, how is it in regard to captains and officers in the mercantile marine?

Admiral PORTER. They would constitute a force which we would be very glad to draw upon in case of emergency, as we did in the last war. Our naval force is very small, a mere nucleus. Every naval officer in time of war becomes an instructor. That was part of his occupation in the last war. Most of our officers were volunteers from the merchant service; hardy, brave fellows, but without education as to the duties of vessels of war, which it requires a pretty long time to learn. But in a war with a foreign nation we could not have a better class of men for the purpose of sending home prizes, or doing other subordinate duty. I am sorry to say, however, that the best class of men in our mercantile marine are fast disappearing. When we had sailing-vessels across the Atlantic, our packets were the most superior vessels in the world, and I do not think that even the best naval officers were better men than the captains of those ships. They were the best class of merchant seamen in the world. They are all disappearing. There is no field for them. They do not command steamships, and have no opportunity of displaying what they are, or of learning anything. I think that on that account it would be very advantageous for us to have a better system. All our good seamen have left our service and have gone into the service of foreign companies, almost losing their identity, and hardly knowing that they have got a flag. They have sailed so long with the English, the French, the Germans, and the Dutch, that they hardly fraternize with their own countrymen.

The CHAIRMAN. What would be the effect of going abroad to buy ships, instead of building them here?

Admiral PORTER. The first effect would be a very big political controversy.

The CHAIRMAN. I mean, what would be its effect upon the character of our mercantile marine and of our navy in time of war?

Admiral PORTER. If we were to go into that business altogether, it would break up the ship-building in this country, and that would be very impolitic. Our policy is to keep up our ship-building interests. There are only one or two ships on the stocks in New York now, and I have seen one hundred and fifty of them at a time.

Mr. CALKIN. There is only one ship on the stocks in New York.

Admiral PORTER. I do not think there is one at all in Boston. I was down the coast last summer, from Portland through the different cities, examining navy-yards and dry-docks and ship-yards, and I do not recollect seeing any more than that one ship building anywhere. That is a very sad picture.

Mr. CALKIN. There are one or two iron ships building at Wilmington, Delaware.

Admiral PORTER. Yes, and at this time they ought to be building a hundred ships for the home-trade. The only vessels that pay now are the old rat-traps that we sell out of the navy at a very low price, and on which profit may be made. As to making the profit that the European steamships make, they do not begin to do that anywhere in this country. To put our people in a fair position for the foreign trade, I think we ought to allow them to buy ships abroad to the extent of about twelve ships for the European trade, and twelve for the China trade, and then shut up on that business, and allow our own ship-builders drawbacks on all the articles used in the ship-building, iron, copper, cordage, hemp, and labor. The high duties not only affect the merchant service, but affect the navy. Every piece of iron that we use in the navy we have to pay duty on, because the American iron is charged for exactly the same as the English would cost with the duty on, and this takes away one-third of the appropriations of the navy. The department has, therefore, to ask for larger appropriations, as one-third of the money that Congress appropriates for the navy, goes off in duties.

The CHAIRMAN. I understood you to say that you think it will be very injurious to all the interests of our merchant marine, and to our means of defense in time of war, to depend upon foreigners for our ships?

Admiral PORTER. I think so. That would not do. But I say I would like to see enough of ships allowed to be bought on the Clyde, under proper naval inspection, to enable us at once to compete with Europe. I am quite satisfied that, if we had that privilege, we would drive just so many foreign ships from the ocean. We can beat them all in running ships and taking care of passengers. Every American crossing the ocean likes to travel under his own flag, instead of with foreigners. Then again, all Americans like to glorify on the 4th of July, and they find it very difficult to do that on board of a foreign ship. We have, I suppose, 30,000 Americans travelling back and forward every year for pleasure, and these 30,000 people are worth considering. I do not think, however, that it would be a good thing to have indiscriminate purchasing of vessels abroad. I think it should be under the control of Congress. If we had, it would destroy American ship-building forever. I think the other plan is preferable, to let the ship-builders have a very liberal drawback, and I think that with that they could build ships for pretty much what they did before the war.

Mr. MORRELL. Could it not be done by calculating the cost of duties and making an allowance to cover it of so much per ton?

Admiral PORTER. Yes; there would be no trouble about that. It is very easy to arrive at the cost of a ship. You can arrive at it within twenty dollars. When we build a ship of war, we can tell within twenty dollars what it costs, for every pound is weighed, and every foot of timber is measured.

Mr. MORRELL. In case it should be deemed wise to make an appropriation for building such vessels, would you have them built in the navy-yards or in private yards?

Admiral PORTER. I would have them built in private yards. I would not have them mixed up at all with navy-yards. They would cost more in the navy yards, because there would be a great deal better work put in them. They cannot build a bad ship in the navy-yards, they do not know how.

Mr. WASHBURN. If drawbacks were allowed on all materials entered into the construction of ships, could we build vessels as cheap as they build them on the Clyde?

Admiral PORTER. No, sir; labor here costs double what it costs on the Clyde.

Mr. WASHBURN. Then, if we cannot build as cheap, we cannot run steamships without subsidies.

Admiral PORTER. Not at all; I do not think that possible.

Mr. WASHBURN. How much subsidy do you suppose should be given to steamships?

Admiral PORTER. I would give them all the letter pos age.

Mr. WASHBURN. Would any one undertake to build and run a line of steamships for that?

Admiral PORTER. Yes, I think so. I think they ought not to have a dime beyond that. I have spent four years myself in running merchant steamships. I ran for three years to Chagres, and I carried a ship round the world, without any subsidy at all. Before the rebellion, I took the Golden Age to Australia, and there were in that time twelve vessels running between Sidney and Melbourne. In six months I ran every ship of them off. The last trip I made I carried seven hundred passengers, while the London, the best ship they had, carried only nineteen; the Golden Age was run by American officers who took trouble to please the passengers. In that way I know exactly how it pays to carry letters. We carried from London, at the time I left, forty-two thousand letters, the cheapest of them twenty eents, and many of them a dollar. The postage all went into the hands of the British government, and we received, I think, only about two thousand dollars for carrying the whole concern.

The CHAIRMAN. Has England any system of naval reserves in her merchant marine?

Admiral PORTER. Yes; a very large system. Every man of the British navy is amenable to a certain law, by which he is obliged to serve in case of war. England has in her merchant service a large reserve ot men, who are always obliged to be ready to present themselves at a moment's notice. She can raise eighty thousand seamen at a very short time. They are in the merchant marine in the time of peace, and the moment they are called upon in the time of war, they are obliged to go. They are conscripted without any bounty at all.

The CHAIRMAN. So that she has a very much larger contingent naval force than her naval force proper?

Admiral PORTER. Yes. Her naval reserve, which she can get within two weeks, amounts to twenty thousand men. Her merchant marine is far superior to ours. In the first place, no man will be shipped in the English merchant marine unless he can show an honorable discharge from the last vessel he left. They get good pay, and are better taken care of than our sailors. They are getting the same class of men in their service that we used to have. Their steamships are kept up exactly on the same principle as a vessel of war; their officers are uniformed the same as the officers of the navy, and they are all under naval regulations. Within the last ten years Great Britain has made the most wonderful strides in that direction.

Mr. HOLMAN. What is your opinion as to the extent to which iron will enter into the construction of ships hereafter?

Admiral PORTER. I think that the steamers that cross the ocean should not be built of anything else but iron. I think that if we can get these drawbacks you will find iron ships going up everywhere, and that no wooden ones will be built. The life of a wooden ship is only ten or twelve years, at the most. We have an old iron ship at Norfolk that was introduced in the navy in 1846. She was a failure. She was got up by some officer who did not understand exactly what he was about.

Her hull is as good to-day as the day she was built, but she is of no use at all as a sea-going vessel.

Mr. HOLMAN. What will probably be the policy of the government in regard to building ships for war purposes hereafter?

Admiral PORTER. We will probably build clippers of wood, but not steamers. Steam takes away all life from a wooden vessel. At present we do not allow our ships of war to use steam at all. They are ordered to take tugs when they are going to sea, and they make their voyages under sail. The engine is put away, and, except in great emergencies, they are not allowed to burn coal. The result is that they come back with the engines in perfect order, and the hull not injured by heat. Under that arrangement, wooden ships will last for years. We have now at the Naval Academy a wooden ship, the Constitution, that was built in 1796, and she is as good as the day she was built; and we have also the Macedonian, lying alongside of her, built by the British, in 1810 or '12. She is a teak-built ship, and she is as good as the day she was built.

The CHAIRMAN. Do you know anything about the composite ships, built of iron frames and wooden planking?

Admiral PORTER. They do not last at all. Wood and iron do not go together at sea. There is always an acid in the wood, and in a short time that acid eats a big hole in the iron. If you are going to build an iron ship, the best way is to build it of all iron, except the decks.

Mr. HOLMAN. You spoke of there being thirty good ships in our navy; are they all wooden ones?

Admiral PORTER. Yes, sir; they are all wooden. We have no iron sailing-vessels.

Mr. HOLMAN. What will be the policy of the government hereafter in building vessels intended for general war purposes?

Admiral PORTER. The policy will be to build two classes of vessels; one of iron vessels for harbor defense, and one class for going to sea. That policy we have never tried yet. The European governments have made mistakes in regard to building iron war-vessels. They tried everything, and have failed so far as making a perfect vessel of war, and the prospects are now that we will go to work and take advantage of all their mistakes. When the English do use wood, they use the teak wood. They get it from China at a very heavy expense, and an English ship will cost three times as much as any ship we ever build. Their last ships, built all of iron, cost some five or six hundred thousand pounds sterling.

Mr. HOLMAN. All the commercial powers, including England, France, and Russia, not only experiment with iron sea-vessels, but have them in the service?

Admiral PORTER. Yes; they use them altogether; they very seldom use anything else. There is only one objection to an iron vessel; that is, that she fouls her bottom so much. The English have overcome that in a great measure, I think, by making a planking under her and coppering that.

Mr. HOLMAN. What would be the effect of a policy of this kind. First, to permit only American built ships to be used in the domestic trade; secondly, to allow American ship-builders a drawback on materials used; and, thirdly, to allow Americans to purchase ships abroad, with a tax on such foreign ships of, say fifteen per cent.

Admiral PORTER. The difficulty would be first in the labor. The labor is much more expensive here than it is abroad, and there would be that much in favor of a foreign ship-builder. Labor in England averages one dollar and a half a day, and here it averages three dollars. If the American ship-builder gets a drawback on all the materials, you put him at once on an equality with the English ship-builder, except in regard to labor.

The CHAIRMAN. Is not our labor more efficient?

Admiral PORTER. No, sir; we do not build as good engines here as they do in England.

Mr. HOLMAN. Looking at this question as one of national concern in respect of employing merchant vessels for war purposes; how far would the allowing this policy of purchasing vessels abroad by American citizens contribute to that object, in case of war?

Admiral PORTER. It would contribute very greatly. As I said before, if we had had thirty or forty such vessels as are now trading to New York, during the war, every port in rebeldom would have been closed, not a bale of cotton would have got out, nor would anything have got in.

Mr. HOLMAN. Is there any other nation that adopts such an exclusive policy as we have adopted heretofore with reference to giving registry to foreign vessels?

Admiral PORTER. I do not think that any nation does. All other nations are more liberal. Our policy has been always to encourage ship-building. The result has been that we have built the finest ships in the world. Until latterly, I have not seen any ships to compare with them.

Mr. HOLMAN. Has not the policy of using iron instead of wood produced a revolution in ship-building?

Admiral PORTER. It has in England, because iron there is so much cheaper than wood. If they could get wood as cheap as we can, they would use it.

Mr. HOLMAN. Do you think that the building of wooden vessels in this country will be continued?

Admiral PORTER. Yes; except steamers. We get white oak, and red oak, and hackmatack, and locust cheaply. It is only when we come to live oak timber that it is found expensive; but this other timber is very much cheaper than iron.

Mr. HOLMAN. Can we successfully compete with other nations in the commerce of the world except with steamships?

Admiral PORTER. Yes; under the fostering care of the government. We could, if the government would look out for the mercantile interests of the country, as the governments of Great Britain and France do. Ten years ago France had comparatively no commerce, and she has now got a commerce of two and a half millions of tons. I remember well that it was very seldom you could see a large French ship. Now you find French commerce all over the world. Ten years ago a Frenchman could not run a steamship; he did not know anything about it. We always associated a Frenchman aboard a ship as a "sea-sick Frenchman," and as not fit to be trusted with a passenger ship. But now the French Messagerie line has run all the British lines off where it is in competition with it. The French have started a line to Australia, and are now prepared to start a line from California to China, which will run our Pacific mail steamship line right off.

Mr. HOLMAN. Are the French ships most built in France, or are they purchased abroad?

Admiral PORTER. All the French steamships that are running here are purchased in England. The French government allows every latitude in that way, and is encouraging its commerce without reference to ship-building.

Mr. HOLMAN. And the French government is paying heavier subsidies than the English?

Admiral PORTER. Yes; the French exact higher rates of postage. The Postmaster General here has not been able to make a satisfactory arrangement with the French government for the reduction of postage. The French claim not only half of the postage on this side, but half on the other side; and they charge double the amount of postage that is charged by any other nation, and thus they make foreigners pay their subsidies.

Mr. HOLMAN. Is not the largest portion of our tonnage employed in the domestic trade?

Admiral PORTER. Yes, sir. Our tonnage is now very much less than it used to be. We were nearly up to Great Britain in amount of tonnage, but we have lost nearly a million of tons.

Mr. HOLMAN. If we cannot adopt some mode by which the building of ships in this country may be encouraged, is it not then a simple question of whether the foreign commerce of the country shall be carried on altogether in foreign bottoms, or whether American citizens shall be permitted to purchase vessels abroad and put them under the American flag?

Admiral PORTER. As the general thing, perhaps, the latter would be a good plan; but I myself should not favor a rule that would allow that thing to be universal. While getting possession of the ocean again we must still protect ship building.

Mr. HOLMAN. Is not that an alternative? Unless we can adopt a policy that will revive the ship-building interest, is it not a question of whether the foreign commerce of the country shall be carried on in foreign vessels, or carried on in vessels built abroad and owned by American citizens, run under the American flag?

Admiral PORTER. As a matter of course. The first object is to increase the commerce of the country, because upon commerce depends the paying off the national debt, and every additional steamer that is put on adds so much more to our commerce.

Mr. HOLMAN. So that we have an object in increasing our commerce, apart from, and without reference to, ship-building?

Admiral PORTER. Yes; of course.

The CHAIRMAN. Do you believe that there is any difficulty in renewing our commerce as fast as is required by building our ships at home?

Admiral PORTER. No; provided you hold out an inducement for people to build, have drawbacks, and allow for labor.

The CHAIRMAN. Can our commerce be renewed within a reasonable time, and as fast as is required, if inducements are held out to ship-builders?

Admiral PORTER. Yes; with the exception that I have mentioned. We are now at that point that I think we should allow a certain number of vessels to be purchased abroad for the purpose of supplying our immediate wants. They would amount to about twelve.

Mr. MORRELL. Cannot these vessels be built in this country and put upon the lines almost as quickly as they can be procured abroad?

Admiral PORTER. No; they cannot begin to do it here, unless you allow them drawbacks, and drawbacks on labor.

Mr. MORRELL. By allowing drawbacks, would it not be better, instead of buying so many vessels abroad, to encourage the building of them in this country, and could you not get vessels built here to answer every purpose?

Admiral PORTER. They have greater facilities abroad. The great machine shop of this country is bound to be on the banks of the Delaware, at Chester, Pennsylvania, and at Wilmington, Delaware. I am personally interested, for I own a large piece of water front in Chester, where they are getting up these machine shops; but I must say, notwithstanding, that I do not think they can build steamships here as they can in England. They would make a failure at first, if they attempted to rush the thing through. But, if you go to work and give these people the right of purchasing 12 or 14 ships to start upon, and then give the builders of this country drawbacks, and let them go to work, I think that, in the course of three or four years, we would be able to compete with Great Britain.

Mr. WASHBURN. Suppose we should agree to grant a drawback to everybody who would build ships in this country; suppose we should say to the people of Baltimore, Philadelphia, Boston, and New York, "Go to work and establish lines of steamers, to leave twice or three times a week—for instance, to leave Boston on Monday, New York on Wednesday, and Philadelphia on Saturday—and you shall have the mails," would capitalists organize and establish steamship lines?

Admiral PORTER. I think so.

Mr. WASHBURN. Then how long would it take to get steamships for the purpose in this country?

Admiral PORTER. Two or three years. You cannot do it in any less. You cannot begin to show in less than three years. It takes a long time to build the engines, and these ships have to be large vessels.

Mr. WASHBURN. Could you not lend them some of your engines out of the navy?

Admiral PORTER. They would not have them. The most that we have been offered for four ships that cost the government nearly a million, is one hundred thousand dollars each; and I do not think the people who offered it were in earnest then.

Mr. CALKIN. Supposing that we should subsidize lines from Baltimore, Philadelphia, New York, and Boston, and that an American steamer left New York on Monday, with a foreign steamer leaving on Tuesday, and a Philadelphia steamer leaving on Wednesday, would you say that the New York merchant should not be allowed to send his letters by the steamer leaving on Tuesday?

Admiral PORTER. No, he could send them as he liked.

Mr. CALKIN. That is where the rub comes in about allowing mail money. We cannot secure the full mails for American ships.

Admiral PORTER. The merchant has to be governed by circumstances. The thing will work some day in the same way in favor of the American ships when we drive off foreign vessels, there must be a beginning and a tussle for the prize.

Mr. WASHBURN. The swiftest ships will take the mails?

Admiral PORTER. Yes; they are the ones that will take the mails.

Mr. CALKIN. You cannot build ships to beat these foreign propellers?

Admiral PORTER. You cannot build ships to do as well as they do now; but offer bounty and you will see a difference.

Mr. CALKIN. I know that gentlemen say they can make better time with side-wheel steamers.

Admiral PORTER. I do not believe that. Sometimes it is not so much in the ship as in the captain. It is the bold running that does the work. Put an American captain upon one of those steamships, and in from nine to twelve months he will beat the foreign vessels every trip.

Mr. CALKIN. You made a statement that the mail money would be a sufficient subsidy for steamship lines?

Admiral PORTER. I did not say that it would be a sufficient subsidy, but I said that they would be satisfied with it, and would commence with it.

Mr. CALKIN. Why could not the American steamship lines compete with the foreigners before the war?

Admiral PORTER. Because I think the American lines ran the wrong class of vessels. I knew the Collins line very well, and I know that they could not run a day in competition with the present line of steamships. They burned an immense quantity of coal; they were fitted out and fitted up in the most sumptuous manner; they had large crews, a large number of officers and a large number of engineers, for they had most powerful engines. They were run at the full speed, and the company had not enough ships on the line to enable them to have proper relays, so that they began to deteriorate very rapidly, and they ran them out in a very short time. They had very large buildings in New York, a great many officers, and a great many people connected with them. All these had to be paid. Then there were a great many dead-heads; so that I used to be astonished how they kept running at all. I think that I could have carried on the business at one-third the amount that it cost to carry it on. Everybody had a chance at these steamships.

Mr. CALKIN. You mean to say distinctly that the American steamship lines before the war were badly managed?

Admiral PORTER. I think they were.

Mr. CALKIN. And then also the subsidy to the Collins's line was withdrawn?

Admiral PORTER. Yes.

Mr. CALKIN. You also remember the man who was most prominent in the withdrawing of that subsidy?

Admiral PORTER. I do not.

Mr. CALKIN. Mr. Vanderbilt did more to break up the American line to Europe than any other man.

Mr. MORRILL. Can you tell us the comparative cost of running side-wheel steamers and screw steamers.

Admiral PORTER. The cost is very much less with propellers. If you have a fair wind, or a wind abeam, and have enough of it, you need not use your steam scarcely.

Mr. MORRELL. They are run with much greater economy?

Admiral PORTER. Very much greater; and then they have very much more storage room. I know they say there are some places where they can run a side-wheel steamer cheaper than a propeller; but I doubt it. That is from San Francisco to China. A gentleman was trying to convince me of that the other day.

Mr. JUDD. If the government should enter upon this system of subsidies, how would it affect naval estimates?

Admiral PORTER. It would save the government millions of dollars in case of war, because I do not want better ships than those steamships are; and then they are kept in order all the time. It is to the interest of the owners to keep them in perfect order. There is not a ship running on those lines that is not put into thorough order whenever she comes into port. We can take such ships, run bulkheads across them, and fit them for sea as privateers, in a week.

Mr. JUDD. And the Navy Department, if the system were entered upon, would not, as a rule, need to be constructing additional vessels?

Admiral PORTER. We would have to construct a certain number. My purpose is to keep the navy down to one hundred and eighty vessels. It is now two hundred. During the war we had a thousand vessels. Eight hundred of that thousand were merchant ships that had been bought by the department. We built very few good ones. The British government has a contract with these subsidized lines under which it can take the ships for government purposes when it needs them. I never had an idea what the British steam commerce was until I went up the Balaklava, during the Crimean war, just before the fall of Sebastopol; and I suppose that there were at that time in the different ports about there, three or four hundred of the most magnificent steamships, taken at a moment's notice by the government, and on which the government had not to pay a dollar of repairs. I went over in one of them, an ordinary ship, and she went at the rate of 14 miles an hour.

The CHAIRMAN. You spoke of the failures that were made in constructing vessels for the navy when the war broke out. Is not that inevitable after a long period of peace, from depending entirely upon the Naval Department for constructing war vessels, and would not that be obviated by providing for the supervision of the building of mercantile vessels by a naval officer?

Admiral PORTER. The government would have no right to do that, except in cases where it gave contracts on subsidies. Not only that, but there are just as clever constructors in the merchant marine as in the navy. Some of the best constructors in the world are those who had charge of our merchant marine.

The CHAIRMAN. The navy, of course, is only brought into use in time of war, which occurs at long intervals, while the merchant marine is in constant use, and is consequently brought to greater perfection. The point I want to get at is this—whether by the government pursuing the same policy which the English government pursues in respect to its merchant marine, having it under its supervision, and having the vessels constructed under the supervision of naval officers, that would not contribute greater efficiency to the navy.

Admiral PORTER. No doubt of that. But we could not carry that out with the whole merchant marine, because it would be very distasteful to merchants. Many ships must be built for carrying merchandise.

The CHAIRMAN. I mean only as applied to such number of vessels as would be wanted to make an efficient navy.

Admiral PORTER. It ought to be done in regard to subsidized vessels, but not to the whole merchant marine. Merchants would not be at all pleased to have such interference. Sailing-vessels, for instance, have to be built for carrying purposes, and are entirely unfit for war purposes; and some classes of steamers have also to be built for carrying purposes that would be entirely useless as vessels of war. Therefore, as to those classes of vessels, merchants would not consider it a favor for the government to interfere with their building. A naval officer would have his ideas which would be entirely different from those of the constructor. The naval officer would have an eye to the carrying of guns and to speed, while the merchant would have an eye simply to the quantity of cargo the vessel could carry.

The CHAIRMAN. I am only speaking of this policy so far as it would give us an efficient navy at the least cost to the government; so that the government could always have a navy at hand.

Admiral PORTER. The ships that would be employed by the government under contract for carrying the mails are the only ones as to which you could put such a law into operation with effect.

The CHAIRMAN. Has France good facilities for ship-building?

Admiral PORTER. Yes, sir; their commerce is increasing very rapidly.

They build very handsome, beautiful wooden ships. They build iron ships, too. They have very fine machine shops in France. All their naval vessels (and their navy amounts to 490,000 tons) are built at home.

Mr. CALKIN. Have they really improved upon our models?

Admiral PORTER. Very much. There are no models for men-of-war equal to the French models. The French ships have been always famous as fleet sailers. The first great model of a ship ever made was made by a Frenchman. In the old time, whenever an Englishman captured a French frigate and put an English crew on board of her, she could run away from the whole British fleet. They build some of the best vessels in the world.

Mr. WASHBURN. I understand you to say that the iron-clad ships of England and France are failures.

Admiral PORTER. We think so. Here is the Monarch, coming to this country with the body of George Peabody. She cannot get into any of our ports, except Portland, Maine; and that fact is a failure to commence with. We are very glad to have English ships built in that way. None of those large vessels can come into our ports, and therefore they cannot do us any harm. They have great speed, but they cannot fight with their guns in a sea-way. They roll thirty degrees, whereas our monitors only roll seven degrees. Our monitors, as harbor defenses, are a success, and other governments are coming round to the monitor system. It is the only true principle. The Dunderberg was the finest ram that we had, and is now the best ram the French have in their navy.

The CHAIRMAN. I understand you to say that you think the most economical and best policy would be for the government to maintain a comparatively small navy in time of peace, and to depend upon the merchant marine as an auxiliary force?

Admiral PORTER. No; that would not be my policy. If I had the money I would have a good deal larger navy, one superior to any nation. But we have proposed the navy to be kept at one hundred and eighty vessels, which is a very small navy for this country; but it is about as much as the people would stand. We could not get along with a much smaller naval force, and could add to its effectiveness by having mail steamers properly built, which we can use in time of emergency. That is what this country has got to do. We have not only to depend upon merchant vessels, but upon officers in the merchant marine, in case of a long war, because a large portion of our people cannot be made to understand the necessity of a great nation like ours keeping up a respectable navy.

The CHAIRMAN. How much would the government have saved directly, in cost, if it had had thirty or forty of the class of vessels that you speak of, and could have brought them into use at once?

Admiral PORTER. The government would have saved thirty or forty millions right off, because we run into a good many wild schemes in building vessels. We cannot tell all that it would have saved. It would have stopped the rebels from getting their supplies as they did. The blockade runners laughed at everything we had in the shape of vessels.

The CHAIRMAN. I understood you to say that the navy cost $480,000,000 during the war, and that we did not then get an efficient navy?

Admiral PORTER. Yes; it cost us $480,000,000.

The CHAIRMAN. Could not the half of that have been saved, if we had had thirty or forty fast mercantile steamships?

Admiral PORTER. They would have saved a great deal. I cannot say how much.

LETTERS FROM AMERICAN SHIP-BUILDERS AND OWNERS.

A circular letter embracing the following interrogatories, and also requesting their views on the general subjects under investigation, was addressed to a large number of merchants, ship-owners, and builders, representing the navigation interests of the country:

What is the present condition of ship-building at your town as compared with the period from 1854 to 1860?

What are the present average rates of wages paid to first-class mechanics on ship-work?

What were the average rates of same from 1854 to 1860?

What is the present cost per ton for building sail-vessels and of steamers?

Cost of same from 1854 to 1860?

What was the cost of materials for each ton from 1854 to 1860?

What is the cost per ton of same at the present time?

Amount of duty on materials in a thousand-ton ship from 1854 to 1860; also amount of same at the present time?

How are vessels built and owned in your town; are builders and masters generally owners in the vessels which they build and sail?

Could you build vessels at the present time in competition with the foreign builder, providing you could obtain the materials free of duty?

To ——— ———.

From the numerous replies received the committee have selected the following, as giving a fair representation of the views entertained by the representatives of the important interests under review:

KITTERY, MAINE, *December* 4, 1869.

DEAR SIR: Yours of the 25th ultimo was duly received, and the following are the answers we give to the questions you propose:

Question. What is the present condition of ship-building at your town as compared with the period from 1854 to 1860?

Answer. From 1854 to 1860, as for many years previous, ship-building was a steady and lucrative business, giving employment to about all the mechanics on the river. At present, it is in a state of complete stagnation.

Question. What are the present average rates of wages paid to first-class mechanics on ship-work?

Answer. Two dollars and fifty cents per day.

Question. What are the average rates for same from 1854 to 1860?

Answer. One dollar seventy-five cents per day.

Question. What is the present cost per ton for building sail-vessels and steamers? Cost of same from 1854 to 1860?

Answer. The present cost of building sail-vessels ready for sea is about seventy-five dollars per ton. Steamers, exclusive of machinery, sixty-five dollars per ton. The cost of sail-vessels from 1854 to 1860 was about fifty-eight dollars per ton.

Question. What was the cost of materials for each ton from 1854 to 1860?

Answer. About forty-one dollars per ton.

Question. What is the cost per ton for the same at the present time?

Answer. About fifty-three dollars per ton.

Question. Amount of duties on materials in a thousand-ton ship from 1854 to 1860; also amount of same at the present time?

Answer. The amount of duties on a thousand-ton ship from 1854 to 1860 was about one thousand dollars; at the present time we think it would amount to from seven to eight thousand dollars.

Question. How are vessels built and owned in your town; are the builders and masters generally owners in vessels they build and sail?

Answer. All the vessels we have built the past dozen years, have been owned by the builder, master, merchants, and mechanics, in pieces varying from one sixty-fourth to one-eighth. It is seldom any one owns over one-eighth.

Question. Could you build vessels at the present time in competition with the foreign builder, providing you could obtain the materials free of duty?

Answer. As we have to pay one-third of the amount we receive for the hull and spars of vessels for labor, we could not compete with the foreign builder, even with that materials free of the duty.

Yours truly,

NEAL, MATHEWS & BROOKS.

Hon. JOHN LYNCH,
Washington, D. C.

EASTPORT, *December* 1, 1869.

DEAR SIR: Your favor of 25th ultimo received, and contents noted. In reply to your several interrogatories, I will reply to your first, viz, What is the present condition of ship-building at your town, as compared with the period from 1854 to 1860?

Answer. Full sixty-five per cent. less tonnage built by me.

2. What are the present average rates of wages paid to first-class mechanics on ship work?

Answer. Two dollars and seventy-five cents per day.

3. What are the average rates of same from 1854 to 1860?

Answer. One dollar and seventy-five cents per day.

4. What is the present cost per ton for building sail-vessels?

Answer. Sixty-two dollars per ton for sail-vessels at present time. (Steamers do not build.)

5. Answer. Cost of construction of vessels from 1854 to 1860, fifty dollars per ton.

6. In reply to your inquiry about how the vessels are built and owned, I will state that associated owners, and generally masters, are interested.

7. In reply to your inquiry whether I could build vessels in competition with foreign builders, providing I could obtain the material free of duty, I will state that I could, providing of same class of vessels.

Very truly yours,

CALEB S. HUSTON.

Hon. JOHN LYNCH, *Chairman.*

CAPE NEDDICK, *Maine.*

SIR: Yours of the 25th instant is received. I built a vessel in this town in 1854 for thirty-four dollars per ton; paid first-class carpenters two dollars per day; ship-timber, paid nine dollars per ton; copper, paid twenty-one cents per pound; iron, (English,) paid sixty dollars per ton.

In 1860 timber was bought for fourteen dollars per ton; iron, one hundred and forty dollars per ton; copper, forty-five cents per pound; employed first-class carpenters at three dollars and a half and four dollars per day.

There have been but two vessels built here in this town since 1860, owing to the high duty on material. The same class vessels could not have been built in 1860 for sixty-five dollars per ton.

From the Piscataqua to Monsum Rivers there are five ship-building towns in the county of York. In Kennebunk, in 1854, there were seven large ships built; there were two built in Wells the same year, and one in Cape Neddick; two large ships in the town of Kittery, in 1854. All the above-named towns are now idle, except Kennebunk, where there is one ship on the stocks. Ship merchants build and repair in British dominions, on account of high duty on material.

Very respectfully,

JOHN BREWSTER.

Hon. JOHN LYNCH,
Washington, D. C.

P. S.—If it had not been for what work there was done in the navy yard at Portsmouth, I do not know what the ship carpenters would have done this fall.

WISCASSET, MAINE, *December* 6, 1869.

DEAR SIR: As chairman of Special Committee on Navigation Interests, it is perhaps pertinent for you to have all and any facts that bear unfavorably on the interest of navigation, and, without further preface, would bring to your notice one of the special restraints.

Our ship Richard III cleared at Wiscasset 28th October for Charleston, S. C., having in as cargo a small amount of hay and potatoes, on ship's account, consigned to order. It had beeen our intention to send the ship off Charleston Bar, there to be met with letter from a Charleston merchant by pilot-boat off the port, either to proceed south or go into Charleston. On the 30th October, the morning on which she sailed, our information was such that we dispatched the ship direct to New Orleans, where she arrived on 25th November, and on entering at customs on 26th November, was fined twenty dollars for not clearing for New Orleans. I have been a manager of ship property for twenty-five years; my father, for twenty-five years before me. Free from illicit trade or evasion of proper dues, it has been our only business, and we ought to know whether we are pursuing right or not. We have often had our ships, both coastwise and foreign, when they had no cargo to bind them to enter a particular port, seek such ports as circumstances or convenience might bring them to, and heretofore no intimation of fine or restriction. It is quite new to us, if such really is a rule or law, and, if of late enactment, it calls for a change.

In your investigations of the decay of the once great American navigation interest, it will not seem strange to you when I tell you that our own interest in ten ships, in the general freighting business, has got reduced to two ships, or that we lack the energy of former days. We are as ready now as ever to bring home to our country the pay for freighting our own exports and imports, as well as do the freighting business for any other nation that wants skillful, enterprising, courageous men, and when we can figure a remuneration will be on hand.

Apologizing for taking up so much of your time, I remain, very respectfully, yours,

JOSEPH TUCKER.

Hon. JOHN LYNCH,
Chairman Committee on Navigation, Washington.

DAMARISCOTTA, MAINE, *December* 1, 1869.

DEAR SIR: Your valued favor of the 25th ultimo came to hand by due course of mail, and contents noted.

In reply, will make answer to the inquiries as best I can from a hasty examination of records and my own personal knowledge.

1. Ship building has fallen off at this place since 1854 about nine-tenths, as you will notice by list inclosed of vessels recorded at our custom-house in that year, showing over ten thousand tons, and this present year only about seven hundred tons, being nearly a total suspension of the business.
2. Average wages, first-class workmen, this year, about $2 50 per day.
3. From 1854 to 1860 a wide range in wages was given; say average for 1854 was $3 per day; 1857, $1 50 and $1 75, advancing since 1857 to the present rates.
4. The cost per ton varies on larger and smaller sized vessels; say, a bark of six hundred tons, two decks, will cost more per ton than a ship of one thousand tons, same materials, as the larger the vessel the less cost per ton; think average first-class this year about $75 per ton, fitted for sea. Soon after the close of the war, some cost as high as $90 and $100 per ton. Steamers we have never built here.
5. A ship of seven hundred and fifty tons cost here in 1854 about $65 per ton, and in 1857 one of twelve hundred tons cost about $52 per ton; since 1857 to date prices increased.
6. Cost of material per ton, cannot state from 1854 to 1860.
7. Present cost of material twenty-five per cent. more than from 1854 to 1860.
8. Cannot state amount of duties on material.
9. Builders and masters are the owners; more so at present than formerly, when a profit in manufacturing was realized. The outright sale of a vessel now from the builder is a very rare occurrence, and no man can with any certainty build to sell and realize his money back again, at the high cost. Running the chances in sailing them is the only inducement to try and get a small return; take the risk, and get about the insurance.
10. Have no doubt, could material entering into the building of vessels be free of duty, we could compete with any nation in the world, and no one thing can ever help us more as a ship-building community.

Hoping the above may meet the most of your inquiries, I am, very truly yours,

JOSEPH DAY.

Hon. JOHN LYNCH,
Washington, D. C.

Under date of December 28, Mr. Day writes additional facts, of which the chief portions are here given:

In the year 1854 I bought into a ship by previous agreement of about seven hundred and fifty tons, at the bills, costing, ready for sea, some $65 per ton, being the most expensive year up to that time known here in building, causing many failures in our State among builders. Freighting declined, and hardly fifty per cent. of cost could be realized to sell a vessel that fall; it seemed the beginning of what has since proved a total failure in that branch of business.

In the year 1857 built the ship Success, of about one thousand two hundred tons, a thorough white oak vessel, costing, when ready for sea, about $52 per ton, being a very cheap year to build, as you will notice in previous letters, as to workmen's wages; other things entering into construction being in about the same proportion. Still, business was very dull when ready for sea.

In the year 1866 built a bark of about seven hundred tons, a first-class white oak vessel in every respect, costing, when fitted for service, about $85 per ton. This also was a very expensive year, and in the three vessels named, together, since they began to run, (and they have been managed by thorough merchants, and good masters as will average,) after deducting expenses, insurances, wear and tear, &c., the owners all would have been thousands of dollars better off to-day had these investments never existed.

The first cause of decline, in a measure, can be traced to the uncertainty hanging over our national affairs between the North and the South, and the lack of confidence in the country as to results of the impending crisis. Our senators and representatives in Congress were at a loss how to advise, throwing doubt and uncertainty upon all operations. After the conflict began in earnest, privateers, English influences, and other complications, finished what was left of hope in the interest of our commerce, and I truly believe no class of industry has had so much to contend with throughout this long dearth of some sixteen years, with so little encouragement from any source, as the ship-owning and building class. Sailing expenses, including insurances of the various kinds of risks, &c., have been so much above what the rates of freights would warrant, these items, in connection with the high costs of construction, with other causes before cited, have caused the whole life of navigation in this country to be crushed out, and it now remains to be seen what can be done to repair the great waste and depreciation of our commerce. Other nations have the start of us in every way in amount of tonnage and in doing the carrying trade of the world.

Our government should consider well the importance of its situation as regards an efficient merchant marine when it has realized the effects of such an arm as has heretofore existed in our country.

It will demand the greatest encouragement even to get the breath of life in it; but when once more firmly established, (having the original first cause of decline now firmly settled,) it will, as ever previous to the years above mentioned, take care of itself as the one most important branch of our national wealth and glory.

Think no trade has called so little for aid or protection at any time from the government as the ship-building and ship-owning interest previous to the present emergency.

BOSTON, *November* 29, 1869.

DEAR SIR: We beg leave to acknowledge receipt of your esteemed favor, 25th instant, and are glad to have the opportunity of presenting our views, and we earnestly solicit your considerate attention. There are but two causes of the decline and depressed condition of our commerce, viz:

First. The destruction of our vessels by the rebel cruisers during the war, and the sale of a large number to foreign merchants, when the premium on the gold enabled our ship-owners to realize a handsome profit.

Second. The increased cost of building, and of manning, victualing and furnishing the vessels. There is such a difference that we cannot successfully compete with other nations either in building or sailing our vessels. Our own ports are full of foreign ships. We venture the assertion that the total commerce of the country (inland navigation excluded) has not paid five per cent. per annum since the war.

These, in our opinion, are the causes of the decline; and the measures that should be adopted by Congress to revive these interests are quite obvious to us, and we do not see as any difference of opinion can exist among ship-owners.

1. A remission of the duties upon all foreign materials used in the construction of ships, whether for new vessels or repair, and when used for that purpose.

This would enable us to build or repair ships as low as any other nation. Iron ships and steamers are built in large numbers in England, and are rapidly taking the place of wooden vessels. They now command higher rates of freight in nearly all the ports of the world, and especially for carrying grain and the products of the Indies. This discrimination in the duty upon iron would enable us to build iron vessels at a cost not greatly in excess of what can be done in Europe, whereas now the duty is equal to prohibition.

2. In this connection, we would suggest a law granting American registers to iron steamers and sailing vessels when built in foreign ports, and by the payment of a tax, say five to ten per cent. on the cost; and for this reason, that even with a remission of the duty, we have not the facilities for building a large number, and our experience is limited. Such a law would benefit our commerce for the present, and until we have had more practical experience in constructing iron vessels.

3. A drawback on duties levied upon stores and goods when purchased for con-

sumption on board said vessel, and when said vessel is bound to any foreign port. And we think it would be well to include such distant ports in our own country as San Francisco. This is a law in England. The goods have to be purchased in bond, and do not include merchandise on which duty has already been paid.

4. Repeal of the tax of thirty dollars per ton, payable every year.

5. The repeal of some of the laws relating to American seamen. These laws, as you are aware, were enacted during the infancy of the republic, and when our commerce was but limited. They are entirely impracticable in the existing state of things. A very large proportion of the seamen now shipped on board of American vessels are foreigners, and the law requiring or authorizing our consuls to compel the payment of three months' extra pay to crews in certain cases, is greatly to the disadvantage of the ship-owner, and does not meet the expectation of the law. This law was passed, as we understand, to provide for the support and payment of the passage home of any American seaman who had been improperly treated on the voyage, or who should be unable to discharge his duties by reason of disability or sickness. The class of seamen now employed are very different in these times, and are quite unscrupulous, often incompetent, and nearly all foreigners. The consuls are sometimes only too ready to accede to their demands, and we have suffered to the extent of several thousand dollars the past few years by the payment of three months' extra wages, often advanced to a whole crew of twenty men, and that in gold, when the articles provided especially for their wages in United States currency. We protest against such conduct on the part of our consuls abroad.

It is true, and we know of cases where the seamen have actually feigned sickness for the purpose of robbing the owners of three months' extra pay, and they have obtained it. We have had proof in several instances the crews of our own vessels have formed a conspiracy to complain to the consul on arrival of bad treatment, and thus obtain the extra pay, and they have only been too successful.

We have lately had a case where the master shipped four seamen in a foreign port, and the consul, by accident, neglected to give him the articles for the four men. On the arrival of the ship at Havre, the consul compelled the payment of three months' extra pay, though the master produced the account of the consul at the port of departure, showing that the men in question were duly shipped, and in conformity with law. But as he did not have the articles the law was sufficient to compel the payment.

These laws should certainly be changed, so as to meet the necessity of the times, and you will be entitled to the hearty thanks of every ship-owner in the United States, if you will but give this matter your attention and consideration.

We have thus at some length given our views upon the questions you name. We are happy to be able to present them to you, assured, as we are, that you will give them that consideration which their importance demands. We hope Congress will realize the necessity of doing something early in the session for the relief of our ship-owners. The building of ships is now nearly suspended, awaiting the action of Congress. The argument that if we are enabled to build vessels more cheaply, that it will depreciate the value of what vessels we now have, is too shallow to require any comment. As large ship-owners, we prefer depreciation, if such would be the result, to utter annihilation, which will be the case if some relief is not granted.

These views we believe to be entirely sound.

We have the honor to remain, very respectfully, your obedient servants,

THAYER & LINCOLN.

Hon. JOHN LYNCH,
Chairman Committee on Navigation Interests.

Memorial.

To the honorable the Senate and House of Representatives in Congress assembled:

The memorial of the undersigned, builders, owners, and shippers, engaged in commerce, respectfully represents:

That the commerce of the country is prostrated; that the foreign carrying trade is seeking other than American bottoms, and that the skilled labor in this branch of industry has to look for employment from other sources.

The reasons for this state of things will be found in the fact that *labor* and *materials* in this country are higher than in most commercial countries. The *labor*, because the necessities of the government have made large taxation necessary, and the *materials* on account of a high tariff. The commerce of any one nation having to compete with that of the world in all the great markets of production, it follows that our government must afford some relief, or else ours will continue to languish and diminish.

They therefore respectfully petition that your honorable bodies would pass a law remitting the duties upon articles used in the construction of vessels; and, as in duty bound, will ever pray.

BOSTON, *November* 29, 1869.

MY DEAR SIR: In answer to your favor of 20th I respectfully submit a short memorial which I drew up for circulation some months ago, and which I believe covers the gist of the whole matter.

After the breaking out of the rebellion, and when several confederate pirates were afloat, the government gave ship-owners to understand that they could not protect their interests upon the ocean or in distant seas because they required all the available vessels for blockade service.

This led to a transfer, or partial transfer, of many vessels to a foreign flag.

When peace was conquered an attempt was made through Congress to restore the vessels thus transferred to their own flag, and which was refused.

The effect of that refusal was to keep quite a large tonnage of American-built and American-owned vessels under a foreign flag, and in fact making it a necessity in the prosecution of their business by American merchants and growing out of their ownership to sustain a foreign flag.

I was never satisfied myself with the debate or the decision of Congress upon this question. I know, from personal observation, that some of the very best ship-masters felt unwilling to continue during the rebellion in ships under the American flag, because the government did not propose in the first instance to give them proper protection, for the reasons herein recited; and secondly, they were liable to have their vessels burned under them, and they landed penniless on some distant shore, to find their way home as opportunity might offer.

These several reasons have reduced American tonnage, and have prevented American ship-builders from competing with those of other nations.

There has been a strong effort upon the part of British builders to magnify vessels built of iron over those built of wood. True to their instincts, English insurers have done all in their power to keep up the delusion.

England is a country of cheap iron. We are a country of cheap and good wood.

My own opinion, distinct from one of prejudice, is in favor of wood. If our people would study these questions in the light of patriotism they could effectually, with the proper aid of government, restore the commerce of the country to our own flag, and thus aid the construction of magnificent wooden ships.

I am, with great respect, your very obedient servant,

GEO. B. UPTON.

Hon. JOHN LYNCH, *Chairman, &c.*

BOSTON, *December* 22, 1869.

MY DEAR SIR: I am this morning in receipt of your kind favor of the 18th. I am in favor of wooden ships for foreign commerce, for these simple reasons:

First. In case of stranding or severe wrecking at sea, they are much more easily repaired. Of all the ports of the world, in South America, the East Indies, and China, few or none have the necessary tools or workmen for an extensive repair of iron vessels while there is hardly one that cannot repair a wooden ship.

Second. A wooden ship, under the same circumstances, will bring or carry her cargo better than an iron one. Wood is a good non-conductor; iron condenses. The damage by sweat is very great, and is one, moreover, that insurers do not cover. Iron ships, for the reason named, are more apt to sweat the cargo than those built of wood.

Third. Wooden ships can be more safely navigated than those built of iron. I am aware of the improvements in correcting the compass, still the fact exists and cannot be gainsaid, that in this respect wood has an advantage over iron.

Fourth. The United States have the best and cheapest wood in the world for ship-building. At a gold basis, and with a reasonable concession of duties upon articles which enter into the fitting and sailing, we can build wooden ships of the best class at about thirty per cent. less rates than the Clyde can build those of iron.

For these simple reasons, I have always maintained that it was for our interest to build and carry on our business in wooden ships. They are tools of trade. As a question of political economy, the cheapest tool which does the work well is the true one to procure, and although I am in favor of having and of giving encouragement to skilled workmen in all branches of industry, iron as well as wood, I do not think the time has arrived when we can economically use iron either alone or as a composite in ship-building.

I am, with great respect, your most obedient servant,

GEO. B. UPTON.

Hon. JOHN LYNCH, *Chairman, &c.*

BOSTON, *December* 3, 1869.

DEAR SIR: In reply to your request in letter of the 25th ultimo we think the government wrong in not taking some fair and liberal measures immediately after the war for the increase of our mercantile marine. At this late date we can see no other strictly safe and sure course to re-establish our commerce, viz:

1. Than by granting the privilege of purchasing tonnage in any part of the world; that of foreign construction bearing an equitable duty on cost when taking the flag.
2. A drawback on all materials used in construction of vessels.
3. Outfits for vessels taken from bonded stores exempted from duty.

Yours, very respectfully,

THOMAS B. WALES & CO.

Hon. JOHN LYNCH,
Chairman Committee on Navigation Interests.

BOSTON, *December* 6, 1869.

SIR: When I received your favor of the 25th ultimo I was not in condition to attempt an answer. Since then I have seen a copy of a long article by the Hon. E. H. Derby, of this city, which is to appear in the coming Atlantic Magazine; also, a pamphlet by Captain John Codman, addressed to you; and also the report of the commissioner of the New York Chamber of Commerce, the writer of which, Mr. A.A. Low, is well qualified to speak on the subject. I concur almost without reserve in these several papers, and I think they embody the views of merchants. Only one point of peculiar interest to me has not been touched upon, and to this I propose to confine my remarks. It had much to do with the decadence of American commerce.

It is this: the government by force of circumstances failed to give protection to our commerce. In a great emergency like that which came so suddenly upon us in 1861 it was quite natural, not to say necessary, for the government to turn its attention exclusively to blockading the ports of the enemy, and leave the shipping to take care of itself. If it could have turned its attention to protecting our foreign commerce it would have been obliged to send out vessels wholly unfit for the purpose. The government had not then and has not now any efficient cruising ships. The class of vessels built during the latter part of the war (of the type of the Madawaska, Wampanoag, &c., known as the "canoe ships," intended for great speed) are perfectly useless as cruisers to go in search of Alabamas; millions of dollars were wasted in their construction, and millions may be wasted in keeping them in order *to do nothing useful.* I do not hesitate to say that it would be good economy to burn every one of them rather than to finish, repair, and employ them. I think this sweeping statement will be found confirmed by a report of distinguished naval officers and an engineer, made by order of the Secretary of the Navy, and probably accessible to your committee. There are a few, very few, fair-sailing, fair-steaming, and fairly economical ships in the navy, as the Hartford and Brooklyn, and some that I cannot identify under their new names. There is an intermediate class, like the Ticonderoga, Monongahela, Lackawanna, and Detroit, mounting five heavy guns, and of thirteen hundred to fifteen hundred tons, old measurement, which came much nearer to being useful cruising ships than the "canoe ships;" but by reason of an incompetent jury-rig, they are, or were, wholly unfit to make long cruises without frequent coaling.

The large class of vessels, like Colorado, Minnesota, Franklin, and Wabash, mounting forty guns, and averaging about thirty-six hundred tons, old measurement, are very fine vessels for flag-ships on foreign stations in time of peace, but they are too large and too expensive for cruising ships, and they are wholly unfit to contend with iron-clads. As an illustration of the want of economy sometimes practiced, I would remark that I have recently seen under repairs at this station a ship built at Philadelphia in 1864-'5—I believe either the Shenandoah or Ticonderoga. She has been almost entirely rebuilt, and it would be interesting and instructive to know how much has been expended on her. I think the most cursory observer who saw her plank off would say that it would have been good economy to take her to sea and sink her in preference to repairing her.

With this sketch of the inefficiency of our navy in ships adapted to keeping the sea for any considerable time, mostly under canvas, for the protection of our commerce and for hitting the first hard blows at the commerce of the enemy, it is quite apparent that at the beginning of the war our government could not have effectually protected our foreign commerce, and could not to-day should a war occur. One great cause, therefore, for the decadence of American commerce on the ocean was the want of due protection. Another prominent cause was the want of due encouragement to private enterprise to fit out vessels to capture the enemy's cruisers. Had any sufficient inducement been held out, regularly commissioned vessels would have been fitted out by private enterprise.

The remedy for this short list of evils is very simple. It is to construct a fleet of fast-sailing, efficient screw steamers, with full supply of canvas, such as we see under all but our own flag, crossing the ocean in nine and ten days—ships with light armaments, not fit to encounter iron-clads or old-style fighting ships, or to batter forts, but ships well adapted to catch the commercial ships of an enemy, and to escape from a superior force; and for government to grant subsidies to those who should build mail packets fit for conversion for these purposes.

Such ships would afford valuable training schools for seamen, and to this end every encouragement should be given to young men to enlist on board of them. They would afford excellent training schools for young officers, and in time of peace as well as in time of war, would prove very valuable auxiliaries to promote and protect commerce.

I am, very respectfully, your obedient servant,

R. B. FORBES.

Hon. JOHN LYNCH,
Chairman, &c., Washington, D. C.

BOSTON, *December* 20, 1869.

MY DEAR SIR: I am in receipt of your note of the 25th ultimo asking my opinion on the "causes of the decline and present depressed condition of the ship-building and general navigation interests of the country, and the means of legislation necessary to revive those interests."

My business engagements have been such as to prevent me from making an earlier reply, and I must now give you my views briefly. But little, however, need be said, as I think it will be sufficient to review the history of our affairs for the last ten years, with this subject in mind, to see clearly what have been the causes of our present difficulties. As to the remedies, it may not be easy to speak confidently. The chief of them, however, will appear quite plain.

Before the war of the rebellion, in the course of years, our commercial enterprise had placed our country in the front rank among nations. The amount of tonnage of our sea-going vessels was more than one-seventh part greater than that of England at the beginning of the year 1861, and rapidly increasing. The demands of foreign commerce had directed attention to the business of ship-building, and this branch of industry had grown up to great importance, engaging the capital, skill, and energies of a large number of our citizens, and resulting in securing to our ships a reputation before all others in the world for beauty and speed. When the war of the rebellion broke out our government was not only unprepared to protect her commerce abroad, but was, for the time at least, mainly dependent upon the building establishments which had grown up under private hands for those ships which were needed to enforce the blockade of the rebel ports and meet the attacks of their armed vessels; while the rebels, with the substantial aid and comfort given by our foreign rivals, were enabled to sweep the ocean nearly without hinderance. No vessel was safe but under a foreign flag. Under this state of things, what with the capture and destruction of many of our vessels by the "confederate allies," and the natural decay and loss, (amounting to about ten per cent. annually,) the decline of our navigation interests such as we have experienced was inevitable; and it would take years of prosperity, under the most favorable circumstances, for us to regain the position which we thus lost. But our circumstances are not favorable.

The wants of the government during the recent war had to be met by a system of taxation depressing to every branch of business, more or less, but especially heavy upon that which we are now considering. It is not necessary to specify the particulars. The builder of a ship must now pay very heavy duties and taxes upon every article used in and upon it. The purchaser and owner will pay about seventy per cent. upon her outfit, and thirty cents per ton annually for a license. No hopes can be entertained of a revival of these interests under such influences. The disabilities of our present position must be removed by action of the national government.

England in 1853, and France in 1856, saw the necessity for doing something for the encouragement of navigation among their citizens. They saw the United States taking the lead in commercial affairs, and about to do the greater part of the carrying trade of the world. England at once took off all duties upon everything belonging to the building of a ship, and on all outfits taken out of bond at the time. Ship-building was then in as depressed a condition there as it now is with us. At the time when her mechanics struck for higher wages, she passed the neutral law, by which any one of her citizens could build a ship wherever he might choose, and by paying one shilling per ton, could procure her registry precisely as if she had been built at home. France passed a similar law. In fact, we are the only maritime nation that has not done the same. England, moreover, went further than this, and enacted a law whereby a foreigner (an American for instance) might take charge of an English ship without denying allegiance to his own country, and, if necessity required, he might call on either country for protection of his rights with reference to it. The mercantile marine of a country is one of the greatest elements of its strength. No nation can be really great or strong without it. It seems to me that on national grounds, as well as on the plainest principles of economy, that our government should take especial care of these interests, on which her standing among the nations so materially depends.

The course necessary to be pursued seems to me plainly indicated in the policy which our great rival has pursued so successfully.

I would recommend in the interests of the ship-builder, the merchant, and the whole country, the passage of a law remitting all duties and taxes on whatever enters into the construction or outfit of vessels; the enactment of such measures as will allow one of our citizens to build, buy, or equip, in any part of the world, any vessel whatever to be used in legitimate commerce, and to take out an American register for the same by payment of some specific tax upon her cost or tonnage, say twenty-five cents per ton. This would create a competition, not however *specially* injurious to any of our interests, but resulting in the *general* good. The skill, energy, and greater efficiency of our mechanics would be more than an offset to the cheap labor, cheap iron, and cheap coal of England. We should soon be building ships for the world, as we did from 1846 to 1859. I have myself built for England, France, Germany, Peru, and Chili. England has taken our place now. Shall she keep it?

Next in the interests of our commerce, (as I have before had occasion to state to another department of the government,) I should recommend to Congress such enactments as shall give liberty of a free exchange of all productions and commodities in the shape of *raw materials*. The restrictions placed upon a free trade should be, as far as possible and as soon as possible, removed. In a moderately fair field we have no cause to fear any rivals. American ship-masters and officers are, as a class, superior to all others, and so generally acknowledged to be such that, if there is a freight to be had, the American will command it in preference to others.

Another recommendation I would make with regard to our steam navigation: This is a branch of our marine of great and increasing importance, and should receive some special encouragement. A subsidy law for United States mail steamers, so liberal in its provisions as to secure the services of our own citizens in the carrying of foreign mails, is very desirable.

I have thus hastily given my views upon the subject presented. So confident am I of their correctness that, if I myself were the United States government, and my pocket the treasury, I should not hesitate immediately to adopt all the provisions which I have recommended.

I am, sir, most truly yours,

ISAAC TAYLOR.

Hon. JOHN LYNCH,
Chairman of Committee, Washington, D. C.

The following is from a letter of Donald McKay, ship-builder, of East Boston:

* * * * * * * *

I annex a list of duties (in gold) upon various articles entering into the construction of a new ship of one thousand tons:

Article	Duty
Iron, 120,906 pounds	$1,209 06
Iron spikes, 9,966 pounds	249 15
Galvanized spikes, 2,409 pounds	60 23
Castings, 14,408 pounds	216 12
Chain cables and rigging chains, 58,300 pounds	1,457 50
Anchors, 10,700 pounds	240 75
Metal and nails for do., 20,338 pounds	711 83
Salt, 1,200 bushels	216 00
Manilla, 12,423 pounds	310 57
Hemp, 28,774 pounds	863 22
Duck for sails and house-tops, including spare sails, 7,150 yards	714 90
Clinch rings, 1,800 pounds	36 00
Foreign white pine lumber and decking	825 00
Foreign hackmatack knees	330 00
Copper bolts, composition, castings, paints, oils, crockery, cabin trimmings, nails, and sundry outfits	1,225 00
Total dutiable articles for 1,000-ton ship (gold)	8,665 33

As a partial relief to the ship-building interest, I would suggest that Congress permit a drawback of duties paid on materials entering into the construction of new vessels, (which at the present date on a thousand-ton ship proves to be between eight and nine thousand dollars, as shown above,) and this privilege is accorded to the ship-owners and ship-builders of Great Britain, enabling them to compete with all other commercial nations, and their drawback extends to all articles of construction, equipment, and stores used in building and fitting out of new vessels.

Interested persons can obtain from the honorable Secretary of the Treasury, for purposes of comparison, the registered amount of tonnage built each of the past twenty years. There have been so few vessels built for our merchants in recent years that the average age of American sea-going ships is over ten years, and on this account our insurance companies meet with many losses, and yet the ship-owner now pays double the old rate of marine insurance.

DONALD McKAY.

OFFICE OF W. H. WEBB, SHIP-BUILDER,
No. 200 Lewis Street, New York, December 29, 1869.

DEAR SIR: In the absence of Mr. W. H. Webb, who is at present in California, we have to acknowledge your letter of the 20th instant, since receipt of which we have consulted some of our largest insurance companies in this city on the points you raise, that in the absence of Mr. Webb we might forward you the opinions of men in whom he would repose confidence, leaving Mr. Webb to write you his own ideas at a little later day, as we shall send your letter on to him.

These gentlemen, such as Mr. Dennis, of the Atlantic Mutual Company, Mr. Phulixion, of the Sun Mutual Company, neither knowing the other was consulted, expresses identically the same opinion, that they would rate the composite and the iron ship of similar quality at same rate, insure them at same cost, take as much on the one as on the other, and they would expect the one ship to class as long and last as long as the other. As iron ships "sweat" a good deal, their conversation left us to believe that, until that fault is got over, the composite ships would be on the whole more favorably regarded by them.

In reply to a question put by the Treasury, asking if, in his opinion, the composite class of vessels would succeed here, Mr. Webb replied so recently as November 3, of the present year. "Yes, without doubt; our great command of wooden materials in this country enabling us to compete more successfully in building this class of vessels, as against foreign ship-building, than with those wholly built of iron."

Hoping that, until Mr. Webb is able to address you, this may be of some service, we remain, very respectfully,

C. METZGAR,
N. M. GILLAN,
Joint Attorneys for Wm. H. Webb.

Hon. JOHN LYNCH, *Washington, D. C.*

SAN FRANCISCO, *January* 10, 1870.

DEAR SIR: Your valued favor of the 20th ultimo has been forwarded to me here by my attorneys at New York.

I can do but little more at this distance from home than indorse, which I do fully, their reply under date of 29th ultimo, a copy of which I have before me.

At this port I learn that the English-built iron ship is quite as favorably considered as the American-built wooden ship for shipments to Europe, but I attribute much of this to the unfortunate fact that most of those shipments from this port, as well as from the Atlantic ports, now are controlled by agencies of foreign houses, or foreigners themselves established in our country.

I may add, in regard to the building of composite ships in our own country, that if the tariff on materials used, other than wood, was removed, or an equivalent granted in some other manner, we could succeed eventually, as against all Europe, in producing not only a better but cheaper composite vessel; but we need aid from the government to enable the ship-building interest of the country to engage in this, to us, new branch of our business, and one which requires a larger investment of capital than heretofore employed in the building of wooden vessels.

I am confident that composite ships can be built in this country to advantage, and such as would have advantages in several respects over those wholly built of iron, certainly as regards comfort of passengers in hot climates, the preservation of cargoes, as well as economy in the running, and the safety of passengers and freight when stranded.

Trusting the above will satisfy your inquiry, I am yours, very respectfully and truly,

W. H. WEBB.

Hon. JOHN LYNCH,
Washington, D. C.

NEW YORK, 38 *John st., December* 4, 1869.

SIR: I take the liberty of placing before you my views of the disadvantages the American ship-builders, shipwrights, and other mechanics are at this time laboring under, caused by the heavy duties and taxes paid on all material used in building and repairing vessels, and as your committee have obtained so much valuable information on the subject of *building* both wooden and iron vessels, I will not dwell on this point, but will endeavor to more fully demonstrate the fact, that the *building* of vessels is but a part of the disadvantages which the mechanics of this country have to contend with.

It is a well known fact that the lifetime of a vessel is from ten to fifteen years, and that she has to be repaired a number of times during this period, and in many cases the outlay for repairs is nearly equal to the first cost. For instance, a wooden vessel has to be recaulked and remetaled every two years, and rebuilt at least on an average every seven years. An iron vessel requires to be docked at least every six months for the purpose of cleaning and painting. You will at once perceive that repairs on *iron* vessels are not so expensive as on the wooden vessels, but at the same time you will observe that the iron vessel requires more careful attention and is much oftener docked.

Another great detriment to the shipwrights, and other mechanics of this country, is that the greater portion of the foreign freighting business is carried on by foreigners, and these foreign vessels will not make their repairs in this country, as a matter of economy, on account of the high prices of material, such as iron, and other metals, cordage, &c., caused by the high tariff. This takes away from our dry-docks and mechanics that employment and revenue which we did have when our American vessels controlled foreign freighting business or the greater portion of it. It is also a well known fact, that there are no repairs made on these foreigners in this country, unless they are so disabled that it is impossible for them to get home, and even then the repairs made are only temporary. As an illustration, I will here mention the case of the steamship City of Cork, of the Inman Line, which vessel struck on a rock when entering the harbor of Halifax, Nova Scotia, in July, 1868, and came to New York and was docked in one of the docks which I built for the "Erie Basin Dry-dock and Warehouse Company." Her stern was badly damaged, but it was only temporarily repaired with wood and iron to make her safe to reach Liverpool, where the repairs could be made thoroughly, and employment given to their own mechanics, and also allow them to make a handsome saving over our prices. This is but one instance of many I could name, whereby our docks and mechanics are deprived of employment on account of great cost of material, when it is an acknowledged fact that our mechanics can execute fifty per cent. more work in a given time than European mechanics; still our government gives no aid to our commercial interest, either in the way of subsidies or special protection, to enable us to run a line of steamers, or to compete with the foreign ship-builders, or our merchants and others interested in dry docks and mechanical pursuits, for the heavy duty on sheathing metal and copper drives by necessity many of our American vessels to Europe to be remetaled, and as a natural result our dry docks and mechanics remain idle. To give you a more clear idea of the determination of foreigners not to give employment or spend any money in this country, I will state the following fact: The ship Mayflower, hailing from Liverpool, arrived at Portland, Maine, in August last, with a cargo of coal, and leaking so badly that it was necessary to keep a steam-pump going most of the time. He refused to make repairs there, but sailed for Halifax, Nova Scotia, so that he could employ his own countrymen. I think you will at once see that there is as much lost to the shipwright, dry docks companies, and other mechanics, in repairing vessels, as there is in building. My opinion is, if the duty is removed from all material used in the construction, repairs, and sailing ships, within a short time, we shall as heretofore be able to compete with, if not rival the world in building as well as sailing both wooden and iron vessels, for we have the material and ability to do so, and trust our representatives in Congress will give us that aid and protection which will enable us to realize our highest expectations.

I have the honor to remain your most obedient servant,

JAS. E. SIMPSON,
President Portland Dry Dock and Warehouse Company.

Hon. JOHN LYNCH,
Chairman Congressional Committee on Ship-building.

NEW YORK, *January* 13, 1870.

SIR: In reply to your communication of the 11th instant, we would give as our estimate of the cost of victualing and manning an American ship of 1,000 tons register, say $1,100 per month. It would be difficult, however, to estimate the cost per 100 tons register, to apply to vessels of all sizes, as a vessel of 500 tons requires as many officers as one of 1,500 tons, (with the exception of the third mate,) and pays nearly as high wages. Frequently, too, vessels of the same tonnage have a difference of two or three sailors in the number of their crews, as some are more heavily sparred than others, and require more men to handle them.

An average crew for an eastern ship of 1,000 tons register, would cost, at the present rates of wages, about as follows, viz:

Master, ($125 to $200, according to qualifications,) say	$150
Mate, $50; second mate, $40	90
Cook, steward, and carpenter, each $35	105
15 sailors, each $30	450
	795
Making twenty-one persons, "all told." Victuals average fifty cents per day	315
	1,110

Some ships carry three or four boys or "ordinary seamen," at one-half or two-thirds the wages of "able-bodied seamen," and ships bound on long voyages can obtain sailors now at twenty-five dollars per month, but in the Atlantic trade the current rate is thirty dollars per month, as above stated.

We annex memorandum of the actual cost of manning three vessels of different sizes, now in this port, and all hailing from Maine; and should you require any additional information, we are always at your service.

Your obedient servants,

RICH. P. BUCK & CO.

Hon. John Lynch,
Chairman Com. on Nav. Interests.

Bark of 563 tons:

Master	$150
Mate	50
Second mate	35
Cook and steward, (one man for both)	40
Eight seamen, at $30	240
	515
Victualing twelve persons at fifty cents per day, average	180
	695

Ship of 1,308 tons:

Master	$150
Mate	60
Second mate	40
Cook	35
Steward	40
Carpenter	35
Fifteen sailors, at $30	450
	810
Victuals for twenty-one	315
	1,125

Ships of 1,506 tons:

Master	$200
Mate	60
Second mate	45
Third mate	35
Carpenter	40
Cook	35
Steward	35
Eighteen sailors, at $30	540
	990
Victualing twenty-five persons	375
	1,365

The master of the latter ship was formerly in one of 1,116 tons, new measurement, and although nearly 400 tons smaller, she required and carried the same crew as this new one.

NEW YORK, *January* 20, 1870.

DEAR SIR: We have delayed answering your favor of the 15th instant, in order to obtain reliable information respecting the sailing of French vessels. The only French captain we can find has a vessel of about 400 tons. Her crew list is as follows:

	Francs.
Captain	400
First mate	150
Second mate	75
Cook and steward, (one person)	70
Carpenter	70
Six seamen, at 50 francs	300
Two apprentices	70
One boy	25
	1,160
At 5¼ francs per dollar in gold	$221
Victualing per month 1,200 francs, equal	229
Gold	450
Add 25 per cent. premium on gold	112
Equal in United States paper	562

Estimate for a French ship of 1,000 tons:

	Francs.
Captain	600
Mate	200
Second mate	100
Third mate	70
Carpenter	70
Cook	70
Steward	70
Twelve seamen	600
Three boys	100
	1,880
At 5¼ francs per gold dollar	$358
Victuals per month, 2,000 francs	381
Gold	739
Add 25 per cent. premium on gold	185
United States currency	924

Estimate for a British ship of 1,000 tons:

	£	s.
Captain	16	0
Mate	7	0
Second mate	5	0
Third mate	3	5
Carpenter	5	10
Cook	3	5
Steward	3	15
Twelve men, at £2 15*s*	33	0
Three boys, at 15*s*	2	5
	79	00
At $6 currency per pound sterling, (being $4 80 gold, and 25 per cent. premium)	$474	
Victualing, twenty-two persons at 15 cents per day, £41 5*s*., equal	247	
United States paper currency	721	

A bark now here, hailing from Sunderland, pays the following, (she is 546 tons register:)

	£	s.
Captain, £14; mate, £6 10s	20	10
Second mate, £4 10s.; carpenter, £5 10s	10	0
Cook, £3 5s.; steward, £3 15s	7	0
Eight able seamen, at £2 15s.; and three boys, at 15s	24	5
	61	15

At $6 United States currency per pound	$370 50
Victuals, seventeen persons, at 15*d.* per day	191 25
United States currency	561 75

Hoping this information will reach you in season to be of service, we remain, your obedient servants,

RICHARD P. BUCK & CO.

Hon. JOHN LYNCH,
Chairman, &c., Washington, D. C.

P. S.—Light dues are still collected by England, and we find from our vessels accounts that they amount to five or six pence sterling per ton in the Bristol channel. There are other local charges of this kind on the English coast and the British possessions.

NEW YORK, *January* 13, 1870.

DEAR SIR: In reply to your note to our senior, Mr. A. A. Low, we beg to say that our experience gives about $125 per ton per month, or $1,250 per month for vessels of 1,000 tons each for victualing and manning. For such vessels we have—

Master, say	$150
First mate	60 to 70
Second mate	35 to 40
Steward	40
Cook	40
Sailmaker	40
Carpenter	35
Sixteen able seamen	25
Four ordinary seamen	15
Four boys	5

Average wages, about $900 per month.
Average victualing, about $350 per month.

Very truly yours, &c.,

A. A. LOW & BRO.

JOHN LYNCH, *Chairman.*

AMERICAN SHIP-BUILDING.

The following letter is from a gentleman who was formerly an English iron-master, and now in business in Philadelphia. He has a practical knowledge of the subject upon which he writes:

From the morning papers of the 25th of October it appears that the congressional committee appointed to investigate the cause of the decline of the mercantile navy of the United States, and the best method of restoring prosperity to the ship-building interest, have adjourned to meet in Philadelphia on the first Thursday in December next; that the questions before the committee were narrowed down to distinct propositions, which will probably be recommended to Congress. These are the remission of all duties on materials entering into the construction of ships; the permitting foreign ships to be purchased and admitted to American register; and the granting of subsidies to steamship lines; and lastly, offering a premium for building ships in this country, by allowing a drawback on the imported materials used.

On a subject of such national importance, and one involving such immense interests, there must naturally be a great diversity of opinion, and any information that may show the subject in a new light may, perhaps, be deemed acceptable. With this view the following observations are thrown together to endeavor to show that it is not the comparatively low standard of wages in Europe alone that prevents iron for ship-building purposes being produced in this country on equal terms with that brought from Europe.

It is chiefly the lack of organization, and the situations of the different establishments, that prevent ship plate-iron being cheaply produced. It is a fact beyond dispute, that pig-iron can be made as cheap, and coal can be obtained cheaper on the Ohio than on the Tees, in England. Why, then, cannot iron for ship-building be made, and ships be built on the Ohio at the same price by ton with American iron, as at the Atlantic ports with European iron, even if no duty is paid on it? Simply for want of the organization used in England, and the policy used in France.

* * * * * * * * * * *

The pig-iron is dear on account of the relative position of the ore, coal, and transport to the mills; here again profit must be made on the pig-iron, after the miner has made his on the ore and coal, and the railway company made theirs on the transport; thus everything used is to the disadvantage of the ship-builder, and vessels cannot be built at a low price. The question is, how and when can this be altered? To this no satisfactory answer can be given as long as ships are built on the eastern coast of the States; and to solve the difficulty a new location must be chosen, where iron-ore and coal are found in a near proximity to a navigable river, that pig-iron can be made as cheap as in England, and where coal can be obtained for manufacturing the same at as low a price as it costs at works there, and where ships can be built and launched as cheap, except the difference in the price of labor; but this difference can be compensated by the fact of the superiority of American iron over English, which will enable vessels to be built of lighter iron, and consequently a greater tonnage for their weight than British built ships.

The proposition about to be made may at first appear to be impractical to those accustomed to launch their vessels in salt water, but on considering the improvements of the age, and the facility with which ships are now by machinery lifted out of the water, the proposition will show no difficulties which may not be overcome.

The best locality for building iron ships in the United States will be found to be on the Mississippi or Ohio Rivers, above Cairo, and the situation where iron for building the same can be made as cheap as in England is on the Ohio.

Here, then, in the center of the States, iron ships can be built to any extent or burden, and be towed down to New Orleans, either alone or partially supported on lighters, according to their size, and thence to New York or elsewhere to receive their engines and full rigging, or their engines can be sent to and fixed in New Orleans.

To carry out the foregoing suggestions it would be necessary to form a company of the most practical men for each department, with ample capital to carry out the whole plan.

It is the magnitude and extent of the grand rivers of this continent which enables one to see the foregoing plans as quite practicable, although at first sight they deviate from the old beaten track, yet on the slightest reflection by practical men, the whole project will be accepted, as the only means that can be devised of enabling America successfully to compete with Europe in establishing an *independent* mercantile navy. Let us for an instant refer to what has lately been proposed to assist the shipping interest. First, the remission of duties on materials entering into the construction of ships.

By building ships with iron from Europe the States will be *dependent*, and continue so, for its ship-building material, as no attempt would be made to produce native material on the east coast, while foreign iron could be purchased cheaper than it could be made there. Then, again, purchasing foreign ships; this might be done at a cheaper rate than they are now built here, but is it the policy of this country virtually to employ European ship-builders in Europe to build vessels which can, by a proper systematic arrangement, be built as cheaply by Americans in this country? The answers to these questions are evident.

But other questions may be asked. Can pig-iron be made on the Ohio, and coal worked for converting it into ship-plates at the same price as iron and coal costs in England? The answer is decidedly yes, and scores of places could be pointed out on the Ohio where pig-iron can be made and coal delivered quite as cheap as in England, and why this is not generally known could easily be explained, if necessary. This subject is one of the greatest national importance, and should be investigated by those who are interested in the prosperity of the country, before measures are taken which will only *partially* assist in improving the condition of ship-owners, and which can never satisfy the nation. With such enormous deposits of iron-ore and coal throughout the country in situations most favorable for working them, is it policy to let them remain undisturbed, and purchase ships, with gold, from other nations, or employ capital at home in developing the resources of the country, and give employment to thousands of its inhabitants?

JOHN PLAYER,
3904 *Walnut street, Philadelphia.*

Hon. JOHN LYNCH,
Chairman Committee on Ship-building, &c.

WILMINGTON IRON WORKS,
Wilmington, Del., January 18, 1870.

DEAR SIR: Your favor of 13th was received, and I take pleasure in replying to your interrogatories to the best of my ability.

In the United States, where no positive practice regulates the standard of dimensions of the parts and pieces of an iron vessel, but the whole question of strength of detail is left to the experience and knowledge of the builder, or, more frequently, to the crude ideas of the party for whom the ship is to be built, it has always been the custom of the builder to determine his price by the amount of iron and other material to be used. Hence you will readily understand how two ships of the same tonnage may cost different figures.

In England and France, where insurance depends upon the kind of construction, the builders have all fallen into one class of specifications, in which the size of the vessel determines the proportions of each piece or part, and consequently a price per ton can easily be given which will fit all cases.

Supposing that your inquiry relates to strictly first-class ships, I have to say that the labor upon a sailing-ship of 1,000 tons, (hull and cabins only,) the material being iron, can be done for $58,000, and that the material of all kinds can be purchased for $42,000 to $46,000.

For a steamship of like capacity the cost would not differ materially in the items of labor and material, of course, exclusive of machinery.

For a screw steamship of 1,000 tons there would be required an engine of sixty inches diameter and sixty inches stroke, which, with boilers of adequate capacity, with all the details complete, would cost $48,500.

For a side-wheel ship of 1,000 tons, there would be required a lever-beam engine of fifty-six inches diameter, ten feet stroke, which, with boilers, &c., complete, would cost $51,000.

The masts, sails, rigging, furniture, outfit, and stores of a sailing-ship of 1,000 tons would cost from $15,000 to $18,000.

For a steamship the figures would not materially differ; the diminished cost of masts, rigging and sails would be made up nearly by the stores and fixtures for the machinery department.

Will be pleased to further serve you if in my power.

Very truly yours,

WM. G. GIBBONS.

Hon. JOHN LYNCH, *Washington, D. C.*

CHICAGO, *December* 20, 1869.

DEAR SIR: I hereby acknowledge the receipt of your communication of the 11th instant, requesting answers to certain interrogatories, for the use of the committee named.

I have carefully considered the subject alluded to, and beg leave to make the following statement in answer thereto:

The present condition of ship-building in Chicago, as compared with the period from 1854 to 1860, may be described by the word "abandoned," with the exception of a few tugs, canal-boats, dredges, and scows, built for local uses. Ship-building has been almost entirely given up since the war. From 1854 to 1860 it was practicable to build vessels with profit in Chicago, and several propellers and schooners were built during this period.

The present average rate of wages for "new work" may be set at $3. I think men could be got for less this winter, if any new vessels were to be built. As there are no vessels building this quotation may be more nominal than real. The wages on repairs, or "old work," are $3 50 for ten-hour days, and $3 for eight-hour days in winter; and wages on "old work" are always and everywhere about fifty cents a day greater than on "new work."

The average rates of wages, from 1854 to 1860, were from $2 to $2 25 per day.

The cost per ton for building the hulls of sail-vessels or steamers would be, probably, if any were building, from $40 to $45. The cost of same, from 1854 to 1860, was from $30 to $35. The cost per ton for the sails and rigging usually amounted to about one-half the price of the hulls: say, hull, two-thirds sails and outfit rigging one-third the whole price of vessel.

The cost of materials for each ton of hull, from 1854 to 1860, was from $8 to $10. The cost of same per ton, at the present time, would be $12 to $15. (The cost of rope and canvas is, I think, greater proportionately than formerly.)

It might be useful to state, in this connection, that about ten days' labor may be regarded as entering into the production of one ton of the hull of lake shipping, old measurement, upon which the foregoing approximations have been based. As the new measurement is about twenty-five per cent. less than in the old, in the case of lake sail-vessels, seven and a half days may be taken when the new measurement is used.

The amount of duty on materials in a thousand-ton ship, or in each ton of a ship, built in this port, might at first sight be deemed to depend upon the extent to which articles of foreign growth or manufacture enter into her construction. And here, where the wood and iron of the hull is of home production, and the rope, canvas, ground tackle, or machinery, may be wholly or partially imported, it might appear that duties had but slight influence in adding to the cost of vessels; but, nevertheless, it is true that duties do add to the cost of vessels in every case where it would be cheaper to import the materials, could they be brought in free of duty. American ship-builders had become rivals with those of England for the construction of the fleets of the world. Vessels had become articles of export to all nations, as well as carriers of commerce between them all; and duties laid upon the materials entering into their construction was of the nature of a bounty paid to our rival from whom many of those materials must come. It is not material, therefore, to enter upon the determination of the precise degree of impolicy embodied in this most impolitic measure of levying duties upon so grand an article of export as the noble ship that careers over the course of ocean like a thing of life.

Vessels, when built in Chicago, are generally constructed on contract for the owners. The masters are frequently part owners.

I think vessels could be built in this port for Chicago vessel-owners, in competition with provincial builders, providing we could obtain the materials free of duty, and this for the following reasons: First, the cost of materials being the same to our builders in the provincial port, the expense of transportation only need be added to place them under the hands of our builders in their own yards. Against this disadvantage we should offset the cost and inconvenience of owners going to a foreign port to superintend a vessel's construction. Second, the greater skill of American mechanics may be fairly placed against the lesser wages of the Canadian workman, with the controlling advantage in our favor, that the style of model and workmanship of our builders better suits the taste of our owners than the style of provincial builders.

But were the *vessels* to be imported free of duty rather than the materials, then would our builders and workmen go to the provinces and build all our vessels; and, thereafter, a ship-yard on the American shore of the lakes would be a place non-existent, with its mysteries forgotten and unknown to our people, and the history of its achievements become as obscure and mythical as that of the "mound builders" anciently inhabiting this region of country.

I am, sir, yours respectfully,

WILEY M. EGAN.

Hon. JOHN LYNCH,
Chairman Committee on Navigation Interests.

BUFFALO, *December* 15, 1869.

DEAR SIR: Yours of 8th instant is at hand, and contents noted, and in reply would say:

1st. The ship-building is very much less now than it was from 1854 to 1860. 2d. The present average wages, $3 50 to $3 90 per day. In 1854 to 1860, they were $2 to $2 25 per day. The cost, what we call old measurement, was in 1854 to 1860, $28 to $30 per ton; at present it is $48 to $50 per ton. Flitch, which is for frames, six inches, in 1854 to 1860 cost $12 to $14; now costs $22 to $26 per thousand. Ship plank, 1854 to 1860, cost $16 to $20 per thousand; now costs $30 to $50 per thousand. Duty on material in 1854 to 1860 and at present time ———. There is now a government tax of about $300 on small class vessels, when the keel is first laid on blocks, which there was not in 1854 or 1860.

At present, as in 1854 to 1860, ship-builders, in some cases, own interest in vessels; also, some masters. It costs so much at present to build, that the most of them are not able to own ships or vessels.

An 800-ton vessel all ready for sea, at present would cost about $60,000 to $65,000. In 1854 to 1860, same vessel would cost $38,000 to $40,000. We could build as cheap or cheaper than any other nation, with same price of material and duty off, as I think our mechanics do more work in a day than they do in Canada. Our people are more active. The several trade unions in United States are a drawback on all ship and other work, as we are troubled with strikes. Our vessels here on the lakes are far superior to the Canada vessels in model, strength, and speed. The reason is, I think, that we have better ship draughtsmen. In 1853, I built a steam propeller at a cost of $36,000, and the same propeller would now cost about $75,000 to $80,000. I have sailed from a boy until 1855, and owned and do now own steam and sail vessels, and I find that for the last seven or eight years vessels have not made any money, and would be pleased to sell out if I could do so. Find that rope is twenty-five cents per pound, and in 1854 to 1860 it cost ten cents per pound, and most everything else in same proportion. We now pay government tax of thirty cents per ton, which all goes to enhance cost of vessels. Thirty cents per ton is called tonnage dues, and income on profits when there is any.

Hoping the above will be what you inquired for, I am, yours respectfully,

FRANK PEREW.

JOHN LYNCH, Esq.

CUSTOM-HOUSE, COLLECTOR'S OFFICE,
Portsmouth, N. H., January 4, 1870.

SIR: From information received from communication with prominent ship-builders of this place, I am enabled to reply to the questions submitted in your letter of the 15th ultimo, as follows, viz:

Question 1. What is the present condition of ship-building at your town, as compared with the period from 1854 to 1860?

Answer. During the period from 1854 to 1860, there were in our city five ship-yards in successful operation, producing ships equal if not superior to any afloat. At that time, ship-building was *the business of our city*. At the present time there are only two yards in operation, and these are doing a very small business, comparatively.

Question 2. What are the present average rates of wages paid to first-class mechanics on ship-work?

Answer. The present rate of wages to first-class mechanics on ship-work is $2 50 per day—working hours from sunrise to sunset in the winter season, and in the summer ten hours for a day.

Question 3. What were the average rates of same from 1854 to 1860?

Answer. The average rate from 1854 to 1860 was $2 per day.

Question 4. What is the present cost per ton for building sail-vessels, and of steamers?

Answer. The present cost per ton for building sailing-vessels, ready for sea, averages $75; for steamers, exclusive of machinery, $65.

Question 5. Cost of same, from 1854 to 1860?

Answer. The average cost of sailing-vessels, from 1854 to 1860, was about $60 per ton; steamers, $55 per ton.

Question 6. What was the cost of materials for each ton, from 1854 to 1860?

Answer. Average cost of materials for sailing-vessels, about $42 per ton; steamers, $40.

Question 7. What is the cost per ton of the same, at the present time?

Answer. Cost of materials for sailing-vessels, about $52 per ton; steamers, $45.

Question 8. Amount of duty on materials in a thousand-ton ship, from 1854 to 1860?

Answer. About twelve hundred dollars.

Question 9. Also, amount of the same at the present time?

Answer. Seven thousand five hundred dollars.

Question 10. How are vessels built and owned in your town? Are builders and masters generally owners in the vessels which they build and sail?

Answer. Vessels are owned mostly in small shares, by the builders, masters, and men of small means.

Question 11. Could you build vessels at the present time in competition with the foreign or provincial builder, providing you could obtain the materials free of duty?

Answer. If ship-building materials were free from duty, we could, in a very short period, compete with foreign builders.

Very respectfully, your obedient servant,

JOHN H. BAILEY, *Collector*.

Hon. JOHN LYNCH, M. C.,
Chairman Congressional Committee, &c.

AUGUSTA, MAINE, *February* 5, 1870.

DEAR SIR: The ship-building business in our place has dwindled down next to nothing. In 1854, there were twelve ships built on one river, (Damaris cotta,) besides other smaller vessels; 1869, one barque; and this year, one schooner, is all that I know of.

No one thinks of building now, except he has money equal to the cost, and knows no other business. Wages for common carpenters are about $2 per day of ten hours. In 1854, wages were about $3 25, but the money panic in the fall of 1854,'55, and '56, carried wages down to about $1 75.

The present cost of an A 1 ship, (sail,) 1,000 tons, fitted for sea, is about $75 per ton. Cost of the same 1854, thence up to 1860, was about $50 to $55 per ton.

I have no experience in steamers. The cost for the materials in a ship of 1,000 tons, at present time, is about $52 50 per ton; 1854 to 1860, about $36 per ton.

The duties on a thousand ton ship, at present time, are about $8 or $9 per ton.

Duties on same in 1854 to 1860, about $1 to $1 50 per ton. The above estimates are on old measure. Vessels are generally owned and sailed by the builders and masters in this vicinity.

Maine is suffering in this respect more than any other State, as you will see by the Secretary of the Treasury's report. But, as things now are, our yards are deserted; carpenters migrating West, and the men otherwise becoming depleted, so that in case of a sudden war, we shall neither have skilled ship-carpenters nor American sailors. In the last rebellion we could not have existed as a nation without either class of those men.

We then had well-trained sailors ready to defend the flag. Our government cannot make so profitable an investment for its defense, as to foster its navigation by granting a drawback for duties, and remit the taxes on ships. It would be absurd to permit foreign-built ships to be imported free, and sailed under the American flag, while our ship-builders are being starved by high duties and taxation.

Respectfully,

B. D. METCALF.

Hon. JOHN LYNCH.

LETTERS FROM UNITED STATES CONSULS.

The following inquiries were addressed, through the State Department, to consuls of the United States at various ports of Europe and British America, in regard to—

Cost in Great Britain of wooden ships per ton, fitted for sea, in 1860.

Same of iron ships per ton, fitted for sea, in 1860.

Same of wooden steamers per ton, fitted for sea, in 1860.

Same of iron steamers per ton, fitted for sea, in 1860.

Also, cost of each of foregoing at present time.

Rates of wages of first-class mechanics on ship-work, in London, on the Clyde, and on the Tyne, in 1860; rates of same at present time.

Rates of insurance in wooden and iron steamships, sailing vessels, &c.; regulations adopted by English government to ascertain amount of material entering into the construction of ships, which are exempt from duty; advantages possessed by ship-owners and builders in Great Britain over the same class in the United States; character of officers and crews of English vessels, as compared with those of the United States.

What measures are adopted to secure efficiency in the merchant marine service, and in what regard is the merchant marine held as a means of national defense?

The amount of subsidies paid to various lines of English ocean steamers?

To what extent are iron superseding wooden vessels?

* * * * * * * * *

Mr. Morse to Mr. Fish.

No. 47.]

UNITED STATES CONSULATE GENERAL,
London, December 27, 1869.

SIR: In reply to a series of questions in reference to the interests of the American mercantile marine, addressed to me, through the Department of State, by Hon. John Lynch, "Chairman of the Committee on American Navigation Interests," and Nathan Sargent, esq., commissioner of customs, I have the honor to submit the following report. Without answering in their order each interrogatory, I have, for the economy of time and space, endeavored to respond to the inquiries of each gentleman as fully as my means of information will permit.

In answer to the request for an "English Report," showing the number, tonnage, &c., of the vessels belonging to the British navy, and which of them were built in *private*, and which in government dock-yards, I forward herewith the official quarterly "Navy List" for October. This "Navy List" is published by authority of the government, and gives many particulars as to the character and efficiency of all serviceable vessels in the British navy, and may be relied on for accuracy. But there is no official or unofficial report or document informing us how many, and which of these vessels were built in government and which in private yards, and I had to procure the information from other, though equally reliable, sources.

The following list is a full and complete record of all the serviceable vessels of every class, including transports, or troop ships, now comprising the British naval vessels. It gives their names, tells whether they are screw, paddle-wheel, or sailing; the tonnage, horse-power of each, and the number of guns carried by each one. It states of what materials each is constructed, whether of wood or iron, or of iron frame and teak wood planking, (called composite,) and which of them are armor-plated. It states which of them were built in government and which in *private* dock yards. I have separated those built in government from those built in private yards, first giving the names and particulars of those built in government, followed by those built in *private* yards. The following list was furnished me by high authority, and is entirely correct. (See Appendix, table.)

The whole number of serviceable fighting ships in the British navy is three hundred and ninety-four. Of this number thirty are gun-boats of small size; two hundred and fifty-six of the whole number were built in government dock-yards, and one hundred and thirty-eight in private yards. Only nine of those built in government yards are constructed of iron, eight are composite, and all the rest were built of wood. Twelve of these government-built wooden ships and eight of the nine iron ones are iron-clad or armor-plated. Of the one hundred and thirty-eight ships built in private yards fifty-five are iron ships of a large class, twenty-five of which are armor-plated; three of the wooden ships built in private yards are also armor-plated, making twenty-eight iron-clads built in private yards, and twenty in government yards. It will thus be seen that there are now in the British navy forty-eight large, sea-going iron-clads. The aggregate tonnage of these forty-eight ships is 170,000 tons. They average 3,541 tons each, and carry 653 guns. Several of these iron-clads are yet incomplete, but ready for sea. The forty-eight will cost £16,000,000, or nearly $78,000,000.

Iron war ships and armor-plated ships are of recent date, and when the admiralty decided to introduce iron ships into the navy, iron steamers and sailing ships had for some years been in use in the mercantile marine, and these several private yards, well equipped for the construction of iron vessels of any class, whether sailing or steam, while yards had not then been fitted for such purposes, and could not readily respond to the call of the government for iron war ships, even if it were the policy of the government to rely on its own yards for its supply. Although some of the government yards are now equipped for building iron ships, and no doubt could now supply all the wants of the government, unless perhaps in cases of sudden emergency, yet we see that only nine of the sixty-four iron ships belonging to the British navy were built in government yards, and of the thirty-three iron armor-plated ships, only eight were built in the navy yards and twenty-five in private yards.

There are now building fourteen iron armor-plated ships for the government, all of large size. Seven of these iron-clads are building in government, and seven in private yards, and the engines for all these ships are being constructed at private works, and all but one are on the improved expansion plan with surface condensers. All marine engines of any importance, required for the British navy, are made at the works of private engine-builders. Up to the year 1868, Penn & Maudslay, two of the leading engine-builders, whose works are located in London, built nearly all the engines for government ships, whether the ships were built in private or government yards. Now, as a general rule, the war ships built for the government in the yards of Napier or Laird have their engines built also in the yards of these gentlemen. Though this is not always the case, for Penn & Maudslay are still the chief builders of government engines. Within the last few years, Rowenhill & Humphreys have built occasionally. I may add that iron armor-plated war steamers have frequently been and continue to be built in the private yards of this country for nearly all the maritime nations of Europe except France, and she has had troop ships built here, and some of her largest and best merchant steamers are Clyde-built.

SUBSIDIZED LINES OF MAIL STEAMERS.

I have procured and forwarded, as desired, the post office reports for the last ten years, but they do not give the full information asked for, but from other reliable sources of information, I find the existing contracts with steamboat companies for carrying the mails to be as follows:

CONTRACT WITH THE CUNARD LINE.

In December, 1868, a contract was made with the managers of the Cunard line to carry a mail twice a week to the United States, every Saturday to New York, and every Tuesday to Boston, for £70,000 per annum. Under this contract the company carries the mails on the outward voyage only. This contract runs to the year 1876, and can be terminated any time thereafter on giving twelve months' notice.

CONTRACT WITH THE INMAN LINE.

On the 9th of March, 1869, a contract was made with William Inman, manager of the Inman line, to carry one mail each week to New York, for £35,000 per annum. Like the contract with the Cunard line, the Inman contract can be terminated after the year 1876, on giving twelve months' notice.

NORTH GERMAN LLOYD'S LINE.

In December, 1868, a contract was made with the North German Lloyd's line to carry a weekly mail from Southampton to New York for the postage, 1*s*. per ounce for letters, 3*d*. per pound for newspapers, and 5*d*. per pound for books.

TO BERMUDA AND ST. THOMAS.

In December, 1867, a contract was made with the Cunards to carry a mail every *fourth* week from Halifax to Bermuda and St. Thomas for £19,500 per annum.

BRAZIL, ETC.

In June, 1868, a contract was made with the Royal Steam Packet Company to carry a mail once a month from Southampton to Brazil and the river Plate, touching at Lisbon, St. Vincent, (Cape de Verde,) Pernambuco, Bahia, Rio de Janeiro, Montevideo, and Buenos Ayres, for £33,500 per annum. This contract can be terminated at the close of the year 1874, on giving twenty-four months' previous notice.

FROM LIVERPOOL TO BUENOS AYRES, ETC.

In July, 1868, a contract was entered into with the "Liverpool, Brazil, and River Plate Steam Navigation Company," to carry a mail once a month from Liverpool to Buenos Ayres, touching at Rio de Janeiro and Montevideo, on the outward voyage, and at Montevideo, Rio de Janeiro, and Bahia, on the home voyage, for the postage, at the rate of 2*s*. 6*d*. (60 cents) per ounce on letters, newspapers, 3*d*. (6 cents) per pound, and on books, 5*d*. (10 cents) per pound.

LIVERPOOL TO MONTEVIDEO, ETC.

One other contract was made with the "Pacific Steam Navigation Company" to carry a mail once a month from Liverpool to Montevideo, touching at Bordeaux, Lisbon, Rio de Janeiro, and St. Vincent, for the postage at the same rates as those last named.

LIVERPOOL TO PUERTO CABELLO.

In July, 1869, an agreement was made with the "West India and Pacific Steamship Company," to carry a mail from Liverpool, on the 5th of each month, to Puerto Cabello, touching at La Guayra.

LIVERPOOL TO TAMPICO, ETC.

From Liverpool, on the 10th of each month, to Tampico, Port-au-Prince, and Vera Cruz.

LIVERPOOL TO SANTA MARTHA.

From Liverpool, on the 20th of each month, to Santa Martha.

FROM FALMOUTH TO BUENOS AYRES, RIO DE JANEIRO AND MONTEVIDEO.

During the present year a contract was made with the "London, Belgium, Brazil and River Plate Royal Mail Steamship Company" to carry a mail from Falmouth, on the 3d of each month, to Buenos Ayres, Rio de Janeiro, and Montevideo. These last four postal services are performed for the postage money received on letters, newspapers, and books, at 2*s*. 6*d*. (60 cents) per ounce for letters, 6 cents per pound on newspapers, 10 cents per pound on books.

WEST INDIES.

In June, 1868, a contract was entered into with the "Royal Mail Steam Packet Company," to carry a mail from Southampton on the 2d and 17th of each month, to the Islands of Antigua, Barbadoes, Demerara, Dominica, Grenada, Guadaloupe, Havana,

Jacmel, (Hayti,) Jamaica, Martinique, Porto Rico, St. Kitts, St. Lucia, St. Thomas, St. Vincent, Tobago, and to Trinidad. Also, to Aspinwall, Carthagena, Grey Town, Santa Martha, Tampico, and Vera Cruz, on the continent. For performing this mail service the company receive £172,914 per annum, $830,362. In addition to this sum the company receive £2,000 per annum for landing the West India mails at Plymouth, on the return voyage. This contract can be terminated in 1874, on giving twenty-four months' previous notice.

PANAMA AND THE PACIFIC COAST.

A contract with the "Pacific Steam Navigation Company" was made in July, 1864, to carry a mail twice a month, on the 10th and 25th of each month, from Panama to ports on the Pacific coast, for £18,250 per annum. This contract runs to 1872, when it may be terminated, on giving previous notice.

LOCAL LINES IN WEST INDIES.

Contracts with two local lines have been made, one to carry a mail four times a month between St. Kitts, Nevis, and Montserrat, for £490 per annum, and one twice a month between St. Thomas, Puerto Rico, and Havana, for £2,000 per annum.

WEST COAST OF AFRICA.

In July, 1866, a contract was made with the "African Steamship Company" to carry a mail once a month to Madeira, Teneriffe, Bathurst, Sierra Leone, Monrovia, Cape Palmas, Cape Coast Castle, Oneva, Jellah Coffee, Lagos, Benin, Bouny, Old Calabar, Camavoons, and Fernando Po, for the sum of £20,000 per annum, contract terminable in 1872, provided twenty-four months' previous notice has been given.

CAPE OF GOOD HOPE.

In June, 1868, a contract was made with the "Union Steamship Company" to carry a mail twice a month to the Cape of Good Hope, touching at St. Helena and Ascension, for a sum equal in amount to the Sea and British inland postage on the mail matter conveyed.

TO ALEXANDRIA, SUEZ, AND INDIA.

On the 19th of November, 1868, the post office department entered into a contract with the "Peninsula and Oriental Steam Navigation Company" to convey a mail once a week to and from Southampton, Gibraltar, Malta, and Alexandria; and between Marseilles and Alexandria, and between Suez and Bombay.

Also, once a fortnight, between Suez and Calcutta, Bombay and Hong Kong, Hong Kong and Shanghai, Shanghai and Yokohama, for the sum of £400,000 ($1,944,000) per annum. This contract expires in 1880, if twenty-four months' previous notice has been given.

With the same company to carry a mail every four weeks between Point de Galle and Sidney, for £130,000, ($631,800.)

DOVER AND CALAIS.

With the Southeastern Railway Company for a daily mail, between Dover and Calais, for £6,000 per annum.

NUMBER OF SUBSIDIZED LINES AND AMOUNT OF SUBSIDY.

Here are *twelve* lines of steamers under contract for carrying the mails, for which they are paid an annual subsidy of £903,750, or $4,392,244, and four other important lines running to the West Indies and South and Central America, subsidized by having granted to them the postage on all the mail matter they convey.

In addition to the contracts above specified, contracts have been made for a mail service between Halifax and Newfoundland, New Orleans and Balize, British Honduras, and between New York and Bahamas. The negotiations of these contracts have been left to the local governments, the home government pledging itself to pay *one-half* the cost of each service.

It is hardly necessary here to repeat the well-known fact, that the establishment and support of these transatlantic lines of steamers, and the local lines in the West Indies and along the Atlantic and Pacific coasts of Central and South America, has brought by far the largest part of the trade of those countries to this side of the Atlantic. If we wish to extend our trade with these countries, we must offer greater facilities for conducting it, and not oblige traders to go to the most distant markets, because the means of communicating with them are more frequent, regular, and rapid.

PRICE OF WOOD AND IRON SHIPS IN GREAT BRITAIN.

On the subject of the value of new wood and iron first-class English and Scotch built sea-going steamers and sailing-ships, much depends on the service for which they are intended, the materials out of which they are constructed, the standing of the builder, and the character of the outfits. The price depends on these several points and the classification or standing with underwriters on the nature of the materials and manner of construction. I have conversed with ship-owners and builders on the subject, and have the figures of some of them in writing. From one of the most reliable houses in London, as surveyors and valuers of shipping, I have received the following statement of the prices of wood and iron sailing-ships and of iron steamers for the years 1860 and 1869:

SHIPS BUILT OF WOOD, 1860.

	1869	
Classed for fourteen years, £16 16*s*. to £18 18*s*	£15	
Classed for thirteen years, £16 16*s*. to £17 17*s*	14	to 15
Classed for ten years, £12 to £13 10*s*	11	to 12
Classed for nine years, £11 to £12	10	to 11
Classed for eight years, £10 to £10 10*s*	9 10*s*.	to 10

At the above prices the ships will have their bottoms covered with yellow metal and be furnished with a complete East India outfit, which includes a double suit of sails, spare spars, &c.

The best colonial-built ships can be bought here now for about £7 ($34) per ton, and second-hand American and colonial-built at a much lower rate.

COMPOSITE SHIPS.

Composite sailing-ships and steamers, built of iron, except the planking, which is generally of teak-wood, on account of its great durability, were a commercial experiment in 1860. They have proved a success, and are much approved of for the India and China trade, especially for the tea trade. They are iron ships in all respects except their planking. Wood is used for the outside covering, because it can be easily coppered or yellow-metaled, and the ship or steamer thus prevented from becoming foul from barnacles, sea-weed, &c. I am not aware that a wood bottom is preferred for any other reason. But now that a cheap and durable remedy is said to have been discovered and coming into use, which prevents the bottoms of iron vessels from fouling, it is not probable that composite ships will form a much larger proportion of the mercantile tonnage than they do at the present time. The authority already quoted names from £13 to £16 per ton as the average price of fair and good composite sailing-ships, classed for fourteen, fifteen, and sixteen years, ready for sea with India outfit.

A ship-owner informed me that he had built two composite ships the present year for the China trade, which had cost him, coppered, with India outfit, about £17 per ton. But he called them "fancy ships, and unusually expensive." Into one of these ships he put auxiliary steam-power at an additional expense of about £8,000, which, with latest improved engines, moved the ship through the water, on her trial trip, at the rate of about eight knots per hour, on only *nine tons* of coal per day. Steam power on these auxiliary ships is used only on going into and out of port, and in calms and continuous head winds and bad weather, when found more economical or safe than to depend on sails. When sails only are used, the screw is hoisted out of water, and the space in which it played is filled up with a piece of wood fitted for the purpose. There are comparatively but few composite ships built, and these are generally built with a view to some special service.

The authority heretofore quoted, and several ship-owners and builders whom I have consulted on the subject, all agree that the price per ton of a first-class iron sailing-ship, with India outfit, ranged, in the year 1860, from £17 to £18 per ton. But such was the demand for iron steamers from the years 1860 to 1864, caused in part, and very largely, too, by the American war, that the price for sailing-ships was run up to £20 and £21 per ton. Since 1864, the price has gradually fallen to from £12 to £14 10*s*. per ton, according to their classification and style of finish. The classification depends on the character of the materials used, the workmanship, and, to some extent, on the reputation of the builder and the place where built.

A first-class iron ship, that will class A 1 at Lloyds for twenty years, can now be built and fitted for sea for less money than the best English-built wood ship, which, when built in the best manner, under Lloyds' survey, can never be classed A 1 for more than fourteen years. The iron ship, ordinarily, will cost but little for repairs, and at the end of twenty years may continue on in the same class for twenty years more, while the wood structure, during the period of her first classing, is liable to, and very often does, become rotten in various parts of her hull, making extensive and expensive repairs a necessity. She will also require to be newly coppered about every third year. Wood ships generally depreciate in value about one-half in ten years, and then pass into the second, and on to the third class, with increased expenses for repairs and insurance, while her earnings are less, when she soon disappears from the records of shipping. The iron ship of the same age, in the mean time, continues on in her A 1 classification, with but little comparative depreciation in value. At the same time the iron ship has a preference over her wooden competitor of from three to seven shillings sterling per ton (the amount of preference depending on the nature of the cargo) in the leading freight markets, because both ship and cargo insure for less, and she delivers her cargo in better condition.

Iron ships now take the most valuable cargoes, when such ships can be obtained, and the less valuable is left for the wooden ship, such as coals, chalk, lumber, guano, jute, seeds, rice, and bulky raw material of inconsiderable comparative value. On cargoes of low value the insurance on the ship is higher, because in case of such disasters as are brought under general average, cargoes of low value contribute less to repairs than more valuable ones, and the loss falls more heavily on the ship than it would had she been loaded with a cargo of greater value.

The preference given in this country to iron sailing-ships for the foreign freighting business is clearly shown by the character of the tonnage annually constructed for such service. During the year 1868 five hundred and ninety-six wooden sailing vessels of every description were built in this country. The aggregate tonnage of these vessels was 87,151 tons, giving an average of 146 tons each. One hundred and one of these vessels were of 300 tons burden and upward, very few reaching 400 tons. They were principally small, for fishing and coasting, and the largest ones for some special trade, and were built in old yards in sections of the country where iron ships are not usually built. During the same time, the year 1868, one hundred and sixty-two iron sailing-ships were built in Great Britain, the entire tonnage of which was 131,731 tons, averaging 813 tons each. At the same time twenty-nine composite sailing-ships were built, the united tonnage of which was 18,805 tons, and averaging 700 tons each. There are one hundred and ninety-one large sea-going iron and composite sailing ships built in this country in one year, the aggregate tonnage of which was 150,536 tons; while during the same period very few, if any, "deep-sea" wooden ships were built which come up to the average size of one of these one hundred and ninety-one iron and composite ships. The result of the operations of the present year will no doubt show a still wider difference in favor of iron ships.

In addition to the sailing vessels above particularized, there were built in the British Possessions during the same year seven hundred and one wood sailing vessels, the tonnage of which was 141,313 tons, averaging 201 tons each; five hundred and five of these vessels were built in the British North American Possessions, the tonnage of which was 129,720 tons, averaging 250¾ each.

If any stronger facts are necessary to show of what material deep-sea vessels must hereafter be constructed to command a participation in the carrying trade of the world on equal terms, they may be found in the character of the steam vessels built in the United Kingdom during the year 1868. In this year only thirty-nine wooden steamers were built, altogether only 1,134 tons, and averaging but 29 tons each. They were mere launches, river yachts, and perhaps three or four small tugs, *not a freight or passenger steamer among them,* showing that iron only is now used in this country for the construction of freight and passenger steamers.

Continuing our analysis of ship-building in this country for the past year, it is shown that there were built in private yards, and registered as British vessels, one hundred and ninety-three mercantile iron steamers, the aggregate tonnage of which was 77,376 tons, and averaging over 400 tons each. Many of them were large first-class ocean steamers, for passenger and freighting service. During the same year only five composite steamers were built. By this official record, we see the time has already come when not a solitary wooden sea-going steamer is built in this country, and probably no large first-class wooden sailing-ship. Many of these large steamers have but moderate passenger accommodations, and were built mainly for the purpose of carrying cargo.

Notwithstanding the great revelation which iron and steam have so rapidly introduced into the commercial marine of Great Britain, the success of the Suez canal, it is believed, will necessitate further changes. The completion of this great work lessens by one-half the distance to India, and by thousands of miles the passage to China, Australia, and all ports east of the Red Sea. The questions which have thus been forced on the consideration of commercial men here are: Will not the most of the trade which has heretofore gone round the capes pass through the canal, and be carried on mainly by steamers, instead of so largely by sailing-ships, as is now done? Looking forward to such results, some merchants are now hesitating about the wisdom of adding further to their sailing-ships for the eastern trade, while a few others, I learn, have already begun steamers on a new model, with greater length, greater breadth of beam, and less depth of hold than the old models, for the same trade via the Suez canal. It is very probable that this new route, to all the countries lying beyond the Red Sea as far as Australia, is destined to bring about great and rapid changes in the currents of trade and commerce to those countries. Instead of the long, slow route over which their trade has heretofore been conducted, and until recently almost entirely by sailing-vessels, this canal will open a short route, and place the most valuable and probably the principal part of the trade at the command of steamers better adapted for carrying cargo than any heretofore constructed. Should these anticipations be realized, a large amount of sailing tonnage will be released, to seek employment in other channels of trade. Such an amount of sailing tonnage thrown upon freight markets already *overstocked* with ships seeking business will cause a greater reduction in the profits of capital invested in this kind of property. I think it is a conceded fact among commercial men in the United States that capital invested in sailing-ships, taken as a whole, has for the last six or eight years been less remunerative by at least twenty per cent. than for a series of years prior to the time when this new revolution in ocean commerce, caused by iron and steam, had shown its strength and power to ride. Such, also, is the opinion of the same class of men in this country. But in England it is not so much felt, because capitalists are content with a lower rate of interest on their investments. Yet in effecting this great change in the commerce of the seas from wood sailing-ships to iron and steam, the loss in the depreciation of ship property, as well as the commercial advantages, will be greater to this country than to any other, and probably as great as to all others, because she now has a larger number of large sea-going wooden ships seeking business than all other nations combined, which their owners would now be glad to dispose of at a price very far below the value which would have been set on tonnage of the same amount, character, and age, six or eight years ago. Since the year 1854, the tonnage of Great Britain has increased fifty per cent., while in nearly all other European countries tonnage has actually diminished or remained nearly stationary. The United Kingdom alone had last year 8,168 vessels, large and small, engaged in an exclusively foreign trade. The tonnage of these vessels amounted to 4,265,349 tons, and they averaged 522 tons each; 862 of these vessels were steamers, the united measurement of which was 619,199 tons, which would do the work of 2,000,000 tons of sailing-vessels, and the proportion of steam tonnage is rapidly increasing from year to year. In proportion as steamers enter into the carrying trade, the tonnage necessary to carry on that trade will diminish, because steamers on the best models and most improved engines will perform about three times the labor of sailing-vessels.

While there is no doubt but that for certain branches of the carrying trade wood ships will continue to be built for a time and used, the transformation from wood to iron and steam is sure to go on until the principal part of the commerce between nations will be carried on through their agencies, and the adoption of any measures, public or private, intended to promote the restoration of our commerce, which look to anything short of the change, of at least that portion of our mercantile marine required for international commerce, from wood to iron and steam, will surely fail of their object. It is not temporary relief to "tide over" temporary disaster that is required to meet the necessities which are upon us; but change, radical change in structure, to effect which government and people must act in harmony; the government to extend all proper encouragement and inducements for commercial men to meet promptly the emergency that is forced upon us, and the merchant and ship-builder to set about in good earnest the reconstruction of our mercantile fleets. Our remedy is not to be found in a restoration of the past; that era of ocean commerce is fast passing away, and a new and more progressive one has overtaken us. We must move on with it and deal with facts and events as they meet us to-day or give up all idea of recovering our old ocean supremacy, retire substantially within our coast lines, and yield this great and noble field of enterprise, once so gallantly contested and won, to be controlled and monopolized by other heads and hands.

I am asked to state "what regulations have been adopted by the British government to ascertain the amount of materials entering into the construction of ships which are exempt from duty?"

No regulations of such a character are required, because there is no duty assessed on any article that goes into the construction of vessels or steamers of any kind. Not only are all such materials free, but all vessels bound on foreign voyages are permitted to take a supply of such dutiable articles as may be needed for the ship's use from bonded warehouses free of duty.

"What advantages are possessed by ship-builders and ship-owners in Great Britain, over the same class in the United States?"

Here ocean commerce is held to be one of the great branches of national industry and sources of wealth, and ranks with manufactures and agriculture. It is the pride of a commercial people, and the whole nation is united in watching over it, and in trying to gain for it every advantage that sagacity, wealth, talent, mechanical skill, science, and ample protection on every sea can command.

The Board of Trade is a department of the government, and is always in charge of able and experienced men, who have been long in its employ, and has the commercial marine under its special care.

The merchant shipping act extends legal protection in a thousand ways, whenever needed, to ship, cargo, and sailor. This important law is often amended or revised with great care and labor, as a wider experience and a change of circumstances or new features appear to make revisions desirable. The latest revision was reported at the last session of Parliament, and will, no doubt, after some amendments, be passed into law at the next coming session. Again, the consular corps of this country are generally trained men. They are selected for their supposed fitness for the places they are wanted to fill, and the study of how best to extend and secure British trade and commerce is made one of their chief studies. No nation is so watchful over everything that affects its trade and commerce as the English nation, and the whole nation is reaping the benefit of this care and vigilance, constantly exercised in every available manner.

The preparation of a yard, buildings, machinery, &c., for the construction of iron vessels, requires a much greater outlay of capital than what is necessary for building vessels of wood. But capital has always been ready to open as many of these expensive yards as the demand for ships required. It is said the yard belonging to the Thames Iron Ship-building Company cost half a million sterling, nearly $2,500,000 in gold. The Minotaur, one of the largest armor-plated ships in the British navy, was built there. It has within its limits two dry-docks, built of stone, of a capacity sufficient to receive ships of the largest class, the heaviest rolling machinery, forging, planing and slotting machines, iron spar-yard, and, in fact, every convenience necessary for constructing and completing five or six large ships, steam or sailing, at the same time. There are several yards similar in character on the Thames, several on the Mersey, several in the north of England, and a much larger number on the Clyde than in any other locality. With this constant national attention in every necessary form, these many large well organized and equipped yards in complete readiness for every department of iron ship-building, with an abundance of native iron and coal delivered in them at low rates, and everything free from taxation, it will be perceived that ship-builders and owners in Great Britain have already gained advantages over us which only time, close and careful attention, all proper encouragement, and a full determination to succeed will enable us to reach. Besides transforming the vast mercantile fleet of this country from wood to iron and steam, more or less mercantile steamers, sailing-ships, and ships of war are continually in progress of construction for the maritime nations of Europe, China, Japan, and the British possessions.

The geographical position of England and the position held by her in relation to the trade, capital, and commercial enterprises of Europe and the whole Eastern hemisphere, is of such a controlling character as naturally to conduct a large portion of the trade of those countries to her. Ten years ago much of this trade was done by American ships which were chartered by English merchants, but English iron and composite ships now take the most profitable part of this trade; and although American ships still get a portion of the second-class business, the number thus employed is fast diminishing.

The labor of all grades and classes of artisans employed in the construction of ships in England and Scotland is cheaper than in the United States, ranging in London from 4*s.* to 7*s.* 6*d.* per day; on the Clyde about 1*s.* less per day, and in the north of England still lower. But this does not afford the English builder much if any advantage, because in America mechanics perform more labor in a given time than the same class of workmen do in this country.

"Character of officers and crews of English vessels as compared with those of the United States."

There is an acknowledged difference, in favor of the American officer, in the preparatory education of American and English ship-masters. While the American is as good a seaman, he is to a certain extent also a merchant. He is very frequently a part owner in the ship he commands, and when abroad seeking business is to a great extent intrusted by the other owners with the general management of the ship and business connected with her, such as looking up business, deciding on what offers to accept, and protecting her interests in all ways. The English ship-master is rarely a part owner, or intrusted with any such responsibilities. He is generally a good seaman and obeys the instructions laid down for his guidance. His duty is to sail the ship, keep her in good order, and deliver cargoes in good condition. The business is entirely in the hands of the owners and ship-brokers. As a general rule American ship-masters make greater dispatch, sail their ships with a less number of men, feed them better, and their port charges are less. Before an English master can take charge of a ship, he has to pass a rather rigid examination before a board of examiners appointed by the Board of Trade, and receive a certificate from them of competency and good character. For any misconduct or incompetency as master, this certificate may be suspended or taken from him. It is said the rigid enforcement of this law has produced a decided reform in the service.

A majority of the seamen in our mercantile service are foreigners. We have no licensed shipping officers and no provisions of law for their protection until they sign the shipping articles and go on board ship. No certificates of competency as seamen and of good conduct are given them on their discharge, and they are left while in port to the tender mercies of landlords and shipping-masters and their runners. They are frequently robbed of the proceeds of their last voyage, and their advance wages for the next, and delivered aboard ship by those who control them, destitute and helpless, like any marketable commodity. In all these respects the English sailor is carefully protected by law and the constant watchfulness of government officials. In the leading ports he has, when in them, a good, well-regulated boarding-house to go to, with books, papers, amusements, savings banks, medical attendance, &c., forming a part of the establishment, and, what is perhaps of more importance, shipping officers *licensed* and controlled by the government. At these government shipping offices all seamen for the British mercantile service *must* be shipped. They have, before they can be shipped, to produce their recommendations from the captains of the last ships on which they served, and to the shipping office pay the small fee of one shilling, (twenty-five cents,) and it is made unlawful to exact any larger sum. I went over this subject with some care in a dispatch to the Department of State, dated May 12, 1866, and numbered 375. This dispatch was called for and published, with another on the subject of commerce, by the fortieth Congress, second session, Executive Document No. 283, and may be found on page 22 of this document. As I have not time to go over the question in detail before this paper ought to be sent forward, now too long delayed by illness and pressing official duties, I must respectfully refer the honorable committee and the Commissioner of Customs to that paper for further information on the subject. The revised merchant shipping act, which will come before the next session of Parliament for adoption, contains a clause permitting foreign ships to enjoy the benefits of these government shipping offices in English ports. This will be an excellent thing for American ships and seamen in British ports, and all masters should be compelled to ship such men as they may want through these licensed shipping offices, instead of through irresponsible private shipping offices, on which foreign ships in British ports now depend, and where sailors are so often deceived, robbed, and ill-treated. It is to be hoped that some efficient measures will soon be established by law to give American and foreign seamen an equally good protection within the limits of the United States.

The establishment of the coast guard corps of mariners, and navy pensions, are the chief inducements to encourage seamen to enter the government service when called for. For more full information on this branch of their inquiry, I must again respectfully ask to refer the committee to the published dispatch (No. 375) heretofore mentioned. I will investigate this question further, and if I find any additional facts worth reporting I will communicate them hereafter.

French Lloyds is more favorable to American ships than the English, because the construction of American ships conforms more nearly to the surveys and specifications laid down by French Lloyds. No American-built ship, whether English-owned or otherwise, can be brought within the requirements of English Lloyds, yet American ships can be classed as A 1 there, by having the letter F placed against them, signifying *foreign* built.

There are no fixed and established "printed rates of wages paid English seamen, firemen, and engineers" in the mercantile service. Such wages fluctuate according to supply and demand. The rates of wages of all persons serving in the navy, from seamen upward, are established and may be found printed in the "Navy List," two copies of which I herewith forward. I think quite full answers to the inquiries put to me will be found embodied in this paper; but if any point has been overlooked, or any further information from me desired, I will endeavor to supply such omissions on further calls, with as little delay as practicable.

I have the honor to be your obedient servant,

F. H. MORSE, *Consul General.*

Hon. HAMILTON FISH,
Secretary of State.

P. S.—I will make the price of iron steamers the subject of another communication, I hope, by next post.

A 1.

UNITED STATES CONSULATE GENERAL,
London, January 15, 1870.

DEAR SIR: In answer to your inquiry in regard to composite vessels, I would say they have only one advantage over iron, which is more than overcome by several disadvantages, and the one advantage I feel quite confident is only temporary. It is, they can be easily coppered and thus kept clean longer without docking than an iron ship with the ordinary coating on her bottom. But this is not found from experience of sufficient advantage to give them a preference over iron. The first cost of the composite vessel is greater than if built of iron. The wood bottom wears out quicker, and must be replaced with new at heavy expense. Then there is the additional outlay for sheathing with copper, or yellow metal, which must be renewed every two or three years. The iron ship had to be docked and scraped, or washed down as her bottom becomes foul, but a cheap coating, put on with a brush, like paint, is coming into use here, which it is said after trial keeps the bottom more free from sea-weed and barnacles than copper. This coating has to be renewed about once in fifteen or eighteen months.

You will bear in mind that a composite vessel is built entirely of iron, except that the planking is of wood, secured to the iron frame by through bolts and nuts screwed on to their inside ends, and by washers and rivets. This planking, on the iron plating of an iron frame is the most simple part of the structure, and when the machinery is provided for the preparation of the other parts of the vessel, and the frame up, complete in all its parts, except planking or plating, the difficulty is over, and putting on the outside covering becomes a very simple and easy matter. Composite, though excellent vessels, are not gaining in this country anything like the rapidity that iron is. I have not yet obtained full statistics for the year just closed, but I think it will be found that the number of iron ships over composite, will be comparatively greater than the year before last, which shows that the experience of persons engaged in maritime commerce is setting their judgments in favor of iron ships.

It must be evident to all who have given any thought to the subject that we cannot expect a revival of our shipping interest without some measures of relief and encouragement from government; in regard to the mode of applying which, men differ according to the standpoint from which they view the subject. If the object be *merely to possess* iron ships and steamers, without any other object in view, no matter where built, the way is easy to gain such possessions. Open the door and admit a foreign supply. But if nothing else is done, the certain effect of such a policy will be, as long as it may be continued, to prevent the establishment of iron ship-building yards within our own country. The object should be, not merely to possess, but also and *chiefly* to create facilities and encouragement for opening yards and constructing iron steamers and sailing ships on our own soil. It is, I think, an admitted fact that there is now more tonnage at the command of merchants who have freights to offer than is, in the present condition of trade, necessary to do the carrying trade of the world; and therefore capital invested in sailing ships does not *now*, taken as a whole, pay well. It is true that some steam lines make large dividends, and some sailing ships kept in certain trades are doing a fair business, but, taken as a whole, the shipping interest has not been for the last few years a remunerating business.

If this view be correct, and the iron ship-builders could have *free materials* and could put a ship afloat at as low a price as it can be done in Great Britain, I should not look for an immediate and general revival of our shipping interests, especially for general freighting service. A few yards would probably be started, and ships and steamers be built for special service. Government could also greatly encourage iron ship-building by giving a liberal subsidy to a few leading lines of postal steamers, on the express condition that all the regular steamers on the lines should be either iron or composite steamers of the highest class, and at least one-half or more of the number on each line should be built in the United States. The great end to be kept in view and *gained* should be the development, to the highest state of perfection, the art of iron ship-building among ourselves, and free us from dependence on foreign countries for our mercantile marine and means of transport, and give us facilities for building the most efficient *sea-going ships-of-war* in time of need. Any measures which look *only* to the increase of our mercantile marine by the purchase of foreign-built ships will render no aid in placing us in such an independent position, but will tend rather to hold us back from it.

I forward with this note a letter from Sunderland, in the north of England, where the largest number of the wood-ships built in this country are constructed. This will give you the price of steamers, sailing-ships, and the rate of wages in that part of the kingdom. I also send a list of ships, over a certain size, built there during the year 1869. You will notice only *six* wooden sailing ships on the list, and not one of them comes up to the average of the whole number of iron sailing ships built in the United Kingdom during the year 1868. And what is more discouraging for wooden ships, the writer says in a letter to me, dated 30th December, 1869,

"A great many wooden vessels that were finished *last year* (1868) are still lying *unsold*, as they have gone off very slowly this year, while on the contrary a great many iron vessels have been contracted; for in fact, nearly all the iron vessels that have been built have been invariably sold before they were finished."

If I can do anything more here to aid the object for which you are laboring please inform me, and it shall be promptly and cheerfully done.

I have been relying on one of the principal London ship-building firms, for a statement in reference to ship-building on the Thames, similar to the one from Sunderland, but it has not yet been sent to me. On its receipt, I will forward it immediately.

I am, sir, your obedient servant,

F. W. MORSE,
Consul General.

Hon. JOHN LYNCH, *M. C.*

B 1.

SUNDERLAND, *January* 3, 1870.

DEAR SIR: We now have the great pleasure of handing you copy of a letter received by us this morning from one of our eminent ship-builders, in which you will find a more detailed account of wages, and also in prices of iron sailing vessels and cargo boats, as follows:

"Replying to yours of 9th instant, we have pleasure in furnishing you with the following particulars for your American friends, viz:

"The rate of wages paid to iron shipwrights and artizans in several years:

Years.	Platers.		Smiths.		Riveters.		Caulkers.		Drillers.		Carpenters.		Joiners.	
	s.	*d.*	*s.*	*d.*	*s.*	*d.*	*s.*	*d.*	*s.*	*d.*	*s.*	*d.*	*s.*	*d.*
1860	4	8	4	2	4	0	4	0	3	0	5	0	4	0
1861-2	5	0	4	6	4	6	5	0	3	6	5	0	4	0
1863	5	0	5	0	4	8	5	0	3	6	5	0	5	0
1864	5	6	5	6	5	0	5	0	3	4	5	6	5	0
1869	4	6	4	6	4	2	4	6	3	4	5	0	4	6

The prices of A A iron sailing ships of highest class at Lloyd's, and with East India outfit: In 1861, £15 10*s.* per register ton; in 1862 and 1863, £17 17*s.* 6*d.* per register ton; in 1869, £14 per register ton.

The price for nine years on A B cargo steamers, fitted complete, with engines and boilers ready for sea: In 1861, £18 per register ton; in 1862 and 1863, £19 2*s.* 6*d.* per register ton; in 1869, £16 per register ton.

"I hope this information may be what your friends require; any further I can give I shall be happy to do.

"Please note that all the information we have given you about steamers has been for what we call cargo boats; that is, steamers of large carrying capacity but with only moderate horse-power; while for ocean-going steamers the price is about £25 per register ton, and the price of this description of steamer varies very little, as the cost of fitting these vessels up for passengers, the engines &c., are always much about the same; thus for a boat of 2,000 tons register, fitted up with full passenger accommodation, with engines on board of large horse-power to give the boat great speed, and all the other requisites required for this class of boats, the price would be about £50,000.

Trusting this information will be of service to you.

We are, dear sir, yours truly,

PEACOCK BROTHERS.

F. H. MORSE, Esq., *London.*

B 2.

Vessels built at Sunderland, England, during the year 1869.

	Number.	
Iron ships	28	
Iron steamships	9	
Total iron ships	—	37
Composite ships	12	
Composite steamships	1	
Total	—	13
Wooden sailing ships	—	6
Total		56

		Tonnage.
Vessels from 480 to 1,000 tons burden	42	28,114
Vessels from 1,000 tons and upward	14	18,179
Total tonnage		46,293

C.

2 COWPER'S COURT, CORNHILL,
London, December 7, 1869.

SIR: In reply to your favor of yesterday's date we have much pleasure in giving you the following information, as to the value of wood and iron ships, as in the year 1860 and at the present time:

In the case of sailing-ships the price varies according to the standing and repute of the builder, and the character of the outfit.

The same remark applies to steamers, besides which the fittings and outfit of passenger boats must be considered, and also the higher prices of engines, by the first engineering firms, on the Thames and Mersey.

	1860.	1869.
Wood ships with East India outfit and yellow metaled:		
Fourteen years class	£18 18 to £16 16 0	£15 00 to £00 00 0
Thirteen years class	17 17 to 16 16 0	15 00 to 14 00 0
Ten years class	13 10 to 12 00 0	12 00 to 11 00 0
Nine years class	12 00 to 11 00 0	11 00 to 10 00 0
Eight years class	10 10 to 10 00 0	10 00 to 9 10 0
Composite vessels, East India outfit and yellow metaled:		
Sixteen years class	Very few built.	16 00 to 13 00 0
Fifteen years class		
Fourteen years class		
Iron ships, East India outfit:		
Twelve years class	18 00 to 17 00 0	[A] 14 10 to 13 00 0
Nine years class	17 00 to 16 00 0	[A] 13 00 to 12 00 0
Screw steamers, including average power to tonnage, cargo boats, and small passenger accommodation	21 00 to 20 00 0	16 00 to 10 00 0
With larger passenger accommodation and greater power	35 00 to 25 00 0	30 00 to 20 00 0

Paddle steamers of greater power in proportion to tonnage, say difference in horse-power at £40 to £30 per horse-power.

Wood vessels that have been built on speculation and have remained some time on builders' hands may now be bought at a considerable reduction on prices quoted above, the demand for wood vessels being now very limited.

Wood steamers have been entirely superseded by iron, excepting a few tug-boats.

Tendering our services at any time,

We are, sir, yours respectfully,

GEO. BAYLEY & WM. RIDLEY.

Hon. F. H. MORSE,
Consul General United States.

No. 1025.]

UNITED STATES CONSULATE,
Liverpool, December 18, 1869.

SIR: I have the honor to acknowledge the receipt of your dispatch inclosing a letter from the Hon. John Lynch, chairman of the Committee on American Navigation in the House of Representatives, requesting information about the cost of ships, wages to workmen, &c., in Great Britain in 1860 and 1869.

I have found quite a discrepancy in the costs of building vessels, owing partly, no doubt, to the competition among builders both now and in 1860. With regard to wooden vessels, there were very few built in Great Britain in 1860, and less at the present time. So far as I can learn, there are no wooden steamers built at the present time. Price of wooden sailing-ships in Great Britain, in 1860, from £18 to £21 per ton. Price of wooden sailing-ships in 1869 from £15 to £16.

The price for wooden steamers in 1860 is given to me at £30 per ton. All say there are none now building.

Price of iron sailing-ships in 1860 may be given at about £19 per ton.

Price of iron sailing-ships in 1869, £15 10*s*.

Price of iron steamers of average engine power, in 1860, £26 10*s*.; in 1869, £22 10*s*.

The above prices are, assuming the vessel to be in every case of about 1,000 tons, builders' measurement, supplied with an East India outfit, but without passenger accommodation, and the steamers to have engines of 150 nominal horse-power. Larger vessels would be dearer, and smaller ones cheaper, than the rates given.

The wages of mechanics on ship work in Liverpool, in 1860, was fixed by the Ship-Carpenters' Association, a kind of trades union. The foreman received nine shillings, and ordinary workmen seven shillings per day. These are the wages paid at the present time.

The rates for insurance in Liverpool, for first-class vessels, were as follows:

British-built vessels, in 1860, about seven guineas per cent. per annum. In 1869, about ten guineas.

Colonial-built vessels, in 1860, nine guineas per cent. per annum. The same in 1869, about twelve guineas per cent. per annum.

On steamers, wood and iron, in 1860, from five to six guineas per cent. per annum. The same in 1869, from eight to nine guineas per cent. per annum.

The only advantage possessed by ship-builders and owners in Great Britain over the same class in the United States, is cheaper labor and cheaper iron. In this country there is a redundance of labor, consequently labor is cheap. The redundancy is so great that very nearly one man out of every twenty, taking England and Wales together, is a pauper, that is, has to be provided for in whole or in part at the public expense, to keep him from starving. The effect of this is felt not only in the construction of vessels, enabling builders to build cheaper, but to the owners as well in conducting their commercial pursuits, enabling them to run their vessels at less cost, and, as a general thing, with a better class of sailors. As an instance, wages of able seamen in New York, at present time, are about $30 per month in currency, while in Liverpool they are only £2 10*s*., or equal to $12 10 in gold, or about $16 or $17 in currency. Iron is also cheaper in this country, which is accounted for by the same reason, viz, that labor is cheaper, thereby enabling those engaged in the iron business to produce iron cheaper than it can be made in the States.

I have the honor, &c.,

THOMAS H. DUDLEY.

Hon. HAMILTON FISH,
Secretary of State.

UNITED STATES CONSULATE,
Quebec, November 24, 1869.

SIR: Your favor under date of October 30th has been acknowledged. I have given the shipping interests of Quebec considerable attention the past year, and am now able to make the following communication on the subject of your letter:

1. *Wooden sea-going sailing-vessels.*—The present cost of building this class, including both material and labor, is about the same as in 1860. The price of material is higher, while labor is lower than in 1860.

2. *The cost of same.*—Vessels of nine hundred tons cost about $38 per register ton; vessels of fourteen hundred tons, $36 per ton. This does not include the yellow metal for sheathing, the cost of which is $3 per ton. Vessels are usually sold in Europe before they are sheathed.

3. *Value of same in England.*—At no time have Quebec-built vessels been held in very high repute in England; to-day they cannot be sold at remunerative prices. They sell in England for about seven pounds sterling per register ton, to which may be added about five dollars per ton for outward freight. Ship-owners do not like wooden vessels. Iron and composite are taking the place of wood in Europe, except in some special branch of the service, such as the freighting of lumber, &c. But iron and composite have never been built at Quebec or in Canada.

4. *Steamers.*—There never was but one wooden sea-going steamer built here—that was many years ago. There are —— ocean steamers sailing from this port, and quite a number down the river to the ports below. All of them are of iron, and built on the Clyde, in Scotland. Among the latter are the Gaspe, formerly Emma, City of Quebec, formerly Dunbarton, and the Seacrit, all old blockade-runners in the rebel service.

5. *Tariff of* 1868.—Previous to 1868, all materials for ship-building purposes imported into Canada were subject to duties, but with a drawback to the full amount of duties paid. The act of May 22, 1868, so far as it relates to the ship-building interests, was drafted by J. W. Dunscomb, esq., collector of customs at Quebec, assisted by McKay & Warner, Americans, and large ship-builders here. It was the intention of these gentlemen, and also of the government, to have all material imported for ship-building free of duty, but, through some mistake, a few minor articles were not included, such as a certain class of nails, &c. All other articles were made free entirely, except cables of hemp or grass, cordage, varnish; when for ships only, free, otherwise fifteen per cent. duty.

6. *Cost of material.*—In order to shorten this communication, I will refer you to my report on the shipping interests of Quebec, to Hon. J. A. Graham, Acting Register of the Treasury, under date of October 20, 1869.

7. *Wages of laborers in ship-yards.*—I will refer you to my report to Mr. Graham.

8. *Composite vessels* are those with iron frames with planking of wood.

9. *Ships now building at Quebec.*—There are seventeen in all, including three half composite, for market of 1870.

10. *Character of officers and crew.*—About the same as in the United States.

11. *General information.*—The labor per ship of about one thousand tons classed A 1, at Lloyds, will amount to ten dollars per ton.

I fully believe that iron is to take the place of wood, eventually; that iron steamships will take the place of sailing, for nearly all freights except lumber. The great majority of ships to-day from Europe (England and France) to the East Indies are iron propellers. You may place the advantages of iron over wood for means of transportation in a greater ratio than you would water over land.

In the classing of vessels, Lloyds have heretofore given Quebec ships A 1, seven years. I am now advised that in order to advance the interest of the Dominion, they will give eight years in 1870.

You will find the wages of seamen, from the master down to the boy, in my report to Mr. Graham above referred to.

* * * * * * * * * * *

I am, sir, your obedient servant,

CHARLES ROBINSON,
United States Consul.

Hon. JOHN LYNCH, M. C.,
Chairman Committee on American Navigation.

UNITED STATES CONSULATE,
Kingston, Ontario, November 29, 1869.

SIR: In obedience to a request contained in yours of October 30, I have the honor to submit the following report:

1. Cost in Kingston of wooden sailing-vessels per ton, fitted for lake navigation, in 1860, (old custom-house measurement,) two hundred and fifty tons and under, $50; over that tonnage, $45 per ton.

2. Wooden steamers, for passengers, in 1860, $100 per ton.

3. There is but slight, if any, difference in the cost of building the foregoing at the present time.

4. First-class mechanics, in ship-yards, in 1860, received from $1 50 to $1 75 per day. The same prices are paid now as near as may be.

5. Steamers to class A 1. Insurance for the season six per cent.; sailing-vessels, one per cent less.

6. I am not aware of any regulation by this government to ascertain the amount of material entering into the construction of vessels, except the required oath of the builder or owner.

7. All material imported for vessel-building by the builder or owner comes into the province free of duty, while there is a heavy duty on all material entering the United States for the same purpose, thereby giving to the builder or owner here a decided advantage.

8. Character of officers and crews of Canadian vessels rates as near as possible the same as on American vessels of same classes.

At the present time, compared with 1860, pitch, tar, and oakum are a shade lower in price, and timber a shade higher.

From the best information I can get these trifling variations in price about neutralize, thereby making the cost now about the same as in 1860.

For a short time during the late rebellion oakum, pitch, and tar were at fabulous prices, but at the close of the war dropped back to the old prices.

All of which is most respectfully submitted.

I am, sir, very respectfully, your obedient servant,

S. B. HANA,
United States Consul.

Hon. JOHN LYNCH, *Chairman, &c., Washington, D. C*

CONSULATE OF THE UNITED STATES OF AMERICA,
Halifax, N. S., December 2, 1869.

SIR: I have the honor to acknowledge the receipt of your communication, making certain inquiries in relation to the ship-building interests of Nova Scotia, and in compliance with your request have much pleasure in furnishing the following information:

1. The cost in Nova Scotia of wooden ships, iron fastened, per ton, fitted for sea, in 1860, was fifty-five dollars; and of coppered and copper-fastened, about sixty-five dollars per ton, register tonnage.

2. There is no material difference in the cost of building this class of ships at the present time, the increased price of some of the raw materials being equivalent to the abolition of the duty of five per cent. on imported articles.

3. No wooden steamers are built in Nova Scotia.

4. The rates of wages of first-class mechanics on ship work, in 1860, were from $1 50 to $1 75 per day, and at the present time are about the same.

5. Steamships crossing the Atlantic are generally insured in England. The rate of insurance on such steamers is about nine per cent. per year, or one-half per cent. per voyage.

6. On sailing vessels, the rates of insurance here on voyages from Halifax to England are from two and a half to three per cent.; on voyages to the West Indies, from one and three-fourths to two per cent.; and to the United States, one per cent.

7. No specific regulations are adopted by the government to ascertain the amount of materials exempt from duty entering into the construction of vessels. The articles are admitted free merely upon the oath of the importer that they are *intended solely to be used in the construction of vessels.* But by act of Parliament the importation of goods so exempt from duty, and all matters relating thereto, are subject to such regulations as may be prescribed by the governor and council for the purpose of preventing fraud or abuse under pretext of such exemption.

8. The advantages possessed by ship-builders and ship-owners in Nova Scotia over the same classes in the United States arise from the lower rates of wages, the cheaper raw materials, and the exemption from duty of all imported articles required in the construction of ships.

These advantages are partially counterbalanced by the greater durability of American-built vessels, owing to the better quality of the timber used in their construction.

Formerly the duty in Nova Scotia on ship-building materials was five per cent., but under the present Canadian tariff they are admitted duty free.

There has been no material change in the price of labor and ship-building materials in this province since 1866, and I respectfully refer you for many particulars relating thereto to my report on that subject made in that year, and published (page 219) in the appendix to the report of the Special Commissioner of Revenue.

But a small number of American vessels have been registered in Nova Scotia.

While the admission of American vessels to registry in the British North American provinces is of but little practical importance to American citizens, the admission of foreign vessels to registry in the United States necessarily involves the opening of our coasting trade to foreign competition.

This would be most injurious to the ship-building interests of our country.

It is not, therefore, it appears to me, by admitting foreign vessels to registry upon an equal footing with our own, and thus opening our extended coasting and inland trade to foreign competition, that the shipping and ship-building interests of the United States are to be restored to their former state of prosperity, but by the reduction of duties on all imported materials for the construction of ships, and by liberal subsidies, under judicious regulations, to ocean mail steamers.

I have the honor to be, sir, your obedient servant,

M. M. JACKSON,
United States Consul.

Hon. JOHN LYNCH,
Chairman of the Committee on American Navigation Interests

UNITED STATES CONSULATE,
St. John, New Brunswick, November 29, 1869.

SIR: I have the honor to acknowledge the receipt, this 18th day of November, of your letter, dated October 30, 1869, forwarded me through the Department of State, asking certain information concerning ship-building interests of the province.

Inquiry of the same character having lately been made of this office by the Treasury Department, I am therefore enabled to answer your questions without much delay.

The cost of wooden ships and wooden steamers built in this province in 1860 and 1869 is the same. A comparison of ships and steamers built then and now show no difference in cost per ton worth noting. Sailing vessels of from 1,200 to 1,500 tons register, complete with anchors and sails, ready for sea, can be built for $40 per ton. They are what the Liverpool market term soft-wood ships. Frames are spruce; stanchions, keelsons, waterways, stringers and rails are hard wood; that is, hackmatack or pitch pine. They class 3-3; 1-1. Seven years French Lloyds, wooden steamers, for use on the St. John's River and Bay of Fundy, are built here at a cost, when ready for sea, fitted complete, of $90 to $95 per ton register; the largest being about 650 tons register, with 150 horse-power, cabins and saloon, built of hackmatack and Bay spruce. No steamers are built but those required for local traffic.

The rate of wages for ship-carpenters have varied but little in ten years. I am informed by different parties that the difference has not exceeded ten cents per day at any time within ten years last past. First-class ship mechanics get from eight to nine shillings a day, that is, $1 60 to $1 80.

Rate of insurance on sailing vessels is twelve per cent. per annum, to go anywhere, except Gulf of St. Lawrence in winter season. Rates of insurance on steam vessels are the same as on sailing vessels. Fire rates are from two to two one-half per cent.

There are no regulations whatever adopted, by which the amount of material entering into the construction of vessels which are exempt from duty can be ascertained. The Dominion government, in their tariff of customs, exempt certain articles intended for the construction of vessels. There being no check other than the oath of the importer that the articles are imported for the purpose of ship-building, it is impossible to ascertain what part or how much of such importations actually enter into the construction of shipping. An examination of the customs records shows the entire importation of these exempted articles to be for ship-building purposes.

The advantages claimed by New Brunswick ship-builders over those of the United States are numerous, the most important being cheapness of timber, low wages of ship-carpenters and laborers, free entry of all foreign material entering into the construction, use of less timber and bolting, giving a lighter and stronger vessel than the American build. (This is a question of construction, and one worthy our American ship-builders' attention.) Building their vessels under the inspection and scrutiny of London Lloyds and French Lloyds, giving them a preference in market over those not classed, or those classed in American Lloyds. The ship-owners of the province get their vessels at very low prices, because of there being no foreign demand for colonial ships. That although the spruce ships may not be as durable as our oak, still their greater buoyancy gives great advantage in carrying dead freights. The difference they claim to be twenty-five per cent. in their favor, and more than compensates for difference in durability. My knowledge of officers and crews being confined almost entirely to those of American shipping, I am unable to contrast them with those of New Brunswick. As far as my observation goes, I think our officers superior in education and general business capacity, but the New Brunswick skipper is generally a thorough sailor and of steady habits. As to the crews of the different vessels, it would be hard to make a distinction. The only nationality attaching to any of them being the flags under which they sail from time to time. When we find an American sailor who has a pride in his nationality, he is generally a very superior man to those of any other country. That he is a better sailor, I cannot say.

In former years the colonial ship-builders found market for their vessels in Liverpool, which often gave them fair profits, and again, heavy losses were suffered. Their ships went to market, like any other article of sale, the prices depending upon the demand. They were built of hackmatack, pitch-pine and oak, and under the scrutiny of Lloyds, London, the most of them receiving their (Lloyds) classification of seven years, A 1, which was indispensable, in case of sale in that market. The demand for this class of vessels having ceased, the builders are engaged in the construction of the spruce or soft-wood vessel, depending upon the citizen, merchant, and ship-broker of the province as purchasers. The demand is quite limited, and for three years the business has been rapidly declining. The few ships built pay the builder no profit, notwithstanding the advantages they have in cheap material, labor, &c. They are generally built under the inspection of French Lloyds. Ship-owners inform me their spruce vessels are giving better satisfaction than expected, and so well pleased are they, that they declare their intention of confining their future investments to that class. They cost about five dollars per ton less than the hackmatack ship, and carry fully sixteen per cent. more guano or coals.

In giving the cost of these vessels at $40 per ton, I intend it as a fair average. It would probably give a clearer understanding to the committee to give the different kinds of vessels and cost of each. Small vessels, single deck, to class in French Lloyds A 1, five years, will cost $34 to $37 per ton. Vessels classed A 1, 3-3, five years, will cost from $38 to $39 per ton. Vessels classed A 1, 3-3, six years, will cost $39 to $40 per ton. Vessels classed A 1, 3-3, seven years, will cost $42 to $44 per ton. The vessels of the five-year class may be built of timber wholly the growth of the province. In the six year class, the rudder, stock, and windlass, must be southern oak, and the stems, stern-posts, aprons, knight-heads, bills, corners, &c., must be either oak or hackmatack. In the seven-year class, southern oak for all cases where hackmatack or oak is required in the six-year class, also, tamarack or pitch-pine beams, pitch-pine or oak keelsons, waterways, stringers, rails, &c., &c. All of these vessels, when running from two hundred to four hundred tons register, more or less iron knees are required under every beam. Above six hundred tons, in addition to the knees, iron straps on the outside, or an equivalent in the ceiling, with edge bolting, &c. Ships may be built in this province from one to two dollars per ton less, but only when the object is production at the lowest possible cost.

In building spruce ships, much depends upon the condition of the timber and the care in putting it together, it being very essential, indeed, indispensable to long service, that the timber be cut in the winter season; that every part have thorough ventilation, and so salted that the salt remains where placed and not allowed to collect on the bottom. When ready for sea a spruce ship should never be allowed to cruise in tropical climates until she has had a year's service in northern waters. When carefully and properly built and cared for, spruce vessels are known to have sailed, discharging their cargoes in good condition, from sixteen to twenty years. Again, when constructed of timber cut in bad season and probably sent south, while green, they have become utterly worthless in five years.

That the committee may have some of the reasons advanced by the builders here of their advantages in construction over our American builders, in a form more ship-shape than I can give, I enclose extract of letter recived from Mr. Tucker, the very intelligent and long experienced agent of Lloyds, London, who has made the construction of ships a study for forty years, and who has been the agent of the committee of Lloyds in this province for fifteen years, in which time he has introduced many and radical reforms in the construction of sailing vessels.

I am sir, very respectfully, your obedient servant,

D. B. WARNER,
United States Consul.

Hon. JOHN LYNCH,
Chairman Committee on Navigation Interests.

[Extract.]

* * * * * Permit me to state that since the appointment of surveyors to these provinces by the committee of Lloyds, London, so great has been the reduction in cost of construction of our vessels, while the improvements have been considerable, from a personal knowledge, and I believe it is generally concorded. Ships of any required model and build to class A 1 in the society of Lloyds' register, London, can be constructed in the Dominion of Canada for one-fourth less cost than they can be turned out of any building yard in the States of America. As a consequence, the reduction of expenses in construction being so important, comparatively, where colonial vessels are returning interest upon the outlay to their respective owners, the mercantile vessels of the United States are, as a general thing, running to a disadvantage; in fine, are yielding no profitable return to those who may be interested.

It is also generally admitted that vessels constructed of tamarack or spruce have a material advantage over others, because of their buoyancy, while they are equally as durable when properly cared for; this species of timber not being of the same specific gravity compared with that which enters into the construction of ships built in the United States. Our colonial vessels, as a consequence, when either light or laden, do not become so deeply immersed, sailing, it is estimated, about one-sixth lighter, admittedly carrying a heavier dead weight and measurement cargo, tonnage being compared, *and have a much more free* board than ships built wholly of oak.

Again, your builders adhere to the ancient method of building ships with wood lodging and vertical knees, which are pretty to look at, because of the diffuse quantity of short bolts introduced for fastening, considered by those practically acquainted with ships, but very indifferent security, those knees not only increasing the weight, the former of no longitudinal strength, occupying a large space of the ship's carrying capacity, also preventing that free passage of air so essentially necessary in all vessels, of whatever may be their material, thus causing, it may fairly be presumed, the ships to prematurely decay.

In the better class of colonial vessels, especially those constructed to class at Lloyds, wood vertical knees to beam ends have, as a general thing, become obsolete, and in many instances both vertical and lodging knees of wood are dispensed with, and in lieu thereof, shelves and water-ways are worked equal in transverse sectional area to the respective beams at their ends. Iron hanging knees and knee riders are substituted, the latter embracing all the points of the frame, bolted through and through, the bolts being spaced less than every twenty-one inches apart, the whole length of rider, thereby giving those vessels an advantage over yours in regard to connection, general strength throughout, better ventilation, and larger carrying capacity.

It would also be needless for me to state other than that our better class of vessels are more liberally supplied with ground tackling and general equipments, those important essentials required to be, by Lloyds' register, rigidly tested at public machines recognized by them. While stating those advantages and requirements I admit that there are many fine points about your American-built ships to be admired: their very fine model, the application of modern appliances to reduce labor and facilitate the working of ships, their general smooth finish, the generally acknowledged accommodation for the mariner who traverses the storm-tossed deep, and the general stores supplied, excepting anchors and chain cables, which although of the most vital importance for the safety of both life and property, those, as a general thing, are found light and untested. * * * * *

UNITED STATES CONSULATE,
Prince Edward Island, November 22, 1869.

SIR: In reply to your letter of October 30, 1869, this day received, I have the honor to state:

1. The cost in Prince Edward Island of wooden ships, *fitted for sea*, was £9 4*s*. 6*d*., or $29 52 per ton, medium tonnages, in 1860.
2. Steamers are not built on the island.
3. The cost of wooden ships, fitted for sea, is, at this time, £10, or $32, per ton.
4. The rate of wages for first-class mechanics, on ship work, was, in 1860, 7*s*. 6*d*, or $1 20 per diem.
5. Wages of same class, at present time, 6*s*. 6*d*. to 7*s*., or $1 04 to $1 12, per diem.
6. Rate of insurance on steamships and sailing-vessels from eight to ten per cent.
7. There is no government regulation for ascertaining the amount of materials used in the construction of vessels which are exempt from duty.
8. The character of officers and crews of Prince Edward Island vessels is very inferior to that of the same classes on vessels of the United States.
9. I would mention, in explanation of the cost of construction, as above given, that the *pound currency* of this island is equal to *three dollars and twenty cents* of federal money.

I have the honor to be, very respectfully, your obedient servant,

E. PARKER SCAMMON,
United States Consul.

Hon. JOHN LYNCH, M. C.,
Chairman Committee on Navigation Interests.

CONSULATE GENERAL OF THE UNITED STATES OF AMERICA,
Frankfurt am Main, December 31, 1869.

To the Hon. Committee on American Navigation Interests:

During the present month I had the honor to receive from the Department of State, a dispatch inclosing certain inquiries, by your committee, concerning the navigation interests of Prussia. Sensible of the importance of the subject under your consideration, not only as it affects all persons directly engaged in ship-building and commerce, but also as it bears upon the finances and vital interests of the government, I have endeavored to furnish full and satisfactory information upon the matters involved in your inquiries, however it may affect your object.

Prior to the year 1866, Prussia was a member of the old Germanic Diet, and up to that time, neither Prussia alone, nor the Diet exhibited any inclination or ability either to extend its commerce, or to establish a navy and increase its maratime strength. The secession of Prussia and the events of the year 1866 attending and consequent thereon, scattered that confederation. A North German Union was formed of the several northern powers of Germany; the other powers remaining isolated. Prussia is the head, and principal power of the twenty-two distinct independent governments constituting the North German Union, as it alone contains 24,000,000 of the 30,000,000 inhabitants of the whole Union, and covers five-sixths of the whole territory of the Union.

The principal ports of the North German Union are the free cities of Bremen and Hamburg. The merchant marine is mostly confined to those free cities, and there is but little merchant marine in any port of Prussia. Each power of the Union may regulate its own merchant marine independently of all the other powers of the Union, but it can have no separate navy. The navy belongs to the Union as a whole. I shall, therefore, in answering your inquiries, inform you upon the subject-matters of inquiry not only as they affect Prussia, but also as they affect the North German Union as a confederation.

The inland location of the states of the North German Union would seem not to admit of a large merchant marine or require a powerful maratime force, still individuals are greatly increasing the former, and the government immensely enlarging the latter, and all tending to a great maritime power.

These tables* show in detail the present amount of the merchant marine according to the last public accounts and the latest information that can be had. Only ordinary merchant vessels are built in Prussia. The most valuable and largest of ocean steamers are still built upon the river Clyde.

To the second inquiry: "What encouragement the Prussian government offers to ship-builders and ship-owners by way of bounties, drawbacks, and exemption from taxation. If material entering into the construction of ships is exempt from duty, or a drawback is allowed upon it, what regulations are adopted by the government to ascertain the amount used," I reply that no bounties, drawbacks, or exemption from duties or taxation are provided either by Prussia or the North German Union.

There is a general complaint among those interested in the merchant marine that their interests are neglected by the government in favor of the navy. As an evidence of the feeling upon this subject, I call your attention to the discussion, at the last meeting of the German Nautical Association, of the new law of the federal council of the North German Union, requiring a more technical school education, and more thorough qualifications of captains and inferior ship officers, and subjecting them to more rigid technical examinations, without regard to practical knowledge. This association is composed of the leading ship-owners, ship-builders, underwriters, and captains of Hamburg and Bremen. The association expressed their dissatisfaction with the apparent disregard by the government of the merchant service, and severely denounced the tendency of Prussia to shape all naval matters and regulations to the interest of the navy on the ground of the pretended great necessity of making the "Union" a powerful maritime power, to the neglect and injury of the merchant marine service of the ports of the country. They ask the question—"What importance as a maritime power had Prussia previous to the annexation of Schleswig-Holstein and Hanover?" The answer was, "That except on the Baltic, where Denmark, Sweden, and Russia also dominated, Prussia had no maritime power at all; while the Hanseatic flag, that of Hamburg, Bremen, and Lubec, had carried the German name to every quarter of the globe." It thus appears that the ship-builders and ship-owners receive not only no encouragement, but that the government is more intent upon aggrandizing its own power upon the sea, as well as upon the land, than advancing the commerce and shipping of its ports.

To the third inquiry: "Whether shipstores are allowed to be taken in bond for consumption on the voyage?" I answer that no dutiable shipstores are allowed to be taken on board, under any privilege of exemption from duty, by any law of Prussia or of the "Union."

To the fourth inquiry: "What subsidies are paid to lines of Prussian steamers?" I answer that no subsidy is paid to any line of steamers by the North German Union or by Prussia, and it is not supposed that the free cities of Hamburg or Bremen pay any subsidy or allow any privilege or exemption from duty to any line of steamers leaving said ports.

The Bremen and Hamburg steamship companies have contracts with the North German Union for carrying the mails, but they are paid only for the exact services performed, and at very low rates of compensation.

To the last inquiry: "What measures are adopted to improve the character of and secure efficiency in the merchant marine service, and what relation does this service hold to the navy of Prussia?" I reply that the North German Union have not had time to adopt measures, which experience, the essential portions of which are herewith given, might show to be useful to itself or instructive to others.

Some of the ports have established schools for the study of navigation, which have attained distinction. There are laws regulating the sea-worthiness of vessels, also laws respecting ship-building.

The relation of the merchant marine service to the navy is best answered by a translation of those articles of the constitution of the North German Union referring to navigation, viz:

"SECTION 53. The federal navy is a united one, under the supreme command of Prussia. The organization and composition of the same is incumbent upon his Majesty, the King of Prussia, who appoints all the officers of the navy, and to whom the latter, together with the marine troops, must take the oath of allegiance.

"The ports of Kiel and Jahde are federal war ports.

"The cost and expense incurred in the foundation and maintenance of the navy and the institutions connected therewith will be borne by the federal treasury.

* The report of Mr. Webster was accompanied by an elaborate set of tables, translated from a work of Dr. Engels, chief of the Prussian statistical bureau.

"The entire marine population of the Union, the body of engineers, and marine mechanics included, is dispensed from the service in the army, but obliged to serve in the federal navy.

"The distribution takes place in proportion to the existing marine population, so that the number to be furnished by each government will be deducted from the quota to be furnished for the army.

"SEC. 54. The merchant men of all the federal States form a joint merchant marine.

"The Union will fix the mode of ascertaining the tonnage of sea vessels, regulate the issue of bills of tonnage, and ships' certificates, and the conditions of licenses of sea vessels.

"The merchant men of all the federal states are uniformly admitted and received at the seaports, and on all natural and artificial water roads of the several federal states. The imports on vessels or cargoes for the benefit of any institution shall not exceed the cost of same."

I have thus endeavored to give the desired information upon the subject-matter of your inquiries. I fear that you will derive but little light from the information that will enlighten your investigations. The government aims to enhance itself, and magnify its strength and power as a nation, more than to aid the individual or develop the industry and wealth of the country. Neither is government aid much needed where every kind of material is so cheap, and labor so poorly paid. If the merchant marine is allowed to develop itself, wherever commerce demands or justifies its establishment in the ports of Germany, and is not burdened by government, it will regulate itself, and will compensate all persons employed in its interests. The kingdoms of Bavaria and Wurtemberg and the grand duchies of Baden and Hesse-Darmstadt being still independent, and forming no part of the Union, are not referred to in this communication.

I trust that a satisfactory result will follow as the reward for your arduous labors.

I have the honor to be your obedient servant,

WM. PREUTIN WEBSTER,
Consul General.

Hon. JOHN LYNCH,
Chairman Committee on American Navigation Interests.

Sea vessels and river steamers in the old Prussian provinces. State at the end of the year 1867.

NUMBER AND QUALITY OF MERCHANTMEN IN THE BEGINNING OF THE YEAR 1868.

	Number of vessels.	Lasts.
SAILING VESSELS.		
Sea vessels of a tonnage of more than 40 lasts *	960	183,742
Coasting vessels of less than 40 lasts	422	9,746
STEAMERS.		
Sea steamer	28	3,959
Steam tow-boats, river-steamer	84	1,677
Total	1,464	199,124

Of the above steamers there were:

	Tonnage of lasts.	Horse-power.
26 sea screw-steamers	3,788	1.667
2 paddle steamers	171	240
21 tow-boats and river screw-steamers	500	372
63 tow-boats and river paddle-steamers	1,177	2,399
112 steamers	5,636	4,678

Changes in the state of 1363 *to* 1867.

	Of the vessels built at home there were built in—				
	1863.	1864.	1865.	1866.	1867,
For domestic ship owners	93	76	85	73	43
Sea vessels over 40 lasts	63	48	64	56	37
Coasting vessels	14	14	12	16	4
Steamers	16	12	9	1	2
For the royal government	......	1	......	......	1
For foreign account	7	8	6	8	8
Total	100	85	91	81	52

In the beginning of the year 1868 there were building on Prussian and Pomeranian wharves 31 sea vessels, 5 coasting vessels, and 2 steamers; that is to say, just as many as in the preceding year.

	During the years—				
	1863.	1864.	1865.	1866.	1867.
There were bought in other states	17	10	3	3	5
Of which there were stranded and brought off	2	3	2	1	2
Sold to other states	13	15	17	17	14
Wrecked	1	1	6	2	2

Sea and river vessels of the province of Hanover. State at the end of the year 1865.

NUMBER AND QUALITY OF MERCHANTMEN AT THE END OF THE YEAR 1865.

	Number.	Tonnage in lasts.*	Manning.
Sea vessels	862	64, 371	5, 324
River and coasting vessels	2,462	30, 175	5, 556

* A last is like two tons, or 4,000 pounds.

Changes in the state, 1862 *to* 1866.

Province of Hanover.	Sea vessels.	Tonnage in lasts of 4,000 pounds.
1862	843	54, 169
1863	842	60, 251
1864	814	60, 101
1865	862	64, 371
1866	859	62, 123

The five principal ports of the province were at the end of the year 1866 in possession of 377 sea vessels, of a tonnage of 37,954 lasts, viz:

	Vessels.	Tonnage of lasts.
Harburg	17	2, 759
Geestemünde	44	10, 567
Emden	84	5, 397
Leer	50	3, 202
Papenburg	182	16, 029

River and watching revenue vessels.

Year.	Vessels.	Lasts.*
1862	2,748	31,173
1863	2,776	31,229
1864	2,792	30,863
1865	2,762	30,175
1866	2,809	31,034

* A Prussian last is equal to two tons.

Of the same were steamers, viz:

	Vessels.	Tonnage of lasts.
1862	10	410
1863	11	471
1864	11	443
1865	13	560
1866	16	753

As regards ship-building, there were finished in the course of—

	Sea vessels.		River and watch vessels.	
	No.	Tonnage of lasts.	No.	Tonnage of lasts.
1862	93	9,246	130	2,483
1863	112	12,221	125	1,928
1864	70	9,128	100	1,228
1865	74	8,858	106	1,207
1866	66	7,910	95	1,159

Schleswig-Holstein merchant marine. Changes in the state of 1860 *to* 1866.

In the year	Number of vessels.	Tonnage of lasts.*	In the year	Number of vessels.	Tonnage of lasts.*
1860	2,549	63,408	1864	2,552	66,596
1861	2,590	63,814	1865	2,531	68,173
1862	2,633	65,766	1866	2,527	69,865
1863	2,639	67,582			

* A Prussian last is equal to two tons.

State of the merchant marine of the North German Union on the 1st *of February,* 1869.

States to which the vessels belong.	Vessels.	Tonnage in tons.	Amongst them sea-steamers.	Tonnage in tons.
1. Prussia:				
Province of Prussia and Pomerania	1,382	403,000	29	8,000
Province of Hanover	1,310	133,500	2	800
Province of Sleswig-Holstein	919	114,500	5	5,600
Total	3,611	651,000	36	14,400
2. Hamburg	467	245,300	35	36,900
3. Bremen	307	244,700	20	39,200
4. Mecklenburg	449	172,600	1	200
5. Oldenburg	231	57,100	.....	.....
6. Lübeck	43	10,500	21	5,500
In all	5,108	1,381,200	113	96,200

B.—*Tabular statement of new built men-of-war up to the 31st of December*, 1868.

No.	Class.	Name.	Number of guns.	Horse-power.	Tonnage.	Commencem'nt of building.	Date of launching.	Expended for—	Up to 1867, inclusive.	In 1868.
1	Iron-clad screw-frigate.	King William	23	1, 150	5, 938	1866	Apr. 25, 1868	1. Hulk (body) of the vessel, including boats and round-wood.		
								2. The fitting-out (equipment)		
								3. Machines and machine-inventory		
								4. Armature		
									$1, 573, 679 74	
2	Iron-clad screw-frigate.	Crown Prince	16	800	3, 404	Spring of 1866.	May 16, 1867	1. Hulk (body) of the vessel, including boats and round-woods.		$5, 586 69
								2. The fitting-out (equipment)		2, 268 84
								3. Machines and machine-inventory		
								4. Armature		182, 732 87
									1, 210, 142 47	190, 589 23
									1, 400, 738 60	
3	Iron-clad screw-frigate.	Frederic Charles	16	950	4, 044	Spring of 1866.	Jan. 16, 1867	1 Hulk (body) of the vessel, including boats and round-woods.		42, 200 56
								2. The fitting-out (equipment)		2, 207 52
								3. Machines and machine-inventory		
								4. Armature		182, 732 87
									1, 224, 221 68	227, 041 66
									1, 458, 563 36	
4	Decked screw-corvette.	Elizabeth	26	400	2, 640	May 1, 1866	Oct. 18, 1868	1. Hulk (body) of the vessel, including boats and round-woods.	93, 707 91	142, 098 15
								2. The fitting-out (equipment)	413 91	21, 103 06
								3. Machines and machine-inventory	32, 930 30	112, 393 72
								4. Armature		6, 018 12
									128, 074 75	281, 625 24
									408, 679 99	

UNITED STATES VICE-CONSULATE,
Copenhagen, December 7, 1869.

SIR: Your letter, dated the 5th of last month, (addressed to George P. Hansen, formerly a United States consul, but now returned to the United States,) expressing a desire to obtain information respecting the ship-building and navigation interests of this country, has been transmitted to me by the Department of State, and, in reply thereto, I shall endeavor to give you an explanation as satisfactory as I have been able to obtain it, giving my reply in the same order as your different questions are made.

The annexed register of ships belonging to this country has been issued in the beginning of this year, and shows very near the present state of the Danish merchant marine, (of course with the exception of some alterations through ships lost, ships built or bought from foreigners, or ships having shifted owners, since the register issued.)* The building of sailing-ships is in a tolerable efficiency, especially in *the province ports*, because the work is cheaper *there* than in *this city*, but steamship building is only carried on at this port, at a moderate scale, however, there being only one establishment for such building, and the same is working at high prices. The merchant marine steam service, on account thereof, is frequently supplied by the purchase or chartering of foreign steamers.

The government offers no encouragement to ship-builders and ship-owners by way of bounties, drawbacks or exemption from taxation. Ship-owners' business, however, is *free;* that is to say, not subject to any concession such as many other lines of merchants' business, but it is, of course, the same as all other situations, subject to income tax when such is imposed. Foreign material entering into the construction of ships built for account of *Danish* citizens is subject to duty according to the tariff annexed, (oak timber only is free of duty.) But vessels built in Denmark for *foreigners'* account, or *foreign* vessels repairing average suffered or other damages, are in that respect *better* situated, as they may obtain a permission to take such articles as metal sheathing and bolts, chains, anchors, sails, and cordage, &c., out of bond. (The prerogative thus allowed foreigners arises from a desire to attract work and secure the labor to Danish citizens.) The material taken out of bond is not treated "ad valorem," but in conformity with the said tariff annexed. Ships' stores for consumption on the voyage are allowed to be exported out of bond.

There are no subsidies paid by the government to lines of Danish or foreign steamers, nor of sailing-ships, except a trifling remuneration of postage for letters carried, brought as well as sent; but steamers enjoy a separate favor, having only to pay port charges according to the quantities of goods loaded or discharged, and reduced into tons, or, better, into Danish lasts; consequently, they do not pay in proportion to their registered tonnage.

There are no measures adopted to improve the character of, and secure efficiency in the merchant marine service, and that service bears no relation to the navy of Den, mark. If the royal marine department occasionally is in want of ship-room for any kind of transport, the department charters ships in the same way as private charterers.

Being at present aware of no further suggestions or facts deserving to be mentioned, I only add translations of the laws concerning the registration and measurement of ships, and remain, sir, very respectfully, your most obedient servant,

L. MEETSCHER,
United States Vice-Consul.

Hon. JOHN LYNCH,
Chairman Committee on Navigation Interests.

WASHINGTON, D. C., *February* 5, 1870.

SIR: I have the honor to acknowledge the receipt of your letter of the 4th instant asking me to send to the special committee of investigation on the causes of the decay of American commerce any communication as to what, in my judgment, has created those causes, at least, in that part of the country with which I am acquainted, and suggesting, at the same time, what steps I would consider best adapted to remove them, and to establish in their stead an invigorating impulse by which American commerce would acquire that development and influence which the extent and importance of the agriculture and industry of this republic give it a right to expect.

Among various causes, too extensive to enumerate in the space of an ordinary communication, I beg to state that, in my opinion, the following are the most important, viz:

I. Neither the American government nor any portion of the American people, constituted as a body, have ever done nor directly attempted anything to secure the object they desire to attain.

*Accompanying this communication were Danish official documents, which have been omitted.

II. The commerce of those localities in the West Indies with which I am acquainted has always been allowed to follow its primitive course without any efforts from the capitalists or the government of this country to take advantage of their proximity, in order to alter that course and try to give it a direction to these shores.

III. Instead of that, capitalists of Liverpool, Glasgow, Antwerp, Bremen, Hamburg, Paris, Havre, Marseilles, both as individuals and as corporations, make yearly advances for the productions to be shipped from most of those islands and from Central and South America, and secure thereby, at very advantageous profits, the consignment of such produce.

IV. France and England, especially the latter, have several lines of steamers touching at the various ports, largely subsidized, and offering great accommodations for freight and passengers.

V. The governments of England and France watch with a jealous eye over their vessels in those distant ports, and whether justly or not, they never allow the slightest interference wtth them, be it in time of peace or not, thus securing them, at all times and under every circumstance, the facility of taking and landing freight. That policy has been carried so far that most of the merchants in those unsettled countries rather prefer, for security's sake, to have their freight under English or French flags.

These are the principal causes, according to my judgment, which have unfavorably influenced the development and progress of American commerce both in South America and in the West Indies.

A contrary course would insure a contrary result:

I. The American government should lead, by initiatory measures, the American capitalists to invest their capital in the trade of those countries.

II. The American capitalists should, like the European, make advances to these different localities, in order to secure their consignment in return.

III. The American government, alike with England and France, should encourage the establishment of frequent communications by steam with all these countries.

IV. The American agents in all the different ports, while the country is in a state of war, should be instructed not to allow any intereference with American vessels without due, formal, and immediate redress from the party, whomsoever it be, that may have caused such interference.

A few years of this policy would, I believe, give an unprecedented forward impetus to the development and growth of American commerce in this hemisphere.

Though I feel confident that none of the above considerations could have escaped the sagacity and attention of the committee, yet I send them with pleasure as a proof of my sincere desire to be always ready to give my service, however limited it be, for the good and prosperity of the American people.

I have the honor to be, sir, your obedient and humble servant,

A. TATE.*

Hon. JOHN LYNCH.

UNITED STATES CONSULATE AT BREMEN,
January 18, 1870.

SIR: In compliance with your favor of November 5, 1869, transmitted to me through the Department of State, Washington, D. C., making inquiries concerning ship-building and navigation interests of Germany, I have the honor to submit the following facts collected from statistics and other sources of information upon this subject, viz:

The German government offers no inducement to German ship-builders, but the material entering into the construction of ships is exempted from duty, or a drawback is allowed on it upon the following conditions: The builder can import, free of duty, all raw materials which are used for the construction of vessels, or in case the material is partly or wholly manufactured here, the government remits the duty which was originally paid on the imported raw metal.

The ship-builder who claims these advantages for building or repairing vessels, before commencing, has to give notice to the custom officer in whose district the vessel is to be repaired or built, by presenting a declaration, giving an exact description of the vessel, as well as the metal articles which will be used for building and outfitting, either in their manufactured condition imported, or the amount of foreign metal used for manufacturing same.

Those articles marked, which the ship-builder imports from foreign countries in a manufactured or half-manufactured condition, must be presented to the collector of his district in the mentioned declaration, stating the various shapes and condition in which said articles or materials are to be imported, which articles are entered according to the weight and number of pieces in the *Conto-register*, and marked with a stamp in order to pass the custom-house duty free. To control this, the custom officer inspects the vessel

* Recently minister plenipotentiary from the Republic of Hayti to the government of the United States.

while she is built, or after her completion, and if these inspections prove that the declaration is made correct, said articles or material are cancelled out of the *Conto-register*.

Should the articles manufactured here, but from material imported from other countries, be used, the builder has to state the amount, quality, and kind of material for every article in his declaration; on this it passes the custom-house, every piece being stamped, weighed, and entered in the *Conto-register* by the custom officers. The number of pieces and the weight of the articles manufactured from these materials is also taken on their completion by the custom officer and compared with the *Conto-register* and if found correct said materials are exempted from duty.

The bars imported for the use of building coppered vessels, are entered in the same manner, but when the bolts are cut out in the dock it must be done in the presence of an officer of customs, who has to count and weigh such bolts, and see that they are used for the vessel, and on his certificate the bars are exempted from duty.

All declarations must be sworn to by the ship-builder, and should it be proved that fraud was intended, the builder is deprived of these advantages forever, besides paying the penalty.

Ship stores are allowed to be taken in bond for consumption without being subject to any duty.

No subsidies whatever are paid to lines of German steamers.

Masters are required to take on board his vessel one apprentice for every one hundred "lasts" (a last equal to 4000 pounds) measurement of his vessel. These apprentices, after having served a term of years, are advanced to the grade of regular sailors, in which capacity they are required to serve three years, at which time they can make application for admittance to the navigation school, where they have to pass severe examinations before they can be commissioned as second and first officers or commanders. As every able-bodied man is required to enter in the army on arriving at the age of twenty years, so is every seaman at the same age required to enter the navy.

I remain, sir, very respectfully, your obedient servant,

R. M. HAUSON,
United States Consul.

Hon. JOHN LYNCH,
Chairman Committee on American Navigation Interests, Washington, D. C.

APPENDIX.

STATISTICAL TABLES.

No. I.—*List of steamships and vessels of the British navy.*

BUILT IN GOVERNMENT DOCK YARDS.

Description.	Names.	No. of guns.	Tons.	Horse-power.	Of what built.
Screw	Aboukir	86	3, 091	400	Wood,
Screw	Achilles	26	6, 121	1, 250	Iron armor-plated.
Paddle	Advice	......	197	100	Wood.
Screw	African	......	36	20	Iron.
Double screw	Agamemnon	71	3, 102	600	Wood.
Paddle	Alberta	......	391	160	Wood.
Screw	Albion	72	3, 117	400	Wood.
Screw	Alert	17	751	100	Wood.
Screw	Algiers	73	3, 340	600	Wood.
Screw	Anson	54	3, 336	800	Wood.
Screw	Arethusa	35	3, 141	500	Wood.
Paddle	Argus	6	981	300	Wood.
Screw	Ariadne	26	3, 214	800	Wood.
Screw	Atlas	54	3, 318	800	Wood.
Screw	Aurora	35	2, 558	400	Wood.
Screw	Brcchante	28	2, 667	600	Wood.
Paddle	Barracouta	6	1, 053	300	Wood.
Screw	Barrosa	17	1, 700	400	Wood.
Paddle	Basilisk	6	1, 031	400	Wood.
Double screw	Beacon	4	465	120	Composite gun vessel.
Screw and paddle	Bee	......	42	10	Wood.
Screw	Bellerophon	14	4, 270	1, 000	Iron armor-plated.
Double screw	Bittern	3	663	160	Gun vessel.
Screw	Blanche	6	1. 268	350	Wood.
Sail	Boscawen	20	2, 213	....	Wood.
Double screw	Boxer	4	465	120	Composite gun vessel.
Sail	Brilliant	16	954	....	Wood.
Screw	Brisk	16	1, 087	250	Wood.
Screw	Bristol	31	3, 027	600	Wood.
Sail	Britannia	115	3, 995	....	Wood.
Screw	Briton	10	1, 322	350	Wood.
Screw gun vessel	Bullfinch	3	663	160	Wood.
Screw	Bulwark	81	3, 716	800	Wood.
Paddle	Buzzard	2	980	300	Wood.
Screw	Cæsar	76	2, 767	400	Wood.
Screw	Cadmus	16	1, 466	400	Wood.
Screw	Caledonia	30	4, 125	1, 000	Armor-plated.
Sail	Cambridge	20	3, 101	....	Wood.
Screw	Cameleon	7	952	200	Wood.
Paddle	Carron	......	267	150	Wood.
Sail	Castor	22	1, 293	....	Wood.
Screw	Centurion	68	2, 590	400	Wood.
Screw	Challenger	18	1, 462	400	Wood.
Screw	Chanticleer	7	950	200	Wood.
Screw	Charybdis	18	1, 506	400	Wood.
Screw	Clio	18	1, 472	400	Wood.
Screw	Columbine	3	672	150	Wood.
Paddle	Confiance	......	295	100	Wood.
Screw	Conqueror	74	2, 845	500	Wood.
Screw	Constance	35	3, 213	500	Wood.
Screw	Cordelia	11	579	150	Wood.
Screw gun vessel	Cormorant	4	695	200	Wood.
Double Screw	Cracker	4	467	120	Composite gun vessel.
Screw	Cruiser	5	752	60	Wood.
Double screw gun vessel	Curlew	3	665	160	Wood.
Sail	Daedalus	16	1, 082	....	Wood.
Screw	Danae	6	1, 287	350	Wood.
Screw	Daphne	4	1, 081	300	Wood.
Paddle	Dasher	2	260	100	Wood.
Screw	Dauntless	31	1, 575	580	Wood.
Paddle	Dee	1	704	220	Wood.
Screw	Defiance	45	3, 475	800	Wood.

No. I.—*List of steamships and vessels of the British navy*—Continued.

BUILT IN GOVERNMENT DOCK YARDS.

Description.	Name.	No. of guns.	Tons.	Horse-power.	Of what built.
Screw	Devastation	......	4, 406	800	Turret ship, armor-plated.
Screw	Diadem	22	2, 483	800	Wood.
Screw	Dido	6	1, 268	350	Wood.
Screw	Donegal	81	3, 245	800	Wood.
Screw	Doris	24	2, 483	800	Wood.
Screw	Druid	10	1, 322	350	Wood.
Screw	Dryad	4	1, 086	300	Wood.
Screw	Duke of Wellington	49	3, 771	700	Wood.
Screw	Duncan	69	3, 727	800	Wood.
Sail	Durham	20	1, 627	....	Wood.
Double screw	Dwarf	4	465	120	Composite gun vessel.
Paddle	Echo	......	295	140	Wood.
Screw	Edgar	54	3, 094	600	Wood.
Paddle	Elfin	......	98	40	Wood.
Double screw	Elk	4	465	120	Composite gun vessel.
Screw	Emerald	28	2, 913	600	Wood.
Paddle	Enchantress	1	835	250	Wood.
Screw	Endymion	......	2, 486	500	Wood.
Screw	Enterprise	21	993	160	Armor-plated.
Sail	Excellent	......	2, 311	....	Wood.
Screw	Exmouth	76	3, 109	400	Wood.
Screw	Falcon	17	751	100	Wood.
Screw	Favorite	10	2, 094	400	Armor-plated.
Screw	Fawn	15	751	100	Wood.
Sail	Fisgard	42	1, 069	....	Wood.
Double screw	Flirt	4	464	120	Composite gun vessel.
Sail	Flora	10	1, 634	....	Wood.
Double screw	Fly	4	464	120	Composite gun vessel.
Screw	Forte	24	2, 364	400	Wood.
Screw	Fox	2	1, 131	200	Wood.
Screw	Frederick William	74	3, 241	500	Wood.
Screw	Galatea	26	3, 227	800	Wood.
Screw	Gannet	3	579	150	Wood.
Screw	Gibraltar	81	3, 729	800	Wood.
Paddle	Gladiator	6	1, 210	430	Wood.
Screw	Glasgow	28	3, 037	600	Wood.
Double screw	Glutton	2	2, 709	....	Turret ship, armor-plated.
Screw	Goliath	60	2, 596	400	Wood.
Screw	Greyhound	5	880	200	Wood.
Screw	Hannibal	73	3, 136	450	Wood.
Screw	Hastings	50	1, 760	200	Wood.
Paddle	Helicon	2	837	250	Wood.
Screw	Hercules	14	5, 234	1, 200	Iron, armor-plated.
Screw	Hero	71	3, 148	600	Wood.
Sail	Hibernia	104	2, 530	....	Wood.
Screw	Hood	54	3, 308	600	Wood.
Screw	Howe	84	4, 245	1, 000	Wood.
Paddle	Hydra	1	818	220	Wood.
Screw	Icarus	3	580	150	Wood.
Screw	Immortalité	28	3, 059	600	Wood.
Sail	Impregnable	78	2, 406	....	Wood.
Screw	Inconstant	16	4, 066	1, 000	Iron, cased with wood.
Sail	Indus	......	2, 098	....	Wood.
Double screw	Iron Duke	14	3, 774	800	Iron, armor-plated.
Screw	Irresistible	4	2, 642	400	Wood.
Screw	James Watt	71	3, 083	600	Wood.
Screw gun vessel	Jasewr	5	427	80	Wood.
Screw	Jason	17	1, 711	400	Wood.
Screw	Juno	6	1, 462	400	Wood.
Screw gun vessel	Landrail	5	427	80	Wood.
Double screw gun vessel	Lapwing	3	663	160	Wood.
Sail	Liberty	12	428	....	Wood.
Screw	Liffey	30	2, 654	600	Wood.
Paddle	Lightning	2	296	100	Wood.
Screw	Lion	60	2, 611	400	Wood.
Screw	Liverpool	30	2, 656	600	Wood.
Paddle	Locust	1	284	100	Wood.
Screw	London	72	2, 687	500	Wood.
Screw	Lord Clyde	24	4, 067	1, 000	Armor-plated.
Screw	Lord Warden	18	4, 080	1, 000	Armor-plated.
Screw	Lyra	7	488	60	Wood.
Double screw gun vessel	Magpie	3	665	160	Wood.
Screw	Marlborough	98	4, 000	800	Wood.
Sail	Martin	10	481	....	Wood.
Paddle	Medusa	2	889	312	Wood.
Screw	Melpomene	28	2, 861	600	Wood.
Screw	Mersey	36	3, 733	1, 000	Wood.
Screw	Miranda	15	1, 039	250	Wood.
Screw turret ship	Monarch	7	5, 102	1, 100	Iron, armor-plated.
Screw	Mutine	17	882	200	Wood.

No. 1.—*List of steamships and vessels of the British navy*—Continued.

BUILT IN GOVERNMENT DOCK YARDS.

Description.	Name.	No. of guns.	Tons.	Horse-power.	Of what built.
Screw gun vessel	Myrmidon	4	695	220	Wood.
Sail	Nankin	50	2,049	....	Wood.
Screw	Narcissus	35	2,665	400	Wood.
Screw	Nassau	5	695	150	Wood.
Screw	Neptune	78	2,830	500	Wood.
Screw	Nereus	6	1,094	....	Wood.
Screw	Newcastle	28	3,035	600	Wood.
Screw	Newport	5	425	80	Wood.
Screw	Niger	13	1,072	350	Wood.
Screw	Nile	78	2,622	500	Wood.
Screw gun vessel	Nimble	5	428	80	Wood.
Screw	Niobe	4	1,083	300	Wood.
Screw	Nymphe	4	1,084	300	Wood.
Screw	Ocean	24	4,047	1,000	Armor-plated.
Screw	Octavia	35	3,161	500	Wood.
Screw	Orlando	46	3,740	1,000	Wood.
Paddle	Osborne	......	1,536	450	Wood.
Screw	Pallas	6	2,372	600	Armor-plated.
Screw gun vessel	Pandora	5	426	80	Wood.
Screw	Pearl	17	1,469	400	Wood.
Double screw	Penelope	11	3,096	600	Iron, armor-plated.
Screw	Perseus	15	955	200	Wood.
Screw	Peterel	3	669	150	Wood.
Screw	Phæton	28	2,396	400	Wood.
Screw	Phœbe	30	2,896	500	Wood.
Double screw gun vessel	Plover	3	663	160	Wood.
Paddle	Porcupine	3	382	132	Wood.
Sail	President	31	1,537	....	Wood.
Screw	Prince Consort	24	4,045	1,000	Armor-plated.
Screw	Prince Regent	78	2,762	500	Wood.
Sail	Prince of Wales	115	2,646	....	Wood.
Sail	Princess Charlotte	12	2,443	....	Wood.
Screw	Princess Royal	73	3.129	400	Wood.
Paddle	Pysche	2	835	250	Wood.
Screw	Pylades	17	1,278	350	Wood.
Screw	Queen	74	3,249	500	Wood.
Screw	Racer	11	579	150	Wood.
Screw	Raccoon	22	1,467	400	Wood.
Screw	Ranger	5	427	80	Wood.
Screw	Rapid	11	672	150	Wood
Screw	Rattlesnake	17	1,705	400	Wood.
Screw	Reindeer	7	953	200	Wood.
Screw	Renown	54	3,319	800	Wood.
Screw	Repulse	12	3,749	800	Armor-plated.
Screw	Research	4	1,253	200	Armor-plated.
Screw	Revenge	73	3,322	800	Wood.
Screw	Rifleman	5	486	100	Wood.
Screw	Rinaldo	7	951	200	Wood.
Double screw gun vessel	Ringdove	3	666	160	Wood.
Screw	Robust	81	3,716	800	Wood.
Screw	Rodney	72	2,770	500	Wood.
Screw	Rosario	3	673	150	Wood.
Sail	Royal Adelaide	26	2,446	....	Wood.
Screw	Royal Albert	107	3,726	500	Wood.
Screw	Royal Alfred	18	4,068	800	Armor-plated.
Screw	Royal George	72	2,616	400	Wood.
Screw	Royalist	3	669	150	Wood.
Screw	Royal Oak	24	4,056	800	Wood.
Screw turret ship	Royal Sovereign	5	3,765	800	Wood.
Screw	Royal William	72	2,849	500	Wood.
Screw ram	Rupert	......	3,159	700	Iron-clad.
Screw	St. George	72	2,864	500	Wood.
Screw	St. Jean d'Arc	81	3,200	600	Wood.
Sail	St. Vincent	26	2,612	....	Wood.
Paddle	Salamander	2	818	220	Wood.
Paddle	Salamis	2	835	250	Wood.
Screw	Satelite	17	1,462	400	Wood.
Screw	Scout	21	1,462	400	Wood.
Screw	Scylla	16	1,467	400	Wood.
Double screw gun vessei	Sea-gull	3	663	160	Wood.
Screw mortar ship	Sea-horse	12	1,258	200	Wood.
Sail	Sea-lark	8	319	....	Wood.
Screw	Severn	28	2,767	500	Wood.
Screw	Shannon	35	2,667	600	Wood.
Screw	Shearwater	3	669	150	Wood.
Screw	Sirius	6	1,268	350	Wood.
Screw	Spartan	6	1,269	350	Wood.
Screw gun vessel	Speedwell	5	428	80	Wood.
Paddle	Sphinx	6	1,061	500	Wood.

No. I.—*List of steamships and vessels of the British navy*—Continued.

BUILT IN GOVERNMENT DOCK YARDS.

Description.	Name.	No. of guns.	Tons.	Horse-power.	Of what built.
Paddle	Spiteful	6	1,054	280	Wood.
Paddle	Spitfire	......	432	140	Wood.
Sail	Squirrel	8	428	....	Wood.
Screw	Sultan	12	5,226	1,200	Iron armor-plated.
Double screw gun vessel	Swallow	3	664	160	Wood.
Screw	Sylvia	5	695	150	Wood.
Screw	Tenedos	6	1,268	350	Wood.
Paddle	Terrible	19	1,850	800	Wood.
Screw	Thalia	6	1,459	400	Wood.
Double screw	Thistle	4	465	120	Composite gun vessel.
Screw turret ship	Thunderer	......	4,406	800	Armor-plated.
Screw	Topaze	31	2,659	600	Wood.
Screw	Trafalgar	60	2,900	500	Wood.
Screw	Undaunted	28	3,039	600	Wood.
Paddle	Valorous	12	1,257	400	Wood.
Screw	Vestal	4	1,081	300	Wood.
Screw	Victor Emanuel	79	3,087	600	Wood.
Screw	Victoria	102	4,127	1,000	Wood.
Paddle	Victoria and Albert	2	2,345	600	Wood.
Sail	Victory	12	2,164	....	Wood.
Sail	Vindictive	2	1,758	....	Wood.
Paddle	Virago	6	1,059	220	Wood.
Paddle	Vivid	......	350	160	Wood.
Double screw gun vessel	Vulture	3	663	160	Wood.
Screw	Wasp	13	974	100	Wood.
Paddle	Widgeon	......	164	90	Wood.
Sail	Winchester	12	652	....	Wood.
Screw	Wolverine	17	1,703	400	Wood.
Double screw gun vessel	Wood-lark	3	663	160	Wood.
Screw	Zealous	20	3,716	800	Armor-plated.
Screw	Zebra	7	951	200	Wood.

STEAMSHIP FOR THE DEFENSE OF THE COLONIES, BUILT IN GOVERNMENT DOCK YARD.

Description.	Name.	No. of guns.	Tons.	Horse-power.	Of what built.
Screw	Nelson	72	2,736	500	Wood.

List of screw steam gunboats from 212 *to* 273 *tons.*

BUILT IN GOVERNMENT DOCK YARDS.

Name.	Horse-power.	Name.	Horse-power.
Bruiser	60	Lark	60
Cherub	60	Minstrel	60
Cromer	60	Netley	60
Janus	40	Orwell	60

No. I.—*List of steamships and vessels of the British navy*—Continued.

BUILT IN PRIVATE YARDS BY CONTRACT.

Description.	Name.	No. of guns.	Tons.	Horse-power.	Of what built.
Screw	Active	8	2,322	600	Iron, cased with wood.
Paddle	Adder	......	241	100	Wood.
Screw	Adventure	2	1,794	400	Iron.
Screw	Agincourt	28	6,621	1,350	Iron, armor-plated.
Screw gun vessel	Algerine	3	299	80	Wood.
Paddle	Antelope	3	650	260	Iron.
Sail	Asia	......	2,289	....	Wood.
Paddle	Asp	......	112	50	Wood.
Screw gun vessel	Assurance	4	681	200	Wood.
Double screw	Audacious	14	3,774	800	Iron, armor-plated.
Double screw	Avon	4	467	120	Composite gun vessel.
Paddle	Bann	......	267	80	Iron.
Paddle	Black Eagle	......	540	260	Wood.
Screw	Black Prince	28	6,109	1,250	Iron, armor-plated.
Screw	Buffalo	2	440	80	Iron.
Paddle	Bustler	......	217	100	Wood.
Paddle	Camel	......	319	150	Wood.
Double screw turret ship	Captain	6	4,272	900	Armor-plated.
Paddle	Caradoc	2	676	350	Iron.
Screw	Chasseur	......	543	70	Iron.
Screw	Chester	......	164	30	Iron.
Screw	Cossack	16	1,296	250	Wood.
Screw gun vessel	Dart	5	428	80	Wood.
Screw	Defense	16	3,720	600	Iron, armor-plated.
Screw	Despatch	......	257	40	Wood.
Screw	Dromedary	2	654	100	Iron.
Sail	Eagle	16	1,723	....	Wood.
Screw	Eclipse	6	1,273	350	Wood.
Sail	Egmont	4	1,780	....	Wood.
Screw	Erebus	16	1,954	200	Iron, armor-plated.
Paddle	Fearless	......	165	76	Wood.
Paddle	Fire Queen	......	313	120	Iron.
Sail	Ganges	20	2,285	....	Wood.
Paddle	Grinder	......	332	150	Wood.
Double screw	Growler	4	464	120	Composite gun vessel.
Paddle	Harpy	1	344	200	Iron.
Double screw	Hart	4	464	120	Composite gun vessel.
Paddle	Hearty	......	221	100	Wood.
Screw	Hector	18	4,089	800	Iron, armor-plated.
Screw	Highflyer	21	1,161	250	Wood.
Screw	Himalaya	2	3,453	700	Iron.
Double screw	Hornet	4	464	120	Composite gun vessel.
Double screw	Hotspur	2	2,637	600	Iron, armor-plated ram.
Screw	Industry	2	638	80	Iron.
Double screw	Invincible	14	3,774	800	Iron, armor-plated.
Paddle	Jackal	2	340	150	Iron.
Screw gun vessel	Lee	5	431	80	Wood.
Screw gun vessel	Leven	3	300	80	Wood.
Paddle	Lucifer	1	387	180	Wood.
Double screw	Lynx	4	464	120	Composite gun vessel.
Screw	Mallacca	13	1,034	200	Wood.
Screw	Manilla	......	295	70	Iron.
Paddle	Manly	......	135	50	Iron.
Screw	Megaera	6	1,395	350	Iron.
Double screw	Midge	4	464	120	Composite gun vessel.
Screw	Minotaur	34	6,621	1,350	Iron, armor-plated.
Screw	Minx	......	303	10	Iron.
Paddle	Monkey	......	212	130	Wood.
Screw gun vessel	Mullet	5	430	80	Wood.
Screw	Northumberland	28	6,621	1,350	Iron, armor-plated.
Paddle	Oberon	3	649	260	Iron.
Paddle	Otter	1	237	120	Wood.
Screw	Pelter	......	250	40	Wood.
Screw	Pembroke	25	1,758	200	Wood.
Screw gun vessel	Penguin	5	431	80	Wood.
Double screw	Pert	4	464	120	Composite gun vessel.
Double screw gun vessel	Philomel	3	664	160	Wood.
Paddle	Pigmy	3	227	100	Wood.
Paddle	Pioneer	2	142	34	Wood.
Screw turret ship	Prince Albert	4	2,537	500	Armor-plated.
Paddle	Princess Alice	......	270	120	Iron.
Paddle	Recruit	4	590	160	Iron.
Paddle	Redpole	1	360	160	Wood.
Screw	Resistance	16	3,710	600	Iron, armor-plated.
Double screw	Rocket	4	464	120	Composite gun vessel.
Screw turret ship	Scorpion	4	1,833	350	Iron, armor-plated.
Paddle	Scotia	......	268	114	Wood.

No. I.—*List of steamships and vessels of the British navy*—Continued.

BUILT IN PRIVATE YARDS BY CONTRACT.

Description.	Name.	No. of guns.	Tons.	Horse-power.	Of what built.
Sail	Seringapatam	......	1, 152	....	Wood.
Screw gun vessel	Serpent	4	695	200	Wood.
Screw	Sharpshooter	6	503	160	Iron.
Paddle	Sheerness	......	233	114	Wood.
Screw	Simoon	4	1, 980	400	Iron.
Screw gun vessel	Slaney	3	301	80	Wood.
Screw gun vessel	Sparrow-hawk	4	676	200	Wood.
Paddle	Sprightly	......	234	100	Wood.
Screw gun vessel	Star	4	695	200	Wood.
Screw gun vessel	Steady	5	431	80	Wood.
Screw	Supply	2	638	80	Iron.
Screw	Swiftsure	14	3, 893	800	Iron, armor-plated.
Screw	Tamar	2	2, 812	500	Iron.
Double screw	Teazer	4	464	120	Composite gun vessel.
Screw	Terror	16	1, 971	200	Iron, armor-plated.
Paddle	Thais	......	302	80	Iron.
Screw	Thunder	14	1, 469	150	Armor-plated.
Screw	Thunderbolt	16	1, 973	200	Iron, armor-plated.
Screw gun vessel	Torch	5	428	80	Wood.
Sail	Trincomalee	16	1, 066	....	Wood.
Paddle	Triton	3	654	260	Iron.
Screw	Triumph	14	3, 893	800	Iron, armor-plated.
Paddle	Trusty	......	319	150	Iron.
Double screw	Turtle	......	37	20	Iron.
Screw	Urgent	4	1, 981	400	Iron.
Screw	Valiant	18	4, 063	[illegible]	Iron.
Double screw	Vanguard	14	3, 774	800	Iron, armor-plated.
Double screw gunboat	Viper	2	737	160	Iron, armor-plated.
Double screw gunboat	Vixen	2	754	160	Iron & wood, armor-plated.
Screw	Volage	8	2, 322	600	Iron cased with wood.
Screw, hydraulic gunboat	Waterwitch	2	777	167	Iron, armor-plated.
Paddle	Weser	......	....	....	Wood.
Paddle	Wildfire	......	186	76	Wood.
Screw turret ship	Wivern	4	1, 899	350	Iron, armor-plated.
Screw	Warrior	32	6, 109	1, 250	Iron, armor-plated.

INDIAN TROOP SHIPS BUILT BY CONTRACT.

Description.	Name.	No. of guns.	Tons.	Horse-power.	Of what built.
Screw	Crocodile	3	4, 173	700	Iron.
Screw	Euphrates	3	4, 173	700	Iron.
Paddle	Hasty	......	120	40	Wood.
Screw	Iumna	3	4, 173	700	Iron.
Screw	Malabar	3	4, 173	700	Iron.
Paddle	Prompt	......	120	40	Wood.
Screw	Serapis	3	4, 173	700	Iron.

HER MAJESTY'S SHIPS FOR THE DEFENSE OF THE COLONIES, BUILT BY CONTRACT.

Description.	Name.	No. of guns.	Tons.	Horse-power.	Of what built.
Double screw turret ship	Abysinnia	4	1, 854	200	Iron, armor-plated.
Double screw turret ship	Cerebus	4	2, 107	250	Iron, armor-plated.
Double screw turret ship	Magdala	4	2, 107	250	Iron, armor-plated.

No. I.—*List of screw steam gun-boats from 212 to 273 tons.*

BUILT IN PRIVATE YARDS BY CONTRACT.

Name.	Horse-power.	Name.	Horse-power.
Albacore	60	Magnet	60
Banterer	60	Onyx	20
Bouncer	60	Opossum	60
Britomart	60	Pheasant	60
Bullfrog	60	Pigeon	60
Bustard	60	Procris	60
Clinker	60	Rainbow	60
Cockatrice	60	Raven	60
Cockchafer	60	Redwing	60
Dapper	60	Skipjack	60
Doterel	60	Skylark	60
Dove	60	Spanker	60
Earnest	60	Speedy	60
Earne	60	Spider	60
Fancy	60	Starling	60
Fervent	60	Staunch 200 tons	25
Firm	60	Stork	60
Forester	60	Surly	60
Forward	60	Thrasher	60
Grasshopper	60	Trinculo	60
Havock	60	Tyrian	60
Heron	60	Watchful	40
Hind	60	Weazel	60
Hunter	40	Whiting	60
Hyena	60	Wizard	60
Jackdaw	60	Woodcock	40
Linnet	60		

No. II.—*Statement of the number, names, tonnage, guns, and location of vessels belonging to and connected with the United States Navy on the 1st day of April,* 1861.

Name.	Guns.	Tonnage.	Where built.	When built.	Situation.	Where.
SHIPS OF THE LINE.						
1. Pennsylvania	120	3,241	Philadelphia	1837	In commission	Receiving ship, Norfolk.
2. Columbus	80	2,480	Washington	1819	In ordinary	Norfolk.
3. Ohio	84	2,757	Brooklyn	1820	In commission	Receiving ship, Boston.
4. North Carolina	84	2,633	Philadelphia	1820	....do	Receiving ship, N. York.
5. Delaware	84	2,633	Gosport	1820	In ordinary	Norfolk.
6. Vermont	84	2,633	Charlestown	1848	....do	Boston.
7. New Orleans	84	2,805	Sackett's Harbor	1815	On the stocks	Sackett's Harbor.
8. Alabama	84	2,633	Kittery	1818	....do	Kittery.
9. Virginia	84	2,633	Charlestown	1818	....do	Boston.
10. New York	84	2,633	Gosport	1818	....do	Norfolk.
FRIGATES.						
1. Constitution	50	1,607	Charlestown	1797	In ordinary	Annapolis.
2. United States	50	1,607	Philadelphia	1797	....do	Norfolk.
3. Potomac	50	1,726	Washington	1821	....do	New York.
4. Brandywine	50	1,726	....do.	1825	....do	Do.
5. Columbia	50	1,726	....do	1836	....do	Norfolk.
6. Congress	50	1,867	Kittery	1841	In commission	Coast of Brazil.
7. Raritan	50	1,726	Philadelphia	1843	In ordinary	Norfolk.
8. St. Lawrence	50	1,726	Gosport	1847	....do	Philadelphia.
9. Santee	50	1,726	Kittery	1855	....do	Kittery.
10. Sabine	50	1,726	Brooklyn	1855	In commission	Off Pensacola.
SLOOPS OF WAR.						
1. Cumberland	24	1,726	Charlestown	1842	In commission	Hampton Roads.
2. Savannah	24	1,726	Brooklyn	1842	In ordinary	New York.
3. Constellation	22	1,452	Rebuilt, Gosport	1854	In commission	Coast of Africa.
4. Macedonian	22	1,341	Gosport	1836	....do.	In the Gulf.
5. Portsmouth	22	1,022	Kittery	1843	....do	Coast of Africa.
6. Plymouth	22	989	Charlestown	1843	In ordinary	Norfolk.
7. St. Mary's	22	958	Washington	1844	In commission	Pacific squadron.
8. Jamestown	22	985	Gosport	1844	In ordinary	Philadelphia.
9. Germantown	22	939	Philadelphia	1846	....do	Norfolk

No. II.—*Vessels belonging to and connected with the United States Navy, &c.*—Continued.

Name.	Guns.	Tonnage.	Where built.	When built.	Situation.	Where.
SLOOPS OF WAR—Continued.						
10. Saratoga	20	882	Kittery	1842	In commission	Coast of Africa.
11. John Adams	20	700	Rebuilt, Gosport	1831	....do	East Indies.
12. Vincennes	20	700	Brooklyn	1826	In ordinary	Boston.
13. Vandalia	20	783	Philadelphia	1828	In commission	On way to East Indies.
14. St. Louis	20	700	Washington	1828	....do	Off Pensacola.
15. Cyane	20	792	Charlestown	1837	....do	Pacific squadron.
16. Levant	20	792	Brooklyn	1837	....do	Do.
17. Decatur	16	566	....do	1839	In ordinary	San Francisco.
18. Marion	16	566	Charlestown	1839	....do	Portsmouth, N. H.
19. Dale	16	566	Philadelphia	1839	....do	Do.
20. Preble	16	566	Kittery	1839	....do	Boston.
BRIGS.						
1. Bainbridge	6	259	Charlestown	1842	In ordinary	Boston.
2. Perry	6	280	Gosport	1843	....do	New York.
3. Dolphin	4	224	Brooklyn	1836	....do	Norfolk.
STORE VESSELS.						
1. Relief	2	468	Philadelphia	1836	In commission	Coast of Africa.
2. Supply	4	547	Purchased	1846	....do	In the Gulf.
3. Release	1	327	....do	1855	Repairing	New York.
PERMANENT STORE AND RECEIVING SHIPS.						
1. Independence	....	2, 257	Charlestown	1814	In commission	Receiv'g ship, Mare Isl'd.
2. Alleghany	....	989	Pittsburg, Penn.	1847	....do	Receiv'g ship, Baltimore.
3. Princeton	....	900	Rebuilt, Boston	1851	....do	Receiving ship, Philad'a.
4. Warren	....	691	Charleston	1826	....do	Store ship, Panama.
5. Fredonia	....	800	Purchased	1846	....do	Store ship, Valparaiso.
6. Falmouth	....	703	Charlestown	1827	....do	Store ship, Aspinwall.
SCREW FRIGATES.						
1. Niagara	12	4, 580	Brooklyn	1855	In commission	On return from Japan.
2. Roanoke	40	3, 400	Gosport	1855	In ordinary	New York.
3. Colorado	40	3, 400	....do	1855	....do	Boston.
4. Merrimack	40	3, 200	Charlestown	1855	....do	Norfolk.
5. Minnesota	40	3, 200	Washington	1855	....do	Boston.
6. Wabash	40	3, 200	Philadelphia	1855	....do	New York.
7. Franklin	50	3, 680	Kittery	1854	Unfinished	Portsmouth, N. H.
1ST CLASS STEAM SLOOPS.						
Screw.						
1. San Jacinto	13	1, 446	Brooklyn	1850	In commission	Coast of Africa.
2. Lancaster	22	2, 360	Philadelphia	1858	....do	Pacific squadron.
3. Pensacola	19	2, 158	Pensacola	1858	Unfinished	Washington.
4. Brooklyn	25	2, 070	New York	1858	In commission	Off Pensacola.
5. Hartford	16	1, 990	Gosport	1858	....do	East Indies.
6. Richmond	14	1, 929	Norfolk	1858	....do	Mediterranean.
Side-wheel.						
1. Mississippi	11	1, 692	Philadelphia	1841	Repairing	Boston.
2. Susquehanna	15	2, 450	....do	1850	In commission	Mediterranean.
3. Powhatan	11	2, 415	Gosport	1850	....do	New York.
4. Saranac	9	1, 446	Kittery	1848	....do	Pacific squadron.
2D CLASS STEAM SLOOPS.						
Screw.						
1. Mohican	6	994	Kittery	1858	In commission	Coast of Africa.
2. Narragansett	5	804	Boston	1858	....do	Pacific squadron.
3. Iroquois	6	1, 016	New York	1858	....do	Mediterranean.
4. Pawnee	4	1, 289	Philadelphia	1858	....do	Washington.
5. Wyoming	6	997	....do	1858	....do	Pacific squadron.
6. Dacotah	6	998	Gosport	1858	....do	East Indies.
7. Pocahontas	5	694	Purchased	1855	....do	Atlantic coast.
8. Seminole	3	801	Pensacola	1858	....do	Brazilian squadron.

No. II.—*Vessels belonging to and connected with the United States Navy, &c.*—Continued.

Name.	Guns.	Tonnage.	Where built.	When built.	Situation.	Where.
3D CLASS STEAMERS.						
Screw.						
1. Wyandotte	5	464	Purchased	1858	In commission	Off Pensacola.
2. Mohawk	5	464	....do	1858	....do	In the Gulf.
3. Crusader	8	549	....do	1858	....do	Do.
4. Sumter	5	464	....do	1858	....do	Coast of Africa.
5. Mystic	5	464	....do	1858	....do	Do.
Side-wheel.						
1 Water Witch	3	378	Washington	1845	Prepar'g for sea	Philadelphia.
2. Michigan	1	582	Erie	1844	Winter quart'rs	Erie, Pa.
3. Pulaski	1	395	Purchased	1858	In commission	Brazil squadron.
4. Saginaw	3	453	San Francisco	1858	....do	East Indies.
STEAM TENDERS.						
Screw.						
1. John Hancock	3	382	Charlestown	1850	In ordinary	San Francisco.
2. Anacostia	1	217	Purchased	1858	In commission	Used as a transport.
Stevens's war st'r.	6	......	New York	......	....	Unfinished.

RECAPITULATION.

Vessels	88
Tonnage	118,460
Guns	2,409

No. III.—*Statement of the number and names of all vessels built by and for the government, for the Navy Department, since April 1, 1861, with their tonnage, number of guns, where, when, and by whom built, the cost of each, and time occupied in construction.*

[NOTE.—The column "when built" in this statement is the date when each vessel named was launched, (if built by the United States,) and the date of the last regular payment, if built by contract.]

Number.	Name.	Tonnage.	Guns.	Where built.	When built.	By whom.	Cost.	Time occupied in construction. Y.	Time occupied in construction. M.
	Screw sloops.								
1	Madawaska	3,281	15	New York yard; machinery at New York	July, 1865	U. S. gov't; engines, &c., J. Ericsson	$1,673,080 52	3	5
2	Chattanooga	3,233	15	Philadelphia	Mar., 1866	Wm. Camp & Sons	950,159 31	2	4
3	Wampanoag	3,281	15	Navy yard, New York; machinery, New York	Dec., 1864	U. S. gov't; Novelty Works	1,575,643 84	4	6½
4	Piscataqua, sp. d'k	3,177	21	Navy yard, Kittery; machinery, Hartford, Conn	June, 1866	U. S. gov't; engines, &c., Woodruff & Beach	1,177,895 04	3	4
5	Guerriere, spar-d'k	3,177	21	Navy yard, Boston; machinery, Boston	Sept., 1865	U. S. gov't; engines, &c., Globe Works	1,154,325 10	2	8
6	Shenandoah	1,378	7	Navy yard, Philadelphia; machinery, Philadelphia	Dec., 1862	U. S. gov't; engines by Merrick & Sons	379,717 64	1	10
7	Sacramento	1,367	7	Navy yard, Kittery; machinery, Taunton, Mass	Apr., 1862	U. S. gov't; engines, Taunton Manuf'g Co.	393,218 50	1	2
8	Canandaigua	1,395	7	Navy yard, Boston; machinery, Boston	Mar., 1862	U. S. gov't; engines, Atlantic Works	388,541 84	....	9
9	Ticonderoga	1,533	9	Navy yard, New York; machinery, New York	Oct., 1862	U. S. gov't; engines, Morgan Works	425,426 63	1	2½
10	Lackawanna	1,533	7	do ... do	Aug., 1862	U. S. gov't; engines, Allaire Works	451,069 00	1	2
11	Monongahela	1,378	7	Navy yard, Philadelphia; machinery, Philadelphia	July, 1862	U. S. gov't; engines, Merrick & Sons	373,796 39	....	10
12	Ossipee	1,240	6	Navy yard, Kittery; machinery, Mystic Bridge, Conn	Nov., 1861	U. S. gov't; engines, Reliance Machine Co.	363,787 10	1	6½
13	Juniata	1,240	6	Navy yard, Philadelphia; machinery, Wilmington, Del.	Mar., 1862	U. S. gov't; engines, Pusey, Jones & Co.	364,820 26	1	6½
14	Housatonic	1,240	13	Navy yard, Boston; machinery, Boston	Nov., 1861	U. S. gov't; engines, J. Cony & Co	368,817 63	....	9
15	Adirondack	240	12	Navy yard, New York; machinery, New York	Feb., 1862	U. S. gov't; engines, Novelty Works	411,529 48	1	1½
16	Kearsargo	1,031	7	Navy yard, Kittery; machinery, Hartford, Conn	Oct., 1861	U. S. gov't; engines, Woodruff & Beach	286,918 05	....	7
17	Tuscarora	997	10	Navy yard, Philadelphia; machinery, Philadelphia	Aug., 1861	U. S. gov't; engines, Merrick & Sons	280,090 91	....	4
18	Oneida	1,032	7	Navy yard, New York; machinery, New York	Nov., 1861	U. S. gov't; engines, J. Murphy & Co	294,697 54	2	8½
19	Wachusett	1,032	9	Navy yard, Boston; machinery, New York	Oct., 1861	U. S. gov't; engines, Morgan Works	314,362 85	....	8
20	Resaca	900	8	Navy yard, Kittery; machinery, Washington navy y'd	Nov., 1865	U. S. government	360,037 64	1	11½
21	Nantasket	900	10	Navy yard, Boston; machinery not completed	July, 1867	U. S. government	Not compl't'd.	3	10
22	Quinnebaug	831	10	Navy yard, New York	Mar., 1866	U. S. government	296,032 71	2	10½
				Machinery, London		Jackson & Watkins	£13,500 —		
23	Swatara	831	10	Navy yard, Philadelphia; machinery, Washington y'd	May, 1865	U. S. gov't; U. S. government	$327,365 07	1	....
24	Nipsic	593	6	Navy yard, Kittery; machinery, Hartford, Conn	June, 1863	U. S. gov't; Woodruff & Beach	255,943 99	....	9¼
25	Pequot	593	10	Navy yard, Boston; machinery, Hartford, Conn	June, 1863	U. S. gov't; Woodruff & Beach	249,231 99	1	3
26	Maumee	593	6	Navy yard, New York; machinery, New York	July, 1863	U. S. gov't; Stover Machine Co.	258,408 93	2	....
27	Yantic	593	7	Navy yard, Philadelphia; machinery, Philadelphia	Mar., 1864	U. S. gov't; Merrick & Co	206,262 93	....	9
28	Saco	593	10	Navy yard, Boston; machinery, Providence, R. I	Aug., 1863	U. S. gov't; Corliss Steam Engine Co	274,845 14	1	9
29	Nyack	593	6	Navy yard, New York; machinery, South Brooklyn	Oct., 1863	U. S. gov't; South Brooklyn Works	257,952 12	1	7
30	Shawmut	593	8	Navy yard, Kittery; machinery, Providence, R. I	June, 1863	U. S. gov't; Corliss Steam Engine Co	232,639 53	....	8¼
31	Kansas	593	8	Navy yard, Philadelphia; machinery captured	Oct., 1863	U. S. gov't	212,316 78	1	....

	Gunboats.									
32	Aroostook	507	5	Kennebunk, Me.; machinery, New York	Dec.,	1861	N. L. Thompson; Novelty Works	98,814	35	....	5
33	Cayuga	507	6	Portland, Conn.; machinery, Hartford, Conn	Dec.,	1861	Gildersleeve & Son; Woodruff & Beach	97,912	22	....	5
34	Chippewa	507	6	Brooklyn, N. Y.; machinery, New York	Nov.,	1861	Webb & Bell; Morgan Works	101,235	00	....	5
35	Chocura	507	7	Boston; machinery, Boston	Nov.,	1861	Curtis & Tilden; Harrison Loring	99,912	01	....	4½
36	Huron	507	6	do ... do	Nov.,	1861	Paul Curtis; Harrison Loring	101,421	00	....	4
37	Itasca	507	4	Philadelphia; machinery, Philadelphia	Nov.,	1861	Hillman & Streaker; J. P. Morris & Co	98,786	57	....	4
38	Katahdin	507	6	Bath, Me.; machinery, New York	Nov.,	1861	Larrabee & Allen; Morgan Iron Works	98,868	85	....	4½
39	Kanawha	507	4	East Haddam, Conn.; machinery, Bridgeport, Conn	Dec.,	1861	G.E. & W.H.Goodspeed; Pacific Iron Works	97,775	00	....	5
40	Kennebec	507	4	Portland, Me.; machinery, New York	Nov.,	1861	George W. Lawrence; Novelty Works	103,694	76	....	4
41	Kineo	507	6	do ... do	Dec.,	1861	J. W. Dyer; Morgan Works	101,182	30	....	5½
42	Marblehead	507	7	Newburyport, Mass.; machinery, Newburg, N. Y	Nov.,	1861	G. W. Jackman, jr.; Highland Iron Works	97,739	75	....	4½
43	Ottawa	507	5	New York; machinery, New York	Oct.,	1861	J. A. Westervelt; Novelty Works	88,240	37	....	4½
44	Owasco	507	4	Mystic River, Conn.; machinery, New York	Dec.,	1861	Maxon Fish & Co.; Novelty Works	99,750	00	....	5½
45	Panola	507	4	Baltimore, Md.; machinery, Philadelphia	Nov.,	1861	J. J. Abrahams; Charles Reeder	96,735	47	....	5
46	Pembina	507	4	New York; machinery, New York	Oct.,	1861	Thomas Stack; Novelty Works	88,225	00	....	5
47	Penobscot	507	5	Belfast, Me.; machinery, New York	Dec.,	1861	C. P. Carter; Allaire Works	98,241	52	....	5
48	Sagamore	507	4	Boston; machinery, Boston	Nov.,	1861	A. & G. T. Sampson; Atlantic Works	101,681	52	....	4
49	Sciota	507	5	Philadelphia; machinery, Philadelphia	Nov.,	1861	Jacob Birely; J. P. Morris & Co	96,279	43	....	5
50	Seneca	507	5	New York; machinery, New York	Oct.,	1861	Jere. Simonson; Novelty Works	88,248	61	....	4
51	Tahoma	507	6	Wilmington, Del.; machinery, Chester, Pa	Jan.,	1862	W. & A. Thatcher; Reaney, Son & Archbold	100,486	88	....	6
52	Unadilla	507	6	New York; machinery, New York	Oct.,	1861	John Englis; Novelty Works	88,000	00	....	3½
53	Winona	507	7	do ... do	Nov.,	1861	C. & R. Poillon; Allaire Works	101,240	00	....	4
54	Wissahickon	507	4	Philadelphia; machinery, Philadelphia	Nov.,	1861	John W. Lynn; Merrick & Sons	98,771	72	....	4½
	Paddle-wheel steamers, (double-enders.)										
55	Sassacus	974	12	Navy yard, Kittery; machinery, Boston	Dec.,	1862	U. S. gov't; Atlantic Works	249,037	97	....	7
56	Pawtuxet	974	12	Navy yard, Kittery; machinery, Providence, R. I	Mar.,	1863	U. S. gov't; Providence Steam Engine Co.	241,439	39	....	6
57	Tallapoosa	974	10	Navy yard, Boston; machinery, New York	Feb.,	1863	U. S. gov't; Neptune Works	241,856	98	....	6
58	Winooski	974	10	Navy yard, Boston; machinery, Providence, R. I	July,	1863	U. S. gov't; Providence Steam Engine Co.	239,617	47	1	1
59	Mackinaw	974	10	Navy yard, New York; machinery, New York	April,	1863	U. S. gov't; Allaire Works	251,480	07	....	11
60	Shamrock	974	11	Navy yard, New York; machinery, Baltimore	Mar.,	1863	U. S. gov't; Poole & Hunt	268,000	56	2	....
61	Tullahoma	974	10	Navy yard, New York; machinery, New York	Nov.,	1863	U. S. gov't; Stover Machine Co.	256,824	52	4	3½
62	Tacony	974	12	Navy yard, Philadelphia; machinery, Philadelphia	May,	1863	U. S. gov't; Morris, Towne & Co.	266,718	23	....	9
63	Algonquin	974	10	Navy yard, New York; machinery, New York	Dec.,	1863	U. S. gov't; Paul S. Forbes	277,372	24	2	2½
64	Peoria	974	10	do ... do	Oct.,	1863	U. S. gov't; Etna Iron Works	305,199	73	3	9
65	Iosco	974	10	Bath, Me.; machinery, Boston	Mar.,	1863	Larrabee & Allen; Globe Works	164,768	68	....	7
66	Agawam	974	10	Portland, Me.; machinery, Portland, Me	May,	1863	George W. Lawrence; Portland Works	161,345	42	....	8½
67	Pontoosuc	974	12	do ... do	May,	1863	do ... do	163,031	58	....	8½
68	Massasoit	974	10	Boston; machinery, Boston	Mar.,	1863	Curtis & Tilden; Globe Works	160,630	41	....	6½
69	Osceola	974	10	do ... do	June,	1863	Curtis & Tilden; Atlantic Works	160,575	41	....	8½
70	Mattabesett	974	10	Boston; machinery, New York	June,	1863	A. & G. Sampson; Allaire Works	163,595	17	....	9
71	Chicopee	974	10	do ... do	Mar.,	1863	Paul Curtis; Neptune Works	163,239	85	....	6½
72	Ascutney	974	10	Newburyport, Mass; machinery, New York	June,	1863	George W. Jackman, jr.; Morgan Works	176,143	73	....	9
73	Otsego	974	10	New York; machinery, New York	April,	1863	J. A. & D. D. Westervelt; Fulton Works	161,143	44	....	7
74	Metacomet	974	10	New York; machinery, South Brooklyn, N. Y	Mar.,	1863	Thomas Stack; South Brooklyn Works	159,081	27	....	6½
75	Chenango	974	10	New York; machinery, New York	April,	1863	Jere. Simonson; Morgan Works	161,273	71	....	7
76	Lenapee	974	10	New York; machinery, Newburg, N. Y	June,	1863	Edward Lupton; Washington Iron Works	163,423	48	....	9½

No. 111.—*Statement of vessels built for the Navy Department since April* 1, 1861, *&c.*—Continued.

Number.	Name.	Tonnage.	Guns.	Where built.	When built.	By whom.	Cost.	Time occupied in construction.	
								Y.	*M.*
77	Mendota	974	10	Brooklyn, N.Y.; machinery, South Brooklyn, N. Y	April, 1863	F. Z. Tucker; South Brooklyn Works	$159, 631 53	....	7½
78	Mingoe	974	12	Bordentown, N. J.; machinery, Wilmington, Del	Aug., 1863	D. S. Mershon, jr.; Pusey, Jones & Co	152, 236 00	....	11½
79	Wyalusing	874	14	Philadelphia; machinery, Wilmington, Del	May, 1863	C. H. & W. M. Cramp; Pusey, Jones & Co.	162, 914 84	....	8½
80	Pontiac	974	16	Philadelphia; machinery, Philadelphia	May, 1863	Hillman & Streaker; Neafie, Levy & Co	163, 561 00	....	8
81	Eutaw	975	10	Baltimore; machinery, Baltimore	Mar., 1863	John J. Abrahams; Vulcan Iron Works	160, 200 00	....	7
	Paddle-wheel steamers of iron, (double-enders.)								
82	Mohongo	1, 030	10	New York; machinery, Jersey City, N. J	Aug., 1864	Zeno Secor; Fulton Foundry	305, 928 11	1	1
83	Suwanee	1, 030	10	Chester, Penn.; machinery, Chester, Penn	June, 1864	Reaney, Son & Archbold	278, 662 78	....	10
84	Shamokin	1, 030	10	......do......do	Feb., 1865	......do	278, 020 81	1	6
85	Muscoota	1, 030	10	Brooklyn, N. Y.; machinery, Brooklyn, N. Y	Aug., 1864	Thomas F. Rowland; Continental Works	297, 678 80	1	....
86	Winnipec	1, 030	10	Boston; machinery, Boston	May, 1865	Harrison Loring	298, 132 24	1	8¼
87	Ashuelot	1, 030	10	......do......do	July, 1865	Donald McKay	297, 415 92	1	11
88	Monocacy	1 030	10	Baltimore; machinery, Baltimore	May, 1866	A. & W. Denmead & Son	293, 473 98	1	7
89	Wateree	974	12	Chester, Penn.; machinery, Chester, Penn	Aug., 1863	Reaney, Son & Archbold	203, 170 00	....	11½
	Paddle-wheel steamers, (double-enders.)								
90	Octorara	829	11	Navy yard, New York; machinery, New York	Dec., 1861	U. S. government; Neptune Works	173, 071 81	....	7
91	Miami	730	7	Navy yard, Philadelphia; machinery, Philadelphia	Nov., 1861	U. S. government; Merrick & Sons	172, 341 25	....	5
92	Maratanza	786	6	Navy yard, Boston; machinery, Boston	Nov., 1861	U. S. government; Harrison Loring	187, 128 19	....	5
93	Tioga	819	8	Navy yard, Boston; machinery, New York	April, 1862	U. S. government; Morgan Iron Works	199, 852 14	....	7
94	Genesee	803	7	......do......do	April, 1862	U. S. government; Neptune Works	190, 423 63	....	7
95	Sebago	832	10	Navy yard, Kittery; machinery, New York	Nov., 1861	U. S. government; Novelty Works	212, 771 22	....	7¼
96	Mahaska	832	8	......do......do	Dec., 1861	U. S. government; Morgan Iron Works	210, 137 78	....	8
97	Sonoma	955	8	......do......do	April, 1862	U. S. government; Novelty Works	194, 962 34	....	7½
98	Conemaugh	955	9	......do......do	May, 1862	....do......do	193, 416 70	....	8
99	Port Royal	805	8	New York	May, 1862	Thomas Steck	100, 057 00	....	7
100	Cimarron	860	9	Bordentown, N. J	July, 1862	D. S. Mershon, jr	100, 000 00	....	9
101	Paul Jones	863	7	Baltimore; machinery, Chester, Penn	April, 1862	J. J. Abrahams; Reaney, Son & Archbold	102, 603 33	....	5¼
	Tugs.								
102	Pinta	350	2	Chester, Penn	April, 1865	Reaney, Son & Archbold	128, 000 00	1	2
103	Triana	350	2	New York	Nov., 1865	William Perine	128, 000 00	1	11
104	Nina	350	2	Chester, Penn	Sept., 1865	Reaney, Son & Archbold	128, 000 00	1	7
105	Fortune	350	2	Boston	Sept., 1865	James Felton	149, 600 00	1	9

106	Speedwell	350	2	do	Nov., 1865	do	149,600 00	1	7
107	Standish	350	2	do	Jan., 1866	do	106,240 00	2	1
108	Mayflower	350	2	do	Feb., 1866	do	106,240 00	1	9½
109	Palos	350	2	do	July, 1866	do	128,000 00	1	9
110	Leyden	350	2	do	July, 1866	do	128,000 00	1	9
111	Pilgrim	170	2	Wilmington, Del	Jan., 1865	Pusey, Jones & Co.	74,000 00	1	1
112	Maria	170	2	New York	Jan., 1865	William Perine	80,000 00	1	8
	Iron-clad vessels, (sea-going, casemated.)								
113	Dunderberg	5,090	16	New York	Aug., 1866	William H. Webb	1,041,666 67	4	1
114	New Ironsides	3,486	18	Philadelphia	Aug., 1862	Merrick & Sons	814,866 83	....	10
	Iron-clad vessels, (sea-going, single turret.)								
115	Puritan	3,265	2	New York	Oct., 1864	John Ericsson	1,974,622 93	2	5
116	Dictator	3,033	2	do	Dec., 1864	do	1,382,991 24	2	3
	Iron-clad vessels, (double turret.)								
117	Monadnock	1,564	4	Navy yard, Boston; turrets, Boston; machinery, Philadelphia.	....	U. S. government; Atlantic Works; Morris Toune & Co.	981,439 45	2	8
118	Miantonomoh	1,564	4	Navy yard, New York; turrets, New York; machinery, New York.	Aug., 1864	U. S. government; J. B. & W. W. Cornell & Co.; Novelty Works.	1,310,773 08	2	11½
119	Agamenticus	1,564	4	Navy yard, Kittery; turrets, Boston; machinery, Philadelphia.	May, 1864	U. S. government; Atlantic Works; Morris Toune & Co.	1,016,071 18	2	10
120	Tonawanda	1,564	4	Navy yard, Philadelphia; turrets, New York; machinery, Philadelphia.	May, 1864	U. S. government; J. B. & W. W. Cornell & Co.; Merrick & Sons.	1,156,323 82	3	....
121	Onondaga	1,250	4	New York	May, 1863	George W. Quintard	759,673 08	1	2
122	Winnebago	970	4	St. Louis, Mo	Aug., 1863	James B. Eads	384,969 84	1	3
123	Milwaukee	970	4	do	Aug., 1863	do	387,432 88	1	3
124	Chickasaw	970	4	do	Sept., 1863	Thomas G. Gaylord	389,962 70	1	4
125	Kickapoo	970	8	do	Dec., 1863	G. B. Allen & Co	391,828 24	1	6
	Iron-clad vessels, (single turret.)								
126	Canonicus	1,034	2	Boston	Feb., 1864	Harrison Loring	622,963 22	1	5
127	Mahopac	1,034	2	Jersey City, N. J	July, 1864	Secor & Co	635,374 55	1	10
128	Tecumseh	1,034	2	do	Mar., 1864	do	636,941 76	1	6
129	Manhattan	1,034	2	do	May, 1864	do	628,879 27	1	8
130	Saugus	1,034	2	Wilmington, Del	April, 1864	Harlan & Hollingsworth & Co	588,466 62	1	6
131	Tippecanoe	1,034	2	Cincinnati, Ohio	Mar., 1866	Miles Greenwood	633,327 84	1	6
132	Catawaba	1,034	2	do	June, 1865	Alexander Swift & Co., and Niles Works	621,424 54	2	2
133	Oneonta	1,034	2	do	June, 1865	do .... do	621,424 54	2	8
134	Manayunk	1,034	2	Pittsburg, Pa	July, 1865	Snowdons & Mason	626,582 24	2	9
135	Passaic	844	2	Brooklyn, N. Y	Nov., 1862	John Ericsson	423,171 69	....	8

No. III.—*Statement of vessels built for the Navy Department since April* 1, 1861, *&c.*—Continued.

Number.	Name.	Tonnage.	Guns.	Where built.	When built.	By whom.	Cost.	Time occupied in construction. Y.	M.
136	Camancho	844	2	Jersey City, N. J	Jan., 1865	Donahue, Ryan & Secor	$613, 164 98	2	6½
137	Patapsco	844	2	Wilmington, Del	Dec., 1862	John Ericsson	422, 779 95	....	9
138	Sangamon	844	2	Chester, Pa	April, 1863	......do	422, 766 73	1	....
139	Lehigh	844	2	......do	April, 1863	......do	422, 726 28	1	1
140	Montauk	844	2	Brooklyn, N. Y	Dec., 1862	......do	423, 027 49	....	8½
141	Catskill	844	2	......do	Mar., 1863	......do	427, 766 78	....	11½
142	Weehawken	844	2	Jersey City, N. J	Jan., 1863	Secor & Co	436, 007 29	....	8½
143	Nantucket	844	2	Boston	Mar., 1863	Atlantic Works	408, 091 37	....	10½
144	Nahant	844	2	......do	Jan., 1863	Harrison Loring	413, 515 14	....	8
145	Yazoo	614	2	Philadelphia	Sept., 1864	Merrick & Sons	566, 364 26	1	5
146	Waxsaw	614	2	Baltimore	June, 1865	A. & W. Denmead & Sons	592, 587 32	2	1
147	Napa	614	1	Wilmington, Del	Feb., 1865	Harlan & Hollingsworth & Co	506, 366 33	1	9
148	Tunxis	614	2	Chester and Philadelphia, Pa	June, 1864	Reaney, Son & Archbold and William Cramp & Sons	648, 070 99	1	2
149	Umpqua	614	2	Pittsburg, Pa	Mar., 1865	Snowdons & Mason	595, 649 36	1	11
150	Klamath	614	2	Cincinnati, Ohio	July, 1865	Alexander Swift & Co	602, 985 34	2	4
151	Yuma	614	2	......do	July, 1865	......do	602, 985 34	2	4
152	Naubuc	614	1	Williamsburg, N. Y	Feb., 1865	William Perine	513, 975 74	1	10
153	Cohoes	614	2	Green Point, N. Y	June, 1865	M. F. Merritt	594, 012 10	2	2
154	Koka	614	2	Camden, N. J	Aug. 1865	Wilcox & Whiting	545, 694 81	2	3
155	Casco	614	1	Boston	June, 1864	Atlantic Works	529, 996 99	1	2
156	Chimo	614	1	......do	June, 1864	Aquilla Adams	620, 445 52	....	11
157	Etlah	614	2	St. Louis, Mo	Mar., 1865	Charles W. McCord	589, 458 82	1	8
158	Modoc	614	1	New York	Mar., 1865	J. S. Underhill	513, 353 13	1	9
159	Nausett	614	2	East Boston, Mass	May, 1865	Donald M'Kay	578, 110 98	1	11
160	Shawnee	614	2	......do	June, 1864	Curtis & Tilden	581, 818 50	2	3
161	Shiloh	614	2	St Louis, Mo	Mar., 1865	George C. Bestor	589, 428 20	1	9
162	Squando	614	2	East Boston, Mass	April, 1865	McKay & Aldus	589, 535 70	1	11
163	Suncook	614	2	South Boston, Mass	June. 1865	Globe Works	593, 674 30	2	1
164	Wassuc	614	2	Portland, Maine	June, 1865	George W. Lawrence	552, 374 51	1	7½
165	Osage	523	2	St Louis, Mo	May, 1863	James B. Eads	199, 632 62	1	....
166	Neosho	523	4	......do	June, 1863	......do	200, 757 67	1	1
167	Ozark	573	7	Mound City, Ill	Dec., 1863	George C. Bestor	207, 071 50	1	7
168	Marietta	479	2	Pittsburg, Pa	April, 1866	Tomlinson, Hartupee & Co	235, 039 57	3	11
169	Sandusky	479	2	......do	April, 1866	......do	235, 039 57	3	11
	Iron-clad vessels, (casemated.)								
170	Chillicothe	303	2	Cincinnati Ohio	Oct., 1862	Joseph Brown	92, 960 00	....	6
171	Indianola	442	2	......do	Jan., 1863	......do	182, 372 00	....	8

172	Tuscumbia	565	3	do	Mar., 1863	do	229, 669 73	....10½
173	Keokuk	677	2	New York	Apr., 1863	Charles W. Whitney	227, 507 02	.... 12½
	Torpedo vessel.							
174	Spuyten Duyvil	116	......	New Haven, Conn.; machinery, Mystic Bridge, Conn	Jan., 1865	Samuel H. Pook; mystic Iron Works	45, 036 29	1 ....
	Screw sloop.							
175	Idaho	2, 638	8	Brooklyn, N. Y	Mar., 1865	Paul S. Forbes	550, 000 00	2 6
	Powder tugs.							
176	Blue Light	103	......	Navy yard, Portsmouth	——, 1864	United States government	28, 872 20	.... 7½
177	Port Fire	103	......	do	——, 1864	do	28, 872 20	.... 7½
	Iron-clad vessels, (first completed.)							
178	Monitor	776	2	New York	Mar., 1862	John Ericsson	275, 000 00	.... 4¾
179	Galena	738	6	Mystic Bridge, Conn	Apr., 1862	C. S. Bushnell	235, 250 00	 7
		166, 006	1, 110					

RECAPITULATION.

Vessels built in government yards	55	
Vessels built in private yards	124	
Total	179	
Number of vessels built in government yards, the machinery of which was built in private works	49	

BY PURCHASE.

Whole number of vessels purchased by or transferred to navy		497
Disposed of by sale	363	
Lost, destroyed, sunk as obstructions, transferred to army, &c	97	
Still in service	37	
		497
Number of tons		171, 837

No. IV.—*Statement of vessels sold by the Navy Department from April* 1, 1861, *to April* 1, 1865, *inclusive; also from May* 1, 1868, *to date.*

Name of vessel.	Where sold.	When sold.	Amount received.
Calhoun	New Orleans	June, —, 1864	$14,500 00
Chotank	New York	—— —, 1864	700 00
Eugenie	Key West	Nov. —, 1864	....
Falmouth	Aspinwall, N. G	Oct. 28, 1863	....
Isilda	Key West	—— —, 1863	....
Mohawk	Philadelphia	July 12, 1864	5,000 00
Nightingale	Boston, Mass	Feb. 20, 1865	10,000 00
Patroon	Philadelphia	Dec. 30, 1862	11,200 00
Planter*		Sept. 10, 1862	....
Pulaski	Montevideo	—— —, 1863	....
Warren	Panama	—— —, 1862	....
Aroostook	Hong Kong	Sept. —, 1869	16,094 74
Algonquin	New York	Oct. 21, 1869	30,000 00
Alleghany	Norfolk	Sept. 10, 1868	5,250 00
Ascutney	Washington	Oct. 28, 1868	21,687 50
Atlanta	Philadelphia	May 4, 1869	25,700 00
Augusta	New York	Dec. 1, 1868	20,700 00
Boxer	Philadelphia	Sept. 1, 1868	9,900 00
Buckthorn	Pensacola	Sept. 7, 1869	3,000 00
Chenango	Philadelphia	Oct. 28, 1868	21,687 50
De Soto	New York	Sept. 30, 1868	47,600 00
Don	do	Aug. 29, 1868	18,000 00
Florida	Philadelphia	Dec. 5, 1868	19,200 00
Glasgow	Pensacola	June 4. 1869	7,150 00
Grampus	Mound City	Sept. 1, 1868	450 00
Hornet	Philadelphia	June 26, 1869	33,000 00
Huron	New York	May 14, 1869	13,200 00
Lenapee	Portsmouth	Aug. 26, 1868	17,900 00
Mahaska	New Orleans	Oct. 12, 1868	17,000 00
Maratanza	Portsmouth	Aug. 26, 1868	32,700 00
Marblehead	New York	Sept. 30, 1868	14,100 00
Memphis	do	May 8, 1869	55,300 00
Metacomet	Philadelphia	Oct. 28, 1868	21,687 50
Muscoota	Portsmouth	June 17, 1869	50,000 00
Mendota	Philadelphia	May 25, 1868	18,750 00
Newbern	Washington	Sept. 1, 1868	35,000 00
Pansy	Mound City	Sept. 1, 1868	450 00
Penobscot	Portsmouth	Oct. 19, 1869	6,700 00
Peoria	do	Aug. 26, 1868	6,900 00
Pequot	New York	May 6, 1869	7,700 00
Purveyor	do	July 7, 1869	12,000 00
Sassacus	Philadelphia	Oct. 28, 1868	21,687 50
Seneca	Norfolk	Sept. 10, 1868	10,025 00
Shamokin	Washington	Oct. 21, 1869	25,000 00
Shamrock	Philadelphia	Sept. 1, 1868	19,700 00
Tacony	Portsmouth	Aug. 26, 1868	20,000 00
Tullahoma	New York	Aug. 29, 1868	24,500 00
Winnepec	Norfolk	June 17, 1869	50,000 00
Winooski	Portsmouth	Aug. 26, 1868	19,100 00
Yucca	do	Aug. 26, 1868	9,500 00
Unadilla	Hong Kong	Nov. 9, 1869	24,215 16
Total			853,934 90

* Sold to War Department, not paid for.

RECAPITULATION.

Total vessels sold from April, 1865, to May, 1868	420
Total vessels sold from May 1, 1864, to April, 1865, and from April 1, 1865, to date	51
Total vessels sold by Navy Department, April 1, 1861, to date	471
Amount received for vessels sold from April, 1865, to May, 1868	$9,710,575 55
Amount received from vessels sold from April 1, 1861, to April 1, 1865	41,400 00
Amount received from May 1, 1868, to date	812,534 90
Total	10,764,510 45

NOTE.—For the number and names of vessels sold from close of war to May 1, 1868, see Ex. Doc. No. 282, 2d session 40th Congress.

GENERAL RECAPITULATION.

	Number.	Tonnage.	Guns.
Vessels in service April 1, 1861	88	118, 460	2, 409
Vessels built since April 1, 1861	179	166, 000	1, 110
Whole number purchased since April 1, 1861, or transferred to navy	497	171, 837	
Whole number sold	471	....	

Total price paid.......... $10,764,510 45

No. V.—*Number and tonnage of sailing and steam vessels built and first registered in the United Kingdom.*

Calendar years.	SAILING VESSELS.		STEAM VESSELS.		TOTAL.	
	Vessels.	Tons.	Vessels.	Tons.	Vessels.	Tons.
1850	621	119, 111	68	14, 584	689	133, 695
1851	594	126, 914	78	22, 723	672	149, 637
1852	608	136, 749	104	30, 742	712	167, 491
1853	645	154, 956	153	48, 215	798	203, 171
1854	628	132, 687	174	64, 255	802	196, 942
1855	865	242, 182	233	81, 018	1, 098	323, 200
1856	921	187, 005	229	57, 573	1, 150	244, 578
1857	1, 050	197, 554	228	52, 918	1, 278	250, 472
1858	847	154, 930	153	53, 150	1, 000	208, 080
1859	789	147, 967	150	38, 003	939	185, 970
1860	818	158, 172	198	53, 796	1, 016	211, 968
1861	774	129, 970	201	70, 869	975	200, 839
1862	827	164, 061	221	77, 338	1, 048	241, 399
1863	881	253, 036	279	107, 951	1, 160	360, 987
1864	867	272, 499	374	159, 374	1, 241	431, 873
1865	922	235, 555	382	179, 649	1, 304	415, 204
1866	969	207, 678	354	133, 511	1, 323	341, 189
1867	915	185, 771	295	97, 219	1, 210	282, 990
1868	787	237, 687	232	78, 510	1, 019	316, 197

No. VI.—*Table showing the tonnage of United States and British registered vessels, employed in the foreign trade of each country, during the years, respectively,* 1830, 1840, 1850, *and from* 1860 *to* 1868, *both inclusive.*

Year.	UNITED STATES.			GREAT BRITAIN.*					
				In the foreign trade.			Partly in home and partly in foreign trade.		
	Sail.	Steam.	Total.	Sail.	Steam.	Total.	Sail.	Steam.	Total.
1830	575, 056	1, 419	576, 475	....	....	....	....	....	....
1840	895, 610	4, 155	899, 765	....	....	....	....	....	....
1850	1, 540, 769	44, 429	1, 585, 198	2, 143, 234	45, 186	2, 188, 420	222, 341	5, 298	227, 639
1860	2, 448, 941	97, 296	2, 546, 237	2, 804, 610	277, 437	3, 082, 047	226, 556	29, 803	256, 359
1861	2, 540, 020	102, 608	2, 642, 628	2, 866, 218	313, 465	3, 179, 683	219, 522	24, 924	244, 446
1862	2, 177, 253	113, 998	2, 291, 251	2, 993, 696	328, 310	3, 322, 006	246, 479	29, 463	275, 942
1863	1, 892, 899	133, 215	2, 026, 114	3, 246, 526	371, 201	3, 617, 727	284, 413	33, 547	317, 960
1864	1, 475, 376	106, 519	1, 581, 895	3, 532, 242	456, 241	3, 988, 483	268, 125	36, 944	305, 069
1865	1, 504, 575	98, 008	1, 602, 583	3, 629, 023	523, 698	4, 152, 721	282, 295	43, 225	325, 520
1866	1, 294, 637	198, 289	1, 492, 926	3, 612, 973	553, 425	4, 166, 398	278, 167	47, 194	325, 361
1867	1, 369, 917	199, 115	1, 568, 032	3, 641, 662	608, 232	4, 249, 894	199, 846	50, 201	250, 047
1868	1, 343, 793	221, 939	1, 565, 732	3, 646, 150	619, 199	4, 265, 349	240, 921	52, 150	293, 071

* This table includes Channel Island vessels, but not those of the British plantations. The home trade signifies on the coasts of the United Kingdom, or to ports between the limits of the river Elbe and Brest. The foreign trade signifies to ports beyond such limits.

No. VII.—*Total number and tonnage of vessels registered as belonging to the United Kingdom, including Jersey, Guernsey, and the Isle of Man, at the end of each year.*

Calendar years.	SAILING VESSELS.		STEAM VESSELS.		TOTAL.	
	Vessels.	Tons.	Vessels.	Tons.	Vessels.	Tons.
1850	24, 797	3, 396, 659	1, 187	168, 474	25, 984	3, 565, 133
1851	24, 816	3, 475, 657	1, 227	186, 687	26, 043	3, 662, 344
1852	24, 814	3, 549, 968	1, 272	209, 310	26, 086	3, 759, 278
1853	25, 224	3, 780, 092	1, 385	250, 112	26, 609	4, 030, 204
1854	25, 335	3, 942, 513	1, 524	306, 237	26, 859	4, 248, 750
1855	24, 274	3, 968, 699	1, 674	380, 635	25, 948	4, 349, 334
1856	24, 480	3, 980, 494	1, 697	386, 462	26, 177	4, 366, 956
1857	25, 273	4, 141, 274	1, 824	417, 466	27, 097	4, 558, 740
1858	25, 615	4, 205, 270	1, 926	452, 468	27, 541	4, 657, 738
1859	25, 784	4, 226, 355	1, 918	436, 836	27, 702	4, 663, 191
1860	25, 663	4, 204, 360	2, 000	454, 327	27, 663	4, 658, 687
1861	25, 905	4, 300, 518	2, 133	506, 308	28, 038	4, 806, 826
1862	26, 212	4, 396, 509	2, 228	537, 891	28, 440	4, 934, 400
1863	26, 339	4, 731, 217	2, 298	596, 856	28, 637	5, 328, 073
1864	26, 142	4, 930, 219	2, 490	697, 281	28, 632	5, 627, 500
1865	26, 069	4, 936, 776	2, 718	823, 533	28, 787	5, 760, 309
1866	26, 140	4, 903, 652	2, 831	875, 685	28, 971	5, 779, 337
1867	25, 842	4, 852, 911	2, 931	901, 062	28, 773	5, 753, 973
1868	25, 500	4, 878, 233	2, 944	902, 297	28, 444	5, 780, 530

No. VIII.—*Table showing the tonnage, respectively, of American, British, and French vessels which entered and cleared at the ports of countries to which such vessels belonged in trade with other countries.*

Calendar year.	Entered inward.			Cleared outward.		
	American vessels entering at American from foreign ports.	British vessels entering at ports of Great Brit'n from foreign ports.	French vessels entering at ports of France from foreign ports.	American vessels clearing from American for foreign ports.	British vessels clear'g from ports of Great Britain for foreign ports.	French ves'ls clearing from ports of France for foreign ports.
1853	4, 004, 013	3, 363, 121	854, 029	3, 766, 789	3, 457, 058	911, 164
1854	3, 752, 115	3, 313, 549	921, 186	3, 911, 392	3, 362, 083	1, 011, 611
1855	3, 861, 391	3, 633, 153	1, 006, 419	4, 068, 979	3, 882, 017	1, 042, 279
1856	4, 385, 484	4, 433, 792	1, 191, 424	4, 538, 364	4, 521, 818	1, 215, 154
1857	4, 721, 370	4, 772, 769	1, 356, 687	4, 580, 651	4, 630, 230	1, 375, 082
1858	4, 395, 642	4, 506, 100	1, 286, 870	4, 490, 033	4, 367, 855	1, 274, 219
1859	5, 265, 648	4, 603, 266	1, 328, 322	5, 297, 367	4, 631, 670	1, 401, 164
1860	5, 921, 285	4, 778, 019	1, 345, 396	6, 165, 924	4, 801, 042	1, 437, 898
1861	5, 023, 917	5, 419, 459	1, 434, 778	4, 889, 313	5, 182, 862	1, 468, 461
1862	5, 117, 685	5, 526, 295	1, 589, 763	4, 961, 818	5, 546, 183	1, 559, 886
1863	4, 614, 698	5, 866, 184	1, 610, 347	4, 447, 261	5, 722, 643	1, 656, 777
1864	3, 066, 434	6, 462, 606	1, 649, 518	3, 090, 948	6, 460, 578	1, 660, 640
1865	2, 943, 661	7, 022, 948	1, 639, 994	3, 025, 134	7, 116, 057	1, 705, 334
1866	3, 372, 060	7, 989, 264	1, 633, 296	3, 383, 176	7, 895, 770	1, 699, 549
1867	3, 455, 052	8, 706, 255	1, 799, 703	3, 419, 502	8, 388, 346	1, 392, 904
1868	3, 550, 550	8, 721, 022	1, 804, 021	3, 717, 956	8, 603, 691	1, 834, 856

No. IX.—*Table showing the licensed and enrolled tonnage of the United States engaged in the coastwise trade, and the tonnage of the British registered vessels engaged in the home trade, during the years, respectively, from* 1850 *to* 1868, *both inclusive.*

Year.	UNITED STATES.			* GREAT BRITAIN.						Year.
	Licensed and enrolled sail.	Licensed and enrolled steam.	Total licensed and enrolled.	In the home trade.			Partly in the home and partly in the foreign trade.			
				Registered sail.	Registered steam.	Total registered.	Registered sail.	Registered steam.	Total registered.	
1850..	1,468,738	481,005	1,949,743	666,957	54,196	721,153	222,341	5,298	227,639	1850
1851..	1,524,915	521,217	2,046,132	685,641	78,820	764,461	242,656	4,926	247,582	1851
1852..	1,675,456	563,536	2,238,992	701,803	66,606	768,409	147,867	15,244	163,111	1852
1853..	1,789,238	514,098	2,303,336	689,342	85,471	774,813	156,800	7,250	164,050	1853
1854..	1,887,512	581,571	2,469,083	694,712	54,002	748,714	202,124	19,135	221,259	1854
1855..	2,021,625	655,240	2,676,865	691,128	57,415	748,543	210,114	12,562	222,676	1855
1856..	1,796,888	583,362	2,380,250	719,860	67,616	787,476	162,488	16,102	178,590	1856
1857..	1,857,964	618,911	2,476,875	767,925	92,481	860,406	162,112	20,859	182,971	1857
1858..	2,550,067	651,363	3,201,430	788,113	90,739	878,852	138,699	20,604	159,303	1858
1859..	1,961,631	676,005	2,637,636	777,422	90,867	868,289	132,768	21,123	153,891	1859
1860..	2,036,990	770,641	2,807,631	821,079	92,254	913,333	226,556	29,803	256,359	1860
1861..	2,122,589	774,596	2,897,185	832,771	102,795	935,566	219,522	24,924	244,446	1861
1862..	2,224,449	596,465	2,820,914	771,326	104,020	875,346	246,479	29,463	275,942	1862
1863..	2,660,212	439,755	3,099,967	752,589	107,003	859,592	284,413	33,547	317,960	1863
1864..	2,550,690	853,816	3,404,506	789,108	125,808	914,916	268,125	36,944	305,069	1864
1865..	2,525,067	969,131	3,494,198	795,434	134,776	930,210	282,295	43,225	325,520	1865
1866..	1,932,829	885,023	2,817,852	813,909	147,194	961,103	278,167	47,194	325,361	1866
1867..	1,742,689	993,765	2,736,454	839,523	154,244	993,767	199,846	50,201	250,047	1867
1868..	1,808,550	977,476	2,786,026	804,749	153,265	958,014	240,921	52,150	293,071	1868

* NOTE.—This table includes Channel Islands vessels, but not those of the British plantations. The home trade signifies on the coasts of the United Kingdom, or to ports between the limits of the River Elbe and Brest. The foreign trade signifies to ports beyond such limits.

No. X.—*A comparative view of the tonnage of the United States from June* 30, 1850, *to June* 30, 1869, *showing, separately, the tonnage of sailing and steam vessels, and the yearly increase or decrease of each class.*

Fiscal years.	Total tonnage.	Tonnage employ'd in steam navigation.	Yearly increase and decrease of steam tonnage.	Tonnage of sailing vessels, including barges and canal-boats.	Yearly increase and decrease of saili'g tonnage.
	Tons and 95ths.	*Tons and 95ths.*	*Tons and 95ths.*	*Tons and 95ths.*	*Tons and 95ths.*
1851	3,772,439.43	583,607.05	*57,660.15	3,188,832.38	*179,325.05
1852	4,138,440.47	634,240.67	*50,633.62	3,504,199.80	*315,367.42
1853	4,407,011.43	514,097.87	†120,142.80	3,892,913.56	*388,713.76
1854	4,802,902.63	676,607.12	*162,509.25	4,126,295.51	*233,381.95
1855	5,212,001.10	770,285.12	*93,678.00	4,441,715.98	*315,420.47
1856	4,871,652.46	673,077.54	†97,207.58	4,198,574.92	†243,141.06
1857	4,940,843.04	705,784.04	*32,706.50	4,235,059.00	*36,484.08
1858	5,049,808.35	729,398.41	*23,614.37	4,320,409.94	*85,350.94
1859	5,145,037.39	768,436.83	*39,038.42	4,376,600.56	*56,190.62
1860	5,353,868.42	867,937.49	*99,500.66	4,485,930.93	*109,330.37
1861	5,539,812.79	877,203.51	*9,266.02	4,662,609.28	*176,678.35
1862	5,112,164.48	710,462.33	†166,741.18	4,401,702.15	†260,907.13
1863	5,155,055.47	575,510.17	†134,952.16	4,579,545.30	*177,843.15
1864	4,986,399.79	978,177.74	*402,667.57	4,008,222.05	†571,323.25
1865‡	5,096,781.80	1,067,139.91	*88,962.17	4,029,641.89	*21,419.84
1866‡	4,310,775.48	1,083,511.99	*16,372.08	3,227,263.49	†802,378.40
1867‡	3,957,514.62	1,122,979.61	*39,467.62	2,834,535.01	†392,728.48
1868‡	4,318,309.50	1,199,414.89	*76,435.28	3,118,894.61	*284,359.60
1869	4,144,640.76	1,103,568.38	†95,851.89	3,041,072.38	†77,822.61

* Increase. † Decrease.
‡ For 1865, 1866, 1867, and 1868 the tonnage is partly "old" and partly "new" admeasurement.

No. XI.—*A statement exhibiting the amount of registered tonnage of the United States, steam and sail, employed in navigation annually, from* 1850 *to* 1869, *inclusive, and the annual increase or decrease of each class.*

Year ending June 30—	Total tonnage.	Registered sail tonnage.	Annual increase or decrease of sail tonnage.	Registered steam tonnage.	Annual increase or decrease of steam tonnage.
1850	1, 585, 198	1, 540, 769	*122, 697	44, 429	*23, 559
1851	1, 726, 307	1, 663, 917	*123, 148	62, 390	*17, 961
1852	1, 899, 478	1, 819, 774	*155, 857	79, 704	*17, 314
1853	2, 103, 674	2, 013, 154	*193, 380	90, 520	*10, 816
1854	2, 333, 819	2, 238, 783	*225, 629	95, 036	*4, 516
1855	2, 555, 136	2, 440, 091	*201, 308	115, 045	*20, 009
1856	2, 491, 402	2, 401, 687	†38, 404	89, 715	†25, 330
1857	2, 463, 967	2, 377, 094	†24, 593	86, 873	†2, 842
1858	2, 577, 769	2, 499, 742	*122, 648	78, 027	†8, 846
1859	2, 507, 402	2, 414, 654	†85, 088	92, 748	*14, 721
1860	2, 546, 237	2, 448, 941	*34, 287	97, 296	*4, 548
1861	2, 642, 628	2, 540, 020	*91, 079	102, 608	*5, 312
1862	2, 291, 251	2, 177, 253	†362, 767	113, 998	*11, 390
1863	2, 026, 114	1, 892, 899	†284, 354	133, 215	*19, 217
1864	1, 581, 895	1, 475, 376	†417, 523	106, 519	†26, 696
1865	1, 602, 583	1, 504, 575	*29, 199	98, 008	†8, 511
1866	1, 492, 926	1, 294, 637	†209, 938	198, 289	*100, 281
1867	1, 568, 032	1, 369, 917	*75, 280	198, 115	†174
1868	1, 565, 732	1, 343, 793	†26, 124	221, 939	*23, 824
1869	1, 566, 421	1, 353, 169	*42, 825	213, 252	†8, 687

* Increase. † Decrease.

No. XII.—*Table showing the tonnage of the United States, June* 30, 1869.

	TONNAGE.		
	Sailing vessels.	Steamers.	Total.
Registered vessels	1, 353, 169	213, 252	1, 566, 421
Licensed and enrolled vessels	1, 687, 903	890, 316	2, 578, 219
Total	3, 041, 072	1, 103, 568	4, 144, 640

No. XIII.—*Statement showing the number and class of vessels built, and the tonnage thereof, in the several States and Territories of the United States from* 1850 *to* 1869, *inclusive.*

Fiscal years.	CLASS OF VESSELS.					Total No. of vessels built.	Total tonnage.
	Ships and barks.	Brigs.	Schooners.	Sloops and canal-boats.	Steamers.		
1850	247	117	547	290	259	1, 460	272, 218. 54
1851	211	65	522	326	233	1, 357	298, 203. 60
1852	255	79	584	267	259	1, 444	351, 493. 41
1853	269	95	681	394	271	1, 710	425, 571. 49
1854	334	112	661	386	281	1, 774	535, 616. 01
1855	381	126	605	669	253	2, 034	583, 450. 04
1856	306	103	594	479	221	1, 703	469, 393. 73
1857	251	58	504	258	263	1, 334	378, 804. 70
1858	222	46	431	400	226	1, 325	242, 286. 69
1859	89	28	297	284	172	870	156, 601. 33
1860	110	36	372	289	264	1, 071	212, 892. 45
1861	110	38	360	371	264	1, 143	233, 194. 35
1862	62	17	207	397	183	866	175, 075. 84
1863	97	34	212	1, 113	367	1, 823	310, 884. 34
1864	112	45	322	1, 389	498	2, 366	514, 740. 64
1865	109	46	369	853	411	1, 788	383, 805. 60
1866*	96	61	457	926	348	1, 888	336, 146. 56
1867*	95	70	517	657	180	1, 519	303, 528. 66
1868*	80	48	590	848	236	1, 802	285, 304. 73
1869*	91	36	506	816	277	1, 726	275, 230. 05

* New admeasurement.

No. XIV.—*Total summary of the tonnage of the United States, June* 30, 1869, *as reported to the Bureau of Statistics.*

Class.	Vessels.	Tons.
Ships	537	....
Barks	818	....
Brigs	607	....
Schooners	10, 870	....
Sloops	3, 913	....
Total sailing vessels	16, 745	2, 074 811. 09
Total steam vessels	3, 361	1, 046, 015. 98
Total unrigged	6, 287	623, 492. 02
Total number of vessels permanently documented	26, 393	3, 744, 319. 09
Total number of vessels temporarily documented	1, 033	401, 046. 99
Total	27, 426	4, 145, 366. 08

No. XV.—*A table showing the amount of American and foreign tonnage entered the ports of the United States from foreign countries in* 1830, 1840, 1850, *and from* 1860 *to* 1869, *both inclusive.*

Fiscal years.	American tonnage.	Foreign tonnage.	American in excess of foreign tonnage.	For'n in excess of American tonnage.
1830	967, 227	131, 900	835, 327	....
1840	1, 576, 946	712, 363	864, 583	....
1850	2, 573, 016	1, 775, 623	797, 393	....
1860	5, 921, 285	2, 353, 911	3, 567, 374	....
1861	5, 023, 917	2, 217, 554	2, 806, 363	....
1862	5, 117, 685	2, 245, 278	2, 872, 407	....
1863	4, 614, 698	2, 640, 378	1, 974, 320	....
1864	3, 066, 434	3, 471, 219	....	404, 785
1865	2, 943, 661	3, 216, 967	....	273, 306
1866	3, 372, 060	4, 410, 424	....	1, 038, 364
1867	3, 455, 052	4, 318, 673	....	863, 621
1868	3, 550, 550	4, 495, 465	....	944, 915
1869	3, 402, 668	5, 347, 694	....	1, 945, 026

No. XVI.—*Table showing the estimated value of American foreign carrying trade during the ten years from* 1860 *to* 1869, *both inclusive.*

Fiscal years.	Amount of registered tonnage June 30.	Estimated specie value, per ton.	Aggregate specie value of tonnage.	Estimated specie value of gross yearly earnings, being 33⅓ per cent. of value.
1850	1, 585, 198	$38	$60, 237, 524	$20, 079, 175
1860	2, 546, 237	41	104, 395, 717	34, 798, 572
1861	2, 642, 628	41	108, 347, 748	36, 115, 916
1862	2, 291, 251	45	103, 106, 295	34, 368, 765
1863	2, 026, 114	45	91, 175, 130	30, 391, 710
1864	1, 581, 895	45	71, 185, 275	23, 728, 425
1865	1, 602, 583	45	72, 116, 235	24, 038, 745
1866	1, 492, 926	45	67, 181, 670	22, 393, 890
1867	1, 568, 032	45	70, 561, 440	23, 520, 480
1868	1, 565, 732	45	70, 457, 940	23, 485, 980
1869	1, 566, 421	45	70, 488, 945	23, 496, 315

No. XVII.—*Table showing the estimated value of American coastwise and inland carrying trade during the ten years from* 1860 *to* 1869, *both inclusive.*

Fiscal years.	Amount of licensed and enrolled tonnage on June 30.	Estimated specie value, per ton.	Aggregate specie value of tonnage.	Estimated specie value of gross yearly earning, being $33\frac{1}{3}$ per cent. of value.
1850	1, 949, 743	$38	$74, 090, 234	$24, 696, 745
1860	2, 807, 631	41	115, 112, 871	38, 370, 957
1861	2, 897, 185	41	118, 784, 585	39, 594, 861
1862	2, 820, 914	45	126, 941, 130	42, 313, 710
1863	3, 099, 967	45	139, 498, 515	46, 499, 505
1864	3, 404, 506	45	153, 202, 770	51, 067, 590
1865	3, 494, 198	45	157, 238, 910	52, 412, 970
1866	2, 817, 852	45	126, 803, 340	42, 267, 780
1867	2, 736, 454	45	123, 140, 430	41, 046, 810
1868	2, 786, 026	45	125, 371, 170	41, 790, 390
1869	2, 578, 219	45	116, 019, 855	38, 673, 285

No. XVIII.—*Table showing the total foreign commerce of the United States during each year from* 1850 *to* 1869, *inclusive.*

Fiscal years.	Exports and imports in American vessels.	Exports and imports in foreign vessels.	Total.
1850	$239, 272, 084	$90, 764, 954	$330, 037, 038
1851	316, 107, 232	118, 505, 711	434, 612, 943
1852	294, 735, 404	123, 219, 817	417, 955, 221
1853	346, 717, 127	152, 237, 677	498, 954, 804
1854	406, 698 539	170, 591, 875	577, 290, 414
1855	405, 485, 462	131, 139, 904	536, 625, 366
1856	482, 268, 274	159, 336, 576	641, 604, 850
1857	510, 331, 027	213, 519, 796	723, 850, 823
1858	447, 191, 304	160, 066, 267	607, 257, 571
1859	465, 741, 381	229, 816, 211	695, 557, 592
1860	507, 247, 757	255, 040, 793	762, 288, 550
1861	381, 516, 788	203, 478, 278	584, 995, 066
1862	217, 695, 418	218, 015, 296	435, 710, 714
1863	241, 872, 471	343, 056, 031	584, 928, 502
1864	184, 061, 486	485, 793, 548	669, 855, 034
1865	167, 402, 872	437, 010, 124	604, 412, 996
1866	325, 711, 861	685, 226, 691	1, 010, 938, 552
1867	296, 998, 387	580, 022, 004	877, 020, 391
1868	297, 981, 573	550, 546, 074	848, 527, 647
1869	289, 950, 272	586, 492, 012	876, 442, 284
Total	6, 824, 986, 719	5, 893, 879, 639	12, 718, 866, 358

No. XIX.—*Total exports of domestic and foreign merchandise combined.*

Fiscal years.	American vessels.	Foreign vessels.	Total.
1850	$99, 615, 041	$52, 283, 679	$151, 898, 720
1851	152, 456, 689	65, 931, 322	218, 388, 011
1852	139, 476, 937	70, 181, 429	209, 658, 366
1853	155, 028, 802	75, 947, 355	230, 976, 157
1854	191, 322, 266	84, 474, 054	275, 796, 320
1855	203, 250, 562	71, 906, 284	275, 156, 846
1856	232, 295, 162	94, 669, 146	326, 964, 308
1857	251, 214, 857	111, 745, 825	362, 960, 682
1858	243, 491, 288	81, 153, 133	324, 644, 421
1859	249, 617, 953	107, 171, 509	356, 789, 462
1860	279, 082, 902	121, 039, 394	400, 122, 296
1861	179, 972, 733	69, 372, 180	249, 344, 913
1862	125, 421, 318	104, 517, 667	229, 938, 985
1863	132, 127, 890	199, 880, 691	332, 008, 581
1864	102, 849, 409	237, 442, 730	340, 292, 139
1865	90, 017, 756	262, 839, 588	352, 857, 344
1866	213, 671, 466	351, 754, 928	565, 426, 394
1867	179, 788, 851	279, 399, 969	459, 188, 820
1868	175, 016, 348	301, 886, 491	476, 902, 839
1869	153, 148, 248	285, 979, 781	439, 128, 029
Total	3, 548, 866, 478	3, 029, 577, 155	6, 578, 443, 633

No. XX.—*Table showing the amount of foreign merchandise imported into the United States in American and foreign vessels, respectively, during the fiscal years from* 1850 *to* 1869, *both inclusive.* (*Expressed in specie value at foreign ports of exportation.*)

Years.	IMPORTS.		
	In American vessels.	In foreign vessels.	Total in American and foreign vessels.
1850	$139, 657, 043	$38, 481, 275	$178, 138, 318
1851	163, 650, 543	52, 574, 389	216, 224, 932
1852	155, 258, 467	53, 038, 388	*212, 945, 442
1853	191, 688, 325	76, 290, 322	267, 978, 647
1854	215, 376, 273	86, 117, 821	*304, 562, 381
1855	202, 234, 900	59, 233, 620	261, 468, 520
1856	249, 972, 512	64, 667, 430	314, 639, 942
1857	259, 116, 170	101, 773, 971	360, 890, 141
1858	203, 700, 016	78, 913, 134	282, 613, 150
1859	216, 123, 428	122, 644, 702	338, 768, 130
1860	228, 164, 855	134, 001, 399	362, 166, 254
1861	201, 544, 055	134, 106, 098	335, 650, 153
1862	92, 274, 100	113, 497, 629	205, 771, 729
1863	109, 744, 580	143, 175, 340	252, 919, 920
1864	81, 212, 077	248, 350, 818	329, 562, 895
1865	74, 385, 116	174, 170, 536	248, 555, 652
1866	112, 040, 395	333, 471, 763	445, 512, 158
1867	117, 209, 536	300, 622, 035	417, 831, 571
1868	122, 965, 225	248, 659, 583	371, 624, 808
1869	136, 802, 024	300, 512, 231	437, 314, 255
Total	3, 273, 119, 640	2, 864, 302, 484	6, 145, 138, 998

* In the year 1852 $4,640,587, and in 1854 $3,068,287, were imported into San Francisco; class of vessels in which brought cannot be stated.

No. XXI.—*Statement exhibiting the arrival and departure, at certain specified ports, of American and foreign vessels, in certain portions of the foreign trade of the United States, 1856 to 1860, and 1865 to 1869, both inclusive.*

No. I.—DISTRICT OF BOSTON.

ENTERED.

District.	From 1856 to 1860 inclusive.						From 1865 to 1869 inclusive.						Countries.
	American.		Foreign.		Total.		American.		Foreign.		Total.		
	Number.	Tonnage.	Number.	Tonnage.	Number.	Tonnage.	Number.	Tonnage.	Number.	Tonnage.	Number.	Tonnage.	
Boston.....	37	21, 992	1	472	38	22, 464	18	12, 218	12	6, 207	30	18, 425	Dutch E. Indies.
	403	319, 497	— 9	8, 624	412	328, 121	123	113, 858	63	50, 871	186	164, 729	British E. Indies.
	1	311	....	....	1	311	....	....	3	1, 538	3	1, 538	Australia.
	67	55, 924	1	892	68	56, 816	25	23, 376	7	6, 008	32	29, 384	Philippine Islands.
	20	15, 399	1	125	21	15, 524	5	2, 709	12	5, 601	17	8, 310	China.
	....	....	....	....	....	....	....	....	1	757	1	757	Japan.
Total	528	413, 123	12	10, 113	540	423, 236	171	152, 161	98	70, 982	269	223, 143	
Boston.....	49	16, 180	23	9, 599	72	25, 779	11	5, 010	18	6, 949	29	11, 959	France on Med.
	45	15, 943	27	6, 724	72	22, 667	33	10, 097	23	3, 851	56	13, 948	Spain on Med.
	203	81, 246	131	26, 507	334	107, 753	184	79, 124	76	28, 451	260	107, 575	Italy and Sicily.
	5	2, 411	....	....	5	2, 411	....	....	....	....	....	....	Austria.
	102	33, 310	6	1, 645	108	34, 955	33	11, 817	25	7, 971	58	19, 788	Turkey & Greece.
Total	404	149, 090	187	44, 475	591	193, 565	261	106, 048	142	47, 222	403	153, 270	

CLEARED.

District.	Number.	Tonnage.	Number.	Tonnage.	Number.	Tonnage.	Number.	Tonnage.	Number.	Tonnage.	Number.	Tonnage.	Countries.
Boston.....	23	11, 518	5	1, 912	28	13, 430	22	16, 184	3	2, 030	25	18, 214	Dutch E. Indies.
	206	133, 606	1	475	207	134, 081	94	86, 202	16	14, 763	110	100, 965	British E. Indies.
	93	63, 618	1	1, 545	94	65, 163	61	39, 437	39	20, 164	100	59, 601	Australia.
	9	7, 083	....	....	9	7, 083	....	....	....	....	....	....	Philippine Islands.
	38	22, 210	....	....	38	22, 210	21	16, 603	5	3, 976	26	20, 579	China.
	....	....	....	....	....	....	3	1, 731	....	....	3	1, 731	Japan.
Total	369	238, 035	7	3, 932	376	241, 967	201	160, 157	63	40, 933	264	201, 090	
Boston.....	38	10, 661	8	2, 016	46	12, 677	.5	1, 527	5	1, 173	10	2, 700	France on Med.
	24	5, 865	3	871	27	6, 736	30	9, 897	7	1, 865	37	11, 762	Spain on Med.
	30	8, 680	11	3, 281	41	11, 961	10	3, 105	3	919	13	4, 024	Italy and Sicily.
	36	11, 463	6	2, 049	42	13, 512	1	384	1	211	2	595	Austria.
	116	41, 912	4	2, 266	120	44, 178	26	8, 009	13	3, 539	39	11, 548	Turkey & Greece.
Total	244	78, 581	32	10, 483	276	89, 064	72	22, 922	29	7, 707	101	30, 629	

No. XXI.—*Arrival and departure of American and foreign vessels, &c.*—Continued.

No. II.—DISTRICT OF NEW YORK.

Districts.	ENTERED.												Countries.
	From 1856 to 1860 inclusive.						From 1865 to 1869 inclusive.						
	American.		Foreign.		Total.		American.		Foreign.		Total.		
	Number.	Tonnage.	Number.	Tonnage.	Number.	Tonnage.	Number.	Tonnage.	Number.	Tonnage.	Number.	Tonnage.	
New York	28	14, 074	1	360	29	14, 434	10	7, 335	31	14, 535	41	21, 870	Dutch East Indies.
	136	117, 768	25	14, 238	161	132, 006	58	54, 983	170	141, 010	228	195, 993	British East Indies.
	13	5, 196	1	250	14	5, 446	4	3, 178	8	3, 818	12	6, 996	Australia.
	67	67, 049	4	2, 790	71	69, 839	60	63, 275	31	24, 605	91	87, 880	Philippine Islands.
	234	213, 958	16	8, 868	250	222, 826	64	46, 750	227	108, 821	291	155, 571	China.
	....	....	....	....	....	....	11	7, 383	54	23, 314	65	30, 697	Japan.
Total....	478	418, 045	47	26, 506	525	444, 551	207	182, 904	521	316, 103	728	499, 007	
New York	117	56, 724	68	24, 867	185	81, 591	54	26, 714	131	57, 066	185	83, 780	France on Medite'n.
	209	57, 904	116	22, 810	325	80, 714	88	29, 459	141	39, 000	229	68, 459	Spain on Medite'n.
	335	145, 052	237	70, 534	572	215, 586	252	114, 855	480	198, 389	732	313, 244	Italy and Sicily.
	20	8, 718	34	11, 684	54	20, 402	2	949	76	30, 999	78	31, 948	Austria.
	25	9, 072	46	15, 397	71	24, 469	6	2, 150	55	13, 430	61	15, 580	Turkey and Greece.
Total....	706	277, 470	501	145, 292	1207	422, 762	402	174, 127	883	338, 884	1285	513, 011	

Districts.	CLEARED.												Countries.
New York	30	20, 939	2	849	32	21, 788	6	4, 385	10	6, 631	16	11, 016	Dutch East Indios.
	56	41, 617	31	17, 399	87	59, 016	4	2, 925	24	14, 059	28	16, 984	British East Indies.
	186	179, 915	22	12, 122	208	192, 037	42	29, 872	109	61, 512	151	91, 384	Australia.
	2	755	....	....	2	755	1	729	....	....	1	729	Philippine Islands.
	145	124, 818	1	369	146	125, 187	81	71, 974	49	36, 382	130	108, 356	China.
	....	....	....	....	....	....	25	33, 270	6	5, 337	31	38, 607	Japan.
Total....	419	368, 044	56	30, 739	475	398, 783	159	143, 155	198	123, 921	357	267, 076	
New York	150	58, 224	35	9, 421	185	67, 645	134	56, 976	115	37, 357	249	94, 333	France on Medite'n.
	143	38, 548	45	13, 572	188	52, 120	68	23, 434	87	24, 076	155	47, 510	Spain on Medite'n.
	40	12, 986	60	18, 979	100	31, 965	69	37, 509	192	86, 840	261	124, 349	Italy and Sicily.
	10	4, 881	14	5, 021	24	9, 902	2	1, 040	62	18, 662	64	19, 702	Austria.
	51	16, 713	13	3, 766	64	20, 479	16	5, 334	33	8, 043	49	13, 377	Turkey and Greece.
Total....	394	131, 352	167	50, 759	561	182, 111	289	124, 293	489	174, 978	778	299, 271	

No. XXI.—*Arrival and departure of American and foreign vessels, &c.*—Continued.

No. III.—DISTRICT OF PHILADELPHIA.

ENTERED.

District.	From 1856 to 1860, inclusive.						From 1865 to 1869, inclusive.						Countries.
	American.		Foreign.		Total.		American.		Foreign.		Total.		
	Number.	Tonnage.	Number.	Tonnage.	Number.	Tonnage.	Number.	Tonnage.	Number.	Tonnage.	Number.	Tonnage.	
Philadelp'a	13	11, 345	1	1, 007	14	12, 352	2	736			2	736	Br. East Indies.
							1	421			1	421	Australia.
Total....	13	11, 345	1	1, 007	14	12, 352	3	1, 157			3	1, 157	
Philadelp'a	3	624	3	706	6	1, 330	1	295	4	933	5	1, 228	France on Med'n.
	10	2, 350	13	3, 032	23	5, 382	3	921	5	891	8	1, 812	Spain on Med'n.
	97	39, 393	71	22, 201	168	61, 594	76	27, 099	90	25, 660	166	52, 759	Italy and Sicily.
Total....	110	42, 367	87	25, 939	197	68, 306	80	28, 315	99	27, 484	179	55, 799	
CLEARED.													
Philadolp'a	3	2, 613			3	2, 613							British E. Indies.
													Australia.
	1	847			1	847							Philippine Isla'ds.
	6	5, 838			6	5, 838	2	2, 013	1	716	3	2, 729	China.
							1	338			1	338	Japan.
Total....	10	9, 298			10	9, 298	3	2, 351	1	716	4	3, 067	
Philadelp'a	4	1, 705	3	619	7	2, 324	93	36, 206	20	6, 670	113	42, 876	France on Med'n.
			2	326	2	326			8	1, 500	8	1, 500	Spain on Med'n.
			3	919	3	919	24	7, 920	35	10, 402	59	18, 322	Italy and Sicily.
	1	299			1	299	7	2, 569	2	1, 022	9	3, 591	Austria.
							1	248	1	190	2	438	Turkey & Greece.
Total....	5	2, 004	8	1, 864	13	3, 868	125	46, 943	66	19, 784	191	66, 727	

No. XXI.—*Arrival and departure of American and foreign vessels, &c.*—Continued.

No. IV.—DISTRICT OF BALTIMORE.

District.	ENTERED.												Countries.
	From 1856 to 1860, inclusive.						From 1865 to 1869, inclusive.						
	American.		Foreign.		Total.		American.		Foreign.		Total.		
	Number.	Tonnage.	Number.	Tonnage.	Number.	Tonnage.	Number.	Tonnage.	Number.	Tonnage.	Number.	Tonnage.	
Baltimore..	....	....	1	781	1	781	....	....	....	....	....	....	Brit'h East Indies.
Baltimore..	4	2,526	2	498	6	3,024	....	....	1	228	1	228	France on Med'n.
	9	2,040	8	1,028	17	3,068	5	4,354	8	1,683	13	6,037	Spain on Med'n.
	46	16,043	22	4,252	68	20,295	12	3,904	46	13,026	58	16,930	Italy and Sicily.
Total....	59	20,609	32	5,778	91	26,387	17	8,258	55	14,937	72	23,195	

CLEARED.

District.	Number.	Tonnage.	Number.	Tonnage.	Number.	Tonnage.	Number.	Tonnage.	Number.	Tonnage.	Number.	Tonnage.	Countries.
Baltimore..	....	....	3	1,639	3	1,639	....	....	....	....	....	....	British East Ind's.
	2	1,392	....	....	2	1,392	....	....	....	....	....	....	Australia.
	1	910	....	....	1	910			....	....	....	....	Philippine Islands.
	2	3,433	1	1,313	3	4,746	1	679	2	1,309	3	1,988	China.
	....	....	....	....	....	....	8	7,782	1	987	9	8,769	Japan.
Total....	5	5,735	4	2,952	9	8,687	9	8,461	3	2,296	12	10,757	
Baltimore..	22	11,746	2	337	24	12,083	5	2,438	2	1,627	7	4,065	France on Med'n.
	6	2,116	1	189	7	2,305	7	2,121	7	1,031	14	3,152	Spain on Med'n.
	4	1,013	4	659	8	1,672	5	1,383	6	1,156	11	2,539	Italy and Sicily.
	5	2,246	....	....	5	2,246	....	....	1	246	1	246	Austria.
Total....	37	17,121	7	1,185	44	18,306	17	5,942	16	4,060	33	10,002	

No. XXI.—*Arrival and departure of American and foreign vessels, &c.*—Continued.

No. V.—DISTRICTS OF RICHMOND AND CHARLESTON.

ENTERED.

Districts.	From 1856 to 1860, inclusive.						From 1865 to 1869, inclusive.						Countries.
	American.		Foreign.		Total.		American.		Foreign.		Total.		
	Number.	Tonnage.	Number.	Tonnage.	Number.	Tonnage.	Number.	Tonnage.	Number.	Tonnage.	Number.	Tonnage.	
Richmond	1	533			1	533							Spain on Med.
Charleston	1	883	1	1,029	2	1,912							British E. Indies.
Charleston	3	2,144	4	1,216									France on Med.
	5	3,535	49	18,986									Spain on Med.
			4	1,982									Italy.
	1	533											Austria.
			2	967									Turkey.
Total	9	6,212	59	23,151									

CLEARED.

Districts.	Number.	Tonnage.	Number.	Tonnage.	Number.	Tonnage.	Number.	Tonnage.	Number.	Tonnage.	Number.	Tonnage.	Countries.
Richmond	6	4,294											Australia.
Richmond	8	4,414			8	4,414							France on Med.
	4	2,073	2	672	6	2,745			5	1,439	5	1,439	Italy.
	33	18,310	5	3,143	38	21,453			5	1,725	5	1,725	Austria.
Total	45	24,797	7	3,815	52	28,612			10	3,164	10	3,164	
Charleston	1	572			1	572							China.
Charleston	7	2,222	4	913									France on Med.
	13	3,906	377	99,993			1	235	43	9,333			Spain on Med.
	4	1,801	1	290									Italy.
	2	1,209											Austria.
Total	26	9,138	382	101,196			1	235	43	9,333			

No. XXI.—*Arrival and departure of American and foreign vessels, &c.*—Continued.

No. VI.—DISTRICT OF NEW ORLEANS.

District.	ENTERED.												Countries.
	From 1856 to 1860, inclusive.						From 1865 to 1869, inclusive.						
	American.		Foreign.		Total.		American.		Foreign.		Total.		
	Number.	Tonnage.	Number.	Tonnage.	Number.	Tonnage.	Number.	Tonnage.	Number.	Tonnage.	Number.	Tonnage.	
N. Orleans.	7	6,909	3	2,673	10	9,582	1	1.043	3	3,359	4	4.402	British E. Indies.
	1	997	1	1,207	2	2,204	...	...	...	...	...	...	Australia.
Total....	8	7,906	4	3,880	12	11,786	1	1,043	3	3,359	4	4,402	
N. Orleans.	30	30,034	21	9,887	51	39,921	5	3,009	13	5,759	18	8,768	France on Med.
	42	25,083	129	57,461	171	82,544	12	8,942	12	6,284	24	15,226	Spain on Med.
	107	71,762	115	41,350	222	113,112	12	4,275	57	16,626	69	20,901	Italy and Sicily.
	12	11,483	1	548	13	12,031	...	...	...	...	...	...	Austria.
	5	5,418	2	1,572	7	6,990	...	...	...	...	...	...	Turkey & Greece.
Total....	196	143,780	268	110,818	464	254,598	29	16,226	82	28,669	111	44,895	
	CLEARED.												
N. Orleans.	2	2,253	...	...	2	2,253	...	...	...	...	...	...	British E. Indies.
	...	...	...	...	...	...	...	...	...	...	...	...	Australia.
Total....	2	2,253	...	...	2	2,253	...	...	...	...	...	...	
N. Orleans.	68	34,003	28	11,050	96	45,053	3	1,261	4	919	7	2,180	France on Med.
	28	13,607	443	160,454	471	174,061	5	1,960	194	58,274	199	60,234	Spain on Med.
	140	91,433	53	19,688	193	111,121	10	4,606	28	7,042	38	11,648	Italy and Sicily.
	40	25,440	13	5,067	53	30,507	...	...	...	...	...	...	Austria.
	...	...	...	...	...	...	...	...	...	...	...	...	Turkey & Greece.
	276	164,483	537	196,259	813	360,742	18	7,827	226	66,235	244	74,062	

No. XXI.—*Arrival and departure of American and foreign vessels, &c.*—Continued.

No. VII.—DISTRICTS OF SAN FRANCISCO AND PUGET SOUND.

District.	ENTERED. From 1855 to 1860, inclusive. American. Number.	Tonnage.	Foreign. Number.	Tonnage.	Total. Number.	Tonnage.	From 1865 to 1869, inclusive. American. Number.	Tonnage.	Foreign. Number.	Tonnage.	Total. Number.	Tonnage.	Countries.
S. Francisco	12	4, 998	11	3, 820	23	8, 818	2	469	13	4, 736	15	5, 205	Dutch E. Indies.
	8	5, 006	5	2, 025	13	7, 031	...	...	11	6, 628	11	6, 628	British E. Indies.
	32	14, 910	40	17, 436	72	32, 346	40	24, 655	182	89, 651	222	114, 306	Australia.
	12	5, 363	9	2, 827	21	8, 190	9	6, 057	9	7, 236	18	13, 293	Philippine Islands.
	107	90, 999	69	35, 108	176	126, 107	62	55, 081	94	63, 726	156	118, 807	China.
	8	1, 604	1	126	9	1, 730	40	78, 073	28	13, 720	68	91, 793	Japan.
Total	179	122, 880	135	61, 342	314	184, 222	153	164, 335	337	185, 697	490	350, 032	
S. Francisco	...	...	6	2, 132	6	2, 132	...	...	6	2, 821	6	2, 821	France on Med.
	2	461	1	369	3	830	...	...	3	989	3	989	Spain on Modite'n.
Total	2	461	7	2, 501	9	2, 962	...	...	9	3, 810	9	3, 810	
Puget So'nd	1	532	2	961	3	1, 493	...	...	1	336	1	336	Australia.
	...	...	1	424	1	424	...	...	...	...	...	...	France on Med.
	...	...	1	273	1	273	5	3, 469	6	6, 517	11	9, 986	China.
	...	...	...	...	...	...	1	449	1	650	2	1, 099	Japan.
Total	1	532	4	1, 658	5	2, 190	6	3, 918	8	7, 503	14	11, 421	
							CLEARED.						
S. Francisco	8	4, 571	8	3, 458	16	8, 029	1	164	5	2, 067	6	2, 231	Dutch E. Indies.
	56	59, 319	11	4, 668	67	63, 987	6	5, 994	6	2, 861	12	8, 855	British E. Indies.
	70	43, 644	74	32, 140	144	75, 784	23	12, 190	156	64, 596	179	76, 786	Australia.
	41	37, 000	5	1, 835	46	38, 835	11	10, 979	5	1, 745	16	12, 724	Philippine Islands.
	204	213, 841	78	38, 835	282	252, 676	92	88, 503	83	50, 782	175	139, 285	China.
	10	2, 281	...	...	10	2, 281	35	79, 690	6	1, 735	41	81, 425	Japan.
Total	389	360, 656	176	80, 936	565	441, 592	168	197, 520	261	123, 786	429	321, 306	
S. Francisco	...	...	...	...	...	...	1	1, 016	...	...	1	1, 016	Franco on Med.
Pugot So'nd	...	...	...	...	...	...	...	...	4	1, 734	4	1, 734	British E. Indies.
	8	5, 837	6	3, 302	14	9, 139	13	8, 629	21	12, 855	34	21, 484	Australia.
	7	3, 026	8	3, 104	15	6, 130	8	4, 730	24	17, 839	32	22, 569	China.
	...	...	...	...	...	...	1	, 738	...	...	1	738	Philippine Islands
Total	15	8, 863	14	6, 406	29	15, 269	22	14, 097	49	32, 428	71	46, 525	

No. XXII.—*Statement exhibiting the entrances and clearances of vessels from and to each principal foreign country for the two periods, 1850 to 1859, and 1860 to 1869, all inclusive.*

Countries.	ENTERED.								CLEARED.							
	AMERICAN.				FOREIGN.				AMERICAN.				FOREIGN.			
	From 1850 to 1859, inclusive.		From 1860 to 1869, inclusive.		From 1850 to 1859, inclusive.		From 1860 to 1869, inclusive.		From 1850 to 1859, inclusive.		From 1860 to 1869, inclusive.		From 1850 to 1859, inclusive.		From 1860 to 1869, inclusive.	
	No.	Tons.	No.	Tons.	No.	Tons.	No.	Tons.	No.	Tons.	No.	Tons.	No.	Tons.	No.	Tons.
Russia	219	98, 455	219	76, 988	41	15, 674	147	55, 657	220	126, 400	171	81, 452	62	33, 115	188	70, 965
Prussia	12	3, 473	1	916	3	1, 093	2	700	5	1, 633	13	5, 420	35	10, 298	117	38, 674
Sweden and Norway	108	53, 013	53	29, 388	339	110, 279	200	76, 657	76	38, 708	20	9, 213	204	61, 621	56	17, 489
Swedish West Indies	91	12, 629	41	5, 792	6	524	26	3, 669	89	15, 637	41	11, 949	5	738	15	2, 075
Denmark	3	1, 081	7	11, 316	12	3, 229	6	2, 871	19	6, 517	4	1, 358	78	25, 025	31	9, 113
Danish West Indies	690	142, 680	446	110, 045	142	43, 581	325	90, 841	1, 077	203, 553	703	152, 280	165	43, 135	514	88, 762
Hamburg and Bremen	335	303, 519	98	133, 787	2, 662	1, 408, 867	2, 121	2, 587, 261	325	298, 636	143	153, 526	1, 923	1, 088, 603	2, 242	2, 542, 356
Holland	302	164, 823	115	88, 674	393	148, 270	351	167, 134	316	180, 694	173	115, 144	603	229, 936	625	274, 896
Dutch West Indies	716	134, 840	357	73, 589	308	45, 069	498	86, 459	411	80, 969	228	37, 781	39	6, 352	258	49, 725
Dutch Guiana	322	68, 407	152	40, 093	71	12, 066	188	38, 700	250	54, 306	159	33, 913	33	5, 437	174	35, 640
Dutch East Indies	141	66, 316	61	34, 496	22	7, 135	77	33, 119	118	60, 577	63	42, 455	94	42, 927	27	15, 697
Belgium	462	308, 273	175	145, 981	201	92, 126	367	204, 450	502	334, 562	210	150, 612	147	67, 994	805	406, 398
England	9, 064	8, 165, 144	5, 185	5, 350, 347	5, 369	3, 908, 780	7, 344	8, 612, 874	7, 688	7, 495, 089	4, 688	4, 918, 174	4, 364	3, 556, 652	7, 384	8, 621, 982
Scotland	450	241, 095	286	191, 958	1, 164	661, 783	952	790, 456	387	215, 609	246	181, 119	415	281, 987	598	550, 775
Ireland	96	41, 732	112	61, 034	857	376, 121	547	324, 426	289	150, 807	408	231, 176	507	196, 934	2, 829	1, 193, 864
Gibraltar and Malta	111	46, 553	44	22, 817	66	28, 654	56	22, 935	424	105, 920	304	102, 351	69	15, 817	326	87, 323
British North American Possessions*	5, 660	1, 296, 851	9, 331	2, 705, 483	37, 046	3, 742, 190	35, 490	4, 564, 071	7, 231	2, 404, 735	9, 919	3, 375, 986	41, 157	5, 209, 844	38, 055	5, 579, 278
British West Indies	3, 836	731, 544	3, 239	674, 195	3, 044	413, 460	4, 156	708, 998	5, 546	1, 006, 523	3, 564	677, 003	2, 726	365, 634	4, 064	723, 656
British Honduras and Guiana	514	102, 739	620	113, 213	412	63, 673	863	158, 425	907	188, 194	742	152, 942	500	76, 489	876	158, 690
British Possessions in Africa	172	45, 000	284	79, 583	32	8, 121	267	72, 842	243	79, 819	308	94, 157	39	11, 759	229	63, 761
British East Indies	896	614, 501	522	449, 095	72	38, 486	301	240, 880	783	524, 249	250	198, 926	97	48, 649	57	36, 543
Australia	120	43, 576	144	81, 723	173	54, 821	283	134, 637	652	377, 247	393	260, 018	329	103, 436	491	236, 318
France	2, 739	2, 119, 106	1, 264	1, 065, 559	1, 016	365, 502	1, 155	656, 478	3, 331	2, 285, 048	1, 872	1, 405, 876	569	201, 160	1, 052	579, 716
French Possessions in America	427	69, 029	184	36, 299	208	43, 616	359	98, 058	1, 122	182, 179	656	112, 856	325	45, 141	646	103, 775
French Possessions in Africa	5	1, 105	70	20, 256	3	744	29	7, 533	7	1, 353	133	26, 651	15	2, 345	44	8, 541
Spain	988	348, 827	664	264, 499	823	260, 270	608	198, 800	906	302, 369	598	223, 844	1, 951	550, 512	972	330, 537
Canary Islands	77	15, 868	26	9, 396	34	8, 408	26	8, 773	80	20, 109	48	12, 934	38	10, 741	42	10, 850
Philippine Islands	289	203, 437	228	218, 484	40	17, 678	81	56, 450	175	130, 502	47	41, 798	49	19, 040	20	7, 201
Cuba and Porto Rico	20, 295	5, 384, 077	17, 748	5, 521, 950	2, 704	613, 851	7, 337	1, 800, 155	18, 627	4, 868, 503	15, 788	4, 983, 061	1, 061	287, 808	4, 257	1, 095, 500
Portugal and Madeira	156	50, 110	76	29, 525	254	54, 482	221	67, 559	313	87, 478	174	52, 426	307	72, 184	274	78, 512
Azores and Cape de Verde Islands	187	43, 477	123	38, 370	66	16, 921	121	42, 825	211	50, 195	131	31, 305	70	15, 805	138	35, 729
Italy and Sicily	1, 461	560, 839	1, 299	546, 374	1, 009	287, 070	1, 391	456, 164	473	200, 866	357	160, 123	316	95, 993	424	162, 823

* This designation does not include Canada, nothing of the Lake tonnage being included in this statement.

No. XXII.—*Entrances and clearances of vessels from and to each principal foreign country, &c.*—Continued.

Countries.	ENTERED.								CLEARED.							
	AMERICAN.				FOREIGN.				AMERICAN.				FOREIGN.			
	From 1850 to 1859, inclusive.		From 1860 to 1869, inclusive.		From 1850 to 1859, inclusive.		From 1860 to 1869, inclusive.		From 1850 to 1859, inclusive.		From 1860 to 1869, inclusive.		From 1850 to 1859, inclusive.		From 1860 to 1869, inclusive.	
	No.	Tons.	No.	Tons.	No.	Tons.	No.	Tons.	No.	Tons.	No.	Tons.	No.	Tons.	No.	Tons.
Austria	72	40, 805	18	7, 974	59	26, 664	107	41, 867	269	126, 050	57	21, 614	181	69, 058	84	26, 454
Greece	10	2, 421	4	1, 383	13	3, 169	59	11, 904	3	635	1	375	....	....	....	....
Turkey	289	96, 569	144	52, 679	53	19, 668	78	28, 553	233	72, 145	155	53, 248	19	6, 266	68	18, 461
Africa generally	603	137, 364	320	95, 225	38	9, 072	71	21, 311	699	163, 729	290	89, 833	41	8, 185	36	10, 004
Hayti and St. Domingo	2, 961	448, 476	1, 398	239, 322	462	73, 488	1, 370	214, 566	2, 404	350, 977	1, 409	247, 040	365	62, 299	1, 459	240, 930
Mexico	1, 500	376, 137	1, 207	434, 240	757	127, 248	1, 366	256, 276	1, 534	422, 220	1, 346	521, 122	860	160, 855	1, 658	300, 886
Central American States	596	440, 456	215	183, 264	47	9, 489	128	26, 327	702	471, 182	232	204, 230	93	22, 319	142	30, 432
United States of Colombia	1, 893	1, 463, 239	1, 488	2, 053, 515	109	32, 654	181	39, 818	2, 025	1, 522, 700	1, 859	2, 237, 165	120	35, 538	258	68, 323
Venezuela	972	204, 202	253	66, 237	218	40, 226	449	100, 387	706	157, 239	224	56, 557	128	27, 190	469	109, 632
Brazil	3, 010	854, 276	1, 398	523, 876	725	194, 357	2, 203	560, 111	2, 702	744, 087	1, 322	489, 809	168	42, 067	1, 155	266, 712
Uruguay and Argentine Republic	578	179, 116	490	193, 918	193	51, 645	455	167, 682	925	306, 816	833	370, 157	184	50, 314	618	248, 042
Chili	433	183, 170	181	103, 650	494	152, 493	171	80, 060	687	299, 047	239	148, 360	604	191, 604	211	103, 024
Peru	963	677, 637	272	248, 505	249	96, 200	139	70, 007	674	498, 168	382	396, 105	375	169, 521	232	128, 520
Sandwich Islands	620	176, 383	369	157, 061	133	20, 671	64	26, 178	721	221, 874	399	177, 421	225	41, 708	82	31, 563
Other islands of the Pacific	103	20, 537	135	41, 840	56	8, 260	67	11, 516	112	39, 563	138	57, 109	51	7, 279	71	11, 914
China and Japan	713	514, 434	515	469, 537	316	148, 520	574	317, 087	827	663, 812	692	625, 925	297	131, 740	318	193, 606
Whale Fisheries	1, 424	419, 687	954	251, 582	8	947	....	....	1, 824	540, 233	815	210, 215	60	17, 013	....	....
	67, 684	27, 717, 028	52, 535	23, 355, 033	62, 522	13, 867, 315	73, 377	24, 344, 507	69, 850	28, 679, 363	52, 947	23, 944, 114	62, 063	13, 826, 067	74, 691	25, 005, 667

No. XXIII.—*Statement of steamers making regular trips between ports of the United States and foreign ports, in* 1860 *and in* 1869.

TABLE A.

STEAMSHIP LINES FROM NEW YORK TO FOREIGN PORTS.—1860.

Name of line and port of destination.	Names of steamers.	Tonnage.	Material.	Flag.	Total tonnage each line.
Pacific Mail Steamship Line. From New York to Aspinwall.	Atlantic	2,846	Wood.	American	5,569
	Baltic	2,723	..do...	....do.	
Atlantic Mail Steamship Line. From New York to Aspinwall.	Ariel	1,295	Wood.	American	6,074
	North Star	1,868	..do...	....do.	
	Northern Light	1,768	..do...	....do.	
From New York to Havana	Quaker City	1,143	..do...	....do.	
North Atlantic Mail Steamship Line. From New York to Havre.	Adriatic	4,145	Wood.	American	9,630
	Illinois	2,124	..do...	....do.	
	Vanderbilt	3,361	..do...	....do.	
Havre Steam Navigation Company. From New York to Havre.	Arago	*2,240	Wood.	American	4,548
	Fulton	*2,308	..do...	....do.	
North German Lloyds. From New York to Bremen, via Southampton.	Bremen	2,398	Iron..	German	4,764
	New York	2,366	..do...	....do.	
Hamburg and American Steam Packet Company. From New York to Hamburg.	Hammonia	*2,964	Iron..	German	9,350
	Borussia	*2,133	..do...	....do.	
	Bavaria	*2,235	..do...	....do.	
	Teutonia	*2,027	..do...	....do.	
British and North American Royal Mail Steamship Company. From New York to Liverpool.	Africa	2,087	Wood.	British	25,744
	Asia	2,051	..do...	....do.	
	Arabia	2,286	Iron..	....do.	
	Australasian	2,663	..do...	....do.	
	Balbec	940	..do...	....do.	
	Etna	1,968	Wood.	....do.	
	Java	*2,781	Iron..	....do.	
	Jura	2,045	..do...	....do.	
	Kedar	*1,825	..do...	....do.	
	Persia	3,688	Wood.	....do.	
	Damascus	1,116	..do...	....do.	
	Savonia	2,294	Iron..	....do.	
Liverpool, New York, and Philadelphia Steamship Company, "Inman Line." From New York to Liverpool, via Queenstown.	City of Baltimore	*2,323	Iron..	British	13,372
	City of Washington	*2,386	..do...	....do.	
	City of Manchester	*1,895	..do...	....do.	
	City of Edinburgh	2,188	..do...	....do.	
	Glasgow	1,649	..do...	....do.	
	Kangaroo	1,516	..do...	....do.	
	Vigo	1,415	..do...	....do.	
Anchor Line. From New York to Glasgow.	John Bell	1,103	Iron..	British	3,392
	United Kingdom	1,155	..do...	....do.	
	United States	1,134	..do...	....do.	
Galway Line. From New York to Galway.	Prince Albert	431	Iron..	British	7,082
	Parana	2,570	..do...	....do.	
	Golden Fleece	2,328	..do...	....do.	
	Circassian	1,753	..do...	....do.	

* Tonnage under new admeasurement.

NOTE.—It may be proper to state that there may have been other vessels belonging to the above lines in 1860; if so, they did not come to this port in that year.

No. XXIII.—*Statement of steamers making regular trips between ports of the United States and foreign ports, in 1860 and in 1869*—Continued.

STEAMSHIP LINES FROM PORT OF NEW YORK TO FOREIGN PORTS, JANUARY 1, 1870.

Name of line and port of destination.	Names of steamers.	Tonnage.	Material.	Flag.	Total tonnage each line.
New York and Mexican Steamship Line. From New York to Vera Cruz and Sisal, via Havana.	City of Mexico.........screw.	1,200	Wood.	American.....	2,325
	Cleopatra..................do..	1,125	..do...	....do.	
Atlantic Mail Steamship Line. From New York to Havana.	Moro Castle ....side-wheel.	1,680	Wood.	American.....	5,216
	Eagle......................do..	1,385	..do...	....do.	
	Columbia ....do..	1,271	..do...	....do.	
	Missouri ....screw.	1,180	..do...	....do.	
Pacific Mail Steamship Line. From New York to Aspinwall.	Henry Chauncey ..side-wheel.	2,556	Wood.	American.....	12,034
	Arizona ....do..	2,740	..do...	....do.	
	Alaska ....do..	4,011	..do...	....do.	
	Rising Star ....do..	2,727	..do...	....do.	
United States and Brazil Mail Steamship Line. From New York to Rio de Janeiro, via the West Indies.	Merrimack.............screw.	2,031	Iron..	American.....	6,166
	South America ....side-wheel.	2,050	Wood.	....do.	
	North America.........screw.	2,085	..do...	....do.	
New York and Bermuda Steamship Line. From New York to Bermuda.	Fah Kee ....screw.	601	Wood.	American.....	601
Port au Prince Line...........	City of Port au Prince .screw.	371	Iron..	American.....	371
British and North American Royal Mail Steamship Line. From New York to Liverpool.	Russia..................screw.	3,013	Iron..	British........	42,038
	Scotia..............side-wheel.	3,865	..do...	....do.	
	China ....screw.	2,661	..do...	....do.	
	Cuba ....do..	2,781	..do...	....do.	
	Java.......................do..	2,781	..do...	....do.	
	Tarifa ....do..	2,118	..do...	....do.	
	Siberia ....do..	2,538	..do...	....do.	
	Aleppo ....do..	2,103	..do...	....do.	
	Samaria ....do..	2,605	..do...	....do.	
	Tripoli ....do..	2,059	..do...	....do.	
	Palmyra ....do..	1,389	..do...	....do.	
	Atlas* ....do..	1,650	..do...	....do.	
	Kedar ....do..	1,825	..do...	....do.	
	Malta......................do..	2,206	..do...	....do.	
	Marathon ....do..	1,819	..do...	....do.	
	Olympus*...................do..	1,219	..do...	....do.	
	Palestine*.................do..	1,468	..do...	....do.	
	Sidon* ....do..	1,703	..do...	....do.	
	Batavia....................do..	2,235	..do...	....do.	
Liverpool, New York and Philadelphia "Dale Line." From New York to Liverpool.	City of Paris ....screw.	2,646	Iron..	British........	26,874
	City of Antwerp...........do..	2,400	..do...	....do.	
	City of London ....do..	2,807	..do...	....do.	
	City of Dublin............do..	1,997	..do...	....do.	
	City of Baltimore.........do..	2,323	..do...	....do.	
	City of Washington ....do..	2,386	..do...	....do.	
	City of Manchester ....do..	1,895	..do...	....do.	
	City of Limerick ....do..	1,604	..do...	....do.	
	City of Brooklyn ....do..	2,974	..do...	....do.	
	City of New York ....do..	2,094	..do...	....do.	
	City of Cork..............do..	1,540	..do...	....do.	
	Etna.......................do..	2,208	..do...	....do.	
Liverpool and Great Western Steamship Line. From New York to Liverpool.	Manhattan ....screw.	2,965	Iron..	British........	18,594
	Minnesota ....do..	2,965	..do...	....do.	
	Nebraska...................do..	3,392	..do...	....do.	
	Nevada.....................do..	3,125	..do...	....do.	
	Colorado...................do..	3,015	..do...	....do.	
	Idaho......................do..	3,132	..do...	....do.	

* Made no trip in 1869.

No. XXIII.—*Statement of steamers making regular trips between ports of the United States and foreign ports, in* 1860 *and* 1869—Continued.

STEAMSHIP LINES FROM PORT OF NEW YORK TO FOREIGN PORTS, JANUARY 1, 1870.

Name of line and port of destination.	Names of steamers.		Tonnage.	Material.	Flag.	Total tonnage each line.
Anchor Line. From New York to Glasgow, via Londonderry and Liverpool.	Columbia	screw.	1,716	Iron	British	24,640
	Caledonia	do	1,418	do	do.	
	Britannia	do	1,418	do	do.	
	Dacian	do	1,039	do	do.	
[A part of this line during a portion of the year runs to Mediterranean ports.]	Iowa	do	2,030	do	do.	
	Dacian	do	1,039	do	do.	
	Europa	do	1,747	do	do.	
	Cambria	do	2,141	do	do.	
	Tyrian	do	1,039	do	do.	
	Sabrina	do	2,538	do	do.	
	India	do	2,166	do	do.	
	Roxanna	do	915	do	do.	
	Palmyra	do	717	do	do.	
	Statira	do	862	do	do.	
	Acadia	do	755	do	do.	
	Northumbria	do	900	do	do.	
	Anglia	do	2,200	do	do.	
London and New York Steamship Line. From New York to London, via Brest.	Atlanta	screw.	2,110	Iron	British	5,948
	Bellona	do	1,845	do	do.	
	Cella	do	1,993	do	do.	
National Steamship Line. From New York to Liverpool.	England	screw.	3,441	Iron	British	23,301
	The Queen	do	3,560	do	do.	
	Helvetia	do	3,327	do	do.	
	Denmark	do	3,178	do	do.	
	Erin	do	3,336	do	do.	
	Pennsylvania	do	2,873	do	do.	
	France	do	3,586	do	do.	
General Transatlantic Company. From New York to Havre, via Brest.	Europe	side-wheel.	1,929	Iron	French	9,518
	Pereire	screw.	1,809	do	do.	
	St. Laurent	do	2,048	do	do.	
	Ville de Paris	do	1,809	do	do.	
	Lafayette	side-wheel.	1,923	do	do.	
New York and Bremen Steamship Line. From New York to Bremen.	Smidt	screw.	1,797	Iron	North German.	1,797
North German Lloyds. From New York to Bremen.	America	screw.	2,614	Iron	North German.	25,947
	Herman	do	2,747	do	do.	
	Union	do	2,870	do	do.	
	Hansa	do	2,909	do	do.	
	Deutchland	do	2,881	do	do.	
	Weser	do	2,871	do	do.	
	Rhine	do	3,019	do	do.	
	Main	do	3,018	do	do.	
	Doran	do	3,018	do	do.	
Hamburg and American Steam-Packet Company. From New York to Hamburg.	Borussia	screw.	2,133	Iron	North German.	26,681
	Saxonia	do	2,591	do	do.	
	Hammonia	do	2,964	do	do.	
	Allemania	do	2,620	do	do.	
	Bavaria	do	2,235	do	do.	
	Teutonia	do	2,027	do	do.	
	Cimbria	do	2,964	do	do.	
	Holsatia	do	3,026	do	do.	
	Westphalia	do	3,054	do	do.	
	Silesia	do	3,067	do	do.	

NOTE.—Some of the above lines have spare steamers, not in use at present, and not included in foregoing list.

No. XXIV.—*Steamship lines from various ports of the United States to foreign ports.*

Name of line.	To what nation belonging.	In what year started.	Termini of route.		Name of each steamer.	Wood or iron.	Screw or side-wheel.	Tonnage of each steamer.		Total tonnage of each line.	
			In the United States.	In foreign countries.				Tons.	100ths.	Tons.	100ths.
BALTIMORE.											
North German Lloyd Company	North German	1868	Baltimore	Bremen	Baltimore	Iron	Screw	2, 301	63		
					Berlin	do	do	2, 250	81		
					Ohio	do	do	2, 388	42		
					Leipsic	do	do	2, 335	10	9, 275	96
Total to Baltimore										9, 275	96
NEW ORLEANS.											
Liverpool and Southern Steamship Line	British	1867	New Orleans	Liverpool	Crysolite	Iron	Screw	765	34		
					Fire Queen	do	do	1, 129	78		
					Alice	do	do	1, 181	60		
					Alhambra	do	do	1, 033	95		
					Gladiator	do	do	604	13		
					Statesman*	do	do	1, 400	00		
					Olinda	do	do	648	74		
					Historian	do	do	1, 400	00		
					Castilla	do	do	2, 254	00	10, 417	54
Alliance Line	United States	1866	New Orleans	Havana	Alliance	do	do	418	72		
					Beaufort	Wood	do	374	08		
					Lavacat†	Iron	do	499	43		
					Florida	Wood	do	385	86	1, 678	09
Total to New Orleans										12, 095	63
SAN FRANCISCO.											
Pacific Mail Steamship Company	United States	1849	San Francisco	Panama	Golden City	Wood	Side-wheel	3, 589	69		
					Sacramento*	do	do	2, 682	92		
					Colorado	do	do	3, 727	80		
					Montana	do	do	2, 676	82		
					St. Louis	do	do	1, 771	00		
					Constitution	do	do	3, 575	36	18, 023	59

Do	do	1867	do	Hong Kong	Gre't Republic	do	do	3,881	83		
					China	do	do	3,836	12		
					Japan†	do	do	4,351	72		
					America	do	do	4,300	00		
										16,369	67
North Pacific Transportation Company	do		do	Victoria	Moses Taylor	do	do	1,354	00		
					Oriflamme	do	do	1,082	31		
					Active	do	do	510	43		
					California*	do	do	673	51		
										3,620	25
Do	do		do	Mazatlan	Continental	do	do	1,626	23		
					Sierra Nevada	do	do	1,257	27		
										2,883	50
Do	do		do	Honolulu	Idado	do	do	1,077	13		
										1,077	13
Total to San Francisco										41,974	14

* Twenty-four trips. † Twelve trips.

No. XXV.—*Statement of American steam lines making regular trips between ports of the United States and foreign ports.*

Name of line.	To what foreign port.	When established.	Number of steamers.	Number of trips.	Tonnage.
PORTLAND.					
Portland and Halifax	1 Halifax, 1 St. Johns	1867	2	52	1, 096. 71
BOSTON.					
Nickerson & Co.'s line	Charlotte Town	1868	3	About 38	1, 840. 36
I. G. Hall & Co.'s line	St. Johns	1866	1	About 40	449. 27
International Steamship Co., (owned in Portland)	Boston and Portland		3		3, 067. 34
Total Boston			7		5, 356. 97
NEW YORK.					
New York and Mexican Mail Steamship Co	Vera Cruz	1868	2	18	2, 141. 23
New York and Bermuda Steamship Line	Bermuda	1868	1	20	601. 00
Atlantic Mail Steamship Co	Havana		4		5, 544. 16
Pacific Mail Steamship Co	Aspinwall	1849	4	26	12, 034. 00
United States and Brazil Mail Steamship Co	Rio de Janeiro	1865	3	12	6, 435. 17
New York and Port au Prince Line	Port au Prince	1864	1	12	490. 00
Total New York			15		27, 245. 56
NEW ORLEANS.					
Alliance Line	Havana	1866	4	52	1, 678. 09
SAN FRANCISCO.					
Pacific Mail Steamship Co	Panama	1849	6	24	18, 023. 59
Pacific Mail Steamship Co	Hong Kong	1867	4	12	16, 369. 67
North Pacific Transportation Co	Victoria		4		3, 620. 25
North Pacific Transportation Co	Mazatlan		2		2, 883. 50
North Pacific Transportation Co	Honolulu		1		1, 077. 13
Total San Francisco			17		41, 974. 14
Total			45		77, 351. 47

No. XXVI.—*Comparative statement of English steamers entered and cleared at Portland, Maine, during the fiscal year* 1860, *and during the fiscal year* 1869, *for transatlantic ports.*

Names of steamers.	Tonnage.	Class.	Names of steamers.	Tonnage.	Class.
1860.			1869.		
1. Hungarian	1, 487	Iron, screw.	1. Austrian	2, 650	Iron, screw.
2. Anglo-Saxon	1, 165	Iron, screw.	2. Prussian	3, 056	Iron, screw.
3. Nova Scotian	2, 266	Iron, screw.	3. Nova Scotian	2, 265	Iron, screw.
4. North American	1, 816	Iron, screw.	4. Moravian	2, 241	Iron, screw.
5. North Briton	1, 487	Iron, screw.	5. North American	1, 816	Iron, screw.
6. Bohemian	1, 488	Iron, screw.	6. Nestorian	2, 665	Iron, screw.
7. Canadian	1, 310	Iron, screw.	7. Peruvian	2, 566	Iron, screw.
8. Australasian	1, 512	Iron, screw.	8. Hibernian	2, 444	Iron, screw.
Total tonnage	12, 531		9. St. Andrew's	1, 345	Iron, screw.
			10. Damascus	1, 359	Iron, screw.
			11. Scandinavian	3, 400	Iron, screw.
			Total tonnage	25, 807	

No. XXVII.—*Steamship lines.*

RECAPITULATION.

	Number of vessels.	Tonnage.
American line steamers trading with foreign ports, not transatlantic, January 1, 1870	15	27,013
American line steamers trading with foreign ports, not transatlantic, 1860	6	11,643
Increase in American tonnage since 1860	9	15,370
American line steamers trading with transatlantic ports, in 1860	5	14,178
American line steamers trading with transatlantic ports January 1, 1870	None.	None.
Decrease in American tonnage since 1860	5	14,178
British line steamers trading with transatlantic ports, January 1, 1870	64	141,395
British line steamers trading with transatlantic ports in 1860	26	51,610
Increase in British tonnage since 1860	38	89,785
German line steamers trading with transatlantic ports, January 1, 1870	20	54,425
German line steamers trading with transatlantic ports in 1860	6	14,123
Increase in German tonnage since 1860	14	40,302
French line steamers trading with transatlantic ports, January 1, 1870	5	9,518
French line steamers trading with transatlantic ports in 1860	None.	None.
Increase in French tonnage since 1860	5	9,518
Total number of steamers and tonnage coming to New York from transatlantic ports under foreign flags, January 1, 1870	89	205,338
Total number of steamers and tonnage coming to New York from transatlantic ports under foreign flags in 1860	32	65,733
Total increase of foreign tonnage since 1860	57	139,605
Total number of steamers and tonnage coming to Baltimore from transatlantic ports under foreign flags, January 1, 1870	4	9,249
Total number of steamers and tonnage coming to Baltimore from transatlantic ports under foreign flags in 1860	None.	None.
Total increase of foreign tonnage since 1860	4	9,249
Total number of steamers and tonnage coming to Portland from transatlantic ports under foreign flags, January, 1869	11	25,807
Total number of steamers and tonnage coming to Portland from transatlantic ports under foreign flags, January, 1860	8	12,531
Total increase of foreign tonnage since 1860	3	13,276
Total number of steamers and tonnage coming to New Orleans from transatlantic ports under foreign flags, January, 1870	9	10,417
Total number of steamers and tonnage coming to New Orleans from transatlantic ports under foreign flags, January, 1860	None.	None.
Increase of foreign tonnage since 1860	9	10,417
Number of American steamers and tonnage trading between New Orleans and foreign ports, not transatlantic, January, 1870	4	1,678
Number of American steamers and tonnage trading between New Orleans and foreign ports, not transatlantic, January, 1860	None.	None.
Increase of American tonnage since 1860	4	1,678
Number of American steamers and tonnage running between San Francisco and foreign ports, not transatlantic, January, 1870	17	41,974
Number of American steamers and tonnage running between San Francisco and foreign ports, not transatlantic, January, 1860	6	18,023
Increase of American tonnage since 1860	11	23,951
Net increase of foreign tonnage since 1860	73	172,547
Net increase of American tonnage since 1860	19	26,821

No. XXVIII.—*Statement exhibiting the value of total trade of United States with foreign countries, as divided between American and foreign vessels.*

	Countries.	1850 to 1859, inclusive.									
		Imports.			Exports.			Re-exports.			
		American vessels.	Foreign vessels.	Total.	American vessels.	Foreign vessels.	Total.	American vessels.	Foreign vessels.	Total.	
1	Russia and Dependencies	$10,911,419	$1,558,723	$12,470,142	$17,916,616	$3,008,093	$20,924,709	$1,085,667	$295,909	$1,381,576	1
2	Sweden, Norway, and Swedish West Indies.	3,806,081	3,732,802	7,538,883	6,400,063	4,398,923	10,798,986	62,595	217,359	279,954	2
3	Denmark and Danish West Indies	2,060,780	540,157	2,600,937	8,326,040	1,974,788	10,300,828	760,750	139,500	900,250	3
4	Hamburg and Bremen	56,884,454	76,374,581	133,259,035	25,090,953	71,823,285	96,914,238	2,402,581	8,526,133	10,928,714	4
5	Holland and Dutch Colonial Poss'ns	26,220,038	12,293,068	38,513,106	22,644,882	11,937,844	34,582,726	2,638,485	1,372,028	4,010,513	5
6	Belgium	27,050,924	4,790,842	31,841,766	27,699,261	3,304,681	31,003,942	9,585,820	1,312,130	10,897,950	6
7	England, Scotland, and Ireland	719,527,588	397,899,372	1,117,426,960	894,017,515	456,692,446	1,350,709,961	33,904,184	19,271,489	53,175,673	7
8	Canada, and British North American Provinces.	54,983,401	74,048,281	129,031,682	57,522,920	88,425,124	145,948,044	33,037,638	23,698,546	56,736,184	8
9	British West Indies and Possessions in Central and South America.	15,387,383	6,254,620	21,642,003	43,289,783	14,361,163	57,650,946	1,126,822	645,947	1,772,769	9
10	British Possessions in Africa and the Mediterranean.	4,213,569	869,471	5,083,040	6,605,974	1,005,439	7,611,413	773,487	99,271	872,758	10
11	British East Indies and Australia	61,247,701	3,028,422	64,276,123	30,021,785	1,559,335	31,581,120	1,969,475	228,651	2,198,126	11
12	France	307,154,497	52,248,375	359,402,872	294,625,033	12,156,827	306,781,860	12,959,659	1,761,510	14,721,169	12
13	French West Indies and Colonies	775,387	729,284	1,504,671	4,649,695	1,535,211	6,184,906	138,370	304,926	443,296	13
14	Spain and Canary Islands	15,253,726	8,601,525	23,855,251	12,275,879	49,444,552	61,720,431	908,678	181,722	1,090,400	14
15	Spanish West Indies, Cuba, and Porto Rico.	248,689,714	16,367,019	265,056,733	85,516,435	3,067,314	88,583,749	14,653,521	180,175	14,833,696	15
16	Philippine Islands	23,454,922	1,438,460	24,893,382	859,191	9,841	869,032	451,712	20,143	471,855	16
17	Portugal and Portuguese Colonies	1,732,345	2,293,309	4,025,654	4,080,451	1,560,713	5,641,164	121,104	144,585	265,689	17
18	Italy	21,255,963	10,803,711	32,059,674	26,353,055	7,904,806	34,257,861	1,710,031	867,673	2,577,704	18
19	Austria	2,294,908	2,703,300	4,998,208	10,760,411	3,661,752	14,422,163	1,278,885	781,559	2,060,444	19
20	Turkey in Europe, Asia, and Egypt	7,283,056	930,348	8,213,404	5,060,681	280,925	5,341,606	731,068	52,602	783,670	20
21	Hayti and San Domingo	19,825,725	2,067,226	21,892,951	16,572,522	1,907,121	18,479,643	2,333,719	193,817	2,527,536	21
22	Mexico	25,571,834	8,903,499	34,475,333	17,449,132	3,921,333	21,370,465	6,522,870	1,229,134	7,752,004	22
23	Central America	4,955,600	319,089	5,274,689	2,840,316	212,582	3,052,898	442,046	69,407	511,453	23
24	New Granada and Venezuela	42,267,670	6,003,675	48,271,345	23,792,588	979,358	24,771,946	3,147,226	174,245	3,321,471	24
25	Brazil	134,115,226	23,227,697	157,342,923	39,629,190	1,551,107	41,180,297	2,958,112	179,414	3,137,526	25
26	Uruguay	2,800,022	328,610	3,128,632	3,548,375	235,426	3,783,801	206,214	19,545	225,759	26
27	Buenos Ayres, or Argentine Republic	22,771,016	4,582,900	27,353,916	7,655,799	889,079	8,544,878	2,640,175	112,955	2,753,130	27
28	Chili	23,854,924	3,316,495	27,171,419	19,491,556	1,048,870	20,540,426	2,255,710	521,769	2,777,479	28
29	Peru and Ecuador	4,355,019	467,954	4,822,973	5,258,827	955,695	6,214,522	354,466	197,729	552,195	29
30	China and Japan	90,281,227	6,290,495	96,571,722	23,009,677	464,759	23,474,436	8,656,368	1,259,303	9,915,671	30
31	Sandwich Islands and whale fisheries of Pacific.	2,494,981	99,188	2,594,169	5,454,691	239,540	5,694,231	804,160	58,753	862,913	31

32	Liberia and other ports in Africa	12, 227, 408	342, 968	12, 570, 376	14, 584, 726	731, 559	15, 316, 285	843, 397	15, 783	859, 180	32
33	All other countries and ports	1, 069, 169	279, 586	1, 348, 755	3, 082, 741	67, 475	3, 150, 216	229, 358	2, 099	231, 457	33
	Total	1, 996, 777, 677	733, 735, 052	2, 730, 512, 729	1, 766, 086, 763	751, 316, 966	2, 517, 403, 729	151, 694, 353	64, 135, 811	215, 830, 164	
	1860 TO 1869, INCLUSIVE.										
34	Russia and Dependencies	$8, 530, 306	$5, 318, 734	$13, 849, 040	$6, 924, 366	$8, 989, 129	$15, 913, 495	$540, 259	$169, 292	$709, 551	34
35	Sweden, Norway, and Swedish West Indies.	1, 814, 924	4, 897, 015	6, 711, 939	1, 177, 310	1, 549, 743	2, 727, 053	7, 693	33, 393	41, 086	35
36	Denmark, and Danish West Indies	2, 115, 146	2, 221, 728	4, 336, 874	5, 970, 581	6, 664, 263	12, 634, 844	182, 088	209, 700	391, 788	36
37	Hamburg and Bremen	4, 604, 757	182, 503, 706	187, 108, 463	11, 804, 888	204, 855, 892	216, 660, 780	486, 861	22, 819, 861	23, 306, 722	37
38	Holland and Dutch Colonial Possessions.	13, 488, 738	25, 174, 592	38, 663, 330	13, 624, 762	30, 288, 873	43, 913, 635	727, 847	1, 510, 981	2, 238, 828	38
39	Belgium	7, 916, 157	15, 639, 460	23, 555, 617	11, 567, 183	33, 834, 172	45, 401, 355	2, 810, 678	4, 494, 694	7, 305, 372	39
40	England, Scotland, and Ireland	246, 767, 182	1, 143, 005, 737	1, 389, 772, 919	706, 251, 198	1, 200, 383, 469	1, 906, 634, 667	14, 217, 649	57, 714, 563	71, 932, 212	40
41	Canada, and British North American Possessions.	177, 961, 794	140. 787, 859	318, 749, 653	99, 867, 277	133, 683, 724	233, 551, 001	18, 449, 248	10, 140, 912	28, 590, 160	41
42	British West Indies and Possessions in Central and South America.	15, 586, 767	23, 376, 990	38, 963, 757	38, 122, 751	53, 504, 303	91, 627, 054	355, 447	1, 340, 380	1, 695, 827	42
43	British Possessions in Africa and the Mediterranean.	7, 132, 901	9, 594, 217	16, 727, 118	14, 123, 843	11, 895, 559	26, 019, 402	597, 872	269, 821	867, 693	43
44	British East Indies and Australia	46, 992, 917	24, 032, 920	71, 025, 837	28, 126, 819	24, 963, 618	53, 090, 437	504, 485	174, 360	678, 845	44
45	France	107, 638, 050	126, 304, 441	233, 942, 491	230, 728, 724	113, 105, 775	343, 834, 499	5, 916, 379	7, 428, 065	13, 344, 444	45
46	French West Indies and Colonies	1, 169, 167	2, 060, 457	3, 229, 624	6, 380, 553	6, 005, 207	12, 385, 760	231, 062	413, 877	644, 939	46
47	Spain and Canary Islands	14, 593, 252	14, 793, 846	29, 387, 098	10, 176, 507	35, 565, 143	45, 741, 650	317, 589	766, 799	1, 084, 388	47
48	Spanish West Indies, Cuba, and Porto Rico.	286, 820, 075	122, 366, 584	409, 186, 659	111, 665, 896	46, 591, 982	158, 257, 878	18, 931, 816	5, 907, 020	24, 838, 836	48
49	Philippine Islands	18, 710, 666	6, 518, 912	25, 229, 578	957, 882	386, 914	1, 344, 796	5, 513	75, 902	81, 415	49
50	Portugal and Portuguese Colonies	767, 092	2, 482, 512	3, 249, 604	3, 379, 270	5, 219, 511	8, 598, 781	52, 633	200, 500	253, 133	50
51	Italy	20, 157, 692	19, 250, 826	39, 408, 518	16, 715, 596	23, 379, 604	40, 095, 200	491, 704	349, 461	841, 165	51
52	Austria	934, 359	3, 502, 645	4, 437, 004	1, 259, 795	2, 720, 826	3, 980, 621	421, 316	215, 398	636, 714	52
53	Turkey in Europe, Asia, and Egypt	4, 545, 262	2, 643, 405	7, 188, 667	4, 100, 121	1, 763, 996	5, 864, 117	248, 181	246, 101	494, 282	53
54	Hayti and San Domingo	8, 214, 391	7, 238, 388	15, 452, 779	15, 725, 901	17, 360, 010	33, 085, 911	1, 257, 367	1, 406, 949	2, 664, 316	54
55	Mexico	36, 370, 374	20, 121, 820	56, 492, 194	27, 185, 368	31, 177, 071	58, 362, 439	6, 689, 538	6, 379, 479	13, 069, 017	55
56	Central America	2, 787, 888	2, 796, 050	5, 583, 938	2, 512, 364	1, 434, 635	3, 946, 999	207, 526	147, 072	354, 598	56
57	New Granada and Venezuela	42, 308, 606	16, 836, 202	59, 144. 808	35, 136, 877	12, 595, 475	47, 732, 352	1, 746, 101	615, 096	2, 361, 197	57
58	Brazil	71, 908, 700	100, 775, 745	172, 684, 445	29, 086, 697	24, 483, 878	53, 570, 575	1, 046, 674	585, 827	1, 632, 501	58
59	Uruguay	3, 659, 488	6, 429, 092	10, 088, 580	3, 482, 030	2, 089, 963	5, 571, 993	393, 092	234, 014	627, 106	59
60	Buenos Ayres, or Argentine Republic	22, 021, 929	23, [illegible], 739	45, 900, 668	8, 158, 384	7, 732, 288	15, 890, 672	1, 389, 687	490, 509	1, 880, 196	60
61	Chili	10, 739, 244	5, 743, 8[illegible]1	16, 483, 075	12, 359, 444	6, 297, 148	18, 656, 592	1, 367, 473	704, 777	2, 072, 250	61
62	Peru and Ecuador	3, 744, 319	3, 482, 659	7, 226, 978	6, 587, 323	3, 672, 353	10, 259, 676	263, 385	516, 956	780, 341	62
63	China and Japan	57, 970, 599	59, 914, 472	117, 885, 071	55, 922, 151	23, 087, 431	79, 009, 582	11, 456, 017	3, 734, 634	15, 190, 651	63
64	Sandwich Islands and whale fisheries of Pacific.	16, 986, 943	3, 142, 720	20, 129, 663	6, 351, 253	848, 207	7, 199, 460	781, 454	77, 857	859, 311	64
65	Liberia and other ports in Africa	9, 580, 612	2, 363, 404	11, 944, 016	8, 298, 513	1, 477, 115	9, 775, 628	376, 375	39, 639	416, 014	65
66	All other countries and ports	1, 917, 184	1, 253, 232	3, 170, 416	6, 174, 822	4, 632, 354	10, 807, 176	64, 327	41, 879	106, 206	66
	Total	1, 276, 457, 481	2, 130, 452, 940	3, 406, 910, 421	1, 539, 906, 449	2, 082, 239, 631	3, 622, 146, 080	92, 535, 336	129, 455, 768	221, 991, 104	

No. XXIX.—*Imports, exports, and re-exports,* 1850 *to* 1859, *inclusive.*

Countries.	IMPORTS.			EXPORTS.			RE-EXPORTS.		
	American vessels.	Foreign vessels.	Total.	American vessels.	Foreign vessels.	Total.	American vessels.	Foreign vessels.	Total.
Great Britain	$719, 527, 588	$397, 899, 372	$1, 117, 426, 960	$894, 017, 515	$456, 692, 446	$1, 350, 709, 961	$33, 904, 184	$19, 271, 489	$53, 175, 673
West Indies	287, 771, 572	24, 979, 340	312, 750, 912	152, 632, 694	19, 914, 633	172, 547, 327	18, 851, 735	1, 272 398	20, 124, 133
East Indies	69, 468, 670	3, 596, 352	73, 065, 022	8, 952, 090	207, 006	9, 159, 096	2, 385, 453	88, 577	2, 474, 030
China and Japan	90, 281, 227	6, 290, 495	96, 571, 722	23, 009, 677	464, 759	23, 474, 436	8, 656, 368	1, 259, 303	9, 915, 671
South America	234, 451, 386	37, 975, 688	272, 427, 074	101, 285, 834	5, 756, 569	107, 042, 403	11, 745, 191	1, 263, 275	13, 008, 466
	1, 401, 500, 443	470, 741, 247	1, 872, 241, 690	1, 179, 897, 810	483, 035, 413	1, 662, 933, 223	75, 542, 931	23, 155, 042	98, 697, 973

Imports, exports, and re-exports, 1860 *to* 1869.

Countries.	IMPORTS.			EXPORTS.			RE-EXPORTS.		
	American vessels.	Foreign vessels.	Total.	American vessels.	Foreign vessels.	Total.	American vessels.	Foreign vessels.	Total.
Great Britain	$246, 767, 182	$1, 143, 005, 737	$1, 389, 772, 919	$706, 251, 198	$1, 200, 383, 469	$1, 906, 634, 667	$14, 217, 649	$57, 714, 563	$71, 932, 212
West Indies	310, 831, 383	152, 866, 941	463, 698, 324	170, 214, 587	119, 159, 581	289, 374, 168	20, 905, 335	8, 971, 342	29, 876, 677
East Indies	52, 401, 024	28, 772, 297	81, 173, 321	11, 970, 311	7, 458, 468	19, 428, 779	516, 696	10, 191	526, 887
China and Japan	57, 970, 599	59, 914, 472	117, 885, 071	55, 922, 151	23, 087, 431	79, 009, 582	11. 456, 017	3, 734, 634	15, 190, 651
South America	157, 170, 174	159, 928, 753	317, 098, 927	97, 323, 119	58, 305, 740	155, 628, 859	6, 166, 783	3, 274, 090	9, 440, 873
	825, 140, 362	1, 544, 488, 200	2, 369, 628, 562	1, 041, 681, 366	1, 408, 394, 689	2, 450, 076, 055	53, 262, 480	73, 704, 820	126, 967, 300

BUREAU OF STATISTICS, *January* 27, 1870.

FRANCIS A. WALKER,
Deputy Spec. Com'r Revenue.

No. XXX.—*Amounts paid to American and foreign steamships for the sea conveyance of United States mails from 1860 to 1869, inclusive.*

Fiscal year ending—	Vessels.	Paid to vessels under contract.	Postages paid as compensation for the sea conveyance of mails.	Total amounts paid.
June 30, 1860	American	$426, 635 95	$280, 712 53	$707, 348 48
June 30, 1860	Foreign		147, 085 34	147, 085 34
June 30, 1861	American		306, 970 70	306, 970 70
June 30, 1861	Foreign		235, 713 54	235, 713 54
June 30, 1862	American		90, 303 77½	90, 303 77½
June 30, 1862	Foreign		285, 884 23½	285, 884 23½
June 30, 1863	American		55, 663 13	55, 663 13
June 30, 1863	Foreign		332, 184 80	332, 184 80
June 30, 1864	American		54, 545 54	54, 545 54
June 30, 1864	Foreign		371, 740 43	371, 740 43
June 30, 1865	American		65, 555 52	65, 555 52
June 30, 1865	Foreign		405, 479 56	405, 479 56
June 30, 1866	American	112, 500 00	136, 089 33	248, 589 33
June 30, 1866	Foreign		464, 978 60	465, 978 60
June 30, 1867	American	233, 333 33	181, 522 74	414, 856 07
June 30, 1867	Foreign		455, 049 32	455, 049 32
June 30. 1868	American	497, 916 66	132, 095 09	630, 011 75
June 30, 1868	Foreign		387, 304 35	387, 304 35
June 30, 1869	American	683, 333 33	82, 178 54	765, 511 87
June 30, 1869	Foreign		336, 163 24	336, 163 24
Total		1, 953, 719 27	4, 586, 220 31	6, 762, 039 58

RECAPITULATION.—Sum total paid to American and foreign ships, as compensation for the sea conveyance of mails, from 1860 to 1869 inclusive, $6, 762, 039 58.

No. XXXI.—*Statement of the rates of duty upon the descriptions of iron most used in ship-building under various tariffs.*

[Submitted by FRANKLIN SMITH, of Atlantic Iron Works, Boston, October 21, 1869.]

Description.	Gold cost Dec., 1868, per ton 2,240 lbs.; calling exchange 9¼ per cent.	Duty by tariff bill, 1857, ad valorem.	Duty by tariff bill, 1861, per ton 2,240 lbs.; also the same, ad valorem.	Duty by tariff bill, 1864, &c., per ton 2,240 lbs.; also the same, ad valorem.	Duty proposed by House of Representatives, bill 1868, per ton 2,240 lbs.; also the same, ad valorem.
Plates, (most used in ship-building)	$43 80	24 per ct.	$20 00 or 46 per cent.	$33 60 or 77 per cent.	$33 60 or 77 per cent.
Common rounds and squares, ⅝ inch	29 93	24 per ct.	15 00 or 50 per cent.	33 60 or 112 per cent.	50 40 or 168 per cent.
Common rounds and squares, 11-16 inch	29 93	24 per ct.	15 00 or 50 per cent.	33 60 or 112 per cent.	33 60 or 112 per cent.
Common rounds and squares, ¾ to 2 inches.	29 93	24 per ct.	15 00 or 50 per cent.	22 40 or 75 per cent.	22 40 or 75 per cent.
Common rounds and squares, 2⅛ to 3 inches.	29 93	24 per ct.	15 00 or 50 per cent.	33 60 or 112 per cent.	33 60 or 112 per cent.
Flats, 1¼ to 6 inches wide; ¼ to 5-16 thick.	29 93	24 per ct.	15 00 or 50 per cent.	33 60 or 112 per cent.	33 60 or 112 per cent.
Refined of ordinary sizes, rounds and squares, ½, 9-16, and ⅝ inch.	34 80	24 per ct.	15 00 or 43 per cent.	33 60 or 97 per cent.	50 40 or 145 per cent.

No. XXXII.—*Table showing the number and tonnage of sailing and steam vessels built and registered at ports in the British possessions, (exclusive of the United Kingdom,) in each of the years from 1853 to 1868, both inclusive.*

Years.	Isles of Guernsey, Jersey, and Man.						Other British possessions.						Total British possessions.	
	Sailing vessels.		Steam vessels.		Total vessels.		Sailing vessels.		Steam vessels.		Total vessels.			
	Vessels.	Tons.	Vessels.	Tons.	Vessels.	Tons.	Vessels.	Tons.	Vessels.	Tons.	Vessels.	Tons.	Vessels.	Tons.
1853					32	4, 067					597	145, 313	629	149, 380
1854					28	4, 761					752	188, 272	780	193, 033
1855					28	3, 894					744	164, 968	772	168, 862
1856					32	3, 398					694	175, 620	726	179, 018
1857					46	5, 065					721	167, 940	767	173, 005
1858					40	4, 980					633	99, 328	673	104, 308
1859					31	3, 041					605	93, 307	636	96, 348
1860					31	2, 442					675	104, 418	706	106, 860
1861	35	3, 529			35	3, 529	532	111, 856	4	211	536	112, 067	571	115, 596
1862	30	2, 568			30	2, 568	481	114, 200	12	1, 653	493	115, 853	523	118, 421
1863	33	3, 047			33	3, 047	737	228, 910	19	3, 732	756	232, 642	789	235, 689
1864	38	8, 782			38	8, 782	923	224, 541	37	7, 532	960	232, 073	998	240, 855
1865	39	5, 155			39	5, 155	949	206, 666	31	3, 489	980	210, 155	1, 019	215, 310
1866	38	4, 422			38	4, 422	946	171, 793	33	3, 546	981	175, 497	1, 019	179, 919
1867	26	4, 855	2	455	28	5, 310	773	137, 539	24	2, 049	797	139, 588	825	144, 898
1868	17	2, 940			17	2, 940	651	136, 477	33	1, 896	684	138, 373	701	141, 313
Total, 16 years					526	67, 401					11, 608	2, 495, 414	12, 134	2, 562, 815

NOTE.—Previous to 1861 no distinction is made in British statistics between sailing and steam vessels built in British possessions.

No. XXXIII.—*Table showing the imports, domestic exports, and foreign re-exports of the United States in American and foreign vessels, and the same combined, showing the total value of the foreign carrying trade of the United States, in American and foreign vessels, during the fiscal years* 1860, 1866, 1867, 1868, *and* 1869.

1860.

Countries.	IMPORTS.		EXPORTS.		RE-EXPORTS.		TOTAL.	
	American vessels.	Foreign vessels.	American vessels.	Foreign vessels.	American vessels.	Foreign vessels.	American vessels.	Foreign vessels.
BALTIC AND NORTH SEA TRADE.								
Russia, on the Baltic and White Seas	$1, 532, 190	....	$2, 359, 644	$354, 121	$21, 730	$8, 723	$3, 913, 564	$362, 844
Prussia	....	$36, 464	....	46, 991	....	2, 259	....	85, 714
Sweden and Norway	303, 850	210, 341	887, 198	429, 543	220	2, 166	1, 191, 268	742, 050
Denmark	438	16, 071	2, 340	62, 784	....	....	2, 778	78, 855
Hamburg	126, 022	9, 701, 771	289, 679	4, 007, 593	4, 449	2, 764, 105	420, 150	16, 473, 469
Bremen	1, 678	8, 669, 136	1, 766, 307	8, 737, 912	50, 141	758, 522	1, 818, 126	13, 165, 570
Holland	1, 453, 754	1, 416, 205	2, 152, 050	1, 610, 363	86, 772	123, 146	3, 692, 576	3, 149, 714
Belgium	2, 374, 502	184, 371	2, 303, 166	467, 127	1, 412, 915	376, 540	6, 090, 583	1, 028, 038
Total	5, 792, 434	20, 234, 359	9, 760, 384	15, 816, 434	1, 576, 227	4, 035, 461	17, 129, 045	40, 086, 254
EUROPEAN ATLANTIC TRADE.								
England	55, 413, 786	77, 651, 785	122, 444, 668	64, 651, 284	2, 098, 818	3, 732, 430	179, 957, 272	146, 035, 499
Scotland	730, 536	3, 876, 651	1, 879, 245	2, 987, 973	98, 799	38, 407	2, 708, 580	6, 903, 031
Ireland	7, 413	916, 313	3, 406, 470	891, 116	....	111, 711	3, 413, 883	1, 919, 140
France	36, 293, 102	3, 157, 763	53, 985, 152	3, 855, 205	2, 783, 653	220, 906	93, 061, 907	7, 233, 874
Spain	549, 197	102, 397	678, 928	348, 654	6, 328	9, 585	1, 234, 453	460, 636
Portugal	10, 186	136, 627	205, 924	60, 780	1, 558	4, 727	217, 668	202, 134
Total	93, 004, 220	85, 841, 536	182, 600, 387	72, 795, 012	4, 989, 156	4, 117, 766	280, 593, 763	162, 754, 314
MEDITERRANEAN TRADE.								
France	1, 514, 290	2, 254, 394	1, 097, 209	110, 665	72, 470	81, 018	2, 683, 969	2, 446, 077
Spain	1, 452, 127	938, 330	340, 164	5, 067, 571	18, 107	9, 963	1, 810, 398	6, 015, 864
Italy and Sicily	3, 143, 131	1, 591, 387	4, 158, 300	791, 908	109, 784	13, 542	7, 411, 215	2, 396, 837
Austria	296, 366	436, 279	805, 970	80, 980	115, 544	36, 250	1, 217, 880	553, 509
Turkey and Greece	703, 588	473, 022	705, 288	114, 213	60, 942	5, 745	1, 469, 818	592, 980
Total	7, 109, 502	5, 693, 412	7, 106, 931	6, 165, 337	376, 847	146, 518	14, 593, 280	12, 005, 267
EAST INDIA TRADE.								
China	13, 135, 340	431, 247	6, 774, 422	396, 362	1, 599, 971	135, 363	21, 509, 733	962, 972
Japan	55, 091	....	89, 856	....	48, 918	....	193, 865	....

Fiscal year 1860—Continued.

Countries.	IMPORTS.		EXPORTS.		RE-EXPORTS.		TOTAL.	
	American vessels.	Foreign vessels.	American vessels.	Foreign vessels.	American vessels.	Foreign vessels.	American vessels.	Foreign vessels.
EAST INDIA TRADE—Continued.								
Australia	$52, 203	$76, 597	$3, 622, 339	$447, 251	$42, 293	$7, 404	$3, 716, 835	$531, 252
British East Indies	10, 297, 300	395, 042	1, 111, 697		128, 953		11, 537, 950	395, 042
Total	23, 539, 934	902, 886	11, 598, 314	843, 613	1, 820, 135	142, 767	36, 958, 383	1, 889, 266
WEST INDIA TRADE.								
Danish	173, 804	26, 612	1, 102, 197	117, 092	39, 139	4, 996	1, 315, 140	148, 700
Dutch	669, 900	78, 639	542, 932	35, 742	46, 230	443	1, 259, 062	114, 824
British	1, 668, 391	974, 041	4, 541, 176	2, 044, 333	42, 990	122, 553	6, 252, 557	3, 140, 927
French	44, 758	847	488, 641	65, 670	79, 542	3, 832	612, 941	70, 349
Cuba	31, 840, 706	2, 191, 570	11, 300, 194	447, 719	582, 443	52, 513	43, 723, 343	2, 691, 802
Porto Rico	3, 488, 843	1, 024, 092	1, 395, 669	122, 168	257, 042	6, 871	5, 141, 554	1, 153, 131
Hayti and San Domingo	1, 994, 372	351, 449	2, 241, 207	356, 752	216, 937	28, 086	4, 452, 516	736, 287
Total	39, 880, 774	4, 647, 250	21, 612, 016	3, 189, 476	1, 264, 323	219, 294	62, 757, 113	8, 056, 020
SOUTH AMERICAN TRADE.								
New Grenada	3, 722, 059	121, 509	1, 597, 410	45, 390	147, 155	5, 544	5, 466, 624	172, 443
Venezuela	2, 618, 333	265, 131	1, 035, 276	20, 974	90, 304	1, 346	3, 743, 913	287, 451
Brazil	18, 244, 077	2, 970, 726	5, 429, 950	515, 285	320, 311	14, 709	23, 994, 338	3, 500, 720
Uruguay	908, 750		636, 986	24, 340	128, 032		1, 673, 768	24, 340
Buenos Ayres	3, 761, 055	259, 793	718, 386	10, 620	269, 732	970	4, 749, 173	271, 383
Chili	2, 013, 351	59, 561	2, 693, 519	151, 706	353, 412	70, 036	5, 060, 282	281, 303
Peru	280, 810	27, 642	804, 482	65, 299	94, 222	23, 669	1, 179, 514	116, 610
Total	31, 548, 435	3, 704, 362	12, 916, 009	833, 614	1, 403, 168	116, 274	45, 867, 612	4, 654, 250

Fiscal year 1866.

Countries.	Imports, American vessels.	Imports, Foreign vessels.	Exports, American vessels.	Exports, Foreign vessels.	Re-exports, American vessels.	Re-exports, Foreign vessels.	Total, American vessels.	Total, Foreign vessels.
BALTIC AND NORTH SEA TRADE.								
Russia, on the Baltic and White Seas	$438, 330	$392, 425	$609, 989	$1, 937, 144	$27, 394		$1, 075, 713	$2, 329, 569
Prussia	186, 744	2, 535		67, 540			186, 744	70, 075
Sweden and Norway	43, 223	387, 577		149, 882		$7, 091	43, 323	544, 550
Denmark		21, 467		124, 420				145, 887
Hamburg	423, 691	13, 132, 712		13, 440, 087	12, 653	1, 617, 857	436, 344	28, 190, 656
Bremen	165, 897	12, 535, 636	1, 466, 302	11, 424, 771	41, 678	267, 672	1, 673, 877	24, 228, 079

Holland	301, 286	2, 477, 028	690, 389	1, 716, 760	3, 579	19, 703	995, 254	4, 213, 491
Belgium	433, 685	1, 833, 677	842, 492	5, 589, 361	....	468, 879	1, 276, 177	7, 891, 917
Total	1, 992, 956	30, 783, 057	3, 609, 172	34, 449, 965	85, 304	2, 381, 202	5, 687, 432	67, 414, 224
EUROPEAN ATLANTIC TRADE.								
England	19, 033, 476	177, 487, 152	115, 970, 384	211, 298, 381	467, 072	4, 104, 308	135, 470, 932	392, 889, 841
Scotland	175, 515	5, 669, 813	292, 826	4, 149, 102	....	7, 554	468, 341	9, 826, 469
Ireland	72	74, 214	249, 806	5, 724, 190	....	14, 835	249, 878	5, 813, 239
France	5, 617, 016	13, 072, 761	39, 380, 617	18, 386, 733	260, 357	319, 498	45, 257, 990	31, 778, 992
Spain	27, 909	581, 313	116, 218	1, 518, 928	....	....	144, 127	2, 100, 241
Portugal	5, 566	241, 449	64, 493	434, 235	....	19, 486	70, 059	695, 170
Total	24, 859, 554	197, 126, 702	156, 074, 344	241, 511, 569	727, 429	4, 465, 681	181, 661, 327	443, 103, 952
MEDITERRANEAN TRADE.								
France	678, 071	3, 562, 441	1, 851, 901	1, 564, 054	82, 289	....	2, 612, 261	5, 126, 495
Spain	672, 566	1, 393, 221	390, 311	3, 693, 289	....	....	1, 062, 877	5, 086, 510
Italy and Sicily	1, 449, 837	2, 695, 935	1, 127, 801	2, 806, 347	1, 604	2, 846	2, 579, 242	6, 505, 128
Austria	54, 563	381, 595	1, 800	688, 528	20, 000	2, 706	76, 363	1, 072, 829
Turkey and Greece	177, 079	248, 450	212, 885	352, 663	775	4, 522	390, 739	605, 635
Total	3, 032, 116	8, 281, 642	3, 584, 698	10, 104, 881	104, 668	10, 074	6, 721, 482	18, 396, 597
EAST INDIA TRADE.								
China	2, 326, 829	7, 805, 854	4, 703, 419	3, 928, 669	651, 485	866, 251	7, 681, 733	12, 600, 774
Japan	411, 068	1, 404, 296	427, 567	44, 984	45, 487	14, 734	884, 122	1, 464, 014
Australia	44, 945	379, 073	1, 653, 437	4, 397, 095	3, 624	....	1, 702, 006	4, 776, 168
British East Indies	3, 185, 524	2, 996, 144	401, 529	180, 439	850	54, 843	3, 587, 903	3, 231, 426
Total	5, 968, 366	12, 585, 367	7, 185, 952	3, 551, 187	701, 446	935, 828	13, 855, 764	22, 702, 382
WEST INDIA TRADE.								
Danish	174, 960	265, 919	382, 883	781, 489	1, 050	7, 245	558, 893	1, 054, 653
Dutch	99, 851	624, 887	253, 490	878, 287	2, 019	10, 831	355, 360	1, 514, 005
British	1, 444, 352	3, 364, 480	3, 130, 065	6, 392, 717	4, 952	71, 252	4, 579, 369	9, 828, 449
French	110, 656	253, 487	281, 111	417, 367	1, 481	2, 726	393, 248	673, 580
Cuba	22, 302, 694	15, 493, 118	9, 376, 565	5, 617, 981	535, 967	241, 647	32, 215, 226	21, 352, 746
Porto Rico	2, 845, 804	3, 329, 214	1, 701, 186	761, 649	48, 574	63, 335	4, 595, 564	4, 154, 198
Hayti and San Domingo	406, 101	833, 100	1, 476, 028	2, 110, 707	93, 512	136, 281	1, 975, 641	3, 080, 088
Total	27, 384, 418	24, 164, 205	16, 601, 328	16, 960, 197	687, 555	533, 317	44, 673, 301	41, 657, 719
NORTH AMERICAN TRADE.								
New Grenada	1, 584, 820	107, 247	3, 327, 136	395, 911	59, 484	9, 410	4, 971, 440	512, 568
Venezuela	204, 887	2, 271, 562	205, 412	1, 102, 522	35, 609	17, 194	445, 908	3, 391, 278
Brazil	3, 032, 685	13, 798, 738	1, 738, 428	3, 941, 085	26, 851	79, 140	4, 797, 964	17, 816, 963
Uruguay	5, 447	1, 458, 506	233, 070	130, 826	....	....	238, 517	1, 589, 332
Buenos Ayres	1, 060, 109	5, 772, 157	680, 166	1, 059, 806	4, 325	57, 201	1, 744, 600	6, 889, 164
Chili	241, 010	499, 240	703, 139	431, 516	370	26, 359	944, 519	957, 115
Peru	170, 461	636, 777	610, 936	533, 319	8, 234	63, 346	789, 631	1, 233, 442
Total	6, 299, 419	24, 544, 227	7, 498, 287	7, 594, 985	134, 873	252, 650	13, 932, 579	32, 391, 862

Fiscal year 1867.

Countries.	IMPORTS.		EXPORTS.		RE-EXPORTS.		TOTAL.	
	American vessels.	Foreign vessels.	American vessels.	Foreign vessels.	American vessels.	Foreign vessels.	American vessels.	Foreign vessels.
NORTH SEA TRADE.								
Russia	$1, 051, 190	$195, 364	$870, 217	$1, 058, 103	$69, 071	....	$1, 990, 478	$1, 253, 467
Prussia	451, 298	2, 013	....	611, 959	....	....	451, 298	613, 972
Sweden and Norway	149, 384	762, 455	....	125, 267	....	$3, 600	149, 384	891, 322
Hamburg	79, 575	12, 470, 650	114, 172	10, 912, 528	38, 117	1, 766, 820	231, 864	25, 149, 998
Bremen	69, 580	13, 523, 478	2, 693, 525	12, 709, 425	42, 170	374, 171	2, 805, 275	26, 607, 074
Holland	226, 024	1, 359, 336	527, 940	2, 438, 562	....	113, 205	753, 964	3, 911, 103
Belgium	874, 447	2, 338, 121	2, 024, 658	4, 514, 675	277, 119	298, 900	3, 176, 224	7, 151, 696
Total	2, 901, 498	30, 651, 417	6, 230, 512	32, 370, 519	426, 477	2, 556, 696	9, 558, 487	65, 578, 632
EUROPEAN ATLANTIC PORTS.								
England	21, 485, 774	150, 194, 021	78, 305, 268	156, 997, 463	675, 801	5, 560, 380	100, 466, 843	312, 751, 864
Scotland	196, 690	6, 961, 172	146, 896	4, 658, 236	....	191, 722	343, 586	11, 811, 130
Ireland	4, 208	73, 390	485, 859	6, 631, 995	91, 025	198, 210	581, 092	6, 903, 595
France	7, 439, 135	20, 619, 883	27, 309, 473	14, 277, 962	517, 607	1, 213, 600	35, 266, 215	36, 111, 445
Spain	85, 773	419, 229	243, 115	425, 557	1, 236	....	330, 124	844, 786
Portugal	17, 704	244, 039	91, 686	454, 558	750	2, 950	110, 140	701, 547
Total	29, 229, 284	178, 511, 734	106, 582, 297	183, 445, 771	1, 286, 419	7, 166, 862	137, 098, 000	369, 124, 367
MEDITERRANEAN TRADE.								
France	418, 830	2, 729, 886	2, 010, 483	492, 913	74, 809	....	2, 504, 122	3, 222, 799
Spain	844, 474	1, 701, 336	910, 091	3, 927, 986	27, 517	50, 366	1, 782, 082	5, 679, 688
Italy and Sicily	2, 184, 679	3, 104, 208	1, 388, 376	3, 256, 690	5, 669	51, 628	3, 578, 724	6, 412, 526
Austria	5, 427	505, 414	5, 300	156, 333	8, 700	21, 605	19, 427	683, 352
Turkey and Greece	196, 845	362, 120	284, 808	201, 552	4, 315	6, 974	485, 968	570, 646
Total	3, 650, 255	8, 402, 964	4, 599, 058	8, 035, 474	121, 010	130, 573	8, 370, 323	16, 569, 011
EAST INDIA TRADE.								
China	3, 027, 880	9, 084, 560	6, 127, 680	2, 660, 465	607, 572	371, 899	9, 763, 132	12, 116, 924
Japan	454, 783	2, 163, 704	624, 705	65, 431	38, 841	71, 131	1, 118, 329	2, 300, 266
Australia	49, 986	212, 415	1, 974, 293	3, 128, 060	1, 925	22, 212	2, 026, 204	3, 362, 687
British East Indies	3, 614, 503	5, 317, 982	345, 268	35, 873	17, 779	....	3, 977, 550	5, 353, 855
Dutch East Indies	1, 131, 130	1, 513, 056	127, 019	77, 376	5, 140	1, 518	1, 263, 289	1, 591, 950
Total	8, 278, 282	18, 291, 717	9, 198, 965	5, 967, 205	671, 257	466, 760	18, 148, 504	24, 725, 682

WEST INDIA TRADE.								
Danish West Indies	309, 831	332, 040	471, 581	581, 506	20, 137	28, 643	801 549	942, 189
Dutch West Indies	175, 987	520, 249	191, 701	248, 219	454	2, 777	368, 142	771, 245
British West Indies	1, 331, 786	1, 779, 414	2, 918, 549	4, 687, 704	9, 693	77, 465	4, 260, 028	6, 544, 583
French West Indies	36, 250	211, 569	423, 485	241, 491		4, 881	459, 735	457, 941
Cuba	25, 984, 948	13, 339, 817	10, 336, 671	3, 835, 164	1, 378, 666	267, 574	37, 700, 285	17, 442, 555
Porto Rico	2, 532, 908	2, 781, 751	1, 525, 678	497, 968	52, 507	29, 551	4, 111, 093	3, 309, 270
Hayti	449, 924	508, 462	6, 495	46, 393	171, 994	176, 419	628, 413	731, 274
Total	30, 821, 634	19, 473, 302	15, 874, 160	10, 138, 445	1, 633, 451	587, 310	48, 329, 245	30, 199, 057
SOUTH AMERICAN TRADE.								
New Granada	2, 290, 965	243, 255	4, 027, 444	452, 246			6, 318, 409	695, 501
Venezuela	282, 157	1, 714, 818	205, 412	1, 102, 522	4, 435	27, 185	492, 004	2, 844, 525
Brazil	4, 695, 963	14, 436, 988	2, 579, 737	2, 456, 193	91, 440	72, 981	7, 367, 140	16, 966, 162
Uruguay	227, 165	1, 291, 323	245, 047	299, 152	23, 996	28, 813	496, 208	1, 619, 288
Buenos Ayres	2, 660, 192	3, 182, 619	880, 923	1, 459, 666	159, 442	99, 483	3, 700, 557	4, 741, 768
Chili	416, 990	870, 186	2, 793, 010	739, 533	72, 231	10, 236	3, 282, 231	1, 619, 955
Peru	1, 421, 680	280, 307	1, 196, 373	502, 145	13, 034	19, 362	2, 631, 087	801, 814
Total	11, 995, 112	22, 019, 496	11, 927, 946	7, 011, 457	364, 578	258, 060	24, 287, 636	29, 289, 013

Fiscal year 1868.

NORTH SEA TRADE.								
Russia	$1, 105, 024	$348, 414	$793, 111	$1, 387, 672	$33, 220	$31, 554	$1, 931, 355	$1, 767, 640
Prussia	257, 741	191, 721	64, 027	885, 111		224	321, 768	1, 077, 056
Sweden and Norway	290, 326	934, 332		177, 426			290, 326	1, 111, 758
Hamburg	19, 824	8, 599, 166	193, 192	14, 997, 606	568	2, 236, 599	213, 584	25, 833, 311
Bremen	623, 750	12, 692, 536	1, 874, 981	21, 409, 486	30, 109	513, 208	2, 528, 840	34, 615, 230
Holland	118, 199	1, 155, 658	524, 261	4, 100, 193		31, 477	642, 460	5, 287, 328
Belgium	602, 931	2, 559, 652	1, 056, 023	5, 144, 322	5, 155	609, 259	1, 664, 109	8, 313, 233
Total	3, 017, 795	26, 481, 419	4, 505, 595	48, 101, 816	69, 052	3, 422, 321	7, 592, 442	78, 005, 556
EUROPEAN ATLANTIC PORTS.								
England	17, 084, 258	109, 201, 168	66, 551, 753	158, 147, 165	1, 048, 414	4, 541, 086	84, 684, 425	271, 889, 412
Scotland	431, 072	6, 364, 533	898, 785	6, 169, 641	1, 250	105, 038	1, 331, 107	12, 639, 291
Ireland	63, 739	23, 369	377, 800	5, 940, 617			441, 539	5. 963, 986
France	5, 519, 499	17, 925, 316	21, 206, 607	22, 179, 777	210, 871	1, 771, 733	26, 936, 977	41, 876, 826
Spain	155, 894	338, 098	859, 844	1, 243, 668	7, 216		1, 022, 954	1, 581, 766
Portugal	32, 471	194, 493	437, 925	477, 160	4, 122	17, 686	474, 518	689, 339
Total	23, 286, 933	134, 046, 977	90, 332, 714	194, 158, 028	1, 271, 873	6, 435, 543	114, 891, 520	334, 640, 548
MEDITERRANEAN TRADE.								
France	1, 710, 699	1, 766, 437	2, 305, 410	254, 070	2, 417		4, 018, 526	2, 020, 507
Spain	1, 282, 665	1, 102, 710	748, 573	4, 787, 467	15, 795		2, 047, 033	5, 890, 177
Italy and Sicily	2, 374, 050	2, 135, 583	2, 253, 491	2, 742, 312	12, 004	12, 214	4, 639, 545	4, 890, 109

Fiscal year 1868—Continued.

Countries.	IMPORTS.		EXPORTS.		RE-EXPORTS.		TOTAL.	
	American vessels.	Foreign vessels.	American vessels.	Foreign vessels.	American vessels.	Foreign vessels.	American vessels.	Foreign vessels.
MEDITERRANEAN TRADE—Continued.								
Austria	$58, 242	$566, 325	....	$267, 837	....	$2, 558	$58, 242	$836, 720
Turkey and Greece	364, 091	441, 082	$583, 442	136, 111	$21, 391	5, 153	968, 924	582, 346
Total	5, 789, 747	6, 012, 137	5, 890, 916	8, 187, 797	51, 607	19, 925	11, 732, 270	14, 219, 859
EAST INDIA TRADE.								
China	3, 040, 047	8, 344, 977	8, 498, 372	1, 023, 414	2, 157, 674	12, 030	13, 696, 093	9, 380, 421
Japan	747, 171	1, 682, 011	725, 428	54, 740	85, 722	150	1, 558, 321	1, 736, 901
Australia	37, 260	47, 865	2, 938, 624	1, 910, 360	18, 532	22, 618	2, 994, 416	1, 980, 843
British East Indies	2, 864, 303	4, 611, 991	594, 466	88, 065	4, 909	....	3, 463, 678	4, 700, 056
Dutch East Indies	1, 326, 811	576, 564	83, 514	60, 749	....	....	1, 410, 325	637, 313
Total	8, 015, 592	15, 263, 408	12, 840, 404	3, 137, 328	2, 266, 837	34, 798	23, 122, 833	18, 435, 534
WEST INDIA TRADE.								
Danish West Indies	342, 245	266, 662	629, 453	519, 938	13, 719	13, 632	985, 417	800, 232
Dutch West Indies	225, 273	583, 638	162, 136	333, 957	1, 003	10, 736	388, 412	928, 331
British West Indies	1, 413, 270	1, 546, 695	3, 369, 682	3, 304, 554	48, 701	33, 949	4, 831, 653	4, 885, 198
French West Indies	46, 055	172, 898	717, 966	186, 760	7, 387	1, 008	771, 408	360, 666
Cuba	36, 973, 281	13, 777 446	12, 321, 355	2, 934, 488	3, 188, 943	203, 642	52, 483, 579	16, 915, 576
Porto Rico	3, 917, 011	2, 430, 012	2, 543, 039	448, 169	71, 847	19, 686	6, 531, 897	2, 897, 867
Hayti	341, 425	418, 662	28, 912	35, 198	134, 461	167, 249	504, 798	621, 109
Total	43, 258, 560	19, 196, 013	19, 772, 543	7, 763, 064	3, 466, 061	449, 902	66, 497, 164	27, 408, 979
SOUTH AMERICAN TRADE.								
New Granada	3, 497, 636	154, 083	3, 855, 514	221, 445	....	....	7, 353, 150	375, 528
Venezuela	284, 210	2, 249, 234	280, 315	1, 861, 292	24, 003	18, 984	588, 528	4, 129, 510
Brazil	6, 408, 198	17, 274, 687	3, 025, 411	2, 619, 613	133, 680	64, 179	9, 567, 289	19, 958, 479
Uruguay	495, 848	683, 672	331, 605	465, 756	2, 842	20, 803	830, 295	1, 170, 231
Buenos Ayres	2, 689, 083	2, 118, 791	1, 256, 736	1, 292, 502	172, 109	97, 769	4, 117, 928	3, 509, 062
Chili	330, 947	620, 820	545, 861	978, 751	30, 161	26, 226	906, 969	1, 625, 797
Peru	1, 003, 987	761, 410	1, 239, 342	363, 585	15, 429	47, 999	2, 558, 758	1, 172, 994
Total	14, 709, 909	23, 862, 697	10, 534, 784	7, 802, 944	378, 224	275, 960	25, 622, 917	31, 941 601

Fiscal year 1869.

NORTH SEA TRADE.								
Russia	$402, 768	$435, 309	$887, 727	$3, 320, 430	$13, 548	$10, 288	$1, 304, 043	$3, 766, 027
Prussia	302, 427	245, 107	235, 654	1, 942, 379			538, 081	2, 187, 486
Sweden and Norway	331, 955	771, 636	18, 188	148, 786			350, 143	920, 442
Hamburg	50, 587	8, 917, 820	263, 789	12, 687, 663		1, 048, 703	314, 376	22, 654, 186
Bremen	309, 740	15, 444, 915	234, 049	24, 508, 280	19, 158	318, 340	562, 947	40, 271, 535
Holland	615, 308	2, 076, 015	510, 283	3, 425, 880	746	88, 847	1, 126, 337	5, 590, 742
Belgium	454, 219	2, 535, 720	892, 638	5, 516, 343	31, 245	287, 678	1, 378, 102	8, 339, 741
Total	2, 467, 004	30, 426, 542	3, 042, 328	51, 549, 761	64, 697	1, 753, 856	5, 574, 029	83, 730, 159
EUROPEAN ATLANTIC PORTS.								
England	16, 813, 321	138, 724, 121	42, 792, 736	147, 663, 959	379, 653	4, 849, 455	59, 985, 710	291, 237, 535
Scotland	424, 621	7, 021, 630		4, 843, 942		160, 688	424, 621	12, 026, 260
Ireland	99, 730	112, 233	1, 081, 987	5, 417, 130		369	1, 181, 717	5, 529, 732
France	5, 281, 413	30, 356, 911	25, 854, 961	16, 595, 178	125, 835	1, 295, 702	31, 262, 209	48, 247, 791
Spain	1, 662, 251	1, 896, 137	1, 614, 306	5, 981, 988	2, 367	13, 491	3, 278, 924	7, 891, 616
Portugal	34, 196	185, 834	433, 088	450, 341	17, 320	25, 025	484, 604	661, 200
Total	24, 315, 532	178, 296, 866	71, 777, 078	180, 952, 538	525, 175	6, 344, 730	96, 617, 785	365, 594, 134
MEDITERRANEAN TRADE.								
Italy and Sicily	2, 786, 720	3, 423, 143	2, 473, 070	3, 209, 881	6, 547	16, 677	5, 266, 337	6, 649, 701
Austria	37, 403	938, 235	144, 700	478, 032		19	182, 103	1, 416, 286
Turkey, Greece, and Egypt	550, 587	478, 673	217, 685	435, 510	53, 984	47, 906	882, 256	962, 089
Total	3, 374, 710	4, 840, 051	2, 835, 455	4, 123, 423	60, 531	64, 602	6, 270, 696	9, 028, 076
EAST INDIA TRADE.								
China	5, 361, 187	7, 847, 934	8, 881, 139	1, 377, 039	2, 115, 693	1, 861	16, 358, 019	9, 226, 834
Japan	1, 224, 541	2, 020, 776	2, 791, 217	45, 503	1, 109, 887	9, 454	5, 125, 645	2, 075, 733
Australia	43, 917	83, 736	2, 129, 496	2, 489, 817	18, 243	40, 409	2, 191, 656	2, 613, 962
British East Indies	4, [illegible], 401	4, 210, 309	347, 959	123, 060	7, 476	4, 009	5, 148, 836	4, 337, 378
Dutch East Indies	481, 775	1, 465, 426	94, 723	37, 779	325		576, 823	1, 503, 205
Total	11, 904, 821	15, 628, 181	14, 244, 534	4, 073, 198	3, 251, 624	55, 733	29, 400, 979	19, 757, 112
WEST INDIA TRADE.								
Danish West Indies and Denmark	399, 255	239, 295	693, 577	980, 538	18, 499	20, 622	1, 111, 331	1, 240, 455
Dutch West Indies and Guiana	198, 569	800, 530	285, 424	640, 627	7, 323	22, 272	491, 316	1, 463, 429
British West Indies	3, 008, 731	3, 673, 660	4, 657, 789	4, 484, 555	47, 384	54, 376	7, 713, 904	8, 212, 591
French West Indies	385, 700	311, 252			7, 473	5, 380	393, 173	316, 632
Cuba	42, 495, 084	15, 706, 290	9, 878, 183	2, 765, 772	6, 903, 655	161, 132	59, 276, 922	18, 633, 194
Porto Rico	4, 114, 355	3, 293, 545	2, 003, 612	666, 352	68, 200	45, 837	6, 186, 167	4, 005, 734
Hayti	276, 897	452, 735	531, 927	817, 511	40, 135	89, 327	848, 959	1, 359, 573
Total	[illegible]	24, 477, 307	18, 050, 512	10, 355, 355	7, 092, 669	398, 946	76, 021, 772	35, 231, 608

19 N I

Fiscal year 1869—Continued.

Countries.	IMPORTS.		EXPORTS.		RE-EXPORTS.		TOTAL.	
	American vessels.	Foreign vessels.	American vessels.	Foreign vessels.	American vessels.	Foreign vessels.	American vessels.	Foreign vessels.
SOUTH AMERICAN TRADE.								
New Granada	$5, 128, 748	$162, 958	$4, 809, 329	$90, 746			$9, 938, 077	$253, 704
Venezuela	375, 470	2, 056, 290	152, 802	1, 039, 086	$2, 282	$26, 894	530, 554	3, 122, 270
Brazil	7, 287, 539	17, 624, 911	2, 804, 297	3, 106, 268	97, 961	60, 553	10, 189, 797	20, 791, 732
Uruguay	747, 096	725, 512	287, 935	548, 177	55	58, 215	1, 035, 086	1, 331, 904
Buenos Ayres	2, 392, 945	2, 770, 021	934, 309	1, 300, 780	173, 575	98, 850	3, 500, 829	4, 169, 651
Chili	876, 090	310, 892	906, 631	1, 062, 949	30, 550	85, 355	1, 813, 271	1, 459, 196
Peru	271, 839	1, 114, 471	1, 120, 450	436, 084	82, 809	34, 102	1, 475, 098	1, 584, 657
Total	17, 079, 727	24, 765, 055	11, 015, 753	7, 584, 090	387, 232	363, 969	28, 482, 712	32, 713, 114

XXXIV.—*Comparative table showing the value of imports into, and exports from, the United States and Great Britain, respectively, during the years* 1867 *and* 1868.

	1867.	1868.
Imports into the United States, (specie value)	$417, 831, 571	$371, 624, 808
Imports into United Kingdom, (specie value)	1, 331, 886, 383	1, 426, 317, 063
Exports from the United States:		
Domestic exports, (mixed gold and currency value)	438, 577, 312	454, 301, 713
Foreign produce re-exported, (mixed gold and currency value)	20, 611, 508	22, 601, 126
Total United States, (mixed gold and currency value)	459, 188, 820	476, 902, 839
Exports from the United Kingdom:		
Domestic exports, (specie value)	875, 855, 707	869, 640, 610
Foreign and colonial produce re-exported, (specie value)	217, 186, 119	232, 807, 107
Total United Kingdom, (specie value)	1, 093, 041, 826	1, 102, 447, 717

NOTE.—In this table each year ends in the case of Great Britain, December 31, and in the case of the United States, June 30.

INDEX.

TESTIMONY.

Testimony—Continued.

LETTERS FROM AMERICAN SHIP-BUILDERS AND OWNERS.

LETTERS FROM UNITED STATES CONSULS.

STATISTICAL TABLES.

www.ingramcontent.com/pod-product-compliance
Lightning Source LLC
LaVergne TN
LVHW020228110826
845151LV00003B/856

* 9 7 8 1 4 2 5 5 3 1 0 2 7 *